The Art of Graphics
for the IBM PC

The Art of Graphics
for the IBM PC

Jim McGregor and Alan Watt

University of Sheffield

ADDISON-WESLEY PUBLISHING COMPANY

Wokingham, England · Reading, Massachusetts · Menlo Park, California
New York · Don Mills, Ontario · Amsterdam · Bonn · Sydney
Singapore · Tokyo · Madrid · Bogota · Santiago · San Juan

Phototypeset by MCL Computerset Ltd., Ely, Cambs.
Printed in Great Britain by The Bath Press.

First printed 1986, Reprinted 1987 (twice)

British Library Cataloguing in Publication Data
McGregor, James J.
The art of graphics for the
IBM PC.
1. Computer graphics 2. IBM Personal Computer
—Programming
I. Title II. Watt, Alan H.
006.6 T385

ISBN 0-201-18089-8

Library of Congress Cataloging in Publication Data
McGregor, James J., 1946–
The art of graphics for the IBM PC.

Bibliography: p.
Includes index.
1. IBM Personal Computer—Programming. 2. Computer graphics. I. Watt, Alan H., 1942– II. Title.
QA76.8.I2594M417 1986 006.6'765 85-28767
ISBN 0-201-18089-8

To
S.H. Wards of Sheffield
and
J. Smiths of Tadcaster
whose fine products occasionally assisted
in the production of the manuscript

ACKNOWLEDGEMENTS

The authors gratefully acknowledge the assistance of the following people: Steve Maddock who assisted with the development of the programs; and the staff of Addison-Wesley for their encouragement and editorial assistance, particularly Debra Myson-Etherington.

The idea of using an asymmetric triangle to illustrate the symmetry of network or wallpaper groups is due to Professor Martin J. Buerger of MIT, Cambridge (Massachusetts). Figure 4.17 is used with his kind permission. Figures 3.14a, 3.14b, 3.15a and 3.15b are taken from *On Growth and Form* by D'arcy Thompson and are reproduced by permission of Cambridge University Press. Figure 7.1 is reproduced courtesy of the Boeing Corporation.

NOTE ON ILLUSTRATIONS

All of the screen images have been photographed on an IBM PC or on other micros with equivalent facilities. The programs listed in the text will produce similar illustrations on the IBM PC.

Preface

Computer graphics is one of the most rewarding areas of programming. This is hardly surprising considering that the predominant human sense is sight. It is natural that the use of graphical displays provides the most effective means of communication between computer and human user.

Once confined to wealthy research establishments, elaborate colour graphic displays are now commonly available on microcomputers, enabling a microcomputer programmer to use some of the most advanced graphics programming techniques currently available. The aim of this book is to make these techniques accessible and to examine some interesting applications.

As well as the standard fundamental techniques, such as two- and three- dimensional transformations, the book features extensive coverage of a number of interesting and unusual application areas including innovative material developed by the authors.

On the conventional side, topics covered include: structured programming in computer graphics; interactive graphics and the design of CAD programs; two-dimensional linear and non-linear manipulations; three-dimensional linear and non-linear manipulations; three-dimensional data representation and input; full hidden surface removal; and mathematical patterns.

More unusual application areas discussed are: design and generation of wallpaper and frieze patterns; interactive tessellation art; recursive and natural patterns; three-dimensional decorative techniques; and a systematic approach to computer-generated art.

The text and programming techniques should be comprehensible to anyone with a little experience on the IBM PC. Mathematical techniques are treated using a 'recipe' approach and the formulae presented can be used without a detailed understanding of the derivation or theory.

Sheffield
July 1986

Jim McGregor
Alan Watt

Contents

1 Computer calligraphy and program structure

The most common approach, although by no means the only approach, to programming a computer to produce graphics displays is to consider the 'drawing beam' on the monitor as a pen. We define calligraphy as artistic script produced with a brush or pen, and a calligraphic facility in a computer display is a mechanism that allows us to imitate this process with a program.

When we are writing or drawing with a pen on paper we either move the pen on the paper making a visible line, or we move the pen off the paper to draw a line from a new position. In a computer program we can imagine a spot that either moves leaving a trace or trail, or just moves its position. The spot is exactly equivalent to our pen point.

In a BASIC program on the IBM PC we can use one of a number of utilities to draw a visible line. The particular one we choose will depend on exactly what we want to do, but possibly the most versatile and common is LINE.

```
LINE (x1,y1) - (x2,y2)
```

will draw a line from point $(x1,y1)$ to $(x2,y2)$. An abbreviated form:

```
LINE -(x,y)
```

will draw a line from the current position of the spot to point (x,y). When we want to move the spot to a new start position, without leaving a visible trace, we can use:

```
PSET (x,y)
```

which plots a single point or pixel at point (x,y). This chapter deals with these basic facilities, elaborations of them and how program structures are used to control these facilities to build up a computer image. We shall start by explaining how raster displays work. A rudimentary understanding of the hardware details will greatly assist your general understanding of computer graphics.

1.1 RASTER SCAN DISPLAYS

It is unlikely that the explosive growth in home microcomputers would have come about without colour graphics display facilities. In the first half of the decade, beginning around 1980, the raster scan colour display system reigns supreme and is the most common method in use for displaying computed information. It is so culturally universal that a large majority of computer users will not have experience of any other device, with the possible exception of the line printer.

One of the predominant factors in the rapid growth in popularity of home microcomputers is the availability of arcade games, and these of course rely heavily for their popularity on fast and convincing graphics. The tremendous impact of video games on popular culture is difficult to overestimate. When one particular game reaches its zenith of popularity it becomes the progenitor of a new generation of games that exploit yet another graphics trick.

Something of the madness that infects millions of arcade game fanatics can be gleaned from the following quotation from 'The winner's book of video games' by Craig Kubey, published in 1982.

> 'Most of them are what one would expect in any war that engages millions of soldiers: they are young men. Still, this is an all out Armageddon and, more and more, the young men are being joined by women of all ages, by mere children, and by men of middle age and beyond. Who are these warriors, these courageous fighters defending their nations and loved ones against onslaughts from across the ocean and from the far reaches of the galaxy? They are the men and women who command the control panels of today's video games. Yes, they're called games. But games seems the wrong word to describe a phenomenon never before seen on the planet Earth. Games is fine for hopscotch and checkers. But not for these machines called Asteroids, Space Invaders, Defender, Missile Command, Pac-man, Galaxian, Phoenix, Star Castle, Scramble, Armor Attack, Battlezone, Centipede, Berzerk and Gorf'.

Arcade games are basically reaction games ('dialogue' games such as the Adventure family and strategy games like chess do not seem to have reached the same level of popularity). A reaction game is a graphics display that changes under pre-planned program control as well as keyboard control. In a common family of games a landscape moves from right to left at a rate determined by a key. A (stationary) spaceship then appears to move. As well as controlling the rate at which the landscape moves the keyboard may cause the spaceship to move up and down (gaining and losing height as it 'moves') as well as the usual menu of firing guns, dropping bombs, etc.

The popularity of such games depends almost entirely on the quality of the display produced. The complex and fast graphics they require has only become available in the mass market since the drop in cost of mass semiconductor memory.

Basic line drawing with LINE
Although this chapter is generally concerned with the program structure of graphics programs we need to start off by describing LINE in some detail and introducing the important facility – WINDOW.

As already mentioned the general form of LINE is

```
LINE (x1,y1) - (x2,y2)
```

At this stage you should try experimenting with:

```
10 SCREEN N
20 LINE (X1,Y1) - (X2,Y2)
```

by setting 'N', '(X1,Y1)' and '(X2,Y2)' to different values and getting some feel for the way in which the facility behaves, and how changing the screen affects the line that is drawn. When the computer is in SCREEN 1 we can imagine the screen to be marked out like a piece of graph paper with 319 squares across the screen and 199 squares down the screen – the origin being in the top left hand corner (Figure 1.1). Thus the point (50,190) is 50 units across and 190 units down. The statement:

```
LINE (50,190) - (70,120)
```

draws a line from point (50,190) to (70,120). There are three different resolutions possible: low, medium and high. For the moment we will confine our considerations to the medium resolution screen.

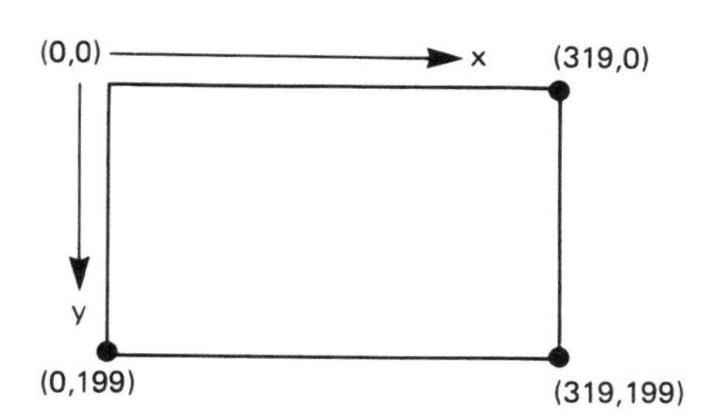

Figure 1.1
Medium resolution (320×200) SCREEN 1 coordinate system

There are in fact three further parameters that can be given to the LINE statement. The first of these optional parameters that comes after the start and stop point specifies the colour of the line:

```
LINE (start) - (stop), color
```

A full discussion of the 'colour scheme' of the machine is given later, as this is more complicated than appears at first sight. For example, differences are involved between screen modes, and there are important facilities on the PCjr for changing colour, which can be used in animation. For the moment it is important to note that the colour of the line plotted by LINE can be changed by altering the colour parameter. To demonstrate this, try the following:

```
10 CLS
20 SCREEN 1
30 LINE (100,100) - (180,180), 1
```

You should see a cyan diagonal line appear on the screen. Changing line 30 to:

```
30 LINE (100,100) - (180,180), 2
```

will result in the line changing to magenta, and:

```
30 LINE (100,100) - (180,180), 3
```

changes the line to white. This parameter, then, controls the actual colour of the line. We can also control the background colour, but we will deal with this later.

The second optional parameter instructs the computer to draw four lines, forming a rectangle, using the start point and the stop point as opposite corners. The parameter is B or BF:

```
LINE (start) — (stop), color, B
                              BF
```

Try changing line 30 to:

```
30 LINE (100,100) - (180,180), 2, B
```

This is really just a shorthand notation for four statements:

```
LINE (100,100) — (100,180), 2
LINE —(180,180), 2
LINE —(180,100), 2
LINE —(100,100), 2
```

If 'BF' is now used instead of 'B' the box is drawn and filled in colour. Program 1.1 draws three filled boxes. Note that the boxes overlap and that the first colour on the screen is 'painted over' by the second and the second is painted over by the third. The colours are laid down on the screen in the same order that the statements are executed in the program. Examine the effect achieved by swapping line 30 and line 50.

The third optional parameter in LINE is line style:

```
LINE (start) — (stop), color, B , linestyle
                              BF
```

```
10 CLS
20 SCREEN 1
30 LINE (100,100)-(180,180),1,BF
40 LINE (50,50)-(130,130),2,BF
50 LINE (0,0)-(80,80),3,BF
```

Program 1.1 Draws three filled boxes.

This lets you choose either a continuous line or a broken line for plotting. The broken line can be one of a large number of specified patterns. (If you find the way these broken patterns are specified a little tricky refer to Appendix 2.) 'linestyle' is a 16-bit integer constant whose individual bits are used to control the style of the line being plotted. For a conventional dotted line with equal marks and spaces, you would use:

1010101010101010

This integer is best specified in hexadecimal notation and the 'hex' form is

&HAAAA

Now try executing:

```
10 SCREEN 1
20 CLS
30 LINE (100,100) – (180,180), 1, B, &HAAAA
```

This time you should see a cyan box whose outline appears in dotted lines. The computer simply uses the repetitive pattern:

10101010...

to determine when to plot and when not to plot: 1 means plot and 0 means don't plot. Table 1.1 lists some line styles (or binary patterns) and their equivalent hex constants.

Table 1.1 Some line styles and their equivalent hex constants

Binary pattern corresponding to line style	*Hexadecimal constant*
10101010...........	&HAAAA
11101110...........	&HEEEE
1111110011111100	&HFCFC
00010001...........	&H1111
0000001100000011	&H0303
0000111100001111	&H0F0F

Note that the scheme must fit into 16 bits. The following line style does not fit into 16 bits:

111000111000111000111000...

If you attempt this pattern by using:

&HE38E

the pattern repeats from the first bit after it gets to the 16th. As the pattern is a multiple of 6 this causes a break in its regularity. This, of course, need not be considered an error – it could be used as a pattern in its own right.

Screen resolution and mode selection

Although it is not strictly necessary to acquire an understanding of the display electronics in your computer to write a graphics program, a rudimentary knowledge will make it easier for you to understand why graphics statements are organized in the way they are. It will also make you appreciate the limitations of the machine.

In a so-called raster scan display a picture or image on the screen is organized as a collection of individual elements called 'pixels' (short for picture elements – a term that originated from the field of image processing). The number of pixels into which a screen is divided determines the accuracy or resolution that we see on the screen. Information about the colour of each pixel is stored in a partition of the same memory used by your program. The picture on the screen is created by hardware that repeatedly scans this partition of memory, sometimes called the screen memory or refresh memory, and colours the corresponding points or pixels on the screen. This scan takes place 50 or 60 times a second and any change made to the stored image causes an immediate change on the screen. Thus the screen is just a visual reflection of the screen memory contents.

As there is a direct correspondence between the information that a screen display can produce and the memory required to store or 'hold' this information, the number of pixels on the screen and the number of colours per pixel directly affect the amount of memory required. For example, if we divide the screen into four (very large) pixels and let each of these pixels represent one of 16 colours, we would require:

4 (pixels) × 4 bits (16 colour codes) of memory

On the IBM PC in medium resolution we have 320×200 pixels where each pixel can be one of four colours. This requires:

320×200×2 bits = 16 Kbytes of the main memory

You can see that there is a battle for main memory between the number of pixels on the screen (the spatial resolution of the display), the number of colours that a pixel can be and the program itself. However, with most microcomputer graphics systems it is possible to juggle the number of pixels and colours and use more or less memory accordingly. If we are working with large programs, then there has to be a compromise between the memory occupied by the program and the memory occupied by the screen. A program that is too large to be run in a high resolution mode may run in a medium resolution mode with a consequent reduction in graphics detail (Figure 1.2). As we go from a high resolution to a low resolution screen, characters get bigger and lines get thicker. This is because the pixels that make up the display get larger (there are fewer of them on the screen).

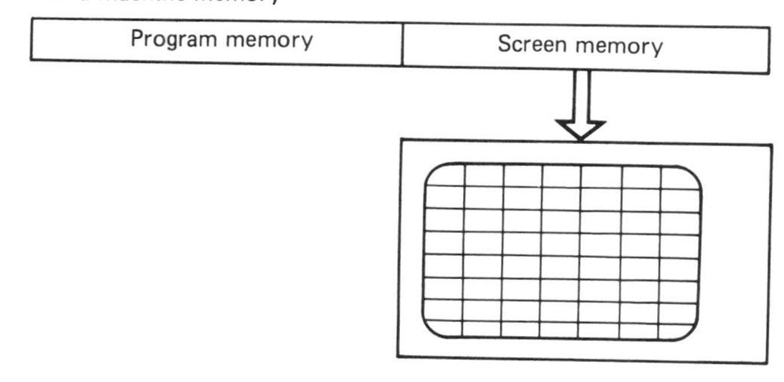

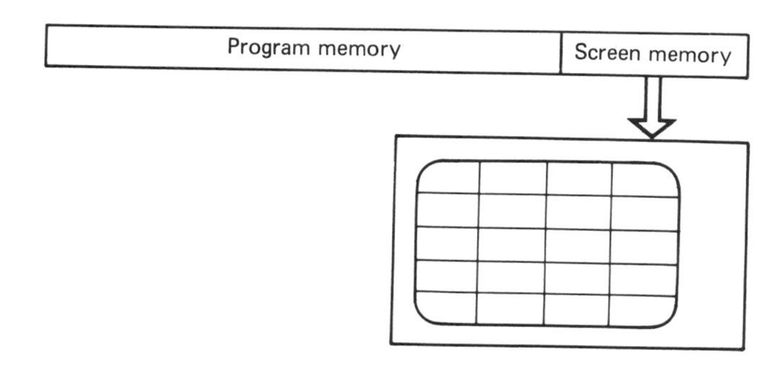

Figure 1.2
The number of pixels on the screen determines the spatial resolution of the display. The higher the resolution the more screen memory is required

Another factor that has to be considered is the number of colours that a pixel can be. Even when you are plotting a single point on a blank screen, the memory required is that for all the pixels on the screen times the number of bits required to represent their possible colours. It does not matter to the computer whether the screen is displaying one point or a very complex pattern – the same amount of memory is needed in each case. This is a fact of life in raster graphics. (In the other major type of system, vector graphics, the amount of memory required to store a picture is a function of the picture complexity.)

A two-colour pixel (or on/off pixel) needs one bit of memory; a four-colour pixel needs two bits; a 16-colour pixel needs four bits, and so on.

We will now look at how the PC and PCjr options work. Particular screen resolutions, or screens for short, are selected by using the SCREEN statement. Table 1.2 contains a summary of the screens available and the memory requirement associated with each. All seven screens are available on the PCjr, but only the first three are available on the PC.

Table 1.2 PC screens and memory requirements

Screen	*Memory requirement*	*Description*
0	WIDTH 40: 2K WIDTH 80: 4K	Selects the mode for printing text at the current width set by the WIDTH statement. (WIDTH 80 needs a machine with 128K of memory.)
1	320×200×2 (16K)	Medium resolution graphics mode (320×200 pixels). Each pixel can be one of four colours.
2	640×200×1 (16K)	High resolution graphics mode (640×200 pixels). Each pixel can be one of two colours.
3	160×200×4 (16K)	Low resolution graphics mode (160×200 pixels). Each pixel can be one of 16 colours. (PCjr only.)
4	320×200×2 (16K)	Medium resolution graphics mode (320×200 pixels). Each pixel can be one of four colours. (PCjr only.)
5	320×200×4 (32K)	Medium resolution graphics mode (320×200 pixels). Each pixel can be one of 16 colours. (128K, PCjr only.)
6	640×200×2 (32K)	High resolution graphics mode (640×200 pixels). Each pixel can be one of four colours. (128K, PCjr only.)

From Table 1.2 you can see that spatial resolution, or number of pixels on the screen, are basically juggled against the number of colours per pixel. Another aspect that you may have noticed is that when the spatial resolution is changed it is only the horizontal dimension that is altered – the vertical dimension remains constant at 200 pixels. This is a significant drawback with current microcomputer graphics systems and is a consequence of the technology that converts the screen memory contents into an image on a TV or monitor screen. To make the vertical dimension greater than, say, 250 requires a significant leap in costs. You will find that all home microcomputers and most PCs suffer from this disadvantage.

In SCREEN 0, the WIDTH statement can be used to switch between 40 character width and 80 character width:

```
WIDTH 40
WIDTH 80
```

The WIDTH statement can also force changes from one screen to

```
10 SCREEN 3 : CLS
20 LINE (50,50)-(150,150),1,B
30 INPUT ANY$
40 SCREEN 1 : CLS
50 LINE (50,50)-(150,150),2,B
60 INPUT ANY$
70 SCREEN 2 : CLS
80 LINE (50,50)-(150,150),3,B
```

Program 1.2 The same LINE statements at different resolutions. (Omit lines 10 to 30 on the PC.)

another. If, for example, the program is in SCREEN 1, executing WIDTH 80 would force it into SCREEN 2.

Program 1.2 demonstrates the effect of drawing a box at different resolutions. (Omit lines 10 to 30 on the PC.) The same LINE statement, with a colour change, is used in each SCREEN. A pause between modes is effected by using:

```
INPUT ANY$
```

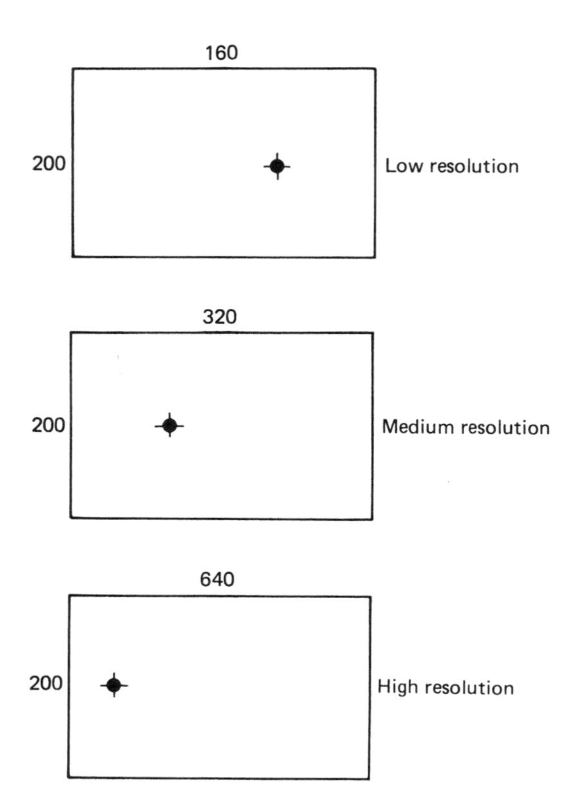

Figure 1.3
The position of the point (100,100) in each of the three screen coordinate systems

```
10 SCREEN 3 : CLS
20 LINE (0.5*50,50)-(0.5*150,150),1,B
30 INPUT ANY$
40 SCREEN 1 : CLS
50 LINE (50,50)-(150,150),2,B
60 INPUT ANY$
70 SCREEN 2 : CLS
80 LINE (2*50,50)-(2*150,150),3,B
```

Program 1.3 Compensating for different resolutions. (Omit lines 10 to 30 on the PC.)

to which you can respond by pressing the ENTER key. This program illustrates two important points:

1. The boxes change position in each mode.
2. The boxes change shape in each mode.

Each mode has its own coordinate system based on the pixel resolution. So using the same pair of coordinates in each LINE statement causes the box to shift (Figure 1.3). Secondly the 'aspect ratio' changes and the boxes change shape. (The aspect ratio is the ratio of the horizontal dimension of a pixel to the vertical dimension.) The aspect ratio depends not only on the screen coordinate system but on the aspect ratio of the screen itself. Note that we get close to a square in medium resolution mode (320×200) so, in such a mode (SCREENs 1, 4 and 5), no aspect ratio correction is required. (The screen aspect ratio may vary slightly from one TV to another.) In high resolution modes (SCREENs 2 and 6) the rectangle is twice as high as it is wide and so the x value needs multiplying by 2. In low resolution mode on the PCjr (SCREEN 3), the rectangle is twice as wide as it is high and the x value needs multiplying by 0.5.

Try running Program 1.3, which incorporates these corrections, and you should get a square in each screen mode. Now if you think that the business of having to remember different correction factors when you are plotting in different modes is rather tedious, you are

```
10 SCREEN 3 : CLS
20 PSET(100,100),1
25 CIRCLE(100,100),50,1,,,2
30 INPUT ANY$
40 SCREEN 1 : CLS
50 PSET(100,100),2
55 CIRCLE(100,100),50,2,,,1
60 INPUT ANY$
70 SCREEN 2 : CLS
80 PSET(100,100),3
85 CIRCLE(100,100),50,3,,,0.5
```

Program 1.4 A pixel at different resolutions.

correct. In the next section we will be looking at a facility that allows us to unify our coordinate system and free ourselves from the screen coordinate system. In other words, although it is necessary for you to know about the screen coordinate systems you will not normally be plotting directly in these systems.

For the moment note that for direct plotting in these systems correction factors are required to be applied to the x value. These are:

Low resolution (160×200) – multiply x value by 0.5

Medium resolution (320×200) – no correction required

High resolution (640×200) – multiply x value by 2

The next program (Program 1.4) demonstrates how an actual pixel changes shape in the three resolutions. (Omit lines 10 to 30 on the PC.) A single point is plotted on the screen using:

```
PSET (x,y), color
```

in low, medium and high resolution. You may not be able to appreciate much difference in the individual pixels – it depends on the quality of your monitor. A pixel in high resolution should be half as long as a pixel in medium resolution. A pixel in medium resolution should be half as long as a pixel in low resolution on the PCjr. All pixels are the same height.

Also in Program 1.4 a circle has been drawn around each pixel using CIRCLE – this will be dealt with later.

The WINDOW statement

The WINDOW statement is one of the most useful and powerful graphics statements. It performs two extremely important functions and you will tend to use it in most graphics programs that you write. The two functions are:

1. It frees the programmer from the tedium of having to work in different coordinate systems for different graphics modes.
2. It allows the programmer to easily place the graphics origin anywhere on the screen – say, for example, the centre or the bottom left hand corner.

Taken together these two functions really mean the same thing – the programmer can set up his or her own coordinate system. A programmer will invent or design a coordinate system that is related to the graphics task being programmed. Figure 1.4 shows three graphics environments that possess widely different coordinate systems. Figure 1.4a is mathematical. To plot graphs of harmonic functions, such as a sine wave, the y-axis may be required to range from -1 to + 1 and the x-axis from 0 to 720, with the origin halfway down the left hand edge of the screen. In Figure 1.4b the graphics environment is a map of a street system. Here a 100 metre grid

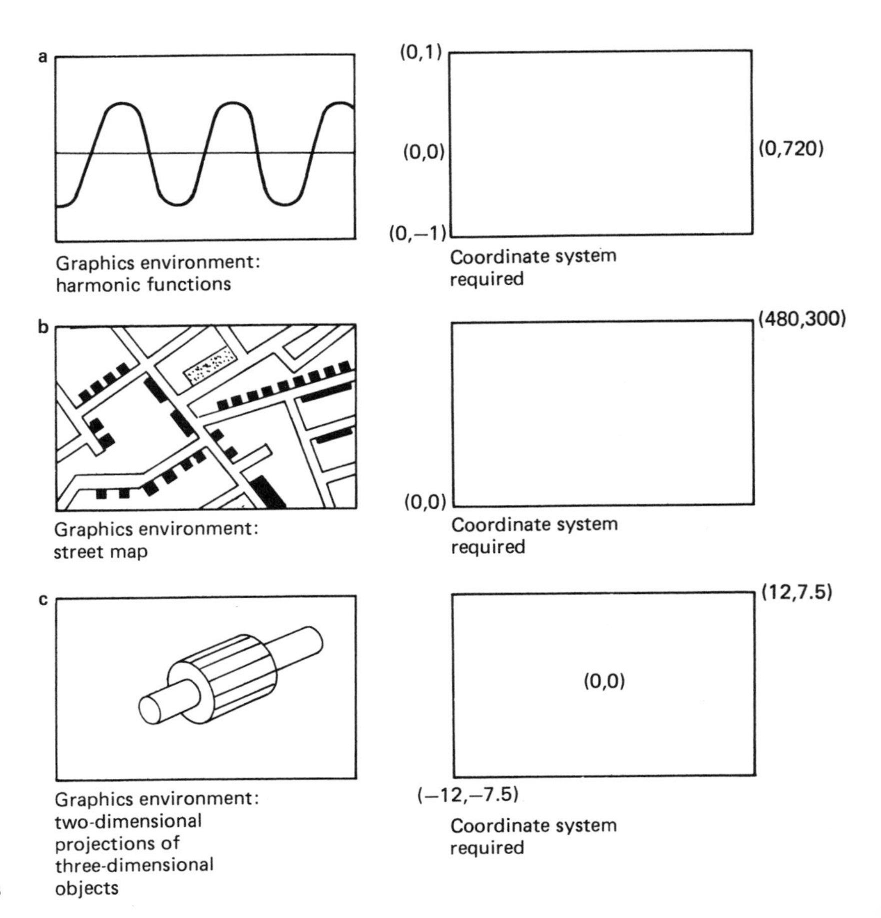

Figure 1.4
Three 'graphics environments' and the required coordinate systems

system may be required with the origin in the bottom left hand corner. In Figure 1.4c the graphics environment consists of a two-dimensional projection of a three-dimensional object. Here it is conventional to have the origin in the centre of the screen. The axis would be scaled according to the size of the object, say in centimetres. Now these different coordinate systems are known as world coordinates and are completely arbitrary coordinate systems designed by the programmer. A programmer can then write a graphics program entirely in the coordinate system of his or her choice and use the WINDOW statement to make the computer convert or map the coordinate system on to the screen.

The WINDOW statement is supplied with two parameters defining two points that completely define the programmer's world coordinate system. These are the bottom left hand corner and the top right hand corner. The WINDOW statements required in the examples of Figure 1.4 are:

```
WINDOW (0,-1) - (720,1)
```

```
  5 PI = 3.141593
 10 SCREEN 1 : CLS
 20 WINDOW (0,-1)-(720,1)
 25 LINE (0,-1)-(0,1) : LINE (720,0)-(0,0)
 30 FOR I = 0 TO 720
 40   ANGLE = I*PI/180
 50   LINE -(I,SIN(ANGLE))
 60 NEXT I
 70 INPUT ANY$ : CLS
 80 WINDOW (0,0)-(480,300)
 90 LINE (0,0)-(240,150),1,B
100 INPUT ANY$ : CLS
110 WINDOW (-12,-7.5)-(12,7.5)
120 LINE (0,0)-(5,0) : LINE -(3,5) : LINE -(0,0)
```

Program 1.5 Three different WINDOW statements.

for the harmonic function world coordinate system,

```
WINDOW (0,0) - (480,300)
```

for the street map world coordinate system,

```
WINDOW (-12,-7.5) - (12,7.5)
```

for the three-dimensional object world coordinate system. In the second and third case we want the scale of both the x-axis and the y-axis to be approximately the same. The x-axis range is thus greater than the y-axis range by an amount that depends on the screen aspect ratio. This is the ratio of the width of the screen to the height. The precise value depends on the TV or monitor that you are using, but on ours, this ratio is approximately 24/15.

Program 1.5 illustrates the use of these three WINDOW statements. The first part of the program draws a sine wave (just accept the FOR and NEXT statement for the time being). The second part of the program draws a square to simulate what we might do in a street map environment. In the third part a triangle is drawn. The program as it stands is written with a medium resolution screen. Now change line 10 to a high resolution screen (SCREEN 2) and re-run the program. You can see from this that the size and shape of the three images remain identical. All that happens is that the lines get finer. Changing to low resolution (SCREEN 3) on the PCjr makes the lines thicker. Notice that, in the case of the sine wave at low or medium resolution, the curved lines are noticeably more jagged and the finite steps are more clearly visible. Drawing diagonal lines at a finite resolution always results in jagged edges. In computer graphics a great deal of research has been devoted to making these jagged edges less noticeable (without increasing the resolution).

Now a practical point – you will find that when you use the

```
 10 SCREEN 2 : CLS
 20 WINDOW (-640,-400)-(639,399)
 30 LINE (300,300)-(-200,200)
 40 LINE -(-300,-300)
 50 LINE -(200,-200)
 60 LINE -(300,300)
100 END
```

Program 1.6 Draws a parallelogram.

WINDOW statement initially, you will inevitably make mistakes in its specification. Say, for example, you write:

```
WINDOW (0,1) - (720,-1)
```

instead of the correct WINDOW statement

```
WINDOW (0,-1) - (720,1)
```

in the foregoing example. As soon as you attempt to plot (using LINE) in the illegal window, you will get an 'overflow' error message. If you get an overflow error from a line that contains a plotting instruction, it will almost certainly be an error in the WINDOW statement.

Up to now LINE has been used mainly to draw vertical or horizontal lines. Program 1.6 draws a parallelogram instead of a square. You can see that the sloping lines are drawn as a series of steps. Remember that eventually the effect of the program is to switch on, or colour, individual pixels. Behind the scenes a system utility converts the line drawing command into a series of pixels selected 'nearest' to the line (Figure 1.5). This process results in the characteristic steps whose noticeability depends on the slope of the line. Try altering the coordinates in Program 1.6 and observe how the 'steps' in the sloping lines change.

There are applications where the programmer wants to alter individual pixels in the screen memory, but when using LINE he or she simply specifies a destination point and the computer decides the best pixels to switch on between the current position and the

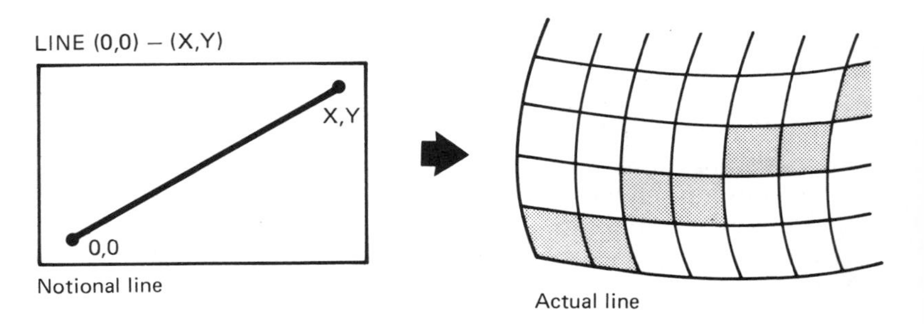

Figure 1.5
A line appears on the screen as a series of steps

destination point. Individual pixels can be controlled by using PSET, as was done in Program 1.4.

This, of course, refers only to straight lines. How are curves drawn? They are drawn by approximating them with short straight line segments produced by the LINE facility, as was done with the sine wave example in Program 1.5. The shorter the line segments are the better they approximate the curve. This technique is illustrated in Figure 1.6 where a circle is drawn using 6, 12, 24 and 36 line segments. There is an obvious improvement in going from 6 segments to 12 line segments. There is little or no improvement in going from 24 to 36. Here we are up against the resolution of the system. The slope and length of a line segment may be such that it does not cross a pixel boundary. This noticeable effect is characteristic of low resolution display systems and limits the implementation of complex line images.

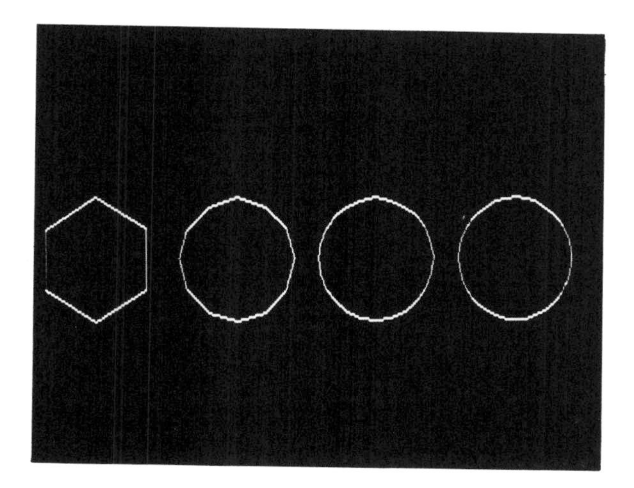

Figure 1.6
A circle drawn by using 6, 12, 24 and 36 line segments

1.2 PROGRAM STRUCTURES AND LINE IMAGES

In this section, we move on to describe the various forms of simple BASIC program structures that are used to draw line images. Wherever possible we shall use a coordinate system with an origin at the centre of the screen and with x and y extents matching the aspect ratio of the screen (Figure 1.7). In the next few sections we will demonstrate the use of appropriate programming structures in controlling the graphics facilities such as LINE to build up computer line images. A very few control statements or combinations of control statements will cover most graphic applications and throughout this text we will be exploiting those features of BASIC that enable transparent or readable programs to be written. This means making extensive use of the subroutine facility which enables a structured programming approach.

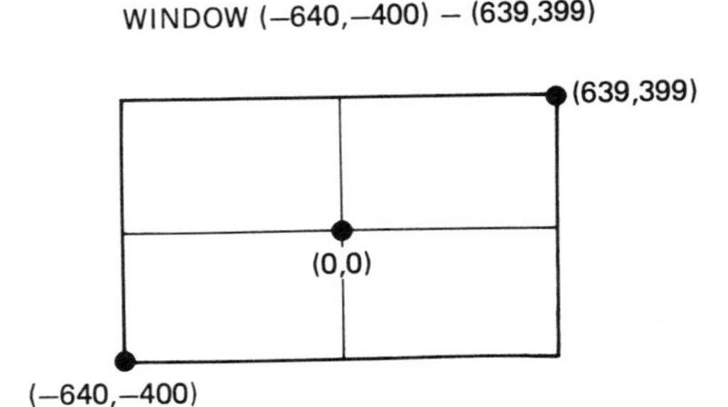

Figure 1.7
The coordinate system set up by WINDOW, which is used in a large number of programs

Deterministic loops – FOR statements

The FOR statement control structure is used to repeat an operation or a series of operations a pre-determined number of times. One of the most common graphics applications of this structure is in generating an approximation to a curve by drawing a number of short line segments. For example, to generate the circles shown in Figure 1.6 we would use Program 1.7. This program generates a 'circle' by plotting a regular polygon of 36 sides.

It uses a 'polar coordinate' system – a point is represented by the two values r and theta, and we convert r and theta into cartesian coordinates, x and y, using:

$$x = r\cos(\text{theta})$$
$$y = r\sin(\text{theta})$$

Increments in 'theta' result in new (x,y) coordinates, one (x,y) pair for each vertex on the polygon as shown in Figure 1.8. In this program the CIRCLE statement could have been used. However, the generation of circles by programming is a useful introduction to polar coordinates which will be used elsewhere in the text. Also CIRCLE has certain disadvantages in its use with WINDOW.

```
 10 SCREEN 2 : CLS
 20 WINDOW (-640,-400)-(639,399)
 30 PI = 3.141593
 40 R = 200 : PSET(200,0)
 50 FOR THETA = 0 TO 360 STEP 10
 60    RADIANS = THETA*PI/180
 70    X = R*COS(RADIANS) : Y = R*SIN(RADIANS)
 80    LINE -(X,Y)
 90 NEXT THETA
100 END
```

Program 1.7 A polygon that approximates a circle.

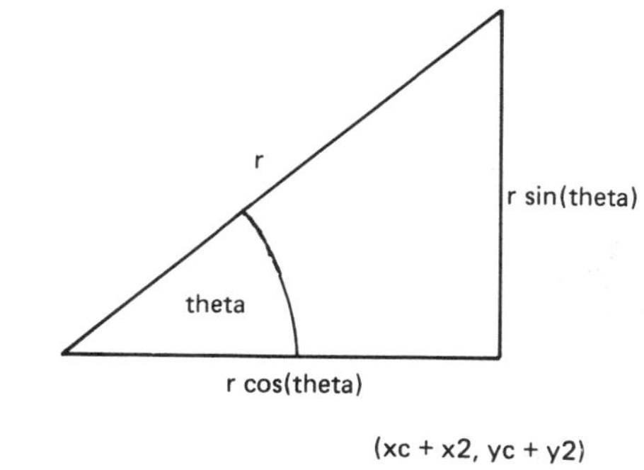

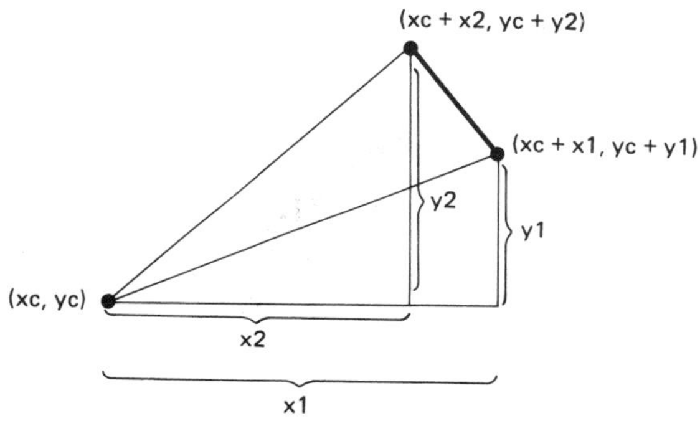

Figure 1.8
Polar coordinate system

```
 10 SCREEN 2 : CLS
 20 WINDOW (-640,-400)-(639,399)
 30 PI = 3.141593
 40 INPUT SX,SY,R
 50 CLS
 60 XC = SX : YC = SY
 70 PSET (XC+R,YC)
 80 FOR THETA = 0 TO 360 STEP 10
 90   RADIANS = THETA*PI/180
100   X = R*COS(RADIANS) : Y = R*SIN(RADIANS)
110   LINE -(XC+X,YC+Y)
120 NEXT THETA
130 FOR CIRC = 0 TO 320 STEP 60
140   CIRCRADIANS = CIRC*PI/180
150   XC = SX+R*COS(CIRCRADIANS)
160   YC = SY+R*SIN(CIRCRADIANS)
170   PSET (XC+R,YC)
180   FOR THETA = 10 TO 360 STEP 10
190     RADIANS = THETA*PI/180
200     X = R*COS(RADIANS) : Y = R*SIN(RADIANS)
210     LINE -(XC+X,YC+Y)
220   NEXT THETA
230 NEXT CIRC
```

Program 1.8 Nested FOR statements.

Figure 1.9
Output from Program 1.8 (nested FOR statements)

Nested FOR statements

A common structure that is a development of a simple FOR statement is a nested FOR statement. Here one FOR statement is contained or nested within another. Program 1.8 demonstrates this structure. The outermost FOR statement controls the position at which the object (or circle) is drawn. The innermost FOR statement controls the drawing of a single circle. The output from this program is shown in Figure 1.9.

Non-deterministic loop – WHILE-WEND

A non-deterministic loop is a loop control structure that causes the repetition of statements within the loop body as long as the expres-

```
 10 CLS
 20 INPUT "File name",FILE$
 30 SCREEN 2 : CLS
 40 WINDOW (-640,-400)-(639,399)
 50 FILENUM = 3
 60 OPEN FILE$ FOR INPUT AS #FILENUM
 70 INPUT #FILENUM,X,Y
 80 PSET (X,Y)
 90 WHILE NOT EOF(FILENUM)
100    INPUT #FILENUM,X,Y
110    LINE -(X,Y)
120 WEND
130 CLOSE
140 END
```

Program 1.9 Draws a picture using a list of coordinates stored in a file.

Figure 1.10
Output from Program 1.9: an image generated from a WHILE structure

sion following the WHILE is TRUE. The commonest graphics application of this structure is in drawing a line image, from a list of (x,y) coordinates, contained in a file or in a set of DATA statements. Program 1.9 demonstrates the idea. The picture must be in the form of a continuous line drawing, and the first two coordinates in the file must be the position where the drawing is to begin. Figure 1.10 shows an image generated by Program 1.9. Again the image is drawn as a series of short line segments representing curves. This time the endpoints of the line segments are not calculated but are contained in a file. (The coordinates contained in the file were produced using a digitizer, a device described in Chapter 2.)

Subroutines

Subroutines are used in general to make the development of a program easier and to enhance its readability. If we take the nested loop structure of Program 1.8 and define the innermost loop as a subroutine, then the program is much easier to read. Also, in a longer program, we may want to draw a circle in many positions. Clearly it makes sense in this context to encapsulate those instructions that draw the circle inside a separate program module and refer to this module when required. Program 1.10 incorporates this idea. The operation of drawing a circle is now referred to in the (main) program as a module – a subroutine – and the definition of that module is contained elsewhere as a subroutine definition. In graphics programming the use of subroutines is very natural. Often complex images are made up of subimages. For example, the front elevation of a house may be a rectangle containing a door and four windows. It is natural and transparent to implement the subpictures as subroutines. The structure of the picture or image is then reflected in the structure of the program.

```
 10 SCREEN 2 : CLS
 20 WINDOW (-640,-400)-(639,399)
 30 PI = 3.141593
 40 INPUT SX,SY,R
 50 CLS
 60 XC = SX : YC = SY
 70 GOSUB 150  'draw a circle
 80 FOR CIRC = 0 TO 320 STEP 60
 90   CIRCRADIANS = CIRC*PI/180
100   XC = SX+R*COS(CIRCRADIANS)
110   YC = SY+R*SIN(CIRCRADIANS)
120   GOSUB 150  'draw a circle
130 NEXT CIRC
140 END

150 'SUBROUTINE draw a circle
160   PSET (XC+R,YC)
170   FOR THETA = 10 TO 360 STEP 10
180     RADIANS = THETA*PI/180
190     X = R*COS(RADIANS) : Y = R*SIN(RADIANS)
200     LINE -(XC+X,YC+Y)
210   NEXT THETA
220 RETURN
```

Program 1.10 Uses a subroutine to draw a circle.

Nested subroutines – image hierarchy and complexity

A rather more convincing demonstration of the utility of subroutines is contained in Program 1.11, which produces the apparently complex image shown in Figure 1.11. An examination of this program will show that it is hierarchical in nature. There are various levels of subroutines reflecting the hierarchy in the image.

Figure 1.11
Output from Program 1.11

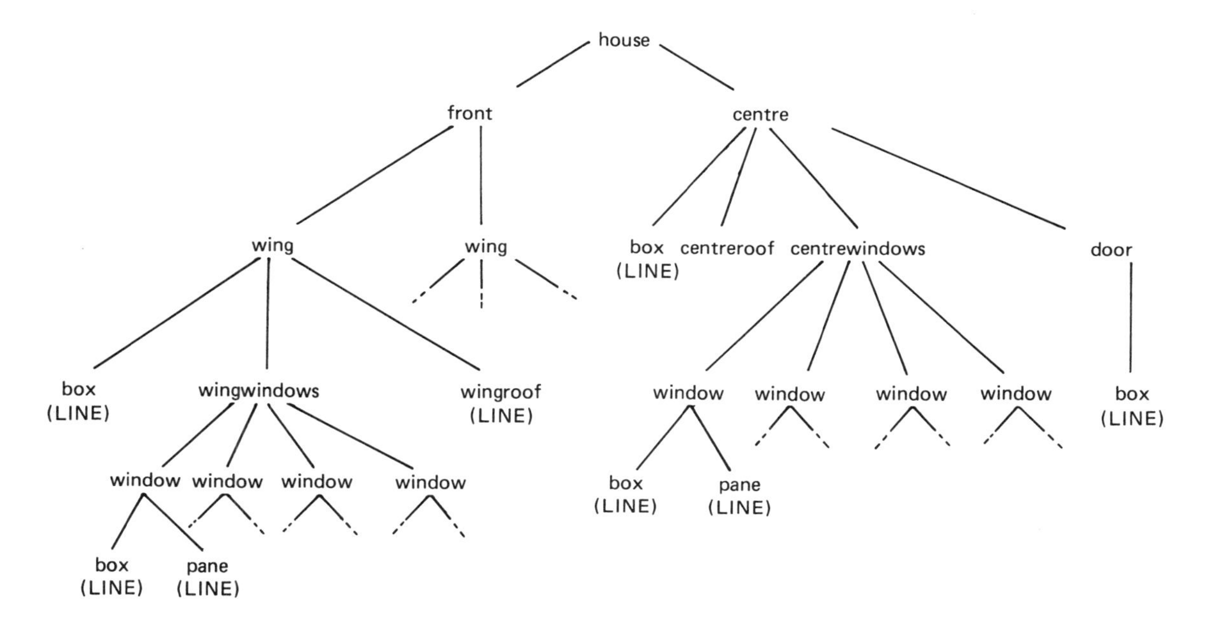

Figure 1.12
The hierarchy of subroutine calls in the house drawing program (Program 1.11)

Only those subroutines at the bottom of the hierarchy contain LINE commands. The program is best examined together with the tree diagram shown in Figure 1.12. The subroutine that draws a house initiates the process. This contains a call to a subroutine that draws a front and one that draws a centre. The subroutine that draws a front contains two calls to the subroutine that draws a wing. Eventually a path terminates by the call of a subroutine that contains LINEs and PSETs.

The process of setting up a hierarchical programming structure to reflect the hierarchy in the image has two advantages. Firstly, it enables a methodical and structured approach to the task of generating this particular image. Secondly, and more importantly, it facilitates structural alterations. We could use a version of the same program to create a different house using the same building blocks. Similar houses could be drawn by simply changing some of the information input to the top of the subroutine tree. This would alter the detailed design and style. More significant changes could be made by altering the structure of the program and thus the house.

Although Program 1.11 illustrates image hierarchy and the equivalent hierarchy in subroutines, a number of other points concerning subroutines should be noted.

Firstly, different variables have a different status in the program. Some variables are used to feed necessary information into a subroutine. For example, on each call of the subroutine 'draw a wing', the two variables 'WINGSTARTX' and 'WINGSTARTY' are given values indicating where the wing is to be drawn. Such variables are often referred to as 'parameters'.

```
 10 SCREEN 2 : CLS
 20 WINDOW (0,0)-(1279,1023)
 30 GOSUB 560  'initialise
 40 GOSUB 60  'draw house
 50 END

 60 'SUBROUTINE draw house
 70   GOSUB 100  'draw front
 80   GOSUB 160  'draw centre
 90 RETURN

100 'SUBROUTINE draw front
110   WINGSTARTX = STARTX : WINGSTARTY = STARTY
120   GOSUB 220  'draw wing
130   WINGSTARTX = STARTX+CENTRELENGTH+WINGLENGTH : WINGSTARTY = STARTY
140   GOSUB 220  'draw wing
150 RETURN

160 'SUBROUTINE draw centre
170   LINE (STARTX+WINGLENGTH,STARTY)-(STARTX+WINGLENGTH+CENTRELENGTH,
        STARTY+HEIGHT),,B
180   GOSUB 860  'draw centre roof
190   GOSUB 290  'draw centre windows
200   GOSUB 650  'draw door
210 RETURN

220 'SUBROUTINE draw wing
230   LINE (WINGSTARTX,WINGSTARTY)-(WINGSTARTX+WINGLENGTH,WINGSTARTY+HEIGHT),,B
240   GOSUB 430  'draw wing windows
250   WINGSTARTY = WINGSTARTY+HEIGHT
260   GOSUB 610  'draw wing roof
270   CIRCLE (WINGSTARTX+WINGLENGTH/2,WINGSTARTY+HEIGHT/8),30
280 RETURN

290 'SUBROUTINE draw centre windows
300   WINDOWSTARTX = STARTX+WINGLENGTH+CENTRELENGTH/10
310   WINDOWSTARTY = STARTY+HEIGHT/7
320   WINDOWWIDTH = CENTRELENGTH/7 : WINDOWHEIGHT = HEIGHT/3
330   GOSUB 740  'draw window
340   WINDOWSTARTY = WINDOWSTARTY+11*HEIGHT/24
350   GOSUB 740  'draw window
360   WINDOWSTARTX = WINGLENGTH+STARTX+3*CENTRELENGTH/7
370   GOSUB 740  'draw window
380   WINDOWSTARTX = STARTX+WINGLENGTH+9*CENTRELENGTH/10-CENTRELENGTH/7
390   GOSUB 740  'draw window
400   WINDOWSTARTY = STARTY+HEIGHT/7
410   GOSUB 740  'draw window
420 RETURN

430 'SUBROUTINE draw wing windows
440   WINDOWSTARTX = WINGSTARTX+WINGLENGTH/5
450   WINDOWSTARTY = WINGSTARTY+HEIGHT/7
460   WINDOWWIDTH = WINGLENGTH/5
470   WINDOWHEIGHT = HEIGHT/3
```

Program 1.11 Draws a Georgian house.

```
 10 CLS
 20 INPUT "File name",FILE$
 30 SCREEN 2 : CLS
 35 WINDOW (-640,-400)-(639,399)
 40 XS = 0 : YS = 0
 50 FILENUM = 3
 70 FOR MOTIF = 1 TO 3
 80   GOSUB 200  'draw motif
 90   XS = XS+100 : YS = YS+100
100 NEXT MOTIF
110 END

200 'SUBROUTINE draw motif at XS, YS
210   OPEN FILE$ FOR INPUT AS #FILENUM
214   PSET (XS,YS)
220   WHILE NOT EOF(FILENUM)
230     INPUT #FILENUM,X,Y
240     LINE -(X+XS,Y+YS)
250   WEND
260 CLOSE FILENUM
270 RETURN
```

Program 1.12 Uses a subroutine that draws a picture from a file.

Other variables provide local workspace in which a subroutine can store temporary values while it is being obeyed. For example, the subroutine 'draw a window' uses several variables in this category.

In the next example (Program 1.12) we have encapsulated the WHILE structure of Program 1.9 in a subroutine. This draws a line image from a file relative to a start point and introduces the idea of drawing a picture or subpicture at many different points on the screen.

The subroutine draws a line image from a start point that is supplied as input information in the form of global variables. In Figure 1.13 the start coordinates are calculated so that they lie on the circumference of a circle, lie on the locus of a spiral, lie on a sine wave or form a checkerboard pattern. Note that the spiral pattern also needs a change of scale between each drawing sequence. Program 1.12, as listed, draws three images on a diagonal line.

IF statements

A common use of IF THEN statements in graphics programming is in menu selection. This idea will be further developed in Chapter 2 when we come to look at interactive graphics. The idea is demonstrated in Program 1.13 which should be self-explanatory.

Another common use of IF statements in computer graphics is illustrated in Program 1.14. This is a generalization of Program 1.9

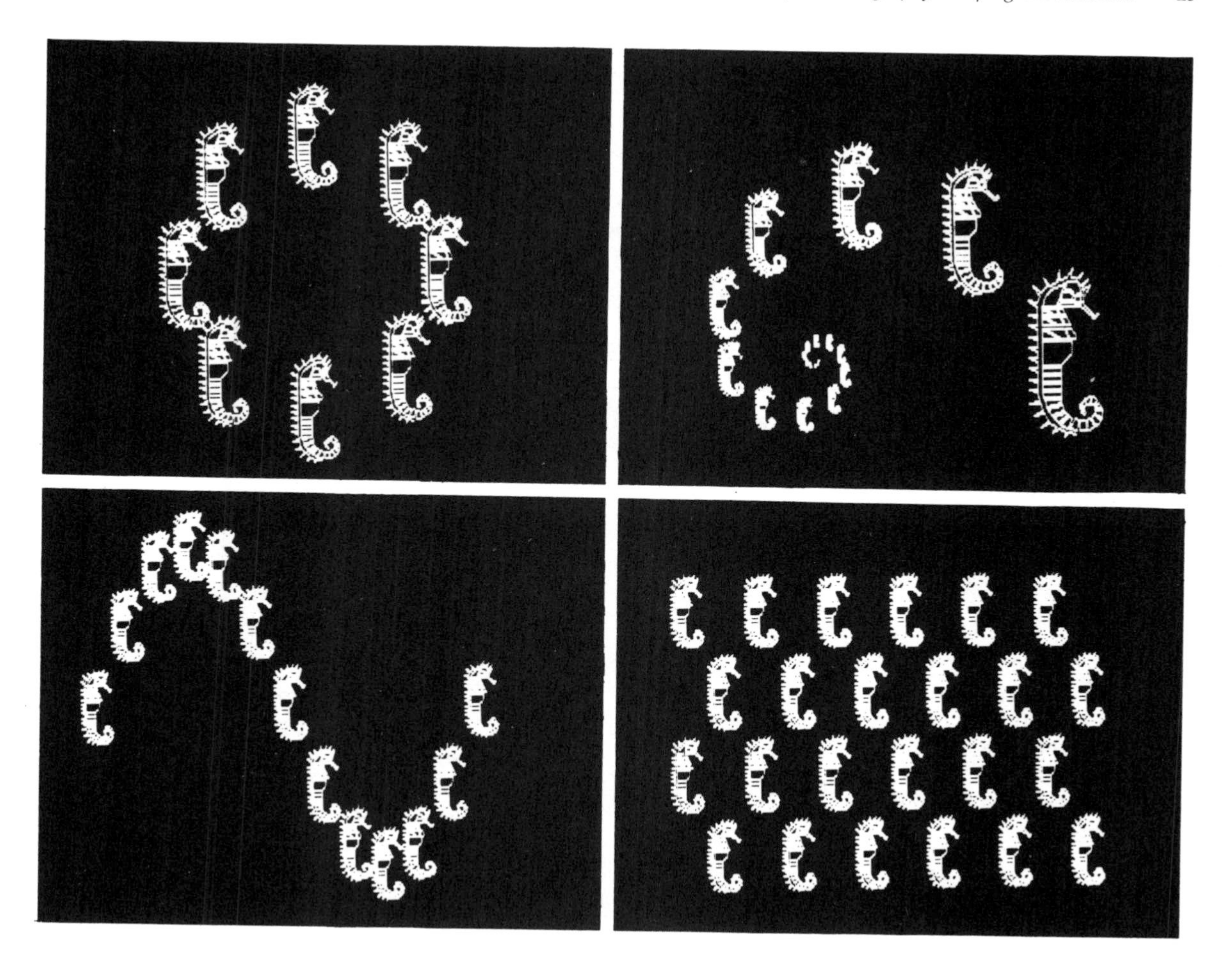

Figure 1.13
Output from Program 1.12: a sea horse drawing subroutine is supplied with positional information

and draws an image from a data set that consists of triples – a pair of coordinates together with a code indicating whether the point has to be moved to or drawn to. Instead of being constrained to representing a continuous line drawing, the data can now represent a general image that may contain moves to new sections as well as line segment sets representing continuous lines.

```
10 SCREEN 2 : CLS
20 WINDOW (-640,-400)-(639,399)
30 INPUT SELECTION$
40 IF SELECTION$ = "c" THEN GOSUB 200  'draw a circle
50 IF SELECTION$ = "t" THEN GOSUB 300  'draw a triangle
60 IF SELECTION$ = "r" THEN GOSUB 400  'draw a rectangle
```

Program 1.13 Simple menu selection.

```
 10 CLS
 20 INPUT "File name",FILE$
 30 SCREEN 2 : CLS
 40 WINDOW (-640,-400)-(639,399)
 50 FILENUM = 3
 60 OPEN FILE$ FOR INPUT AS #FILENUM
 90 WHILE NOT EOF(FILENUM)
100   INPUT #FILENUM,OP,X,Y
110   IF OP = 0 THEN PSET (X,Y) ELSE IF OP = 1 THEN LINE -(X,Y)
120 WEND
130 CLOSE
140 END
```

Program 1.14 Draws a picture from a file (which includes codes for move or draw).

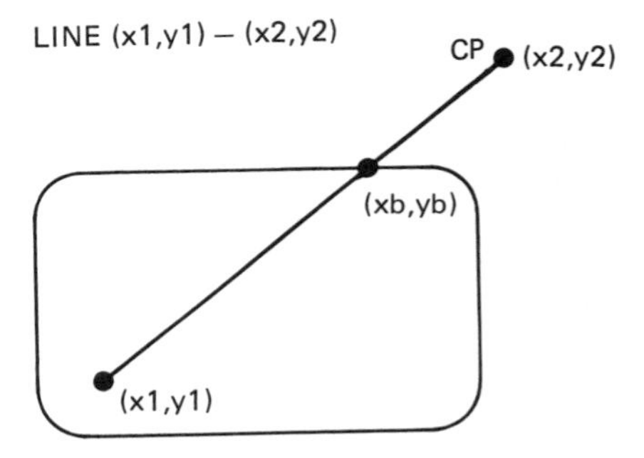

Figure 1.14
Clipping handled by the graphics system: the user specifies a line from (x1,y1) to (x2,y2), and the graphics system calculates (xb,yb) and sets the C(urrent) P(osition) to (x2,y2)

1.3 WINDOWS AND VIEWPORTS

In this section we will examine the graphics concept of a viewport and look at the relationship between a viewport and the facility already introduced – WINDOW. In IBM PC BASIC there is a facility, WINDOW, that allows us to work in context-dependent 'world' coordinates. WINDOW was introduced as a facility to avoid the inconvenience of working in the screen coordinate system. How-

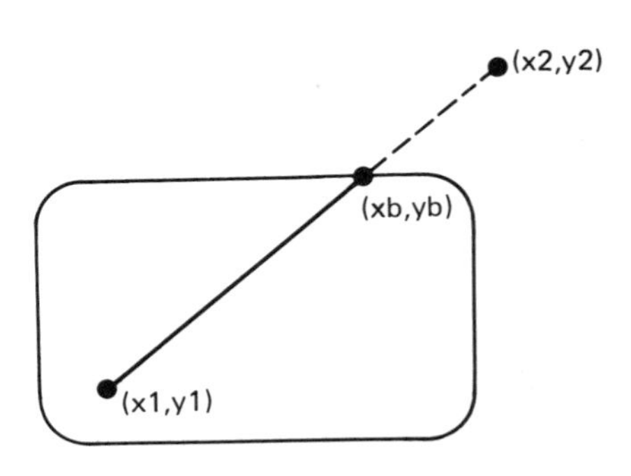

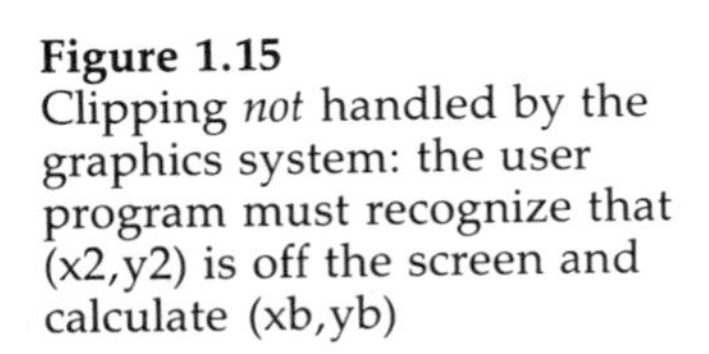

Figure 1.15
Clipping *not* handled by the graphics system: the user program must recognize that (x2,y2) is off the screen and calculate (xb,yb)

Figure 1.16
WINDOW transformation of the scene in Figure 1.10

ever, WINDOW does more than that – it also provides a clipping facility. Any points, referenced by a program, that are outside the range of the defined world coordinate system are automatically catered for, and the intersection of any lines to such points and the screen boundary are calculated. This is illustrated in Figure 1.14. It is a very useful facility in advanced computer graphics. If the facility was not available, as is the case with many microcomputers, then the programmer must either ensure that he or she keeps within the screen limits, or he or she must calculate the intersections of lines with the screen boundary – a distinctly non-trivial task (Figure 1.15). It is this clipping feature that gives the window facility its name. The window defines what the programmer wants to see on the screen. He or she then looks through a window (the screen) into an unbounded world coordinate system.

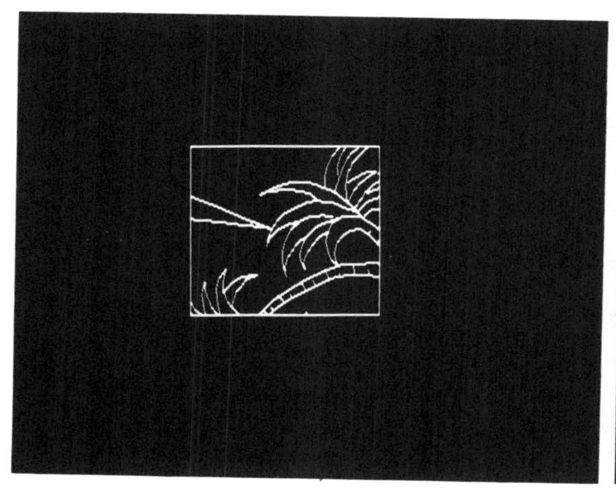

Figure 1.17
Different windows, same viewport

Figure 1.18
Same window, different viewports

A viewport, on the other hand, establishes where the window contents have to appear on the screen. The viewport can be made smaller than the screen and still contain the window contents. This concept is illustrated in Figure 1.10 which shows a scene plotted from DATA statements. Figure 1.16 shows two different windows of the scene obtained by using WINDOW. Figure 1.17 shows these two windows mapped into a much smaller viewport. Figure 1.18 shows the same window appearing twice on the screen using different viewports.

Having explained the difference between windows and viewports we will now look at how these are implemented in IBM PC BASIC. To do this we will develop an example in three stages. Program 1.15 is simple enough and draws a square using a subroutine module. The point (0,0) is near the centre of the screen and the DATA statements are defined to draw a square centred on (0,0). These are the world coordinates and WINDOW is defined accordingly.

```
 10 SCREEN 1 : CLS
 20 WINDOW (-245,-150)-(245,150)
 30 GOSUB 100  'draws a square
 40 END

100 'SUBROUTINE draws a square
110   READ X,Y : LINE -(X,Y),0
120   FOR I = 1 TO 4
130     READ X,Y : LINE -(X,Y),1
140   NEXT
150   DATA -50,-50,50,-50,50,50,-50,50,-50,-50
160 RETURN
```

Program 1.15 Draws a square.

Figure 1.19
Rotating squares

Program 1.16 draws the ubiquitous pattern of rotating squares (Figure 1.19). An initial square is drawn as before and each subsequent square is reduced in size and rotated by 10° about the point (0,0). The program structure is effectively a nested loop. One loop which draws the lines is nested inside the main program loop which draws the squares. The main program loop increases 'THETA' and reduces 'SCALE'. To get the rotated square 'X' and 'Y' are operated on by 'SCALE' and 'THETA'. These formulae can be accepted

```
 10 PI = 3.141593
 20 SCALE = 1.7
 30 SCREEN 1 : CLS
 31 THETA = 0
 40 WINDOW (-245,-150)-(245,150)
 50 FOR SQUARE = 1 TO 20
 60   GOSUB 100  'draws a square
 70   THETA = THETA + 10 : SCALE = SCALE*0.85
 80 NEXT SQUARE
 90 END

100 'SUBROUTINE draws a square
105   RESTORE
110   FOR I = 1 TO 5
130     READ X,Y
140     XT = SCALE*(X*COS(THETA*PI/180)+Y*SIN(THETA*PI/180))
150     YT = SCALE*(Y*COS(THETA*PI/180)-X*SIN(THETA*PI/180))
160     IF I = 1 THEN PSET (XT,YT),0 ELSE LINE -(XT,YT),1
170   NEXT
180   DATA -50,-50,50,-50,50,50,-50,50,-50,-50
190 RETURN
```

Program 1.16 Draws the rotating square pattern.

Figure 1.20
Rotating squares in six different viewports

without worrying about the mathematics. Note the IF statement that controls the use of PSET or LINE. This problem has been made quite easy by using a world coordinate system centred on the origin. Now look at Figure 1.20. This is a complete pattern made up of an

```
 10 PI = 3.141593
 20 SCREEN 1 : CLS
 30 WINDOW (-245,-150)-(245,150)
 40 FOR YV = 0 TO 66  STEP 66
 50   FOR  XV = 0 TO 132 STEP 66
 60     VIEW (XV,YV)-(XV+160,YV+100)
 70     SCALE = 2 : THETA = 0
 80     FOR SQUARE = 1 TO 10
 90       GOSUB 150  'draws a square
100       THETA = THETA + 10 : SCALE = SCALE*0.85
110     NEXT SQUARE
120   NEXT XV
130 NEXT YV
140 END

150 'SUBROUTINE draws a square
160   RESTORE
170   FOR I = 1 TO 5
180     READ X,Y
190     XT = SCALE*(X*COS(THETA*PI/180)+Y*SIN(THETA*PI/180))
200     YT = SCALE*(Y*COS(THETA*PI/180)-X*SIN(THETA*PI/180))
210     IF I = 1 THEN PSET (XT,YT),0 ELSE LINE -(XT,YT),1
220   NEXT
230   DATA -50,-50,50,-50,50,50,-50,50,-50,-50
240 RETURN
```

Program 1.17 Draws the rotating square pattern in different viewports.

Figure 1.21
Rotating squares in overlapping viewports

array of the patterns produced by Program 1.16. Each pattern is smaller than before. To generate this array we simply use six different viewports and place the window contents in each viewport. Program 1.17 produced the pattern. The structure of this program is a quadruple nested FOR loop with the innermost loop contained in a subroutine. The innermost and next innermost loops draw the pattern, as before, using the world coordinate system with (0,0) at the centre of the screen. The outermost two loops control the (x,y) positions of each of the six viewports. These are set up using:

```
VIEW (x1,y1) - (x2,y2), attribute, boundary
```

`(x1,y1)` are the upper left coordinates of the viewport.

`(x2,y2)` are the lower right coordinates of the viewport.

These can be followed by the optional parameters:

`attribute` the colour code that can be used to fill the complete viewport.

`boundary` the attribute of a colour that can be used to draw a boundary line around the viewport.

Changing the x,y values in WINDOW and VIEW gives us Figure 1.21, which is completely different from Figure 1.20. This is because we have set up overlapping viewports. As each viewport is filled it wipes out part of an existing viewport.

Another example of the use of viewports is given by Program 1.20. First consider Program 1.18. This generates and plots a simple harmonic function – a sine wave. The y value for the graph is given by a call to the standard function 'SIN'. The x value, used as a function argument, is set by a FOR loop. In Program 1.19 four exponentially damped sine waves of different damping factor are

```
 10 PI = 3.141593
 20 SCREEN 2 : CLS
 30 WINDOW (0,-400)-(1279,399)
 40 LINE (0,-300)-(0,300)
 50 LINE (1280,0)-(0,0)
 60 YSCALE = 200
 70 FOR X = 0 TO 1279 STEP 10
 80   RADIANS = X*PI/180
 90   Y = SIN(RADIANS)
100   LINE -(X,Y*YSCALE)
110 NEXT X
120 END
```

Program 1.18 Draws a sine wave.

plotted. Each sine wave appears in a different viewport. Program 1.20 is the same as Program 1.19 except that suitable legendry has been addded. Legendry and graphs is a topic that is fully explored in detail later.

Zooming and panning

As we have seen, if a window smaller than the image or the scene is

```
  5 PI = 3.141593
 10 SCREEN 2 : CLS
 20 YSCALE = 225 : XSCALE = 0.25
 30 OX = 0 : OY = 0 : A = 2
 40 GOSUB 120  'draw the graph
 50 OX = 0 : OY = 100 : A = 1
 60 GOSUB 120  'draw the graph
 70 OX = 320 : OY = 0 : A = 0.5
 80 GOSUB 120  'draw the graph
 90 OX = 320 : OY = 100 : A = 0.25
100 GOSUB 120  'draw the graph
110 END

120 'SUBROUTINE draw the graph
130   VIEW (OX,OY)-(OX+319,OY+99)
140   WINDOW (0,-200)-(319,200)
150   LINE (0,-180)-(0,180)
160   LINE (290,0)-(0,0)
170   FOR I = 1 TO 1000 STEP 10
180     RADIANS = I*PI/180
190     Y = SIN(RADIANS)*EXP(-A*I/200)
200     LINE -(I*XSCALE,Y*YSCALE)
210   NEXT I
220 RETURN
```

Program 1.19 Draws four damped sine waves in different viewports.

```
  5 PI = 3.141593
 10 SCREEN 2 : CLS
 20 YSCALE = 225 : XSCALE = 0.25
 30 OX = 0 : OY = 0 : A = 2 : TY = 2 : TX = 15
 40 GOSUB 130  'draw the graph
 50 OX = 0 : OY = 100 : A = 1 : TY = 14 : TX = 15
 60 GOSUB 130  'draw the graph
 70 OX = 320 : OY = 0 : A = 0.5 : TY = 2 : TX = 55
 80 GOSUB 130  'draw the graph
 90 OX = 320 : OY = 100 : A = 0.25 : TY = 14 : TX = 55
100 GOSUB 130  'draw the graph
110 ANY$ = INKEY$ : IF ANY$ ="" THEN 110
120 END

130 'SUBROUTINE draw the graph
140   VIEW (OX,OY)-(OX+319,OY+99)
150   WINDOW (0,-200)-(319,200)
160   LOCATE TY,TX
170   PRINT "a = ";A;
180   LINE (0,-180)-(0,180)
190   LINE (290,0)-(0,0)
200   FOR I = 1 TO 1000 STEP 10
210     RADIANS = I*PI/180
220     Y = SIN(RADIANS)*EXP(-A*I/200)
230     LINE -(I*XSCALE,Y*YSCALE)
240   NEXT I
250 RETURN
```

Program 1.20 Adds legendry to the damped sine waves.

specified, the image is clipped. If we then specify a viewport equal to the screen area and display the contents of the window, the clipped image is magnified. Repeating this process for successively smaller windows is equivalent to the cinematic effect of 'zooming in'. Alternatively, we can 'zoom out' by applying the reverse process.

We can apply a zoom transformation easily by using the default viewport – the whole screen – and re-displaying the image:

```
WX1 = -640 : WY1 = -400 : WX2 = 640 : WY2 = 400
FOR ZOOM = 1 TO 4
  WINDOW (WX1/ZOOM, WY1/ZOOM) - (WX2/ZOOM, WY2/ZOOM)
  CLS : GOSUB 1000  'draws the image
NEXT ZOOM
```

Figure 1.22 shows the effect of this operation. The cinematic effect of 'panning' is achieved by defining a series of (smaller than full size) windows in some given direction. For horizontal panning we would

Figure 1.22
Four 'frames' in zoom sequence

define another window to the left of the first, etc.

```
WX1 = -340 : WY1 = -400 : WX2 = 940 : WY2 = 400
FOR PAN = 0 TO 3
  WINDOW (WX1-PAN*200, WY1) - (WX2-PAN*200, WY2)
  CLS : GOSUB 1000  'draws the image
NEXT PAN
```

Figure 1.23 shows the effect of panning achieved by using this program outline.

1.4 TREND GRAPH PROGRAM TECHNIQUES

In this section, we will look at how numerical data can be displayed in graphical form using the familiar frameworks of trend graphs and histograms. Computer graphics is now used universally, not only in

Figure 1.23
Four 'frames' in a panning sequence

business and scientific programs dealing with numerical data, but in games and recreational programs. In the case of numerical data the power of flexible graphics displays is self-evident. It is much easier to interpret large volumes of numerical data when the data is presented pictorially. Overall trends are easily spotted and the relationship between data items is easily seen. The addition of colour to such a display adds yet another dimension. The simplest and most familiar data display is a trend graph and this will be dealt with first.

Program 1.21 is a simple program that plots an unlabelled trend graph. Twelve sales figures for 12 months are read from a DATA statement and are used to construct a piecewise linear graph where each point in the data is joined to the previous part by a straight line. A WINDOW statement is used to enable plotting in the world coordinate system, which in this case is 1–12 (months) in the posi-

```
480   GOSUB 740  'draw window
490   WINDOWSTARTX = WINDOWSTARTX+2*WINGLENGTH/5
500   GOSUB 740  'draw window
510   WINDOWSTARTY = WINDOWSTARTY+11*HEIGHT/24
520   GOSUB 740  'draw window
530   WINDOWSTARTX = WINGSTARTX+WINGLENGTH/5
540   GOSUB 740  'draw window
550 RETURN

560 'SUBROUTINE initialise
570   STARTX = 50 : STARTY = 200
580   WINGLENGTH = 300 : HEIGHT = 480
590   CENTRELENGTH = 480
600 RETURN

610 'SUBROUTINE draw wing roof
620   LINE (WINGSTARTX,WINGSTARTY)-(WINGSTARTX+WINGLENGTH/2,WINGSTARTY+HEIGHT/3)
630   LINE -(WINGSTARTX+WINGLENGTH,WINGSTARTY)
640 RETURN

650 'SUBROUTINE draw door
660   DWIDTH = CENTRELENGTH/3.5 : DHEIGHT = HEIGHT/2.1
670   LX4 = STARTX+WINGLENGTH+CENTRELENGTH/2-DWIDTH/2 : LY4 = STARTY
680   LINE (LX4,LY4)-(LX4+DWIDTH,LY4+DHEIGHT),,B
690   LINE (LX4+DWIDTH/5,LY4+DHEIGHT/6)-(LX4+2*DWIDTH/5,LY4+13*DHEIGHT/15),,B
700   LINE (LX4+3*DWIDTH/5,LY4+DHEIGHT/6)-(LX4+4*DWIDTH/5,LY4+13*DHEIGHT/15),,B
710   LINE (LX4,LY4+DHEIGHT)-(LX4+DWIDTH/2,LY4+8*DHEIGHT/7)
720   LINE -(LX4+DWIDTH,LY4+DHEIGHT)
730 RETURN

740 'SUBROUTINE draw window
750   LINE (WINDOWSTARTX,WINDOWSTARTY)-(WINDOWSTARTX+WINDOWWIDTH,
        WINDOWSTARTY+WINDOWHEIGHT),,B
760   XPANE = WINDOWWIDTH/4 : YPANE = WINDOWHEIGHT/5
770   LY2 = WINDOWSTARTY
780   FOR PANE = 1 TO 5
790     LY2 = LY2+YPANE : LINE (WINDOWSTARTX,LY2)-(WINDOWSTARTX+WINDOWWIDTH,LY2)
800   NEXT PANE
810   LX2 = WINDOWSTARTX
820   FOR PANE = 1 TO 3
830     LX2 = LX2+XPANE : LINE (LX2,WINDOWSTARTY)-(LX2,WINDOWSTARTY+WINDOWHEIGHT)
840   NEXT PANE
850 RETURN

860 'SUBROUTINE draw centre roof
870   LY5 = STARTY+HEIGHT+HEIGHT/3 : LDY = HEIGHT/30
880   LX5 = STARTX+WINGLENGTH/2 : LDX = WINGLENGTH/20
890   LENGTH = CENTRELENGTH+WINGLENGTH
900   FOR I = 1 TO 10
910     LINE (LX5,LY5)-(LX5+LENGTH,LY5)
920     LX5 = LX5+LDX : LY5 = LY5-LDY
930     LENGTH = LENGTH-2*LDX
940   NEXT I
950 RETURN
```

```
 10 SCREEN 1
 20 CLS
 30 LINE -(0,0),0
 40 WINDOW (1,0)-(12,5000)
 50 LINE  (1,0)-(12,0),1
 60 LINE (1,0)-(1,5000),1
 70 PSET (1,0)
 80 FOR MONTH = 1 TO 12
 90   READ SALES
100   LINE -(MONTH,SALES),2
110 NEXT MONTH
120 DATA 1023,2056,4132,4188,3021,4032,2020,1003,500,405,700,1051
```

Program 1.21 Draws an unlabelled trend graph.

tive x direction and 0–5000 (sales) in the positive y direction. Even an unlabelled graph is easier to interpret than a list of 12 figures – it is immediately apparent in this case that there is a depression at the fifth month (Figure 1.24). In this program it is known *a priori* that the maximum sales figure does not exceed 5000 and the WINDOW statement can be set up accordingly.

A common situation is that this is not known and the data has to be examined in advance before the graph can be plotted. Program 1.22 deals with this situation. Here we assume that the maximum value of 'SALES' is not known in advance. This has to be found and inserted into the WINDOW statement. This is done by initially scanning through the data and using an IF statement to compare each value of 'SALES' with the maximum value so far found. When the loop is complete the largest sales figure will be stored in

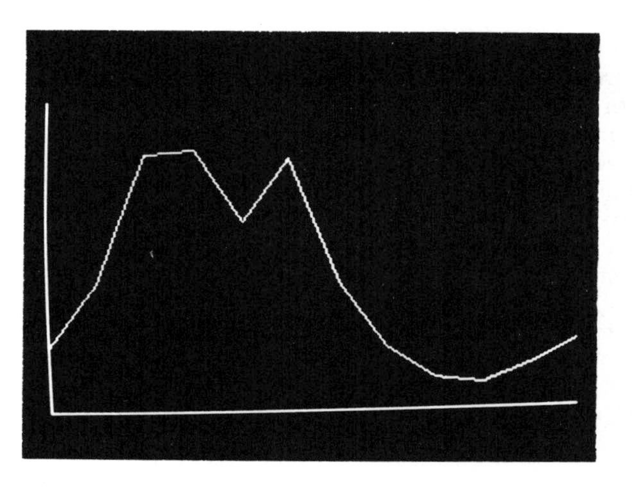

Figure 1.24
A simple trend graph

```
10 SCREEN 1
20 CLS
25 MAXSOFAR = 0
30 FOR MONTH = 1 TO 12
40   READ SALES
50   IF SALES > MAXSOFAR THEN MAXSOFAR = SALES
60 NEXT MONTH
70 LINE -(0,0),0
80 WINDOW (1,0)-(12,MAXSOFAR)
90 LINE  (1,0)-(12,0),1
100 LINE (1,0)-(1,5000),1
110 PSET (1,0)
120 RESTORE
130 FOR MONTH = 1 TO 12
140   READ SALES
150   LINE -(MONTH,SALES),2
160 NEXT MONTH
170 DATA 1023,2056,4132,4188,3021,4032,2020,1003,500,405,700,1051
```

Program 1.22 Uses a WINDOW statement that depends on the data.

'MAXSOFAR' and this can be used in the WINDOW statement. This is a simple example of matching the scale of a graph to the magnitude of the data. In a more general case neither the maximum *y* value nor the minimum *y* value (here assumed zero) will be known. A similar calculation can be performed for the minimum *y* value and inserted into a WINDOW statement. In most trend graph applications the extent of the *x* coordinate is known. For example, if time is the *x* variable, data may have been collected at hourly, daily or weekly intervals. In a population study, age may be the *x* variable.

Labelling trend graphs

The next consideration in trend graphs is labelling. This is a little problematic because, although a world coordinate system can be used to plot the actual graph and axes, a SCREEN-dependent coordinate system must be used to position characters on the screen

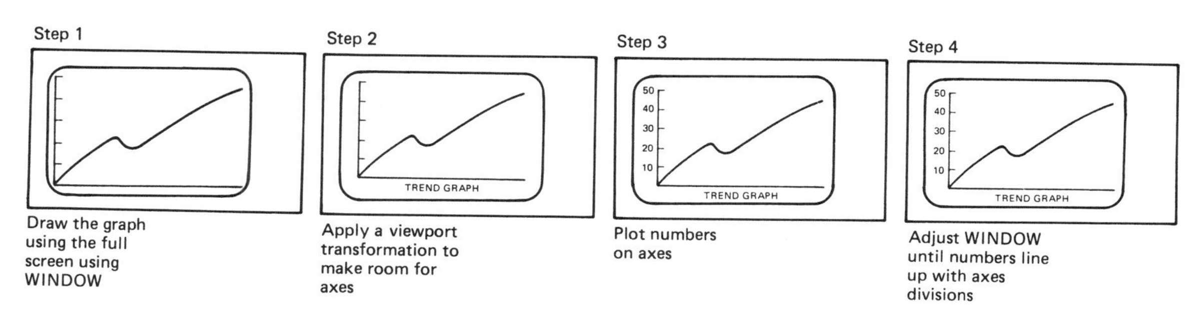
Step 1
Draw the graph using the full screen using WINDOW
Step 2
TREND GRAPH
Apply a viewport transformation to make room for axes
Step 3
50
40
30
20
10
TREND GRAPH
Plot numbers on axes
Step 4
50
40
30
20
10
TREND GRAPH
Adjust WINDOW until numbers line up with axes divisions

Figure 1.25
Programming steps in plotting a trend graph

(using LOCATE). The easiest approach to accurately label the axes with numbers is to draw the graph first of all using the world coordinate system. This can then be 'shrunk' into an appropriate viewport using VIEW to make room for axes labelling. LOCATE and PRINT can then be used to label the axes. If the divisions on an axis are clearly indicated with small marks, it can then be verified that the characters line up with the marks. If they do not, then the character positions are adjusted, if possible, by changing LOCATE, and then fine tuning is achieved by altering the WINDOW statement. This process is summarized in Figure 1.25.

```
 10 SCREEN 2
 20 CLS
 30 KEY OFF
 40 WINDOW (1,0)-(12,5000)
 50 VIEW (50,0)-(575,170)
 60 LINE (1,0)-(12,0),1
 70 LINE (1,0)-(1,5000),1
 80 PSET (1,0)
 90 FOR MONTH = 1 TO 12
100   READ SALES
110   LINE -(MONTH,SALES)
120 NEXT MONTH
130 DATA 1023,2056,4132,4188,3021,4032,2020,1003,500,405,700,1051
140 GOSUB 170  'add legendry
150 WHILE K$="" : K$=INKEY$ : WEND
160 END

170 'SUBROUTINE adds legendry to graph
180   FOR MONTH = 1 TO 12
190     LOCATE 23 ,MONTH*6
200     PRINT USING "##";MONTH
210     LINE (MONTH,0)-(MONTH,100)
220   NEXT MONTH
230   LOCATE 24,35 : PRINT "MONTH";
240   ROW = 1 : LOCATE ROW
250   FOR SALES = 5000 TO 1000 STEP -1000
260     PRINT SALES
270     ROW = ROW+4
280     LOCATE ROW
290     LINE (1,SALES)-(1.1,SALES)
300   NEXT SALES
310   LINE (7,3000)-(11,4500),1,BF
320   LOCATE 4,50
330   PRINT "RIPOV"
340   LOCATE 5,50 : PRINT "Double glazing"
350   LOCATE 6,50 : PRINT "1984 sales"
360 RETURN
```

Program 1.23 Adding labelling to the trend graph.

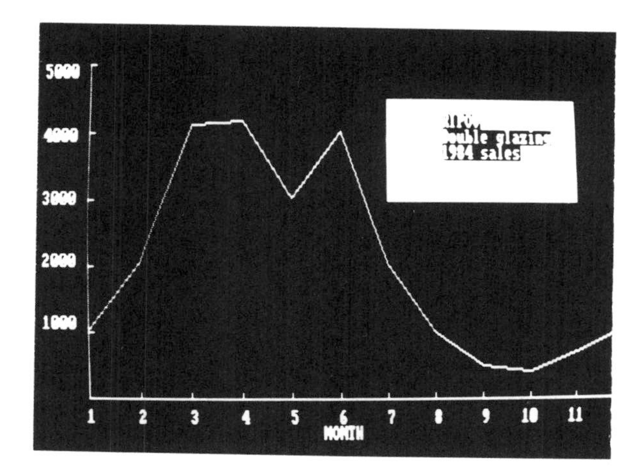

Figure 1.26
A trend graph with labelled axes

Program 1.23 is the same as Program 1.21 except that both axes are appropriately labelled using the aforementioned technique. The WINDOW statement is used to establish the world coordinate system. The graph is plotted and displayed in a viewport that leaves a margin down the left side of the screen and a margin along the bottom of the screen for the numerical labels. These are set up in a subroutine using LOCATE. In Program 1.23 SCREEN 2 has been used, and the use of LOCATE constrains the coordinate system to 24 rows and 80 columns. Remember also that the text coordinates in LOCATE are:

```
LOCATE row, col
```

and this refers to an origin in the top left hand corner of the screen. Also the sense of 'X' and 'Y' (now column and row) are reversed. Figure 1.26 shows the output from the program. Any inconsistency between the numeric labels and the axis division marks can now be adjusted by using the VIEW statement. This system of adding characters is less than perfect and not a little tedious. Ideally we would like to position characters in the world coordinate system and then have them processed by WINDOW and VIEW. Unfortunately, however, there is no alternative to working in the world coordinate system for graphics and the text coordinate system for text. In fact using VIEW brings in yet another coordinate system, because the parameters for VIEW have to be given in the SCREEN-dependent coordinate system.

Multiple trend graphs

In this section we will look at various techniques that can be employed to handle multiple trend graphs. The first thing we can do is to display, say four, graphs in the four quadrants of the screen. Program 1.24 does this and Figure 1.27 shows the output from the

```
 10 SCREEN 1
 20 CLS
 30 KEY OFF
 40 WINDOW (1,0)-(12,5000)
 50 VIEW (0,0)-(150,90)
 60 LOCATE 4,12
 70 GOSUB 180  'draws first graph
 80 VIEW (160,0)-(310,90)
 90 LOCATE 4,32
100 GOSUB 180  'draws the second graph
110 VIEW (0,100)-(150,190)
120 LOCATE 16,12
130 GOSUB 180  'draws the third graph
140 VIEW (160,100)-(310,190)
150 LOCATE 16,32
160 GOSUB 180  'draws the fourth graph
170 END

180 'SUBROUTINE draws a complete graph
190   READ YEAR
200   LINE (7,2800)-(12,4500),1,BF
210   PRINT YEAR
220   LINE (1,0)-(12,0),1
230   LINE (1,0)-(1,5000),1
240   PSET (1,0)
250   FOR MONTH = 1 TO 12
260     READ SALES
270     LINE -(MONTH,SALES),2
280   NEXT MONTH
290 RETURN

300 DATA 1984, 1023,2056,4132,4188,3021,4032,2020,1003,500,405,700,1051
310 DATA 1985, 1027,3054,4900,4700,3500,3600,2700,1500,1700,300,900,2000
320 DATA 1986, 700,2900,4300,4500,3900,4200,3500,1740,2000,1500,500,200
330 DATA 1987, 300,1500,3500,3200,3900,4200,3200,1005,2500,1400,200,20,680
```

Program 1.24 Draws four trend graphs.

program. A subroutine that has the same structure as Program 1.21 draws a complete graph. This is called four times to draw four complete graphs. Each time a different call to VIEW sets up a different viewport and each graph is 'shrunk' into a screen quadrant. Also, between subroutine calls, LOCATE is used to set up a text position for a PRINT statement inside the subroutine that prints a graph label (a year). The label for each graph is placed at the beginning of each of four DATA statements (one for each graph).

Program 1.25 (a PCjr program) shows another common technique. This time the four graphs are superimposed in four different colours and the whole screen area is used. SCREEN 5 (a 16-colour mode) is used and this allows the use of four graph colours plus one

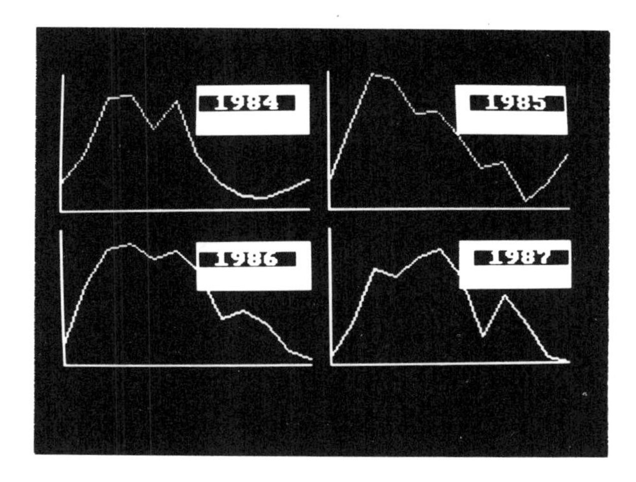

Figure 1.27
Multiple trend graphs

colour for the axis. A similar technique to that of Program 1.25 can be used on the PC, but of course only three colours (plus background) can be used.

Note the use of the CLEAR statement in line 10 of Program 1.25. SCREEN 5 is a 320×200 pixels, 16-colour mode and requires 32K of memory. This amount of screen memory is not normally available. (16K is the default value.)

```
CLEAR,,,32768
```

sets up a screen memory partition of 32K as required for SCREEN 5 (or SCREEN 6) on the PCjr.

Program 1.26 (PCjr only) uses a different technique that allows the screen memory to be divided into separate pages. A page is the term used to describe a memory partition that will store one screen. The amount of memory in a page is thus dependent on the screen mode. In a medium resolution four colour screen, the memory required is

$$320 \times 200 \text{ pixels} \times 2 \text{ bits} = 16 \text{ Kbytes}$$

Four pages of screen memory are used and a different graph is plotted in each page. A desired page can then be instantaneously chosen by simply pressing an appropriate key. Figure 1.28 shows the output from each page. If you run the program you will find that each graph takes just under a second to plot. It then 'disappears' (the fourth graph remains on the screen). Pressing keys 1, 2, 3 or 4 will then make the first, second, third or fourth graph appear instantaneously. This has the effect of selecting or 'making visual' one of the four pages, each of which contains a single graph (Figure 1.29). Plotting in separate pages is effected by using the optional parameters in SCREEN. Program 1.26 uses SCREEN 4 (320×200

```
 10 CLEAR,,,32768!
 20 SCREEN 5
 30 CLS
 40 KEY OFF
 50 COLOR 15
 60 WINDOW (1,0)-(12,5000)
 70 LINE (1,0)-(12,0)
 80 LINE (1,0)-(1,5000)
 90 PSET (1,0)
100 COLOR 12
110 GOSUB 190  'draws first graph
120 COLOR 10
130 GOSUB 190  'draws the second graph
140 COLOR 14
150 GOSUB 190  'draws the third graph
160 COLOR 11
170 GOSUB 190  'draws the fourth graph
180 END
```

Program 1.25 Draws four graphs in different colours on the same axis. (PCjr only.)

```
 10 CLEAR,,,65536!
 20 SCREEN 4 : CLS
 30 KEY OFF
 40 WINDOW (1,0)-(12,5000)
 50 SCREEN 4,,0 : CLS
 60 GOSUB 150  'draws first graph
 70 SCREEN 4,,1 : CLS
 80 GOSUB 150  'draws the second graph
 90 SCREEN 4,,2 : CLS
100 GOSUB 150  'draws the third graph
110 SCREEN 4,,3 : CLS
120 GOSUB 150  'draws the fourth graph
130 GOSUB 330  'selects one graph
140 END

150 'SUBROUTINE draws a complete graph
160   LINE (1,0)-(12,0)
170   LINE (1,0)-(1,5000)
180   PSET (1,0)
190   READ YEAR
200   LOCATE 2
210   PRINT YEAR
220   LOCATE 3,4 : PRINT "Type 1,2,3 or 4 for graph or -1 to quit"
230   FOR MONTH = 1 TO 12
240     READ SALES
```

Program 1.26 Draws four graphs in four separate pages of screen memory. (PCjr only.)

```
190 'SUBROUTINE draws a complete graph
200   READ YEAR
210   LOCATE 2
220   PRINT YEAR
230   FOR MONTH = 1 TO 12
240     READ SALES
250     LINE -(MONTH,SALES)
260   NEXT MONTH
270   PSET(1,0)
280 RETURN

290 DATA 1984, 1023,2056,4132,4188,3021,4032,2020,1003,500,405,700,1051
300 DATA 1985, 1027,3054,4900,4700,3500,3600,2700,1500,1700,300,900,2000
310 DATA 1986, 700,2900,4300,4500,3900,4200,3500,1740,2000,1500,500,200
320 DATA 1987, 300,1500,3500,3200,3900,4200,3200,1005,2500,1400,200,20,680
```

```
250     LINE -(MONTH,SALES)
260   NEXT MONTH
270   PSET(1,0)
280 RETURN

290 DATA 1984, 1023,2056,4132,4188,3021,4032,2020,1003,500,405,700,1051
300 DATA 1985, 1027,3054,4900,4700,3500,3600,2700,1500,1700,300,900,2000
310 DATA 1986, 700,2900,4300,4500,3900,4200,3500,1740,2000,1500,500,200
320 DATA 1987, 300,1500,3500,3200,3900,4200,3200,1005,2500,1400,200,20,680

330 'SUBROUTINE displays a selected graph
340   LOCATE 1,1 : INPUT "", GRAPH
350   LOCATE 1,1 : PRINT " ";
360   WHILE GRAPH <> -1
370     ON GRAPH GOTO 390,400,410,420
380     PRINT "wrong graph number" : STOP
390     SCREEN 4,,,0 : GOTO 430
400     SCREEN 4,,,1 : GOTO 430
410     SCREEN 4,,,2 : GOTO 430
420     SCREEN 4,,,3 : GOTO 430
430     'END CASE
440     LOCATE 1,1 : INPUT "", GRAPH
450     LOCATE 1,1 : PRINT " ";
460   WEND
470 RETURN
```

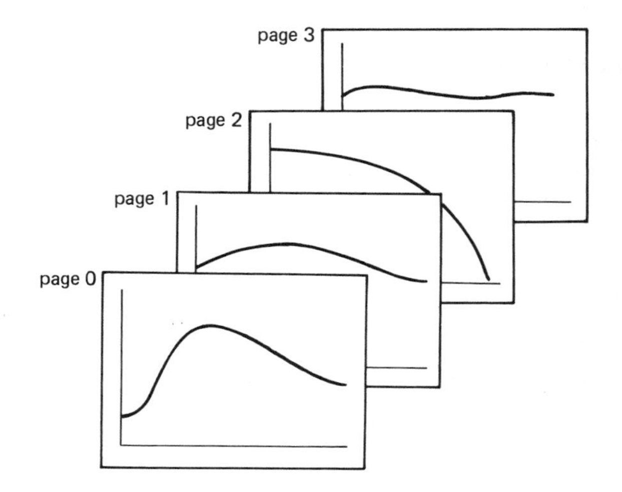

Figure 1.28
Screen memory can be quadrupled into separate pages and a graph plotted in each page

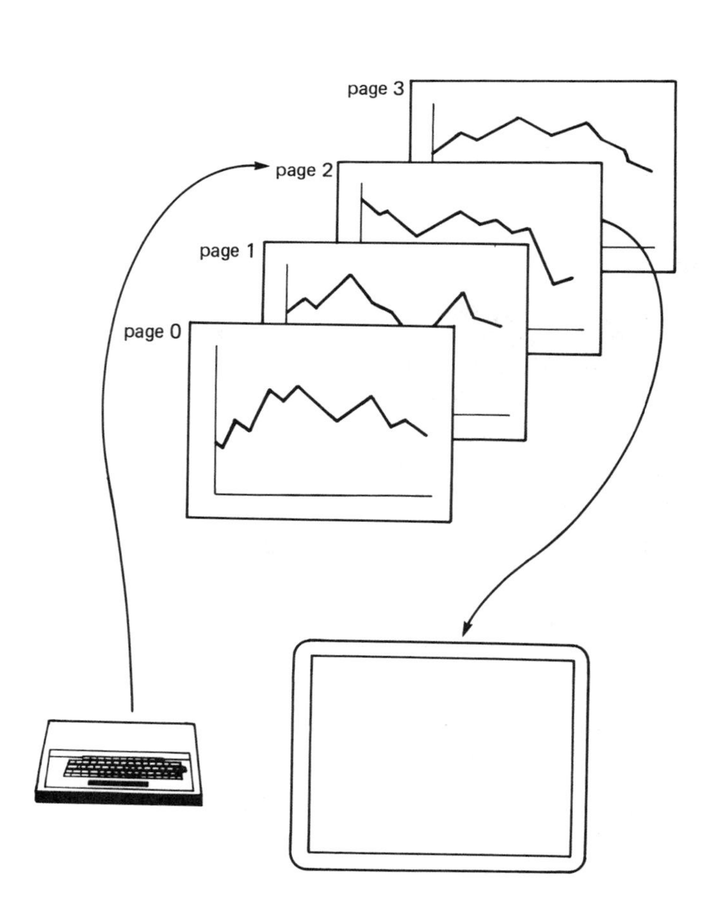

Figure 1.29
Page selection can easily be controlled from the keyboard. Here page 2 is made the visible page

pixels × 4 colours). A screen requires 16K of memory and if we are going to use four pages we need 64K. Line 10 is thus:

```
CLEAR,,,65536
```

As before, a subroutine call plots a complete graph. To direct each graph separately into each of the four pages we use:

```
SCREEN 4,,0 : CLS
```

which sends subsequent output to page 0,

```
SCREEN 4,,1 : CLS
```

which sends subsequent output to page 1,

```
SCREEN 4,,2 : CLS
```

which sends subsequent output to page 2, and

```
SCREEN 4,,3 : CLS
```

which sends subsequent output to page 3. Note that the message 'Type 1, 2, 3 or 4' is common to all screens and this message together with the axes plotting must be plotted four times – once in each page. The CLS is necessary in each case to clear the screen of any previous graph. To display the graph resident in page 0 we use:

```
SCREEN 4,,,0
```

to display the graph resident in page 1 we use:

```
SCREEN 4,,,1
```

to display the graph resident in page 2 we use:

```
SCREEN 4,,,2
```

and to display the graph resident in page 3 we use:

```
SCREEN 4,,,3
```

In the program a separate subroutine incorporates these commands in a 'case' structure that is controlled by typing keys 1, 2, 3 or 4 to display the first, second, third or fourth graph. The structure also services a signal, (-1), that terminates the process. A case structure selects one out of several alternative courses of action. One way of implementing it in IBM PC BASIC is by using the ON GOTO statement. In the program the case structure is inside a WHILE loop. This kind of facility is particularly useful in a lecture or demonstration where instantaneous switching between images is clearly advantageous. The plotting time in this example is small – this is because the image is not complex. Plotting time is a function of image complexity – or simply the number of line segments that have to be plotted. With a set of very complex images this page switching facility is extremely useful.

This technique of page switching can be used on the PC, but only with pages of text in screen 0.

The effect of page switching can be achieved in another way on the PCjr, by using palette changing techniques. These are fully described in Chapter 2.

The SCREEN statement

Now that two of the optional parameters in the SCREEN statement have been demonstrated, the applications study will be interrupted to explain the complete set of SCREEN statement parameters. The general form of the SCREEN statement is:

```
SCREEN mode, burst, apage, vpage, erase
```

`mode` — this is the mandatory parameter that selects the screen mode.

`burst` — is 0 or 1 (or in general an expression that evaluates to 0 or 1). The purpose of this parameter is to enable and disable colour. However, this parameter can be used only if you have a composite monitor rather than an RGB monitor. With a composite monitor (in certain modes) the colour image can be converted into an image of varying grey scale. In text mode (mode 0), 0 disables colour and 1 enables colour. In medium resolution (mode 1 or mode 4), 0 enables colour and 1 disables colour. This parameter has no effect for modes 2, 3, 5 or 6.

`apage` — stands for active page and is an integer in the range 0 to n. Its use has already been illustrated and a page scheme is set up by considering the memory space available and the current SCREEN mode. 'apage' determines which of the $n+1$ pages the output is sent to. If omitted, the default is the current active page. (This parameter is effective only in mode 0 on the PC.)

`vpage` — stands for visible page and is an integer in the range 0 to n, as for 'apage' above. 'vpage' selects which page is to be displayed on the screen. The visible page may be different from the active page. If omitted, the default value is the value of 'apage'. (This parameter is effective only in mode 0 on the PC.)

`erase` — is an integer expression in the range 0 to 2 and indicates how much or how little of the screen memory should be erased.

- 0 means do not erase the screen memory even if 'mode' changes.
- 1 means erase the union of the new page and the old page if 'mode' changes

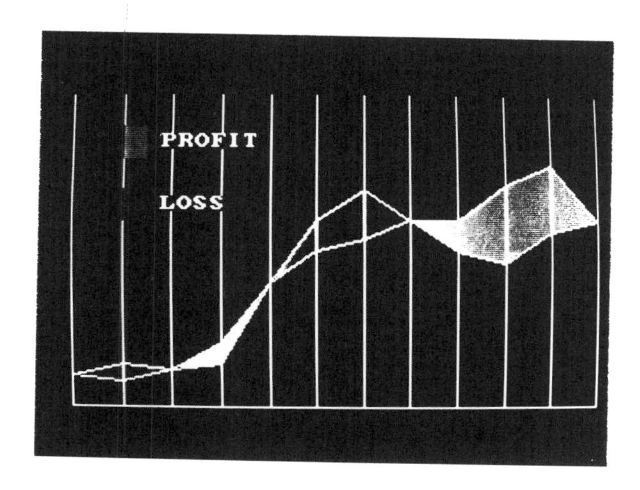

Figure 1.30
Colour fill between two trend graphs

2 means erase all of the screen memory if 'mode' changes. (This parameter is not available on the PC.)

Trend graphs and colour fill

The next example shows the effective use of colour fill with trend graphs. Colour fill is achieved by using the PAINT statement. The use of this statement, sufficient for trend graph applications, is described below. More detail on PAINT is given in Chapter 2. Two sets of data representing monthly costs and sales are plotted initially as two trend graphs. Because the lines cross over, closed regions are defined between each graph (Figure 1.30). Each region is defined by a cost boundary that is greater than the sales boundary, or vice versa, and a region can thus be filled with an appropriate colour – say green for profit (monthly sales greater than monthly costs) and red (monthly costs greater than monthly sales). Program 1.27 implements this idea. Vertical month lines are drawn over the entire screen to aid interpretation. Sales and cost data are stored this time in an array. This is necessary because they have to be compared on a month by month basis and they appear in separate DATA statements. For each month, a pair of IF statements determines whether the region is to be filled in red or green. For example, the 'green' paint statement is:

```
PAINT (MONTH, (COST(MONTH) + SALES(MONTH))/2), 1, 3
```

This gives a start coordinate for PAINT, along the month line at a y position midway between the two curves. Of course, for regions that spread over many months, many of the PAINT statements are redundant because the region has been filled by previous PAINT statements.

```
10 DIM SALES(12),COST(12)
20 SCREEN 1 : CLS
30 COLOR 0,0
40 KEY OFF
50 GOSUB 250  'draw the axes
60 FOR MONTH = 1 TO 12
70   READ SALES(MONTH)
80   LINE -(MONTH,SALES(MONTH))
90 NEXT MONTH
100 PSET (1,0)
110 FOR MONTH = 1 TO 12
120   READ COST(MONTH)
130   LINE -(MONTH,COST(MONTH))
140 NEXT MONTH
150 FOR MONTH = 1 TO 12
160   IF SALES(MONTH) > COST(MONTH) THEN
        PAINT(MONTH,(COST(MONTH)+SALES(MONTH))/2),1,3
170   IF COST(MONTH) > SALES(MONTH) THEN
        PAINT(MONTH,(COST(MONTH)+SALES(MONTH))/2),2,3
180 NEXT MONTH
190 GOSUB 330  'draws the month lines
200 GOSUB 400  'draws the legendry
230 WHILE ANY$="" : ANY$=INKEY$ : WEND : SCREEN 0
240 END
```

Program 1.27 Colour fills between two trend graphs.

Program 1.28 is the same as Program 1.27 except that a pattern is used to fill the regions. String variables 'PAINTATT1$' and 'PAINTATT2$' are defined as follows:

```
PAINTATT1$ = CHR$(&H44)
PAINTATT2$ = CHR$(&H88)
```

These give alternating on/off values for colours 1 and 2. SCREEN 1 is a four-colour mode and uses two bits per pixel. Alternating colour 1 with colour 0 requires:

decimal	1 0 1 0
binary	01000100
hex	&H44

Alternating colour 2 requires:

decimal	2 0 2 0
binary	10001000
hex	&H88

Note that the colour key boxes cannot now be filled using LINE and BF. Instead LINE has to be used with B and PAINT used again with the appropriate string variable to fill each box.

```
250 'SUBROUTINE draws the axes
260   WINDOW (1,0)-(12,5000)
270   LINE (1,0)-(1,5000)
280   LINE (1,0)-(12,0)
290   PSET (1,0)
300 RETURN

310 DATA 500,400,600,1040,2000,2500,2700,3000,3000,3600,3900,3000
320 DATA 500,700,600,700,2000,3000,3500,3000,2500,2300,2800,3000

330 'SUBROUTINE draws month lines
350   FOR MONTH = 2 TO 12
360     PSET(MONTH,0)
370     LINE -(MONTH,5000)
380   NEXT MONTH
390 RETURN

400 'SUBROUTINE draws legendry
410   LINE (2,4000)-(2.5,4500),1,BF
420   LOCATE 4,7 : PRINT "PROFIT"
430   LINE (2,3000)-(2.5,3500),2,BF
440   LOCATE 9,7 : PRINT "LOSS"
450 RETURN
```

Basic histograms

The common alternative to trend graphs is the histogram or bar graph. Here, instead of the data points being joined together to form a graph, we draw a bar whose height is equal to the data value it represents. Program 1.29 draws a histogram for two sets of data – sales and costs. Colour Plate 1a shows the output from the program. The sales data is drawn using green bars and the cost data using red bars displaced slightly to the right. Each green bar is drawn by:

```
LINE (MONTH, 0) - (MONTH+0.5, SALES), 1, BF
```

and each red bar by:

```
LINE (MONTH + 0.25, 0) - (MONTH+0.75, COST), 2, BF
```

The program structure is the same as for the trend graph display except that the bar drawing statements replace the trend line drawing statement. The green and red bars need not, of course, be displaced. They could be superimposed. This, however, makes the interpretation of data pairs which are almost equal quite difficult. In this example the data for month 10 would appear as a thin green line on top of the red bar.

The next example, Program 1.30, is a histogram or bar chart

```
 10 DIM SALES(12),COST(12)
 20 SCREEN 1 : CLS
 30 COLOR 0,0
 40 KEY OFF
 50 GOSUB 250  'draw the axes
 60 FOR MONTH = 1 TO 12
 70   READ SALES(MONTH)
 80   LINE -(MONTH,SALES(MONTH))
 90 NEXT MONTH
100 PSET (1,0)
110 FOR MONTH = 1 TO 12
120   READ COST(MONTH)
130   LINE -(MONTH,COST(MONTH))
140 NEXT MONTH
141 PAINTATT1$ = CHR$(&H44)
142 PAINTATT2$ = CHR$(&H88)
150 FOR MONTH = 1 TO 12
160   IF SALES(MONTH) > COST(MONTH) THEN
        PAINT(MONTH,(COST(MONTH)+SALES(MONTH))/2),PAINTATT1$,3
170   IF COST(MONTH) > SALES(MONTH) THEN
        PAINT(MONTH,(COST(MONTH)+SALES(MONTH))/2),PAINTATT2$,3
180 NEXT MONTH
190 GOSUB 330  'draws the month lines
200 GOSUB 400  'draws the legendry
230 WHILE ANY$="" : ANY$=INKEY$ : WEND : SCREEN 0
240 END

250 'SUBROUTINE draws the axes
260   WINDOW (1,0)-(12,5000)
270   LINE (1,0)-(1,5000)
280   LINE (1,0)-(12,0)
290   PSET (1,0)
300 RETURN

310 DATA 500,400,600,1040,2000,2500,2700,3000,3000,3600,3900,3000
320 DATA 500,700,600,700,2000,3000,3500,3000,2500,2300,2800,3000

330 'SUBROUTINE draws month lines
350   FOR MONTH = 2 TO 12
360     PSET (MONTH,0)
370     LINE -(MONTH,5000)
380   NEXT MONTH
390 RETURN

400 'SUBROUTINE draws legendry
410   LINE (2,4000)-(2.5,4500),1,B : PAINT (2.25,4250),PAINTATT1$,1
420   LOCATE 4,7 : PRINT "PROFIT"
430   LINE (2,3000)-(2.5,3500),2,B : PAINT (2.25,3250),PAINTATT2$,2
440   LOCATE 9,7 : PRINT "LOSS"
450 RETURN
```

Program 1.28 Uses a pattern for colour fill.

```
 10 SCREEN 1
 20 CLS
 30 COLOR 0,0
 40 KEY OFF
 50 WINDOW (1,0)-(12.75,5000)
 60 VIEW (25,0)-(290,170)
 70 LINE  (1,0)-(12,0)
 80 LINE (1,0)-(1,5000)
 90 PSET (1,0)
100 FOR MONTH = 1 TO 12
110   READ SALES
120   GOSUB 410  'draws a bar
130 NEXT MONTH
140 FOR MONTH = 1 TO 12
150   READ COST
160   GOSUB 440  'draws a bar
170 NEXT MONTH
180 DATA 1023,2056,4132,4188,3021,4032,2020,1003,500,405,700,1051
190 DATA 546,1567,2789,3180,2500,3409,1560,600,450,368,566,867
200 GOSUB 230  'add legendry
210 WHILE ANY$="" : ANY$=INKEY$ : WEND : SCREEN 0
220 END

230 'SUBROUTINE adds legendry to graph
240   FOR MONTH = 1 TO 12
250     LOCATE 23,MONTH*3
260     PRINT USING "##";MONTH
270   NEXT MONTH
280   LOCATE 24,17 : PRINT "MONTH";
290   ROW = 1 : LOCATE ROW,1
300   FOR SALES = 5000 TO 1000 STEP -1000
310     PRINT SALES
320     LINE (1,SALES)-(13,SALES)
330     ROW = ROW+4
340     LOCATE ROW
350   NEXT SALES
360   LINE (8,4000)-(9,4300),1,BF
370   LOCATE 4,27 : PRINT "SALES"
380   LINE (8,3500)-(9,3800),2,BF
390   LOCATE 6,27 : PRINT "COSTS"
400 RETURN

410 'SUBROUTINE draws a bar at the required height
420   LINE (MONTH,0)-(MONTH+0.5,SALES),1,BF
430 RETURN

440 'SUBROUTINE draws a bar at the required height
450   LINE (MONTH+0.25,0)-(MONTH+0.75,COST),2,BF
460 RETURN
```

Program 1.29 Superimposes two histograms (sales and costs).

```
 10 DIM SALES(12),COST(12)
 20 SCREEN 1 : CLS
 30 COLOR 0,0
 40 KEY OFF
 50 WINDOW (1,-5000)-(12.75,5000)
 60 VIEW (25,10)-(290,170)
 70 LINE (1,0)-(12,0)
 80 LINE (1,-5000)-(1,5000)
 90 PSET (1,0)
100 FOR MONTH = 1 TO 12
110   READ SALES(MONTH)
120   GOSUB 540  'draws a bar
130 NEXT MONTH
140 FOR MONTH = 1 TO 12
150   READ COST(MONTH)
160   GOSUB 570  'draws a bar
170   PAINTATT1$ = CHR$(&H44)+CHR$(&H11)
180   PAINTATT2$ = CHR$(&H88)+CHR$(&H22)
190 NEXT MONTH
200 FOR MONTH = 1 TO 12
210   DIFF = SALES(MONTH)-COST(MONTH)
220   GOSUB 600  'draws a bar
230 NEXT MONTH
240 DATA 1023,2056,4132,4188,3021,4032,2020,1003,500,405,700,1051
250 DATA 546,3500,4500,3180,2500,3409,1560,600,450,368,566,867
260 GOSUB 290  'add legendry
270 WHILE ANY$="" : ANY$=INKEY$ : WEND : SCREEN 0 : WIDTH 80
280 END

290 'SUBROUTINE adds`legendry to graph
300   ROW = 2 : LOCATE ROW
310   FOR SALES = 5000 TO 1000 STEP -1000
320     PRINT SALES
330     LINE (1,SALES)-(13,SALES)
```

Program 1.30 Draws a profit and loss histogram.

variant of the colour filled trend graph. Again the idea is to show a positive or negative difference (representing profit and loss) between two sets of data. This time the bar chart is divided into a positive (top) and negative (bottom) region (Colour Plate 1b). Sales bars (green) are plotted upwards from the centre and cost bars (red) are plotted downwards. The difference is calculated and a patterned colour fill is superimposed on the bar chart. The pattern is green if the difference is positive and red if it is negative.

Program 1.31 (output shown in Colour Plate 1c) is another common variant of histogram plotting. Each bar is now represented by a rectangular solid. This form appears to emphasize height differences compared with the flat bar chart but, of course, there is no more information on the chart – it is just a different way of

```
340      ROW = ROW+2
350      LOCATE ROW
360    NEXT SALES
370    ROW = 22 : LOCATE ROW
380    FOR SALES = -5000 TO -1000 STEP 1000
390      PRINT SALES
400      LINE (1,SALES)-(13,SALES)
410      ROW = ROW-2 : LOCATE ROW
420    NEXT SALES
430    LINE (8,4300)-(9,4600),1,BF
440    LOCATE 3,27 : PRINT "SALES"
450    LINE (8,3300)-(9,3600),2,BF
460    LOCATE 5,27 : PRINT "COSTS"
470    LINE (8,2300)-(9,2600),,B
480    PAINT (8.5,2500),PAINTATT1$,3
490    LOCATE 7,27 : PRINT "PROFITS"
500    LINE (8,1300)-(9,1600),,B
510    PAINT (8.5,1400),PAINTATT2$,3
520    LOCATE 9,27 : PRINT "LOSSES"
530 RETURN

540 'SUBROUTINE draws a bar at the required height
550    LINE (MONTH,0)-(MONTH+0.5,SALES(MONTH)),1,BF
560 RETURN

570 'SUBROUTINE draws a bar at the required height
580    LINE (MONTH,0)-(MONTH+0.5,-COST(MONTH)),2,BF
590 RETURN

600 'SUBROUTINE draws a bar at the required height
610    LINE (MONTH,0)-(MONTH+0.5,DIFF),3,B
620    IF DIFF > 0 THEN PAINT(MONTH+0.25,DIFF/2),PAINTATT1$,3
                   ELSE PAINT(MONTH+0.25,DIFF/2),PAINTATT2$,3
630 RETURN
```

representing exactly the same information. The front of each solid bar is colour filled using LINE and BF but the side and top of the solid require PAINT. The faces of the bars are rendered in different colours.

Pie charts

Another extremely common form of data representation is the pie chart. This is best used to convey information about percentages and is used almost exclusively for this purpose. For maximum effectiveness the pie chart should not be divided into more than about five or six slices. Program 1.32 (Figure 1.31) shows a possible scheme. The program reads a list of percentages from a DATA statement. Using a start angle of 45°, circle segments are then

```
10 SCREEN 1
20 CLS
30 KEY OFF
40 COLOR 0,1
50 WINDOW (1,0)-(13,5000)
60 VIEW (20,0)-(300,160)
70 LINE (1,0)-(12,0)
80 LINE (1,0)-(1,5000)
90 PSET (1,0)
100 FOR MONTH = 1 TO 12
110   READ SALES
120   GOSUB 320  'draws a bar
130 NEXT MONTH
140 DATA 1023,2056,4132,4188,3021,4032,2020,1003,500,405,700,1051
150 GOSUB 180  'add legendry
160 WHILE ANY$="" : ANY$=INKEY$ : WEND : SCREEN 0 : WIDTH 80
170 END

180 'SUBROUTINE adds legendry to graph
190   FOR MONTH = 1 TO 12
200     LOCATE 22,MONTH*3
210     PRINT USING "##";MONTH
```

Program 1.31 Draws a 'solid' histogram.

```
10 SCREEN 1
20 PI = 3.14159 : R = 70 : SLICE = 0
30 CLS
40 READ PERCENT
50 WHILE PERCENT <> -1
60   SLICE = SLICE+1
70   ANGLE = PERCENT/100*360
80   RADANGLE = PI/180*ANGLE
90   STARTANGLE = STOPANGLE
100  STOPANGLE = STARTANGLE+RADANGLE
110  PAINTANGLE = STARTANGLE+RADANGLE/2
120  PAINTX = 160+R/1.3*COS(PAINTANGLE)
130  PAINTY = 100-R/1.3*SIN(PAINTANGLE)
140  IF STOPANGLE > 2*PI THEN STOPANGLE = STOPANGLE-2*PI
150  CIRCLE(160,100),R,,-STARTANGLE,-STOPANGLE,1
160  COLOR = SLICE MOD 3+1
170  C1 = COLOR+COLOR*16 : C2=COLOR*4+COLOR*64
180  IF SLICE<4 THEN COLOR$ = CHR$(C1+C2)
     ELSE IF SLICE<7 THEN COLOR$=CHR$(C1+C2)+CHR$(0)
          ELSE COLOR$=CHR$(C1)
190  PAINT (PAINTX,PAINTY),COLOR$,3
200  READ PERCENT
210  CHARX = PAINTX\10+3 : CHARY = PAINTY\10+3
220  LOCATE CHARY,CHARX : PRINT "SLICE";SLICE
230 WEND
240 DATA 15,20,15,15,10,15,10,-1
```

Program 1.32 Draws a pie chart.

```
220    NEXT MONTH
230    LOCATE 24,17 : PRINT "MONTH";
240    ROW = 1 : LOCATE ROW,1
250    FOR SALES = 5000 TO 1000 STEP -1000
260      PRINT SALES
270      LINE (1,SALES)-(13,SALES)
280      ROW = ROW+4
290      LOCATE ROW
300    NEXT SALES
310 RETURN

320 'SUBROUTINE draws a bar at the required height
330    LINE (MONTH,0)-(MONTH+0.5,SALES),1,BF
340    LINE (MONTH+0.5,0)-(MONTH+0.9,150),1
350    LINE -(MONTH+0.9,SALES+150),1
360    LINE -(MONTH+0.5,SALES+150),1
370    LINE -(MONTH+0.5,SALES+150),1
380    LINE -(MONTH,SALES),1
390    LINE (MONTH+0.5,SALES)-(MONTH+0.9,SALES+150),1
400    PAINT (MONTH+0.7,SALES/2),2,1
410    PAINT (MONTH+0.5,SALES+50),3,1
420 RETURN
```

drawn. The percentage value from the data is mapped into an angle for a circle segment:

```
ANGLE = PERCENT/100*360
```

and this value is used in CIRCLE to draw a segment. (Remember that for radial lines to be drawn, a minus sign is inserted before the start and stop angle in the CIRCLE statement.) A point from which

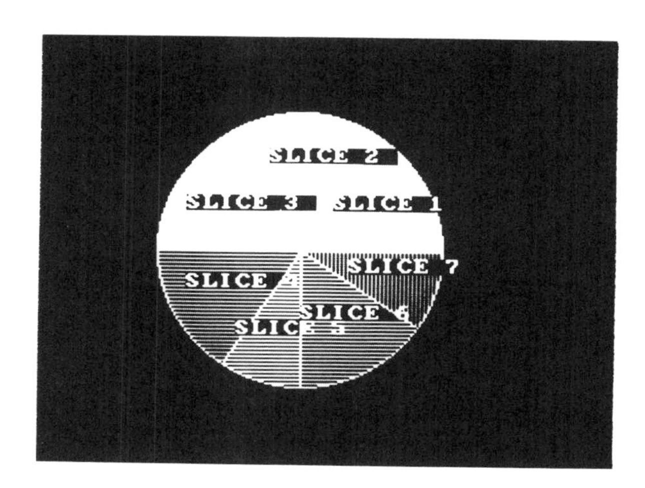

Figure 1.31
A simple pie chart

to paint each segment is calculated by considering a radial line that bisects the segment. These coordinates are also used to work out a position for the text label associated with each slice. Now although the program is general in that it will handle any number of slices it is impossible to give a general scheme for text printing because the angle of the slices can vary by so much. The scheme given in Program 1.32 will work providing each slice is greater than about 20°.

2 *Raster-ops, palettes and interactive drawing and painting*

In this chapter, we examine the facilities needed in a graphics system to enable the computer to be used as a drawing aid for an artist or as a tool in Computer Aided Design (CAD). The provision of such facilities relies heavily on the availability of graphics features such as logical plotting operations and the ability to instantaneously change the colour of objects on the screen. These facilities are a small subset of the facilities, available on advanced graphics systems, called 'raster-ops' and 'video look-up tables'. In the first two sections of this chapter, we present a summary of these two facilities. We then look at how they can be used to enhance 'normal' line drawing and provide facilities such as multi-plane images and instantaneous switching between images. Use of the video look-up table is fairly restricted on the PC and some of the techniques we describe in this chapter are available only on the PCjr. However, these techniques are extremely important in computer graphics generally, and they should be of interest to users of the PC.

Later in the chapter, we look at algorithms for 'painting' regions on the screen and mixing colours. We finish the chapter by looking at some of the commonly available graphics peripherals that can be used to make life easier for the user of an interactive graphics system. (Much of the material in this chapter is summarized in Appendix 1 for easy reference.)

2.1 GET AND PUT (PC AND PCJR)

In PC or PCjr BASIC, the PUT statement not only enables the rapid transfer of 'subpictures' on to the screen, but also allows the selection of one of several different logical operations for combining the colours in the subpicture with the existing colour on the screen. The modern technical term for such logical operations is 'raster-ops'.

The subpicture handled by PUT must be stored in an array and it is initially placed there by drawing it somewhere on the screen and then copying it into the array using the GET statement (Figure 2.1).

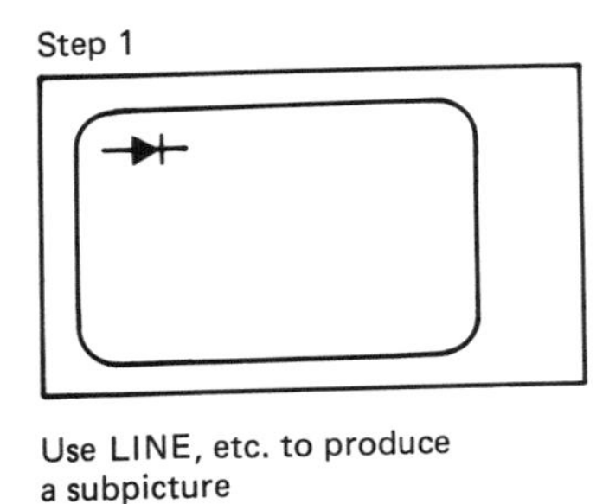

Step 1
Use LINE, etc. to produce
a subpicture

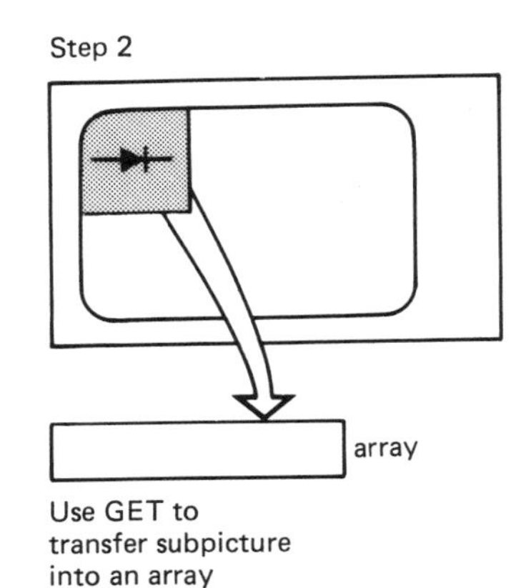

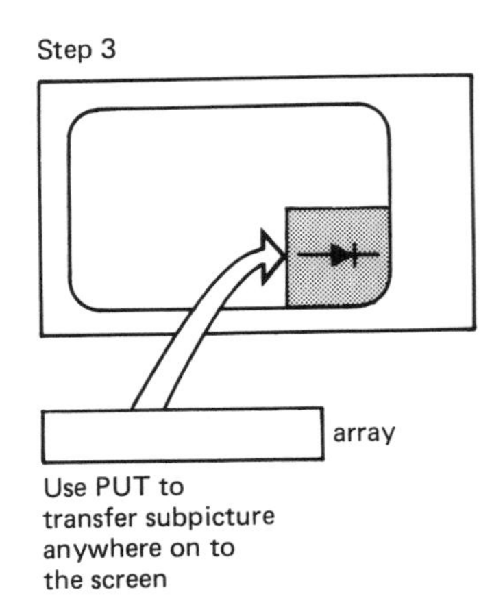

Figure 2.1
The utilities PUT and GET: sequence of use

When the subpicture is drawn for the first time, the full range of graphics statements, such as LINE and CIRCLE, can be used.

The format for GET is:

```
GET (x1,y1) - (x2,y2), arrayname
```

`(x1,y1)` and `(x2,y2)` specify the coordinates of opposite corners of a rectangular area on the screen which is transferred into the named array.

`arrayname` names the array into which the information is transferred.

Note that the way in which the coordinates are specified is exactly the same as for LINE. Also note that the entire contents of the rectangular area are stored in the array. The colour code for each pixel is stored. This means that the size of array required depends on the size of the area and on the SCREEN mode being used. The required array size in bytes is given by:

```
4 + INT((x*bits_per_pixel + 7)/8)*y
```

where 'x' and 'y' are the dimensions of the rectangular area and 'bits per pixel' depends on the SCREEN:

1 bit for a 2 colour SCREEN
2 bits for a 4 colour SCREEN
4 bits for a 16 colour SCREEN (PCjr only)

If 'x' is a multiple of 8 (or a multiple of 4 in a mode with more than 2 colours), then the above expression reduces to:

```
4 + x*y*bits_per_pixel/8
```

For example, consider a 32×32 area in SCREEN 1. The number of bytes required is 4 + 256. A single-precision (real) array holds four bytes per element. Location 0 of the array provides the first four bytes and the rest of the array requires 256/4 elements:

```
DIM PICTURE(64)
```

Alternatively, we can make the array bigger than this. If a program is not short of storage space, it is usually easier to declare a large array than it is to calculate the exact size of array required.

Once a subpicture has been copied from the screen, it can be rapidly displayed at any point on the screen using PUT. The format of the PUT statement is:

```
PUT (X,Y), arrayname, action
```

On the PCjr, '(X,Y)' always specifies the top left corner of the area of the screen in which the image from the named array is to be displayed. On the PC, when using SCREEN coordinates, '(X,Y)' also specifies the position of the top left corner of the image. However, if a WINDOW statement has been obeyed that sets up a non-screen coordinate system on the PC, then '(X,Y)' specifies the position of the bottom left corner of the image. This means that any program using PUT with a WINDOW statement has to be varied, depending on which machine we are using. Any such variation will be indicated in the program listings. (This inconsistency may of course be removed in later versions of BASIC.)

The action specified by the third parameter of PUT affects the way in which the subpicture from the array is displayed on the screen. When a subpicture in an array is PUT to the screen, each pixel colour in the subpicture is combined with the existing colour on the screen in the corresponding pixel. The 'action' parameter specifies the way in which this is done.

Table 2.1 contains a summary of the five different plotting actions that can be specified in PUT. Figure 2.2 illustrates the way in which these work. For a discussion of the different logical operations see Appendix 2. Table 2.2 summarizes the contexts in which different logical plotting actions are frequently used. These will all be extensively illustrated throughout the present chapter.

Table 2.1 The various logical plotting actions

PSET	a pixel colour in the array overwrites the corresponding pixel in the screen.
PRESET	the logical inverse of the pixel colour in the array overwrites the corresponding pixel in the screen.
OR	the new colour at a pixel results from performing an OR operation between the pixel colour in the array and the existing pixel colour in the screen.
AND	as for OR, but the logical operation is AND.
XOR	as for OR, but the logical operation is XOR (exclusive OR).

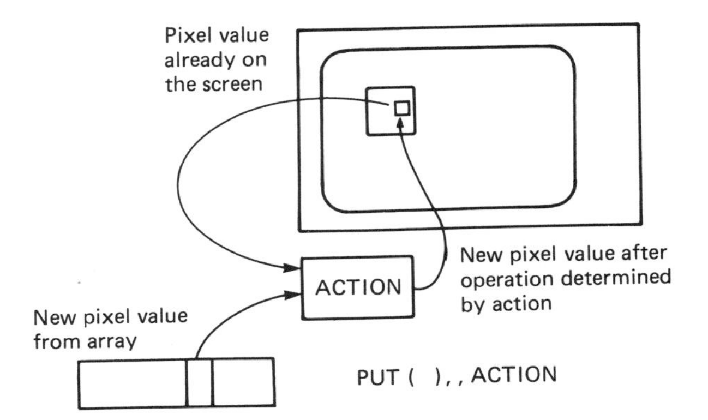

Figure 2.2
When PUT is used, each new pixel value together with the existing pixel value is operated on

Running Program 2.1 should give you a good grasp of the way in which information on the screen changes when plotting is done under the control of the various logical operations. The program runs in SCREEN 1 where the colour of each pixel is represented by a two-bit colour code. Initially, the screen is divided into four quadrants and each quadrant is filled with one of the four colours available. The code for each colour is displayed as a bit pattern in the centre of each quadrant. The user then selects a colour and a plotting action and the program colour fills a rectangle in the centre of the screen using the colour and action selected. This demonstrates the effect of the given action when plotting takes place over each possible existing colour on the screen. The new colour that appears in a region depends on up to three things:

1. The raster-op or logical action selected.
2. The colour selected (but not in the case of PSET).
3. The existing colour on the screen (but not in the case of PSET).

Table 2.2 Applications of the various logical plotting actions

OR	is used in modes with more than one bit per pixel if the screen memory is to be treated as if it contains more than one image plane. Use of OR enables the plotting of information in a specified plane.
AND	is used in multiple image-plane applications to delete information from a selected plane.
XOR	has the interesting property that two successive plots of the same object will restore information on the screen to its previous state. This is important in interactive graphics applications where lines or objects in different colours are moved about the screen without deleting existing information on the screen.

```
 10 KEY OFF
 20 DIM COLARRAY(2000)
 30 SCREEN 1 : CLS
 40 LINE (0,20)-(159,99),0,BF
 50 LINE (0,20)-(159,99),3,B
 60 LINE (0,100)-(159,179),1,BF
 70 LINE (0,100)-(159,179),2,B
 80 LINE (160,100)-(319,179),2,BF
 90 LINE (160,100)-(319,179),1,B
100 LINE (160,20)-(319,99),3,BF
110 LINE (160,20)-(319,99),0,B
120 LOCATE 1,14 : INPUT "col,op$ ";COL,OP$
130 IF COL = 0 THEN GET (0,20)-(159,99),COLARRAY
140 IF COL = 1 THEN GET (0,100)-(159,179),COLARRAY
150 IF COL = 2 THEN GET (160,100)-(319,179),COLARRAY
160 IF COL = 3 THEN GET (160,20)-(319,99),COLARRAY
170 LOCATE 6,6 : PRINT USING "#";POINT(80,50)\2;POINT(80,50) MOD 2
180 LOCATE 21,6 : PRINT USING "#";POINT(80,150)\2;POINT(80,150) MOD 2
190 LOCATE 21,33 : PRINT USING "#";POINT(240,150)\2;POINT(240,150) MOD 2
200 LOCATE 6,33 : PRINT USING "#";POINT(240,50)\2;POINT(240,50) MOD 2
210 IF OP$ = "PSET" THEN PUT (80,60),COLARRAY,PSET
220 IF OP$ = "XOR" THEN PUT (80,60),COLARRAY,XOR
230 IF OP$ = "OR" THEN PUT (80,60),COLARRAY,OR
240 IF OP$ = "AND" THEN PUT (80,60),COLARRAY,AND
250 LOCATE 11,16 : PRINT USING "#";POINT(140,90)\2;POINT(140,90) MOD 2
260 LOCATE 16,16 : PRINT USING "#";POINT(140,110)\2;POINT(140,110) MOD 2
270 LOCATE 16,24 : PRINT USING "#";POINT(180,110)\2;POINT(180,110) MOD 2
280 LOCATE 11,24 : PRINT USING "#";POINT(180,90)\2;POINT(180,90) MOD 2
290 LOCATE 23,1
300 END

310 'SUBROUTINE caption
320   LOCATE PX,PY
330   PRINT USING "#";POINT(GX,GY)\2;POINT(GX,GY) MOD 2
340 RETURN
```

Program 2.1 Demonstration of the effect of plotting with different logical operations.

Colour Plate 2 demonstrates some of the possibilities.

Note the way in which GET is used to create an array containing the appropriate colour. The block of screen memory is copied into the array from one of the four quadrants of the screen. PUT is then used to plot this block in the centre of the screen.

2.2 THE VIDEO LOOK-UP TABLE ON THE PC AND PCJR

A colour, for character printing or plotting, is referred to by means of a 'logical colour code' that specifies the bit pattern to be inserted in the screen memory for each pixel that is coloured. The logical colour code or 'attribute' can be used, for example, as the second parameter

Table 2.3 The sixteen actual colours

Actual colour numbers and corresponding colours	
Colour number	*Colour name*
0	black
1	blue
2	green
3	cyan
4	red
5	magenta
6	brown
7	white
8	grey
9	light blue
10	light green
11	light cyan
12	light red
13	light magenta
14	yellow
15	high-intensity white

of a LINE statement to select the colour of the line or box that is to be drawn.

An important facility in modern computer graphics is the ability to change the actual screen colours associated with the logical colour codes stored in the screen memory. This is done by using the video look-up table mentioned at the beginning of this chapter. The extent to which we can do this on the PC is limited, but on the PCjr there are 16 'actual colours' that can appear on the screen in any mode. These colours are numbered from 0 to 15 as listed in Table 2.3. In professional computer graphics systems, 256 colours is normal.

In SCREENS 3 and 5 on the PCjr, the 16 colour attributes initially correspond directly to the 16 actual colour codes. In a four-colour mode such as SCREEN 1 (PC and PCjr), the initial arrangement is as given in Table 2.4. Colour attribute 0 represents black (actual colour

Table 2.4 Default actual colour settings for the four colour codes available in a four-colour mode (e.g. SCREEN 1)

Colour code numbers	*Default actual colours*	
Foreground	*Colour*	*Number*
0	black	0
1	cyan	3
2	magenta	5
3	white	7

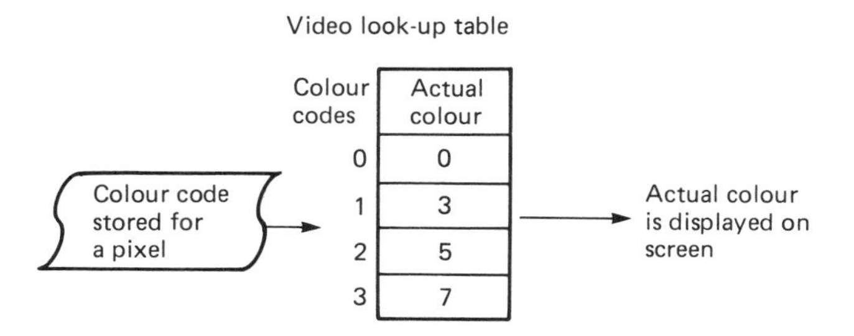

Figure 2.3
The video look-up table is used to convert a colour code stored in the screen memory into an actual colour to be displayed on the screen

0). However, colour attribute 1 represents cyan (actual colour 3), colour attribute 2 represents magenta (actual colour 5) and colour attribute 3 represents white (actual colour 7). In order to handle this correspondence, the graphics processor chip stores a 'video look-up table' containing the actual colour number that corresponds to each logical colour attribute that is available in the current screen mode. When the screen memory is being scanned by the graphics processor, the colour code at a pixel is used to find the corresponding actual colour from this video look-up table and it is this actual colour that defines the combination of 'Red–Green–Blue' signals to be sent to the monitor (see Figure 2.3).

If we can change the entries in the video look-up table, we can make a given colour code correspond to any one of the actual colours available.

Palette changing on the PCjr

In cartridge BASIC on the PCjr, the PALETTE statement is used to change the actual colour associated with a given colour code. This is implemented 'behind the scenes' by changing an entry in the video look-up table.

This process is demonstrated by Program 2.2 (PCjr only) which first colours a square in the centre of the screen in dark blue (attribute 1 set to actual colour 1). Each time a key is pressed, the program asks the user for a new actual colour and uses a PALETTE statement to change the actual colour associated with colour code 1. Note that a PALETTE colour change is almost instantaneous. It takes effect in the time taken for one scan of the screen memory (one fiftieth of a second). All that is needed behind the scenes to implement a change is to change the contents of a single entry in the video look-up table. During the next scan of the screen memory, all pixels containing the logical colour code that was affected will appear on the screen in the new actual colour.

Using a combination of PALETTE statements enables us to select any combination of actual colours for use in a mode. For example, in a two-colour mode, a drawing that appears initially in white on a black background can be instantaneously changed to black on a

```
 10 SCREEN 1 : CLS : WINDOW (0,0)-(1279,799)
 20 LINE (340,312)-(940,712),1,BF
 30 ACTUAL = 1 : PALETTE 1,1
 40 GOSUB 150  'caption
 50 KEYS$ =""
 60 WHILE KEYS$ <> "q"
 70   LOCATE 1,2 : INPUT "New actual color ";ACTUAL
 80   LOCATE 1,2 : PRINT SPC(30)
 90   PALETTE 1,ACTUAL
100   GOSUB 150  'caption
110   LOCATE 23,1 : PRINT "Q to Quit, any other key to continue"
120   KEYS$ = INPUT$(1) : LOCATE 23,1 : PRINT SPC(36)
130 WEND
140 SCREEN 0 : END

150 'SUBROUTINE caption
160   LOCATE 7,12 : PRINT "COLOR CODE 1"
170   LOCATE 9,12 : PRINT "ACTUAL COLOR ";ACTUAL;" "
180 RETURN
```

Program 2.2 Demonstration of palette changing. (PCjr only.)

white background with:

```
PALETTE 0,7
PALETTE 1,0
```

In a four-colour mode, we can select any combination of four colours. For example:

```
PALETTE 0,4
PALETTE 1,14
PALETTE 2,2
```

sets attributes 0, 1 and 2 to red, yellow and green respectively,

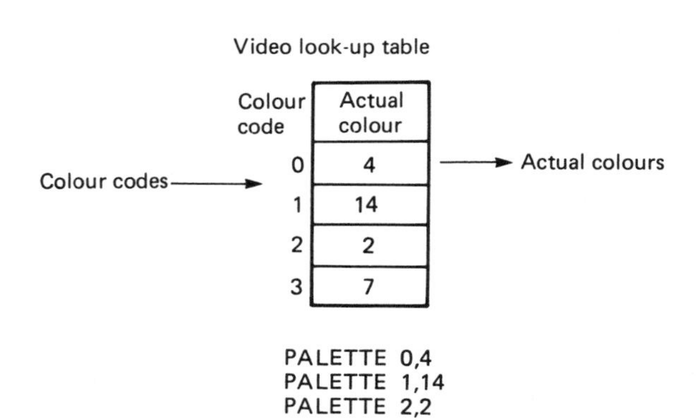

Figure 2.4
The state of the video look-up table after the three PALETTE statements are obeyed

leaving attribute 3 set to white. Figure 2.4 indicates the state of the video look-up table after these three statements have been obeyed.

Palette switching on the PC
In PC BASIC, the PALETTE statement is not available and the contents of the video look-up table can be changed only in a very limited way.

The only two graphics modes available on the PC are SCREEN 1 and SCREEN 2. SCREEN 2 is a two-colour mode and these colours are fixed as black and white. SCREEN 1 is a four-colour mode in which the colour codes or attributes are 0, 1, 2 and 3. As explained earlier, the default actual colour settings for these are black, cyan, magenta and white. The only way in which this palette can be changed is by using the COLOR statement to change the actual background colour or to select the other fixed palette of foreground colours.

In SCREEN 1, the COLOR statement has the form:

```
COLOR background, palette
```

The first parameter can be an actual colour number in the range 0 to 15 and this instantaneously sets the background colour of the screen. The second parameter selects one of two foreground palettes numbered 0 or 1. Palette 1 is the default palette in which the three foreground colours are cyan, magenta and white. Palette 0 sets the three foreground colours to green, red and brown.

The PALETTE statement is used extensively in most of the example programs in the next few sections of this chapter. Because of the restrictions mentioned, these programs will run only in PCjr BASIC.

2.3 IMAGE SWITCHING – NON-OVERLAPPING IMAGES (PCJR ONLY)

One of the commonest uses of the palette-changing facility described in the previous section is in the instantaneous switching between different images on the screen.

A picture that has been plotted using a particular colour code can be 'switched off' by setting the actual colour associated with the colour code to be the same as the background colour. The picture can be instantaneously 'switched on' by setting the colour code back to an actual colour that contrasts with the background.

If several images are drawn on the screen using different colour codes, then we can switch any picture on or off instantaneously by changing the actual colour associated with the appropriate code. We first deal with the simple case where the images to be selectively switched on and off do *not* overlap. In the next section, we deal with the problems that arise when the images do overlap.

When the images do not overlap, we simply use a different colour code for each image. For example, Program 2.3 plots three different sales graphs in three quadrants of the screen. The program uses SCREEN 1 where four different colour codes are available. One of these codes has to be used for the background and this leaves us with three codes, one of which is used for each sales graph.

The user at the keyboard can then switch any one of the graphs on or off. Typing a '1' will switch one graph on or off. Keys '2' and '3'

```
 10 DIM ACTUAL(3)
 20 SCREEN 4 : KEY OFF
 30 FOR COL = 1 TO 3
 40   ACTUAL(COL) = 0 : PALETTE COL,0
 50 NEXT COL
 70 OX = 0 : OY = 0 : COL = 1 : YEAR = 1982 : GOSUB 200  'draw graph
 80 OX = 160 : OY = 0 : COL = 2 : YEAR = 1983 : GOSUB 200  'draw graph
 90 OX = 0 : OY = 100 : COL = 3 : YEAR = 1984 : GOSUB 200  'draw graph
100 GOSUB 400  'switching
110 SCREEN 0 : END

200 'SUBROUTINE draw graph
210   VIEW (OX,OY)-(OX+159,OY+99)
220   WINDOW (-1,-50)-(13,8500)
225   COLOR COL
230   LINE (0,0)-(0,8000)
240   LINE (0,0)-(12,0)
250   READ MONTHLYSALES
260   PSET(1,MONTHLYSALES)
270   FOR MONTH = 2 TO 12
280     READ MONTHLYSALES
290     LINE -(MONTH,MONTHLYSALES)
300   NEXT MONTH
305   LOCATE OY\8+2,OX\8+3 : PRINT YEAR
310 RETURN

320 DATA 1023, 2056, 4132, 6415, 7685, 7844,
         6923, 7246, 6012, 4433, 5412, 3224
330 DATA 1145, 3347, 4245, 6654, 7755, 6877,
         5789, 7456, 5321, 4455, 3567, 3678
340 DATA  996, 2676, 2567, 3215, 4985, 5864,
         5778, 5266, 4562, 4433, 3412, 2284

400 'SUBROUTINE switching
410   WHILE COMMAND$ <> "q"
420     COMMAND$ = INKEY$
430     WHILE COMMAND$ = "" : COMMAND$ = INKEY$ : WEND
440     COL = INSTR("123",COMMAND$)
450     IF COL > 0 THEN ACTUAL(COL) = 7-ACTUAL(COL) : PALETTE COL,ACTUAL(COL)
460   WEND
470 RETURN
```

Program 2.3 Switching between three graphs. (PCjr only.)

have a similar effect on the other two graphs. (Type 'q' to quit the program.)

Switching between non-overlapping images plotted in different colours is often illustrated using the popular 'bouncing ball' demonstration. Program 2.4 runs in SCREEN 5. It plots 15 balls in different vertical positions on the screen, each ball being plotted using a different colour code. Each colour code is set to black when a ball has been drawn using that code. The program then cycles through the 15 different colour codes setting each one to white in turn and then back to black. The order in which this is done gives the effect of a bouncing ball.

When you run this program, you should see from the initial time it takes to draw the 15 copies of the ball that any attempt to animate the ball by simply drawing and deleting would be hopelessly slow.

```
 10 KEY OFF
 20 CLEAR,,,32768!
 30 SCREEN 5 : CLS : WINDOW (0,0)-(1279,799)
 40 X = 644 : Y = 775 : R = 23
 50 FOR COLORCODE = 1 TO 15
 60   PALETTE COLORCODE,7
 70   CIRCLE (X,Y),R,COLORCODE  : PAINT (X,Y),COLORCODE,COLORCODE
 80   PALETTE COLORCODE,0
 90   Y = Y-50
100 NEXT COLORCODE
110 PREVCODE = 0
120 WHILE INKEY$ = ""
130   FOR CODE = 1 TO 15
140     PALETTE PREVCODE,0
150     PALETTE CODE,7
160     PREVCODE = CODE
170     D = 15-CODE\2 : GOSUB 280  'delay
180   NEXT CODE
190   FOR CODE = 14 TO 2 STEP -1
200     PALETTE PREVCODE,0
210     PALETTE CODE,7
220     PREVCODE = CODE
230     D = 15-CODE\2 : GOSUB 280  'delay
240   NEXT CODE
250 WEND
260 PALETTE
270 END

280 'SUBROUTINE delay
290   FOR T = 1 TO D
300     S = T*S
310   NEXT T
320 RETURN
```

Program 2.4 Bouncing ball: non-overlapping images. (PCjr only.)

2.4 IMAGE PLANE SWITCHING – OVERLAPPING IMAGES (PCJR)

Now consider what happens if two overlapping images are to be selectively switched on and off. One way of arranging to switch rapidly between different images is to use separate pages of screen memory as demonstrated in Program 1.26. However, this technique does not allow both images to be switched on at once. Here, we examine an alternative technique that involves storing different images in the same page of screen memory.

Figure 2.5 represents the situation where two images overlap. If image1 is switched on, we must also switch on the overlapping region. Similarly, if image2 is switched on, we must switch on the overlapping region. In order to do this, we need three different colour codes, one for pixels contained only in image1, one for pixels contained only in image2 and a third code for pixels in the overlapping region.

Separate bit planes

The most convenient way to organize the available colour codes is to use a separate 'bit-plane' for each image.

In SCREEN 1, we have two-bit colour codes, but instead of using the SCREEN 1 screen memory as a single plane of two-bit colour codes we can envisage it as two separate planes of one-bit codes. We can now think in terms of plotting image1 in one plane and image2 in the other plane. The four possible bit combinations at a pixel position are:

0 = 00 = image1 and image2 background
1 = 01 = image1 foreground
2 = 10 = image2 foreground
3 = 11 = image1 and image2 foreground

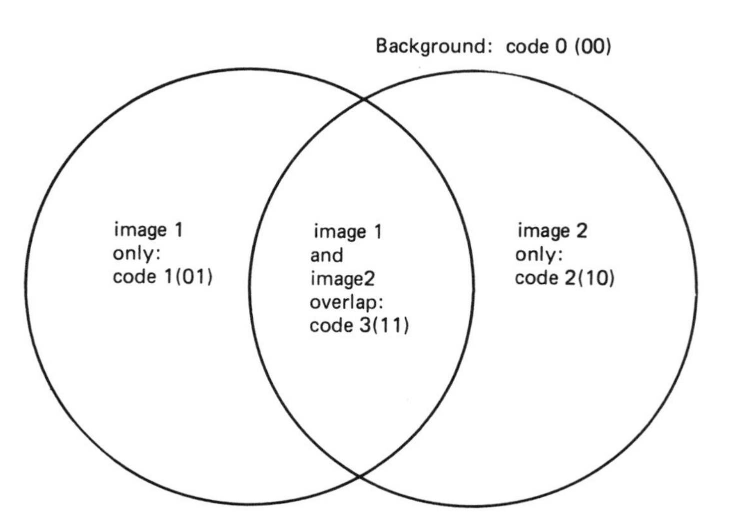

Figure 2.5
Two overlapping images to be selectively switched on and off and the colour codes (and bit patterns) to be used for different regions

Switching between two planes
Starting with the easier consideration of switching between planes (assuming that both images are already built up) we would proceed as follows:

To DISPLAY image1:

```
PALETTE 0, backgroundcolimage1
PALETTE 1, foregroundcolimage1
PALETTE 2, backgroundcolimage1
PALETTE 3, foregroundcolimage1
```

Image2 is thus set to the background colour selected for image1 and becomes invisible.

To DISPLAY image2:

```
PALETTE 0, backgroundcolimage2
PALETTE 1, backgroundcolimage2
PALETTE 2, foregroundcolimage2
PALETTE 3, foregroundcolimage2
```

Now image1 is set to the background colour selected for image2 and becomes invisible.

Plotting in separate planes
To plot in the image1 plane, without affecting existing image2 points, we have to proceed as follows for each pixel:

0 = 00 becomes 01
1 = 01 remains 01 (image1 point already there)
2 = 10 becomes 11 (image2 point already there)
3 = 11 remains 11 (image2 and image1 point already there)

The third column gives the codes required after plotting. This is produced by ORing (inclusive) 01 with the second column. The only plotting statement in PCjr BASIC that allows this OR action is PUT. PUT can be applied only to an image stored in an array and the image to be plotted in the image1 plane must first be drawn on its own in colour 1 and then placed in an array using GET.

Similarly to plot in the image2 plane without affecting image1 points:

0 = 00 becomes 10
1 = 01 becomes 11
2 = 10 remains 10
3 = 11 remains 11

The image must first be plotted on its own in colour 2, placed in an array using GET and then plotted in the required position using OR.

Program 2.5 plots the same three sales graphs as Program 2.3. It also plots, on the same sets of axes, three graphs showing costs. The program then allows the user to switch all the sales graphs on or off using key '1' and all the costs graphs on or off using key '2'. A common background colour is used for both sets of graphs – this is necessary if both graphs are allowed to be switched on at once. If only one set of graphs was to be switched on at a time, then we could use a different background colour for each set of graphs. The sales graphs are plotted normally (all in colour 1), each one in the appropriate quadrant of the screen. The costs graphs are then superimposed as image2, using the OR technique just described. Each cost graph is plotted temporarily in the blank quadrant of the screen in

```
 10 DIM SELECTCOL(2),GRAPH(1000)
 20 SELECTCOL(1) = 2 : SELECTCOL(2) = 4
 30 SCREEN 4 : KEY OFF
 40 PALETTE
 50 STATUS = 0
 60 SX = 0 : SY = 0 : YEAR = 1982 : GOSUB 350  'sales
 70 CX = 0 : CY = 0 : YEAR = 1982 : GOSUB 440  'costs
 80 SX = 160 : SY = 0 : YEAR = 1983 : GOSUB 350  'sales
 90 CX = 160 : CY = 0 : YEAR = 1983 : GOSUB 440  'costs
100 SX = 0 : SY = 100 : YEAR = 1984 : GOSUB 350  'sales
110 CX = 0 : CY = 100 : YEAR = 1984 : GOSUB 440  'costs
120 PALETTE 1,0 : PALETTE 2,0 : PALETTE 3,0
130 GOSUB 530  'switching
140 SCREEN 0 : END

150 'SUBROUTINE drawgraph
160   VIEW (OX,OY)-(OX+159,OY+99)
170   WINDOW (-1,-50)-(13,8500)
180   COLOR COL
190   LINE (0,0)-(0,8000)
200   LINE (0,0)-(12,0)
210   READ MONTHLYSALES
220   PSET(1,MONTHLYSALES)
230   FOR MONTH = 2 TO 12
240     READ MONTHLYSALES
250     LINE -(MONTH,MONTHLYSALES)
260   NEXT MONTH
270   LOCATE OY\8+2,OX\8+3 : PRINT YEAR
280 RETURN

290 DATA 1023, 2056, 4132, 6415, 7685, 7844,
         6923, 7246, 6012, 4433, 5412, 3224
300 DATA 1023, 2055, 4130, 6215, 6500, 7015,
         6005, 6205, 5800, 4015, 4550, 2775
310 DATA 1145, 3347, 4245, 6654, 7755, 6877,
         5789, 7456, 5321, 4455, 3567, 3678
320 DATA  800, 3000, 4600, 6650, 7750, 6255,
         5235, 6775, 4665, 4005, 3100, 3758
```

Program 2.5 Switching between overlapping images. (PCjr only.)

colour 2, and GET is used to copy it into an array. PUT is then used with the OR action to superimpose the costs graph on the corresponding sales graph.

The data has been chosen to include months for which the sales and costs graphs overlap completely in order to illustrate clearly how the program treats such overlapping regions. When a set of graphs is switched on, the actual colour associated with the overlapping region (colour code 3) is set to the actual colour for the graphs being switched on. Thus the overlapping region is displayed in the

```
330 DATA  996, 2676, 2567, 3215, 4985, 5864,
         5778, 5266, 4562, 4433, 3412, 2284
340 DATA  900, 2175, 2005, 2875, 4205, 5185,
         5295, 5105, 4125, 3935, 2995, 2500

350 'SUBROUTINE sales
360   COL = 1
370   OX = 160 : OY = 100 : GOSUB 150  'drawgraph
380   LOCATE 14,35 : PRINT "sales"
390   VIEW : WINDOW
400   GET (160,100)-(319,199),GRAPH
410   LINE (160,100)-(319,199),0,BF
420   PUT (SX,SY),GRAPH,OR
430 RETURN

440 'SUBROUTINE costs
450   COL = 2
460   OX = 160 : OY = 100 : GOSUB 150  'drawgraph
470   LOCATE 15,35 : PRINT "costs"
480   VIEW : WINDOW
490   GET (160,100)-(319,199),GRAPH
500   LINE (160,100)-(319,199),0,BF
510   PUT (CX,CY),GRAPH,OR
520 RETURN

530 'SUBROUTINE switching
540   WHILE COMMAND$ <>  "q"
550     COMMAND$ = INKEY$
560     WHILE COMMAND$ = "" : COMMAND$ = INKEY$ : WEND
570     COL = INSTR("12",COMMAND$)
580   IF COL = 0 THEN RETURN
590     STATUS = STATUS XOR COL
600     ACTUAL = STATUS AND COL
610     PALETTE COL, SELECTCOL(ACTUAL)
620     IF ACTUAL = 0 THEN OVERLAP = STATUS ELSE OVERLAP = COL
630     PALETTE 3, SELECTCOL(OVERLAP)
640   WEND
650 RETURN
```

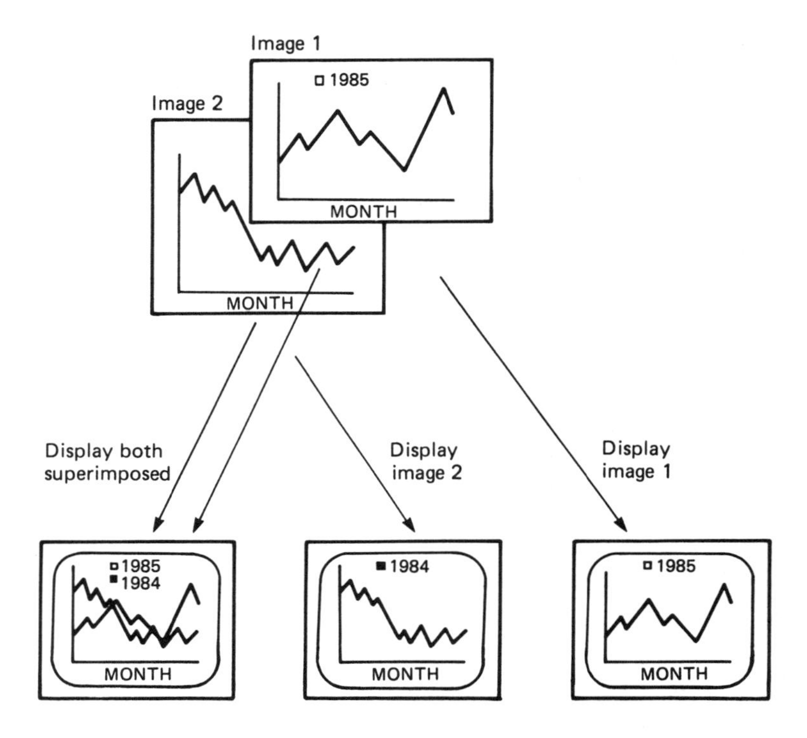

Figure 2.6
Selective display of two graphs stored in two separate image planes

colour for the last set of graphs switched on. The axes in the combined graphs are also in colour 3 and behave in the same way as other overlapping regions.

When a set of graphs is switched off, the actual colour selected for the overlapping region depends on whether or not the other set of graphs is switched on. If it is, then the overlapping region is set to the actual colour for the other graphs, otherwise it is set to the background colour. The process is illustrated in Figure 2.6.

An interesting technique, used to keep track of the status of the screen, is to use a variable 'status'. We imagine this variable as a pattern of two bits indicating what combination of the two sets of graphs is currently switched on:

status = 0 (00) both sets of graphs off.
status = 1 (01) sales graphs on, costs graphs off.
status = 2 (10) costs graphs on, sales graphs off.
status = 3 (11) both sets of graphs on.

This variable is adjusted when a set of graphs is switched on or off, by using logical operations which affect the bit-pattern representation of the value of the variable. This is achieved in much the same way as the logical plotting operations affect the bit-pattern representation of the colour code at a pixel.

Plane switching and animation

Instantaneous switching between separate image planes is an important technique in animation. We have already mentioned that a sequence of normal plot and delete operations would be too slow for animation. An example of the use of palette changing in the

```
 10 CLEAR,,,32768!
 20 KEY OFF
 30 DIM BALL%(16386)
 40 SCREEN 5 : CLS : WINDOW (0,0)-(1279,799)
 50 X = 516 : Y = 778 : R = 128
 60 COLORCODE = 1
 70 FOR IMAGE = 1 TO 4
 80   CIRCLE (128,228),128,COLORCODE,,,1
 90   PAINT (128,228),COLORCODE,COLORCODE
100   GET (0,100)-(256,356),BALL%
110   PUT (X,Y),BALL%,OR
120   Y = Y-160
130   COLORCODE = COLORCODE*2
140 NEXT IMAGE
150 CIRCLE (128,228),128,0,,,1
160 PAINT (128,228),0,0
170 FOR CODE = 1 TO 15
180   PALETTE CODE,0
190 NEXT CODE
200 PALETTE 1,7 : PALETTE 3,7
210 WHILE INKEY$ = ""
220   FOR FRAME = 1 TO 6
230     GOSUB 340  'switch
240     D = (ABS(3-FRAME)+1)*4 : GOSUB 290  'delay
250   NEXT FRAME
260 WEND
270 PALETTE
280 END

290 'SUBROUTINE delay
300   FOR T = 1 TO D
310     S = S*D
320   NEXT T
330 RETURN

340 'SUBROUTINE switch
350   ON FRAME GOTO 360,370,380,390,400,410
360   PALETTE 1,0 : PALETTE 2,7 : PALETTE 6,7 : RETURN
370   PALETTE 3,0 : PALETTE 2,0 : PALETTE 4,7 : PALETTE 12,7 : RETURN
380   PALETTE 6,0 : PALETTE 4,0 : PALETTE 8,7 : RETURN
390   PALETTE 8,0 : PALETTE 4,7 : PALETTE 6,7 : RETURN
400   PALETTE 12,0 : PALETTE 4,0 : PALETTE 2,7 : PALETTE 3,7 : RETURN
410   PALETTE 6,0 : PALETTE 2,0 : PALETTE 1,7
420 RETURN
```

Program 2.6 Bouncing ball: overlapping images. (PCjr only.)

bouncing ball animation was demonstrated in Program 2.4. Program 2.6 uses the bouncing ball demonstration again. This time a larger ball is used, and there are only four images of the ball that overlap. The way in which the images overlap and the colour codes used to represent the parts of each image is shown in Figure 2.7.

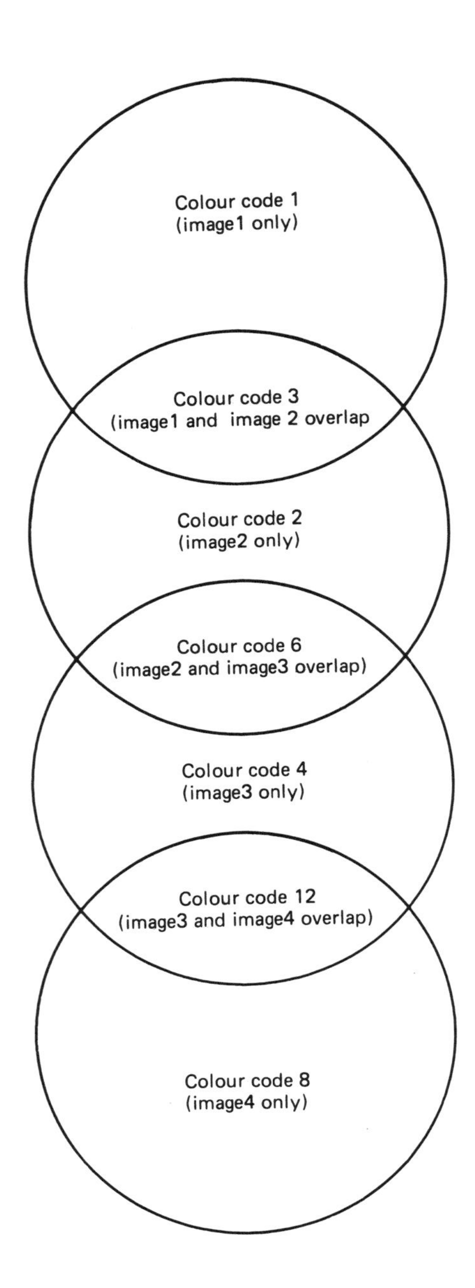

Figure 2.7
Four overlapping images of a ball used in a bouncing ball animation and the colour codes used for different images

Program 2.7 is another example of the use of palette changing in animation. This program animates a bee by giving the impression that its wings are moving (see Figure 2.8). One pair of wings is drawn in colour code 1 and the other pair is drawn in colour code 2. The program repeatedly switches between the two pairs of wings,

```
  5 SOUND OFF : BEEP OFF : KEY OFF
 10 SCREEN 1 : CLS : WINDOW (0,0)-(1279,799)
 20 DIM TOPWINGS%(1070),BOTTOMWINGS%(1346)
 30 PALETTE 3,14 : PALETTE 1,7 : PALETTE 2,7
 40 RESTORE 490
 50 COLOR = 1
 60 GOSUB 280  'draw
 70 GET (325,380)-(670,766),TOPWINGS%
 80 CLS
 90 COLOR = 2
100 GOSUB 280  'draw
110 GET (323,2)-(663,383),BOTTOMWINGS%
120 CLS
130 RESTORE
140 COLOR = 3 : GOSUB 280  'draw
150 VOLUME = 15
160 PUT (325,770),TOPWINGS%,OR
170 PALETTE 1,0
180 PUT (323,382),BOTTOMWINGS%,OR
190 PALETTE 2,0
200 WHILE INKEY$ = ""
210   PALETTE 1,7 : PALETTE 1,0
220   PALETTE 2,7 : PALETTE 2,0
230   VOLUME = VOLUME+RND*3-2
240   IF VOLUME < 5 THEN VOLUME = 5 ELSE IF VOLUME > 15 THEN VOLUME = 15
250   SOUND 140,0.8,VOLUME,0
260 WEND
270 END

280 'SUBROUTINE draw
290   READ POINTS
300   FOR P = 1 TO POINTS
310     READ UPDOWN%,X,Y
320     IF UPDOWN% = 4 THEN PSET(X,Y),COLOR
        ELSE IF UPDOWN% = 5 THEN LINE -(X,Y),COLOR
        ELSE IF UPDOWN% = 6 THEN PAINT(X,Y),COLOR,COLOR
330     IF X < MINX THEN MINX = X ELSE IF X > MAXX THEN MAXX = X
340     IF Y < MINY THEN MINY = Y ELSE IF Y > MAXY THEN MAXY = Y
350   NEXT P
360 RETURN

370 DATA 91
380 DATA  4,687,464,  5,718,499,  5,754,509,  5,775,503,
          5,793,482,  5,807,434,  5,799,388,  5,765,348,
          5,731,344,  5,696,360
```

Program 2.7 An animated buzzing bee. (PCjr only.) *continued*

```
390 DATA  5,685,342,  5,652,317,  5,589,292,  5,546,283,
          5,473,283,  5,428,294,  5,382,325,  5,354,377
400 DATA  5,364,429,  5,421,482,  5,466,496,  5,528,503,
          5,579,499,  5,647,481,  5,688,464
410 DATA  5,682,455,  5,674,400,  5,678,364,  5,685,342,
          5,696,360,  4,652,317,  5,637,358,  5,633,406,
          5,637,455,  5,647,481,  6,657,360
420 DATA  4,579,499,  5,567,439,  5,568,381,  5,576,325,
          5,589,292,  4,528,503,  5,516,460,  5,513,401,
          5,523,341,  5,546,283,  6,540,390
430 DATA  4,466,496,  5,450,427,  5,451,377,  5,460,318,
          5,473,283,  4,421,482,  5,408,424,  5,409,368,
          5,419,314,  5,428,294,  6,425,370
440 DATA  4,761,466,  5,770,465,  5,777,456,  5,783,444,
          5,776,423,  5,765,416,  5,744,433,  5,746,448,
          5,762,464
450 DATA  4,779,448,  5,771,453,  5,766,447,  5,767,433,
          5,778,428
460 DATA  4,807,434,  5,815,417,  5,822,412,  5,815,407,
          5,799,388
470 DATA  4,774,366,  5,762,365,  5,751,380,  5,751,391
480 DATA  4,775,503,  5,792,534,  5,800,560,  5,796,560,
          5,804,560,  4,754,509,  5,747,534,  5,740,560,
          5,736,560,  5,744,560
490 DATA 46
500 DATA  4,621,382,  5,644,413,  5,659,462,  5,669,518,
          5,670,580,  5,667,634,  5,652,689,  5,613,738,
          5,582,760,  5,558,766,  5,540,759,  5,520,737
510 DATA  5,503,702,  5,499,666,  5,499,628,  5,507,588,
          5,516,548,  5,529,512,  5,550,472,  5,571,440,
          5,594,416,  5,608,401,  5,621,380,  5,583,386
520 DATA  5,546,396,  5,515,410,  5,470,437,  5,432,471,
          5,406,501,  5,375,537,  5,347,580,  5,331,620,
          5,325,653,  5,334,681,  5,369,697,  5,405,700
530 DATA  5,450,689,  5,484,669,  5,510,645,  5,540,607,
          5,566,569,  5,583,534,  5,598,496,  5,608,470,
          5,615,440,  5,614,401
540 DATA 50
550 DATA  4,619,386,  5,584,382,  5,540,369,  5,484,340,
          5,445,315,  5,399,282,  5,366,249,  5,347,224,
          5,334,195,  5,328,171,  5,323,147,  5,335,119
560 DATA  5,353,104,  5,380, 97,  5,406, 99,  5,436,109,
          5,469,129,  5,495,150,  5,531,191,  5,562,229,
          5,583,266,  5,597,299,  5,607,331,  5,614,359
570 DATA  5,620,386,  5,586,355,  5,547,313,  5,526,282,
          5,511,251,  5,496,214,  5,485,180,  5,472,144,
          5,466,109,  5,469, 71,  5,479, 44,  5,507, 20
580 DATA  5,553,  2,  5,587, 11,  5,610, 33,  5,625, 52,
          5,640, 87,  5,644,112,  5,650,137,  5,658,174,
          5,663,220,  5,663,260,  5,656,307,  5,643,351
590 DATA  5,633,372,  5,621,386
```

Program 2.7 *continued*

Figure 2.8
Two 'frames' for a buzzing bee

first switching colour code 1 to white with code 2 set to black, and then switching code 2 to white with code 1 set to black. The body of the bee is displayed in colour code 3 which is permanently set to yellow.

We have enhanced the effect produced by this program by adding a continuous humming sound whose volume also varies randomly.

2.5 COMPOSITE IMAGE WITH PRIORITY (PCJR)

With a choice of four colours, the scheme just described can easily be adapted to set up a composite image (foreground, midground and background). Using PUT with the OR action, the foreground and midground planes can be independently accessed. Anything drawn in the midground plane, that is shadowed by anything drawn in the foreground plane, is *automatically* obscured in the composite image. Also, using PUT with the AND action, we can delete from the foreground, delete from the midground, add to the foreground or add to the midground. The foreground/midground priority is automatically taken into account. Common operations that we might want to perform are illustrated in Figure 2.9.

How this is accomplished is now explained. Suppose we are operating in a four-colour mode (this allows two planes plus background). A four-colour mode means that there are two bits per pixel – that is, we can imagine the image memory as two one-bit planes.

If the two planes have 0,0 in a pixel position, then the display image is a background point (Figure 2.10a).

If the two planes have 0,1 in a pixel position then the display image is a foreground point (Figure 2.10b).

1,0 means a midground point (Figure 2.10c).

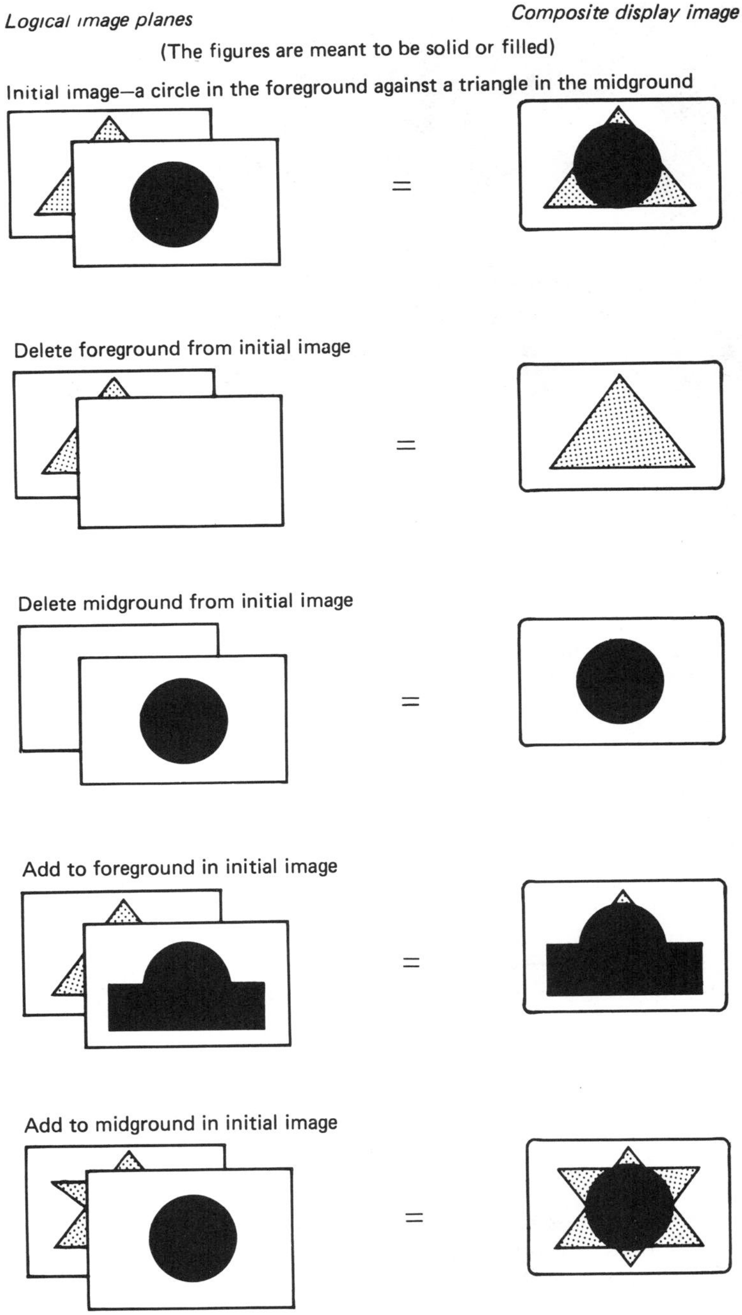

Logical image planes *Composite display image*

(The figures are meant to be solid or filled)

Initial image—a circle in the foreground against a triangle in the midground

=

Delete foreground from initial image

=

Delete midground from initial image

=

Add to foreground in initial image

=

Add to midground in initial image

=

Figure 2.9
Common operations that can be performed with a simple two-level priority scheme for images

Finally 1,1 means a foreground point but this time one that is obscuring a midground point (Figure 2.10d).

Thus we have:

0 = 00 = background point
1 = 01 = foreground point
2 = 10 = midground point
3 = 11 = foreground point (obscuring a midground point)

Note that we use two logical colour codes to represent foreground points. This is because a foreground point can occur in two contexts. It can obscure (only) a background point or it can obscure both a

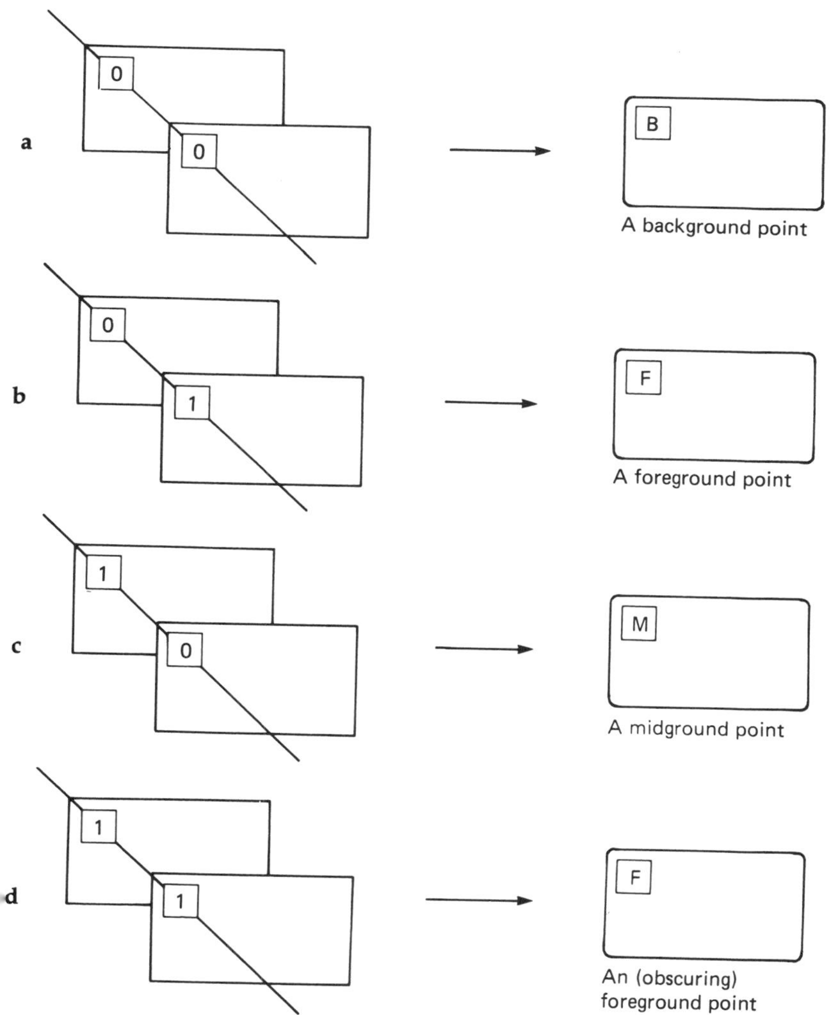

Figure 2.10
Various bit combinations at a pixel and their significance in a midground/foreground priority scheme

Figure 2.11
Examples of drawing and deleting in foreground and midground priority planes:
(a) F plotted in colour 1 using OR;
(b) M plotted in colour 2 using OR;
(c) M revealed by plotting a block of colour 2 using AND

background point and a midground point. There follows a few examples of priority plotting, which can be easily generalized.

To PLOT in the foreground
We use PUT to plot the image in colour 1 with the OR action. Now because

00 background	OR	01 foreground	=	01 foreground

and

10 midground	OR	01 foreground	=	11 foreground (obscuring midground)

background and midground points are obscured by foreground points (Figure 2.11a).

To PLOT in the midground
We use PUT to plot the image in colour 2 with the OR action. Now because

00 background	OR	10 midground	=	10 midground

and

01 foreground	OR	10 midground	=	11 foreground

background points are obscured by midground points as you would expect. Points that are already foreground remain in the foreground colour, *but* with code 11 indicating that they are obscuring a midground point (Figure 2.11b). Thus to build up information in these two planes we use PUT with the OR action. You can see that, after a composite set of planes has been built up, any subsequent additions to the foreground or midground will be incorporated into the composite image according to their respective priority.

To DELETE from foreground and midground
To delete images or parts of images from planes we use PUT with the AND action. When deleting a foreground object, we use PUT to plot a block, containing nothing but colour 2, with the AND action. The colour used happens to be the midground colour but is used here as a 'foreground delete code'. To delete a midground object, we PUT a block of colour 1 using the AND action. For example, when deleting from foreground:

00	AND	10	=	00
background				background

that is, background points remain as background.

01	AND	10	=	00
foreground				background

'ordinary' foreground points revert to background.

```
 10 CLEAR,,,65536! : KEY OFF
 20 DIM PAL%(15)
 30 DIM PIC%(8000),FOREDELETE(20)
 40 CLS
 50 SCREEN 1,,1,0 : CLS : WINDOW (0,0)-(1279,799)
 60 PRINT "2 priority planes demonstration"
 70 SCREEN 1,,0,1 : CLS : WINDOW (0,0)-(1279,799)
 80 PRINT "2 priority planes demonstration"
 90 RESTORE 140
100 FOR P% = 0 TO 15
110   READ PAL%(P%)
120 NEXT P%
130 PALETTE USING PAL%(0)
140 DATA 0,4,14,4,-1,-1,-1,-1,-1,-1,-1,-1,-1,-1,-1,-1
150 RESTORE 1000 : Y = 200 : XSCALE = 3 : YSCALE = 3 :
                   XSTEP = 100 : COL = 1 : GOSUB 240  'word
160 RESTORE 1130 : Y = 220 : XSCALE = 2.8 : YSCALE = 2.8 :
                   XSTEP = 96 : COL = 2 : GOSUB 240  'word
170 LINE (0,0)-(1279,0),2
180 GET (0,0)-(1279,0),FOREDELETE
190 SCREEN 1,,1,1
200 FOR Y = 200 TO 600
210   PUT (0,Y),FOREDELETE,AND
220 NEXT Y
230 INPUT ANY$ : SCREEN 0 : END

240 'SUBROUTINE word
250   CLS
260   READ LETTERS
270   X = (1280-LETTERS*XSTEP*XSCALE)/2
280   OY = Y
290   FOR I = 1 TO LETTERS
```

Program 2.8 Two image planes, foreground and midground. (PCjr only.)

continued

```
 300      OX = X : Y = OY
 310      PSET (OX,OY),0
 320      READ NO
 330      FOR J = 1 TO NO
 340        READ P,RX,RY
 350        X = X+RX*XSCALE : Y = Y+RY*YSCALE
 360        IF P = 0 THEN PSET (X,Y),0
            ELSE IF P = 1 THEN LINE -(X,Y),COL
            ELSE IF P = 2 THEN PAINT (X,Y),COL,COL
 370      NEXT J
 380      X = OX+XSTEP*XSCALE
 390    NEXT I
 400    GET (0,200)-(1279,600),PIC%
 410    SCREEN 1,,1,1 : PUT (0,600),PIC%,OR
 420    SCREEN 1,,0,1 : CLS
 430 RETURN

1000 DATA 4
1010 REM "F"
1020 DATA 11
1030 DATA 1,0,128, 1,80,0, 1,0,-16, 1,-64,0, 1,0,-40, 1,36,0,
          1,0,-16, 1,-36,0, 1,0,-56, 1,-16,0, 2,8,8
1040 REM "O"
1050 DATA 19
1060 DATA 0,0,16, 1,0,96, 1,16,16, 1,56,0, 1,16,-16, 1,0,-96,
          1,-16,-16, 1,-56,0, 1,-16,16, 0,16,8, 1,0,80, 1,8,8,
          1,32,0, 1,8,-8, 1,0,-80, 1,-8,-8, 1,-32,0, 1,-8,8, 2,-8,0
1070 REM "R"
1080 DATA 19
1090 DATA 1,0,128, 1,64,0, 1,16,-16, 1,0,-36, 1,-16,-16,
          1,16,-60, 1,-16,0, 1,-18,60, 1,-30,0, 1,0,-60,
          1,-16,0, 0,16,76, 1,0,36, 1,40,0, 1,8,-8, 1,0,-20,
          1,-8,-8, 1,-40,0, 2,-8,0
1100 REM "E"
1110 DATA 13
1120 DATA 1,0,128, 1,80,0, 1,0,-16, 1,-64,0, 1,0,-40, 1,36,0,
          1,0,-16, 1,-36,0, 1,0,-40, 1,64,0, 1,0,-16, 1,-80,0, 2,8,8
1130 DATA 3
1140 REM "M"
1150 DATA 11
1160 DATA 1,0,128, 1,40,-44, 1,40,44, 1,0,-128, 1,-16,0, 1,0,84,
          1,-24,-24, 1,-20,24, 1,0,-84, 1,-20,0, 2,8,8
1170 REM "I"
1180 DATA 13
1190 DATA 1,0,16, 1,30,0, 1,0,96, 1,-30,0, 1,0,16, 1,80,0, 1,0,-16,
          1,-30,0, 1,0,-96, 1,30,0, 1,0,-16, 1,-80,0, 2,8,8
1200 REM "D"
1210 DATA 14
1220 DATA 1,0,128, 1,64,0, 1,16,-16, 1,0,-96, 1,-16,-16, 1,-64,0,
          0,16,16, 1,0,96, 1,40,0, 1,8,-8, 1,0,-80, 1,-8,-8,
          1,-40,0, 2,-8,-8
```

Program 2.8 *continued*

10	AND	10	=	10
midground				midground

'ordinary' midground points are left unaltered.

11	AND	10	=	10

'obscured' midground points are now revealed (Figure 2.11c). Thus plotting colour 2 with AND can be used to delete colour 1 and reveal anything behind it.

These operations are demonstrated by Program 2.8. The word 'FORE' is first plotted in red in the foreground plane. The word 'MID' is then plotted in yellow in the midground plane. To do this, the word 'MID' is first plotted in a completely separate area of screen memory. GET is then used to copy this complete screen into an array. The contents of the array are then combined with the word 'FORE' in the main screen by using PUT with the OR action.

A block of screen memory 320 pixels wide and one pixel high is constructed in the array 'FOREDELETE' and this array is PUT (with AND) in successive positions up on the screen. This has the effect of gradually deleting the foreground image and revealing any previously hidden parts of the midground image.

Composite image with priority (4 planes plus background)

On the PCjr, in SCREEN 3 and SCREEN 5, we have four-bit colour codes (16 colours) and this gives us many more possibilities. Program 2.9 illustrates one such possibility.

In this program, we have set up four planes plus background:

foreground (magenta)
midground (yellow)
rearground (red)
distant (blue)
background (black)

The different colour codes for a pixel together with their significance are given in Table 2.5. Each bit in a colour code represents one of the four planes.

The OR colour code, for drawing, contains a 1 in the bit position for the plane involved and zeros in the other bit positions. The AND colour code, for erasing, contains a zero bit for the plane in which erasing is taking place and ones for the planes that are to be unaffected. The colour codes needed for drawing (with OR) or erasing (with AND) in each plane, without affecting the other planes, are listed in Table 2.5.

The program plots an image in three of the four available planes, the plane to be omitted being selected by the user at the keyboard. A small car moves across the screen in the plane that contains no image (see Colour plate 3). The car is displayed in each successive position by using PUT with the OR action. Using PUT with the AND action, to plot a block filled with the appropriate 'delete code', erases the car in readiness for displaying it in a new position.

```
10 CLEAR,,,65536!
20 KEY OFF
30 DIM PAL%(15)
40 DIM PIC%(8002),CARDRAWPIC%(79),CARDELPIC%(79)
50 CLS : PRINT "4 priority planes demonstration" : PRINT
60 PRINT "F(oreground)" : PRINT "M(idground)" :
   PRINT "R(earground)" : PRINT "D(istance)" : PRINT : PRINT
70 PRINT "Select plane for animation(F/M/R/D) : ";
80 ANS$ = INPUT$(1)
90 CLS
100 PLANE = INSTR("FMRD",ANS$)
110 IF PLANE = 0 THEN END
120 CARDRAW = 2^(PLANE-1) : CARDELETE = 15-CARDRAW
130 SCREEN 5,,1,0 : CLS : WINDOW (0,0)-(1279,799)
140 SCREEN 5,,0,1 : CLS : WINDOW (0,0)-(1279,799)
150 RESTORE 200
160 FOR P% = 0 TO 15
170   READ PAL%(P%)
180 NEXT P%
190 PALETTE USING PAL%(0)
200 DATA 0,5,14,5,4,5,14,5,1,5,14,5,4,5,14,5
210 IF PLANE <> 1 THEN RESTORE 1000 : Y = 200 : XSCALE = 1 :
      YSCALE = 2 : XSTEP = 200 : COL = 1 : GOSUB 520  'word
220 IF PLANE <> 2 THEN RESTORE 1130 : Y = 280 : XSCALE = 0.9 :
      YSCALE = 1.75 : XSTEP = 190 : COL = 2 : GOSUB 520  'word
230 IF PLANE <> 3 THEN RESTORE 1230 : Y = 360 : XSCALE = 0.8 :
      YSCALE = 1.5 : XSTEP = 180 : COL = 4 : GOSUB 520  'word
240 IF PLANE <> 4 THEN RESTORE 1360 : Y = 440 : XSCALE = 0.7 :
      YSCALE = 1.25 : XSTEP = 170 : COL = 8 : GOSUB 520  'word
250 CX = 0 : CY = 460
260 LINE (0,CY-68)-(1279,CY-68),CARDRAW
270 GET (0,CY-68)-(1279,CY-68),PIC%
280 SCREEN 5,,1,1 : PUT (0,CY-68),PIC%,OR
290 SCREEN 5,,0,1 : CLS
300 COLOR = CARDRAW : GOSUB 460  'draw cardraw
310 GET (200,200)-(267,267),CARDRAWPIC%
320 COLOR = CARDELETE : GOSUB 430  'draw cardel
330 GET (200,200)-(267,267),CARDELPIC%
340 SCREEN 5,,1,1
350 PUT (CX,CY),CARDRAWPIC%,OR
360 FOR STEPINX = 1 TO 34
370   NX = CX+32
380   PUT (CX,CY),CARDELPIC%,AND
390   PUT (NX,CY),CARDRAWPIC%,OR
400   CX = NX
410 NEXT STEPINX
420 INPUT ANY$ : SCREEN 0 : END
```

Program 2.9 Four image planes (foreground, midground, rearground and distant) with car animated in selected plane. (PCjr only.)

```
430 'SUBROUTINE draw cardel
440   LINE (200,200)-(267,267),COLOR,BF
450 RETURN

460 'SUBROUTINE draw cardraw
470   LINE (210,218)-(267,235),COLOR,BF
480   LINE (222,235)-(240,260),COLOR,BF
490   CIRCLE (220,210),7,COLOR : PAINT (220,210),COLOR,COLOR
500   CIRCLE (252,210),7,COLOR : PAINT (252,210),COLOR,COLOR
510 RETURN

520 'SUBROUTINE word
530   CLS
540   READ LETTERS
550   X = (1280-LETTERS*XSTEP*XSCALE)/2
560   OY = Y
570   FOR I = 1 TO LETTERS
580     OX = X : Y = OY
590     PSET (OX,OY),0
600     READ NO
610     FOR J = 1 TO NO
620       READ P,RX,RY
630       X = X+RX*XSCALE : Y = Y+RY*YSCALE
640       IF P = 0 THEN PSET (X,Y),0
          ELSE IF P = 1 THEN LINE -(X,Y),COL
          ELSE IF P = 2 THEN PAINT (X,Y),COL,COL
650     NEXT J
660     X = OX+XSTEP*XSCALE
670   NEXT I
680   GET (0,200)-(1279,600),PIC%
690   SCREEN 5,,1,1 : PUT (0,600),PIC%,OR
700   SCREEN 5,,0,1 : CLS
710 RETURN

1000 DATA 4
1010 REM "F"
         .
         .
         .
       DATA for "FORE" and "MID" as before.
         .
         .
1230 DATA 4
1240 REM "R"
1250 DATA 19
1260 DATA 1,0,128, 1,64,0, 1,16,-16, 1,0,-36, 1,-16,-16, 1,16,-60,
          1,-16,0, 1,-18,60, 1,-30,0, 1,0,-60, 1,-16,0, 0,16,76,
          1,0,36, 1,40,0, 1,8,-8, 1,0,-20, 1,-8,-8, 1,-40,0, 2,-8,0
1270 REM "E"
1280 DATA 13
```

continued

```
1290 DATA 1,0,128, 1,80,0, 1,0,-16, 1,-64,0, 1,0,-40, 1,36,0, 1,0,-16,
          1,-36,0, 1,0,-40, 1,64,0, 1,0,-16, 1,-80,0, 2,8,8
1300 REM "A"
1310 DATA 13
1320 DATA 1,32,128, 1,16,0, 1,32,-128, 1,-16,0, 1,-8,44, 1,-24,0,
          1,-8,-44, 1,-16,0, 0,24,60, 1,8,44, 1,8,-44, 1,-16,0,
          2,-8,-8
1330 REM "R"
1340 DATA 19
1350 DATA 1,0,128, 1,64,0, 1,16,-16, 1,0,-36, 1,-16,-16, 1,16,-60,
          1,-16,0, 1,-18,60, 1,-30,0, 1,0,-60, 1,-16,0, 0,16,76,
          1,0,36, 1,40,0, 1,8,-8, 1,0,-20, 1,-8,-8, 1,-40,0, 2,-8,0
1360 DATA 8
1370 REM "D"
1380 DATA 14
1390 DATA 1,0,128, 1,64,0, 1,16,-16, 1,0,-96, 1,-16,-16, 1,-64,0,
          0,16,16, 1,0,96, 1,40,0, 1,8,-8, 1,0,-80, 1,-8,-8,
          1,-40,0, 2,-8,-8
1400 REM "I"
1410 DATA 13
1420 DATA 1,0,16, 1,30,0, 1,0,96, 1,-30,0, 1,0,16, 1,80,0, 1,0,-16,
          1,-30,0, 1,0,-96, 1,30,0, 1,0,-16, 1,-80,0, 2,8,8
1430 REM "S"
1440 DATA 21
1450 DATA 1,0,16, 1,56,0, 1,8,8, 1,0,24, 1,-8,8, 1,-40,0, 1,-16,16,
          1,0,40, 1,16,16, 1,64,0, 1,0,-16, 1,-56,0, 1,-8,-8,
          1,0,-24, 1,8,-8, 1,40,0, 1,16,-16, 1,0,-40, 1,-16,-16,
          1,-64,0, 2,8,8
1460 REM "T"
1470 DATA 10
1480 DATA 0,32,0, 1,0,112, 1,-32,0, 1,0,16, 1,80,0, 1,0,-16,
          1,-32,0, 1,0,-112, 1,-16,0, 2,8,8
1490 REM "A"
1500 DATA 13
1510 DATA 1,32,128, 1,16,0, 1,32,-128, 1,-16,0, 1,-8,44, 1,-24,0,
          1,-8,-44, 1,-16,0, 0,24,60, 1,8,44, 1,8,-44, 1,-16,0,
          2,-8,-8
1520 REM "N"
1530 DATA 11
1540 DATA 1,0,128, 1,16,0, 1,48,-96, 1,0,96, 1,16,0, 1,0,-128,
          1,-16,0, 1,-48,96, 1,0,-96, 1,-16,0, 2,8,8
1550 REM "C"
1560 DATA 22
1570 DATA 0,0,20, 1,0,88, 1,20,20, 1,40,0, 1,20,-20, 1,0,-24,
          1,-16,0, 1,0,12, 1,-16,16, 1,-16,0, 1,-16,-16, 1,0,-64,
          1,16,-16, 1,16,0, 1,16,16, 1,0,12, 1,16,0, 1,0,-24,
          1,-20,-20, 1,-40,0, 1,-20,20, 2,8,8
1580 REM "E"
1590 DATA 13
1600 DATA 1,0,128, 1,80,0, 1,0,-16, 1,-64,0, 1,0,-40, 1,36,0,
          1,0,-16, 1,-36,0, 1,0,-40, 1,64,0, 1,0,-16, 1,-80,0, 2,8,8
```

Program 2.9 *continued*

Table 2.5 Colour codes for a four-level image priority system and the codes needed for plotting and erasing in different planes

COLOUR CODES

Code	*Binary*	*Actual colour*	*Interpretation*
1	0001	magenta	fore
3	0011	magenta	fore obscuring mid
5	0101	magenta	fore obscuring rear
7	0111	magenta	fore obscuring rear, mid
9	1001	magenta	fore obscuring distant
11	1011	magenta	fore obscuring distant, mid
13	1101	magenta	fore obscuring distant, rear
15	1111	magenta	fore obscuring distant, rear, mid
2	0010	yellow	mid
6	0110	yellow	mid obscuring rear
10	1010	yellow	mid obscuring distant
14	1110	yellow	mid obscuring distant, rear
4	0100	red	rear
12	1100	red	rear obscuring distant
8	1000	blue	distant
0	0000	black	background

PLOTTING COLOURS

	draw (OR)	*erase (AND)*
foreground	1	14
midground	2	13
rearground	4	11
distant	8	7

Another possible priority arrangement would be to have only three priority levels, but with three foreground colours. A possible application and the colour code settings required are listed in Table 2.6.

2.6 BASIC INTERACTION TECHNIQUES (PC AND PCJR)

In this section two interaction techniques are implemented. Both of these use the keyboard, but the principles are the same for either a keyboard or a more convenient device such as a digitizer. Both interaction techniques can be used in picture construction and this forms a part of most CAD systems. Such techniques enable designers to work in a two-dimensional or picture domain. This means, for example, that an electrical engineer can work with circuit diagrams and an architect with elevations, or other projections of

Table 2.6 A three-level image priority scheme with three foreground colours

	3 foreground colours		(spaceships?)
	1 midground colour		(planets?)
	1 rearground colour		(stars?)
	1 background colour		(sky?)

Code	*Binary*	*Actual colour*	*Interpretation*
1	0001	red	fore
2	0010	green	fore
3	0011	yellow	fore
5	0101	red	fore obscuring mid
6	0110	green	fore obscuring mid
7	0111	yellow	fore obscuring mid
9	1001	red	fore obscuring rear
10	1010	green	fore obscuring rear
11	1011	yellow	fore obscuring rear
13	1101	red	fore obscuring mid, rear
14	1110	green	fore obscuring mid, rear
15	1111	yellow	fore obscuring mid, rear
4	0100	blue	mid
12	1100	blue	mid obscuring rear
8	1000	magenta	rear
0	0000	black	background

buildings, rather than just numbers. CAD techniques are an extensive topic by themselves and we shall only be concerned here with picture or line-drawing generation. However, it is not out of place to examine just briefly how such techniques 'fit in' to CAD programs. A CAD program that accepts a picture as input has to deduce certain information from it. An electrical engineer may draw a circuit diagram as input. A simple but somewhat unrealistic example serves to illustrate the point; say he or she inputs a series parallel resistor configuration (Figure 2.12). From this, the CAD program has to deduce that a resistor is connected in series to two resistors in parallel, and that the total resistance is:

```
RT = R1 + R2*R3/(R2 + R3)
```

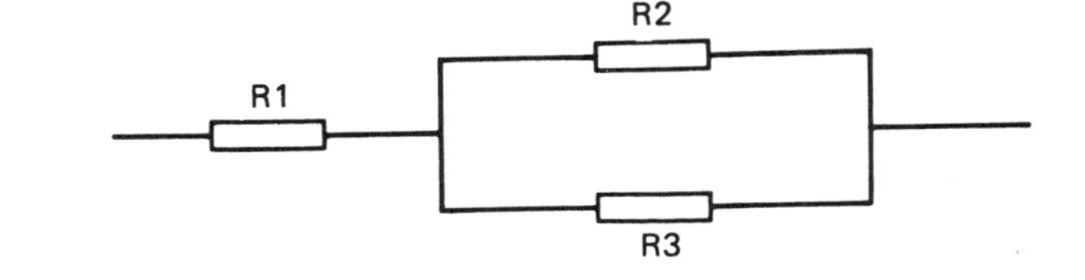

Figure 2.12
A series parallel resistor combination to be constructed on the screen

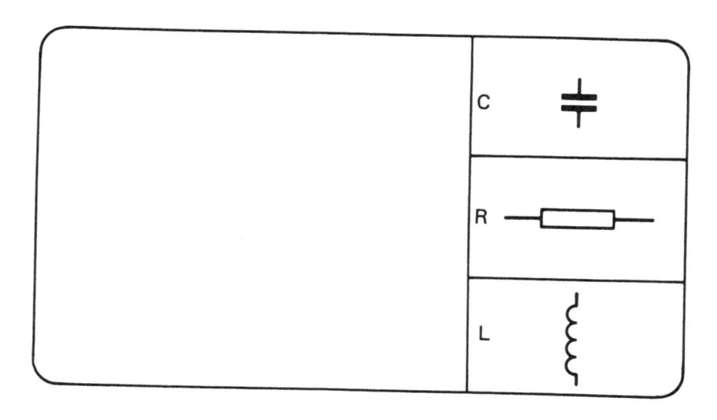

Figure 2.13
A screen layout for picking and dragging

It can then evaluate numerical calculations and output required information, graphically or otherwise, back to the user. The CAD program can also cope with alterations to the diagram – additions, deletions, etc.

The circuit diagram can be built up using a technique known as 'picking and dragging'. A user is presented with a menu of objects, and can pick a particular object and drag it to anywhere on the screen (Figure 2.13).

Other operations that might be available on objects are magnification and rotation. Again, in the case of an electrical circuit diagram, in parallel with the picture-drawing modules there are subroutines that keep track of the spatial relationship between components. The CAD program can then build up a formula reflecting some required attribute or behaviour of the circuit. This may be a transfer characteristic, frequency response, etc. The computer program's view of the problem is numerical or formula based while the engineer's view remains pictorial. This is a tremendous advantage in most design problems.

In the same way an architect may sketch in the elevations of a house and ask for costing, insulation or sunlight calculations.

In the next two sections we look at the front end of such CAD programs, firstly by looking at how we can sketch line drawings on the screen, and secondly how we can pick and drag pre-defined subpictures across the screen.

Cursor drawing

This technique can be used to build up a sketch or line drawing on the screen, made up of line segments whose length and direction are controlled from the keyboard. The program starts by placing two crosses or 'cursors' in the centre of the screen. By using the cursor arrows as direction indicators, we can move the larger of the two cursors anywhere we want.

The larger cursor marks the 'current point' and the smaller cursor

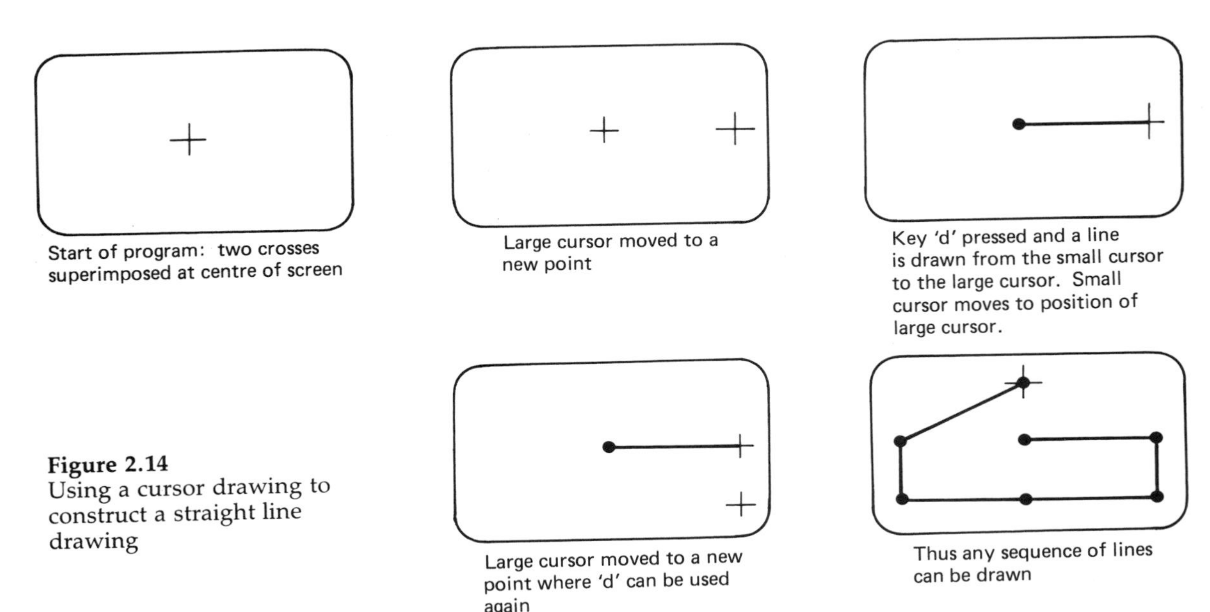

Start of program: two crosses superimposed at centre of screen
Large cursor moved to a new point
Key 'd' pressed and a line is drawn from the small cursor to the large cursor. Small cursor moves to position of large cursor.
Large cursor moved to a new point where 'd' can be used again
Thus any sequence of lines can be drawn

Figure 2.14
Using a cursor drawing to construct a straight line drawing

marks the 'previous point'. Key 'd' can be used to draw a line from the previous point to the current point and key 'm' can be used to 'move' from the previous point to the current point. In either case, both cursors are now at the current point and the larger cursor can now be moved away from this point.

Figure 2.14 illustrates the process of drawing a continuous sequence of lines. The use of the 'm' command in constructing two isolated rectangles is illustrated in Figure 2.15.

Program 2.10 illustrates the technique of cursor drawing. 'XS' and 'YS' always represent the 'previous position' (or the start position of the next line to be drawn); 'X' and 'Y' represent the current position. The main part of the program consists of a WHILE loop that processes commands as long as the key 'q' (quit) has not been typed.

The program always enters the subroutine to process a command having read the next command character. This subroutine first checks for a valid command and then calls the subroutine 'cursors' to delete the cursors in their current position. If 'd' has been pressed, then a line is drawn from (XS,YS) to the current point (X,Y). The current point (X,Y) is then set as the start point for a possible new line. If the command processing subroutine recognizes that one of the cursor arrows has been pressed, then one of the coordinates X,Y is updated by an amount equal to the size of one pixel.

The coordinate increments, 'XSTEP' and 'YSTEP', are set to the dimensions of a pixel in the mode being used. The command processing subroutine terminates by drawing the cursors in the positions now specified by (XS,YS) and (X,Y).

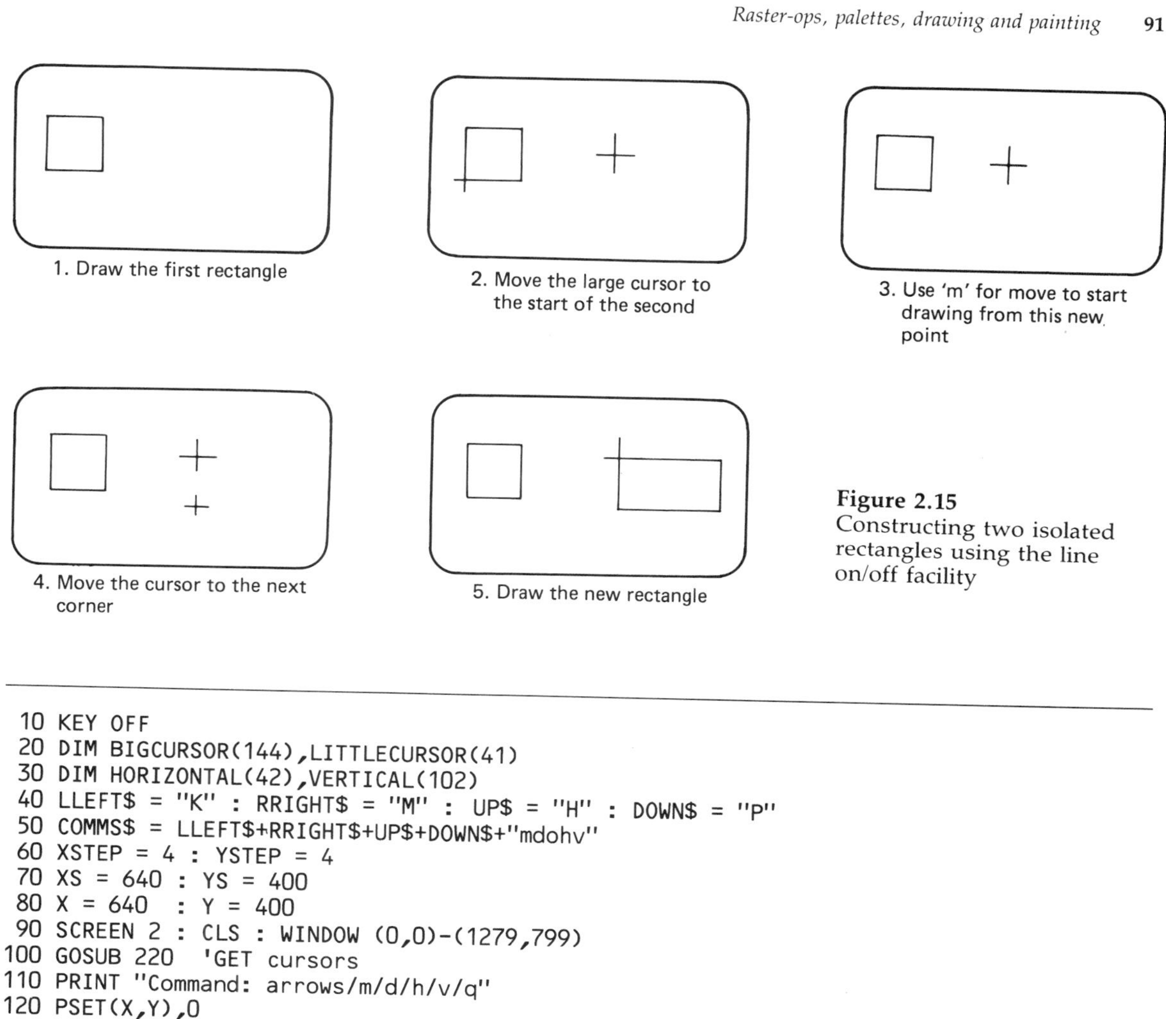

1. Draw the first rectangle
2. Move the large cursor to the start of the second
3. Use 'm' for move to start drawing from this new point
4. Move the cursor to the next corner
5. Draw the new rectangle

Figure 2.15
Constructing two isolated rectangles using the line on/off facility

```
 10 KEY OFF
 20 DIM BIGCURSOR(144),LITTLECURSOR(41)
 30 DIM HORIZONTAL(42),VERTICAL(102)
 40 LLEFT$ = "K" : RRIGHT$ = "M" : UP$ = "H" : DOWN$ = "P"
 50 COMMS$ = LLEFT$+RRIGHT$+UP$+DOWN$+"mdohv"
 60 XSTEP = 4 : YSTEP = 4
 70 XS = 640 : YS = 400
 80 X = 640  : Y = 400
 90 SCREEN 2 : CLS : WINDOW (0,0)-(1279,799)
100 GOSUB 220  'GET cursors
110 PRINT "Command: arrows/m/d/h/v/q"
120 PSET(X,Y),0
130 PUT (X-16,Y-16),BIGCURSOR
    'On the PCjr, use PUT (X-16,Y+16),BIGCURSOR
140 PUT (XS-8,YS-8),LITTLECURSOR
    'On the PCjr, use PUT (XS-8,YS+8),LITTLECURSOR
150 COMMAND$ = INKEY$
160 WHILE COMMAND$ <> "q"
170   GOSUB 370  'process command
180   COMMAND$ = INKEY$
190 WEND
200 GOSUB 330  'cursors
210 END

220 'SUBROUTINE GET cursors
230   LINE (40,40)-(71,40),,,&HCCCC
```

Program 2.10 Cursor drawing.

continued

```
240   LINE (56,24)-(56,55),,,&HAAAA
250   GET (40,24)-(71,55),BIGCURSOR
260   GET (48,32)-(63,47),LITTLECURSOR
270   LINE (640,0)-(640,799)
280   GET (640,0)-(640,799),VERTICAL
290   LINE (0,400)-(1279,400)
300   GET (0,400)-(1279,400),HORIZONTAL
310   CLS
320 RETURN

330 'SUBROUTINE cursors
340   PUT (X-16,Y-16),BIGCURSOR
      'On the PCjr, use PUT (X-16,Y+16),BIGCURSOR
350   PUT (XS-8,YS-8),LITTLECURSOR
      'On the PCjr, use PUT (XS-8,YS+8),LITTLECURSOR
360 RETURN

370 'SUBROUTINE process command
380   IF COMMAND$ = "" THEN RETURN
390   IF LEN(COMMAND$) = 2 THEN COMMAND$ = RIGHT$(COMMAND$,1)
400   IF INSTR(COMMS$, COMMAND$) = 0 THEN RETURN
410   GOSUB 330  'cursors
420   GOSUB 640  'check axis
430   'CASE of command$
440     IF COMMAND$ = "m" THEN GOSUB 560  'move cursor
450     IF COMMAND$ = "d" THEN GOSUB 600  'draw to cursor
460     IF COMMAND$ = LLEFT$ THEN X = X-XSTEP
470     IF COMMAND$ = RRIGHT$ THEN X = X+XSTEP
480     IF COMMAND$ = UP$ THEN Y = Y+YSTEP
490     IF COMMAND$ = DOWN$ THEN Y = Y-YSTEP
500     IF COMMAND$ = "h" THEN HAXIS = NOT(HAXIS)
510     IF COMMAND$ = "v" THEN VAXIS = NOT(VAXIS)
520   'END CASE
530   GOSUB 330  'cursors
540   GOSUB 640  'check axis
550 RETURN

560 'SUBROUTINE move cursor
570   PSET (X,Y),0
580   XS = X : YS = Y
590 RETURN

600 'SUBROUTINE draw to cursor
610   LINE (XS,YS)-(X,Y),1
620   XS = X : YS = Y
630 RETURN

640 'SUBROUTINE check axis
650   IF HAXIS THEN PUT (0,Y),HORIZONTAL
660   IF VAXIS THEN PUT (X,799),VERTICAL
670 RETURN
```

Program 2.10 *continued*

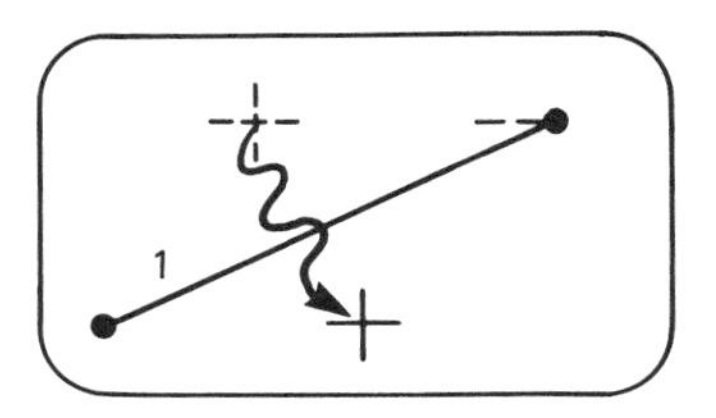

Figure 2.16
The cursor can be swept over the line segment without deleting it

Each cursor is stored as a subpicture in an array that can be plotted using PUT. The important feature of the program is the use of the XOR (exclusive OR) action in the PUT statements used to plot or delete the cursors. XOR is the default action used by PUT if none is specified. Remember that the main property of this plotting operation is that two successive identical plots will restore the screen to its original state. This means that the cursors can be moved over existing lines without permanently wiping part of them out, as would be the case without this facility. Normally, to delete an object we could re-plot the object in the background colour, but this would wipe out intersecting parts of other objects. Using this method, existing information disappears only momentarily while a cursor passes over it. Thus the cursor (Figure 2.16) can be swept over the existing line segment without rubbing it out. This can be explained by reference to the following table.

	1st PUT			*2nd PUT (erase)*	
old	*plotting*	*new*	*old*	*plotting*	*new*
0	1	1	1	1	0
1	1	0	0	1	1

You can see from the bottom row of the table that plotting a 1 on top of a 1 in the first PUT results in a 0 that is restored to a 1 by the 2nd PUT. The top row of the table gives the effect of a normal draw and erase function. The second PUT thus erases or undraws, at the same time restoring any holes in existing lines made by the first PUT.

Figure 2.17 illustrates the use of XOR plotting when dragging a coloured object across another coloured object.

A further drawing aid that is included in Program 2.10 is the ability to switch on or off horizontal and vertical cursor lines. These

Figure 2.17
A moving object (3 colours) being dragged across a fixed object (1 colour). As the moving object passes over the fixed object, pixels change colour as shown

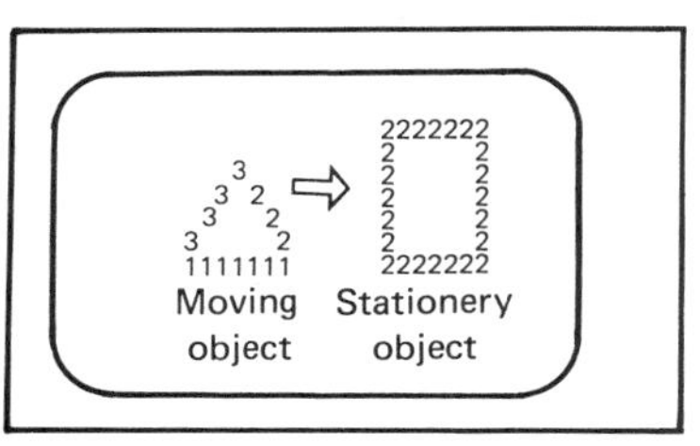

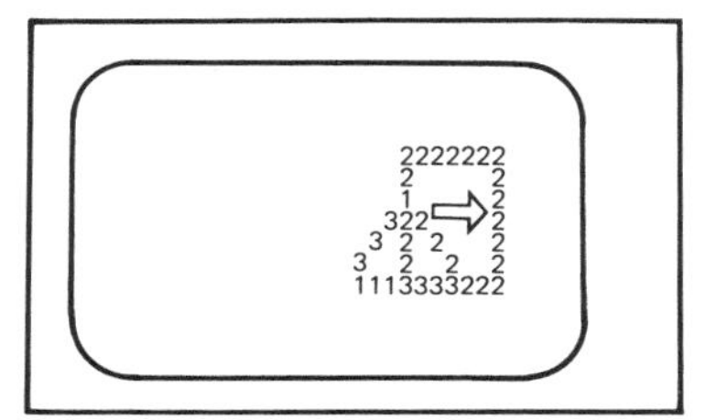

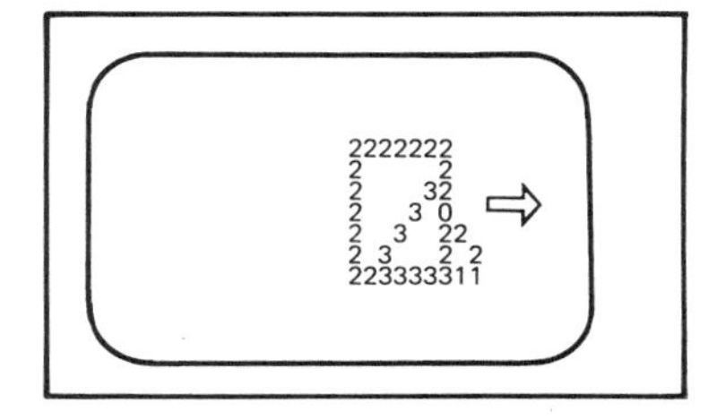

```
 10 DIM CAPACITOR(100),RESISTOR(100),DIODE(100)
 15 LLEFT$ = "K" : RRIGHT$ = "M" : UP$ = "H" : DOWN$ = "P"
 16 MOVECOMMS$ = LLEFT$+RRIGHT$+UP$+DOWN$
 20 SCREEN 2 : CLS
 30 KEY OFF
 40 GOSUB 180  'draws the menu
 50 GOSUB 570  'GETs the menu contents into arrays
 60 GOSUB 800  'GETs object selection
 70 WHILE OBJECT$ <> "q"
 80   X = 100 : Y = 100
 90   GOSUB 750
100   COMMAND$ = INKEY$
110   WHILE COMMAND$ <> "f"
120     GOSUB 620  'process command
130     COMMAND$ = INKEY$
140   WEND
145   GOSUB 791  'PUT object with PSET
150   GOSUB 800  'GETs object selection
160 WEND
170 END

180 'SUBROUTINE draws menu
190   GOSUB 240  'draws capacitor
200   GOSUB 300  'draws resistor
210   GOSUB 350  'draws diode
220   GOSUB 420  'draws remainder of menu
230 RETURN

240 'SUBROUTINE draws capacitor
250   LINE (10,25)-(30,25)
260   LINE (30,10)-(30,40)
270   LINE (40,10)-(40,40)
280   LINE (40,25)-(60,25)
290 RETURN

300 'SUBROUTINE draws a resistor
310   LINE (5,75)-(15,75)
320   LINE (15,80)-(55,70),,B
330   LINE (55,75)-(65,75)
340 RETURN

350 'SUBROUTINE draws a diode
360   LINE (5,125)-(15,125)
370   LINE (15,132)-(15,118)
380   LINE -(30,125) : LINE -(15,132)
390   LINE (30,118)-(30,132)
400   LINE (30,125)-(40,125)
410 RETURN

420 'SUBROUTINE draws remainder of menu
430   LINE (80,0)-(80,150) : LINE (0,0)-(0,150)
440   LINE (0,50)-(80,50)
```

Program 2.11 A simple 'picking and dragging' program.

```
450   LINE (0,100)-(80,100)
460   LINE (0,150)-(80,150)
470   LINE (0,0)-(80,0)
480   LOCATE 19,12
490   PRINT          "   OBJECT      MOVING"
500   PRINT
510   PRINT TAB(12) "c(apacitor)    arrows"
520   PRINT TAB(12) "r(esistor)   f(ix object)"
530   PRINT TAB(12) "d(iode)"
540   PRINT TAB(12) "q(uit)";
560 RETURN

570 'SUBROUTINE  GETs the menu contents into arrays
580   GET (10,10)-(60,40),CAPACITOR
590   GET (5,70)-(65,80),RESISTOR
600   GET (5,118)-(40,132),DIODE
610 RETURN

620 'SUBROUTINE process command
630   IF COMMAND$ = "" THEN RETURN
635   IF LEN(COMMAND$) = 2 THEN COMMAND$ = RIGHT$(COMMAND$,1)
640     IF INSTR(MOVECOMMS$,COMMAND$) = 0 THEN RETURN
650     GOSUB 750  'draws the selected object
660   'CASE of comannd$
680     IF COMMAND$ = LLEFT$ THEN X = X-4
690     IF COMMAND$ = RRIGHT$ THEN X = X+4
700     IF COMMAND$ = UP$ THEN Y = Y-2
710     IF COMMAND$ = DOWN$ THEN Y = Y+2
720   'END CASE
730   GOSUB 750  'draws the selected object
740 RETURN

750 'SUBROUTINE  PUTs the selected object (XOR)
760   IF OBJECT$ = "c" THEN PUT (X,Y),CAPACITOR
770   IF OBJECT$ = "r" THEN PUT (X,Y),RESISTOR
780   IF OBJECT$ = "d" THEN PUT (X,Y),DIODE
790 RETURN

791 'SUBROUTINE  PUTs the selected object (PSET)
792   IF OBJECT$ = "c" THEN PUT (X,Y),CAPACITOR,PSET
793   IF OBJECT$ = "r" THEN PUT (X,Y),RESISTOR,PSET
794   IF OBJECT$ = "d" THEN PUT (X,Y),DIODE,PSET
795 RETURN

800 'SUBROUTINE GETs object selection
810   OBJECT$ = INKEY$
820   WHILE INSTR("qcdr",OBJECT$) = 0 OR OBJECT$ = ""
830     OBJECT$ = INKEY$
840     LINE (80,153)-(175,199),1,B
850     LINE (80,153)-(175,199),0,B
860   WEND
870 RETURN
```

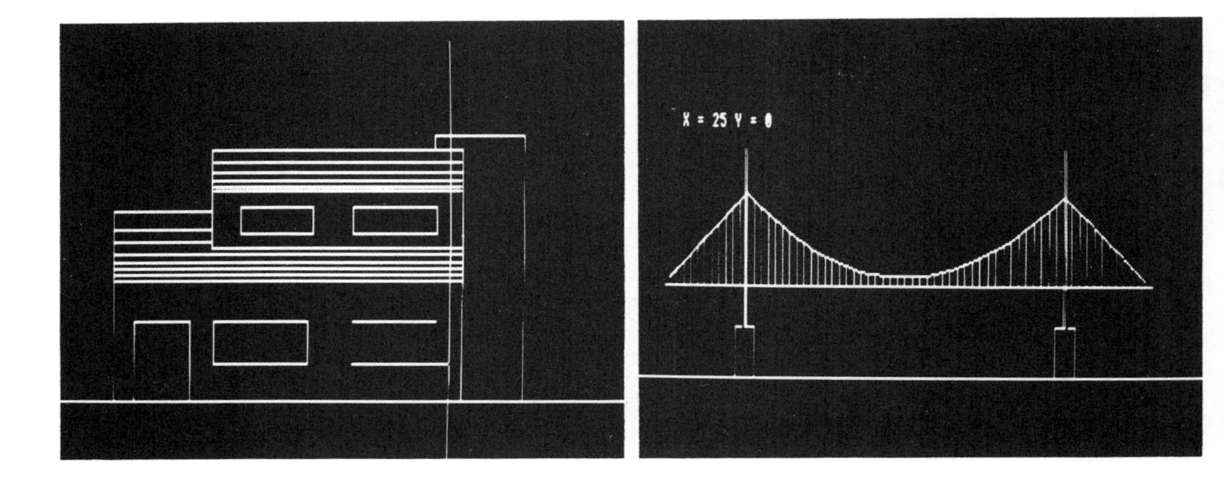

Figure 2.18
Two images constructed by cursor drawing

make it easier to line up different parts of a drawing. 'h' is the on/off switch for the horizontal cursor line and 'v' is the on/off switch for the vertical cursor line. These lines are also stored as arrays for use with PUT and are plotted using the XOR action.

Figure 2.18 shows two images built up using cursor drawing.

Picking and dragging an object

We have already mentioned the use of this particular technique, which involves selecting an object from a menu and moving it under user control to any position on the screen. In Program 2.11 we have set up a menu of objects, one of which is selected by typing 'c', 'd' or 'r'. In practice, if we were using this technique frequently, an object would be selected from the menu by using one of the pointing devices described at the end of this chapter. When an object is selected it is dragged into position and fixed as before. Instead of dragging a cross or cursor, we are now dragging a complete object. The process of dragging an object is identical to the process of dragging the cross in the cursor drawing program. The subroutine that organizes the drawing (or deleting) process selects one out of the three drawing subroutines and the selected object is drawn (or deleted) at the current position (x,y). Figure 2.19 shows the screen during execution of Program 2.11.

Scaling and rotating a dragged object

Other common facilities in picking and dragging programs are magnification and rotation. For example, in the foregoing dragging program, another key option could be 'm' for 'magnify' and 't' (turn) for rotation. Each time such a command is issued, the program would have to switch to a new PUT array that contained a representation of the current object in a different orientation or drawn to a different scale. Such a new array could be generated when it is

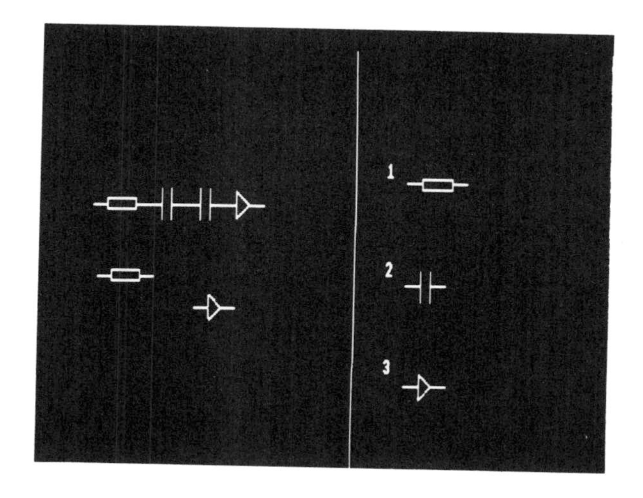

Figure 2.19
The screen during execution of the picking and dragging program (Program 2.11)

required by plotting the object in a separate block of screen memory and using GET. Alternatively, if the number of possible orientations or sizes for each object is limited, then all the PUT arrays can be constructed at the start of the program.

Techniques for carrying out two-dimensional transformations such as rotation and scaling are described in Chapter 3 and techniques for incorporating such techniques in a picking and dragging program are demonstrated in Chapter 5.

Saving a line drawing

An image that has been created by cursor drawing can be saved as a

```
  5 DIM OPERATION(1000),XCOORD(1000),YCOORD(1000) : POINTS = 0
        .
        .
        .

560 'SUBROUTINE move cursor
570   PSET (X,Y),0
580   XS = X : YS = Y
585   POINTS = POINTS+1
586   OPERATION(POINT) = 0 : XCOORD(POINT) = X : YCOORD(POINT) = Y
590 RETURN

600 'SUBROUTINE draw to cursor
610   LINE (XS,YS)-(X,Y),1
620   XS = X : YS = Y
625   POINTS = POINTS+1
626   OPERATION(POINTS) = 1 : XCOORD(POINTS) = X : YCOORD(POINTS) = Y
630 RETURN
```

Program 2.12 Remembering the operations and points used in a cursor drawing program.

file of coordinates. It can be subsequently regenerated by a simple program that reads the coordinates from the file and redraws the image using LINE. The coordinates and codes indicating move or draw can be saved initially in three parallel arrays and, when the drawing is complete, the array contents can be dumped into a file. The coordinate saving could clearly be part of the drawing or moving process (Program 2.12).

Similarly, an image that has been created by picking and dragging an object can be saved, most economically, using three parallel arrays. The program would store, for each object, a pair of coordinates followed by a code indicating the class of object drawn at that position. The program would terminate by outputting the contents of the three arrays to a file. The regenerating program would contain the object-generating subroutines again called from a shape-selection subroutine, the appropriate subroutine for each shape being selected according to the stored code.

2.7 COLOUR PAINTING

Interactive painting in computer graphics is now a well established but rather exotic technique depending on very expensive hardware. It is used in the advertising industry to generate both still and animated images and either these are created by the artist from scratch, or the techniques are used to enhance real images digitized via a TV camera.

Interactive painting means building up a computer image using a light pen or similar device as a brush. A colour can be selected from a menu and used to fill an area of the screen. Various 'textures' might also be available to simulate brush strokes.

On the PC or PCjr, we can go a long way towards these systems. In interactive painting, we require the ability to draw outlines using the techniques covered earlier. We also need to be able to colour these regions from a menu of colours.

Another requirement is to be able to extend the colour range available on a device by mixing or 'dithering' colours – this is covered later in the chapter. In this section, we will examine how to fill regions using just flat colour.

On the PC and PCjr, the PAINT statement provides a fast colouring routine for the BASIC programmer to use. However, writing a colouring algorithm is an interesting problem, and before we look at uses that can be made of the PAINT statement, we will demonstrate how a simple colouring subroutine could be written in BASIC. The program we will write to demonstrate this (Program 2.13) will run very slowly indeed, but it provides a good introduction to the ideas involved.

In interactive painting an outline will normally have been drawn before the colour fill takes place and we want to be able to fill any region no matter how convoluted. We require an algorithm that will allow us to draw a closed region and then select a colour to fill it with.

Algorithms that fill the interior of any closed figure are sometimes called 'flood-fill' algorithms and they work by assuming that the region to be filled is delineated by a boundary of pixels in a non-background colour and that the interior of the region is '4-connected'. This means that all pixels within the region can be reached one from the other by a sequence of any of the movements up, down, left and right. The colour floods from a starting point in the region to a boundary.

Colour Plate 4b shows the algorithm of Program 2.13 in the course of filling a building facade, although we have only included a pair of

```
 10 QSIZE = 200 : DIM QUEUEX(QSIZE),QUEUEY(QSIZE)
 20 R1 = 50 : R2 = 100
 30 SCREEN 1 : CLS : WINDOW (0,0)-(1279,799)
 40 XSTEP = 4 : YSTEP = 4
 50 CIRCLE (640,400),R1
 60 CIRCLE (640,400),R2
 70 STARTX = 640+(R1+R2)/2 : STARTY = 400
 80 GOSUB 110  'fill from
 90 INPUT ANY$
100 SCREEN 0 : END

110 'SUBROUTINE fill from
120   FIRST = 1 : LAST = 0
130   FX = STARTX : FY = STARTY : GOSUB 210  'fill
140   GOSUB 310  'unqueue
150   FX = X : FY = Y+YSTEP : GOSUB 210  'fill
160   FX = X : FY = Y-YSTEP : GOSUB 210  'fill
170   FX = X+XSTEP : FY = Y : GOSUB 210  'fill
180   FX = X-XSTEP : FY = Y : GOSUB 210  'fill
190   IF FIRST <> (LAST+1) MOD QSIZE THEN 140
200 RETURN

210 'SUBROUTINE fill
220   IF POINT(FX,FY) > 0 THEN RETURN
230   PSET (FX,FY)
240   GOSUB 260  'queue
250 RETURN

260 'SUBROUTINE queue
270   LAST = (LAST+1) MOD QSIZE
280   QUEUEX(LAST) = FX
290   QUEUEY(LAST) = FY
300 RETURN

310 'SUBROUTINE unqueue
320   X = QUEUEX(FIRST)
330   Y = QUEUEY(FIRST)
340   FIRST = (FIRST+1) MOD QSIZE
350 RETURN
```

Program 2.13 A simple point queueing colour fill algorithm.

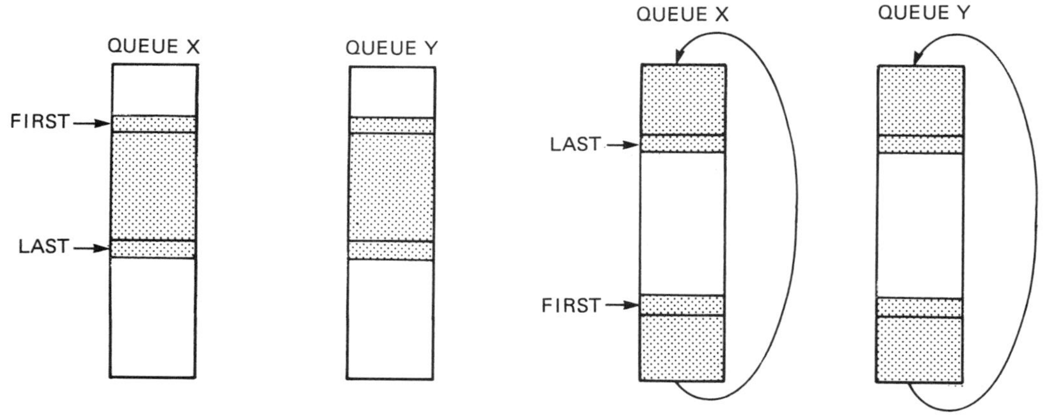

Figure 2.20
Organization of a queue (or FIFO stack): when the end of the arrays is reached, the queue 'wraps around'

circles in the program that drives the algorithm. You can see from the illustration that the filling proceeds with 'diagonal wavefronts'.

The algorithm of Program 2.13 uses a FIFO (first in, first out) buffer or queue. Subroutine 'fill from' is initiated from a start point and that start point is coloured and added to the queue (by calling subroutine 'fill'). 'fill from' then repeatedly takes the first point from the queue and examines each of the neighbouring N, S, E and W pixels (by calling 'fill' for each of these points in turn). Each time 'fill' is called, it colours the point it is given (if it is not already coloured) and adds that point to the end of the queue. Adding a point to the queue in this way ensures that it will subsequently be removed from the queue and its neighbours examined.

The reason the queue is made a FIFO is to ensure that duplicated points are quickly removed from the queue in order to prevent it becoming too large. If, for example, we made the queue an ordinary stack (LIFO or last in first out), as you may see suggested in some computer graphics textbooks, it would gradually fill up and would run out of memory on most micros.

For the queue, we use two arrays, one for x-coordinates and one for y-coordinates. Two variables indicate the positions of the 'FIRST' and 'LAST' items in the queue. The arrays are treated as circular so that when the end of the queue reaches the end of the arrays, the queue is 'wrapped around' and continued into the space that is now free at the start of the arrays (Figure 2.20). Subroutine 'fill from' repeatedly takes the next point from the queue until the queue is empty. Although Program 2.13 is slow, it is worthy of study because of its simplicity. Figure 2.21 presents an illustrated sequence of how the program works for a simple rectangular region. The start point is at the bottom left hand corner.

Most of the flood-fill algorithms used in practice work by queueing (or stacking) complete horizontal strips between two boundary

pixel 1 is filled and added to the queue

1st cycle of loop in fillfrom: pixel 1 is removed from queue and neighbouring points examined

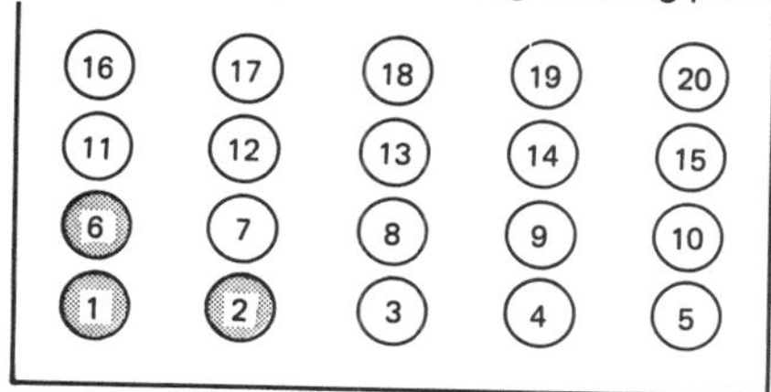

queue is now 6, 2 pixels 6 and 2 are filled

2nd cycle, pixel 6 removed and neighbours examined

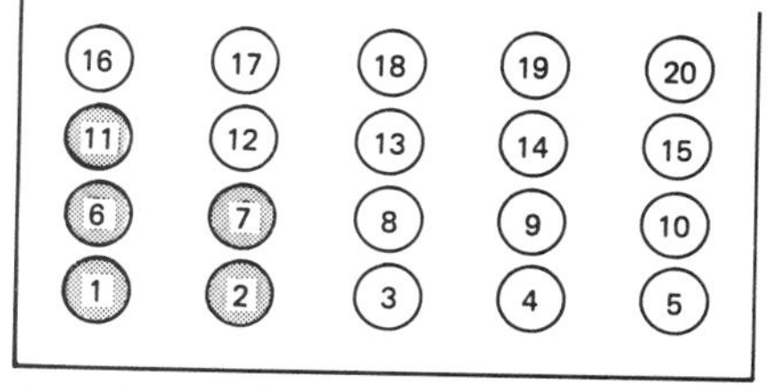

queue is now 2, 11, 7 pixels 11 and 7 are also filled

3rd cycle, pixel 2 removed and neighbours examined

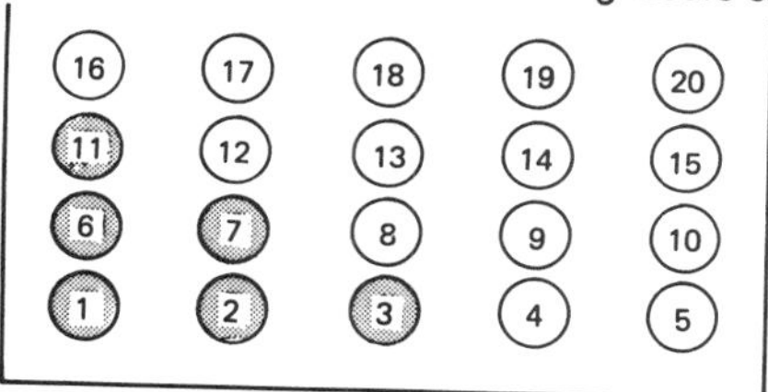

queue is now 11, 7, 3 pixel 3 is filled

4th cycle, pixel 11 removed and neighbours examined

16 17 18 19 20
11 12 13 14 15
6 7 8 9 10
1 2 3 4 5

queue is now 7, 3, 16, 12 pixels 16 and 12 are filled

This sequence continues until the queue is empty

Figure 2.21 A sample colouring sequence produced by the point queueing algorithm

points (Colour Plates 4c and 4d). This makes more efficient use of memory space. However, we will not look in detail at the operation of these algorithms, but will proceed directly to look at the flood-fill algorithm provided in BASIC by the PAINT statement.

The PAINT statement in PC and PCjr BASIC

At its simplest, the PAINT statement has the following form:

```
PAINT (x,y)
```

This starts a flood-fill from the point (x,y) in the current foreground colour. Filling takes place out to a boundary that is drawn in the current foreground colour.

Another form that a simple PAINT statement can take is:

```
PAINT (x,y), paintingcolor
```

where the painting colour is an integer colour code. This fills from the point (x,y) in the painting colour specified. Filling takes place to a boundary that is drawn in the painting colour.

The last form of the PAINT statement that we mention at this stage is:

```
PAINT (x,y), paintingcolor, boundarycolor
```

This again fills from the point (x,y) in the given painting colour, but this form enables us to specify a boundary colour different from the colour in which filling takes place.

Interactive drawing and painting

An interactive design package should combine techniques for producing line drawings with colouring facilities. In Program 2.14, we have shown the changes to Program 2.10 that are needed to do this.

In Program 2.10, we used the cursor arrows to control our 'cursor-drawing' program. There are many more convenient ways for inputting line drawings but we will continue to use the keyboard. Various interactive graphics devices are described at the end of this chapter.

Program 2.14 includes fairly limited colouring facilities. The user can use a key to select one of three colours, b(lue), m(agenta), w(hite), and the region containing the cursor is filled with the selected colour. Note that the region to be filled must be completely surrounded by a boundary. If this is not the case, the colour will 'leak' out through any gaps in the boundary into other regions – a well-known error, graphically known as bleeding.

Colour mixtures – super pixelling (PCjr only)

By mixing colours on the screen in different patterns, the programmer can obtain the effect of many more than the four basic colours available in SCREEN 1 or 4 (or the 16 basic colours available in SCREEN 3 or 5 on the PCjr). A recently coined term for such colour mixing is 'stippling'. The effect is similar to that of colour printing. A small group of pixels of different colours are 'spatially mixed' by the eye. If the basic colours are chosen carefully, this creates the effect of a shade that is different from that of the individual pixels. The

```
 50 COMMS$ = LLEFT$+RRIGHT$+UP$+DOWN$+"mdohvp"
 85 COLS$ = "bmw"
 90 SCREEN 1 : CLS : WINDOW (0,0)-(1279,799)
110 PRINT "Command : arrows/m/d/h/v/q/p"
230   LINE (40,40)-(71,40),,,&HAAAA
455   IF COMMAND$ = "p" THEN GOSUB 680 'paint
610   LINE (XS,YS)-(X,Y),3

680 'SUBROUTINE paint
690   LOCATE 2,1 : PRINT "Color b/m/w "
700   CC$ = INPUT$(1)
710   LOCATE 2,1 : PRINT SPC(15)
720   COLOR = INSTR(COLS$,CC$)
730   IF COLOR = 0 THEN RETURN
740   PAINT (X,Y),COLOR,3
750 RETURN
```

Program 2.14 Alterations needed to include simple colouring facilities in Program 2.10.

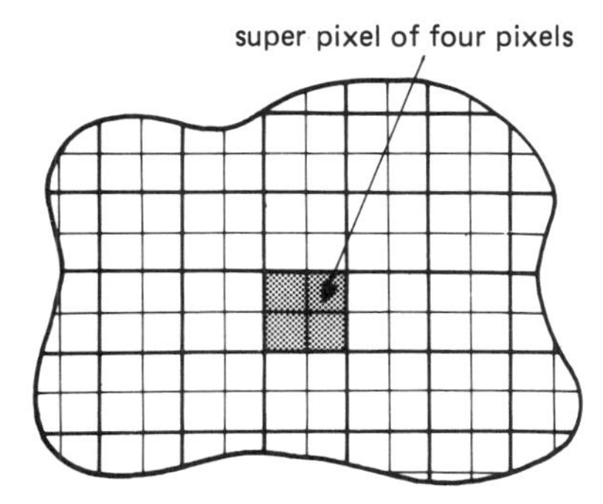

Figure 2.22
'Super pixels'

geometry of the mixing pattern has to be carefully chosen, otherwise 'global' patterns, such as diagonal lines, emerge.

The PAINT statement provides an extremely powerful facility (called 'tiling') for laying down colour mixtures on the screen. Simple use of this facility has already been demonstrated in Program 1.28.

We will restrict the range of mixing patterns we use so as to simplify the explanation of the tiling facility. Even with our restricted range of mixing patterns, we will find that we can extend the range of shades in a four-colour mode, such as SCREEN 1, from 4 to 16, by mixing the three foreground colours in various combinations. Even more shades can be produced if the background colour is included in the mixtures. In a 16-colour mode, many more combinations are possible.

First of all, let us look at the basic mixture patterns that we shall use for combining colours. Any region to be coloured will be divided into blocks where each block measures two pixels by two pixels – a 'super pixel'. This is illustrated in Figure 2.22. By plotting a selection of different colours in a super pixel and repeating this pattern of colours in the other super pixels over the region being coloured, we can create the effect of many different shades.

We shall restrict our consideration to mixtures of the three foreground colours in a four-colour mode such as SCREEN 1. This means that we cannot use colour 0 in our colour mixtures. Colours 1, 2 and 3 can be mixed in any combination we like within a pixel. There are 81 such patterns ($3\times3\times3\times3$) for one super pixel, but many of these patterns are equivalent when spread over a region.

Let us look first at the different ways of combining colours 1 and 2 within a super pixel. These colours are normally set to cyan and magenta and mixing them will give various shades of mauve.

Figure 2.23 shows the 16 theoretically different ways of combining colours 1 and 2 in a super pixel. 'mixture' a is, of course, pure cyan and 'mixture' p is pure magenta.

Now look at mixtures b, c, e and i. Each of these contain three cyan pixels and one magenta. If one of these mixtures is repeated

a	b	c	d	e	f	g	h
1 1	1 1	1 1	1 1	1 2	1 2	1 2	1 2
1 1	1 2	2 1	2 2	1 1	1 2	2 1	2 2

i	j	k	l	m	n	o	p
2 1	2 1	2 1	2 1	2 2	2 2	2 2	2 2
1 1	1 2	2 1	2 2	1 1	1 2	2 1	2 2

Figure 2.23
Different ways of filling a super pixel with colours 1 and 2

over a large region, the overall result is the same – mainly cyan with an occasional spot of magenta. On a high quality monitor, you can see the individual spots of magenta, but on many televisions, the pixels merge together to produce a mauvy-blue effect. Whether the colours mix into a flat shade with individual pixels invisible depends not only on the monitor resolution but also on the contrast between the pairs of colours that are mixed.

Mixtures d, f, g, j, k and m all contain equal proportions of cyan and magenta and these all create an intermediate effect. Whether or not the horizontal, vertical or diagonal stripes of the underlying colours can be seen again depends on the type of television or monitor being used.

Finally, mixtures h, l, n and o each contain three magenta pixels and one cyan one. Thus, out of the 16 different mixing patterns in Figure 2.23, there are really only three different shades apart from the two basic colours being used. In addition, the shades that contain equal quantities of the two basic colours can be categorised into horizontally, vertically or diagonally banded mixtures which will result in differences in texture of the resulting shade.

If we now allow colours 1, 2 or 3 to be mixed within a pixel, then, out of the 81 different ways of combining three different colours, there are 15 different proportions in which the colours can be used and the ways in which we shall obtain these proportions in Program 2.15 are illustrated in Figure 2.24. Thus, in addition to the background colour, we shall provide 15 different foreground shades that can be used in a four-colour mode. With the colour 1 set to cyan, colour 2 set to magenta and colour 3 set to white, these mixtures will include shades of mauve and blue.

Of course, the basic palette can be changed. On the PC, colours 1 to 3 can be set to green, red and brown by using the COLOR statement. On the PCjr, colours 1 to 3 can be set to any three of the 16 actual colours available. This extends the range to many hundreds of possible foreground shades, although only 15 can appear on the screen at once.

In SCREEN 3 or SCREEN 5 on the PCjr, there are 16 basic colours available which makes many more mixes possible. In SCREEN 3, although the pixels are bigger than in SCREEN 1, the results of mixing can be quite effective.

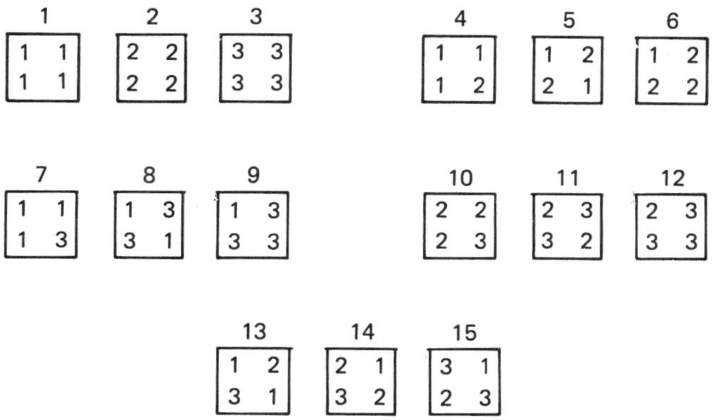

Figure 2.24
Super pixel mixtures used in colour mixing program

Application of colour mixtures

Now we come to the problem of laying down one of these colour mixtures using the PAINT statement.

The final form of the PAINT command (PCjr only) that we will use for doing this is:

```
PAINT (x,y), tilingpattern, background
```

The tiling pattern is a string that describes the way in which a colour mixture is to be constructed. This string is interpreted as a sequence of bytes, each byte describing a combination of colours to be used on successive rows of pixels. Since each character in the string is interpreted as a byte that describes a combination of colours for consecutive pixels, the most convenient way of defining the characters in the string is by writing their ASCII codes in hex form. Thus, to alternate vertical stripes of colours 2 and 3 in a region that is being painted, we require a horizontal row of pixels to contain the sequence of colours:

2 3 2 3 2 3 2 3 ...

In SCREEN 1, each colour is coded as two bits and one byte will specify the sequence of colours in four consecutive pixels. This one byte will be used to describe the grouping of colours:

in binary:	2	3	2	3
in binary:	10	11	10	11
in hex:(&H)	B		B	

The PAINT statement would be:

```
PAINT (X,Y), CHR$(&HBB), 3
```

This gives vertical stripes of colour because the pattern described by the one byte in the tiling pattern is repeated vertically. Filling will take place to a boundary in colour 3.

If we want consecutive rows to contain different patterns, we need to include more than one byte in the tiling pattern. To obtain a checkerboard pattern of colour 2 with colour 3, we need:

2 3 2 3
3 2 3 2

which is in binary:

10 11 10 11
11 10 11 10

giving in hex:

(&H) B B
(&H) E E

```
 35 DIM TIL$(15)
 85 REM **DELETED**
105 GOSUB 740  'initialise mix
109 LOCATE 1,1

680 'SUBROUTINE paint
690   LOCATE 2,1 : INPUT "Color mix (1..15)";MIX
700   LOCATE 2,1 : PRINT SPC(25)
710   IF MIX < 1 OR MIX > 15 THEN BEEP : RETURN
720   PAINT (X,Y),TIL$(MIX),3
730 RETURN

740 'SUBROUTINE initialise mix
750   TIL$(1) = CHR$(&H55)
760   TIL$(2) = CHR$(&HAA)
770   TIL$(3) = CHR$(&HFF)
780   TIL$(4) = CHR$(&H55)+CHR$(&H66)
790   TIL$(5) = CHR$(&H66)+CHR$(&H99)
800   TIL$(6) = CHR$(&H66)+CHR$(&HAA)
810   TIL$(7) = CHR$(&H55)+CHR$(&H77)
820   TIL$(8) = CHR$(&H77)+CHR$(&HDD)
830   TIL$(9) = CHR$(&H77)+CHR$(&HFF)
840   TIL$(10)= CHR$(&HAA)+CHR$(&HBB)
850   TIL$(11)= CHR$(&HBB)+CHR$(&HEE)
860   TIL$(12)= CHR$(&HBB)+CHR$(&HFF)
870   TIL$(13)= CHR$(&H66)+CHR$(&HDD)
880   TIL$(14)= CHR$(&H99)+CHR$(&HEE)
890   TIL$(15)= CHR$(&HDD)+CHR$(&HBB)
900   FOR MIX = 1 TO 15
910     IF MIX MOD 2 <> 0 THEN PMIX = PMIX+2 ELSE PMIX = PMIX +1
920     LINE (1030,799-(MIX*50-50))-(1130,799-MIX*50),3,B
930     PAINT (1080,799-(MIX*50-25)),TIL$(MIX),3
940     LOCATE PMIX,37 : PRINT MIX;
950   NEXT MIX
960 RETURN
```

Program 2.15 Alterations needed to include colour mixing in Program 2.14.

Thus the PAINT statement required would be:

```
PAINT (X,Y), CHR$(&HBB) + CHR$(&HEE), 3
```

More elaborate patterns can be built up by using longer strings, each byte in the string describing another row of four pixels in the tiling pattern. However, the forms that we have introduced so far are enough to implement the colour-mixing scheme described in the previous section.

Program 2.15 shows the modifications to Program 2.14 that are needed to include colour mixing. The program displays a palette of numbered colour mixtures on the right of the screen, and, when the user issues the command 'p' for paint, he or she is asked for a colour number. Painting then takes place using the colour mixture from the displayed palette that has the specified number.

Finally, note that in a 16-colour mode such as SCREEN 3 or SCREEN 5 on the PCjr, each pixel colour requires four bits. This means that a byte in the tiling pattern codes the colours of only two consecutive pixels on the screen. Thus, in SCREEN 3:

```
PAINT (X,Y), CHR$(&H23), 15
```

paints alternating vertical stripes in colours 2 and 3.

```
PAINT (X,Y), CHR$(&H23) + CHR$(&H32), 15
```

paints a checkerboard pattern in colours 2 and 3.

2.8 GRAPHICS INPUT DEVICES

Throughout this chapter, the keyboard has been the main device used to interact with our programs. There are many input devices that are more convenient for interactive graphics programming.

Interactive graphics depends on input devices and such devices can be categorised according to their function in a system. First of all we need to be able to point to a particular position on the screen – for example, to select a particular entity from a menu. We thus need a pointing device. Secondly, we need to input (x,y) coordinates to an interactive system – for example, to define or draw new shapes or to identify a position at which a pre-defined shape is to be drawn. Thirdly, we need a state-selection device to inform an interactive system what state the system is to be in – accepting a menu selection, accepting a stream of coordinates from a digitizer and whether the coordinates are pen-up or pen-down, etc. Most devices will service more than one of these functions. For example, a light pen although predominantly a pointing device can also function as a positioning device (but less conveniently – see later). A graphics tablet is predominantly a positioning device and is only slightly less convenient to use as a pointing device compared with a light pen. A keyboard is predominantly a state-selection device but it can be used as a pointing and a positioning device. However, it is a very inconvenient way of providing these functions.

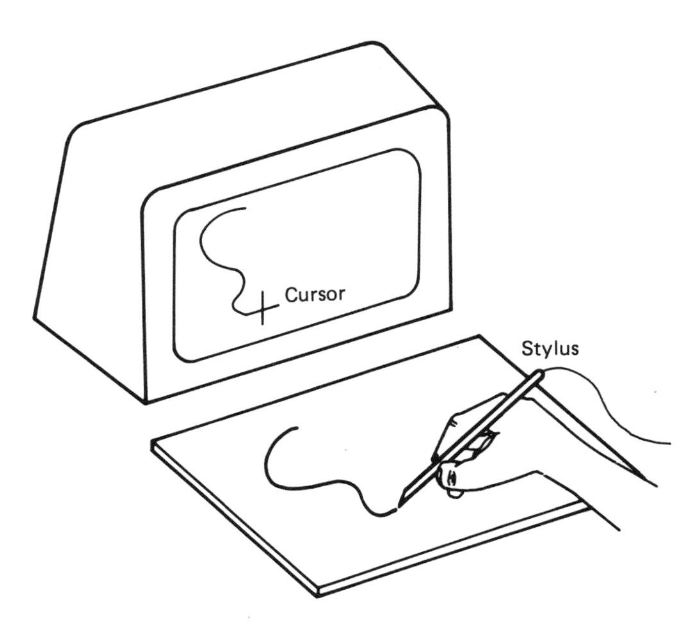

Figure 2.25
Graphics tablet

Graphics tablets

A graphics tablet is one of the most convenient input devices and the term is used to describe any device that consists of a flat surface, separate from the display, over which some kind of stylus is moved (Figure 2.25). It is the most versatile input device and can be used as both a position device and a pointing device. If a puck (see later) is used instead of a stylus, then it can perform all three functions – pointing, positioning and state selection. Although many times more expensive than a light pen it is frequently used in professional computer graphics because of this versatility.

Using a graphics tablet for positioning is much more natural than using a joystick or a light pen because it is equivalent to drawing with a pen on paper. Such devices are of course more expensive than joysticks or light pens. However, there is a whole range of graphics tablet technologies and the cheaper devices are currently about one quarter to one half of the price of a processor. Generally the more expensive a device is the more accurate it is.

Information sent from the device consists of the current (x,y) coordinate of the stylus, or a stream of (x,y) coordinates as the stylus is moved. This stream can be controlled in one of three ways. Firstly, an (x,y) coordinate can be sent to the processor on request. Secondly, an (x,y) coordinate can be sent at equal time intervals, and, thirdly an (x,y) coordinate can be sent every time the stylus is moved more than some distance d. The time interval method is used when a user is drawing on the tablet and the drawing is to be displayed on the screen. The drawing action on the tablet is then mirrored on the screen. The distance interval method is appropriate

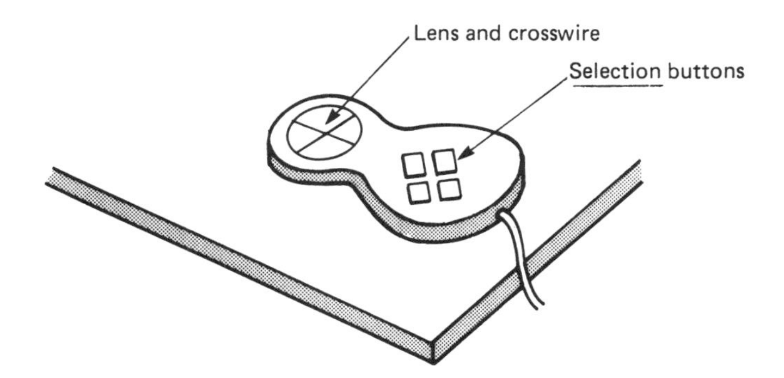

Figure 2.26
A puck combines the function of a positioning device and a state-selection device

when an existing drawing is being digitized. When digitizing a line drawing such as, for example, a map it is impossible for the user to move the stylus over different parts of the drawing at uniform velocity, and distance sampling effectively edits an uneven data stream. Alternatively, a pressure-sensitive switch on the stylus can be used to signal that a point is to be sent. Another logical signal that has to be sent when digitizing is a pen-up pen-down state indication. When a point is sent to the processor the user must state whether this is a pen-up or pen-down point. This facility can be incorporated on the processor keyboard or a flat cross wire cursor device with buttons on it can be used instead of a pen stylus. This device is called a puck (Figure 2.26).

When using a tablet, visual feedback is provided by either mirroring the stylus movement on the screen, if the system is in the pen-down state, or by mirroring the stylus movement by using a cursor. This moves around as the stylus is moved in the pen-up state.

The cheapest tablet technology and the least natural to use is a device made with a pair of potentiometers (Figure 2.27). One poten-

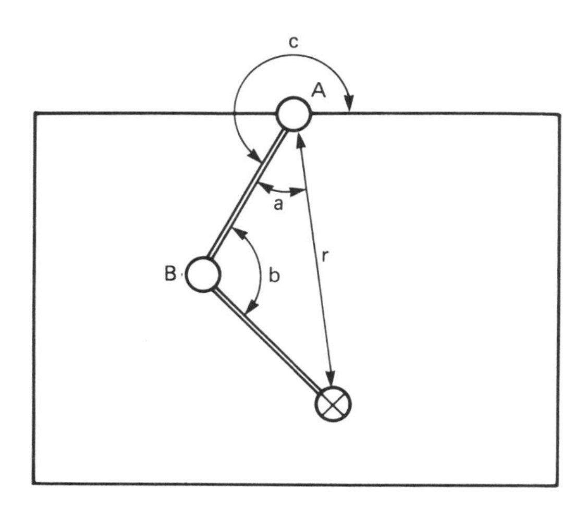

Figure 2.27
An inexpensive graphics tablet design uses two potentiometers

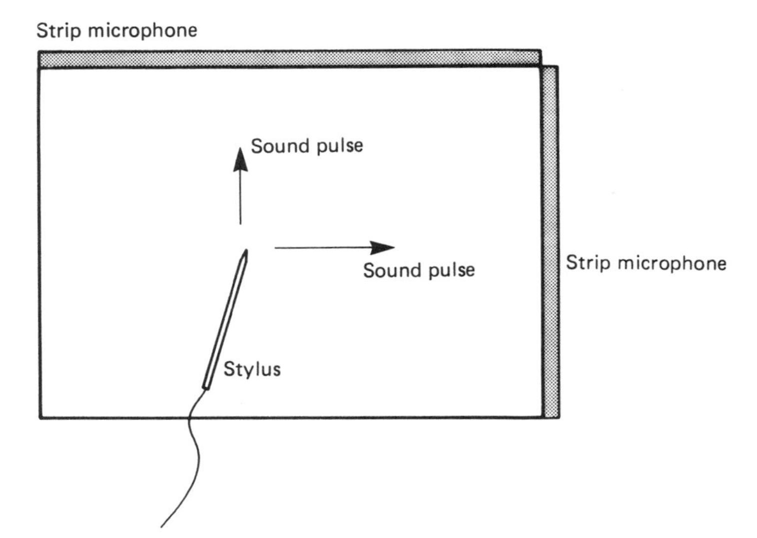

Figure 2.28
Acoustic tablet uses strip microphones and a spark emitting stylus

tiometer (A) is fixed and the other is mounted on the axis that joins two radial arms. The stylus is mounted at the end of the lower radial arm and as it is moved over the surface, angles a, b and c and distance r vary. The angle c is proportional to the voltage from potentiometer A and the angle a can be calculated from angle b which is proportional to the voltage from potentiometer B. r can be computed from the geometry of the system and we can calculate x and y coordinates measured from point A as:

$$x = r \cos (a + c)$$
$$y = r \sin (a + c)$$

This device can easily be built at home. If purchased it will be considerably cheaper than any of the higher technology devices. It

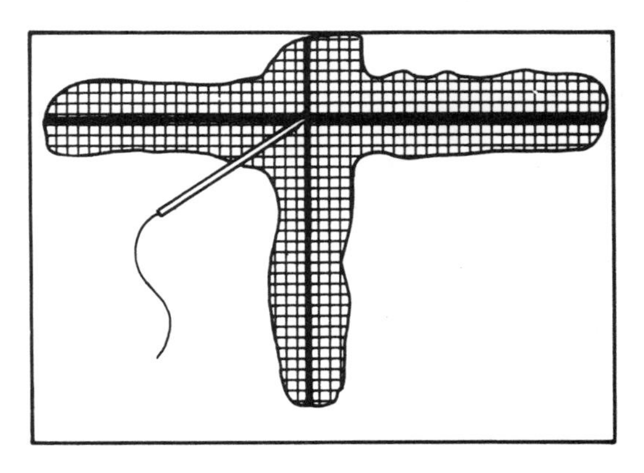

Figure 2.29
The most convenient tablets use a grid of fine wires embedded below (or technology that is equivalent)

does, however, suffer from lack of accuracy and linearity. Because the stylus is rigidly fixed to the lower radial arm it is less natural and thus more difficult to use than a 'free' stylus.

A more expensive device uses acoustic technology (Figure 2.28). Strip microphones are mounted along two sides of the tablet. The stylus emits audible sound pulses by generating a spark at regular intervals. The time delay from the initiation of the spark to the reception of the noise pulse by a strip microphone is proportional to the distance of the stylus from the microphone. The horizontal microphone thus measures the y coordinate and the vertical microphone measures the x coordinate. An advantage of this technology is that it can be extended to three dimensions and three-dimensional range information from a solid body can be input using three mutually perpendicular strip microphones.

Yet another type of tablet, developed originally by the RAND corporation and known as the RAND tablet, uses a grid of fine wires embedded in the surface (Figure 2.29). Each wire carries a uniquely coded signal. The stylus picks up this code and decoding logic identifies which x and y line intersection the stylus is near. This is very accurate but expensive technology. Technology that uses a sensitive tablet is usually the most accurate and convenient and this device was the first sensitive tablet type.

Possibly the most common device in use (apart from the potentiometer type) is one that uses sheet magnetostrictive material. This effectively acts as a matrix of embedded wires but is cheaper to manufacture. Pulses are sent through the material horizontally and then vertically and measurement of time delays provides the coordinate information.

The mouse

Currently, the most popular interaction device used with microprocessors is a mouse. It is a hand-held device that can be moved over any flat surface. Rollers on the base of the device are connected to potentiometers, and the device outputs the magnitude and direction of any change in its position (that is of its rollers).

Unlike the tablet and stylus which give absolute coordinates, the mouse delivers relative coordinates. Its absolute position on the surface is immaterial, and it can be picked up and re-positioned without any change in the coordinates that it reports. Changes occur only when it is moved in contact with the surface.

The reasons for its popularity are: it does not need a special sensitive tablet or a large free area for its operation, it is convenient and easy to use, and it is cheap.

Joysticks

The most popular use of a joystick (Figure 2.30) in microprocessors is to control a computer game. In this context the device is functioning as a positioner, moving a spaceship or whatever over the screen in response to manual movement of the joystick. They can also be

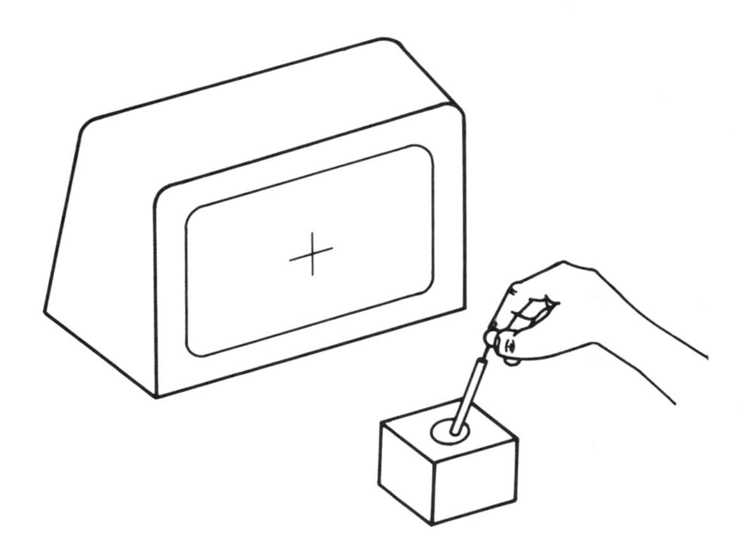

Figure 2.30
A joystick is a common positioning device

used as pointing devices. Although extremely cheap and good positioning devices for computer games, they do not function well as positioning devices in general when a freehand shape is to be input. They are not as natural to use as a stylus or light pen for positioning because the drawing action is completely divorced from the act of drawing on a surface.

Light pens

A light pen is predominantly a pointing device. Unlike the graphics tablet it has no hardware that outputs a stream of (x,y) coordinates. It can, however, function as a positioning device providing a track-

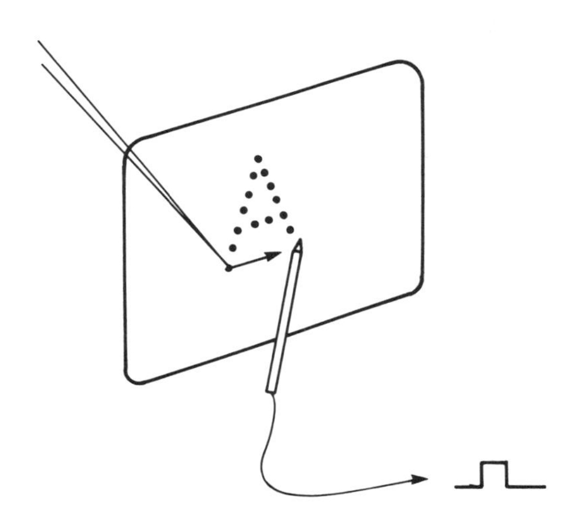

Figure 2.31
Light pen: photo detector in the stylus emits a pulse when the electron beam passes

ing program is running. It is therefore a hardware pointing device and a software positioning device. A light pen is a very cheap and effective pointing device. Its operation is illustrated in Figure 2.31. The light pen contains a photo-detector and is placed at a certain (non-blank) position on the screen. When the raster scan beam comes into coincidence with the light pen a pulse is generated and detected by the processor. The processor compares the time of this with the start of the raster scan and calculates the (x,y) coordinate of the stylus point.

3 Manipulations in the two-dimensional world

In this chapter we will be looking at two-dimensional transformations. The treatment is necessarily mathematical because mathematics gives us an ordered general framework for dealing with transformations. The mathematics used for linear transformations involves matrix notation. Although not difficult the details have been isolated in Appendix 3. As with other mathematical techniques in the book these can be ignored if you are unhappy with them and the end result of the mathematics used as a recipe in the form of a subroutine. The principles are easy to understand and you can become adept at two-dimensional manipulations using a recipe approach.

Non-linear transformations, a topic usually ignored in standard computer graphics texts, are introduced using two intriguing applications: the species 'transformations' of D'arcy Thompson and anamorphic art. Study of this chapter will enable you to explore mathematically based computer art or pattern generation. Subsequent chapters take you deeper into this theme.

3.1 TWO-DIMENSIONAL TRANSFORMATIONS AND MATRIX NOTATION

The easiest two-dimensional transformation to implement and one that you have probably used already is translation or movement in one direction. Translation is one of a set of linear transformations that we can apply to a set of coordinates that specify the vertices or corners of a piecewise linear figure.

In the more general case a set of points S is operated on by a transformation T to produce the set S'. This means that a mathematical operation is carried out on all the points in S, changing their coordinate values to produce points in S' (Figure 3.1).

Depending on the operation used this may change the shape of a figure that is defined by drawing straight lines between the points. In Figure 3.1 the rectangle defined by drawing lines between the

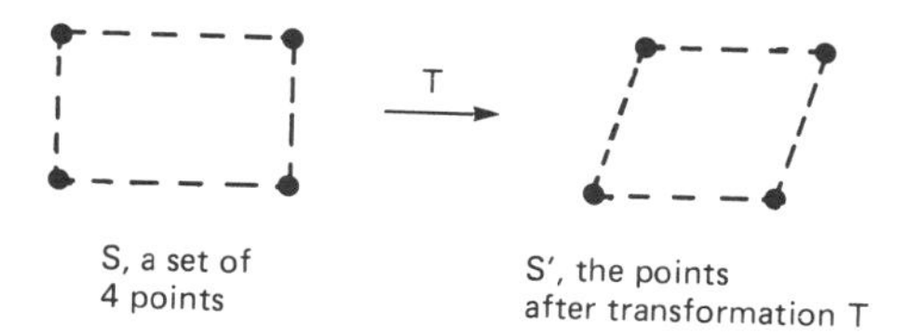

Figure 3.1
Transforming vertices transforms the shape defined by the vertices

vertices is transformed into a parallelogram owing to the transformation of these vertices. Consider a set of coordinate points representing a piecewise linear bird. To draw the six seagulls shown in Figure 3.2a from a single set of (x,y) coordinates in DATA statements we could use Program 3.1.

The program effects five simple transformations of the coordinate set in the DATA statements. To change the translation such that, for

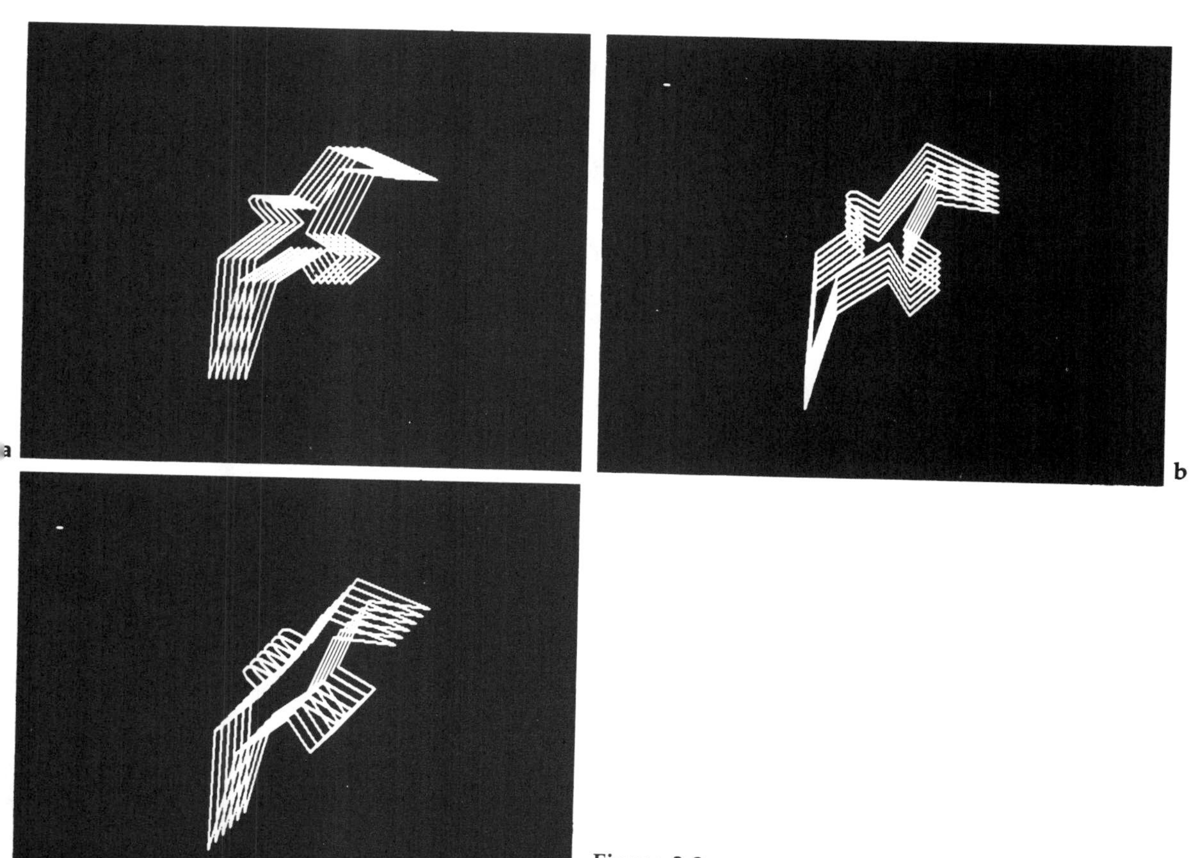

Figure 3.2
Effecting transformations with special programs

example, a vertically displaced set was displayed, we could change lines 100 and 120:

```
100 READ X,Y : PSET (X,Y+I)
120   READ X,Y : LINE -(X,Y+I)
```

This effect is shown in Figure 3.2b. Similarly a diagonally displaced bird could be drawn by incrementing both 'X' and 'Y' (Figure 3.2c). This is, however, an approach that would lead us into a different programming notation for each transformation that we used which would be a rather unsatisfactory state of affairs.

What we will now proceed to develop is a mathematical technique that allows us to specify any transformation as a set of four parameters. We can then have a single subroutine that operates on the data set, using these parameters and producing the desired transformation. (We will then find that this system has certain deficiencies that can be overcome by using six parameters.)

To start with we will ignore translation and consider the other two common transformations, rotation and scaling. To rotate a point (x,y) through a clockwise angle, theta, about the origin, the transformation is:

$$xt = x \cos \theta + y \sin \theta$$
$$yt = -x \sin \theta + y \cos \theta$$

and scaling is given by:

$$xt = x\,S1 \qquad yt = y\,S2$$

```
 10 SCREEN 2 : CLS
 20 WINDOW (-640,-450)-(639,349)
 30 FOR I = 1 TO 100 STEP 20
 40   GOSUB 70  'draw a seagull
 50 NEXT I
 60 END

 70 'SUBROUTINE draw a seagull
 80   RESTORE
 90   READ NOOFPOINTS
100   READ X,Y : PSET (X+I,Y)
110   FOR J = 2 TO NOOFPOINTS
120     READ X,Y : LINE -(X+I,Y)
130   NEXT J
140 RETURN

150 DATA 17,-110,70
160 DATA -120,90,-110,100,-90,100,-30,70
170 DATA 100,240,300,160,130,180,40,0
180 DATA 140,-60,60,-130,0,-40,-140,-130
190 DATA -220,-390,-200,-70,-70,30,-110,70
```

Program 3.1 Repeatedly draws a bird shape with increasing horizontal displacement.

The xt and yt are the transformed values of x and y. $S1$ is the scaling factor in the x direction and $S2$ the scaling factor in the y direction. For example, to magnify a figure uniformly we would use $S1 = S2 = 3$, say. Now we can make the two sets of equations look like each other by re-expressing the scaling equations as:

$$xt = x\,S1 + y\,0$$
$$yt = x\,0 + y\,S2$$

Adding the product of y and 0 and x and 0 has no effect except that the pair of equations for rotation and the pair for scaling are now in the same form. This enables us to write the operations using matrix notation. (Details on matrix notation and matrix manipulation can be found in Appendices 3 and 4). Firstly rotation clockwise:

$$(xt,yt) = (x,y)\begin{bmatrix}\cos\theta & -\sin\theta \\ \sin\theta & \cos\theta\end{bmatrix}$$

and scaling:

$$(xt,yt) = (x,y)\begin{bmatrix}S1 & 0 \\ 0 & S2\end{bmatrix}$$

and this is just a different way of writing the operations expressed as equations above. The notation used for expressing such transformations in matrix form is not standard but is, for better or worse, the *de-facto* standard in computer graphics. We can now represent various linear transformations as 2×2 matrices:

1. Identity (no effect) $\begin{bmatrix}1 & 0 \\ 0 & 1\end{bmatrix}$

2. Rotation (clockwise) $\begin{bmatrix}\cos\theta & -\sin\theta \\ \sin\theta & \cos\theta\end{bmatrix}$

3. Rotation (counter-clockwise) $\begin{bmatrix}\cos\theta & \sin\theta \\ -\sin\theta & \cos\theta\end{bmatrix}$

4. Scaling $\begin{bmatrix}S1 & 0 \\ 0 & S2\end{bmatrix}$

5. Reflection (about the x-axis) $\begin{bmatrix}1 & 0 \\ 0 & -1\end{bmatrix}$

6. Reflection (about the y-axis) $\begin{bmatrix} -1 & 0 \\ 0 & 1 \end{bmatrix}$

7. Y Shear $\begin{bmatrix} 1 & S \\ 0 & 1 \end{bmatrix}$

8. X Shear $\begin{bmatrix} 1 & 0 \\ S & 1 \end{bmatrix}$

Note that we cannot define translation using this system, a point we shall return to in a moment.

```
 10 SCREEN 2 : CLS
 20 PRINT "Transformation matrix"
 30 PRINT : PRINT "   a  c"
 40 PRINT : PRINT "   b  d"
 50 LOCATE 4,4 : INPUT;"",A : INPUT"  ",C
 60 PRINT : INPUT;"   ",B : INPUT"  ",D
 70 PRINT : INPUT"Rectangle or Bird (R/B)";REPLY$
 80 IF REPLY$ = "B" THEN RESTORE 290
 90 WINDOW (-640,-400)-(639,399)
100 GOSUB 200  'draw axes
110 READ NOOFPOINTS
120 READ X,Y : GOSUB 240  'transform
130 PSET (XT,YT)
140 FOR I = 2 TO NOOFPOINTS
150   READ X,Y
160   GOSUB 240  'transform
170   LINE -(XT,YT)
180 NEXT I
190 END

200 'SUBROUTINE draw axes
210   PSET (-640,0) : LINE -(640,0)
220   PSET (0,-400) : LINE -(0,399)
230 RETURN

240 'SUBROUTINE transform
250   XT = A*X+B*Y
260   YT = C*X+D*Y
270 RETURN

280 DATA 5,0,0,180,0,180,300,0,300,0,0
290 DATA 17,-110,70
300 DATA -120,90,-110,100,-90,100,-30,70
310 DATA 100,240,300,160,130,180,40,0
320 DATA 140,-60,60,-130,0,-40,-140,-130
330 DATA -220,-390,-200,-70,-70,30,-110,70
```

Program 3.2 Demonstrates the use of a 2x2 transformation matrix on the bird shape or on a simpler rectangle shape.

Program 3.2 is a program that will accept the four parameters defining a transformation, using the terminology:

$$\begin{bmatrix} a & c \\ b & d \end{bmatrix}$$

for the transformation matrix.

Note that we have just one subroutine and two lines of calculation to perform any of the above transformations. The illustrations in Figure 3.3 show the effect of the transformations on a piecewise linear image made up of the large characters IMAGE.

Now bear in mind that this is only a demonstration program and that normally we would not calculate cosines and sines before supplying these as program input. Rather cos θ and sin θ would be calculated in the course of execution of a program.

Homogeneous coordinates

The above system for effecting two-dimensional transformations has a number of drawbacks. Firstly it excludes an important transformation (translation). Secondly all the transformations are centred at the origin, (0,0). This is fine in the above examples where the bottom left hand corner of IMAGE is at the origin. Consider a rectangle not centred at the origin and subject to a 30° rotation (Figure 3.4). Because the rotation is centred on the origin the rectangle both rotates and translates. When we are rotating a geometrical figure it is far more likely that we require rotation about an arbitrary point, for example, any one of the vertices of the rectangle, or the intersection of its diagonals. Such a transformation is not available in the above system. Similarly reflections are through the x-axis or the y-axis. Reflections through other lines are not available.

Perhaps most absurd of all is scaling. This also involves a translation. Figure 3.5 shows the rectangle offset from the origin and subject to a shrinking. Again it is highly unlikely that we should ever require scaling complicated by a translation proportional to the magnitude of the scaling. Rather we may require 'pure' scaling about a centre point or vertex.

A homogenous coordinate system is a notation that overcomes these difficulties. In a homogeneous coordinate system a point (x,y) becomes $(x/r, y/r, r)$. It is convenient to make $r = 1$, avoiding division, giving the representation of a point as $(x, y, 1)$. Because a point is now a three element row matrix, transformation matrices are now 3×3. This system has the immediate advantage that we can now represent the translation transformation with a 3×3 matrix. We can now write down six common transformation matrices:

1. Translation $\begin{bmatrix} 1 & 0 & 0 \\ 0 & 1 & 0 \\ Tx & Ty & 1 \end{bmatrix}$

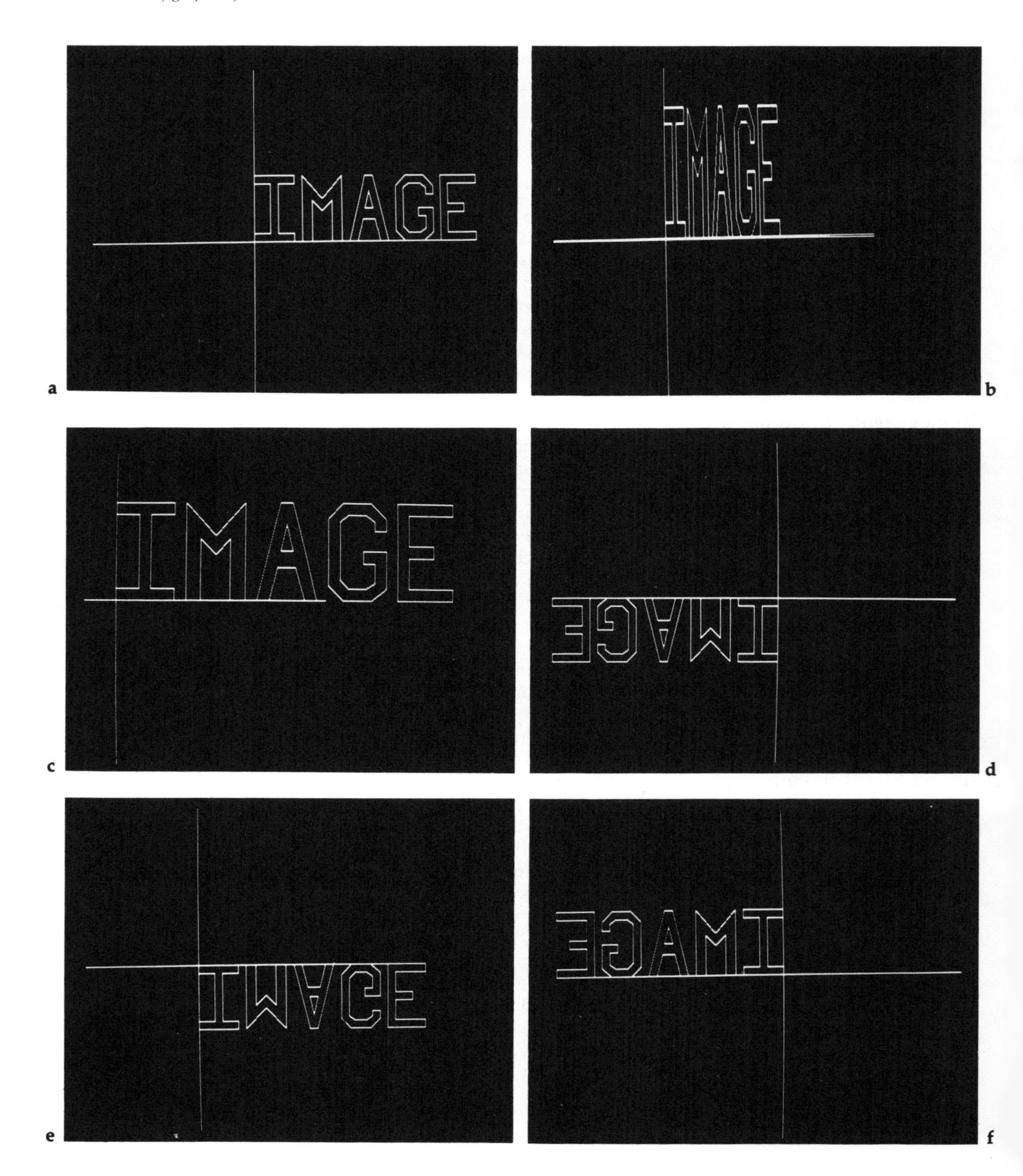
IMAGE
a
IMAGE
b
IMAGE
c
d
e
f

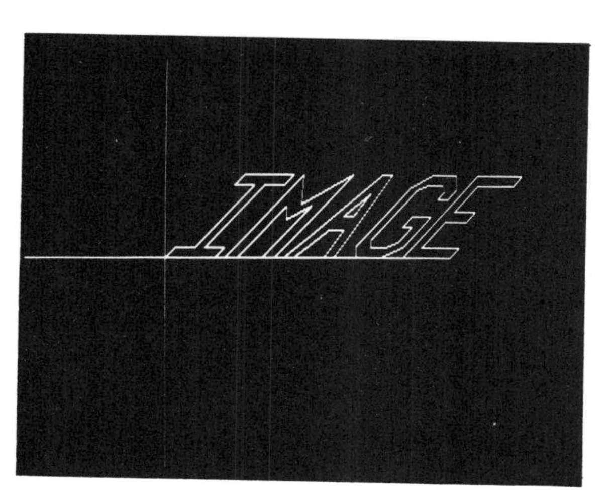

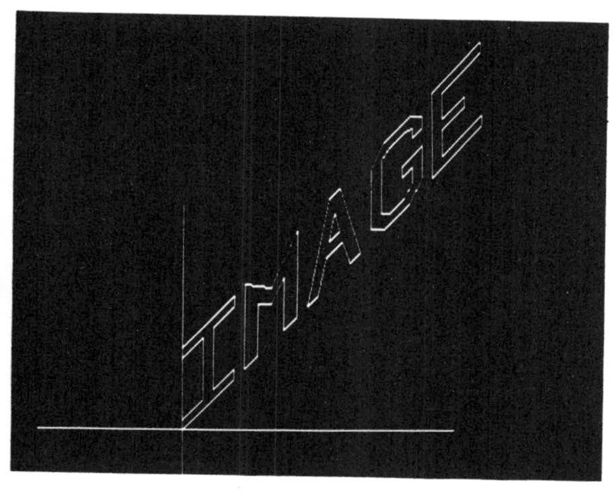

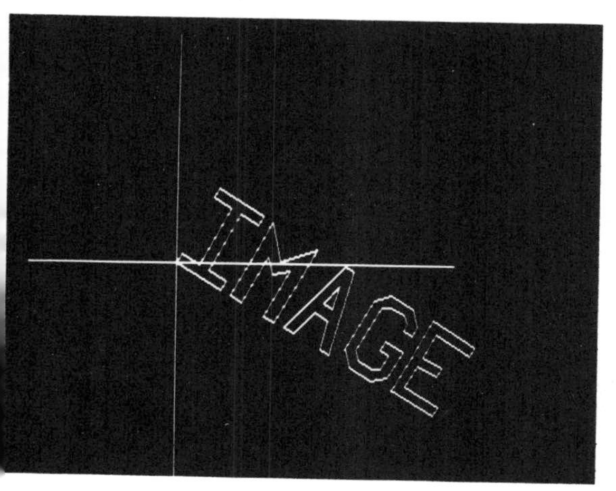

Figure 3.3
Using a general transformation procedure

(a) Identity $\begin{bmatrix} 1 & 0 \\ 0 & 1 \end{bmatrix}$

(b) Scaling $\begin{bmatrix} 0.5 & 0 \\ 0 & 2 \end{bmatrix}$

(c) Scaling $\begin{bmatrix} 1.5 & 0 \\ 0 & 1.5 \end{bmatrix}$

(d) Reflection in x and y $\begin{bmatrix} -1 & 0 \\ 0 & -1 \end{bmatrix}$

(e) Reflection in x-axis $\begin{bmatrix} 1 & 0 \\ 0 & -1 \end{bmatrix}$

(f) Reflection in y-axis $\begin{bmatrix} -1 & 0 \\ 0 & 1 \end{bmatrix}$

(g) X shear $\begin{bmatrix} 1 & 0 \\ 1 & 1 \end{bmatrix}$

(h) Y shear $\begin{bmatrix} 1 & 1 \\ 0 & 1 \end{bmatrix}$

(i) Clockwise rotation $\begin{bmatrix} 0.866 & -0.5 \\ 0.5 & 0.866 \end{bmatrix}$

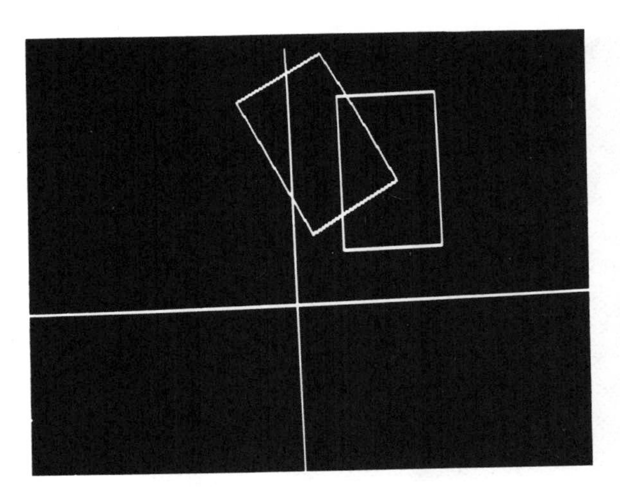

Figure 3.4
A rectangle rotated is also displaced

where Tx is the translation in the x direction and Ty is the translation in the y direction. To check that this works let us translate the point (1, 1, 1)) through a distance of 2 in the x direction:

$$(1, 1, 1)\begin{bmatrix} 1 & 0 & 0 \\ 0 & 1 & 0 \\ 2 & 0 & 1 \end{bmatrix} = ((1\times1 + 0\times1 + 1\times2), (1\times0 + 1\times1 + 1\times0), (1\times0 + 1\times0 + 1\times1))$$

In other words

$$(x, y, 1)\begin{bmatrix} 1 & 0 & 0 \\ 0 & 1 & 0 \\ Tx & Ty & 1 \end{bmatrix} = (x + Tx, y + Ty, 1)$$

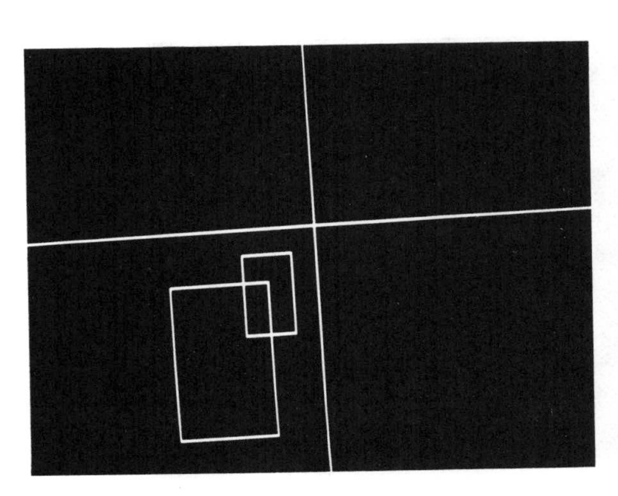

Figure 3.5
A rectangle scaled is also displaced

Some of the other transformations in our new system are:

2. Rotation (clockwise)

$$\begin{bmatrix} \cos\theta & -\sin\theta & 0 \\ \sin\theta & \cos\theta & 0 \\ 0 & 0 & 1 \end{bmatrix}$$

3. Rotation (counter-clockwise)

$$\begin{bmatrix} \cos\theta & \sin\theta & 0 \\ -\sin\theta & \cos\theta & 0 \\ 0 & 0 & 1 \end{bmatrix}$$

These rotations are still centred on the origin.

4. Scaling

$$\begin{bmatrix} Sx & 0 & 0 \\ 0 & Sy & 0 \\ 0 & 0 & 1 \end{bmatrix}$$

5. Reflection (x-axis)

$$\begin{bmatrix} 1 & 0 & 0 \\ 0 & -1 & 0 \\ 0 & 0 & 1 \end{bmatrix}$$

6. X Shear

$$\begin{bmatrix} 1 & 0 & 0 \\ S & 1 & 0 \\ 0 & 0 & 1 \end{bmatrix}$$

To test that these are exactly the same as we had before we can alter the demonstration program to input six parameters and perform the matrix multiplication. The required alterations are captioned Program 3.3. The input parameters represent six of the coefficients of a 3×3 transformation matrix:

$$\begin{bmatrix} a & d & 0 \\ b & e & 0 \\ c & f & 1 \end{bmatrix}$$

So what have we achieved? Very little as yet! Certainly we have represented translation in a matrix system, but we now need nine matrix coefficients instead of four to achieve the same result. (Actually we have only used six of the nine above, but you will see shortly that nine are convenient when combinations of transformations are considered.) However, the fact that we have included translation in our system now gives us a major advantage: we need no longer restrict ourselves to transformations at the origin. Thus homogeneous coordinates provide a rather roundabout way of adding constants to the transformed x and y values. The advantage of this notation is that transformations can still be represented as matrices which will be useful when considering combinations of transformations.

Generalized two-dimensional transformations

Consider the problem of rotation about any point. Say, for example, we wish to rotate a rectangle, in any position, 30° counter-clockwise about its bottom left hand vertex. We can easily do this now in the four steps shown in Figure 3.6.

The three operations would be:

$$T1 = \text{translate} = \begin{bmatrix} 1 & 0 & 0 \\ 0 & 1 & 0 \\ -Tx & -Ty & 1 \end{bmatrix}$$ (move rectangle to the origin)

$$R = \text{rotate} = \begin{bmatrix} \cos(30°) & \sin(30°) & 0 \\ -\sin(30°) & \cos(30°) & 0 \\ 0 & 0 & 1 \end{bmatrix}$$ (rotate rectangle about the origin)

$$T2 = \text{translate} = \begin{bmatrix} 1 & 0 & 0 \\ 0 & 1 & 0 \\ Tx & Ty & 1 \end{bmatrix}$$ (move rotated rectangle back to original position)

Now instead of multiplying each point $(x,y,1)$ by three matrices we can multiply the matrices together to obtain a 'net transformation matrix' (details on matrix multiplication plus a subroutine to perform the multiplication are contained in Appendix 3).

$$\text{net transformation matrix} = T1 \times R \times T2$$

and then multiply each point $(x,y,1)$ by this matrix. A net transformation matrix is always of the form:

$$\begin{bmatrix} a & d & 0 \\ b & e & 0 \\ c & f & 1 \end{bmatrix}$$

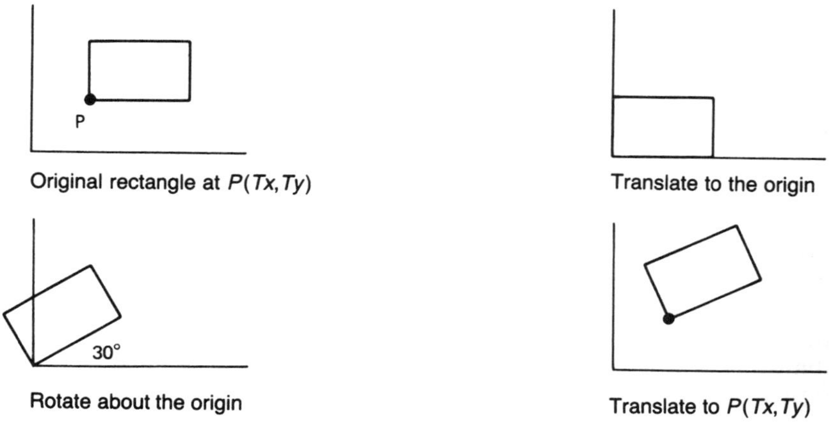

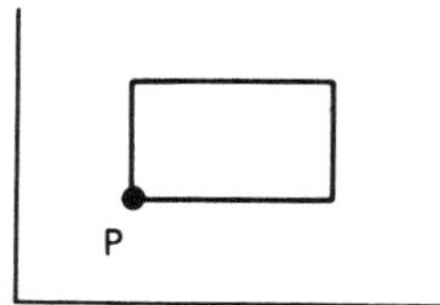

Original rectangle at $P(Tx, Ty)$

Translate to the origin

Figure 3.6
Formation of a net transform for rotation about point P

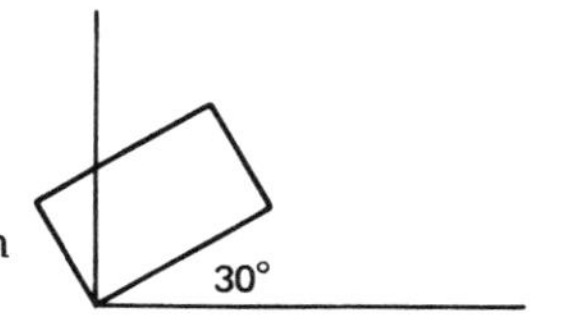

Rotate about the origin

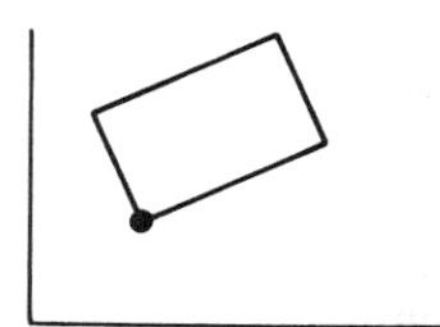

Translate to $P(Tx, Ty)$

and in this case

$$T1 \times R \times T2 = \begin{bmatrix} \cos(30°) & \sin(30°) & 0 \\ -\sin(30°) & \cos(30°) & 0 \\ Tx(1-\cos(30°))+Ty\ \sin(30°) & Ty(1-\cos(30°))-Tx\ \sin(30°) & 1 \end{bmatrix}$$

This is the single matrix required to effect the transformation shown in Figure 3.6. The same approach can be used for scaling.

Say we wanted to shrink the rectangle about its centre point (Figure 3.7). The rectangle has shrunk within itself which is the desired transformation. This should be compared with the 2×2 system shrinking illustration (Figure 3.5) where the effect of applying a shrink transformation was also to translate the rectangle 'outside itself'.

The net transform matrix for scaling is:

$$\begin{bmatrix} S1 & 0 & 0 \\ 0 & S2 & 0 \\ Tx(1-S1) & Ty(1-S2) & 1 \end{bmatrix}$$

A similar approach can be adopted for the other transformations. Any arbitrary combination of translation scaling and rotation will result in a single transformation matrix and this is the advantage of the approach: we only need one matrix for any transformation. For example, we could combine the transformations in Figure 3.8 into a net transformation matrix.

In general, transformations are not commutative, i.e. the order in which the individual matrices are multiplied to form a net transformation matrix is important. $T1 \times R \times T2$ is not the same as $T1 \times T2 \times R$.

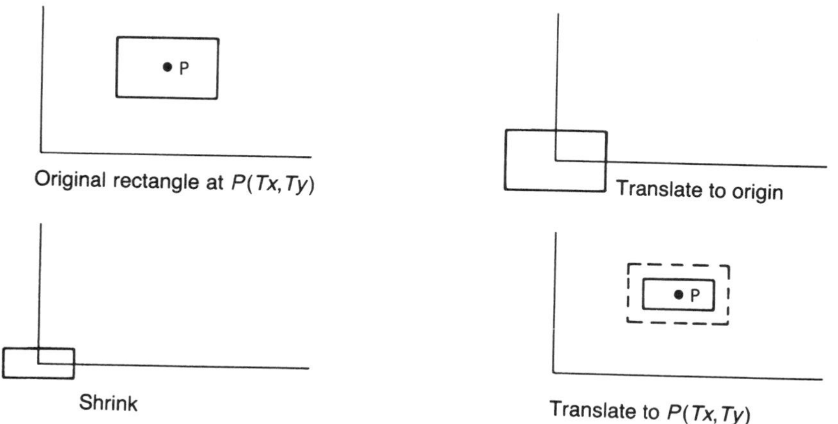

Figure 3.7
Formation of a net transform for shrinking about point *P*

Because net transformation matrices are always of the form:

$$\begin{bmatrix} a & d & 0 \\ b & e & 0 \\ c & f & 1 \end{bmatrix}$$

The multiplication

$$(xt, yt, 1) = (x, y, 1) \begin{bmatrix} a & d & 0 \\ b & e & 0 \\ c & f & 1 \end{bmatrix}$$

reduces to

$$(xt, yt) = (x, y, 1) \begin{bmatrix} a & d \\ b & e \\ c & f \end{bmatrix}$$

and this is implemented in Program 3.3, which is Program 3.2 altered to include homogenous transformations. Thus what we

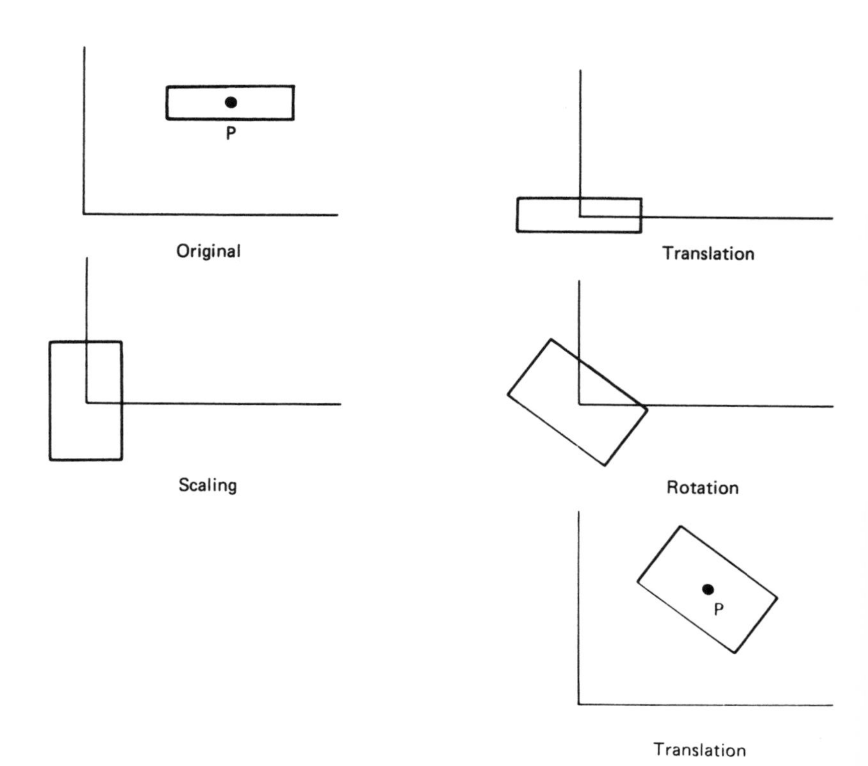

Figure 3.8
Formation of a net transform for scaling and rotation

```
30 PRINT : PRINT "    a  d"
35 PRINT : PRINT "    b  e"
40 PRINT : PRINT "    c  f"
45 LOCATE 4,4 : INPUT;"",A : INPUT"  ",D
50 PRINT : INPUT;"    ",B : INPUT"  ",E
60 PRINT : INPUT;"    ",C : INPUT"  ",F

240 'SUBROUTINE transform
250   XT = A*X+B*Y+C
260   YT = D*X+E*Y+F
270 RETURN
```

Program 3.3 Alterations to Program 3.2 to use a 2x3 transformation matrix (homogeneous coordinates). This permits the inclusion of translations in a transformation.

have achieved with our 3×3 system is a method for producing a net transformation matrix from a series of 3×3 transformation matrices. The process is sometimes called concatenating (joining together) transformations. We need the 3×3 system to perform the concatenation. Concatenation is clearly advantageous because we need only multiply the matrices together once to obtain the net transformation matrix and then multiply each point in the data set by this matrix. As we have seen this final multiplication reduces to just four products and four additions. Such efficiency considerations are critically important in real time animation computers such as flight simulators.

Repeating transformations

Many elaborate designs can be constructed by redrawing a figure in a loop and subjecting it each time to an increasing scaling, rotation, translation or any combination of these. Above we introduced the idea using piecewise linear seagulls together with translation only. In this section we will look at combinations of scaling, rotation and translation operating on the IMAGE characters.

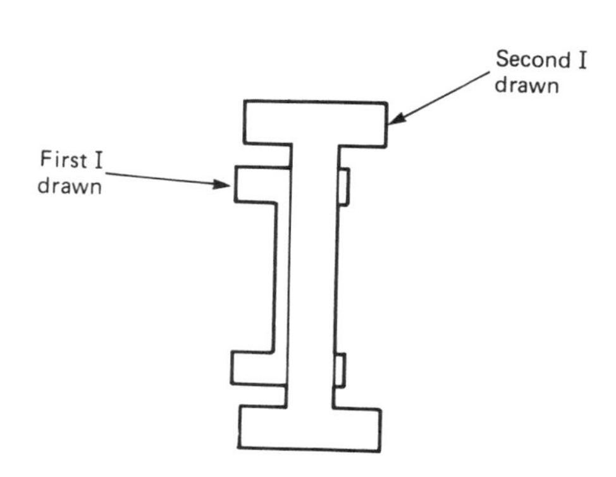

Figure 3.9
Obscuring scheme used for IMAGE designs

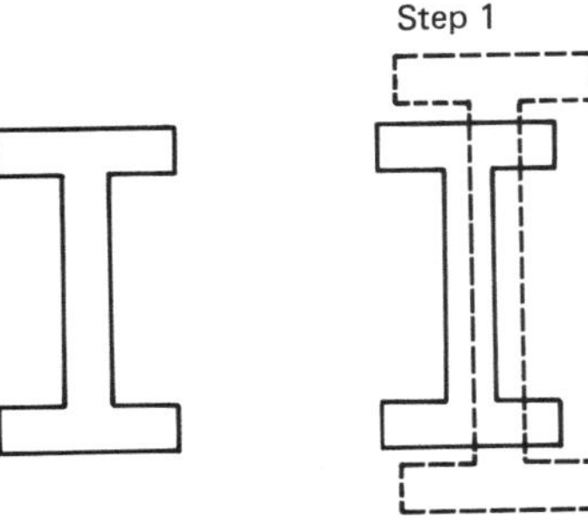
Step 1
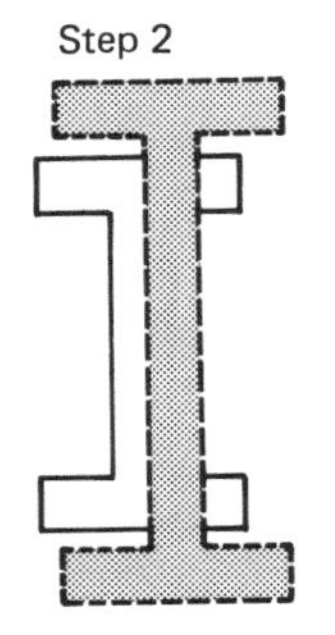
Step 2
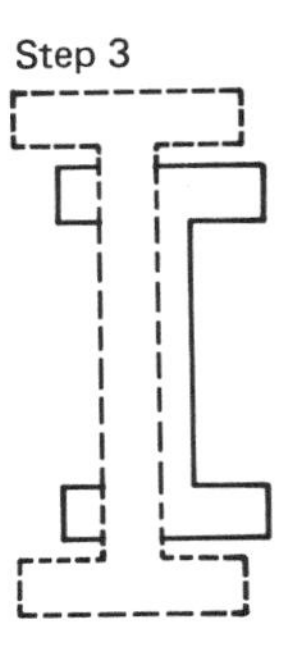
Step 3
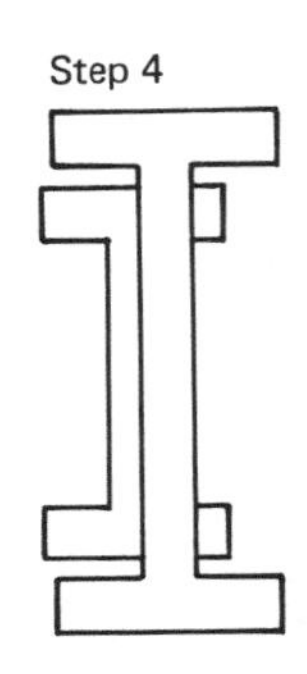
Step 4
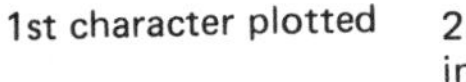
1st character plotted
2nd character plotted in unused colour. 1st character lines still visible in interior of 2nd character
2nd character colour filled in white obliterating the lines from the 1st character
2nd character colour filled in background colour
Final result: 2nd character boundary is redrawn in white

Figure 3.10
Showing the steps in an algorithm for superimposing, while outline characters with background colour interior

Also in this section we introduce a technique for dealing with overlapping patterns like the IMAGE characters. In this context we are going to build up a composite pattern that consists of overlapping IMAGE patterns. The first pattern drawn is to be partially obscured by the second pattern and the second pattern partially obscured by the third and so on. In other words we need to end up with the situation depicted in Figure 3.9.

In Figure 3.9 the interior of the character that has just been drawn obscures or wipes out detail of any previously drawn character on which it is superimposed. This can be achieved in four steps. Firstly the outline of the character is drawn in an unused colour (Figure 3.10). Secondly the character is colour filled in white to its boundary. This second step obliterates any white detail, originating from a

Figure 3.11
Repeated transformations

(a) $Ty = Ty + 60$
$Sx = Sx + 0.25$
$Sy = Sy + 0.35$

(b) $Ty = Ty + 60$
$Sx = Sx + 0.35$
$Sy = Sy + 0.15$

IMAGE

a

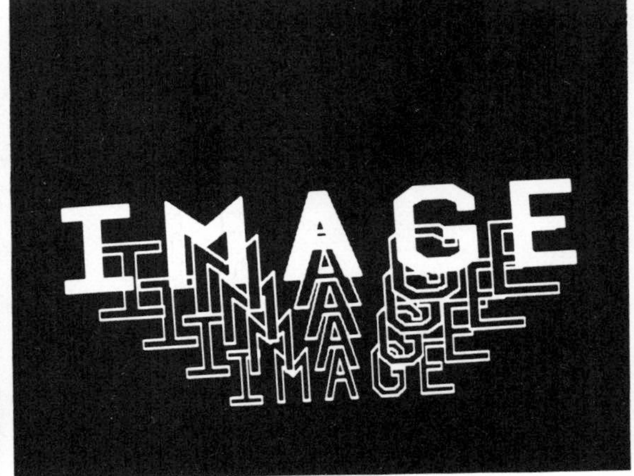
IMAGE

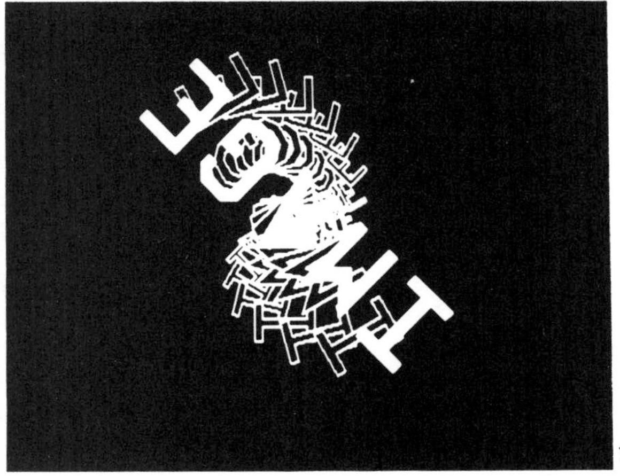

Figure 3.12
Repeated transformations

(a) THETA = THETA + 10
$Sx = Sy = S + 0.2$

(b) THETA = THETA + 10
$Sx = Sy = S + 0.15$

previously drawn character, that appears in the interior of the character. Thirdly the white interior is changed to background colour by initiating a second colour fill in background colour. Step 2 has to be performed before Step 3 can be carried out. Most of the interior following execution of Step 1 is in background colour and you cannot fill a region with a colour if that region already consists mostly of that colour. Finally the character boundary is redrawn in white. Designs using this scheme are shown in Figures 3.11, 3.12 and 3.13. The final IMAGE pattern is filled in foreground colour for effect, otherwise each character ends up with a white outline and background colour interior obscuring all other detail of lower 'priority'. The program that produced Figure 3.11 is Program 3.4. The DATA statements, which contain data for the character outline,

Figure 3.13
Repeated transformations

(a) $Sx = Sy = S + 0.3$
within the 'letter' loop

(b) $Sx = Sy = S + 0.15$
within the 'letter' loop
THETA = THETA + 10
within the 'IMAGE' loop

comprise a control code followed by a pair of relative coordinates. (Relative coordinates are easier to design than absolute coordinates in this context.)

The transformations incorporated in the programs are those for the first image in Figure 3.11. In each case the transformations and loop alterations are shown alongside each photograph. Figure 3.12 shows two more ideas. Rotation in 10° increments has been introduced and this is combined with a uniform scaling to produce the two designs. Figure 3.13 was produced by introducing a structural alteration to the program. In each design the scale factor is increased both between letters and IMAGEs. This means incrementing the scale factor within the 'letter' loop. The design incorporated in Program 3.4 and its alterations are only suggestions and the basic idea can be exploited to produce imitations of most of the caption effects used by television caption designers (Colour Plate 5).

```
 10 SCREEN 1 : CLS
 20 WINDOW (-700,0)-(579,799)
 30 A = 1 : B = 0 : C = 0 : D = 0 : E = 1 : F = 0
 35 TRUE = -1 : FALSE = 0
 40 YSTART = 100
 50 FILLCOLOR1 = 2 : BACKGROUNDCOLOR = 0 : FILLCOLOR2 = 0
 60 FOR IMAGE = 1 TO 5
 70   FILL = TRUE : BORDERCOLOR = 1 : GOSUB 120  'draw
 80   FILL = FALSE : BORDERCOLOR = 3 : GOSUB 120  'draw
 90   F = F+60: A = A+0.25: E = E+0.35
100 NEXT IMAGE
110 END

120 'SUBROUTINE draw
130   RESTORE
140   XSTART = -120*2.5
150   IF IMAGE = 5 THEN FILLCOLOR2 = 3
160   READ LETTERS
170   FOR I = 1 TO LETTERS
180     X = XSTART : Y = YSTART
190     GOSUB 350  'transform
200     PSET (XT,YT),BACKGROUNDCOLOR
210     READ NO
220     FOR J = 1 TO NO
230       READ P,XR,YR
240       X = X+XR : Y = Y+YR
250       GOSUB 350  'transform
260       IF P = 1 THEN LINE -(XT,YT),BORDERCOLOR
                   ELSE PSET (XT,YT),BACKGROUNDCOLOR
270     NEXT J
280     READ XIN,YIN
290     IF FILL THEN X = XSTART+XIN : Y = YSTART+YIN : GOSUB 350  'transform
300     IF FILL THEN PAINT (XT,YT),FILLCOLOR1,BORDERCOLOR
```

Program 3.4 Combining transformations on a simple caption.

3.2 NON-LINEAR TRANSFORMATIONS

The transformations that we have studied up to now have been linear transformations. In simple terms this means that the coordinate pairs representing points or line end points are only ever multiplied by constants. For example, when we magnify an image made up of a set of points joined together with straight lines we multiply the x and y value of each coordinate by the same constant.

In non-linear transformations x and y may be replaced by any functions of x and y. Non-linear transformations can be used to alter not just the size or position or skewness of an image but to change the shape by changing the relative size of different parts of the image. Thus 'drastic' alterations of shape can be achieved and adjusted with non-linear transformations. Non-linear transformations are potentially as useful as linear transformations in mathematically based computer art. They are however a little more

```
310     IF FILL THEN PAINT (XT,YT),FILLCOLOR2,BORDERCOLOUR
320     XSTART = XSTART+120
330   NEXT I
340 RETURN

350 'SUBROUTINE transform
360   XT = A*X+B*Y+C
370   YT = D*X+E*Y+F
380 RETURN

390 DATA 5
400 REM "I"
410 DATA 12
420 DATA 1,0,16, 1,32,0, 1,0,96, 1,-32,0, 1,0,16, 1,80,0,
         1,0,-16, 1,-32,0, 1,0,-96, 1,32,0, 1,0,-16, 1,-80,0, 40,64
430 REM "M"
440 DATA 10
450 DATA 1,0,128, 1,40,-44, 1,40,44, 1,0,-128, 1,-16,0,
         1,0,84, 1,-24,-24, 1,-24,24, 1,0,-84, 1,-16,0, 8,64
460 REM "A"
470 DATA 12
480 DATA 1,32,128, 1,16,0, 1,32,-128, 1,-16,0, 1,-12,44, 1,-24,0,
         1,-12,-44, 1,-16,0, 0,32,60, 1,16,0, 1,-8,36, 1,-8,-36, 25,64
490 REM "G"
500 DATA 23
510 DATA 0,0,20, 1,0,88, 1,20,20, 1,40,0, 1,20,-20, 1,0,-16,
         1,-16,0, 1,0,12, 1,-12,8, 1,-24,0, 1,-12,-8, 1,0,-76,
         1,12,-12, 1,24,0, 1,12,8, 1,0,24, 1,-16,0, 1,0,16,
         1,32,0, 1,0,-48, 1,-20,-16, 1,-40,0, 1,-20,20, 8,64
520 REM "E"
530 DATA 12
540 DATA 1,0,128, 1,80,0, 1,0,-16, 1,-64,0, 1,0,-40, 1,36,0,
         1,0,-16, 1,-36,0, 1,0,-40, 1,64,0, 1,0,-16, 1,-80,0, 8,64
```

difficult to understand. An everyday example of a non-linear transformation is reflection in a distorting mirror. Distorting mirrors distort because their surfaces are curved rather than plane.

In this section we will look at non-linear transformations using the work of the biologist D'arcy Thompson as an example. Another area of interest is the intriguing world of anamorphic art. In Chapter 8 we will look at the use of non-linear transformations in three dimensions.

D'arcy Thompson and transformations in nature

In his remarkable book, 'On Growth and Form', D'arcy Thompson describes how many patterns in nature appear to conform to simple mathematical rules. One of the most frequently referenced chapters in this book is entitled: 'The comparison of related forms'. In this he says:

> 'In a very large part of morphology, our essential task lies in the comparison of related forms rather than in the precise definition of each; and the deformation of a complicated figure may be a phenomenon easy of comprehension, though the figure itself may have to be left unanalysed and undefined. This process of comparison, of recognizing in one form a definite permutation or deformation of another, apart altogether from a precise and adequate understanding of the original 'type' or standard of comparison, lies within the immediate province of mathematics, and finds its solution in the elementary use of a certain method of the mathematician. This method is the Method of Coordinates, on which is based the Theory of Transformations'.

What he is saying is that we may be able to take a shape, say a leaf from a tree of one species, subject it to a transformation, and produce a shape that is a leaf from another species of tree. In his work he restricts himself to 'shapes' by which he means the two-dimensional outline of a three-dimensional object.

Let us look first of all at this idea using a familiar linear transformation and then move on to non-linear transformations. Figure 3.14 shows the original sketches by D'arcy Thompson showing how the outline of the species *Argyropelecus Olfersi* transforms to the outline of *Sternoptyx Diaphana*. This transformation is linear and is the x shear transformation introduced above. The four photographs show the original fish, digitized from the sketch, followed by the output from a program that applies an x shear transformation. The values of S used to produce the three transformed fishes were 0.3, 0.5, and 0.7 respectively. In the program we use a subroutine to draw the fish, a window transformation (that ensures that the origin is the bottom left hand corner of the minimum area rectangle that encloses the fish) and a subroutine that performs the linear transformation.

Now look at Figure 3.15. The original sketch shows a *Diodon* outline being transformed into a *Orthagoriscus* outline using a non-linear transform. We are now multiplying x and y by terms that contain x and y. For example:

```
XNEW = 3*OLDX
YNEW = 2*OLDY
```

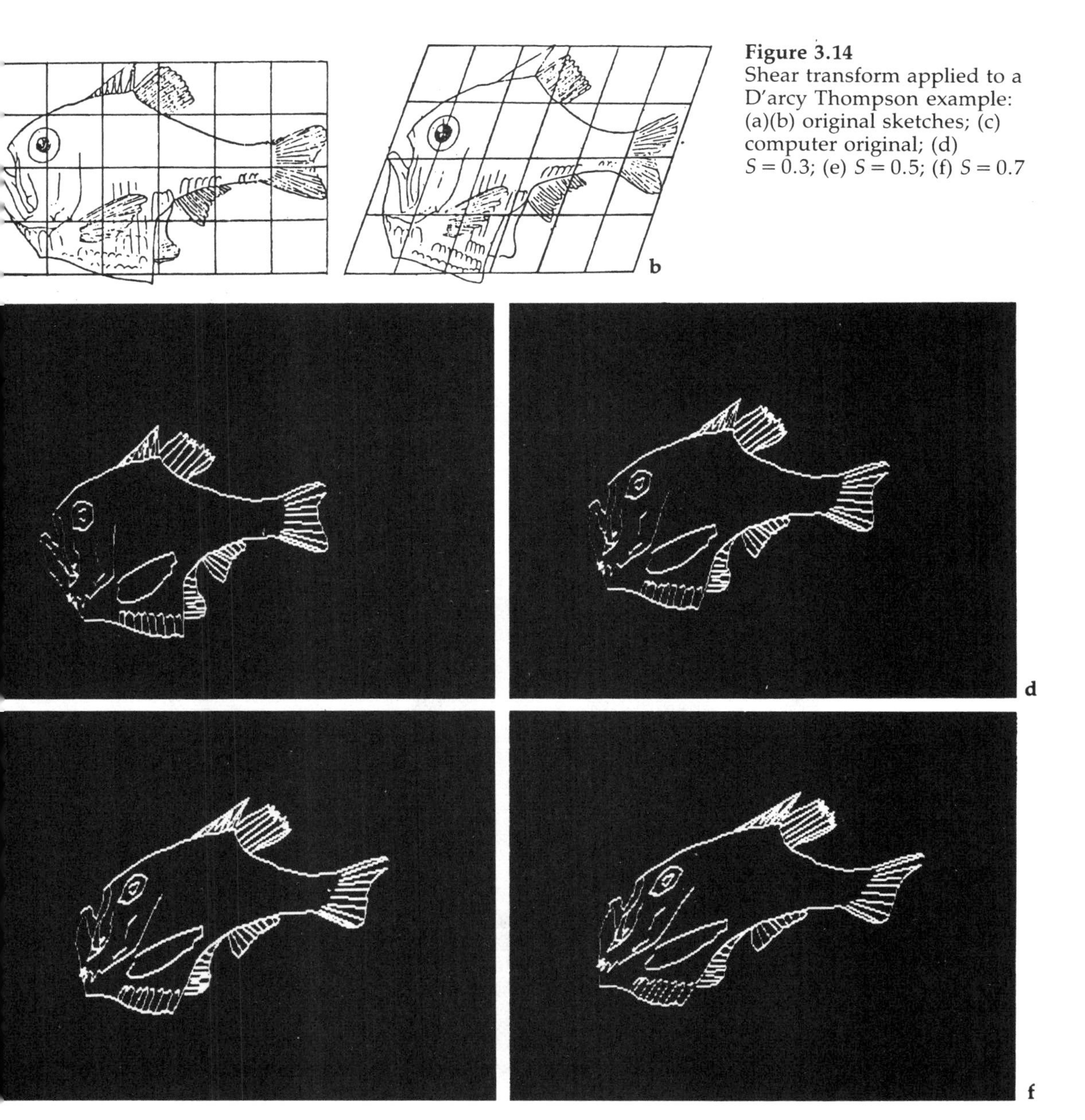

Figure 3.14
Shear transform applied to a D'arcy Thompson example: (a)(b) original sketches; (c) computer original; (d) $S=0.3$; (e) $S=0.5$; (f) $S=0.7$

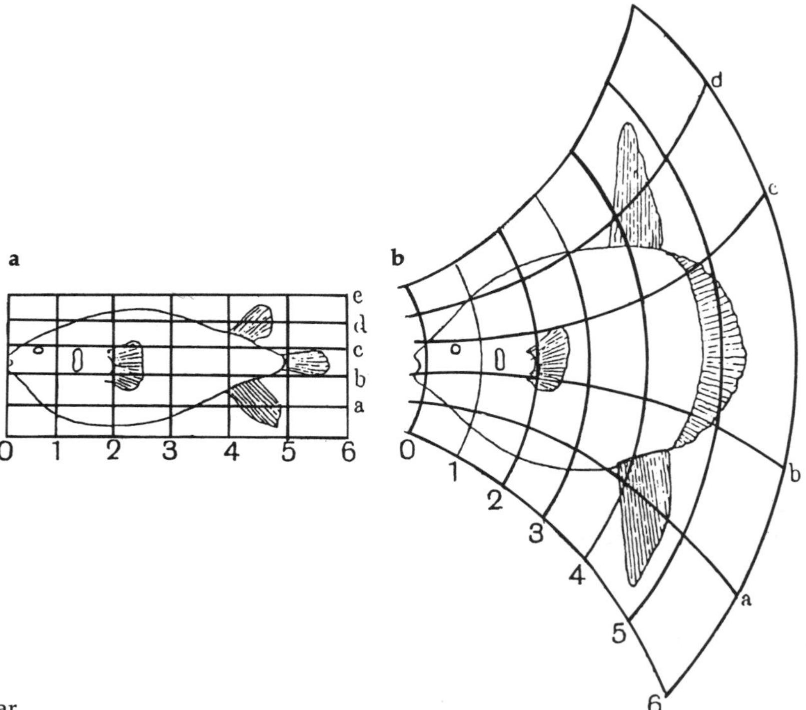

Figure 3.15
Simulation of a D'arcy Thompson sketch using a hyperbolic-ellipse non-linear transform

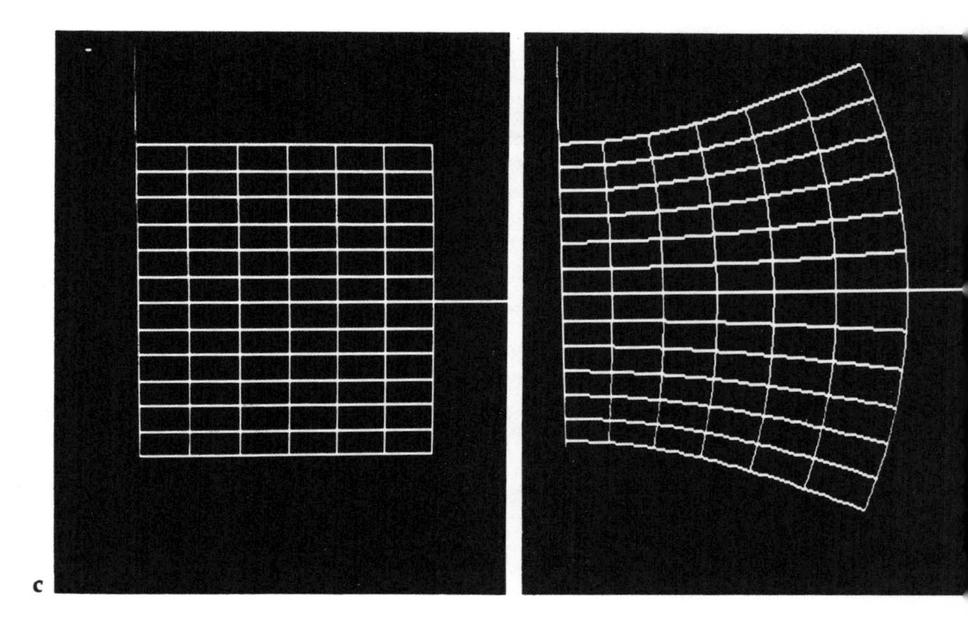

is a linear transformation that we have already met, but:

```
XNEW = 3*OLDX*OLDX
YNEW = 2*OLDY
```

is a non-linear transformation. The non-linear aspect of this transformation can easily be seen by examining Figure 3.15. Here a grid made up of lines of constant x and y has been transformed using this transformation.

Although D'arcy Thompson's illustrations were sketches (he never produced mathematics for his transformations) we can see from the sketch that lines of constant x are mapped into curves, and lines of constant y are mapped into curves that look similar. Now an easy non-linear transformation that fits this observation is a hyperbolic-ellipse transform. Lines of constant x are mapped into segments of ellipses and lines of constant y into hyperbolas. The transformation is:

$$x' = \sinh(x) \times \cos(a \times y)$$
$$y' = \cosh(x) \times \sin(a \times y)$$

Sinh and cosh are hyperbolic sine and cosine functions. Figure 3.16 shows an original *Diodon* outline together with three applications of the transform for values of $a = 1.5$, 2 and 2.5. You can see from this how a brilliant scientific observation conceived in the 1930s could have benefited from the availability of a computer. D'arcy would probably have given his right arm for an IBM PC!

We use exactly the same programming techniques as before. The window transformation now has to position the fish so that the tip of its nose is now on the origin. The transformation subroutine is given as Program 3.5. The functions sinh and cosh are not standard BASIC functions but they can be defined in terms of the BASIC function EXP. The details of the mathematics is unimportant. We are simply using a mathematical recipe to effect a particular non-linear transformation.

Anamorphic art

Another fascinating application of non-linear transformations is anamorphic art (ana = back again, morphe = form). Here the analogy of distorting mirrors is more direct because a distorting mirror (an anamorphoscope) is needed to decode or unscramble the picture.

Anamorphic art has been known for the last three centuries. An anamorphic painting is one that has been distorted by a transformation so that it is difficult to perceive any form in it other than the 'streaks' formed by the transformation. The distortion is removed by viewing the picture via an anamorphoscope. The most common and easily constructed devices are cylinders and cones, and the most common anamorphic pictures are constructed to be decoded by either a cylinder or cone. Colour Plate 6 is a cylindrical anamorphic picture. Cylindrical anamorphic pictures are viewed by placing a cylindrical mirror at the indicated point and looking into the surface of the mirror (Figure 3.17). You can easily construct such a mirror by using a small sheet of Mylar (kitchen foil wrinkles too easily) wrapped around a convenient cylinder (such as a toilet roll centre). This can be used to reconstruct Colour Plate 6 as well as the images shown in Figures 3.20 and 3.21. Anamorphic paintings together with cylindrical and conical mirrors were sold as fashionable toys in the 17th and 18th century. Even pornographic examples

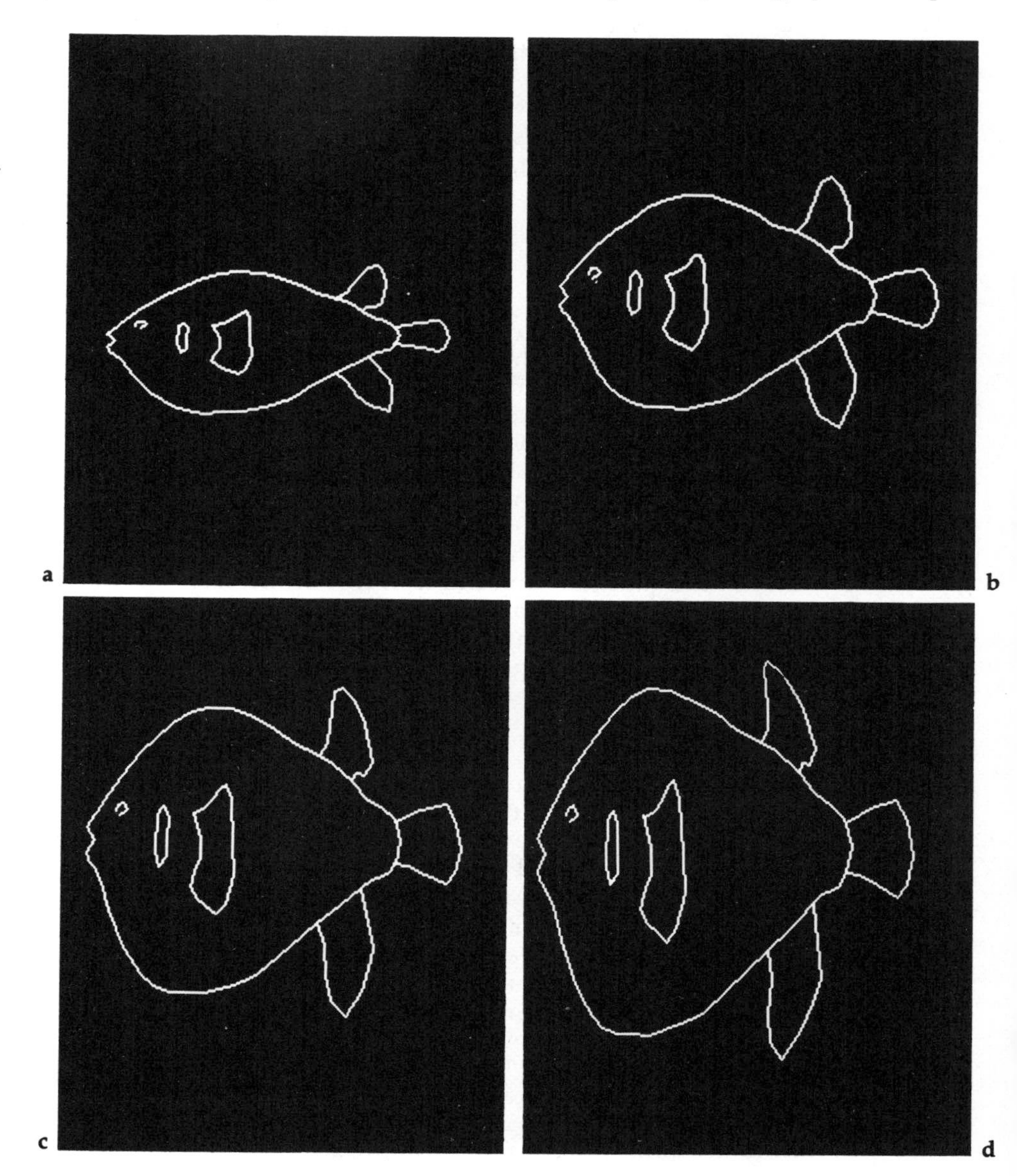

Figure 3.16
Applying the hyperbolic-ellipse transform: (a) computer original; (b) $a = 1.5$; (c) $a = 2$; (d) $a = 2.5$

```
 90 DEF FNSINH(X) = (EXP(X)-EXP(-X))/2
 95 DEF FNCOSH(X) = (EXP(X)+EXP(-X))/2

100 'SUBROUTINE transform
110   XT = FNSINH(X)*COS(A*Y)
120   YT = FNCOSH(X)*SIN(A*Y)
130 RETURN
```

Program 3.5 A hyperbolic-ellipse transformation.

are known and perhaps this was an early use of mathematical transformations to disguise the salaciousness of the material. The eroticism is invisible behind the distortion of a non-linear transformation needing a special device to bring it to life, not unlike the way in which pornography is buried in the ferromagnetic particles of video tapes needing a complex device to unscramble the signal.

Anamorphic transformations have serious applications in cinematography. In 1953 'The Robe' was made by 20th Century Fox. This was the first cinemascope movie to be made. Anamorphic lenses were used to compress the wide angle image on to 35 mm film. A distorted image is recorded on the film. When the film is projected, anamorphic lenses are used to stretch the film on to the wide screen. The image on the film is stored in a distorted or anamorphic form. Similar systems are in use today in cinematography. In still cameras modern wide angle lenses produce a distorted image on the film that is uncorrected. Here the distortion is deemed to be acceptable or even aesthetic and the image does not need any special device to correct it.

In this section we will look at a program to produce a cylindrical anamorphic line image. The intuitive basis of the cylindrical anamorphic transformation can be seen from Figure 3.18 (from Niceron's 'La Perspective Curieuse' – Paris 1638). Lines of constant y

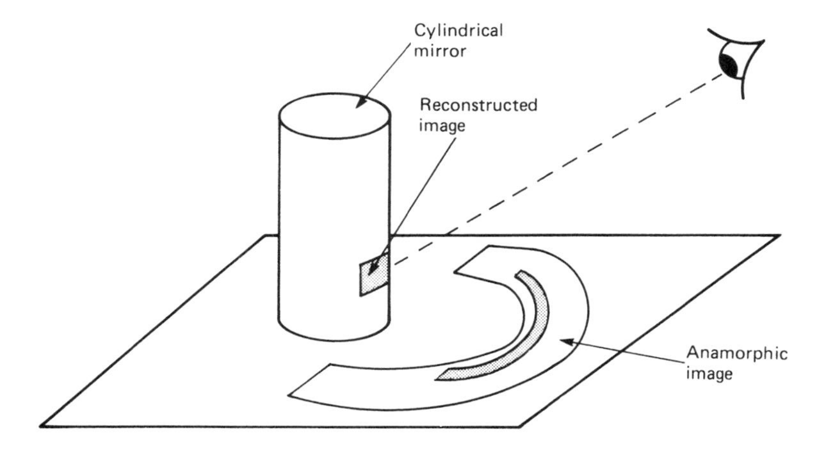

Figure 3.17
Reconstruction of a cylindrical and anamorphic image

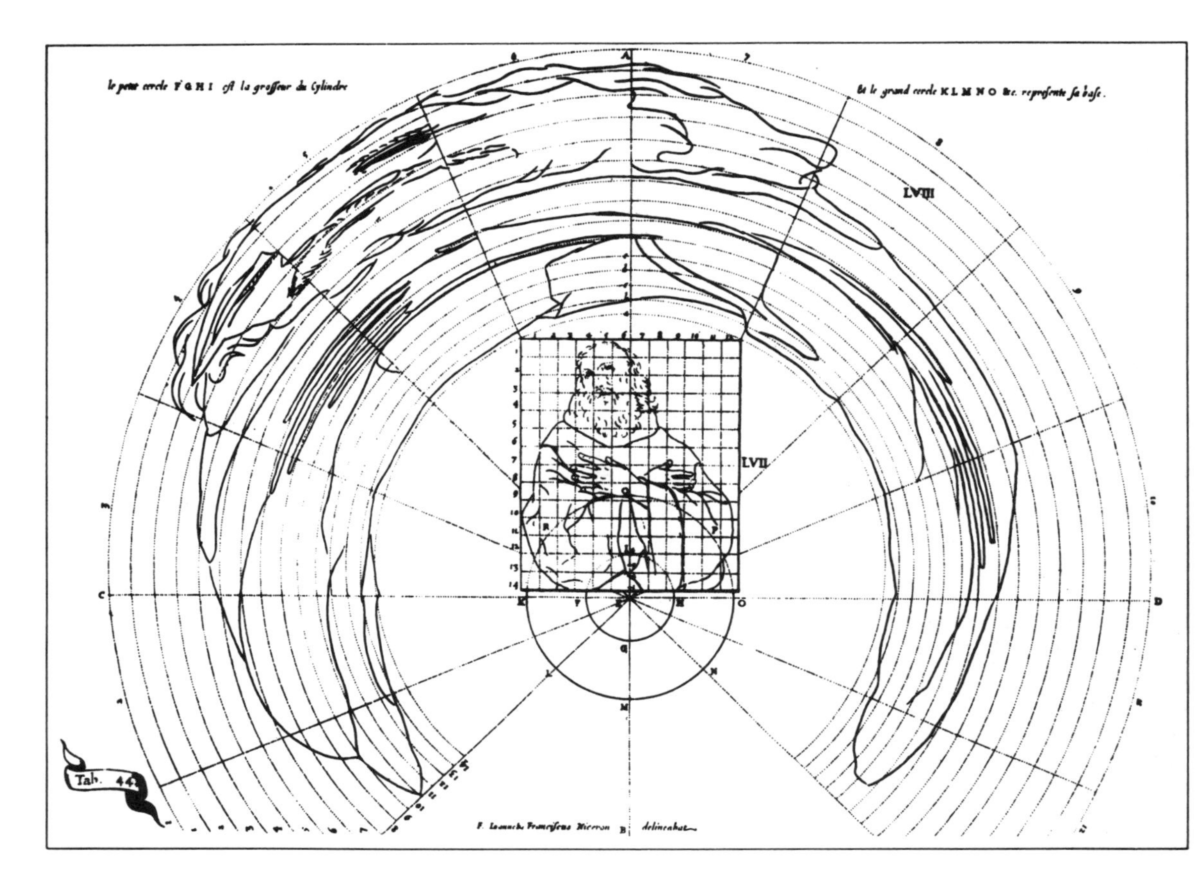

Figure 3.18
Jean Francois Niceron's method of drawing cylindrical anamorphic pictures (1638)

are mapped into 270° segments of concentric circles and lines of constant x into radii. The image fans out in two dimensions, the top of the original mapping into the largest circumference. This is

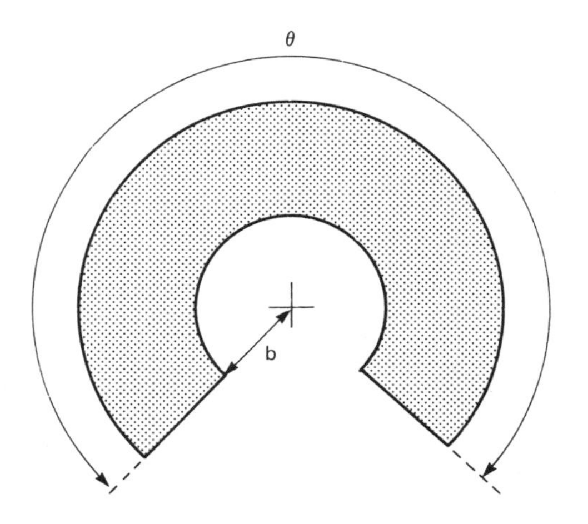

Figure 3.19
The parameters used in the cylindrical anamorphic transformation

because when the reconstructing cylinder is placed at the centre of the anamorphic image the top of the image is furthest away from the cylinder and must map into a larger circumference than the bottom of the image which is nearest to the cylinder.

We already know that to express a coordinate pair (x,y) in terms of (r,θ) we use:

$$x = r \cos \theta$$
$$y = r \sin \theta$$

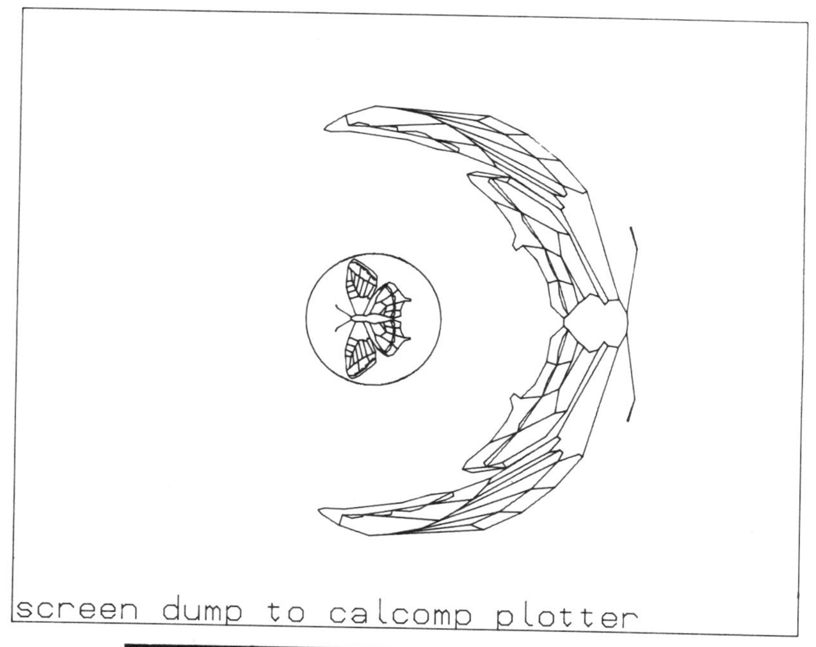

Figure 3.20
Cylindrical anamorphic transformation $a = 1$, $b = 1$, $\vartheta = 4$

The anamorphic transformation is thus:

$$x' = a(y + b)\cos(kx)$$
$$y' = a(y + b)\sin(kx)$$

where a is a scaling factor and b and k are constants (see Figure 3.19) needed to effect the displacement of the anamorphic image out to a finite radius. (So that a hole is left in the middle for the reflecting cylinder.) The constant k is chosen so as to spread the range of x

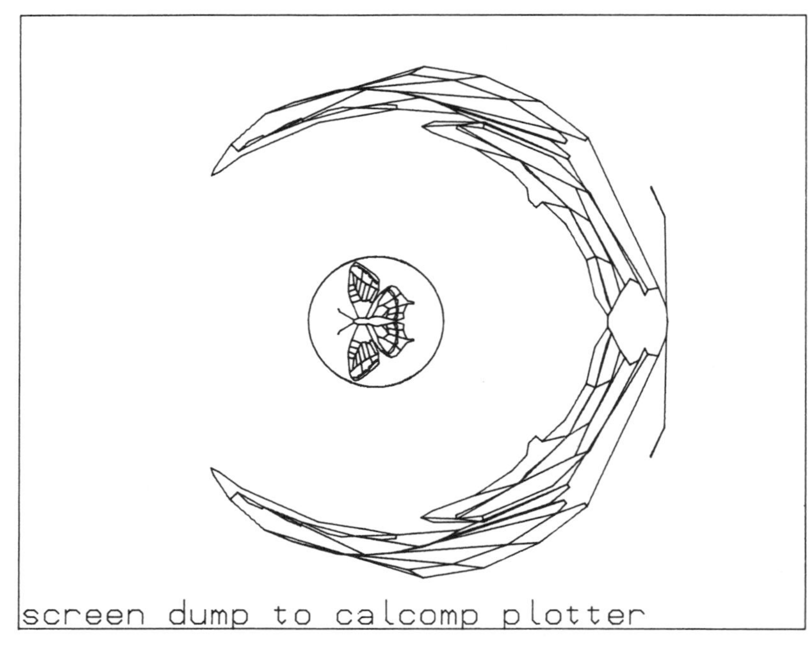

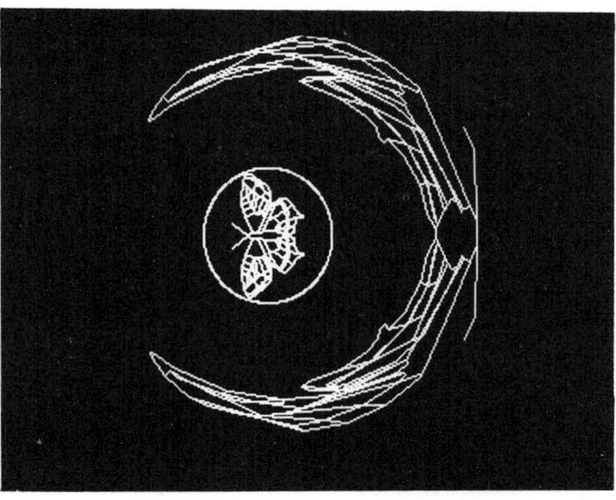

Figure 3.21
Cylindrical anamorphic transformation $a = 1$, $b = 1.3$, $\vartheta = 5$

```
100 'SUBROUTINE transform
110   XT = A*(Y+B)*COS(K*X) : YT = A*(Y+B)*SIN(K*X)
120 RETURN
```

Program 3.6 A cylindrical anamorphic transformation.

values in the original image over an angle of θ in the anamorphic image. Again we are not concerned with mathematical 'propriety'. It is only sufficient that you understand the general principle involved. The subroutine captioned Program 3.6 performs the required transformation. Figures 3.20 and 3.21 show an anamorphic transformation of a butterfly using values for the constants as shown in the captions. The circle shows the ideal radius of the reconstructing cylindrical mirror and within the circle is the image that you should see in the cylinder.

The figures show both screen photographs and output from a high quality incremental plotter for comparison. This allows a hard copy image to be produced that is faithful to the notional coordinate system used in the program (1280×800). The incremental plots were generated by writing a list of coordinates in the BASIC program 1280×800 system to a file and then using that file to drive the incremental plotter. The line plotter illustrations in this book were made using a high quality plotter. If you do not have access to such equipment the images that you produce will be fuzzier and more jagged. However bear in mind that this is owing to the limitation of your display device and that your program is producing coordinate values at the resolution shown in the incremental plotter illustrations.

4 Symmetry and two-dimensional ornamentation

In this chapter we will explore the use of the computer not only to draw decorative motifs but to locate them as part of the grand design of two-dimensional decorative patterns such as those found in wallpapers, fabrics, carpets or porcelain ornamentation. To fully exploit the power of the computer to place motifs (i.e. to design two-dimensional patterns as translations of motifs) we must adopt a scheme for classifying two-dimensional groupings and appreciate the differences between the various ways motifs can be arranged.

The maths introduced in this chapter is fairly simple and is just a scheme for classifying the different symmetries that can occur in two-dimensional patterns. We can then use these formalisms to control the use of the two-dimensional linear transformations and produce elegant patterns. Although symbolic classifications exist for two-dimensional patterns, we can ignore these because all we need is a labelling or classification scheme and an appreciation of the differences between the different pattern schemes. The mathematics of these patterns gives us a method for writing programs that draw the patterns. Just as we need a language to get the computer to draw straight lines in a certain way – so we need a language at a higher level to design the program structures that control the primitive graphics statements. This language is the mathematics of symmetry.

This chapter is mainly devoted to programming structures for the production of 24 examples of pattern classes. There are exactly seven frieze or band groups and 17 wallpaper groups. These seven frieze groups and 17 wallpaper groups specify all the possible ways in which one can arrange motifs so that the final pattern exhibits certain kinds of symmetry. Any repetitive two-dimensional arrangement for placing motifs will fall into one of these categories. In looking at these groups we use a labelling scheme that follows the scheme of Shubnikov (Symmetry in Science and Art – 1974). Although mathematicians adopt a rigorous labelling system using algebraic notation to show the relationships between groups (a subject known as Group theory) we will simply use a numeric scheme: band1, band2, ... band7, net1, net2, ... net17. The symmetry of each pattern will be described, but not mathematically. All that is required is an intuitive appreciation of the groups and their relationship to the program that produced them.

This area of graphics programming is potentially very rewarding. It is rather like composing music. The computer is your instrument producing the final sound, and the mathematics are the rules of harmony that control the type or structure of the music produced. And like musical composition you are limited only by your imagination. The patterns we have produced are just examples that illustrate the underlying principle: you can produce anything that you want. We have tended to stick to traditional motifs and recipes for combining them into a two-dimensional design, but try and be creative and use your own motifs and ideas to get your machine to conjure up unique patterns.

Many beautiful patterns can be created easily. We are using the computer not only for the mundane task of generating and repeating the motifs but to experiment with the various classes. This process (imagining how a finished pattern will look given a collection of motifs and proposed symmetry relationships) is very difficult to perform manually. A great deal of skill and experience as a pattern designer, together with a good knowledge of symmetry is essential. You can however use the computer as a substitute for this experience and experiment freely.

Of course it is unlikely that the designers of such beautiful and intricate patterns as those shown in Colour Plate 7, which are from Jones's massive work (The Grammar of Ornament – London 1856) had any formal knowledge of symmetry. They would use experience passed on from generation to generation, catalogues of motifs and methods built up over many years, a major reflection of their culture. In fact there is apparently no single culture with all 24 groups occurring in its traditional formal ornamentation.

4.1 TYPES OF SYMMETRY

Before looking at the symmetry of band and network patterns we will review some simple concepts of symmetry types.

Symmetry of single motifs – plane of symmetry

The bodies of men, mammals, fish, birds and insects all have a symmetry plane. In a two-dimensional outline this symmetry plane is a line (Figures 4.1 and 4.2). In images classified as having a symmetry plane m two objects are arranged relative to one another as one object and its mirror image. The symmetry plane or line divides the image into an object and its mirror image . In reality the image can be made up of a single object that exhibits symmetry m, as in Figure 4.1 (half the object is the mirror image of the other half), or two objects can be arranged as object/mirror/object (Figure 4.2).

Figure 4.1
A single object that possesses mirror symmetry

Given an object or half an object, an image exhibiting symmetry *m* is obtained by using the linear transformation for reflection about the *y*-axis. Variations of Program 4.1 produced Figures 4.1 and 4.2.

Symmetry of single motifs – axis of symmetry

Figures that possess an axis of symmetry are figures that coincide with themselves when rotated about this axis. Such figures may or may not contain a plane of symmetry. Figure 4.3 is a page from Ernst Haeckel's 'Kunstformen der Natur' (Leipzig 1904) showing micro-organisms with five-fold rotational symmetry. Each time a five-fold figure in Figure 4.3 is rotated through 72° it forms a figure indistinguishable from the original (apart from any imperfections in the sketch or nature). The axis of rotation is a line perpendicular to the plane of the figure or paper and passing through the centre point.

Figure 4.2
A pattern that possesses mirror symmetry made by reflecting an asymmetric motif

```
10 CLS
20 INPUT "File name",FILE$
30 SCREEN 2 : CLS
40 WINDOW (-640,-400)-(639,399)
50 A = 1 : B = 0 : C = 200 : D = 0 : E = 1 : F = 0
60 GOSUB 100  'draw motif
70 A = -1 : C = -200
80 GOSUB 100  'draw motif
90 END

100 'SUBROUTINE draw motif
110   FILENUM = 3
120   OPEN FILE$ FOR INPUT AS #FILENUM
130   WHILE NOT EOF(FILENUM)
140     INPUT #FILENUM,OP,X,Y
150     GOSUB 200  'transform
160     IF OP = 1 THEN LINE -(XT,YT) ELSE PSET (XT,YT)
170   WEND
180   CLOSE #FILENUM
190 RETURN

200 'SUBROUTINE transform
210   XT = X*A+Y*B+C
220   YT = X*D+Y*E+F
230 RETURN
```

Program 4.1 Generating pictures with mirror symmetry.

The smallest angle of rotation that brings the figure into coincidence with itself (72° in this case) is called the elementary angle of rotation. The number of coincidences that occur in one rotation is the order of the axis. The organism labelled (1) in Figure 4.3 possesses both rotational and mirror symmetry. Its rotational symmetry is order five and it can be reflected about a vertical line through its centre. Examples of this type of symmetry abound in nature. Note that organism (8) in Figure 4.3 only possesses mirror symmetry and that part of (9) possesses five-fold rotational symmetry but the whole exhibits mirror symmetry only. Study of Figure 4.4, also from Haeckel's classic work, will give further appreciation of these points. The figures exhibit a combination of mirror symmetry and three, four, five and six-fold rotational symmetry.

To generate a figure possessing axial symmetry of order m using a motif, we need a FOR loop that increments a rotational angle by the elementary angle of rotation. Program 4.2 produced the patterns shown in Figure 4.5. Figure 4.5a is an example of a figure with axial symmetry of order five but no mirror symmetry.

4.2 PROGRAM ORGANIZATION

The remainder of this chapter is devoted to the production of the seven frieze groups and 17 wallpaper groups. The programs that control the arrangement of each of the 24 groups are listed, together with examples produced by the program and examples from Jones. All programs produce patterns from the simple motif which is an asymmetrical triangle. Using a common shape for each group means that we can compare groups and appreciate the differences and similarities between groups without distractions due to the shape of the individual motif. In principle the program required to produce patterns that contain more complex motifs will be identical,

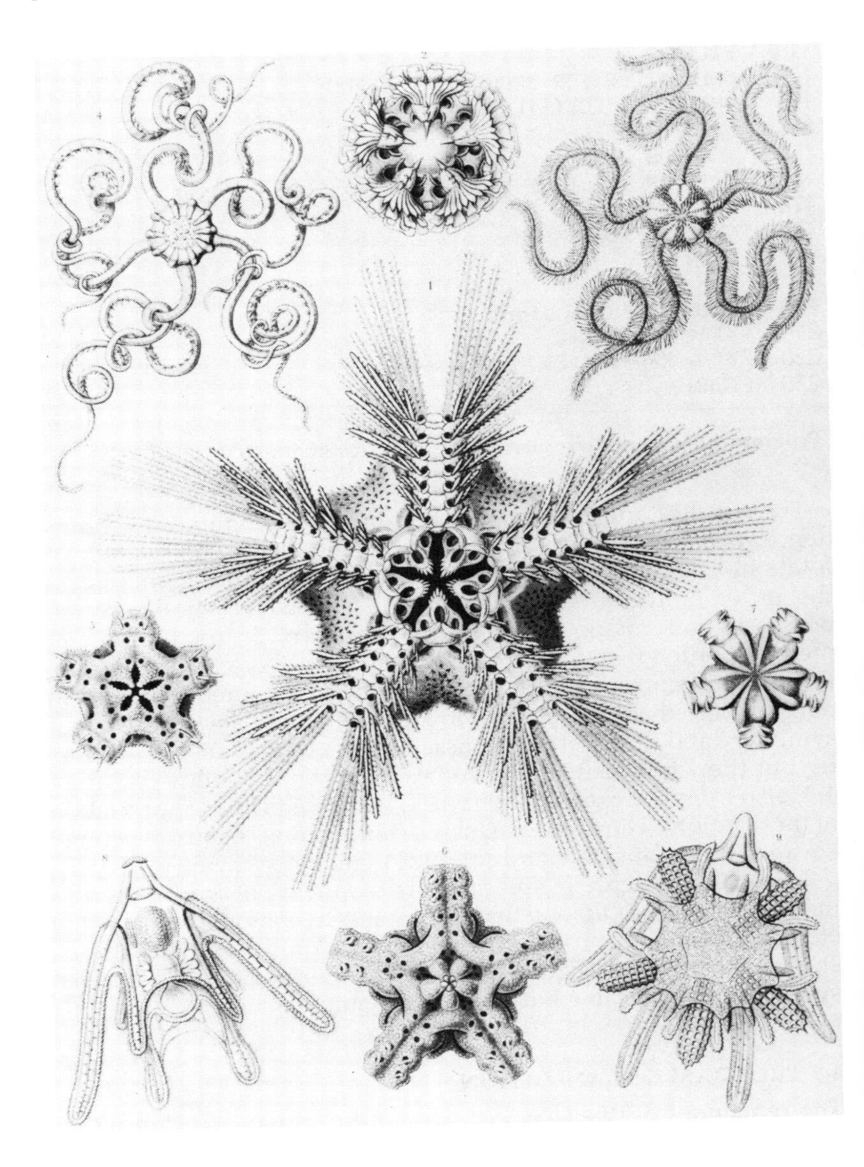

Figure 4.3
Ophiodea

only the subroutine 'draw motif at' will change. The actual motif data used is too long in most cases to be included in the text. You can make up your own using a digitizer or the techniques described in Chapter 2. Alternatively you can use mathematically generated motifs as we have in some cases. All of the mathematically generated motifs are selected from Chapter 10.

As far as handling the data is concerned there are three possible approaches when motifs are being drawn and redrawn. Originally the motif data will be on file and the subroutine 'draw motif at' can

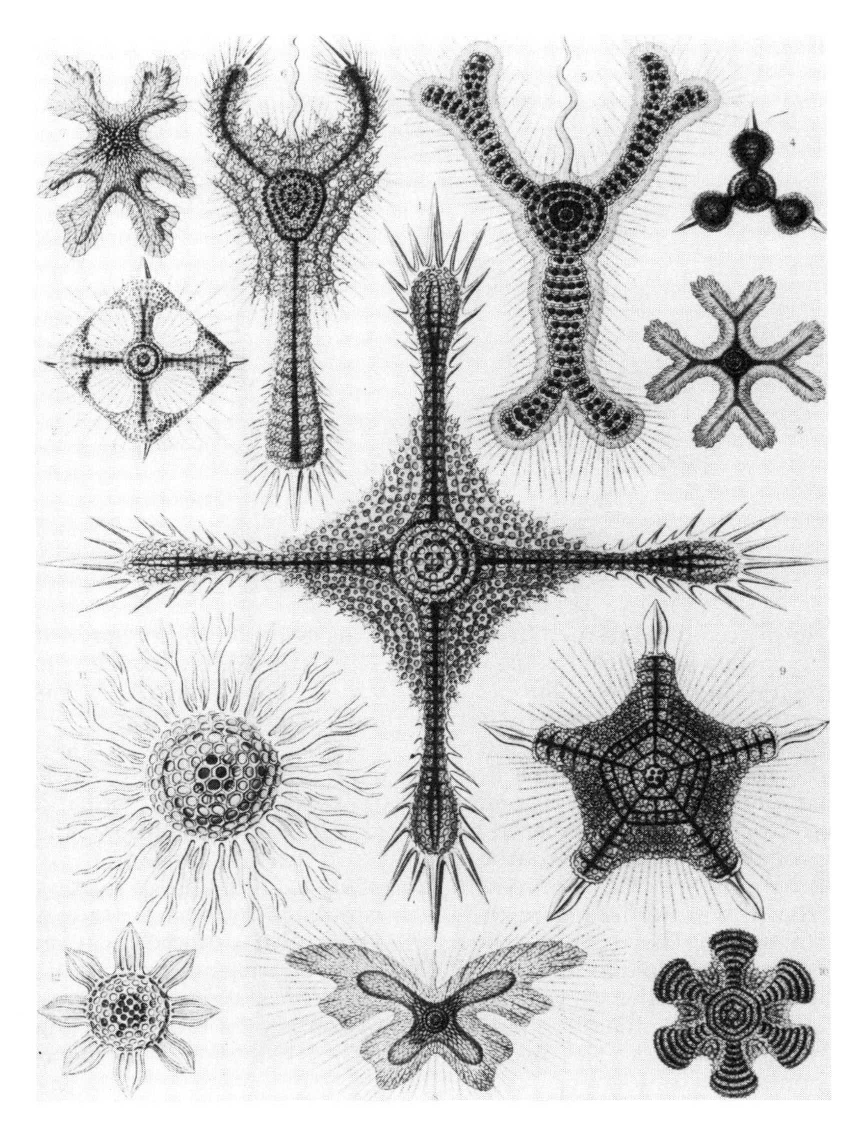

Figure 4.4
Discoidea

```
 10 PI = 3.141593
 20 DEF FNRAD(DEGREES) = DEGREES*PI/180
 30 CLS
 40 INPUT "File name",FILE$
 50 SCREEN 2 : CLS
 60 WINDOW (-640,-400)-(639,399)
 70 R = 300
 80 FOR THETA = 72 TO 360 STEP 72
 90   T = FNRAD(THETA)
100   A = COS(T) : B = -SIN(T) : C = R*COS(PI/2+T)
110   D = SIN(T) : E = COS(T) : F = R*SIN(PI/2+T)
120   GOSUB 150  'draw motif
130 NEXT THETA
140 END

150 'SUBROUTINE draw motif
160   FILENUM = 3
170   OPEN FILE$ FOR INPUT AS #FILENUM
180   WHILE NOT EOF(FILENUM)
190     INPUT #FILENUM,OP,X,Y
200     GOSUB 250  'transform
210     IF OP = 1 THEN LINE -(XT,YT) ELSE PSET (XT,YT)
220   WEND
230   CLOSE #FILENUM
240 RETURN

250 'SUBROUTINE transform
260   XT = X*A+Y*B+C
270   YT = X*D+Y*E+F
280 RETURN
```

Program 4.2 Generating a figure with axial symmetry.

simply read and re-read from the file. This is the simplest approach but is only suitable if the file is on diskette. If the file is a cassette file then it should be read once only and transferred into an array. This method has the advantage that any transformations, such as reflection, need only be calculated once. The motif can be reflected and the reflected version stored in the same array. This approach is adopted in the seven programs that draw the seven frieze or band groups. The file is replaced by a single DATA statement and the programs are organized around arrays. In the 17 wallpaper group programs the other approach is adopted, reading and re-reading from the same file (again the file is simulated by a single DATA statement). This technique is preferred because it is simple but again it is only suitable for diskette files. A third approach is to store the motif data in the program as a set of DATA statements that are created from a file automatically. Here you need a pre-processing program that converts the file data into DATA statements for incorporation in a program.

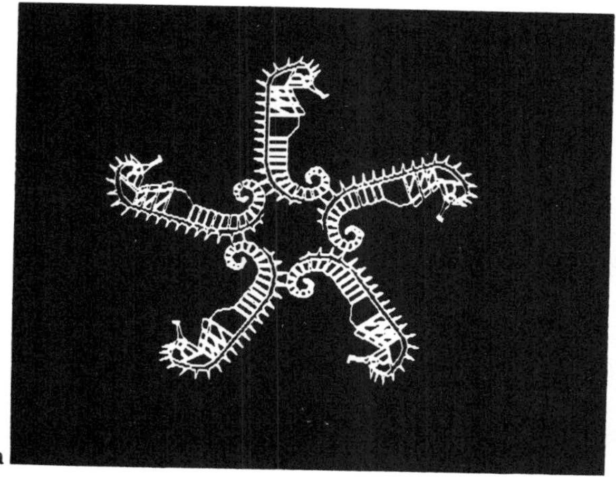

a

b

Figure 4.5
Motifs forming axial symmetry: (a) five-fold; (b) six-fold

Note that in the more complex wallpaper groups some idiosyncratic adjustment is necessary to position the triangles as required. This is because the only sensible position for the point

```
  10 DIM CONTROL(100),X(100),Y(100)
  20 SCREEN 2 : CLS
  40 GOSUB 1000  'initialise
  50 FOR MOTIF = 1 TO NOOFMOTIFS
  60   GOSUB 1100  'draw motif at x,y
  70   X = X+PERIOD
  80 NEXT MOTIF
  90 END

1000 'SUBROUTINE initialise
1010   X = 100 : Y = 400
1020   PERIOD = 200 : NOOFPOINTS = 3 : NOOFMOTIFS = 6
1030   RESTORE
1040   FOR I = 1 TO NOOFPOINTS
1050     READ CONTROL(I), X(I), Y(I)
1060   NEXT I
1070 RETURN

1080 DATA 1,0,30,1,-80,30,1,0,0

1100 'SUBROUTINE draw motif at x,y
1110   WINDOW (-X,-Y)-(1279-X,799-Y)
1115   PSET (0,0)
1120   FOR I = 1 TO NOOFPOINTS
1130     IF CONTROL(I) = 1 THEN LINE -(X(I),Y(I)) ELSE PSET (X(I),Y(I))
1140   NEXT I
1150 RETURN
```

Program 4.3 Band group 1.

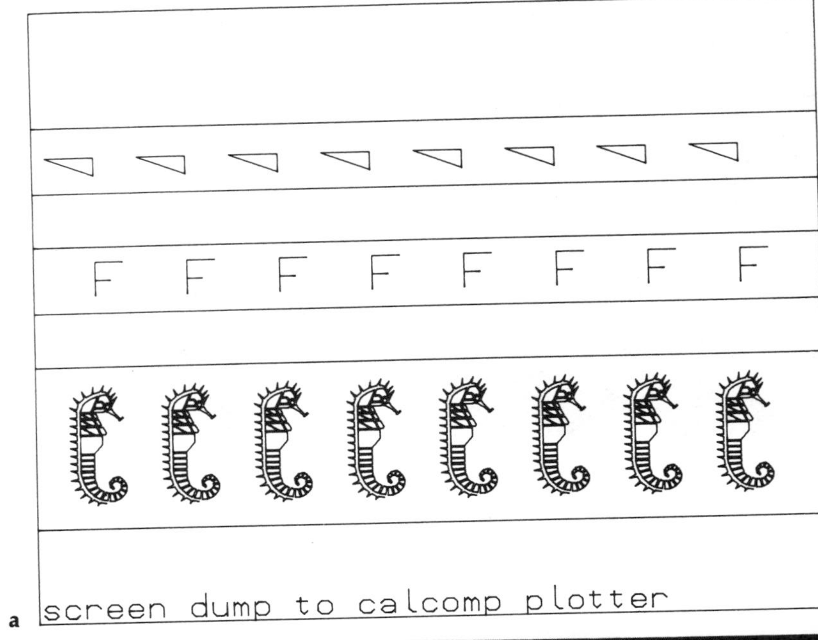

a

b

Figure 4.6
Band group 1

(0,0) of a motif is its centre of gravity or the centre of a minimum area enclosing triangle. This means that when, for example, a triangle is reflected it partially overlaps the original and a displacement is required. The correct displacement for each grouping is a function of motif size and shape, the grouping being used and aesthetic consideration, and cannot be conveniently specified in advance for any motif.

4.3 SYMMETRY OF BANDS OR STRIPS

Our aim in studying symmetry classifications is to use them to write programs that control two-dimensional linear transformations such as translation, rotation, reflection, etc., operating on motifs. In this section we introduce the control of transformations for a class of patterns known technically as one-sided bands or friezes. These are strip patterns used extensively in fabric design and architectura decoration. Their more familiar names are bands or friezes. In a band pattern, a motif or group of motifs is repeated at intervals in one dimension.

Band group 1

The first symmetry class of band patterns that we consider is shown in Figure 4.6. In this figure, and subsequent figures in this section, the plotter output is made up of three elements. The top illustration is a series of right-angled triangles positioned to form the pattern class, followed by a series of the letter 'F'. The next pattern is generated from a digitized motif or motifs (except band group 6 which uses DATA statements). The photo shows an example of the pattern from Jones. Figure 4.6 shows patterns belonging to the first band group. These are patterns with one translation axis and no other type of symmetry. Displacements may take place in direction left or right and the pattern comes into coincidence with itself after it moves through distance a, the elementary translation or period. It is easy to generate this pattern from a single motif and Program 4.3 produced the computer illustrations shown. The required program structure is a FOR loop controlling a translation through the period a for as many instances of the motif as are required.

We can either use our system of homogeneous coordinates for the translation or simply move the origin through the period each time. This is the most efficient mechanism, so it is the one we employ in the program. As we are using the motif over and over again we read the data from a file or DATA statements once only and transfer the motif data into three arrays. It is more efficient to move the origin each time and use the same data because we do not have to get involved in multiplications of (x,y) for the translation transformation. Clearly the efficiency factor becomes more and more important as the 'complexity' of the motif (the number of points in it) increases. There is also the problem with cassette files (already discussed) that this method overcomes.

An interesting point is that mathematically the rosette patterns (Figure 4.5, for example) generated using axial rotation and the band patterns generated using translation are theoretically equivalent. The translation is rotation about an infinitely distant axis. Another point that can be made is that although the direction of the translation may be left or right the translation axis is 'polar'. If we travel along that translation axis for the triangle pattern we encounter a sharp point followed by a blunt end or a blunt end followed by a sharp point depending on our direction of travel. The patterns can be used to give an impression of motion and may be employed, for example, in a corridor in which traffic is unidirectional. You can see this in the 'flow' in Figure 4.6b. The computer generated example is rather static, demonstrating that there is a good deal of aesthetic judgement involved in generating such patterns. The particular frieze shown is Greek in origin. Note that the motifs almost have mirror symmetry.

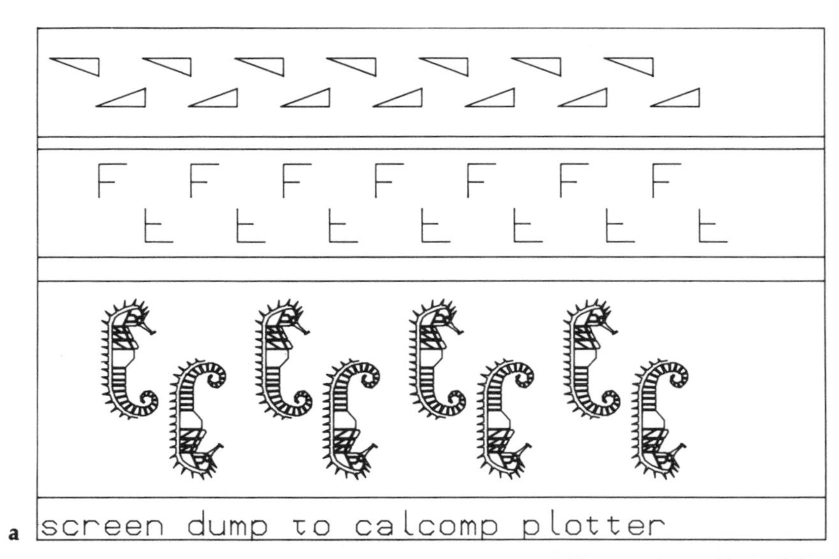

a

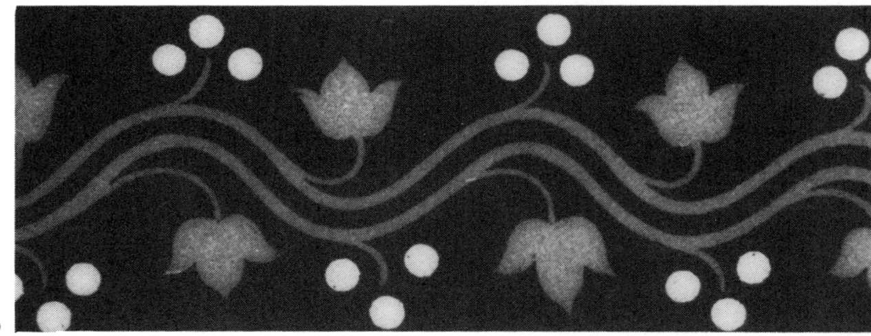

b

Figure 4.7
Band group 2

Band group 2

In the second symmetry class shown in Figure 4.7 there is a glide-reflection plane or mirror-glide plane. A glide-reflection is a combination of a reflection plus a translation. The glide plane coincides with the translation axis and the figure comes into coincidence with itself after translation through a distance *a*/2 and reflection. The translation and glide-reflection axes lie in the same plane.

Shubnikov (in 'Symmetry in Science and Art' 1974) says of this class of pattern: 'Whereas bands with a single symmetry element – a translation axis – are suitable for representing progressive motion in one direction . . . , bands with a translation axis and glide-reflection plane create the impression of sinuous motion like that of a snake'. This facet is not too well demonstrated by the sea horse motif because of its aspect ratio.

The program that generated the computer illustrations is Program 4.4. Again you can see the nature or symmetry of the pattern reflected in the program structure. Again we use a FOR loop to

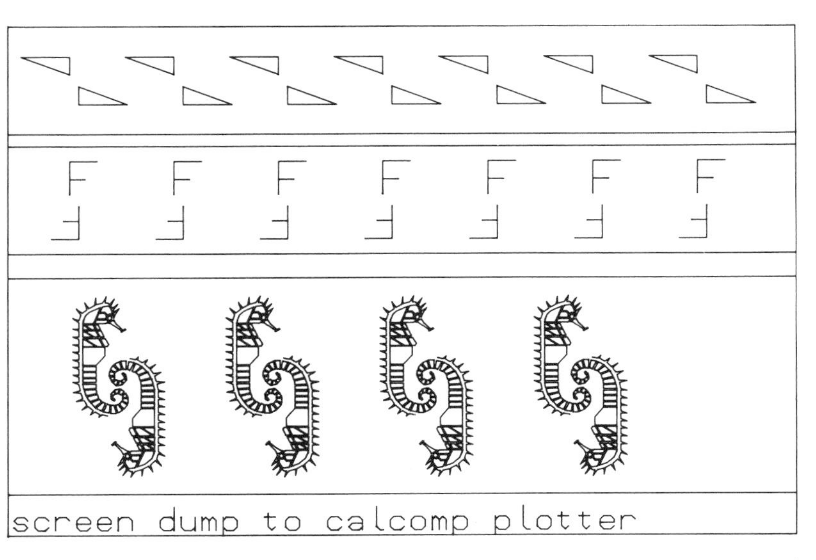

Figure 4.8
Band group 3

repeat the motif. In programming terms it seems most convenient to draw the top motifs then the bottom ones so that two consecutive FOR loops are required. We start the second row of motifs $a/2$ from the first row and subject each to an x-axis reflection. Again from the efficiency point of view we should only perform the reflection once and this is carried out between the FOR loops. Of course using homogenous coordinates we can combine the translation and mirror reflection into one net transformation matrix but for reasons already explained we proceed as in the program. Note also that the two FOR loops that control the drawing of the motifs are identical. We have left the loops like this for emphasis. Later the FOR loops will be contained in a subroutine. The illustration in Figure 4.7b is from Jones and the frieze is Greek.

Band group 3

Now if we return to the first band class and consider a group of motifs that possess axial symmetry of order 2, that is, the elemen-

```
 10 DIM CONTROL(100),X(100),Y(100)
 20 SCREEN 2 : CLS
 40 GOSUB 1000  'initialise
 50 FOR MOTIF = 1 TO NOOFMOTIFS
 60   GOSUB 1100  'draw motif at x,y
 70   X = X+PERIOD
 80 NEXT MOTIF
 90 GOSUB 1000  'initialise
100 Y = Y-100 : X = X+PERIOD/2
110 GOSUB 170  'reflect
120 FOR MOTIF = 1 TO NOOFMOTIFS
130   GOSUB 1100  'draw motif at x,y
140   X = X+PERIOD
150 NEXT MOTIF
160 END

170 'SUBROUTINE reflect
180   FOR I = 1 TO NOOFPOINTS
190     Y(I) = -Y(I)
200   NEXT I
210 RETURN
```

Program 4.4 Band group 2.

```
 10 DIM CONTROL(100),X(100),Y(100)
 20 SCREEN 2 : CLS
 40 GOSUB 1000  'initialise
 50 FOR MOTIF = 1 TO NOOFMOTIFS
 60   GOSUB 1100  'draw motif at x,y
 70   X = X+PERIOD
 80 NEXT MOTIF
 90 GOSUB 1000  'initialise
100 Y = Y-100 : X = X+PERIOD/4
110 GOSUB 170  'rotate
120 FOR MOTIF = 1 TO NOOFMOTIFS
130   GOSUB 1100  'draw motif at x,y
140   X = X+PERIOD
150 NEXT MOTIF
160 END

170 'SUBROUTINE rotate
180   FOR I = 1 TO NOOFPOINTS
190     Y(I) = -Y(I) : X(I) = -X(I)
200   NEXT I
210 RETURN
```

Program 4.5 Band group 3.

```
 10 DIM CONTROL(100),X(100),Y(100)
 20 SCREEN 2 : CLS
 40 GOSUB 1000  'initialise
 50 FOR MOTIF = 1 TO NOOFMOTIFS
 60   GOSUB 1100  'draw motif at x,y
 70   X = X+PERIOD
 80 NEXT MOTIF
 90 GOSUB 1000  'initialise
100 X = X+PERIOD/12
110 GOSUB 170  'reflect
120 FOR MOTIF = 1 TO NOOFMOTIFS
130   GOSUB 1100  'draw motif at x,y
140   X = X+PERIOD
150 NEXT MOTIF
160 END

170 'SUBROUTINE reflect
180   FOR I = 1 TO NOOFPOINTS
190     X(I) = -X(I)
200   NEXT I
210 RETURN
```

Program 4.6 Band group 4.

```
 10 DIM CONTROL(100),X(100),Y(100)
 20 SCREEN 2 : CLS
 40 GOSUB 1000  'initialise
 50 FOR MOTIF = 1 TO NOOFMOTIFS
 60   GOSUB 1100  'draw motif at x,y
 70   X = X+PERIOD
 80 NEXT MOTIF
 90 GOSUB 1000  'initialise
100 GOSUB 170  'reflect
110 Y = Y-100
120 FOR MOTIF = 1 TO NOOFMOTIFS
130   GOSUB 1100  'draw motif at x,y
140   X = X+PERIOD
150 NEXT MOTIF
160 END

170 'SUBROUTINE reflect
180   FOR I = 1 TO NOOFPOINTS
190     Y(I) = -Y(I)
200   NEXT I
210 RETURN
```

Program 4.7 Band group 5.

a

b

Figure 4.9
Band group 4

tary motif coincides with itself after rotation through 180°, we have class 3. Examples of bands with such symmetry are shown in Figure 4.8. Note that the bands tend to impart a feeling of motion in both directions. The program that generated the computer examples is Program 4.5. It has exactly the same structure as the previous program. Rotation is carried out once only between the FOR loops that generate the top and bottom halves of the pattern The illustration in Figure 4.8b is from Jones and again it is Greek.

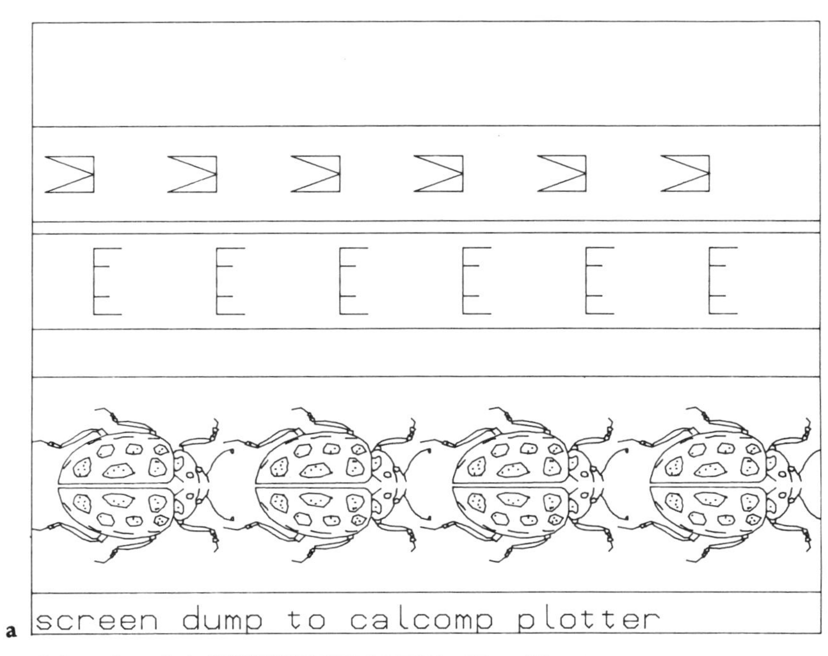

a

b

Figure 4.10
Band group 5

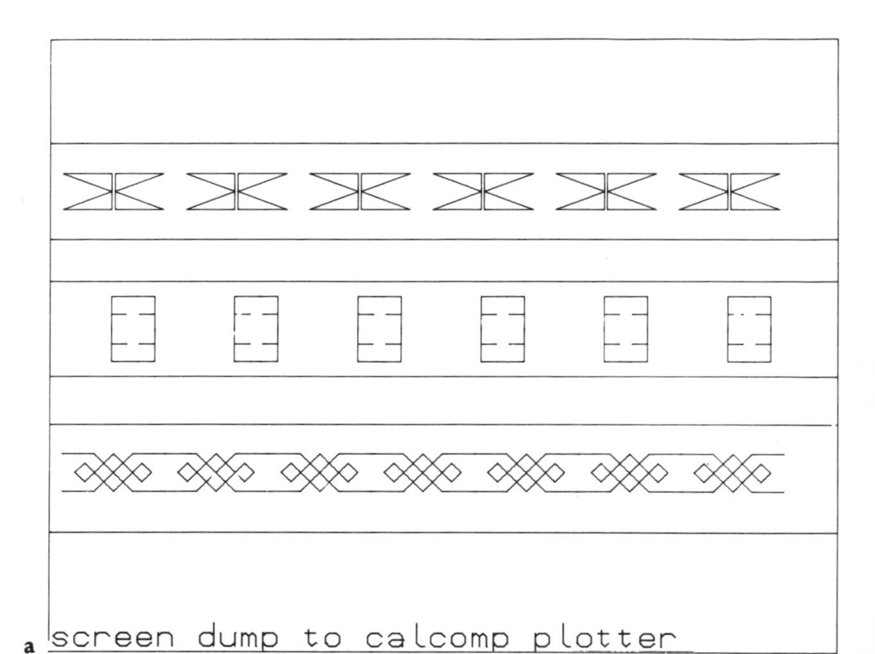

Figure 4.11
Band group 6

Band group 4

The next four symmetry classes involve mirror symmetry planes. This makes a total of seven possible symmetry classes for one-sided bands. The simplest in this category is class 4, examples of which are shown in Figure 4.9. Patterns of this class tend to appear as decorations on horizontal cornices around the top of a room. This group contains a vertical or transverse mirror plane. Program 4.6 generated the computer illustrations. Again it is convenient to have two FOR loops generating the odd-numbered motifs 1, 3, 5, 7 followed by a mirror reflection and a generation of the even-numbered motifs 2, 4, 6, 8, etc. The example in Figure 4.9b is a Greek frieze from Jones.

```
 10 DIM CONTROL(100),X(100),Y(100)
 20 SCREEN 2 : CLS
 30 GOSUB 1000  'initialise
 40 GOSUB 180  'draw a band
 50 GOSUB 1000  'initialise
 60 GOSUB 240  'reflectx
 70 Y = Y-100
 80 GOSUB 180  'draw a band
 90 GOSUB 1000  'initialise
100 GOSUB 290  'reflecty
110 GOSUB 180  'draw a band
120 GOSUB 1000  'initialise
130 GOSUB 240  'reflectx
140 GOSUB 290  'reflecty
150 Y = Y-100
160 GOSUB 180  'draw a band
170 END

180 'SUBROUTINE draw a band
190   FOR MOTIF = 1 TO NOOFMOTIFS
200     GOSUB 1100  'draw motif at x,y
210     X = X+PERIOD
220   NEXT MOTIF
230 RETURN

240 'SUBROUTINE reflectx
250   FOR I = 1 TO NOOFPOINTS
260     Y(I) = -Y(I)
270   NEXT I
280 RETURN

290 'SUBROUTINE reflecty
300   FOR I = 1 TO NOOFPOINTS
310     X(I) = -X(I)
320   NEXT I
330 RETURN
```

Program 4.8 Band group 6.

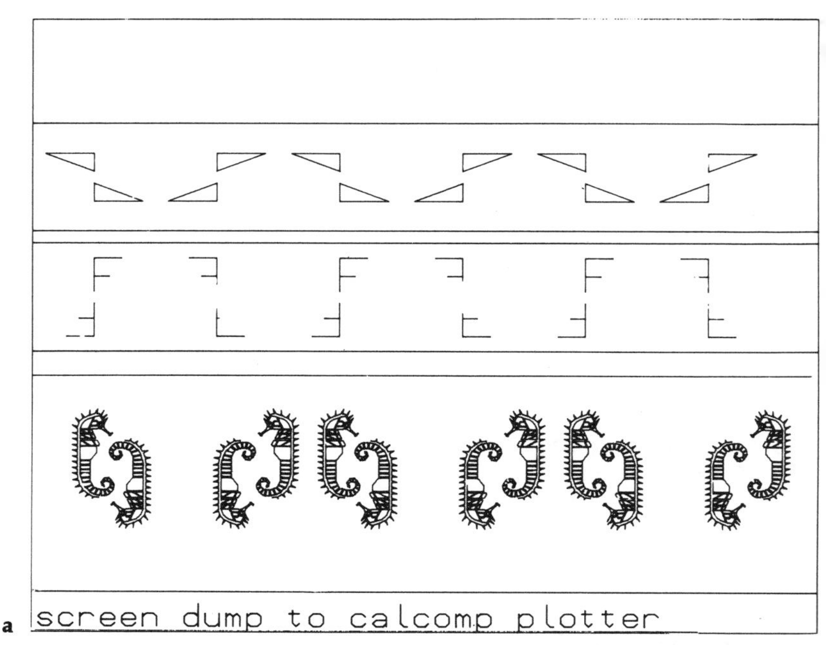

Figure 4.12
Band group 7

Band group 5
The next class, the fifth, is shown in Figure 4.10. Here the mirror plane *m* and the translation axis *a* are parallel. Program 4.7 generated the computer illustrations. These patterns are commonly used vertically in architectural decoration as demonstrated in the examples from Jones. The motif used in the program is a single motif exhibiting mirror symmetry rather than a motif and its reflection.

Band group 6
The sixth class is obtained by taking the fourth class and adding a mirror plane parallel to the translation axis. Examples are shown in Figure 4.11 and the program is Program 4.8. The motifs are generated in four bands and the motif generating FOR loop is now enclosed in the subroutine 'draw a band' which is called four times. The subroutines 'reflectx' and 'reflecty' could of course be combined into one subroutine but these have been left as separate subroutines

for clarity. This time the computer example is generated from a group of DATA statements rather than a digitized motif. A group of three Grecian friezes from Jones is shown in Figure 4.11b.

Band group 7
Finally a seventh class. This has both a vertical axis of symmetry and a transverse mirror plane. Figure 4.12 shows the output from Program 4.9. From a study of the pattern class it may be seen that the easiest way to handle this case is to construct a double size motif containing the original and a rotated version and plot this as a unit. The problem is then reduced to that of class 4. Figure 4.12b shows an example from Jones. This time the pattern is Arabian.

```
 10 DIM CONTROL(100),X(100),Y(100)
 20 SCREEN 2 : CLS
 30 GOSUB 1000  'initialise
 40 GOSUB 180  'draw a band
 50 GOSUB 1000  'initialise
 60 GOSUB 240  'reflectx
 70 X = X+PERIOD : Y = Y-100
 80 GOSUB 180  'draw a band
 90 GOSUB 1000  'initialise
100 GOSUB 290  'reflecty
105 X = X+PERIOD
110 GOSUB 180  'draw a band
120 GOSUB 1000  'initialise
130 GOSUB 240  'reflectx
140 GOSUB 290  'reflecty
150 Y = Y-100
160 GOSUB 180  'draw a band
170 END

180 'SUBROUTINE draw a band
190   FOR MOTIF = 1 TO NOOFMOTIFS
200     IF MOTIF MOD 2 = 1 THEN GOSUB 1100  'draw motif at x,y
210     X = X+PERIOD
220   NEXT MOTIF
230 RETURN

240 'SUBROUTINE reflectx
250   FOR I = 1 TO NOOFPOINTS
260     Y(I) = -Y(I)
270   NEXT I
280 RETURN

290 'SUBROUTINE reflecty
300   FOR I = 1 TO NOOFPOINTS
310     X(I) = -X(I)
320   NEXT I
330 RETURN
```

Program 4.9 Band group 7.

Summary of band pattern symmetry

We can summarize the symmetry of band patterns by using a flowchart classification. Here the patterns are classified by asking three questions. Firstly, is there 180° rotational symmetry? Secondly, is there a vertical reflection? Finally, is there a horizontal or glide-reflection? Figure 4.13 shows the band pattern decision tree.

If you want to develop expertise in generating band patterns, then familiarity with the seven groups is necessary. One of the easiest ways to build up proficiency is to use the decision tree to study examples from everyday life. These are all around us on both the interior and exterior of buildings.

4.4 NETWORK PATTERNS

In this section we will look at how we can generalize into two dimensions and create network patterns by controlling the instancing or placing of motifs in two dimensions. Again it is worth

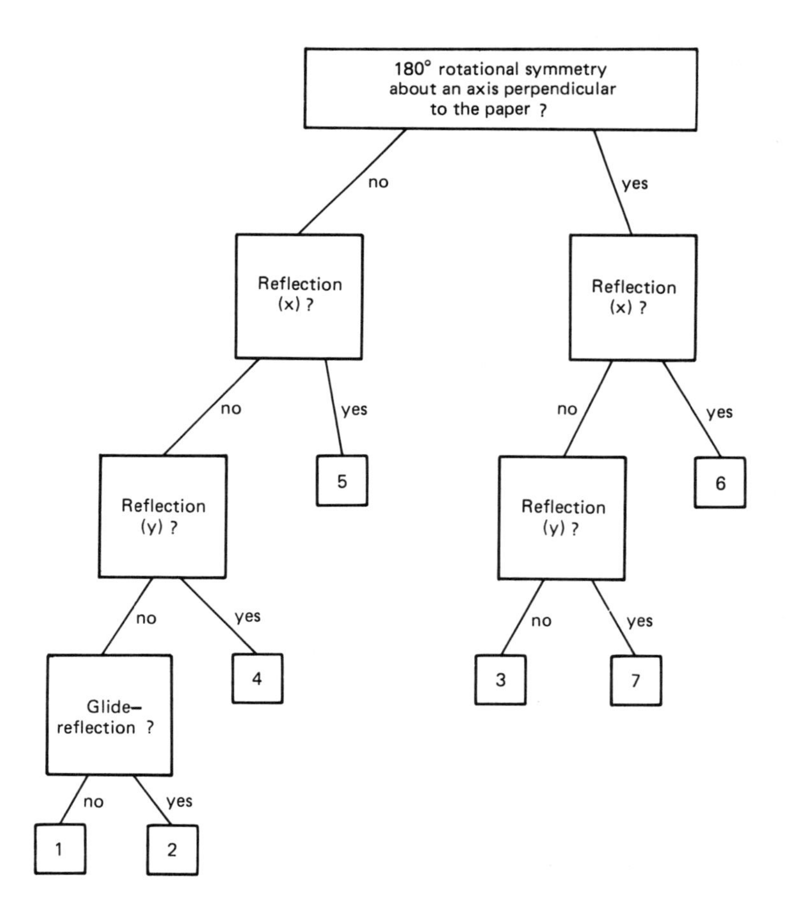

Figure 4.13
Decision tree for classification of band groups

emphasizing that you are only limited by your imagination and by the initial motifs that you choose.

When instancing or placing motifs in one dimension for band patterns, we simply placed motifs, or groups of motifs, at equal intervals. Now when we are instancing or placing motifs in two dimensions we use one of a number of translation nets to control the motif translations. These are parallelogram nets, of which there are five (Figure 4.14). The five categories are square, rectangular, oblique, equilateral and rhombic. Each intersection in a net defines a point in two-dimensional coordinate space where the motif is to be placed. Each net can be defined by the parameters a, b and θ, where a and b are the elementary distances or periods in the two directions or axes and θ the angle between these axes. We can use the five translation nets on our asymmetric motif: the right-angled triangle. Four of these are shown in Figure 4.15. The program that generated this figure is Program 4.10. The program structure is, of course, a nested FOR loop. The innermost FOR loop generating a row or band and the outermost controlling the translation down the vertical axis. Note that the program will handle square, rectangular, equilateral and rhombic nets as it stands. For parallelogram nets lines 60 and 140 need changing. Now although these patterns look different they all form a single symmetry network classification, network group 1. Thus the symmetry class is, in general, independent of the translation net. However if the motif itself possesses axial symmetry, then using different translation nets may result in different symmetry classes. (Compare the sixth and seventh class.)

Another point that we must note at this stage is that we are using network symmetry to place pre-drawn motifs. Using the network to divide up the plane into equal figures without gaps or overlaps is known as tessellating. Mathematically both processes are one and the same but computationally they require completely different

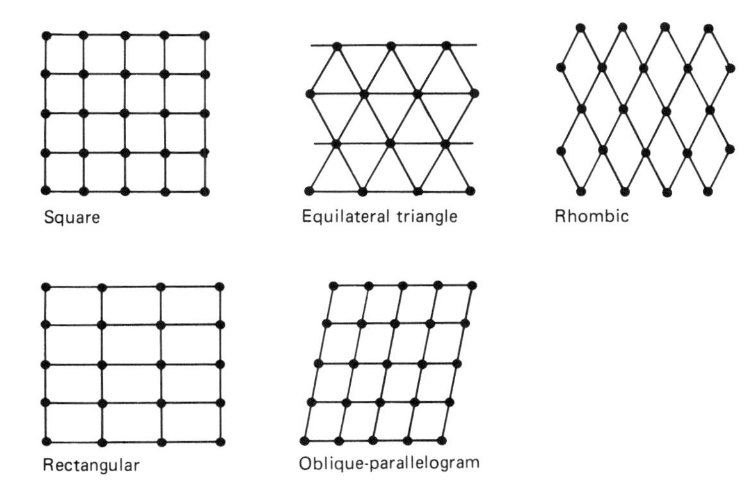

Figure 4.14
The five parallelogram nets for motif placement

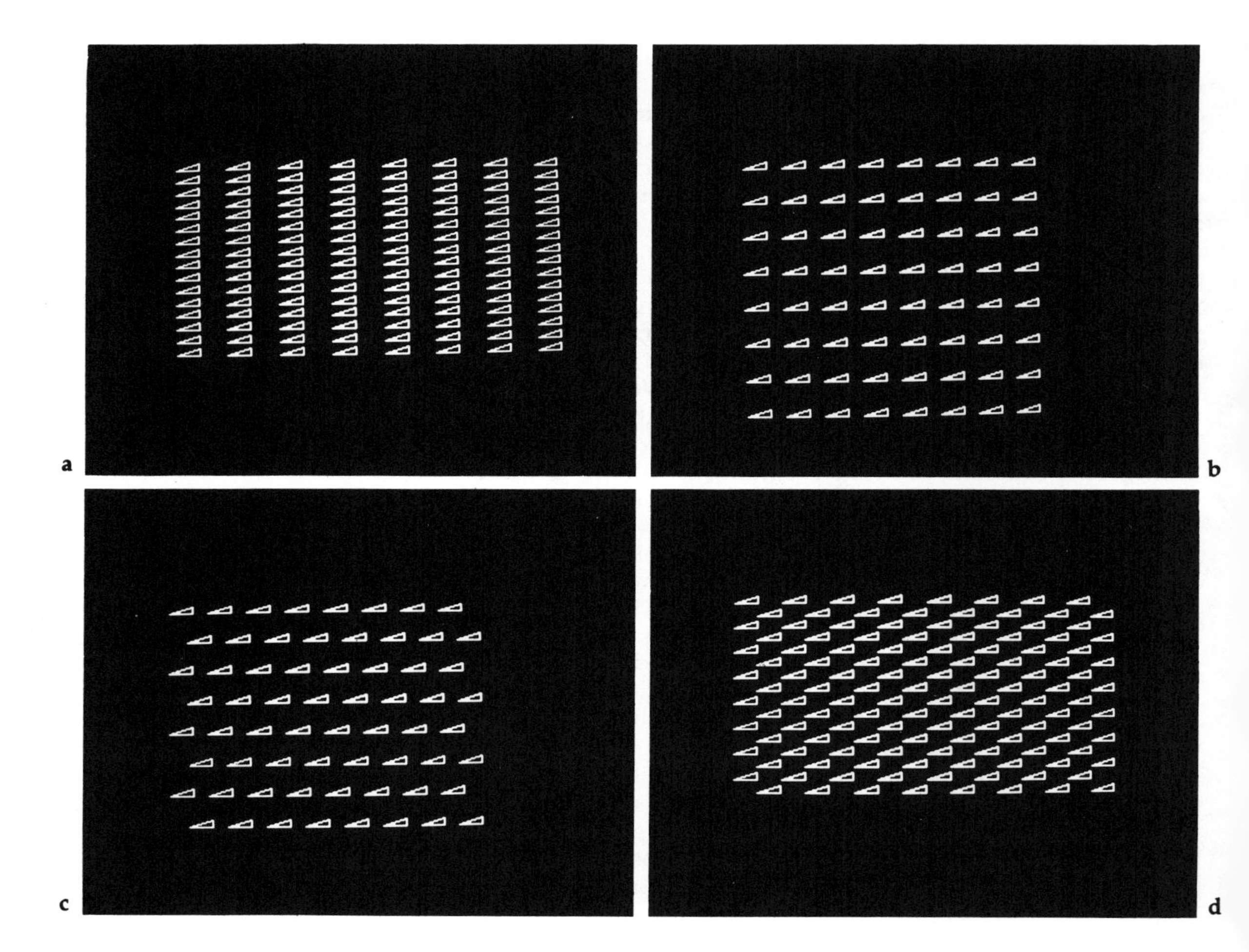

Figure 4.15
Output from Program 4.10:
(a) rectangular 90, 135, 35;
(b) square 90, 100, 100;
(c) equilateral 60, 100;
(d) rhombic 30, 125

Table 4.1 Translation net attributes

Net	*Classification*	*Proportions of unit mesh*
Square	$a \mid a$	$a = b,\ \theta = 90°$
Equilateral Triangle	a/a	$a = b,\ \theta = 60°$
Rhombic	a/a	$a = b,\ \theta \neq 90°$
Rectangular	$a \mid b$	$a \neq b,\ \theta = 90°$
Oblique parallelogram	a/b	$a \neq b,\ \theta \neq 90°$

| means the axes are mutually perpendicular
/ means the axes are oblique

approaches. This difference is illustrated in Figure 4.16. Tessellations are covered fully in the next chapter.

The translation nets themselves possess symmetry. Their attributes are summarized in Table 4.1.

Higher symmetries than those possessed by the net are possible and these depend on the inherent symmetry of the motif. For example, the symmetry of a pattern produced by using the square net may have a higher symmetry than the translation net if the motif possesses symmetry.

We now come to the task of classifying the possible symmetries of network patterns. There are 17 of these and examples of all 17 classes, using the asymmetrical triangle as a motif, are shown

```
 10 PI = 3.141593
 20 DEF FNRAD(DEGREES) = DEGREES*PI/180
 30 DIM CONTROL(100),X(100),Y(100)
 40 SCREEN 2 : CLS
 50 INPUT THETA
 60 IF THETA = 90 THEN INPUT A,YSTEP ELSE INPUT A : YSTEP = (A/2)*TAN(FNRAD(THETA))
 70 GOSUB 240  'initialise
 80 FOR ROW = 1 TO NOOFROWS
 90   FOR MOTIF = 1 TO NOOFMOTIFS
100     GOSUB 170  'draw motif at x,y
110     X = X+A
120   NEXT MOTIF
130   Y = Y-YSTEP
140   IF THETA = 90 THEN X = 100
      ELSE IF ROW MOD 2  = 0 THEN X = 100
      ELSE X = 100+A/2
150 NEXT ROW
160 END

170 'SUBROUTINE draw motif at x,y
180   WINDOW (-X,-Y)-(1279-X,799-Y)
190   PSET (0,0)
200   FOR I = 1 TO NOOFPOINTS
210     IF CONTROL(I) = 1 THEN LINE -(X(I),Y(I)) ELSE PSET (X(I),Y(I))
220   NEXT I
230 RETURN

240 'SUBROUTINE initialise
250   X = 100 : Y = 699 : NOOFPOINTS = 3 : NOOFMOTIFS = 8
260   NOOFROWS = 8
270   FOR I = 1 TO NOOFPOINTS
280     READ CONTROL(I), X(I), Y(I)
290   NEXT I
300 RETURN

310 DATA 1,60,0,1,60,20,1,0,0
```

Program 4.10 Demonstration of different translation nets.

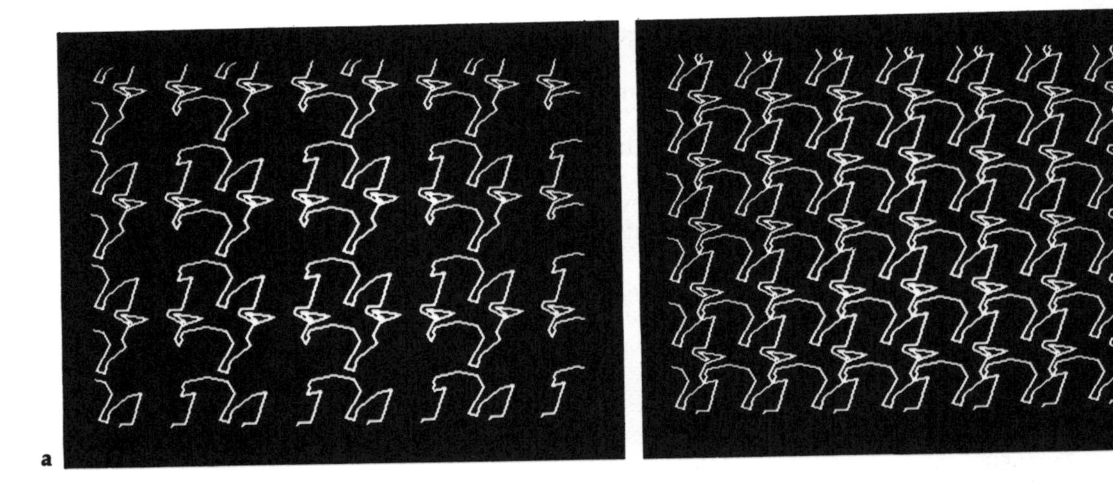

Figure 4.16
(a) Placing motifs on a rectangular net;
(b) Tessellating the plane using the same motif

together in Figure 4.17 for the purposes of comparison. For each class there is a short informal description, a program, an example using the right-angled triangle, a more elaborate computer generated example and, for all cases except one, an example from Jones.

The easiest way to view the process is as follows. To generate each group or class we select a particular translation net and place the motif or cluster of motifs at each point determined by the translation. The different groups are then categorised according to the symmetry exhibited by the motif clusters. The axial or cluster symmetry of the motif group then influences the overall symmetry of the network. A leisurely study of Figure 4.17 will help you to appreciate this point.

Network group 1

This is the simplest network group. It is generated by placing a single motif at each of the specified points in a translation net. Another way of looking at it, is that it is generated by translating band group 1 down a generally oblique axis. Providing the single motif is asymmetric the resulting network possesses no symmetry whatever. This means that if you consider the pattern printed on paper you cannot fold the pattern in any way that superimposes the part of the pattern on itself. Also there is no perpendicular axis about which the pattern can be rotated and come into coincidence with itself after rotation (apart from 360°).

The program for this network group is almost identical to the first band program. We generate a band and repeat this as many times as we require rows. Alternatively we can generate a column and repeat this. To keep the programs reasonably short we will write a program for each group using just one translation net. All 17 programs that follow could be extended to use any allowable translation net. Allowable means that any net that preserves the symmetry group can be used. For example, all five nets can be used in group 1.

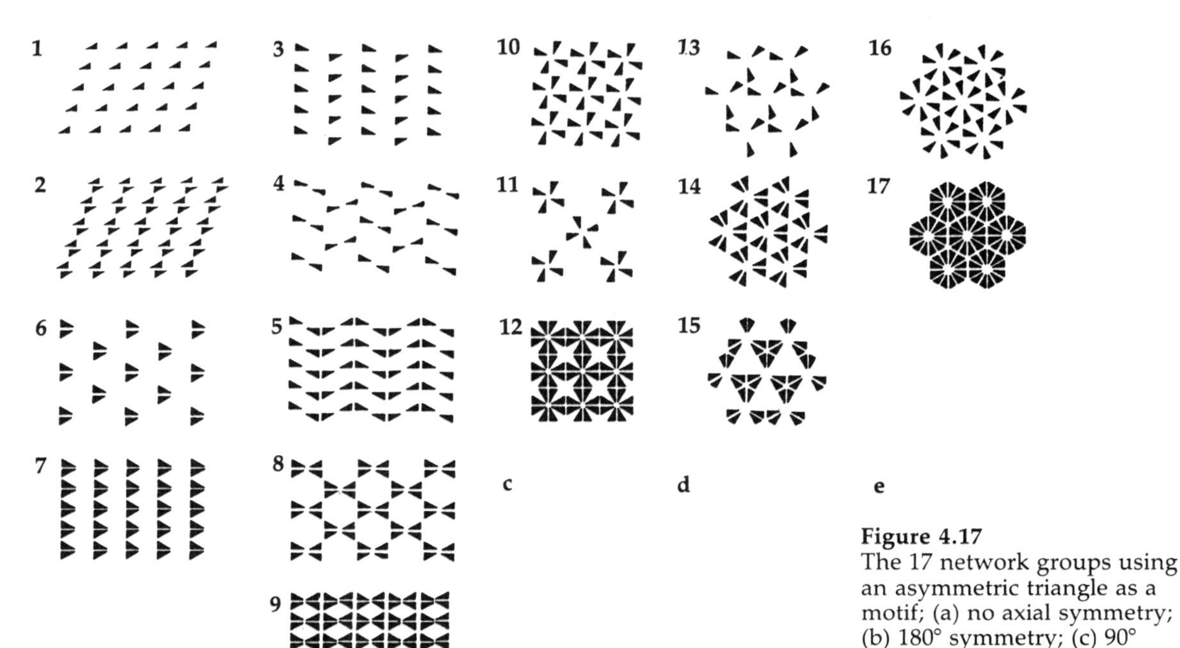

Figure 4.17
The 17 network groups using an asymmetric triangle as a motif; (a) no axial symmetry; (b) 180° symmetry; (c) 90° symmetry; (d) 120° symmetry; (e) 60° symmetry

Program 4.11 generated the computer illustration using the asymmetric triangle and the program remains unaltered to generate the seagulls – only the data changes. The output is shown in Figure 4.18a and b. Figure 4.18c shows a 17th century Persian pattern from Jones that belongs to this network group.

Network group 2

This group can be generated by vertically translating the second band group which was a band with a vertical glide-plane reflection. Again the network itself possesses no lines of symmetry or axial symmetry, but it differs from the first in that the individual motifs are subject to glide-reflections.

The easiest programming approach is to draw one set of motifs in one orientation and follow this with another set that is reflected. The variable TYPE in Program 4.12 distinguishes the motif type. Program 4.12 produced the computer illustrations. Your authors could not find a single example of this network in folk art amongst the sources available to them. The awkwardness of this group can be seen from the fishes shown in Figure 4.19b. It suggests, perhaps, that regardless of motif the result is likely to be disturbing.

Network group 3

This group comes from the translation of the third band group vertically down a generally oblique axis. Again we adopt the pro-

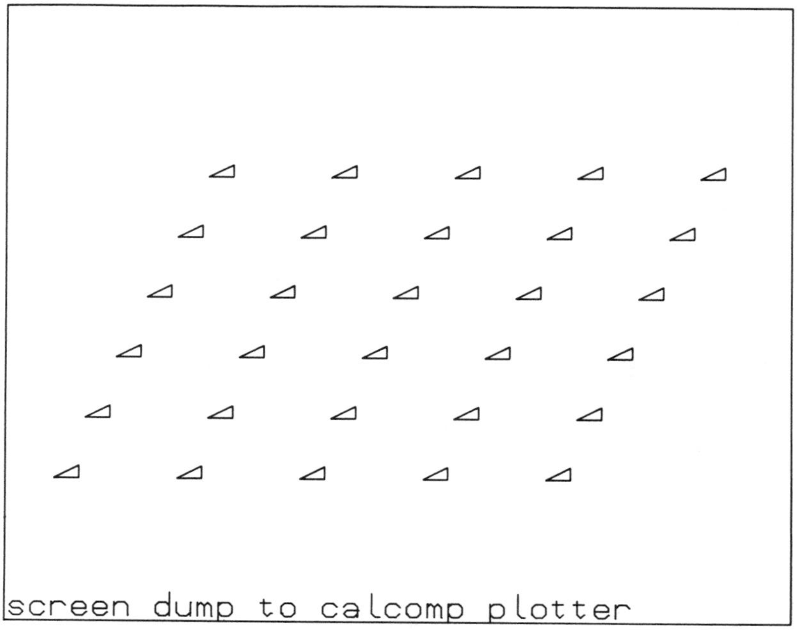

a screen dump to calcomp plotter

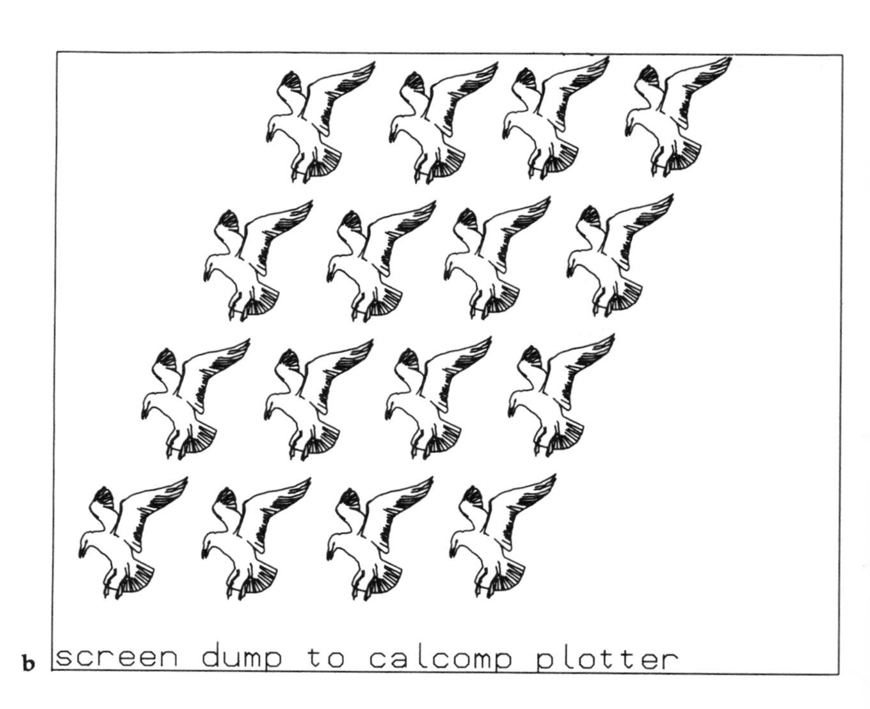

b

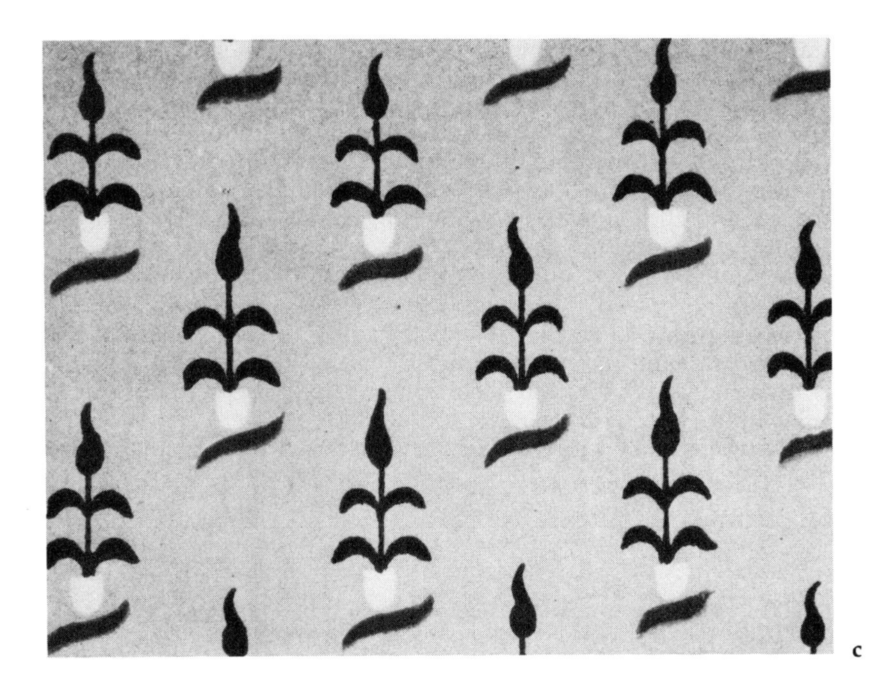

Figure 4.18
c Network group 1

```
 10 SCREEN 2 : CLS
 20 FOR X1 = 100 TO 900 STEP 200
 30   SKEW = 0
 40   FOR YY = 250 TO 750 STEP 100
 50     SKEW = SKEW+30
 60     XX = X1+SKEW
 70     GOSUB 130  'draw motif at xx,yy
 80   NEXT YY
 90 NEXT X1
100 END

110 DATA 0,-20,-10,1,20,-10,1,20,10,1,-20,-10

130 'SUBROUTINE draw motif at xx,yy
140   RESTORE
150   WINDOW (-XX,-YY)-(1279-XX,799-YY)
160   FOR POINTS = 1 TO 4
170     READ OP,X,Y
180     IF OP = 1 THEN LINE -(X,Y) ELSE PSET (X,Y)
190   NEXT POINTS
200 RETURN
```

Program 4.11 Network group 1.

gram structure used previously – rotating and then rotating back again. Again this network group does not possess lines of symmetry. It does however possess axial symmetry. If the whole pattern is rotated through 180° then the network coincides with itself.

Program 4.13 generated the computer illustrations and a comparison of the program structure with the triangle network should prove easy. The example from Jones in Figure 4.20c is Egyptian in origin. It falls into this network group, however, only if we ignore the asymmetry in the bullet shapes in the horizontal bands.

Network group 4

Like the previous group this net does not contain any lines of symmetry but exhibits 180° axial symmetry. It also contains glide-reflections.

The program structure is like the previous two programs except

```
 10 SCREEN 2 : CLS
 20 TYPE = 1
 30 FOR XX = 100 TO 900 STEP 200
 40   FOR YY = 200 TO 700 STEP 100
 50     GOSUB 170  'draw motif at xx,yy
 60   NEXT YY
 70 NEXT XX
 80 TYPE = 2
 90 FOR XX = 200 TO 950 STEP 200
100   FOR YY = 250 TO 750 STEP 100
110     GOSUB 170  'draw motif at xx,yy
120   NEXT YY
130 NEXT XX
140 END

150 DATA 0,-20,-10,1,20,-10,1,20,10,1,-20,-10

170 'SUBROUTINE draw motif at xx,yy
180   RESTORE
190   WINDOW (-XX,-YY)-(1279-XX,799-YY)
200   FOR POINTS = 1 TO 4
210     READ OP,X,Y
220     IF TYPE = 2 THEN A = 1 : B = 0 : C = 0 : D = 0 :
                      E =-1 : F = 0 : GOSUB 260  'transform
230     IF OP = 1 THEN LINE -(X,Y) ELSE PSET (X,Y)
240   NEXT POINTS
250 RETURN

260 'SUBROUTINE transform
270   XT = A*X+B*Y+C : YT = D*X+E*Y+F
280   X = XT : Y = YT
290 RETURN
```

Program 4.12 Network group 2.

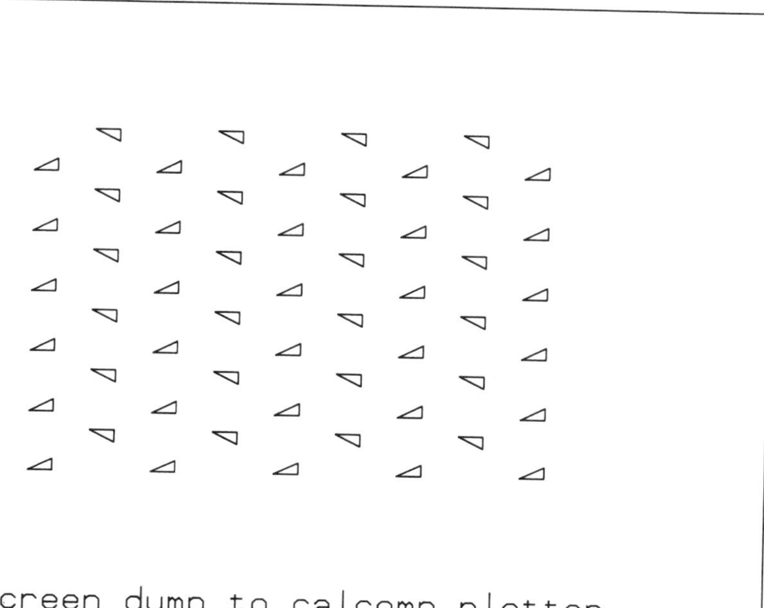

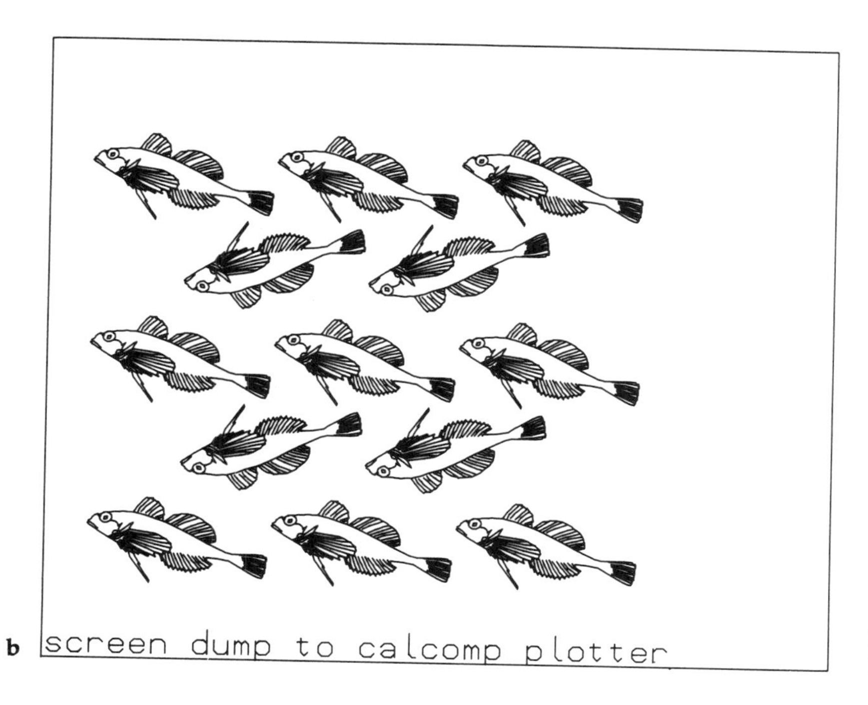

Figure 4.19
Network group 2

a screen dump to calcomp plotter

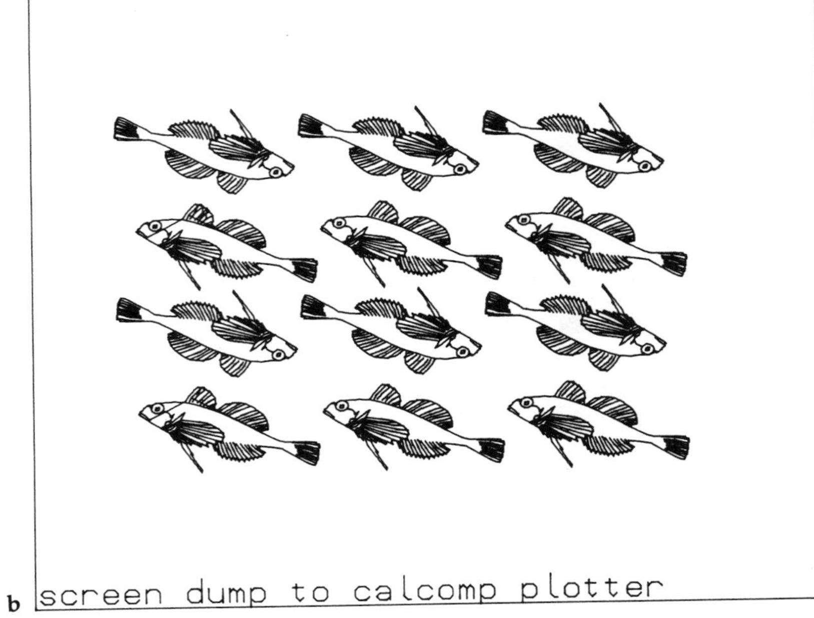

b

c

Figure 4.20
Network group 3

```
 10 SCREEN 2 : CLS
 20 TYPE = 1
 30 FOR XX = 100 TO 900 STEP 200
 40   FOR YY = 200 TO 700 STEP 100
 50     GOSUB 170  'draw motif at xx,yy
 60   NEXT YY
 70 NEXT XX
 80 TYPE = 2
 90 FOR XX = 120 TO 950 STEP 200
100   FOR YY = 220 TO 750 STEP 100
110     GOSUB 170  'draw motif at xx,yy
120   NEXT YY
130 NEXT XX
140 END

150 DATA 0,-20,-10,1,20,-10,1,20,10,1,-20,-10

170 'SUBROUTINE draw motif at xx,yy
180   RESTORE
190   WINDOW (-XX,-YY)-(1279-XX,799-YY)
200   FOR POINTS = 1 TO 4
210     READ OP,X,Y
220     IF TYPE = 2 THEN A =-1 : B = 0 : C = 0 : D = 0 :
                         E =-1 : F = 0 : GOSUB 260  'transform
230     IF OP = 1 THEN LINE -(X,Y) ELSE PSET (X,Y)
240   NEXT POINTS
250 RETURN

260 'SUBROUTINE transform
270   XT = A*X+B*Y+C : YT = D*X+E*Y+F
280   X = XT : Y = YT
290 RETURN
```

Program 4.13 Network group 3.

that now we have four motif 'types'. Program 4.14 produced the computer illustrations. The pattern from Jones in Figure 4.21c is Persian. It is quite difficult to see the relationship between Figure 4.21a and Figure 4.21c and rather than attempt to describe it in words, we leave you to study these two patterns. The difficulty arises because the pattern is a tessellation rather then a motif placement pattern.

This group seems to be quite rare and the example shown in Figure 4.21c appears to be the only one in Jones.

Network group 5

This pattern also contains 180° axial symmetry. Unlike network group 4, however, it contains lines of symmetry. These are all vertical and form a series of parallel vertical lines. If the network is folded down any of these lines it will coincide when superimposed on itself. Note also that the motif clusters are formed from reflections in two directions.

The structure of Program 4.15, which produced the computer illustration, is identical to the previous programs – four motif 'types' are again required. The pattern in Figure 4.22c is from Jones and is Egyptian.

Network group 6

This pattern contains no axial symmetry. If the network is turned through 180° the motif clusters 'point' in the opposite direction. It is best considered in conjunction with network group 7. Look at the difference between these groups in Figure 4.17.

Network group 6, then, is characterized by no axial symmetry but parallel horizontal lines of symmetry. There are also horizontal glide-reflection axes which do NOT coincide with the symmetry lines.

Program 4.16 is structured using two motif 'types' and a 'skew' control. The example from Jones in Figure 4.23c is Egyptian.

Network group 7

This network group is paired with network group 6. It has lines of symmetry in one direction and no axial symmetry. It differs, however, from the previous in that the group contains axes of glide-reflections that DO coincide with the lines of symmetry. It is drawn by Program 4.17.

The example in Figure 4.24c from Jones is Egyptian. It is an example of network group 7 by virtue of the spirals. Had the spirals been concentric circles it would be an example of network group 9.

Network group 8

This network group is best considered paired with network group 9. They both possess horizontal and vertical lines of symmetry. In network group 8 these lines run through the centres of the four-triangle clusters. These centres also form a set of points about which there is 180° rotational symmetry. There is, however, another set of 180° rotational symmetry points. These are on diagonal lines halfway between the motif cluster both horizontally and vertically. The vertical lines that contain these points are NOT lines of symmetry. The group is thus categorised by having lines of reflection and centres of 180° rotational symmetry where NOT ALL of these centres lie on lines of reflection. It is drawn by Program 4.18.

Figure 4.25b is made up of ellipses and cardioids (see Chapter 10 for the appropriate formula). Figure 4.25c is an Indian pattern from Jones.

Network group 9

This network group is paired with network group 8. It differs from this group in that ALL the rotational symmetry centres DO lie on lines of reflection. It is drawn by Program 4.19.

The programming technique is as before. Figure 4.26b is again made from ellipses and cardioids. It should be compared with Figure 4.25b to appreciate the differences in symmetry and also with Figure 4.29b which is the same pattern except that it uses circles instead of ellipses. Figure 4.26c is another Indian pattern from Jones. This is an intriguing example in that it could be misinterpreted as an example of group 8 if you break the rules and treat one petal as belonging to two ellipses.

Network group 10

With network groups 10, 11 and 12 we move on to patterns that have 90° rotational symmetry centres. If the network is rotated about these points it will come into coincidence with itself every 90°. These groups should be studied together and their differences noted. Network group 10 contains no horizontal or vertical lines of symmetry. It cannot be folded down any line and coincide with itself. Except for idiosyncratic adjustments there is nothing new in the structure of Program 4.20.

You can see from Figure 4.27 that the pattern imparts a feeling of rotation. Each motif cluster in Figure 4.27b consists of four separate motifs as in Figure 4.27a. The same program structure generated both patterns. The single motifs in Figure 4.27b are all counterclockwise spirals. Each spiral is rotated through 90° just like the triangle. The spirals then interleave and join up making a pleasing whole. This interleaving and joining is the secret of network pattern making. Some of the computer examples are 'successful' in this respect (Figure 4.27b for example), others are manifestly unsuccessful from an aesthetic point of view (Figure 4.26b for example). It is interesting to note that the more 'successful' a pattern is, the more difficult it becomes to deduce its network group.

The example, Figure 4.27c, from Jones is Egyptian and again imparts a feeling of rotation in one direction.

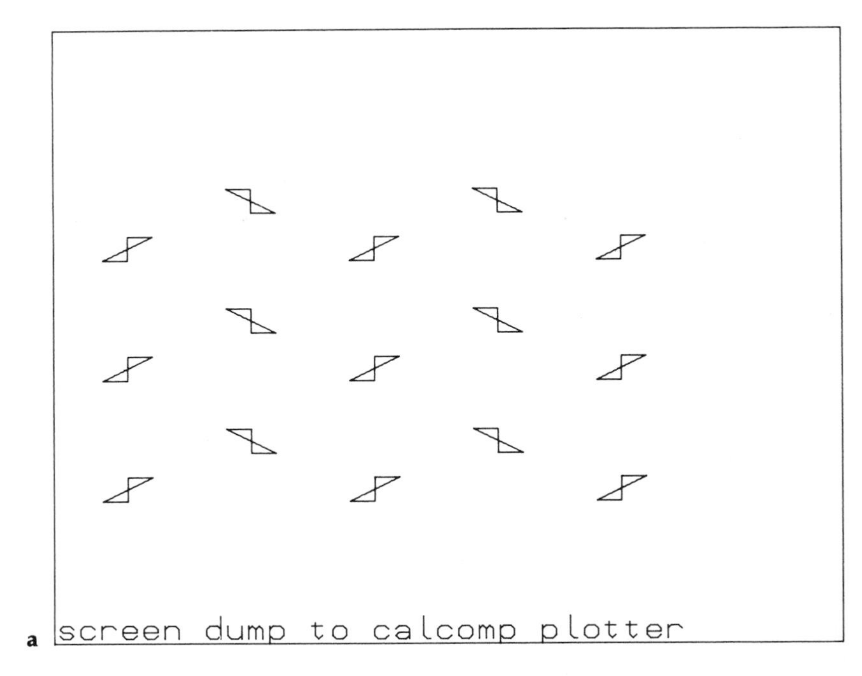
screen dump to calcomp plotter
a

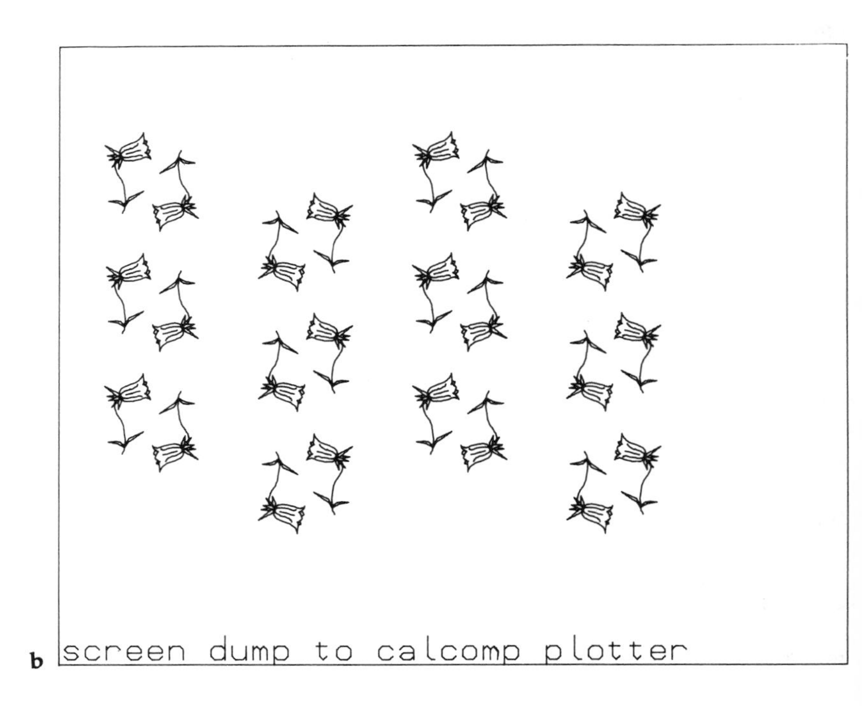
screen dump to calcomp plotter
b

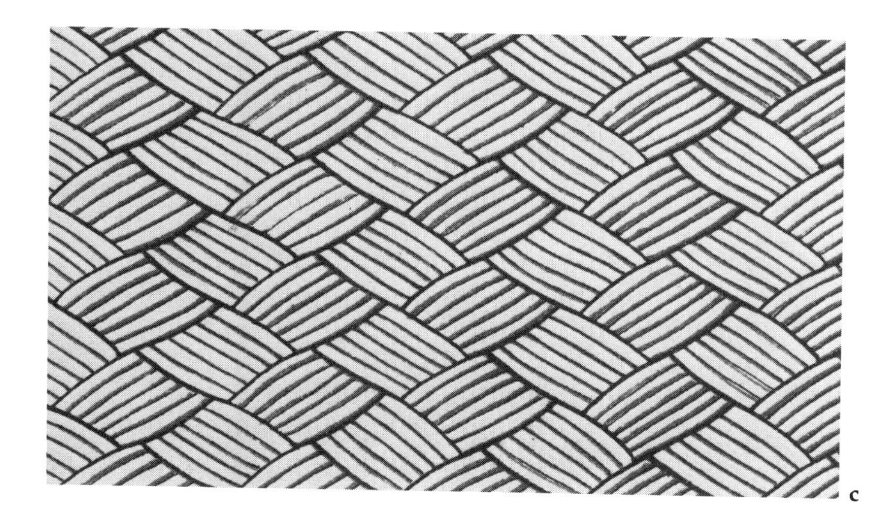

c

Figure 4.21
Network group 4

```
 10 SCREEN 2 : CLS
 20 TYPE = 1
 30 FOR XX = 100 TO 900 STEP 400
 40   FOR YY = 200 TO 700 STEP 200
 50     GOSUB 280  'draw motif at xx,yy
 60   NEXT YY
 70 NEXT XX
 80 TYPE = 2
 90 FOR XX = 140 TO 940 STEP 400
100   FOR YY = 220 TO 750 STEP 200
110     GOSUB 280  'draw motif at xx,yy
120   NEXT YY
130 NEXT XX
140 TYPE = 3
150 FOR XX = 300 TO 900 STEP 400
160   FOR YY = 300 TO 700 STEP 200
170     GOSUB 280  'draw motif at xx,yy
180   NEXT YY
190 NEXT XX
200 TYPE = 4
210 FOR XX = 340 TO 900 STEP 400
220   FOR YY = 280 TO 720 STEP 200
230     GOSUB 280  'draw motif at xx,yy
240   NEXT YY
250 NEXT XX
260 END

270 DATA 0,-20,-10,1,20,-10,1,20,10,1,-20,-10

280 'SUBROUTINE draw motif at xx,yy
290   RESTORE
300   WINDOW (-XX,-YY)-(1279-XX,799-YY)
310   FOR POINTS = 1 TO 4
320     READ OP,X,Y
330     IF TYPE = 2 THEN A =-1 : B = 0 : C = 0 : D = 0 :
                         E =-1 : F = 0 : GOSUB 390  'transform
340     IF TYPE = 3 THEN A = 1 : B = 0 : C = 0 : D = 0 :
                         E =-1 : F = 0 : GOSUB 390  'transform
350     IF TYPE = 4 THEN A =-1 : B = 0 : C = 0 : D = 0 :
                         E = 1 : F = 0 : GOSUB 390  'transform
360     IF OP = 1 THEN LINE -(X,Y) ELSE PSET (X,Y)
370   NEXT POINTS
380 RETURN

390 'SUBROUTINE transform
400   XT = A*X+B*Y+C : YT = D*X+E*Y+F
410   X = XT : Y = YT
420 RETURN
```

Program 4.14 Network group 4.

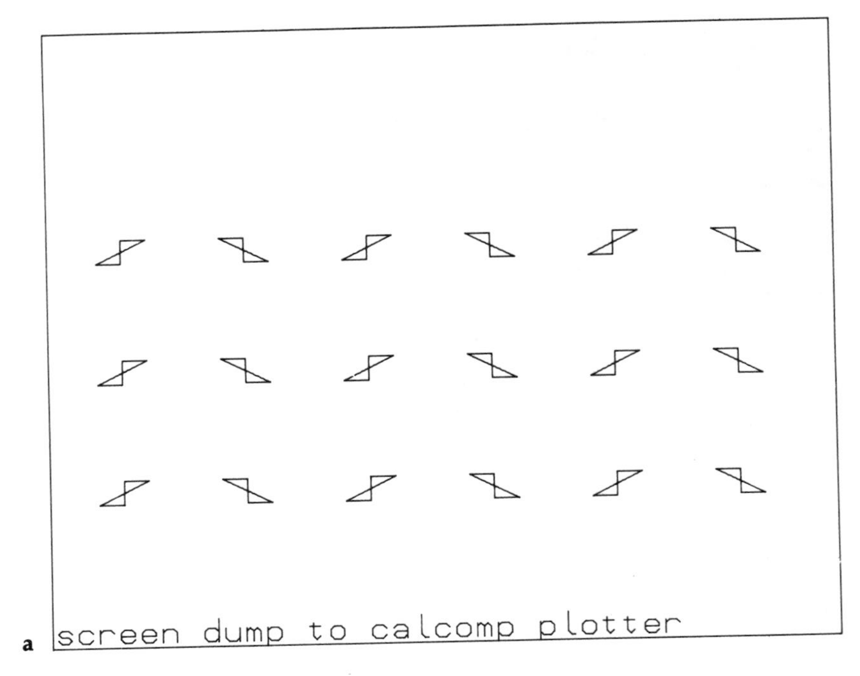
screen dump to calcomp plotter

a

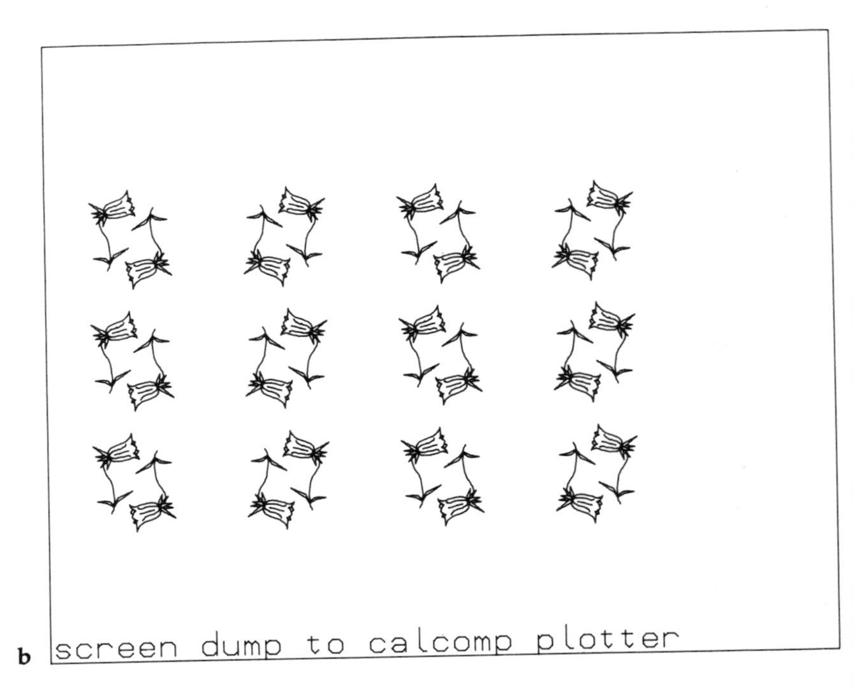
screen dump to calcomp plotter

b

c

Figure 4.22
Network group 5

```
 10 SCREEN 2 : CLS
 20 TYPE = 1
 30 FOR XX = 100 TO 900 STEP 400
 40   FOR YY = 200 TO 700 STEP 200
 50     GOSUB 280  'draw motif at xx,yy
 60   NEXT YY
 70 NEXT XX
 80 TYPE = 2
 90 FOR XX = 140 TO 940 STEP 400
100   FOR YY = 220 TO 750 STEP 200
110     GOSUB 280  'draw motif at xx,yy
120   NEXT YY
130 NEXT XX
140 TYPE = 3
150 FOR XX = 300 TO 1100 STEP 400
160   FOR YY = 220 TO 700 STEP 200
170     GOSUB 280  'draw motif at xx,yy
180   NEXT YY
190 NEXT XX
200 TYPE = 4
210 FOR XX = 340 TO 1140 STEP 400
220   FOR YY = 200 TO 720 STEP 200
230     GOSUB 280  'draw motif at xx,yy
240   NEXT YY
250 NEXT XX
260 END

270 DATA 0,-20,-10,1,20,-10,1,20,10,1,-20,-10

280 'SUBROUTINE draw motif at xx,yy
290   RESTORE
300   WINDOW (-XX,-YY)-(1279-XX,799-YY)
310   FOR POINTS = 1 TO 4
320     READ OP,X,Y
330     IF TYPE = 2 THEN A =-1 : B = 0 : C = 0 : D = 0 :
                         E =-1 : F = 0 : GOSUB 390  'transform
340     IF TYPE = 3 THEN A = 1 : B = 0 : C = 0 : D = 0 :
                         E =-1 : F = 0 : GOSUB 390  'transform
350     IF TYPE = 4 THEN A =-1 : B = 0 : C = 0 : D = 0 :
                         E = 1 : F = 0 : GOSUB 390  'transform
360     IF OP = 1 THEN LINE -(X,Y) ELSE PSET (X,Y)
370   NEXT POINTS
380 RETURN

390 'SUBROUTINE transform
400   XT = A*X+B*Y+C : YT = D*X+E*Y+F
410   X = XT : Y = YT
420 RETURN
```

Program 4.15 Network group 5.

a 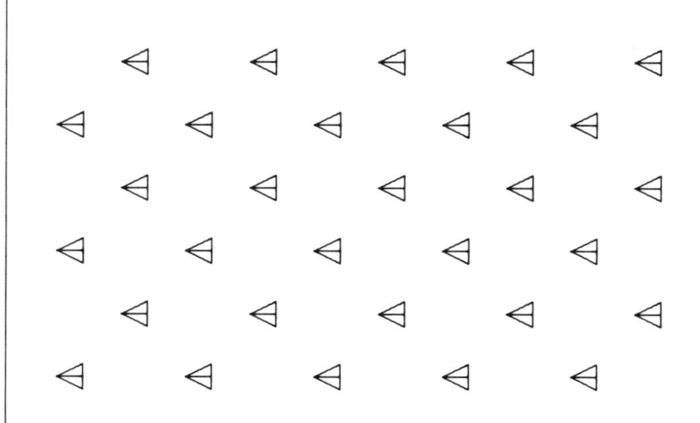
screen dump to calcomp plotter

b 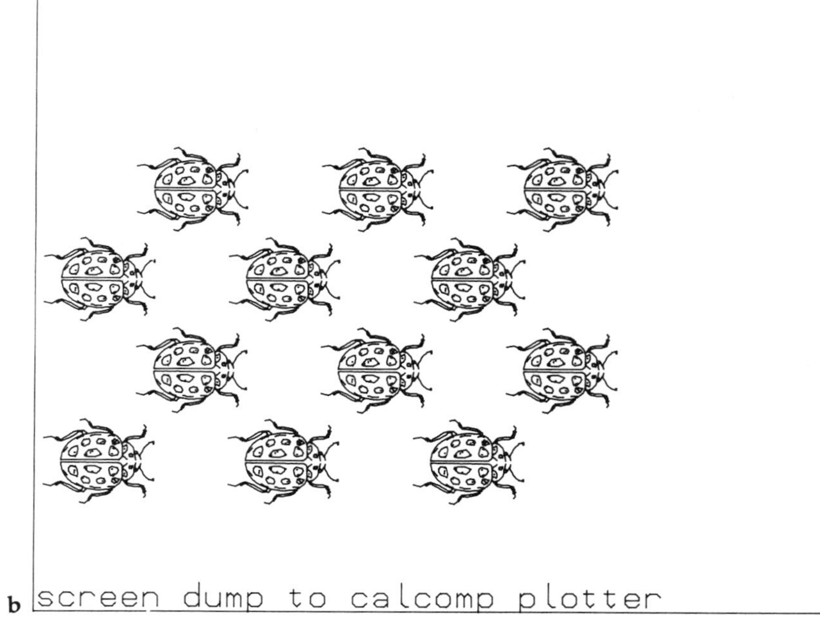
screen dump to calcomp plotter

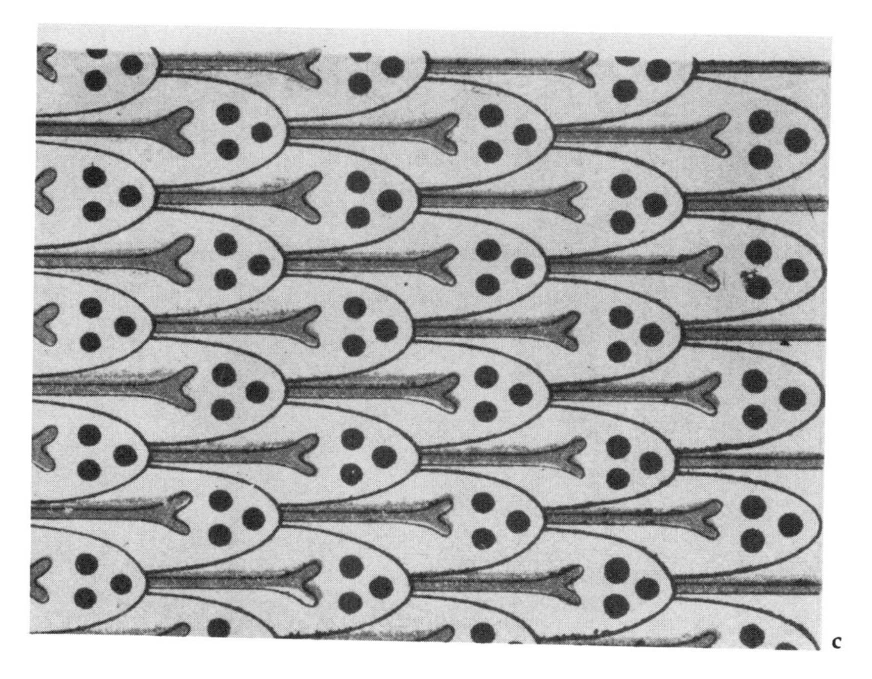

c

Figure 4.23
Network group 6

```
 10 SCREEN 2 : CLS
 20 FOR TYPE = 1 TO 2
 30   FOR X1 = 100 TO 900 STEP 200
 40     SKEW = 0
 50     FOR YY = 200 TO 700 STEP 100
 60       IF YY = 300 OR YY = 500 OR YY = 700 THEN SKEW = 100
 70       XX = X1+SKEW
 80       GOSUB 150  'draw motif at xx,yy
 90       SKEW = 0
100     NEXT YY
110   NEXT X1
120 NEXT TYPE
130 END

140 DATA 0,-20,-10,1,20,-10,1,20,10,1,-20,-10

150 'SUBROUTINE draw motif at xx,yy
160   RESTORE
170   WINDOW (-XX,-YY)-(1279-XX,799-YY)
180   FOR POINTS = 1 TO 4
190     READ OP,X,Y
200     IF TYPE = 2 THEN A = 1 : B = 0 : C = 0 : D = 0 :
                        E =-1 : F =-20 : GOSUB 240  'transform
210     IF OP = 1 THEN LINE -(X,Y) ELSE PSET (X,Y)
220   NEXT POINTS
230 RETURN

240 'SUBROUTINE transform
250   XT = A*X+B*Y+C : YT = D*X+E*Y+F
260   X = XT : Y = YT
270 RETURN
```

Program 4.16 Network group 6.

screen dump to calcomp plotter

a

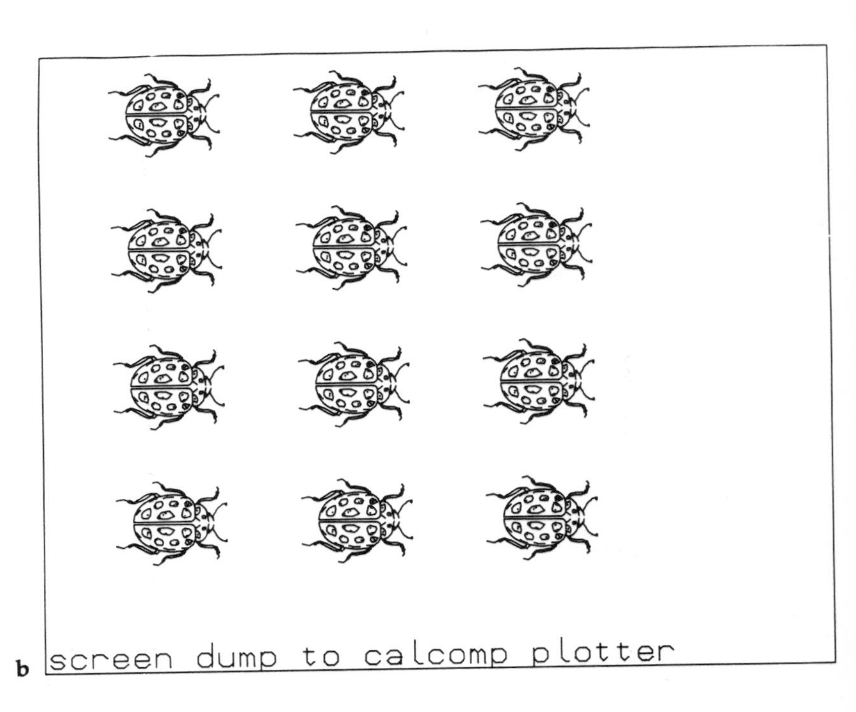
screen dump to calcomp plotter

b

c **Figure 4.24** Network group 7

```
 10 SCREEN 2 : CLS
 20 FOR TYPE = 1 TO 2
 30   FOR XX = 100 TO 900 STEP 200
 40     FOR YY = 200 TO 700 STEP 100
 50       GOSUB 110  'draw motif at xx,yy
 60     NEXT YY
 70   NEXT XX
 80 NEXT TYPE
 90 END

100 DATA 0,-20,-10,1,20,-10,1,20,10,1,-20,-10

110 'SUBROUTINE draw motif at xx,yy
120   RESTORE
130   WINDOW (-XX,-YY)-(1279-XX,799-YY)
140   FOR POINTS = 1 TO 4
150     READ OP,X,Y
160     IF TYPE = 2 THEN A = 1 : B = 0 : C = 0 : D = 0 :
                     E =-1 : F =-20 : GOSUB 200  'transform
170     IF OP = 1 THEN LINE -(X,Y) ELSE PSET (X,Y)
180   NEXT POINTS
190 RETURN

200 'SUBROUTINE transform
210   XT = A*X+B*Y+C : YT = D*X+E*Y+F
220   X = XT : Y = YT
230 RETURN
```

Program 4.17 Network group 7.

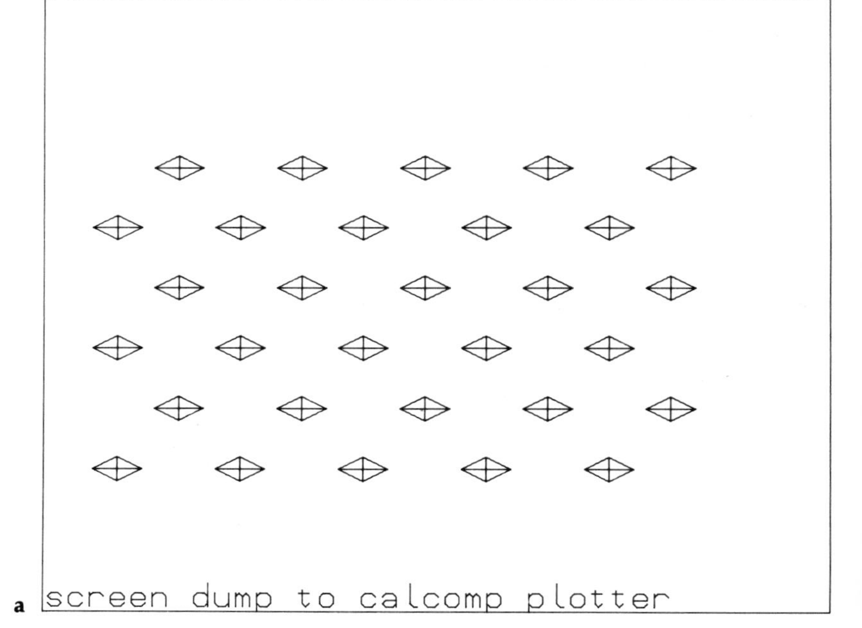
a
screen dump to calcomp plotter

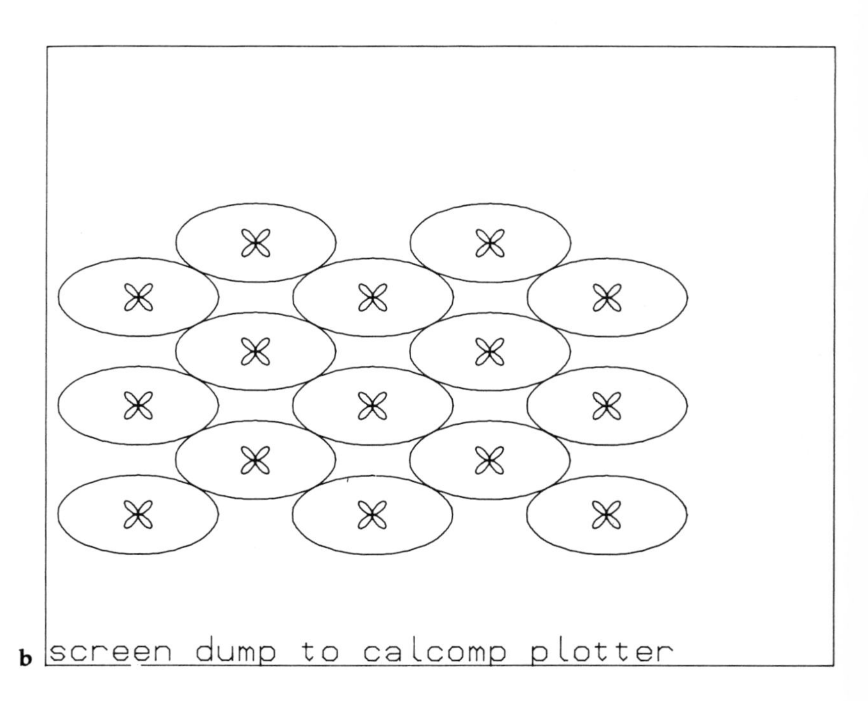
b
screen dump to calcomp plotter

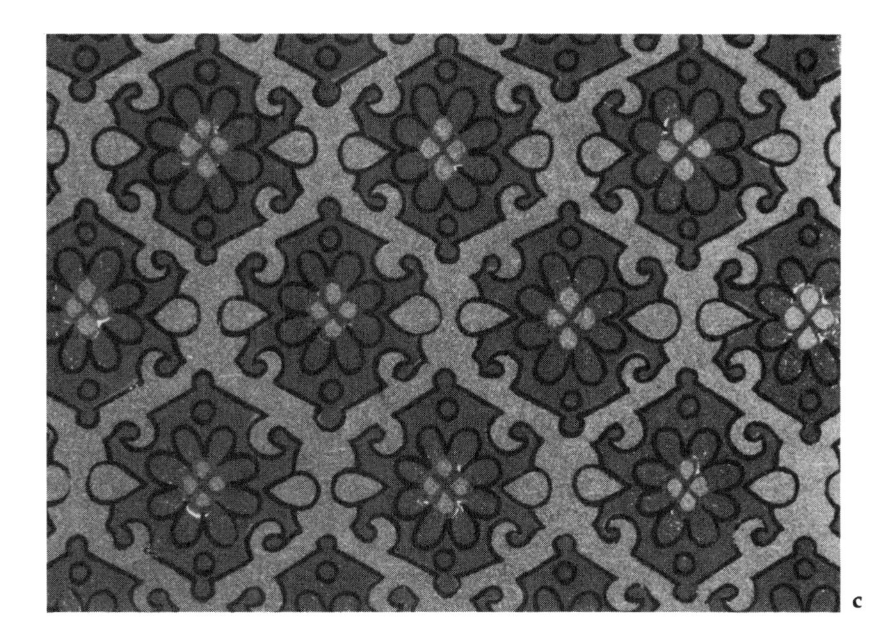

c

Figure 4.25
Network group 8

```
 10 SCREEN 2 : CLS
 20 FOR TYPE = 1 TO 4
 30   FOR X1 = 100 TO 900 STEP 200
 40     SKEW = 0
 50     FOR YY = 200 TO 700 STEP 100
 60       IF YY = 300 OR YY = 500 OR YY = 700 THEN SKEW = 100
 70       XX = X1+SKEW
 80       GOSUB 150  'draw motif at xx,yy
 90       SKEW = 0
100     NEXT YY
110   NEXT X1
120 NEXT TYPE
130 END

140 DATA 0,-20,-10,1,20,-10,1,20,10,1,-20,-10

150 'SUBROUTINE draw motif at xx,yy
160   RESTORE
170   WINDOW (-XX,-YY)-(1279-XX,799-YY)
180   FOR POINTS = 1 TO 4
190     READ OP,X,Y
200     IF TYPE = 2 THEN A = 1 : B = 0 : C = 0 : D = 0 :
                         E =-1 : F =-20 : GOSUB 260  'transform
210     IF TYPE = 3 THEN A =-1 : B = 0 : C = 40 : D = 0 :
                         E = 1 : F = 0 : GOSUB 260  'transform
220     IF TYPE = 4 THEN A =-1 : B = 0 : C = 40 : D = 0 :
                         E =-1 : F =-20 : GOSUB 260  'transform
230     IF OP = 1 THEN LINE -(X,Y) ELSE PSET (X,Y)
240   NEXT POINTS
250 RETURN

260 'SUBROUTINE transform
270   XT = A*X+B*Y+C : YT = D*X+E*Y+F
280   X = XT : Y = YT
290 RETURN
```

Program 4.18 Network group 8.

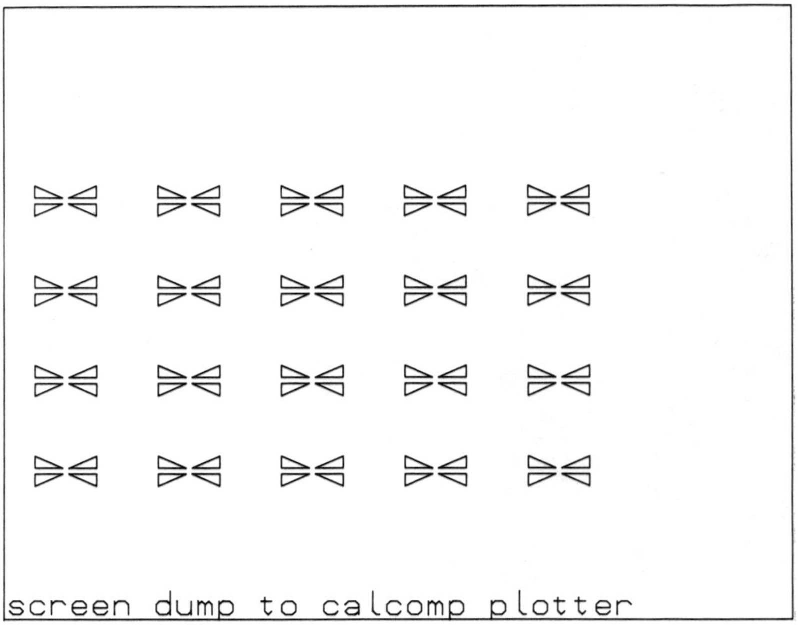

a screen dump to calcomp plotter

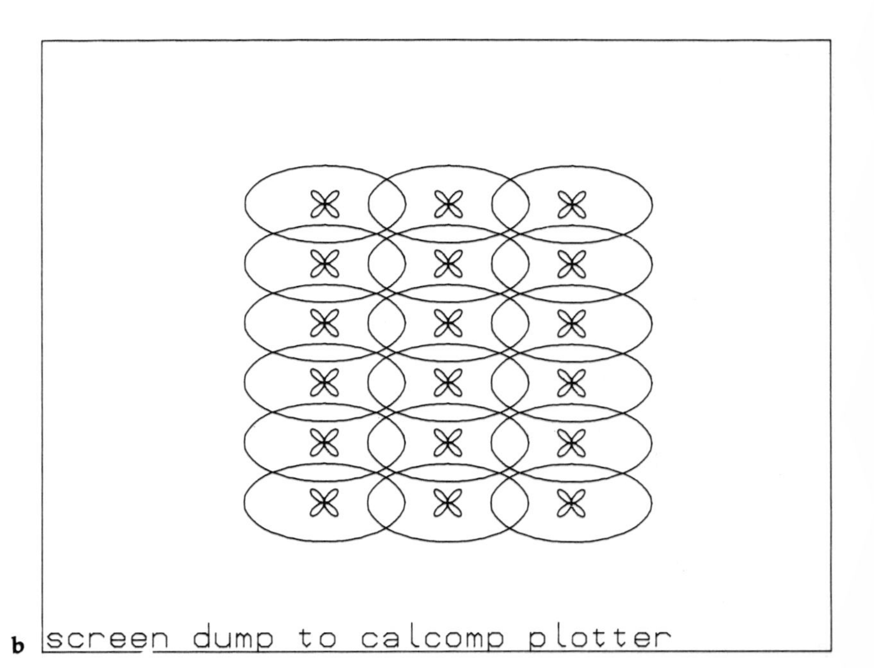

Figure 4.26
c Network group 9

```
 10 SCREEN 2 : CLS
 20 FOR TYPE = 1 TO 2
 30   FOR XX = 200 TO 1000 STEP 200
 40     FOR YY = 200 TO 700 STEP 100
 50       GOSUB 180  'draw motif at xx,yy
 60     NEXT YY
 70   NEXT XX
 80 NEXT TYPE
 90 FOR TYPE = 3 TO 4
100   FOR XX = 150 TO 950 STEP 200
110     FOR YY = 200 TO 700 STEP 100
120       GOSUB 180  'draw motif at xx,yy
130     NEXT YY
140   NEXT XX
150 NEXT TYPE
160 END

170 DATA 0,-20,-10,1,20,-10,1,20,10,1,-20,-10

180 'SUBROUTINE draw motif at xx,yy
190   RESTORE
200   WINDOW (-XX,-YY)-(1279-XX,799-YY)
210   FOR POINTS = 1 TO 4
220     READ OP,X,Y
230     IF TYPE = 2 THEN A = 1 : B = 0  : C = 0 : D = 0 :
                         E =-1 : F =-30 : GOSUB 290  'transform
240     IF TYPE = 3 THEN A =-1 : B = 0  : C = 0 : D = 0 :
                         E = 1 : F = 0  : GOSUB 290  'transform
250     IF TYPE = 4 THEN A =-1 : B = 0  : C = 0 : D = 0 :
                         E =-1 : F =-30 : GOSUB 290  'transform
260     IF OP = 1 THEN LINE -(X,Y) ELSE PSET (X,Y)
270   NEXT POINTS
280 RETURN

290 'SUBROUTINE transform
300   XT = A*X+B*Y+C : YT = D*X+E*Y+F
310   X = XT : Y = YT
320 RETURN
```

Program 4.19 Network group 9.

a screen dump to calcomp plotter

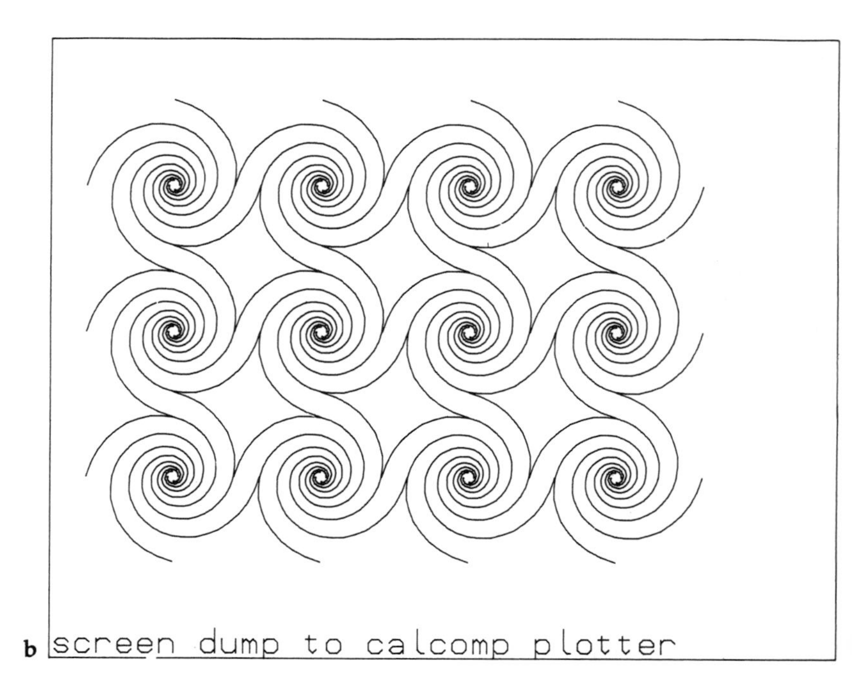

b

Figure 4.27
c Network group 10

```
 10 SCREEN 2 : CLS
 20 FOR TYPE = 1 TO 4
 30   FOR XX = 100 TO 900 STEP 200
 40     FOR YY = 200 TO 700 STEP 130
 50       GOSUB 110  'draw motif at xx,yy
 60     NEXT YY
 70   NEXT XX
 80 NEXT TYPE
 90 END

100 DATA 0,-20,10,1,20,10,1,20,-10,1,-20,10

110 'SUBROUTINE draw motif at xx,yy
120   RESTORE
130   WINDOW (-XX,-YY)-(1279-XX,799-YY)
140   FOR POINTS = 1 TO 4
150     READ OP,X,Y
160     IF TYPE = 2 THEN A =-1 : B = 0 : C = -50 : D = 0 :
                         E =-1 : F = 20 : GOSUB 220  'transform
170     IF TYPE = 3 THEN A = 0 : B = 1 : C =-35 : D =-1 :
                         E = 0 : F =-20 : GOSUB 220  'transform
180     IF TYPE = 4 THEN A = 0 : B =-1 : C =-15 : D = 1 :
                         E = 0 : F = 35 : GOSUB 220  'transform
190     IF OP = 1 THEN LINE -(X,Y) ELSE PSET (X,Y)
200   NEXT POINTS
210 RETURN

220 'SUBROUTINE transform
230   XT = A*X+B*Y+C : YT = D*X+E*Y+F
240   X = XT : Y = YT
250 RETURN
```

Program 4.20 Network group 10.

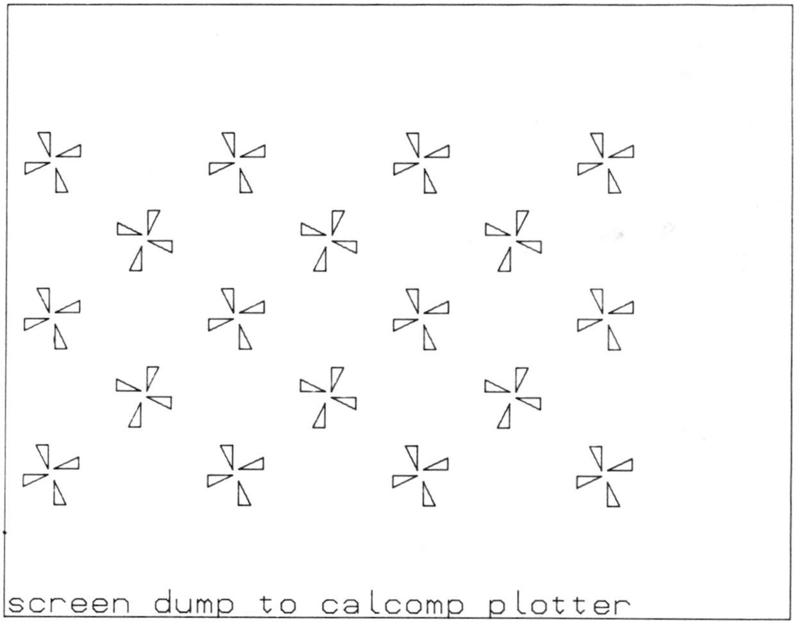

a screen dump to calcomp plotter

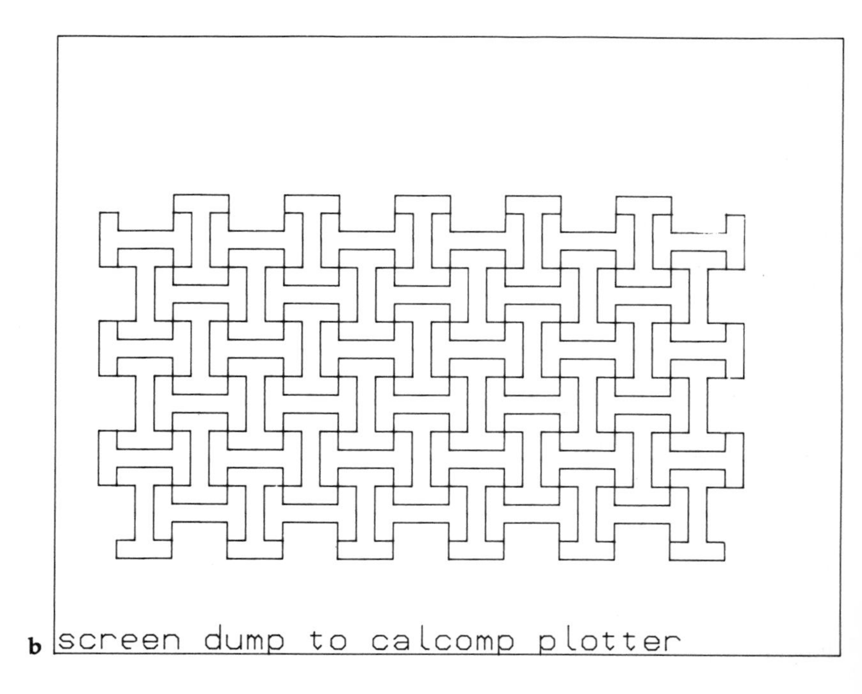

b

c

Figure 4.28
Network group 11

```
 10 SCREEN 2 : CLS
 20 FOR TYPE = 1 TO 4
 30   FOR XX = 100 TO 900 STEP 400
 40     FOR YY = 200 TO 700 STEP 260
 50       GOSUB 180  'draw motif at xx,yy
 60     NEXT YY
 70   NEXT XX
 80 NEXT TYPE
 90 FOR TYPE = 5 TO 8
100   FOR XX = 300 TO 900 STEP 400
110     FOR YY = 330 TO 700 STEP 260
120       GOSUB 180  'draw motif at xx,yy
130     NEXT YY
140   NEXT XX
150 NEXT TYPE
160 END

170 DATA 0,-20,-10,1,20,-10,1,20,10,1,-20,-10

180 'SUBROUTINE draw motif at xx,yy
190   RESTORE
200   WINDOW (-XX,-YY)-(1279-XX,799-YY)
210   FOR POINTS = 1 TO 4
220     READ OP,X,Y
230     IF TYPE = 1 THEN A = 1 : B = 0 : C = 0 : D = 0 : E = 1 : F = 10
240     IF TYPE = 2 THEN A =-1 : B = 0 : C =-50 : D = 0 : E =-1 : F =-20
250     IF TYPE = 3 THEN A = 0 : B = 1 : C =-10 : D =-1 : E = 0 : F =-40
260     IF TYPE = 4 THEN A = 0 : B =-1 : C =-40 : D = 1 : E = 0 : F = 20
270     IF TYPE = 5 THEN A =-1 : B = 0 : C =-50 : D = 0 : E = 1 : F = 10
280     IF TYPE = 6 THEN A = 0 : B =-1 : C =-40 : D =-1 : E = 0 : F =-40
290     IF TYPE = 7 THEN A = 0 : B = 1 : C =-10 : D = 1 : E = 0 : F = 20
300     IF TYPE = 8 THEN A = 1 : B = 0 : C = 0 : D = 0 : E =-1 : F =-20
310     GOSUB 350  'transform
320     IF OP = 1 THEN LINE -(X,Y) ELSE PSET (X,Y)
330   NEXT POINTS
340 RETURN

350 'SUBROUTINE transform
360   XT = A*X+B*Y+C : YT = D*X+E*Y+F
370   X = XT : Y = YT
380 RETURN
```

Program 4.21 Network group 11.

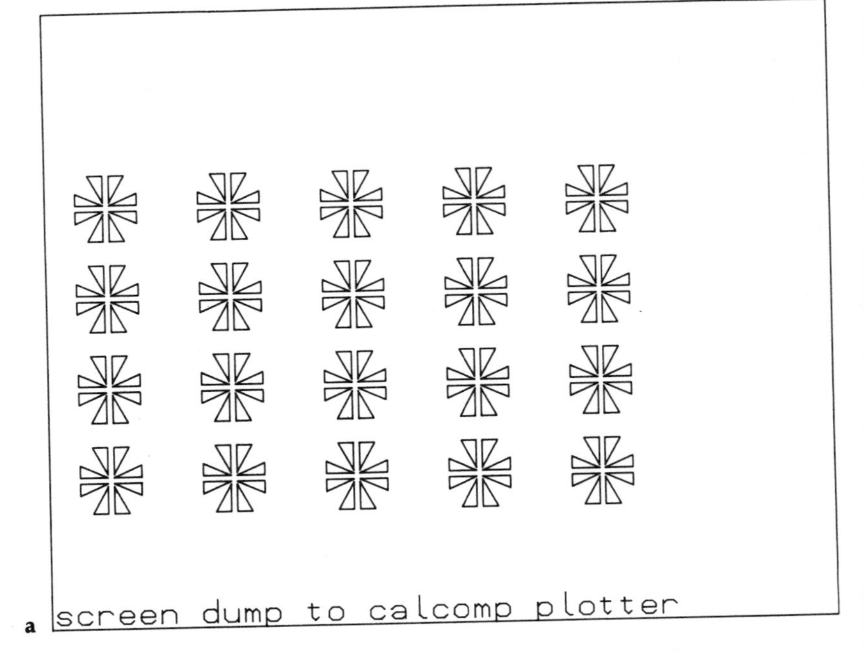
screen dump to calcomp plotter

a

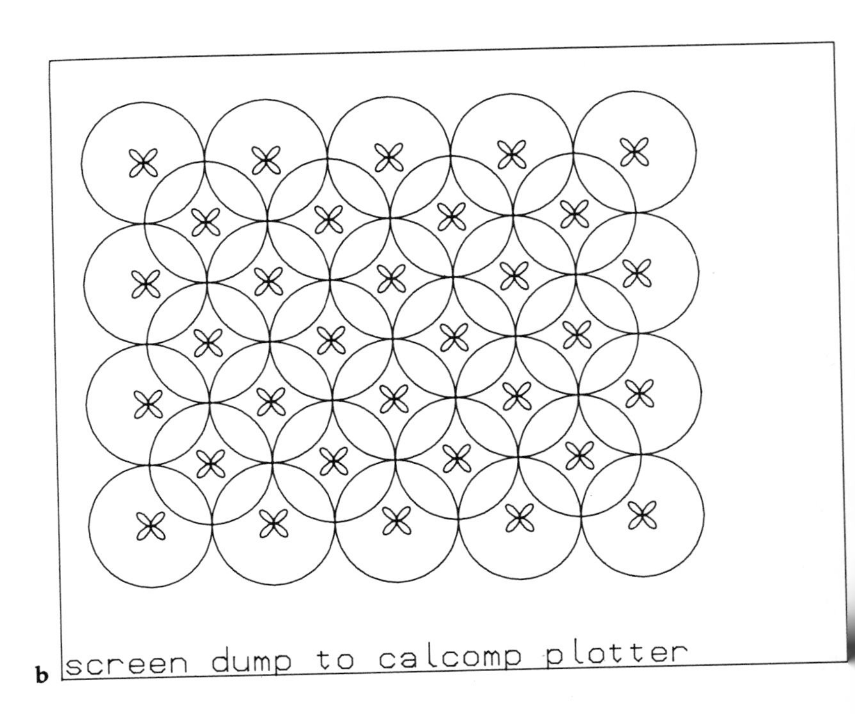
screen dump to calcomp plotter

b

Figure 4.29
c Network group 12

```
 10 SCREEN 2 : CLS
 20 FOR TYPE = 1 TO 8
 30   FOR XX = 100 TO 900 STEP 200
 40     FOR YY = 200 TO 700 STEP 130
 50       GOSUB 110  'draw motif at xx,yy
 60     NEXT YY
 70   NEXT XX
 80 NEXT TYPE
 90 END

100 DATA 0,-20,-10,1,20,-10,1,20,10,1,-20,-10

110 'SUBROUTINE draw motif at xx,yy
120   RESTORE
130   WINDOW (-XX,-YY)-(1279-XX,799-YY)
140   FOR POINTS = 1 TO 4
150     READ OP,X,Y
160     IF TYPE = 1 THEN A = 1 : B = 0 : C = 0 : D = 0 : E = 1 : F = 10
170     IF TYPE = 2 THEN A =-1 : B = 0 : C =-50 : D = 0 : E =-1 : F =-20
180     IF TYPE = 3 THEN A = 0 : B = 1 : C =-10 : D =-1 : E = 0 : F =-40
190     IF TYPE = 4 THEN A = 0 : B =-1 : C =-40 : D = 1 : E = 0 : F = 20
200     IF TYPE = 5 THEN A =-1 : B = 0 : C =-50 : D = 0 : E = 1 : F = 10
210     IF TYPE = 6 THEN A = 0 : B =-1 : C =-40 : D =-1 : E = 0 : F =-40
220     IF TYPE = 7 THEN A = 0 : B = 1 : C =-10 : D = 1 : E = 0 : F = 20
230     IF TYPE = 8 THEN A = 1 : B = 0 : C = 0 : D = 0 : E =-1 : F =-20
240     GOSUB 280  'transform
250     IF OP = 1 THEN LINE -(X,Y) ELSE PSET (X,Y)
260   NEXT POINTS
270 RETURN

280 'SUBROUTINE transform
290   XT = A*X+B*Y+C : YT = D*X+E*Y+F
300   X = XT : Y = YT
310 RETURN
```

Program 4.22 Network group 12.

a screen dump to calcomp plotter

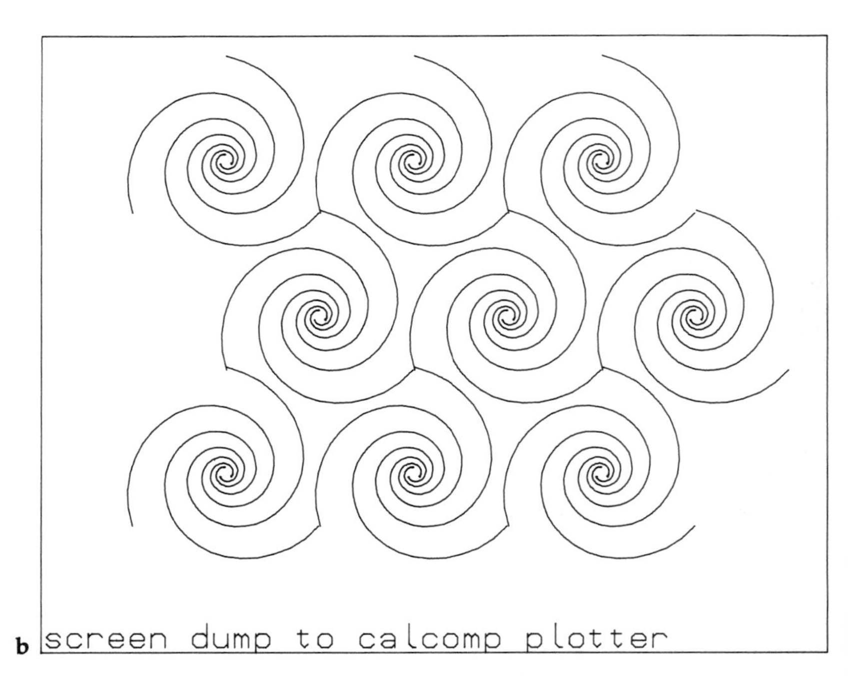

b

c

Figure 4.30
Network group 13

```
 10 SCREEN 2 : CLS
 20 FOR TYPE = 1 TO 3
 30   FOR YY = 200 TO 700 STEP 120
 40     SKEW = 0
 50     IF YY = 320 OR YY = 560  THEN SKEW = 60
 60     FOR X1 = 100 TO 700 STEP 120
 70       XX = X1+SKEW
 80       GOSUB 140  'draw motif at xx,yy
 90     NEXT X1
100   NEXT YY
110 NEXT TYPE
120 END

130 DATA 0,5,5,1,39.64,5,1,39.64,25,1,5,5

140 'SUBROUTINE draw motif at xx,yy
150   RESTORE
160   WINDOW (-XX,-YY)-(1279-XX,799-YY)
170   FOR POINTS = 1 TO 4
180     READ OP,X,Y
190     IF TYPE = 1 THEN A = 1 : B = 0 : C = 0 : D = 0 : E =-1 : F = 0
200     IF TYPE = 2 THEN A =-0.5 : B =-0.866 : C = 0 : D =-0.866 :
                         E = 0.5 : F = 0
210     IF TYPE = 3 THEN A =-0.5 : B = 0.866 : C = 0 : D = 0.866 :
                         E = 0.5 : F = 0
220     GOSUB 260  'transform
230     IF OP = 1 THEN LINE -(X,Y) ELSE PSET (X,Y)
240   NEXT POINTS
250 RETURN

260 'SUBROUTINE transform
270   XT = A*X+B*Y+C : YT = D*X+E*Y+F
280   X = XT : Y = YT
290 RETURN
```

Program 4.23 Network group 13.

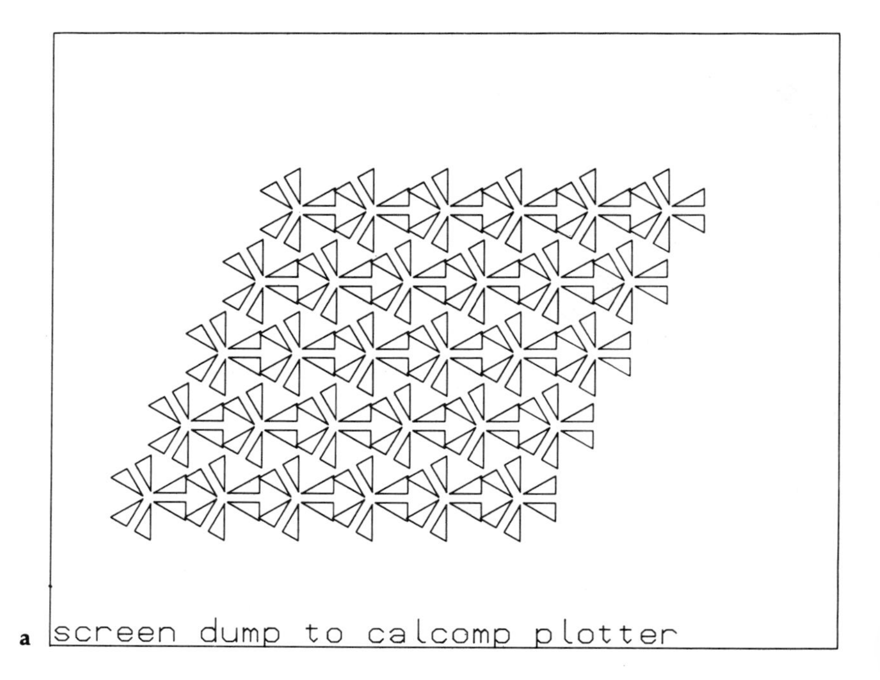
screen dump to calcomp plotter

a

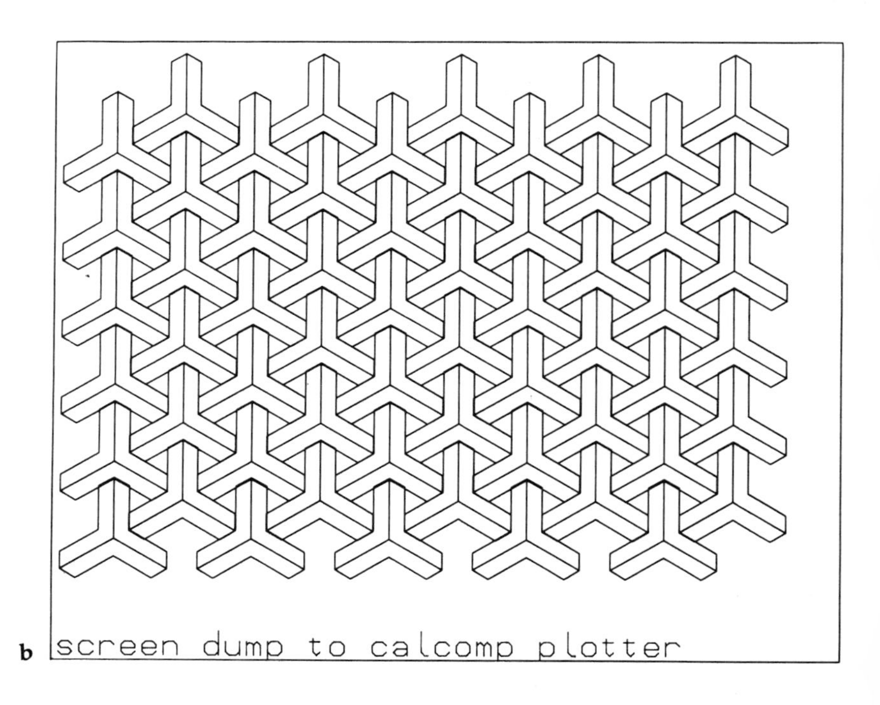
screen dump to calcomp plotter

b

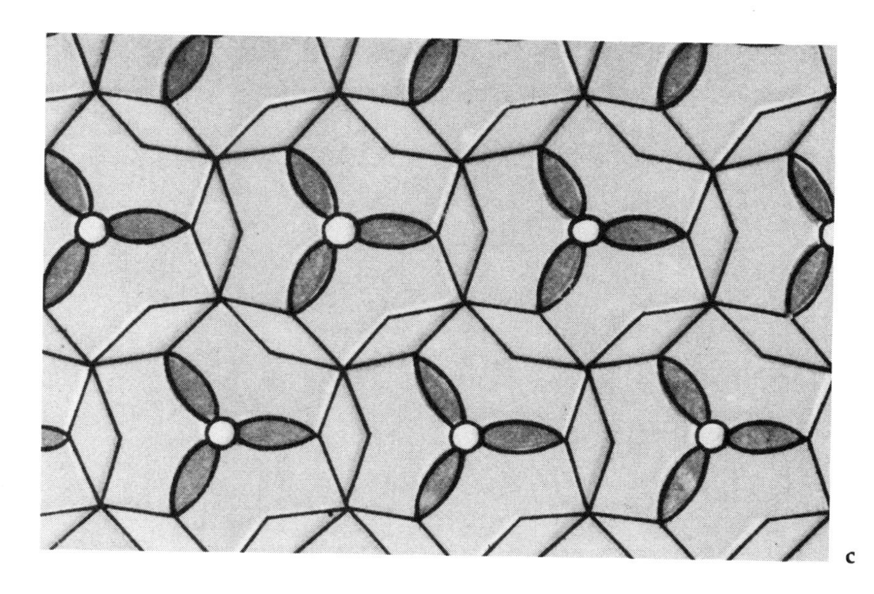

Figure 4.31
c Network group 14

```
 10 SCREEN 2 : CLS
 20 FOR TYPE = 1 TO 6
 30   FOR YY = 200 TO 700 STEP 120
 40     SKEW = 0
 50     IF YY = 320 OR YY = 560  THEN SKEW = 60
 60     FOR X1 = 100 TO 700 STEP 120
 70       XX = X1+SKEW
 80       GOSUB 140  'draw motif at xx,yy
 90     NEXT X1
100   NEXT YY
110 NEXT TYPE
120 END

130 DATA 0,5,5,1,39.64,5,1,39.64,25,1,5,5

140 'SUBROUTINE draw motif at xx,yy
150   RESTORE
160   WINDOW (-XX,-YY)-(1279-XX,799-YY)
170   FOR POINTS = 1 TO 4
180     READ OP,X,Y
190     IF TYPE = 1 THEN A = 1 : B = 0 : C = 0 : D = 0 : E = 1 : F = 0
200     IF TYPE = 2 THEN A = 1 : B = 0 : C = 0 : D = 0 : E =-1 : F = 0
210     IF TYPE = 3 THEN A =-0.5 : B =-0.866 : C = 0 : D = 0.866 :
                         E =-0.5 : F = 0
220     IF TYPE = 4 THEN A =-0.5 : B = 0.866 : C = 0 : D =-0.866 :
                         E =-0.5 : F = 0
230     IF TYPE = 5 THEN A =-0.5 : B =-0.866 : C = 0 : D =-0.866 :
                         E = 0.5 : F = 0
240     IF TYPE = 6 THEN A =-0.5 : B = 0.866 : C = 0 : D = 0.866 :
                         E = 0.5 : F = 0
250     GOSUB 290  'transform
260     IF OP = 1 THEN LINE -(X,Y) ELSE PSET (X,Y)
270   NEXT POINTS
280 RETURN

290 'SUBROUTINE transform
300   XT = A*X+B*Y+C : YT = D*X+E*Y+F
310   X = XT : Y = YT
320 RETURN
```

Program 4.24 Network group 14.

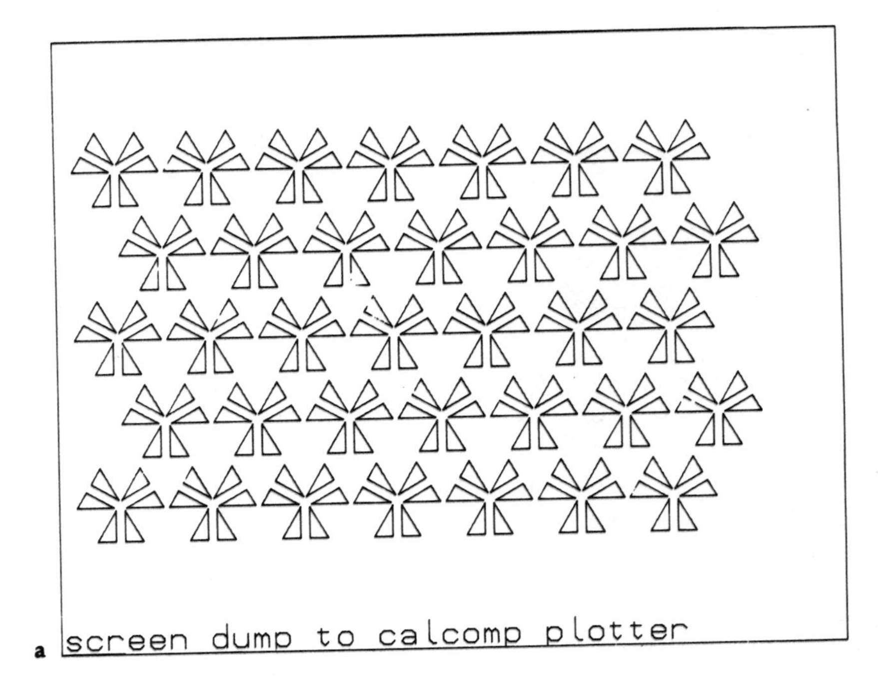
screen dump to calcomp plotter

a

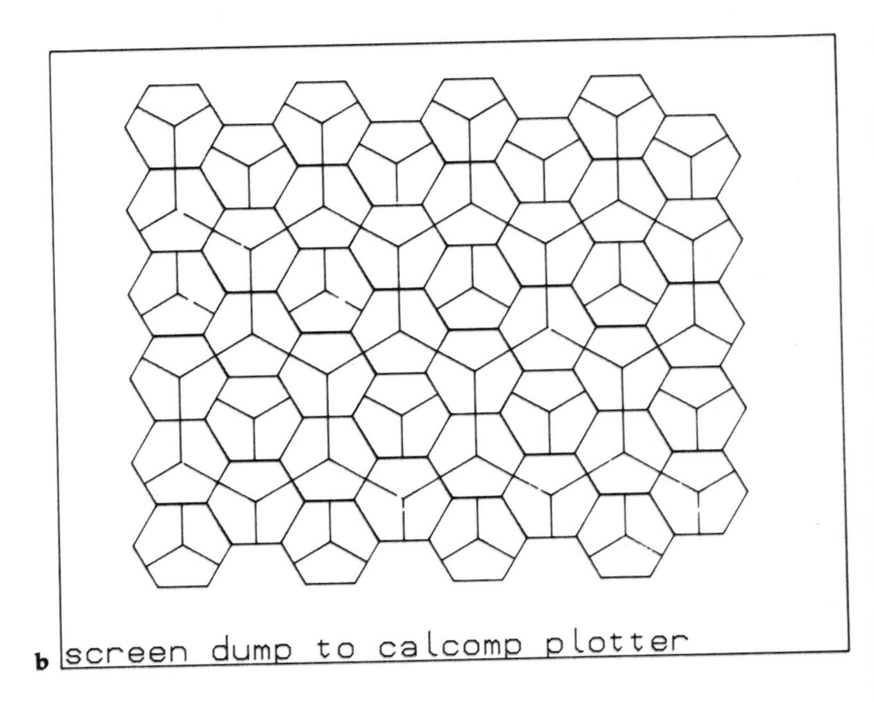
screen dump to calcomp plotter

b

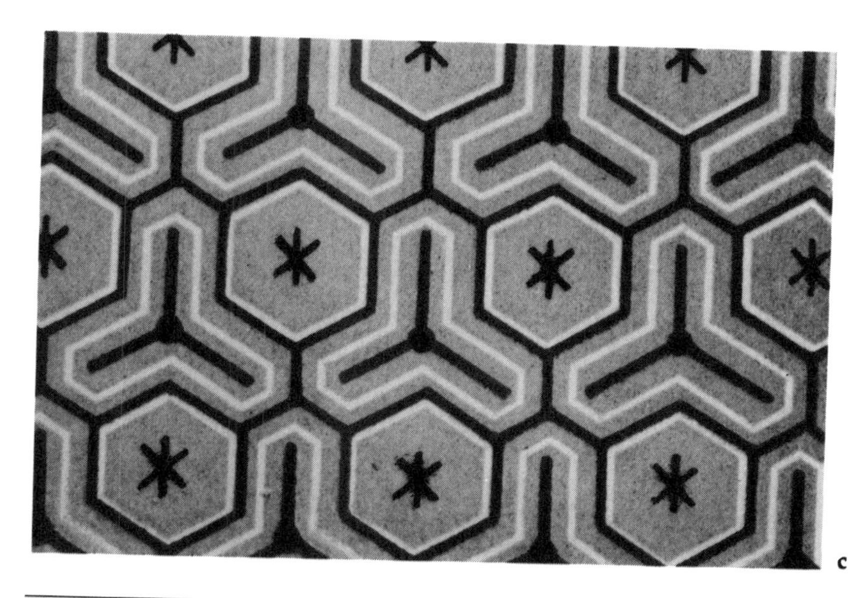

c

Figure 4.32
Network group 15

```
 10 SCREEN 2: CLS
 20 FOR TYPE = 1 TO 6
 30   FOR YY = 200 TO 560 STEP 90
 40     SKEW = 0
 50     IF YY = 290 OR YY = 470  THEN SKEW = 50
 60     FOR X1 = 100 TO 700 STEP 100
 70       XX = X1+SKEW
 80       GOSUB 140  'draw motif at xx,yy
 90     NEXT X1
100   NEXT YY
110 NEXT TYPE
120 END
130 DATA 0,5,5,1,39.64,5,1,39.64,25,1,5,5

140 'SUBROUTINE draw motif at xx,yy
150   RESTORE
160   WINDOW (-XX,-YY)-(1279-XX,799-YY)
170   FOR POINTS = 1 TO 4
180     READ OP,X,Y
190     IF TYPE = 1 THEN A = 0 : B = 1 : C = 0 : D =-1 : E = 0 : F = 0
200     IF TYPE = 2 THEN A = 0 : B =-1 : C = 0 : D =-1 : E = 0 : F = 0
210     IF TYPE = 3 THEN A = 0.866 : B = -0.5 : C = 0 : D = 0.5 :
                         E = 0.866 : F = 0
220     IF TYPE = 4 THEN A = 0.866 : B = 0.5 : C = 0 : D = 0.5 :
                         E = -0.866 : F = 0
230     IF TYPE = 5 THEN A = -0.866 : B = -0.5 : C = 0 : D = 0.5 :
                         E = -0.866 : F = 0
240     IF TYPE = 6 THEN A = -0.866 : B = 0.5 : C = 0 : D = 0.5 :
                         E = 0.866 : F = 0
250     GOSUB 290  'transform
260     IF OP = 1 THEN LINE -(X,Y) ELSE PSET (X,Y)
270   NEXT POINTS
280 RETURN

290 'SUBROUTINE transform
300   XT = A*X+B*Y+C : YT = D*X+E*Y+F
310   X = XT : Y = YT
320 RETURN
```

Program 4.25 Network group 15.

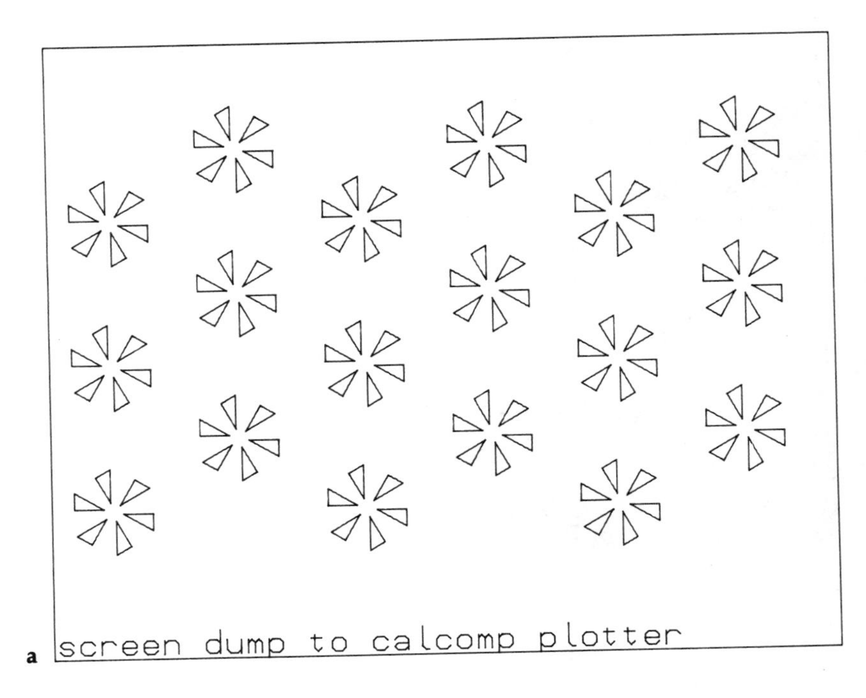
screen dump to calcomp plotter

a

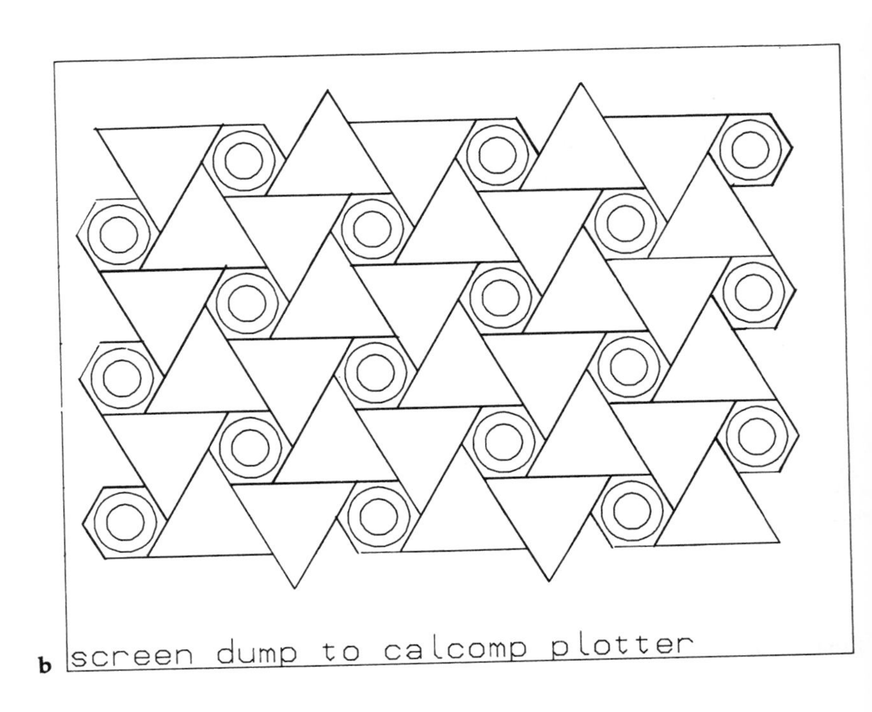
screen dump to calcomp plotter

b

c

Figure 4.33
Network group 16

```
 10 SCREEN 2: CLS
 20 FOR TYPE = 1 TO 6
 30   FOR YY = 120 TO 720 STEP 120
 40     SKEW = 0
 50     IF YY = 240 OR YY = 480 OR YY = 720 THEN SKEW = 206
 60     FOR X1 = 100 TO 1000 STEP 412
 70       XX = X1+SKEW
 80       GOSUB 140  'draw motif at xx,yy
 90     NEXT X1
100   NEXT YY
110 NEXT TYPE
120 END
130 DATA 0,16,-4,1,64,-4,1,64,-32,1,16,-4

140 'SUBROUTINE draw motif at xx,yy
150   RESTORE
160   WINDOW (-XX,-YY)-(1279-XX,799-YY)
170   FOR POINTS = 1 TO 4
180     READ OP,X,Y
190     IF TYPE = 1 THEN A = 1 : B = 0 : C = 0 : D = 0 : E = 1 : F = 0
200     IF TYPE = 2 THEN A = 0.5 : B =-0.866 : C = 0 : D = 0.866 :
                         E = 0.5 : F = 0
210     IF TYPE = 3 THEN A =-0.5 : B =-0.866 : C = 0 : D = 0.866 :
                         E =-0.5 : F = 0
220     IF TYPE = 4 THEN A =-1 : B = 0 : C = 0 : D = 0 : E =-1 : F = 0
230     IF TYPE = 5 THEN A =-0.5 : B = 0.866 : C = 0 : D =-0.866 :
                         E =-0.5 : F = 0
240     IF TYPE = 6 THEN A = 0.5 : B = 0.866 : C = 0 : D =-0.866 :
                         E = 0.5 : F = 0
250     GOSUB 290  'transform
260     IF OP = 1 THEN LINE -(X,Y) ELSE PSET (X,Y)
270   NEXT POINTS
280 RETURN

290 'SUBROUTINE transform
300   XT = A*X+B*Y+C : YT = D*X+E*Y+F
310   X = XT : Y = YT
320 RETURN
```

Program 4.26 Network group 16.

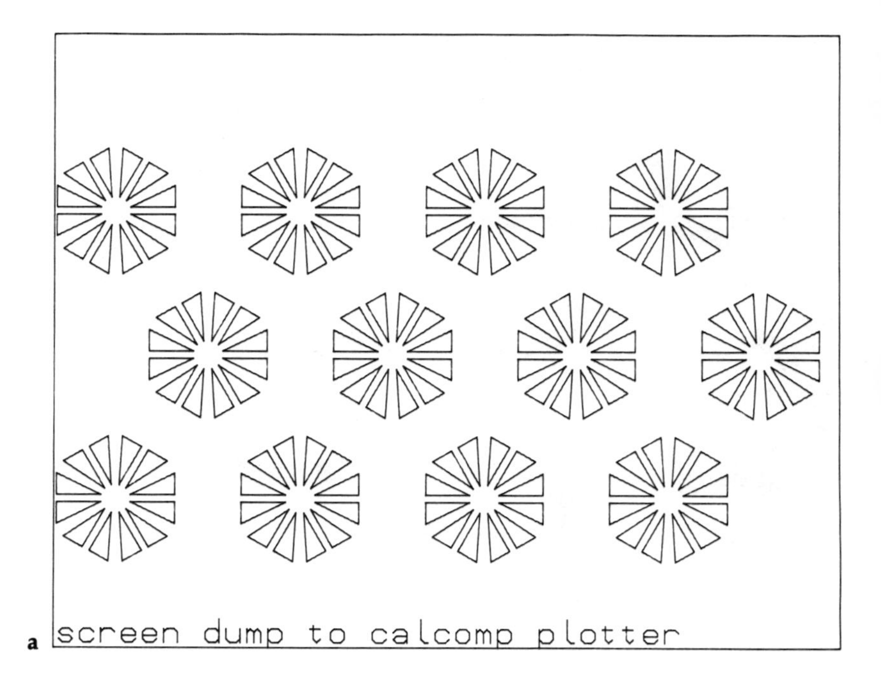
screen dump to calcomp plotter
a

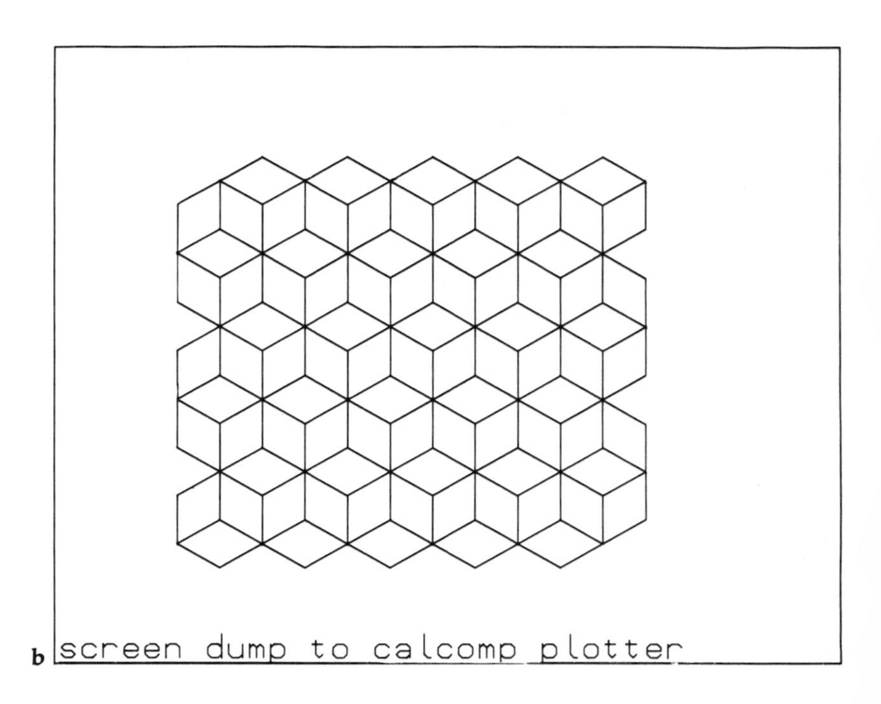
screen dump to calcomp plotter
b

Figure 4.34
Network group 17

```
 10 SCREEN 2: CLS
 20 FOR TYPE = 1 TO 12
 30   FOR YY = 150 TO 750 STEP 240
 40     SKEW = 0
 50     IF YY = 390 THEN SKEW = 150
 60     FOR X1 = 100 TO 1000 STEP 300
 70       XX = X1+SKEW
 80       GOSUB 140  'draw motif at xx,yy
 90     NEXT X1
100   NEXT YY
110 NEXT TYPE
120 END
130 DATA 0,16,-4,1,64,-4,1,64,-32,1,16,-4

140 'SUBROUTINE draw motif at xx,yy
150   RESTORE
160   WINDOW (-XX,-YY)-(1279-XX,799-YY)
170   FOR POINTS = 1 TO 4
180     READ OP,X,Y
190     IF TYPE = 1 THEN A = 1 : B = 0 : C = 0 : D = 0 : E = 1 : F = 0
200     IF TYPE = 2 THEN A = 1 : B = 0 : C = 0 : D = 0 : E =-1 : F = 0
210     IF TYPE = 3 THEN A = 0.5 : B =-0.866 : C = 0 : D = 0.866 :
                         E = 0.5 : F = 0
220     IF TYPE = 4 THEN A = 0.5 : B = 0.866 : C = 0 : D = 0.866 :
                         E =-0.5 : F = 0
230     IF TYPE = 5 THEN A =-0.5 : B =-0.866 : C = 0 : D = 0.866 :
                         E =-0.5 : F = 0
240     IF TYPE = 6 THEN A =-0.5 : B = 0.866 : C = 0 : D = 0.866 :
                         E = 0.5 : F = 0
250     IF TYPE = 7 THEN A =-1 : B = 0 : C = 0 : D = 0 : E =-1 : F = 0
260     IF TYPE = 8 THEN A =-1 : B = 0 : C = 0 : D = 0 : E = 1 : F = 0
270     IF TYPE = 9 THEN A =-0.5 : B = 0.866 : C = 0 : D =-0.866 :
                         E = J.5 : F = 0
280     IF TYPE = 10 THEN A =-0.5 : B =-0.866 : C = 0 : D =-0.866 :
                          E = 0.5 : F = 0
290     IF TYPE = 11 THEN A = 0.5 : B = 0.866 : C = 0 : D =-0.866 :
                          E = 0.5 : F = 0
300     IF TYPE = 12 THEN A = 0.5 : B =-0.866 : C = 0 : D =-0.866 :
                          E =-0.5 : F = 0
310     GOSUB 350  'transform
320     IF OP = 1 THEN LINE -(X,Y) ELSE PSET (X,Y)
330   NEXT POINTS
340 RETURN

350 'SUBROUTINE transform
360   XT = A*X+B*Y+C : YT = D*X+E*Y+F
370   X = XT : Y = YT
380 RETURN
```

Program 4.27 Network group 17.

Network group 11

The difference between network groups 11 and 10 can easily be seen by examining the corresponding triangle figures. Again there are 90° rotational symmetry points. This time there are lines of reflection (these are diagonal in the triangle diagram). The group is thus categorised by 90° rotational symmetry points and by having reflection lines that do NOT contain these points. It is drawn by Program 4.21. The relationship between Figure 4.28a and Figure 4.28b is perhaps not obvious at first sight. Figure 4.28b is a familiar tessellation and is commonly used in modern Western patterns. In Figure 4.28b the reflection lines are horizontal and vertical. The lines joining points of rotational symmetry are also horizontal and vertical. These two sets of lines form two non-overlapping rectangular nets. You should try and see what motif in Figure 4.28b is equivalent to the triangle in Figure 4.28a.

Figure 4.28c is an Egyptian example from Jones and you can see the similarity between this and the computer generated pattern. An interesting point about this pattern is that although the basic generating motifs that determine the symmetry are four spirals, the impression of the pattern is of rectangles with spirals at the corner. This is another case where the actual network symmetry is 'buried' and occupies a place of apparently less significance than some incidental effect that gives the overall aesthetic impact to the pattern.

Network group 12

Out of the set of network groups 10, 11 and 12, this one is conceptually the easiest. It is categorised by having 90° rotational symmetry centres and lines of reflection on these centres. It is drawn by Program 4.22.

Figure 4.29b is identical to Figure 4.26b except that circles are used instead of ellipses. Figure 4.26b, of course, only contains 180° rotational symmetry points. The example from Jones is Persian.

Network group 13

Network groups 13, 14 and 15 all have 120° rotational symmetry points. Network group 13 does not contain any lines of symmetry. Program 4.23 now contains subroutine calls that rotate the motif through angles other than 90° or 180°.

Figure 4.30b is made up from a single spiral rotated through 120° and 240°. It corresponds exactly to the pattern made up of triangular motifs. Figure 4.30c, the example from Jones, is Moorish and taken from the Alhambra.

Network group 14

Network group 14 contains two overlapping nets of 120° rotational symmetry centres. It differs from network group 15 in that one of those nets does NOT coincide with lines of reflection. There are lines of reflection at three different orientations in network group

14. This can easily be seen in Figure 4.31b, the computer example, drawn by Program 4.24, which is based on a traditional Chinese lattice. Again you should study this pattern and try and deduce the elementary motif that corresponds to the triangle. The example from Jones in Figure 4.31c is Persian.

Network group 15

In network group 15, which also contains 120° rotational symmetry, all the rotational centres lie on lines of reflection. The differences between group 14 and group 15 are perhaps best seen by comparing the respective lattices (Figure 4.31b and Figure 4.32b). The triangular motifs from these two groups seem to be more difficult to interpret – perhaps because we are unfamiliar with 120° patterns.

The hexagonal lattice in Figure 4.32b, drawn by Program 4.25, is made up of small hexagons with 120° radial lines drawn within each hexagon. Note the orientation of these Y shapes and how they combine to form larger hexagons.

Network group 16

Network groups 16 and 17 are the two groups with 60° rotational symmetry centres. Network group 16, drawn by Program 4.26, does not contain any lines of symmetry and like group 13, the triangular motifs, of which there are now six instead of three impart a feeling of rotation. This is also conveyed by Figure 4.33b which is generated by placing a pair of concentric circles at each rotational symmetry centre. Added to this is a hexagon with eccentrically extending sides. This was based on the design in Figure 4.33c, a Persian example from Jones.

Network group 17

Finally we come to network group 17. This possesses 60° rotational symmetry centres and lines of reflection. We have used 12 triangles in Figure 4.34a for comparison with Figure 4.33a. Strictly only six isosceles triangles are required.

The computer example in Figure 4.34b is interesting. It was drawn using Program 4.27, is based on a Chinese lattice and the impression is of stacked cubes. The pattern is generated, however, from six radial lines drawn at 60° intervals. The example from Jones is Chinese.

Summary of network pattern symmetry

We can summarize the symmetry of network groups by using a decision tree (Figure 4.35), just as we did for the band groups. This time we start by asking the question: 'Is there axial symmetry, and, if there is, what is the smallest elementary angle?' The second question determines whether there are any reflection lines. At the third level we have to determine whether there are reflections in more than one direction, whether there are glide-reflections and

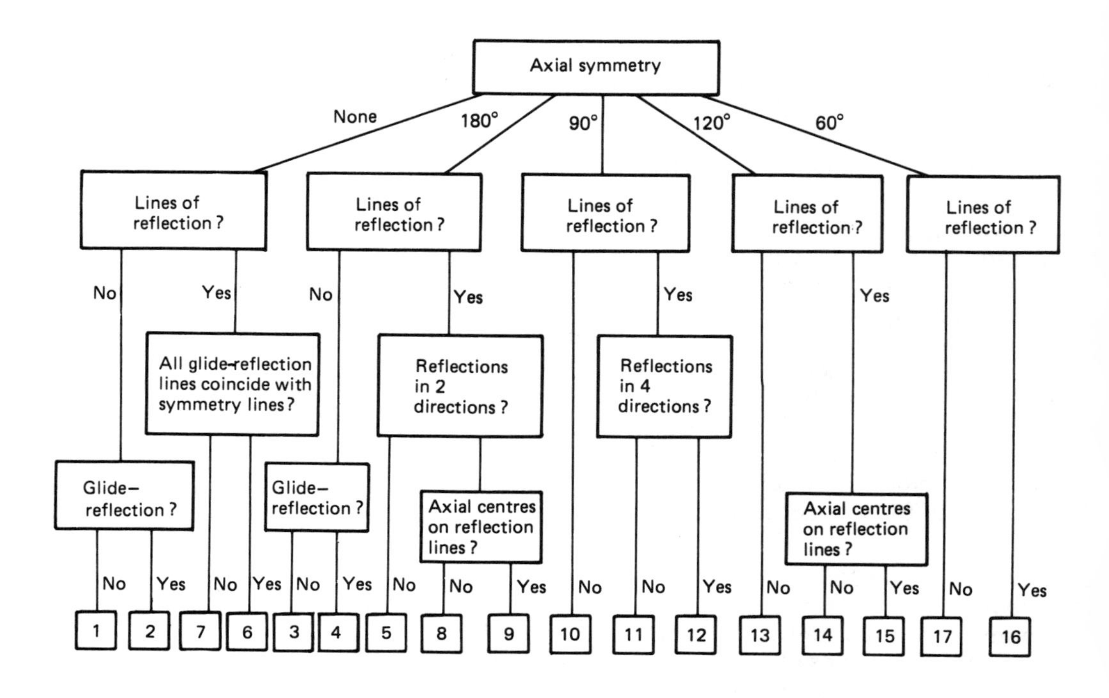

Figure 4.35
Decision tree for 17 network groups

whether the glide-reflection axes correspond with the reflection lines.

Network groups are rather more difficult to categorise than bands but everyday examples of them are far more common. Network patterns abound in wallpapers, fabrics and ornamentation of every description.

5 *Night and day – a journey through the world of tessellations*

People have always been fascinated by shapes or tiles that fit together to cover a plane surface leaving no gaps between the tiles. Such 'tessellations' come in many different forms.

In Chapter 4, we dealt with the programming required to place a motif at certain positions in a plane. Some of these motifs happened to tessellate the plane. Mathematically there is no difference between the symmetry groupings of network patterns that do not tessellate and those that do. However, the programming requires a completely different approach and the two topics are separated into different chapters.

Among the simplest tessellations are those by regular polygons. Figure 5.1 shows a selection of ways of tiling the plane with regular polygons. The tessellations in Figure 5.1 all share an interesting property. In each pattern, every vertex is surrounded by the same combination of shapes and in the same order. In fact the 11 tessellations of Figure 5.1 are the only ones that have this property. Only three of these tilings use repeated copies of a single tile and the rest require the use of two or more different tiles.

Any single equilateral triangle can be used to tessellate the plane, as can any square or any regular hexagon. Equilateral triangles, squares and regular hexagons are the only shapes that can be used in this way. The plane cannot be tessellated by regular pentagons, but there are a number of irregular pentagons that will tessellate the plane. An example of a pentagon that will tessellate is the well-known Cairo tile, so called because many of the streets of Cairo were paved in this pattern (Figure 5.2). The Cairo tile is equilateral but not regular because its angles are not all the same.

The fascination that is aroused by finding a single shape that will tile the plane is well exemplified by the feverish activity that is stimulated amongst amateur mathematicians by articles on the subject. For example, an article in Martin Gardner's column in *Scientific American* in 1975 discussed the problem of classifying the types of pentagon that would tessellate the plane. This article stimulated a

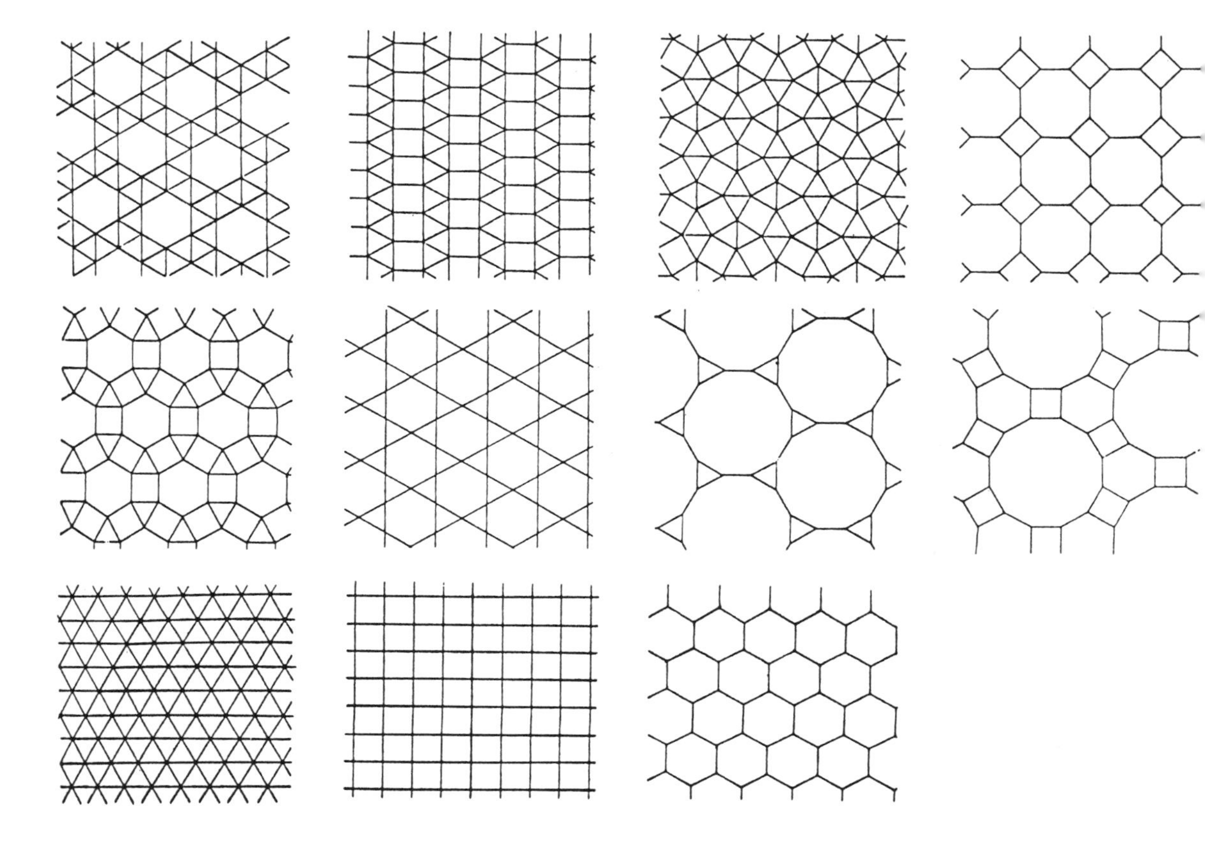

Figure 5.1
Tessellation of the plane
with regular polygons

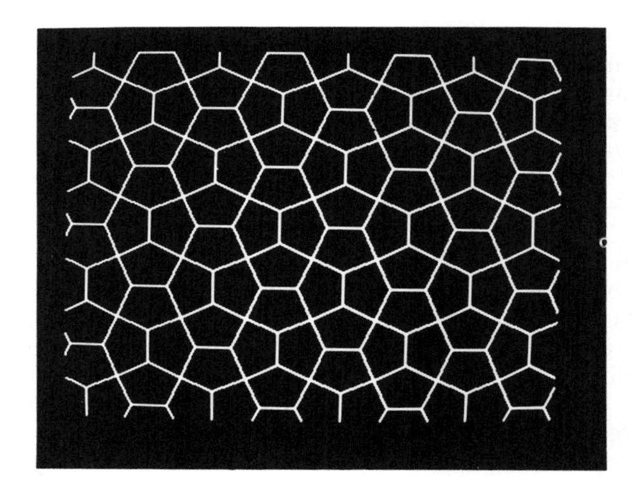

Figure 5.2
The Cairo tile: an equilateral
pentagon that tessellates

number of amateur mathematicians into generating descriptions of previously unknown pentagonal shapes that could be used in such tilings.

The work of M. C. Escher is well known in this area. Many of his pictures involved tilings of the plane with shapes that resembled animals and birds. In some of his works a single shape was used, whereas in others a combination of shapes was used. One well-known picture involves a group of 12 different bird shapes that can be repeated to tessellate.

Many traditional decorations and crafts involve tessellations. A common example is in the design of patchwork patterns where pieces of fabric are sewn together to create attractive patterns. There are many traditional designs and some of these are illustrated in Figure 5.3. The patterns illustrated are used as single motifs on cushions, or they can be extended for use on larger objects such as bedspreads.

Figure 5.3
Traditional patchwork patterns: (a) world without end; (b) clay's choice; (c) falling star; (d) Virginian star

Tessellations are also widely used in floor and wall decorations. A famous example of this appears in the Alhambra in Spain where Escher himself spent some time studying the Moorish tessellations.

In this chapter, we will look at two main ways in which a microcomputer can be used in exploring the world of tessellations. First of all, we shall see how the technique of 'picking and dragging' introduced in Chapter 2 can be used in a program for designing and experimenting with tessellation layouts. Our second main topic will be a study of ways in which simple tile shapes can be deformed into shapes that are more interesting, but which still tessellate the plane. Programming techniques for decorating the shapes that are generated will also be introduced. For examples of the sort of display that can be designed, look ahead to Figures 5.10 and 5.13.

5.1 AN INTRODUCTORY TESSELLATION LAYOUT PLANNER

Program 5.1 is a simple picking and dragging program that can be used to design tessellation layouts. The basic shapes used are described to the program in DATA statements that contain a sequence of relative coordinates for each shape available. (Actually, one of the increment pairs is not yet used, but will be needed later.) The first line of DATA gives the number of different shapes in the set being used, and a string containing the characters that will be used in the program as codes for selecting shapes. Redefining the DATA statements allows the user to experiment with different combinations of basic shapes. Program 5.1 includes the DATA for an equilateral triangle and a hexagon. DATA statements describing some other combinations of shapes appear as Program 5.2.

The program is similar to the picking and dragging program described in Chapter 2, but includes as an additional option rotation of objects (command letter 'c' for clockwise and 'a' for anticlockwise). The method used for doing this was suggested in Chapter 2. Rotations are done in increments that are appropriate for the shapes being used. For example, when tessellations are being planned with equilateral triangles and hexagons, an appropriate rotation step is 60°. Data for each shape includes the number of orientations in which the shape can appear in a tessellation. An appropriate rotation increment is calculated for each shape and a set of 'PUT' arrays is created for each shape. One PUT array is required for each orientation in which a shape can appear. Copies of these PUT arrays are held in the three-dimensional master array 'SHAPES%'.

The first subscript for the array 'SHAPES%' selects a shape and the second subscript selects an orientation for that shape. That part of 'SHAPES%', which is selected by a particular pair of values for these two subscripts, contains a copy of the PUT array which is required for dragging the selected shape in the selected orientation.

Whenever a shape is selected by the subroutine 'pick' (line 700), the required shape (in orientation 0) is transferred to the current

```
 10 PI = 3.141593
 20 DEF FNRAD(DEGREES) = DEGREES*PI/180
 30 FALSE = 0 : TRUE = -1
 40 SCREEN 1 : CLS : XSTEP = 4 : YSTEP = 4
 50 MAXSHAPES = 3 : MAXPTS = 10 : MAXORIENTATIONS = 8
 60 CURRPTS = 0 : CURRORIENTATION = 0 : CURRSHAPE = 0
 70 DIM SHAPESPTS(MAXPTS)
 80 DIM ORIENTATIONS(MAXORIENTATIONS)
 90 DIM CURRMOVEX(MAXPTS),CURRMOVEY(MAXPTS)
100 DIM SHAPESMOVEX(MAXSHAPES,MAXORIENTATIONS,MAXPTS),
        SHAPESMOVEY(MAXSHAPES,MAXORIENTATIONS,MAXPTS)
110 DIM SHAPES%(MAXSHAPES,MAXORIENTATIONS,500),CURRSHAPE%(500)
120 KEY OFF
130 WINDOW (-640,-400)-(639,399)
140 GOSUB 310  'initialise
150 WHILE INSTR(SHAPES$,SELECTION$) = 0 OR SELECTION$ = ""
160   EXTRACOMMS$ = "" : GOSUB 700  'pick
170 WEND
180 WHILE SELECTION$ <> "Q"
190   C$ = INKEY$ : IF C$ = "" THEN 190
200   FIXED = FALSE
210   WHILE NOT(FIXED)
220     GOSUB 780  'process command
230     C$ = INKEY$
240   WEND
250   SELECTION$ = ""
260   WHILE INSTR(SHAPES$+"Q",SELECTION$) = 0 OR SELECTION$ = ""
270     EXTRACOMMS$ = "Q" : GOSUB 700  'pick
280   WEND
290 WEND
300 END

310 'SUBROUTINE initialise
320   CLS
330   READ SHAPES,SHAPES$
340   FOR S = 1 TO SHAPES
350     READ SHAPESPTS(S)
360     READ ORIENTATIONS(S)
370     THETAINC = 360\ORIENTATIONS(S)
380     FOR I = 0 TO SHAPESPTS(S)
390       READ CURRMOVEX(I),CURRMOVEY(I)
400     NEXT I
410     SINE = SIN(FNRAD(THETAINC)) : COSINE = COS(FNRAD(THETAINC))
420     FOR OS = 0 TO ORIENTATIONS(S)-1
430       FOR I = 0 TO SHAPESPTS(S)
440         TX = CURRMOVEX(I) : TY = CURRMOVEY(I)
450         CURRMOVEX(I) = TX*COSINE-TY*SINE
460         CURRMOVEY(I) = TX*SINE+TY*COSINE
470         SHAPESMOVEX(S,OS,I) = CURRMOVEX(I)
480         SHAPESMOVEY(S,OS,I) = CURRMOVEY(I)
490       NEXT I
```

Program 5.1 A tessellation layout planning program that uses 'picking and dragging' to place tiles.

continued

```
500        NX = 0 : NY = 0
510        FOR I = 0 TO SHAPESPTS(S)
520          NX = NX+CURRMOVEX(I) : NY = NY+CURRMOVEY(I)
530          IF I = 0 THEN PSET (NX,NY) ELSE LINE -(NX,NY)
540        NEXT I
550        GET (-121,-121)-(121,121),CURRSHAPE%
560        GOSUB 650  'transfer currshape to master array shapes
570        CLS
580      NEXT OS
590      CLS
600    NEXT S
610    LLEFT$ = "K" : RRIGHT$ = "M"
620    UP$  = "H" : DOWN$ = "P"
630    DRAGCOMMS$ = LLEFT$+RRIGHT$+UP$+DOWN$+"CAF"
640 RETURN

650 'SUBROUTINE transfer currshape to master array shapes
660   FOR I = 0 TO 500
670     SHAPES%(S,OS,I) = CURRSHAPE%(I)
680   NEXT I
690 RETURN

700 'SUBROUTINE pick
710   LOCATE 1,1 : PRINT "Next selection ("SHAPES$+EXTRACOMMS$")";
720   SELECTION$ = INPUT$(1)
730   IF INSTR(SHAPES$+EXTRACOMMS$,SELECTION$) = 0 THEN BEEP : RETURN
740   IF SELECTION$ = "Q" THEN RETURN
750   GOSUB 950  'get tile
760   LOCATE 1,1 : PRINT SPC(30)
770 RETURN

780 'SUBROUTINE process command
790   IF C$ = "" THEN RETURN
800   IF LEN(C$) = 2 THEN C$ = RIGHT$(C$,1)
810   IF INSTR(DRAGCOMMS$, C$) = 0 THEN BEEP : RETURN
820   GOSUB 920  'draw or delete
830   IF C$ = "F" THEN GOSUB 1120 : FIXED = TRUE : RETURN
840   IF C$ = LLEFT$  THEN X = X-XSTEP
850   IF C$ = RRIGHT$ THEN X = X+XSTEP
860   IF C$ = UP$     THEN Y = Y+YSTEP
870   IF C$ = DOWN$   THEN Y = Y-YSTEP
880   IF C$ = "C" THEN CURRORIENTATION = ABS(CURRORIENTATION-1)
                                  MOD ORIENTATIONS(CURRSHAPE) :
                        GOSUB 1020  'transfer master to current
```

Program 5.1 *continued*

shape array, 'CURRSHAPE%'. The subpicture in this array is then dragged around the screen in response to the arrow keys.

Whenever a 'c' (clockwise) or 'a' (anticlockwise) command is processed, the part of the array 'SHAPES%' that contains the current shape in its new orientation is copied into 'CURRSHAPE%' and this is now the subpicture that is dragged around the screen.

```
 890   IF C$ = "A" THEN CURRORIENTATION = (CURRORIENTATION+1)
                                         MOD ORIENTATIONS(CURRSHAPE) :
                         GOSUB 1020  'transfer master to current
 900   GOSUB 920  'draw or delete
 910 RETURN

 920 'SUBROUTINE draw or delete
 930   PUT (X,Y-242),CURRSHAPE%,XOR
     ' 'On the PCjr, use PUT (X,Y),CURRSHAPE%,XOR
 940 RETURN

 950 'SUBROUTINE get tile
 960   CURRSHAPE = INSTR(SHAPES$,SELECTION$)
 970   CURRORIENTATION = 0
 980   GOSUB 1020  'transfer master to current
 990   X = -500 : Y = -150
1000   GOSUB 920  'draw or delete
1010 RETURN

1020 'SUBROUTINE transfer master to current
1030   FOR I = 0 TO 500
1040     CURRSHAPE%(I) = SHAPES%(CURRSHAPE,CURRORIENTATION,I)
1050   NEXT I
1060   CURRPTS = SHAPESPTS(CURRSHAPE)
1070   FOR I = 0 TO CURRPTS
1080     CURRMOVEX(I) = SHAPESMOVEX(CURRSHAPE,CURRORIENTATION,I)
1090     CURRMOVEY(I) = SHAPESMOVEY(CURRSHAPE,CURRORIENTATION,I)
1100   NEXT I
1110 RETURN

1120 'SUBROUTINE fix
1140   NX = X+121+CURRMOVEX(0) : NY = Y-121+CURRMOVEY(0)
1150   PSET(NX,NY)
1160   FOR I = 1 TO CURRPTS
1170     NX = NX+CURRMOVEX(I) : NY = NY+CURRMOVEY(I)
1180     LINE -(NX,NY)
1190   NEXT I
1200 RETURN

4995 REM DATA for H(exagon) and T(riangle)
5005 DATA 2,HT
5015 DATA 6,1, 0,-100, -86.6025404,50, 0,100, 86.6025404,50,
               86.6025404,-50, 0,-100, -86.6025404,-50
5025 DATA 3,2, 57.735027,0, -86.6025404,-50, 0,100, 86.6025404,-50
```

Moving large amounts of information between arrays is fairly slow in BASIC. When you run this program, you will therefore find that there are delays while the various arrays are being initialised and while a particular image is being transferred to the 'CURRSHAPE%' array.

```
4995 'DATA for S(quare), D(iamond), and T(riangle)
                        for World without end pattern
5000 DATA 3,SDT
5010 DATA 4,1,50,-50, -100,0, 0,100, 100,0, 0,-100
5020 DATA 4,4,50,0, -50,-120.710678, -50,120.710678,
                      50,120.710678,   50,-120.710678
5030 DATA 3,2,50,-40.236893, -100,0, 50,120.710678, 50,-120.710678

4995 'DATA for S(quare), R(hombus), and T(riangle)
                        for Clays choice pattern
5000 DATA 3,SRT
5010 DATA 4,1,50,-50, -100,0, 0,100, 100,0, 0,-100
5020 DATA 4,4,50,0, -100,0, 100,100, 100,0, -100,-100
5030 DATA 3,4,33.333333,-33.333333, -100,0, 100,100, 0,-100

4995 'DATA for S(quare), D(iamond), and T(riangle)
                        for Falling star pattern
5000 DATA 3,SDT
5010 DATA 4,1,50,-50, -100,0, 0,100, 100,0, 0,-100
5020 DATA 4,4,14.644661,35.355339, 70.7106781,-70.7106781,
                        -100,0, -70.7106781,70.7106781, 100,0
5030 DATA 3,4,33.333333,-33.333333, -100,0, 100,100, 0,-100
```

Program 5.2 Alternative DATA sets for Program 5.1.

Patchwork tessellations like those in Figure 5.3 can be easily produced by using Program 5.1.

Colour filling tiles

A tile can be easily colour filled by using the PAINT command from a point inside the tile. Such a point is easy to find in the case of a 'convex' shape. (A convex shape is one that 'bulges outwards' everywhere and has no 'bays'.)

A colour fill option that can be switched on or off can be included in Program 5.1 by making the alterations and extensions indicated in Program 5.3. When the colour fill option is on, the user is asked for a colour code to be used when a tile is fixed. As well as drawing round the outline of the tile, the program fills the interior with the selected colour.

(Later in this chapter, an algorithm for finding an interior point for a non-convex shape is introduced.)

Accurate alignment of tiles

If you experiment with Program 5.1, you will find that as you build up a complex pattern, rounding errors and slight misalignments of the tiles will accumulate and become more and more noticeable. This is because it is impossible for the user of the program to accurately align new tiles with the shapes already included in the pattern. Firstly, it is difficult to see when two lines are accurately superimposed. Secondly, dragging a tile proceeds in discrete steps and the coordinates of most of the vertices of previously placed tiles do not necessarily match the possible start points of the tile being dragged.

The solution to this problem is to maintain a list of the existing vertices or corners in the pattern created so far. When a new tile has been dragged into its approximate position, the command to fix it is given. Instead of simply drawing the tile in the position to which it has been dragged, the program should first examine each of the tile's vertices in turn. If a vertex is found that is 'close' to a vertex in the existing pattern, then the vertex in the existing pattern is used as the start point for drawing the new tile. While the tile is being drawn, any other vertex that is close to an existing vertex in the pattern is also replaced by the existing vertex. As the tile is being drawn, new vertices are added to the overall list of vertices. This

```
160 EXTRACOMMS$ = "C" : GOSUB 700  'pick

270 EXTRACOMMS$ = "QC" : GOSUB 700  'pick

325 COLORING = FALSE

745 IF SELECTION$ = "C" THEN COLORING = NOT(COLORING)
750 IF INSTR(SHAPES$,SELECTION$) THEN GOSUB 950  'get tile

1120 'SUBROUTINE fix
1130   IF NOT(COLORING) THEN FILLCOLOR = 0 : CC = 3 : GOTO 1180
1140   CODES$ = "CMW"
1150   GOSUB 1260  'choose color
1160   CC = INSTR(CODES$,COLOR$)
1170   FILLCOLOR = CC
1180   NX = X+121+CURRMOVEX(0) : NY = Y-121+CURRMOVEY(0)
1190   PSET (NX,NY),CC
1200   FOR I = 1 TO CURRPTS
1210   NX = NX+CURRMOVEX(I) : NY = NY+CURRMOVEY(I)
1220   LINE -(NX,NY),CC
1230   NEXT I
1240   PAINT (X+121,Y-121),FILLCOLOR,CC
1250 RETURN

1260 'SUBROUTINE choose color
1270   LOCATE 1,1 : PRINT "Choose colour (";CODES$;")";
1280   COLOR$ = ""
1290   WHILE INSTR(CODES$,COLOR$) = 0 OR COLOR$ = ""
1300     COLOR$ = INKEY$ : IF COLOR$ = "" THEN 1300
1310     IF INSTR(CODES$,COLOR$) = 0 THEN BEEP
1320   WEND
1330 RETURN
```

Program 5.3 Alterations to Program 5.1 to enable tiles to be coloured.

ensures that the vertices of any new tiles added to a pattern exactly match the corresponding vertices of tiles that have already been placed. The alterations needed to implement this extension are presented as Program 5.4.

Another useful facility in a design program of this nature would be the ability to save designs on tape or diskette files. Implementation of a save facility in a picking and dragging program was

```
  65 MAXVERTS = 100 : NOOFVERTS = 0
  66 DIM VX(MAXVERTS),VY(MAXVERTS)
  85 DIM MOVEX(MAXPTS),MOVEY(MAXPTS)

1120 'SUBROUTINE fix
1130   NX = X+121+CURRMOVEX(0) : NY = Y-121+CURRMOVEY(0)
1140   FOR I = 1 TO CURRPTS
1150     MOVEX(I-1) = CURRMOVEX(I)
1160     MOVEY(I-1) = CURRMOVEY(I)
1170   NEXT I
1180   I = 0
1190   DFOUND = FALSE
1200   'loop
1210     NX = NX+MOVEX(I) : NY = NY+MOVEY(I)
1220     GOSUB 1340  'check verts
1230     I = (I+1) MOD CURRPTS
1240   IF I <> 0 AND NOT(DFOUND) THEN 1210
1250   PSET (NX,NY) : S = I+1
1260   'loop
1270     NX = NX+MOVEX(I) : NY = NY+MOVEY(I)
1280     GOSUB 1340  'check verts
1290     IF NOT(DFOUND) THEN GOSUB 1440  'add
1300     LINE -(NX,NY)
1310     I = (I+1) MOD CURRPTS
1320   IF I+1 <> S THEN 1270
1330 RETURN

1340 'SUBROUTINE check verts
1350   IF NOOFVERTS = 0 THEN DFOUND = FALSE : RETURN
1360   E = 30 : J = 0
1370   DFOUND = FALSE
1380   WHILE NOT(DFOUND) AND (J <> NOOFVERTS)
1390     J = J+1
1400     DFOUND = ABS(VX(J)-NX) < E AND ABS(VY(J)-NY) < E
1410   WEND
1420   IF DFOUND THEN NX = VX(J) : NY = VY(J)
1430 RETURN

1440 'SUBROUTINE add
1450   NOOFVERTS = NOOFVERTS+1 : VX(NOOFVERTS) = NX : VY(NOOFVERTS) = NY
1460 RETURN
```

Program 5.4 Extensions to Program 5.1 to align tiles accurately.

discussed in Chapter 2 and we leave this as an exercise for the interested reader.

5.2 NON-PERIODIC TESSELLATIONS

Many of the best-known tessellations are 'periodic'. This means that there is a grouping of tiles that are repeated again and again over the plane. If you can imagine the tiles in a periodic tessellation being outlined on an infinite piece of tracing paper, then the paper can always be moved, without rotation, into a new position where the outlines will again fit exactly. The structure of any periodic tiling matches the structure of one of the wallpaper or frieze patterns described in Chapter 4.

Many shapes that tile periodically will also tile non-periodically. For example, Figure 5.4 shows two periodic tilings and two non-

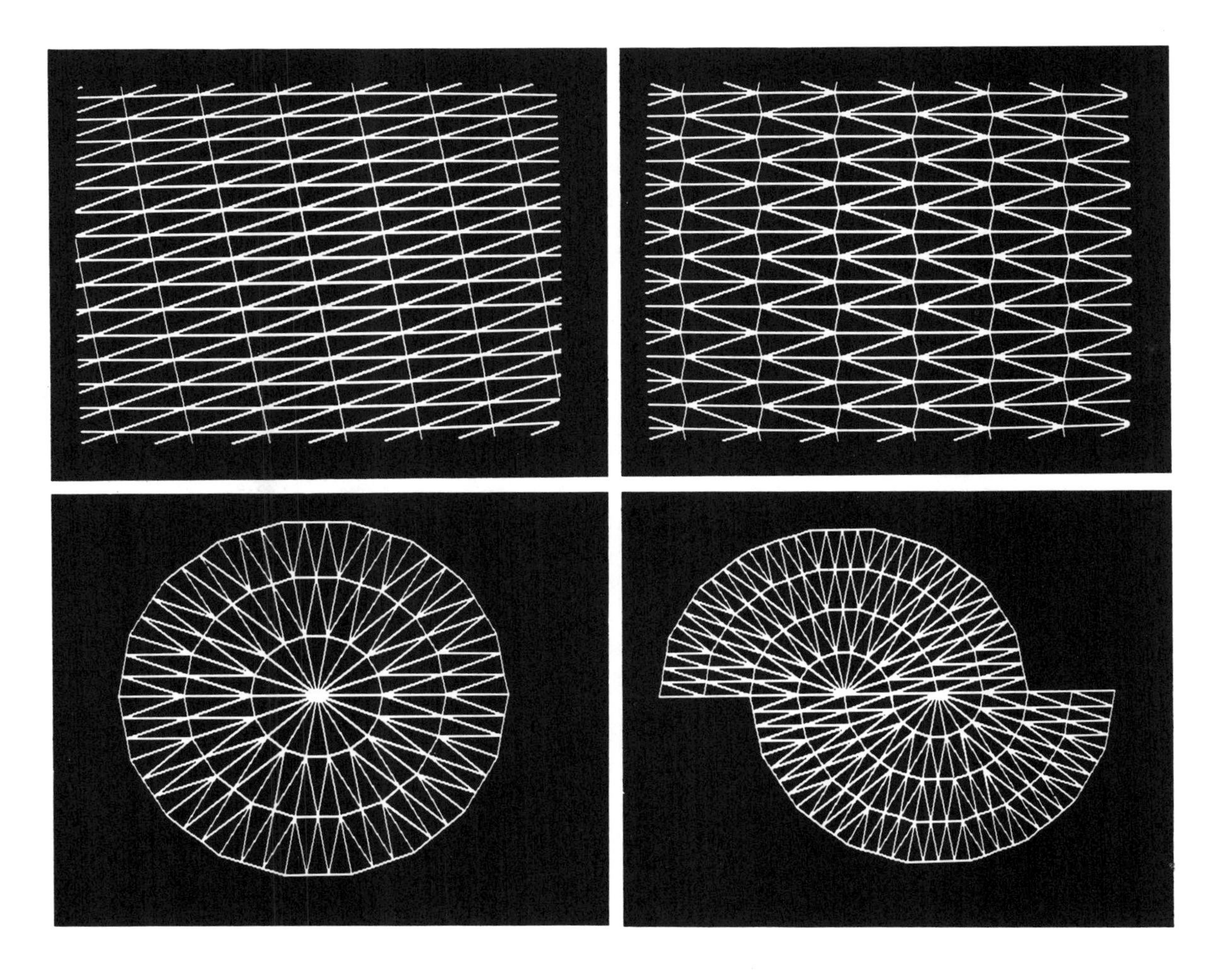

Figure 5.4
Two periodic and two non-periodic tilings of an isosceles triangle

periodic tilings using an isosceles triangle. (Although the circular and spiral patterns in Figure 5.4 are non-periodic, they are obviously highly regular.)

The photographs in Figure 5.4 could have been produced by picking and dragging (Program 5.1) or by inserting the triangle plotting instructions in simple loops with an appropriate rotation factor built in.

Reptiles

An interesting family of tiles, many of which give rise to non-periodic tilings, are the so-called 'reptiles'. These are tiles that can be grouped into larger replicas of themselves. These replicas can be grouped into still larger replicas, and so on.

Figure 5.5 shows how a simple right-angled 'triomino' can act as a reptile. The figure shows three generations of replication, together with an extension of this to a complete tessellation of the screen.

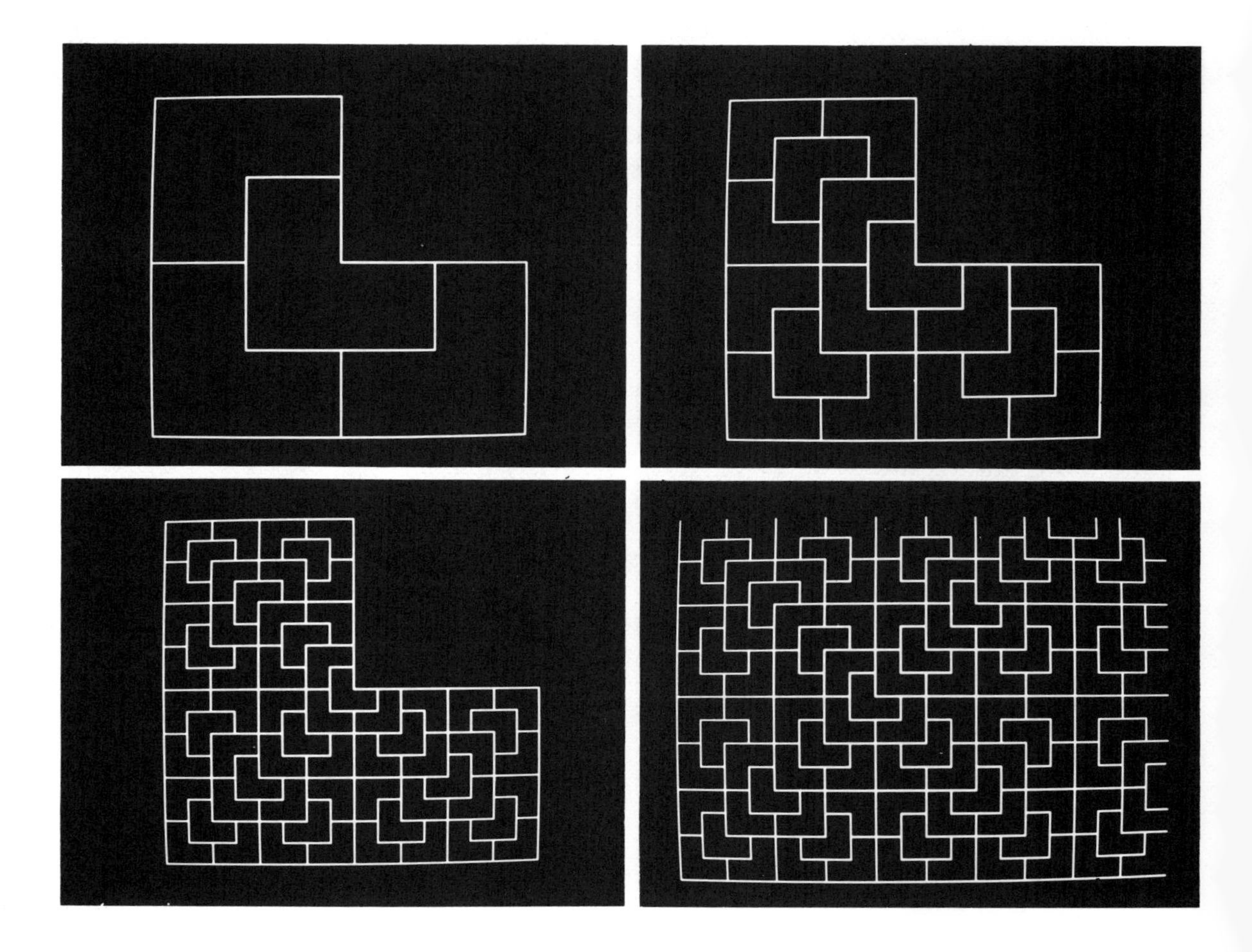

Figure 5.5
A triomino as a replicating tile or reptile (three generations) and a non-periodic tessellation of the screen

Another well-known reptile is the 'sphinx' illustrated in Figure 5.6.

A presentation of the programs used to generate these patterns is delayed until Chapter 6 where we discuss the use of recursion in computer graphics.

Tessellations with Penrose kites and darts

All known examples of single tiles that tessellate in a non-periodic fashion will also tessellate periodically. However, it is possible to construct sets of two or more tiles that tessellate only in a non-periodic fashion. Finding such sets of tiles is by no means an easy problem. Until a few years ago, it was believed that no such set existed.

By far the most interesting and entertaining tiles in this family are the pair of tiles known as the 'kite' and the 'dart'. These were first described by the renowned mathematician, Professor Roger

Figure 5.6
The sphinx tile as a reptile (three generations) and a non-periodic tessellation of the screen

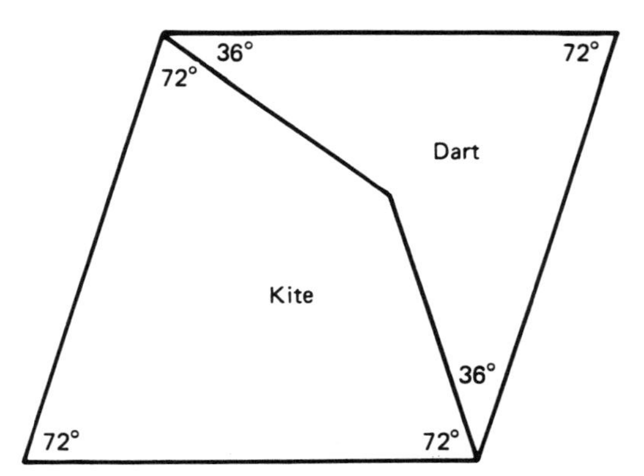

Figure 5.7
Decomposition of a rhombus into a Penrose kite and dart

Penrose. The two tiles are constructed by cutting a 'rhombus' in two as illustrated in Figure 5.7. If a kite and a dart were rejoined into a rhombus then that combination of the tiles easily gives rise to a periodic tessellation. However, we forbid this way of joining the tiles as well as any others that could give rise to a periodic tessellation. The rules are very simple. Permitted joins can be indicated by adding protuberances and matching holes on the pairs of edges that are allowed to meet (see the first two photographs in Figure 5.8). Alternatively, permitted joins can be indicated by labelling the corners of the tiles in such a way that only corners with the same label are allowed to meet (Figure 5.9a).

A rather more attractive method that has been suggested is to draw two coloured arcs on each tile, in two different colours. The arcs can be positioned such that, for each permitted joining of two tiles, two arcs of the same colour meet at the common edge (Figure 5.9b). In a tessellation where the tiles are marked in this way, these arcs join together to produce coloured circles and curves that add to the beauty of the pattern. (See the second pair of photographs in Figure 5.8 and Colour Plate 8.)

Tessellations using Penrose kites and darts have an amazing variety. In fact, it has been shown that the possible tile layouts are not only infinite but are uncountable ('more infinite' than the set of integers). A warning has been given by one writer that, because of this infinite variety, tiling with Penrose kites and darts is habit forming.

The tile design program of the last section can be used to experiment with Penrose patterns. All that is needed is to describe the shape of the kite and the dart in DATA statements. (The DATA statements needed appear as Program 5.5.) A simple extension allows the addition of coloured arcs. Perhaps the reason that the patterns are so pleasing to the eye is because the lengths of the long and short edges are in the 'golden ratio' (1.61803...) much used in classical painting and architecture.

An excellent description of Penrose kites and darts and some of their mathematics and 'folklore' appeared in Martin Gardner's column in *Scientific American (1977).*

5.3 TILE DEFORMATIONS AND THE WORLD OF ESCHER

A fascinating area for experimentation with tessellations is in the generation of unusual shapes that will tessellate. If the shapes resemble animals or birds, they can be decorated with lines to draw attention to this resemblance. Two simple shapes, a cat's head and a whale, are illustrated in Figure 5.10 (also Colour Plates 9 and 10).

We first examine programming techniques for generating unusual shapes that will tessellate and leave the problem of colouring and decorating the shapes until later.

Figure 5.8
Two ways of 'marking' kites and darts to force non-periodic tessellation. The two patterns used are the 'bow tie' and the 'sun': (a)(b) edges that can meet are marked with protruberances and matching dents; (c)(d) tiles are marked with curves that must meet in a tessellation

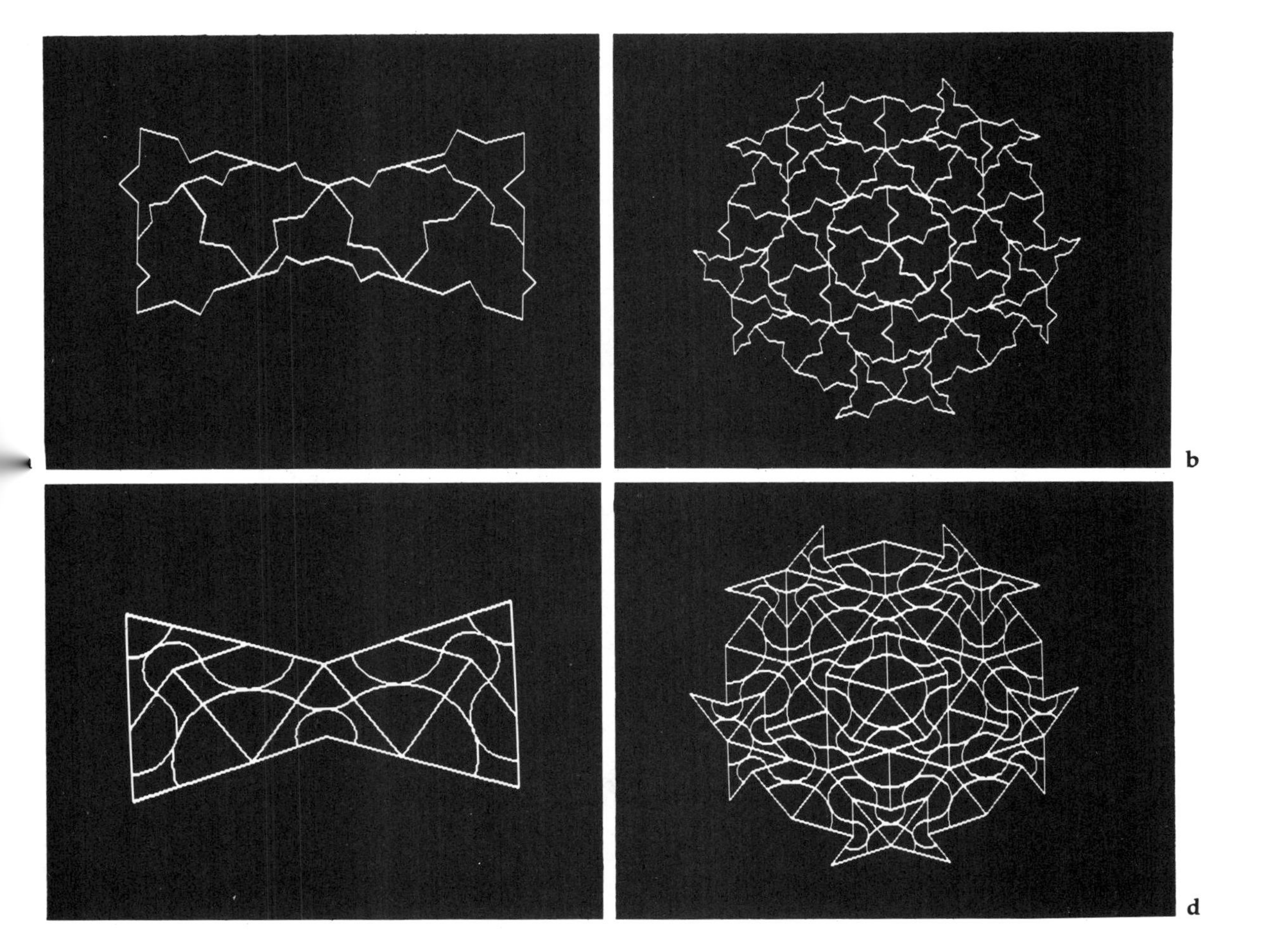

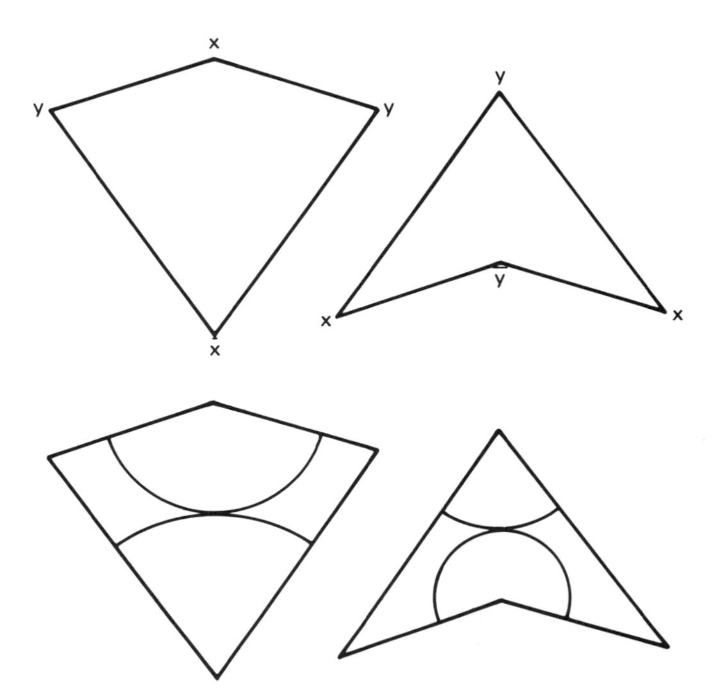

Figure 5.9
Marking Penrose tiles to force non-periodic tessellation: (a) corners labelled x must always meet other corners labelled x, corners labelled y must always meet corners labelled y; (b) curves must always meet in a tessellation

Deforming tile edges

Any shape or set of shapes that will tessellate can be deformed into a new set of shapes that will also tessellate. The basic process that we can use is to replace an edge in one of the shapes by two lines at an angle that connect the two end points of the original edge (Figure 5.11). Whenever this is done, a matching deformation must be carried out on any edge that could meet the deformed edge in a tessellation. We have illustrated this in Figure 5.12 by applying successive deformations to a square that tessellates by simple translation in the x and y directions. After a few deformations, the shape resembles a cat's head. A rather more elaborate sequence of deformations rather loosely based on an Escher drawing are illustrated in Figure 5.13.

```
5000 DATA 2,KD
5010 DATA 4,5,-64,16.823396, 64,-88.0884429, 64,88.0884429,
          -64,20.7948606, -64,-20.7948606
5020 DATA 4,5,-64,-27.220826, 64,20.7948606, 64,-20.7948606,
          -64,88.0884429, -64,-88.0884429
```

Program 5.5 DATA for the Penrose kite and dart.

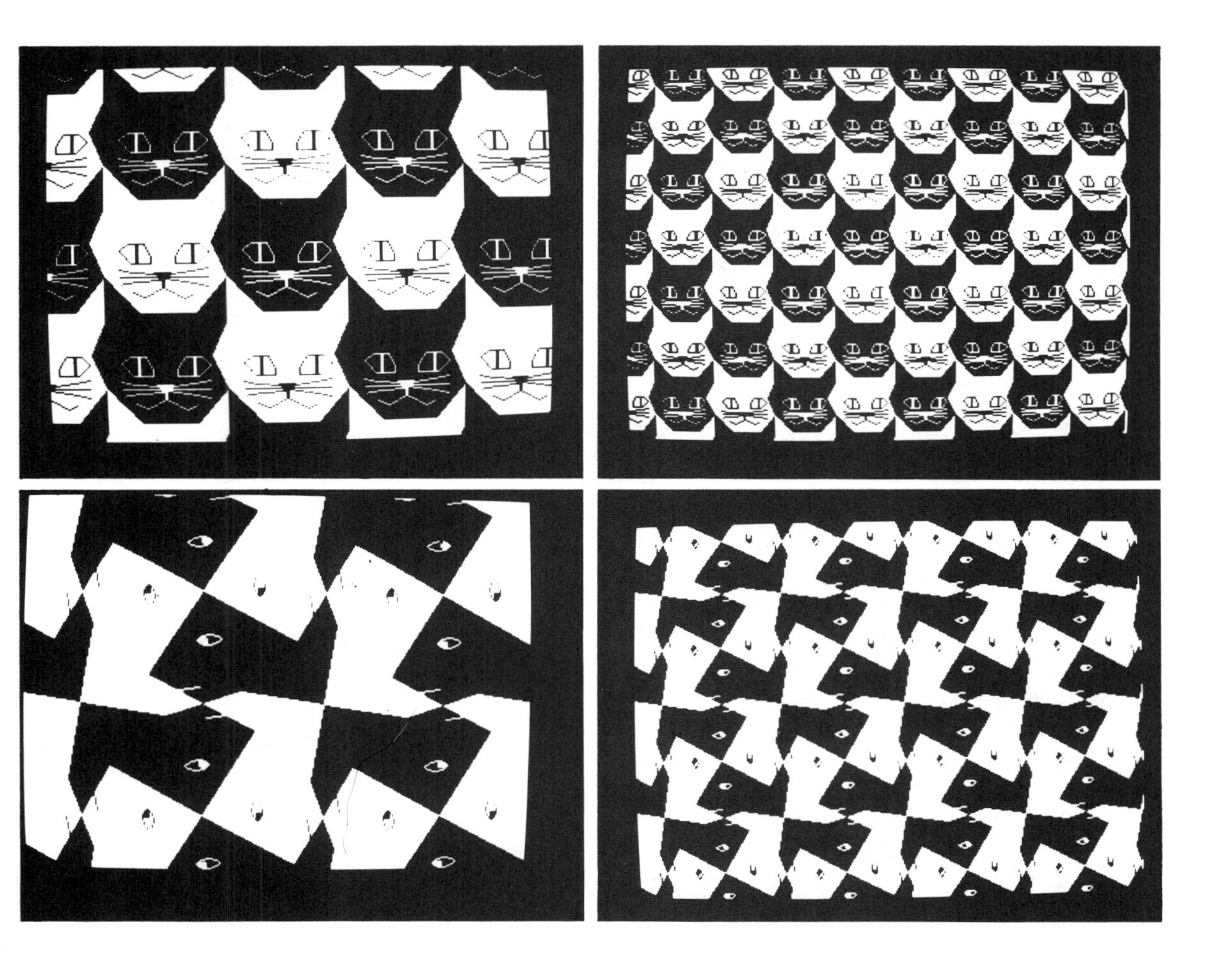

Figure 5.10
Two simple Escher-like tessellations

A simple tile deformation program

In this section, we present an introductory program (Program 5.6) that can be used to experiment with simple tile deformations of the type that we have just described. We limit ourselves here to a single shape that can be tiled by translating it in the x and y directions, like the square that was used in the last section.

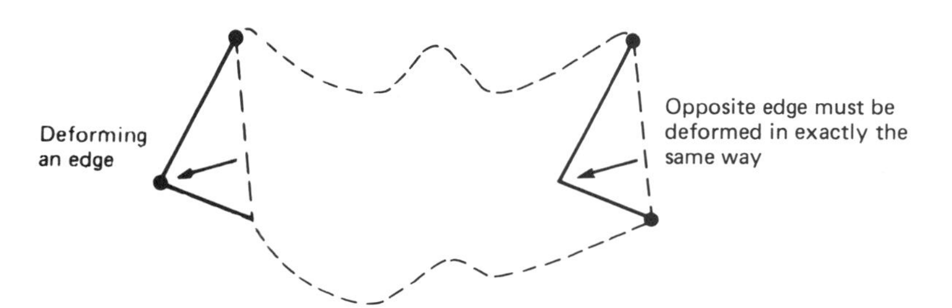
Deforming
an edge
Opposite edge must be
deformed in exactly the
same way

Figure 5.11
Deforming two matching edges

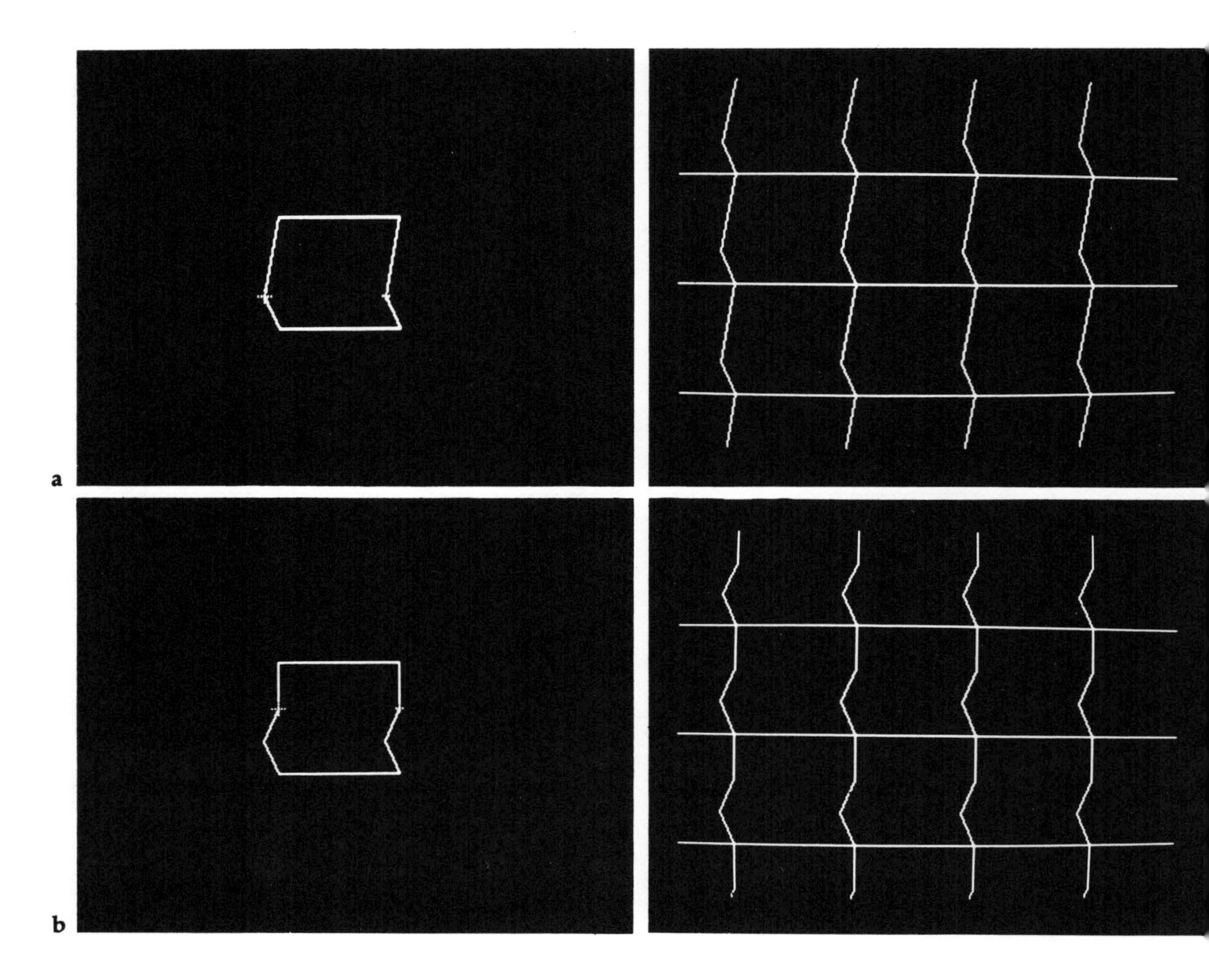

Figure 5.12
Stages in constructing a cat's head tessellation

The structure of the initial shape and details of the translations needed to tessellate it are contained in DATA statements at the end of the program. Before we can present a detailed explanation of the significance of all the values in these DATA statements, we must first look in some detail at the operation of the program.

When deforming a shape, the program uses techniques similar to those used in the drawing programs of Chapter 2. The shape to be deformed is displayed on the screen and a cross marks a point on the circumference of the shape. We will call this point the 'current point'. The user can move the cross round the circumference of the shape, either clockwise or anticlockwise under keyboard control. (We shall use the key 'c' for clockwise movement and 'a' for anticlockwise movement.) In addition to the main cross moved by the user, there is a smaller cross that marks the opposite point. This opposite point will meet copies of the current point when the shape tessellates.

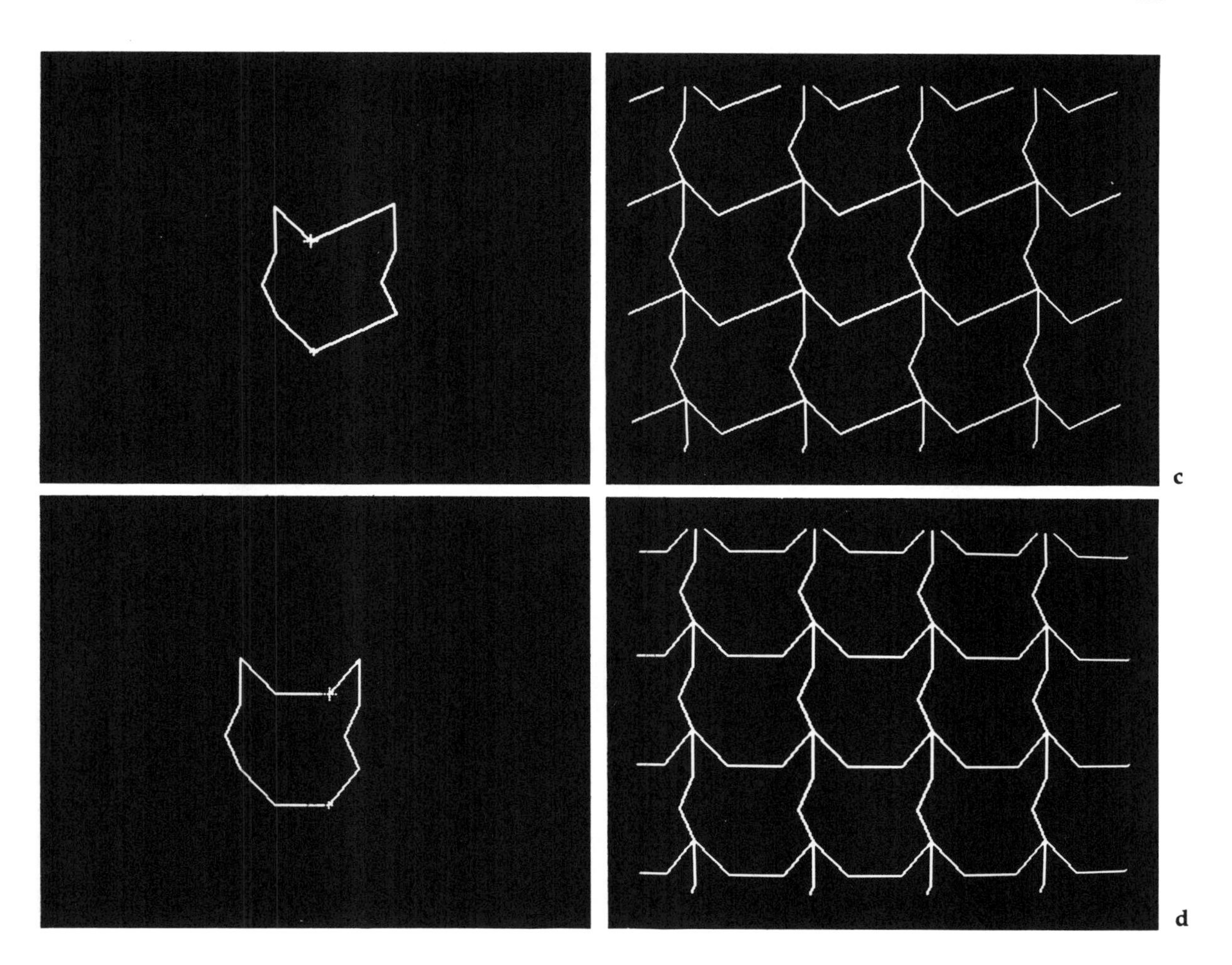

At any stage, the user can opt to deform the tile at the current point (using the key 'd'). When the user indicates that he or she wishes to deform the shape at a point on an edge, a new vertex is created and the program switches to 'deformation mode'. The large cursor now marks the desired position for the new vertex and it can be moved around the screen by using the cursor arrows. While this is happening, the program will automatically create another new vertex, and will move the small cursor in exactly the same way. Thus, if the new vertices are fixed at the cursor positions, the shape's tessellation properties are maintained.

When the large cursor is in the position required, the user can fix the vertex at this position (using the key 'f') and the program automatically fixes the opposite vertex.

The user can also opt to deform from a previously created vertex. The large cursor is dragged to the new position for the vertex and the small cursor moves to match.

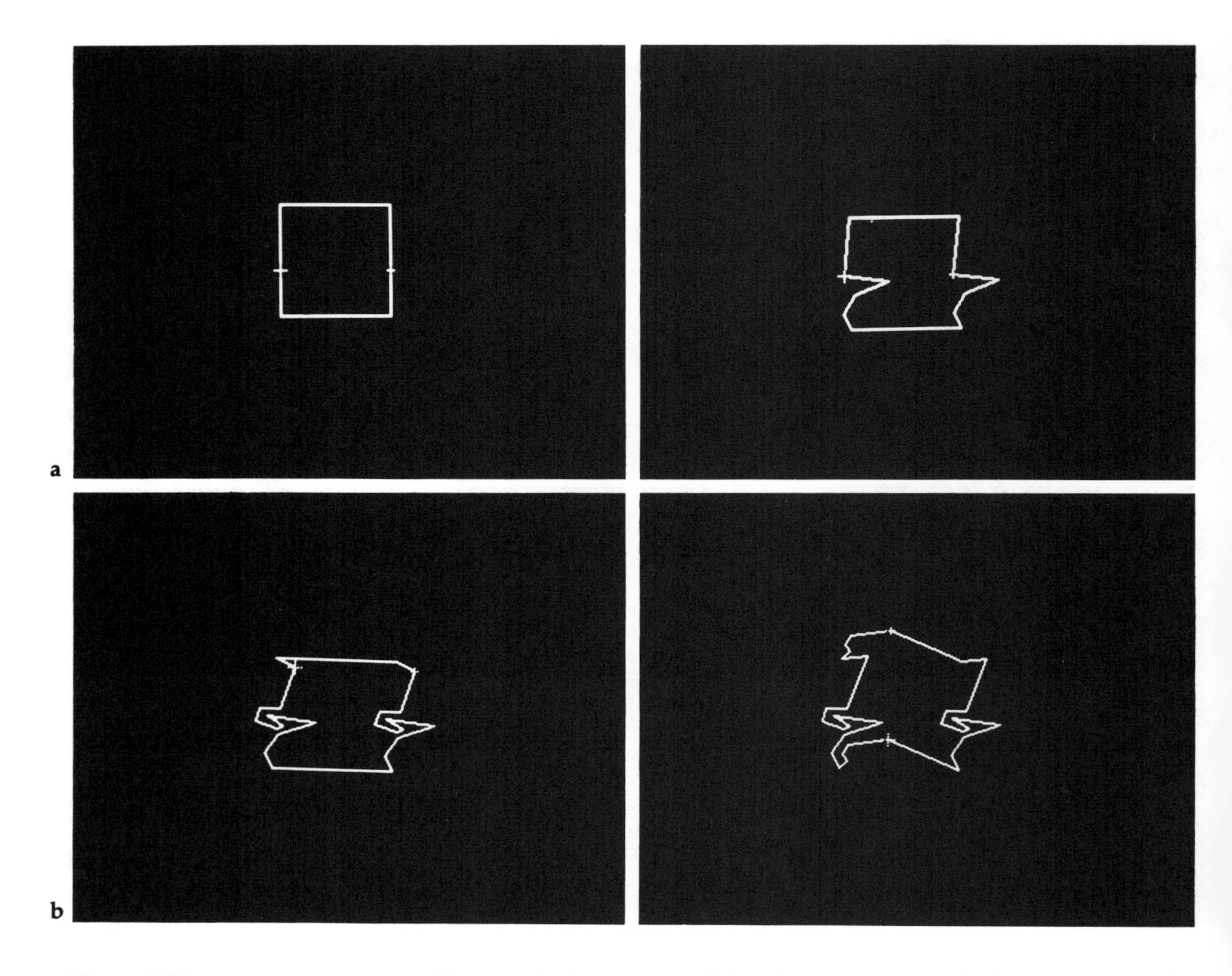

Figure 5.13
Stages in constructing a flying horse tessellation

The original vertices of the shape are regarded as permanently fixed and the shape cannot be deformed by dragging these vertices. This is because the original vertices are usually points where copies of more than two vertices of the original shape meet in a tiling of the plane. In the case of the square, copies of four different corners of our initial square meet at each vertex in a complete tessellation.

Another option available to the user while in the main command mode (that is, when the program is not in deformation mode) is to request a tessellation of the screen so as to see how the shape looks in this context. (The key 't' for tessellate is used.) When this is done, the program requests a scale factor to be used in drawing the shapes during the tiling process. This enables tilings to be tried with large or small copies of the basic shape.

Program operation

The main command loop of Program 5.6 repeatedly calls the

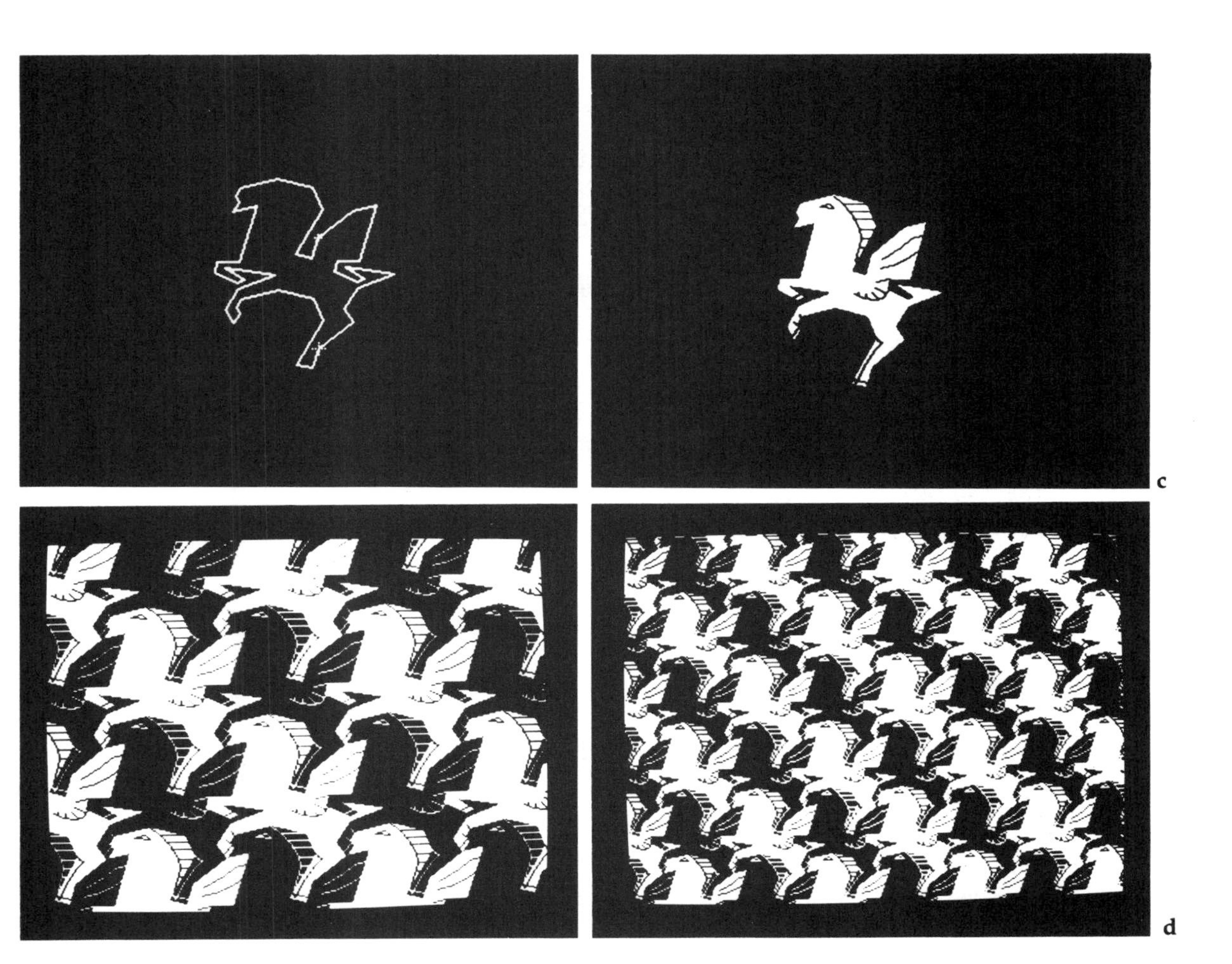
c

d

subroutine 'command'. The variable 'COMMS$' contains a string that is a list of the command keys permitted in the current state of the program. Any key pressed that is not in this list is ignored.

An understanding of the workings of the various subroutines called by 'command' requires an explanation of the data structure used to represent the shape being manipulated by the program.

Information about the vertices of the shape is stored in a set of parallel arrays (Figure 5.14). Similarly, information about lines is stored in another set of parallel arrays (Figure 5.15).

Each vertex is represented by a set of five values stored in corresponding locations in the five vertex arrays. The first two values for a vertex are its x and y coordinates. Coordinates are expressed relative to the bottom left hand corner of the shape. The next two entries for a vertex provide connectivity information. They contain 'pointers' to the 'previous' line (anticlockwise round the boundary of the shape) and to the 'next' line (clockwise round the boundary).

```
  5 KEY OFF
 10 VMAX = 150 : TRUE = -1 : FALSE = 0
 20 DIM BIGCURSOR(144),LITTLECURSOR(41)
 30 DIM X(VMAX),Y(VMAX),PREVL(VMAX),NEXTL(VMAX),CORRV(VMAX)
 40 DIM PREVV(VMAX),NEXTV(VMAX),CORRL(VMAX)
 50 SCREEN 2 : CLS : WINDOW (0,0)-(1279,799)
 60 XSTEP = 4 : YSTEP = 4
 70 GOSUB 140  'initialise
 80 COMMAND$ = INKEY$ : IF COMMAND$ = "" THEN 80
 90 WHILE COMMAND$ <> "q"
100   GOSUB 560  'command
110   COMMAND$ = INKEY$
120 WEND
130 END

140 'SUBROUTINE initialise
150   LINE (40,40)-(71,40),,,&HCCCC
160   LINE (56,24)-(56,55),,,&HAAAA
170   GET (40,24)-(71,55),BIGCURSOR
180   GET (48,32)-(63,47),LITTLECURSOR
190   CLS
200   VP = -1 : LP = -1
210   START = VP+1
220   READ LASTVERTEX,XSTART,YSTART
230   FOR INITV = 0 TO LASTVERTEX
240     VP = VP+1 : LP = LP+1
250     READ X(VP),Y(VP),PREVL(VP),NEXTL(VP),CORRV(VP)
260     READ PREVV(LP),NEXTV(LP),CORRL(LP)
270   NEXT INITV
280   READ YGRIDINC,XSHIFT,XGRIDINC,YSHIFT
290   GOSUB 340  'start planning
300   LLEFT$ = "K" : RRIGHT$ = "M"
310   UP$ = "H" : DOWN$ = "P"
320   DCOMMS$ = LLEFT$+RRIGHT$+UP$+DOWN$+"f"
330 RETURN

340 'SUBROUTINE start planning
350   ATVERTEX = TRUE : VERTEX = START
360   COMMS$ = "qtpcad"
370   GOSUB 430  'draw planning shape
380   PX = X(VERTEX) : PY = Y(VERTEX)
390   CPX = X(NEXTV(CORRL(NEXTL(VERTEX))))
400   CPY = Y(NEXTV(CORRL(NEXTL(VERTEX))))
410   GOSUB 1190  'cursors
420 RETURN

430 'SUBROUTINE draw planning shape
440   CLS
450   WINDOW (-XSTART,-YSTART)-(1279-XSTART,799-YSTART)
460   SX = 0 : SY = 0 : SCALE = 1 : GOSUB 480  'draw shape
470 RETURN
```

Program 5.6 Program that generates unusual shapes that tessellate.

```
480 'SUBROUTINE draw shape
490   LDV = START
500   PSET (SX,SY)
510   FOR LDVCOUNT = 0 TO LASTVERTEX
520     LDV = NEXTV(NEXTL(LDV))
530     LINE -(SX+X(LDV)*SCALE,SY+Y(LDV)*SCALE)
540   NEXT LDVCOUNT
550 RETURN

560 'SUBROUTINE command
570   IF COMMAND$ = "" THEN RETURN
580   IF LEN(COMMAND$) = 2 THEN COMMAND$ = RIGHT$(COMMAND$,1)
590   IF INSTR(COMMS$,COMMAND$) = 0 THEN BEEP : RETURN
600   IF COMMAND$ = "t" THEN GOSUB 660  'tessellate
610   IF COMMAND$ = "p" THEN GOSUB 340  'start planning
620   IF COMMAND$ = "c" THEN GOSUB 880  'clockwise
630   IF COMMAND$ = "a" THEN GOSUB 920  'anticlockwise
640   IF COMMAND$ = "d" THEN GOSUB 1230  'deform
650 RETURN

660 'SUBROUTINE tessellate
670   CLS : INPUT "Scale factor ";SCALE
680   CLS : WINDOW (0,0)-(1279,799)
690   PLANNING = FALSE
700   LEFTX = -SCALE*XGRIDINC/2
710   STOPX = 1279+SCALE*XGRIDINC/2
720   BOTY = -SCALE*YGRIDINC/2
730   STOPY = 799+SCALE*YGRIDINC/2
740   WHILE BOTY <= STOPY AND KEYS$ <> " "
750     SX = LEFTX : SY = BOTY
760     WHILE SX <= STOPX AND KEYS$ <> " "
770       GOSUB 480  'draw shape
780       SX = SX+SCALE*XGRIDINC
790       SY = SY+SCALE*YSHIFT
800       KEYS$ = INKEY$
810     WEND
820     BOTY = BOTY+SCALE*YGRIDINC
830     LEFTX = LEFTX+SCALE*XSHIFT
840     IF LEFTX > 0 THEN LEFTX = LEFTX-SCALE*XGRIDINC :
                          BOTY = BOTY-SCALE*YSHIFT
850   WEND
860   COMMS$ = "srtpq"
870 RETURN

880 'SUBROUTINE clockwise
890   IF ATVERTEX THEN LINEON = NEXTL(VERTEX) : GOSUB 960 : LINESTEP = 0
900   DIR = 1 : GOSUB 1090  'move along
910 RETURN

920 'SUBROUTINE anticlockwise
```

continued

```
930   IF ATVERTEX THEN LINEON = PREVL(VERTEX) :
                GOSUB 960 : LINESTEP = STEPSONLINE
940   DIR = -1 : GOSUB 1090  'move along
950 RETURN

960 'SUBROUTINE move on to line
970   CLINE = CORRL(LINEON)
980   LINESTART = PREVV(LINEON) : LINEFINISH = NEXTV(LINEON)
990   CORRLS = NEXTV(CLINE) : CORRLF = PREVV(CLINE)
1000  XDIFF = X(LINEFINISH)-X(LINESTART)
1010  YDIFF = Y(LINEFINISH)-Y(LINESTART)
1020  XSTEPS = ABS(XDIFF)\XSTEP
1030  YSTEPS = ABS(YDIFF)\YSTEP
1040  IF XSTEPS > YSTEPS THEN STEPSONLINE = XSTEPS+1
                         ELSE STEPSONLINE = YSTEPS+1
1050  XINC = XDIFF/STEPSONLINE
1060  YINC = YDIFF/STEPSONLINE
1070  ATVERTEX = FALSE
1080 RETURN

1090 'SUBROUTINE move along
1100  LINESTEP = LINESTEP+DIR
1110  IF LINESTEP <= 0 THEN LINESTEP = 0 : ATVERTEX = TRUE : VERTEX = LINESTART
                     ELSE IF LINESTEP >= STEPSONLINE
                     THEN LINESTEP = STEPSONLINE :
                     ATVERTEX = TRUE : VERTEX = LINEFINISH
1120  GOSUB 1190  'cursors
1130  PX = X(LINESTART)+LINESTEP*XINC
1140  PY = Y(LINESTART)+LINESTEP*YINC
1150  CPX = X(CORRLS)+LINESTEP*XINC
1160  CPY = Y(CORRLS)+LINESTEP*YINC
1170  GOSUB 1190  'cursors
1180 RETURN

1190 'SUBROUTINE cursors
1200  PUT (PX-16,PY-16),BIGCURSOR
      'On the PCjr, use PUT (PX-16,PY+16),BIGCURSOR
1210  PUT (CPX-8,CPY-8),LITTLECURSOR
      'On the PCjr, use PUT (CPX-8,CPY+8),LITTLECURSOR
1220 RETURN

1230 'SUBROUTINE deform
1240  NEWVERTEX = NOT(ATVERTEX)
1250  IF NEWVERTEX THEN GOSUB 1430
                ELSE IF CORRV(VERTEX) = 255 THEN BEEP : RETURN
1260  V0 = PREVV(PREVL(VERTEX)) : V1 = NEXTV(NEXTL(VERTEX))
1270  X0 = X(V0) : Y0 = Y(V0) : X1 = X(V1) : Y1 = Y(V1)
1280  CV0 = NEXTV(NEXTL(CORRV(VERTEX)))
1290  CV1 = PREVV(PREVL(CORRV(VERTEX)))
1300  CX0 = X(CV0) : CY0 = Y(CV0) : CX1 = X(CV1) : CY1 = Y(CV1)
1310  IF NOT(NEWVERTEX) THEN GOSUB 1610  'delete lines
```

Program 5.6 *continued*

```
1320   COMMAND$ = INKEY$ : IF COMMAND$ = "" THEN 1320
1330   WHILE COMMAND$ <> "f"
1340     GOSUB 1670  'dcomm
1350     COMMAND$ = INKEY$
1360   WEND
1370   GOSUB 1190  'cursors
1380   GOSUB 1800  'draw
1390   GOSUB 1190  'cursors
1400   X(VERTEX) = PX : Y(VERTEX) = PY
1410   X(CORRV(VERTEX)) = CPX : Y(CORRV(VERTEX)) = CPY
1420 RETURN

1430 'SUBROUTINE breakline
1440   NX = PX : NY = PY : NBROKLINE = LINEON : NCV = VP+2 : NCL = LP+2
1450   GOSUB 1510  'new
1460   NX = CPX : NY = CPY : NBROKLINE = CLINE : NCV = VP : NCL = LP
1470   GOSUB 1510  'new
1480   LASTVERTEX = LASTVERTEX+2
1490   ATVERTEX = TRUE : VERTEX = VP-1
1500 RETURN

1510 'SUBROUTINE new
1520   VP = VP+1 : LP = LP+1
1530   X(VP) = NX : Y(VP) = NY
1540   NEXTL(VP) = LP : PREVL(VP) = NBROKLINE
1550   NEXTV(LP) = NEXTV(NBROKLINE) : PREVV(LP) = VP
1560   PREVL(NEXTV(LP)) = LP
1570   NEXTV(NBROKLINE) = VP
1580   CORRV(VP) = NCV
1590   CORRL(LP) = CORRL(NBROKLINE) : CORRL(NBROKLINE) = NCL
1600 RETURN

1610 'SUBROUTINE delete lines
1620   GOSUB 1190  'cursors
1630   LINE (X0,Y0)-(PX,PY),0 : LINE -(X1,Y1),0
1640   LINE (CX0,CY0)-(CPX,CPY),0 : LINE -(CX1,CY1),0
1650   GOSUB 1190  'cursors
1660 RETURN

1670 'SUBROUTINE dcomm
1680   IF COMMAND$ = "" THEN RETURN
1690   IF LEN(COMMAND$) = 2 THEN COMMAND$ = RIGHT$(COMMAND$,1)
1700   IF INSTR(DCOMMS$,COMMAND$) = 0 THEN BEEP : RETURN
1710   IF COMMAND$ = LLEFT$ THEN XDIR = -XSTEP : YDIR = 0
1720   IF COMMAND$ = RRIGHT$ THEN XDIR = XSTEP : YDIR = 0
1730   IF COMMAND$ = UP$ THEN XDIR = 0 : YDIR = YSTEP
1740   IF COMMAND$ = DOWN$ THEN XDIR = 0 : YDIR = -YSTEP
1750   GOSUB 1190  'cursors
1760   PX = PX+XDIR : PY = PY+YDIR
1770   CPX = CPX+XDIR : CPY = CPY+YDIR
1780   GOSUB 1190  'cursors
1790 RETURN
```

continued

```
1800 'SUBROUTINE draw
1810   LINE (X0,Y0)-(X1,Y1),0
1820   LINE -(PX,PY),1 : LINE -(X0,Y0),1
1830   LINE (CX0,CY0)-(CX1,CY1),0
1840   LINE -(CPX,CPY),1 : LINE -(CX0,CY0),1
1850 RETURN

5000 DATA 3,450,350
5010 DATA 0,0,3,0,255, 0,1,2,  0,300,0,1,255, 1,2,3,
          300,300,1,2,255, 2,3,0,  300,0,2,3,255, 3,0,1
5020 DATA 300,0,300,0
```

Program 5.6 *continued*

A 'pointer' to a line is simply the subscript of the set of locations in the line arrays that contain information about the line. The final piece of information for a vertex is a pointer to another vertex that will meet the first vertex in a tessellation. A 'pointer' is again just a subscript for a set of locations in the vertex arrays.

The last piece of information is needed if the user attempts to deform the shape at this vertex. The program must carry out a similar deformation at the corresponding vertex. Deformation is not allowed at the original vertices of the initial shape and this is indicated by giving them a 'corresponding vertex value' of 255.

The information stored for a line is similar. There is a pointer to the 'previous' vertex (anticlockwise), a pointer to the 'next' vertex (clockwise) and a pointer to the 'corresponding line' that will be adjacent to the first line in a tessellation. Thus the connectivity between vertices and lines on the screen is reflected as a set of pointers in the data structure.

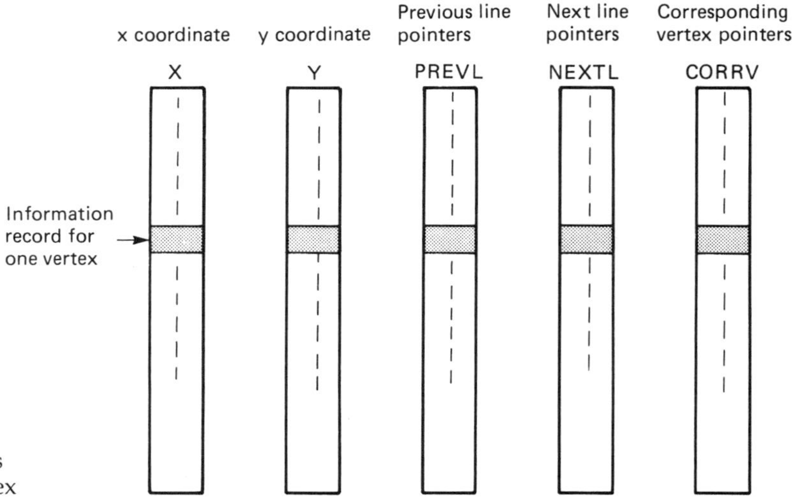

Figure 5.14
The vertex arrays: a set of matching locations contains information about one vertex

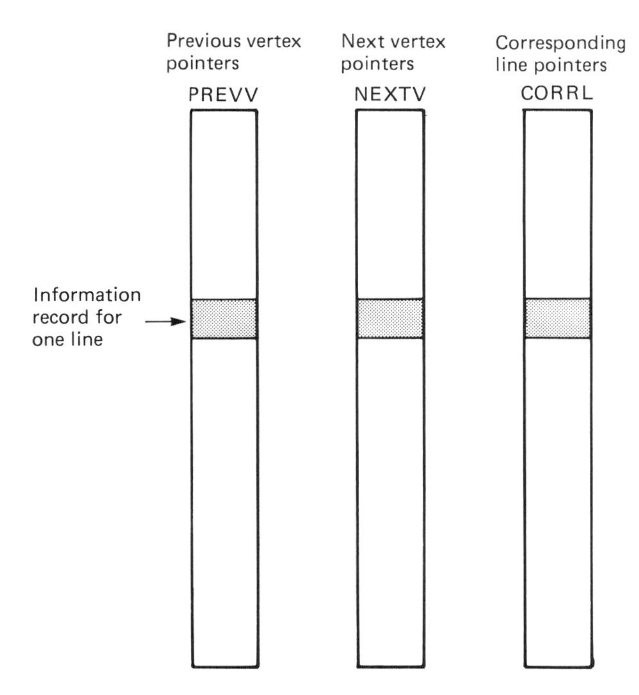

Figure 5.15
The line arrays: a set of matching locations contains information about one line

We can think of a slice across the vertex arrays as a 'record' containing information about a vertex. Similarly, a slice across the line arrays is a record containing information about a line. Figure 5.16 is an illustration of the data structure representation of the initial square from which the cat's head and the horse tessellations were developed.

A number of variables are used to indicate the position of the current point on the perimeter of the shape being planned. The coordinates of the current point are stored as (PX,PY) and the coordinates of the corresponding point are stored as (CPX,CPY).

The value of the variable 'ATVERTEX' is set to TRUE if the cross marking the current point is at a vertex of the shape. This variable is set to FALSE if the cross is somewhere on a line between two vertices.

If the current point is at a vertex, then the variable 'VERTEX' contains a pointer (or subscript) to the locations in the vertex arrays that contain information about the current point.

If the current point is part way along a line, then the variable 'LINEON' contains a pointer to the locations in the line arrays that contain information about the line. It is convenient to have another variable 'CLINE' that contains a pointer to the line corresponding to the first line.

When the current point is on a line, 'XINC' and 'YINC' are the increments for x and y needed to move one step along the line in a

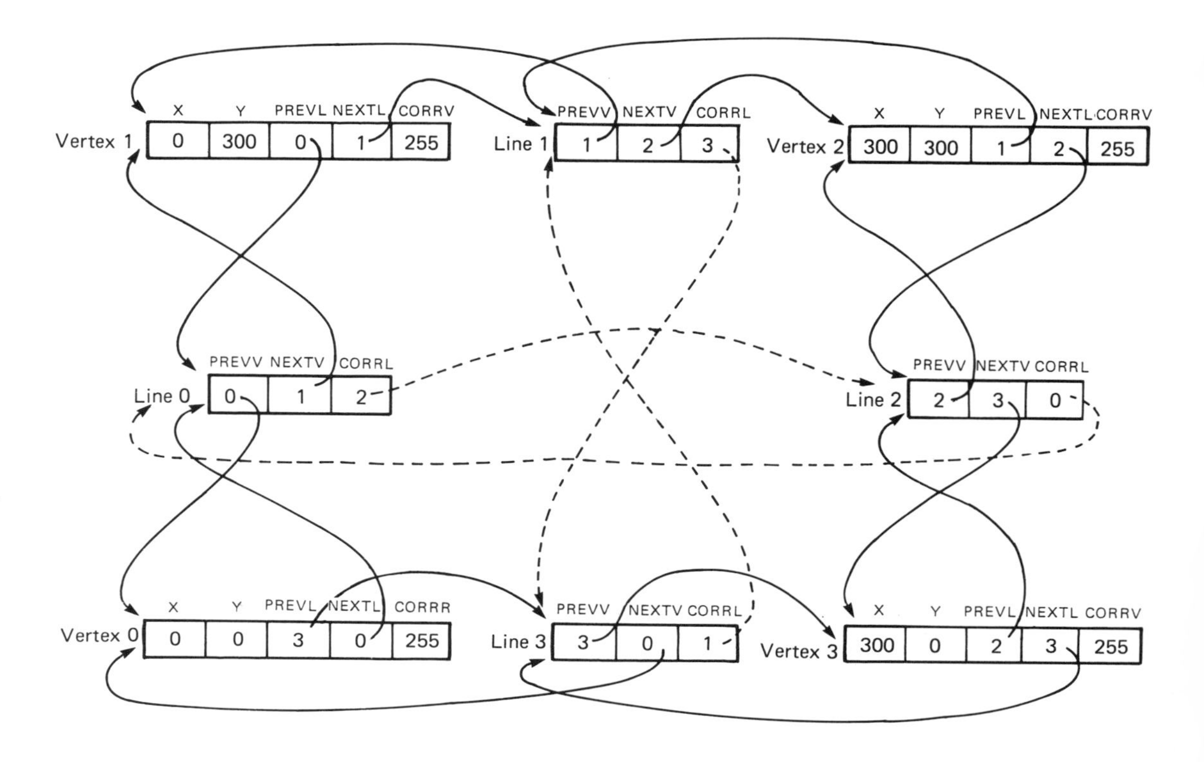

Figure 5.16
Record and pointer structure for an initial square: each record is a slice through either the vertex arrays or the line arrays

clockwise direction. These values depend on the length and orientation of the current line. Values are chosen that make movement take place in steps of approximately one pixel. The position of the current point on the current line is indicated by the value of the variable 'LINESTEP'. This contains a count of the number of steps from the start of the current line to the current point.

The two variables 'LINESTART' and 'LINEFINISH' are pointers to the vertices at either end of the current line, and 'CORRLS' and 'CORRLF' are pointers to the vertices at either end of the corresponding line. Note that when two shapes meet on a line in a tessellation, the direction along the line that represents clockwise movement round one of the shapes always represents anticlockwise movement round the other shape. Thus 'LINESTART' is set to the 'previous' vertex of the current line, but 'CORRLS' is set to the 'next' vertex of the corresponding line. Similarly, 'LINEFINISH' is set to the 'next' vertex of the current line, but 'CORRLF' is set to the 'previous' vertex of the corresponding line.

Let us now examine how these data structures and variables are used by the procedures that implement clockwise and anticlockwise movement around the boundary of the shape (subroutines 'clockwise' and 'anticlockwise'). Each of these subroutines takes one step around the circumference of the shape.

'clockwise' first tests to see whether the current point is at a vertex. If it is, the variable 'LINEON' is set to the next line round from the vertex and the subroutine 'move on to line' is called to set all the relevant variables to appropriate values for that line. A value of zero is then given to 'LINESTEP' to indicate that we are at the start of the line. Whether or not the current point was previously at a vertex, it is now on a line and subroutine 'move along' is called to move the current point one step along the line. 'move along' adjusts the variables appropriately and ensures that movement does not proceed beyond the end points of the line.

The structure of subroutine 'anticlockwise' is similar to the structure of 'clockwise'.

We now consider the details of the process used to deform the outline of the tile. If the deform command is issued when the current point is at a vertex from which deformation is permitted, then no new data structure entries are needed. If the deform command is issued when the current point is part way along a line, then the line must be broken and data structure entries for a new vertex and a new line must be created. The corresponding line must be broken in the same way. When necessary, a call of subroutine 'breakline' creates the new entries in the data structure.

We can now explain the significance of the various values that need to be supplied to the program in DATA statements.

The first value supplied is the number of the last vertex in the initial shape. The corners in the initial shape are numbered from 0 upwards. In Program 5.6, we included the DATA statements for the square used to generate the cat's head and the horse. Here, the number of the last vertex is 3. The next two values indicate where on the screen the shape should be placed in planning mode.

There follows a sequence of values grouped in fives and threes. The first five values are the entries for the vertex array locations that will represent the first vertex (vertex 0). The next three values are the entries for the line array locations that represent the first line (line 0). The next five values represent the next vertex, the next three values represent the next line and so on.

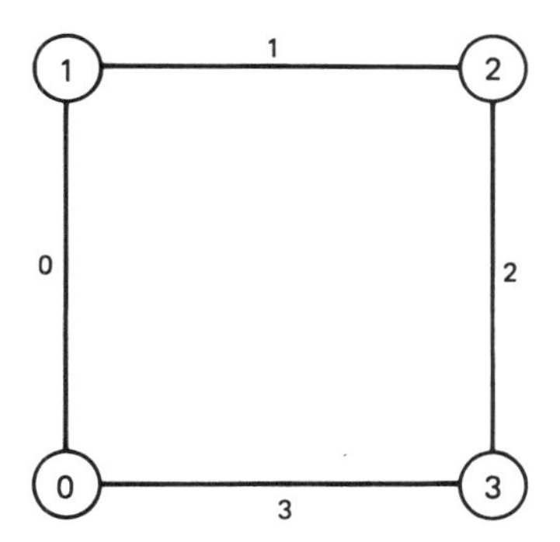

Figure 5.17
Vertex and line numbering system used for the simple square

```
5000 DATA 3,250,350
5010 DATA 0,0,3,0,255, 0,1,2, 200,300,0,1,255, 1,2,3,
          800,300,1,2,255, 2,3,0, 600,0,2,3,255, 3,0,1
5020 DATA 300,200,600,0
```

Program 5.7 DATA for using Program 5.6 to deform a parallelogram.

The vertex and line numbering system used for the square is illustrated in Figure 5.17. Thus the data for the first vertex (vertex number 0) consists of its *x* and *y* coordinates (0,0), the numbers of the previous line and the next line (3,0) and a 'corresponding vertex value' of 255 to indicate that this is a fixed vertex. The three values for the first line (line 0) are the numbers of the previous vertex and the next vertex (0,1) together with the number of the corresponding line (2). The structure created in the vertex and line arrays as a result of this DATA was illustrated in Figure 5.16.

After the vertex and line data, we have four values that are used to describe the layout of the tessellation in which the shape will be used. The first two values are the *y*-grid increment and an associated '*x*-shift' and the next two values are the *x*-grid increment and an associated '*y*-shift'. In the case of the square for which the data appeared in Program 5.6, the *x*-shift and *y*-shift are set to zero and the tessellation is obtained by using simple increments in the *x* and *y* directions. However, to see the need for the *x*-shift value, consider the problem of using a parallelogram as the starting shape. Data for such a shape appears in Program 5.7. The structure of the shape is exactly the same as the previous square and the only difference in the vertex and line information is in the coordinates of the vertices. However, when a step is taken from one row of the tessellation to the next, not only must *y* be increased, but *x* must also be increased

Figure 5.18
Translation increments for a parallelogram

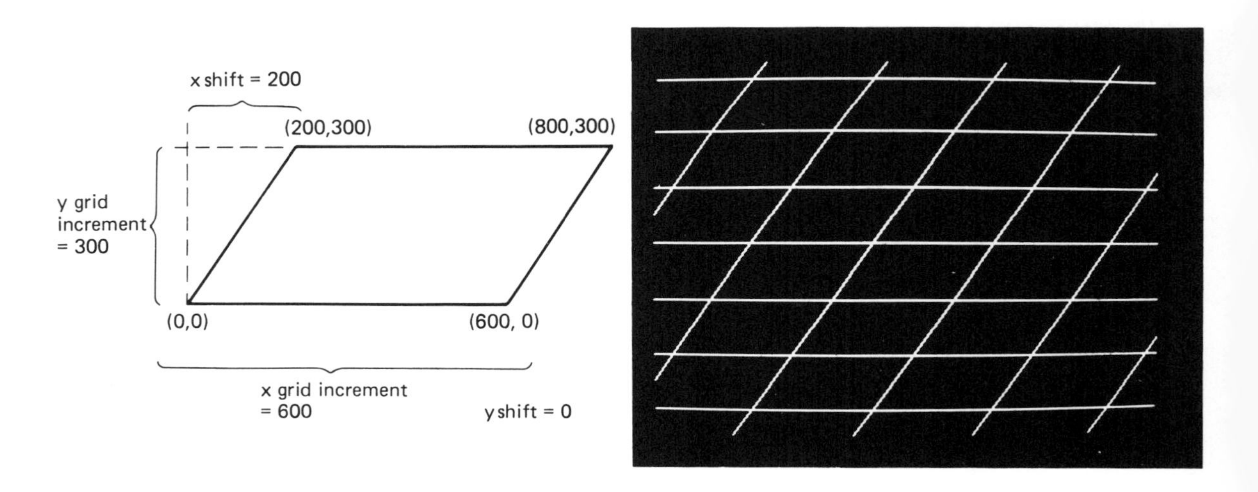

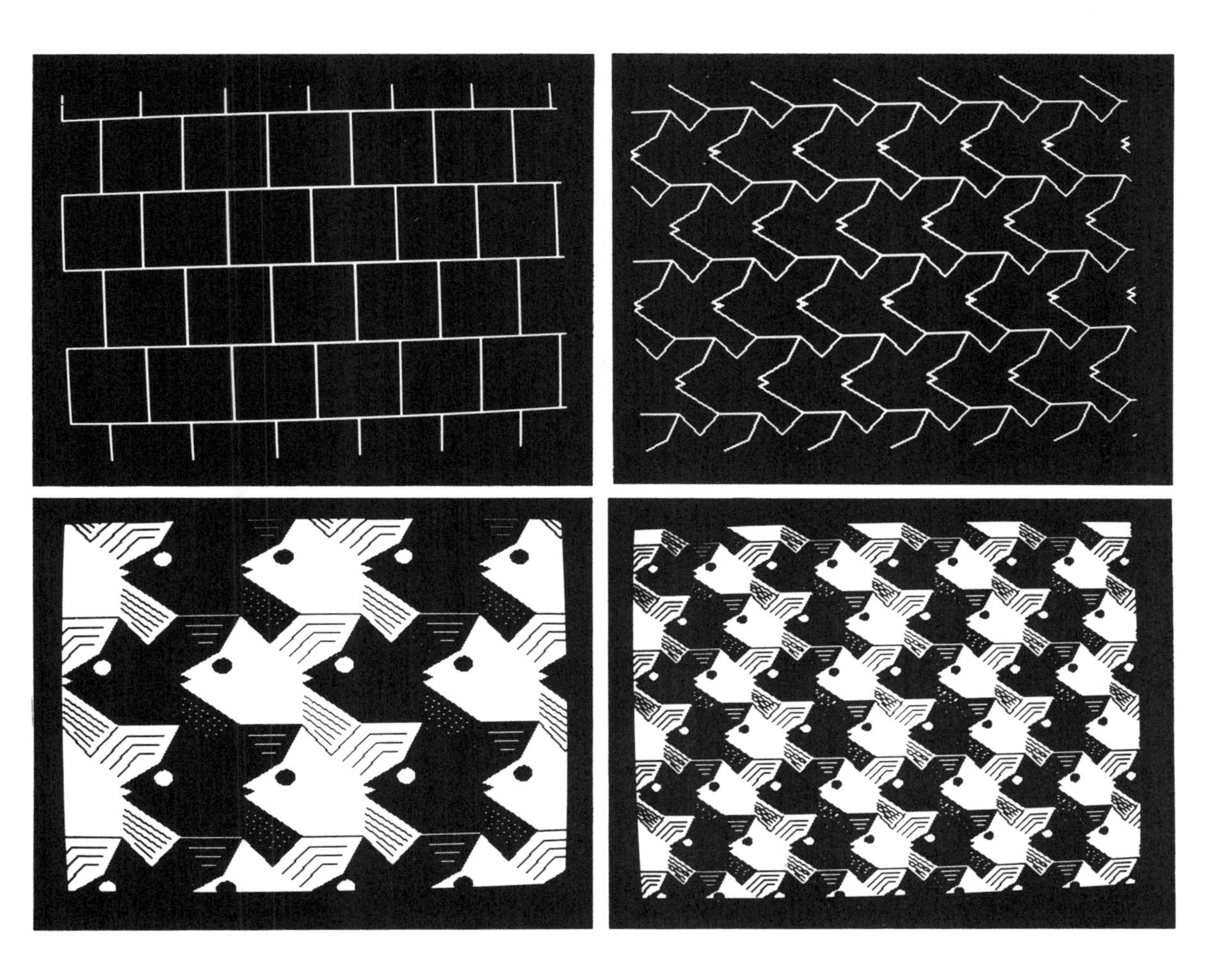

Figure 5.19
A 'flying fish' tessellation generated from the initial square pattern shown

to compensate for the fact that the parallelogram leans to the right (Figure 5.18).

As another example of our initialising DATA statements, we can give the square a rather more elaborate structure in preparation for the generation of the 'flying fish' tessellation illustrated in Figure 5.19. The first picture in Figure 5.19 illustrates the initial layout that we require. Here, the top edge of a square does not meet the complete bottom edge of another single square, but meets half the bottom edge of one square and half the bottom edge of another. If the left half of the top edge of our starting square is deformed, then the right half of the bottom edge must be deformed to match. Similarly, the right half of the top edge corresponds to the left half of the bottom edge. To deal with this, we must treat the square as if it had six vertices and six edges numbered as in Figure 5.20. The DATA statements required to describe this shape and its tessellation pattern are presented as Program 5.8.

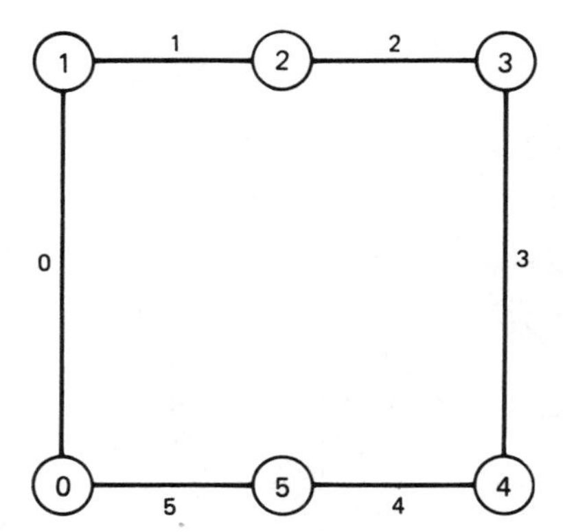

Figure 5.20
Vertex and line numbering used in the initial square that produced the 'flying fish'

5.4 COLOURING AND DECORATING TILES

Many of the tessellations illustrated so far have included tiles that have been filled with contrasting colours and decorated with lines that enhance our interpretation of the tile as an animal or fish. We now look at ways of extending our tile design program so as to permit colour filling and decoration of tiles.

A colour fill algorithm for tiles

Earlier in this chapter, we mentioned that it was easy to find an interior point from which to PAINT a convex polygon. The shapes generated by our tile deformation program are not necessarily convex. They tend to have recesses in the boundary that make it difficult to find such an interior point.

Finding an interior point for an arbitrary polygon is quite a tricky operation. One way of reliably finding an interior point for a complex shape is to find three consecutive points on the boundary that define a triangle which is completely inside the shape. A point within this triangle is then easily calculated as the average of the three vertices and this point is also inside the more complex shape.

It happens that the data structure we have used in the deformation process allows a convenient implementation of an algorithm that searches for such a triangle. To see why, consider the three

```
5000 DATA 5,450,350
5010 DATA 0,0,5,0,255, 0,1,3, 0,300,0,1,255, 1,2,4,
          150,300,1,2,255, 2,3,5, 300,300,2,3,255, 3,4,0,
          300,0,3,4,255, 4,5,1, 150,0,4,5,255, 5,0,2
5020 DATA 300,150,300,0
```

Program 5.8 DATA used in Program 5.6 to produce the 'flying fish' tile.

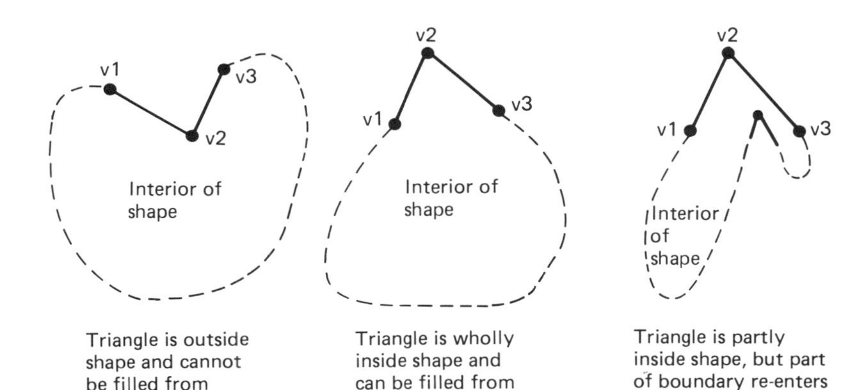
v1
v3
v2
Interior of shape
v2
v1
v3
Interior of shape
v2
v1
v3
Interior of shape
Triangle is outside shape and cannot be filled from
Triangle is wholly inside shape and can be filled from
Triangle is partly inside shape, but part of boundary re-enters the triangle which cannot be safely filled from

Figure 5.21
Various types of triangle v1, v2, v3 on the boundary of a shape that is to be colour filled

shapes illustrated in Figure 5.21. In the first shape, the triangle defined by the three vertices *v1, v2* and *v3* is completely outside the shape and is not suitable. In the second case the triangle *v1, v2, v3* is completely inside the shape and is suitable. In the third case, the triangle is partly inside the shape and partly outside and again is not suitable.

In order to distinguish the three cases illustrated in Figure 5.21, a program needs to know which ordering of the three vertices involved represents the clockwise direction round the boundary. If three adjacent vertices, *v1, v2* and *v3* taken clockwise round the boundary, are such that *v3* is to the left of the line that runs from *v1* to *v2*, then the triangle *v1, v2, v3* is at least partly outside the shape (case 1 in Figure 5.21). If *v3* is to the right of the line that runs from *v1* to *v2*, then the triangle is to the right of the boundary and is at least partly inside the shape (case 2 or 3 in Figure 5.21). In case 2, no other part of the boundary of the shape 're-enters' the triangle, but in case 3 this does happen. Once we have established that a particular triangle may be completely inside the shape, we must make a further test to eliminate the possibility of 're-entrancy' before we fill it. To do this, we need to apply a test to every other vertex on the boundary to see if it lies inside the triangle *v1, v2, v3*. Only if this test succeeds for every other vertex can the triangle be safely filled.

We can easily extend Program 5.6 to use a subroutine that finds an interior triangle and hence an interior point. The alterations needed are presented as Program 5.9. Subroutine 'colourfill' is called from the main command loop of the program in response to the command key 'f'. The algorithm implemented by 'colourfill' works its way round the boundary searching for an interior triangle. The line and vertex pointers that represent the structure of the boundary make moving round the boundary straightforward. When an interior triangle is found, the average of its three vertices defines the interior point required for PAINT.

```
 15 COLFILLX = 0 : COLFILLY = 0

345 FILLED = FALSE

360 COMMS$ = "qtpcadf"

460 SX = 0 : SY = 0 : SCALE = 1 : COLOR = 0 : GOSUB 480  'draw shape

545 IF COLOR = 1 THEN PAINT(SX+COLFILLX*SCALE,SY+COLFILLY*SCALE),1,1

635 IF COMMAND$ = "f" THEN GOSUB 3000  'colorfill

735 R = 0

755   COLOR = R

805     COLOR = (COLOR+1) MOD 2

835   R = (R+1) MOD 2
840   IF LEFTX > 0 THEN LEFTX = LEFTX-SCALE*XGRIDINC :
                           BOTY = BOTY-SCALE*YSHIFT : R = (R+1) MOD 2

3000 'SUBROUTINE colorfill
3010   IF FILLED THEN BEEP : RETURN
3020   V1 = START : V2 = NEXTV(NEXTL(V1)) : V3 = NEXTV(NEXTL(V2))
3030   V1 = V2 : V2 = V3 : V3 = NEXTV(NEXTL(V3))
3040   GOSUB 3190  'right
3050   IF NOT(RIGHT) THEN 3030
3055   FILLED = FALSE
3060   WHILE V1 <> V2 AND NOT(FILLED)
3070     GOSUB 3190  'right
3080     IF RIGHT THEN GOSUB 3260 : IF OKTOFILL THEN GOSUB 3440  'fill
3090     V1 = V2 : V2 = V3 : V3 = NEXTV(NEXTL(V3))
3100   WEND
3110   COMM$ = "qtp"
3120 RETURN
```

Program 5.9 Colour fill extensions to Program 5.6.

Each triangle, defined by three consecutive vertices on the current boundary, is first tested to see if it lies to the right of the boundary (using subroutine 'right'). If it does, all other vertices on the boundary are then checked to see if any lie within the triangle. This test is carried out by subroutine 'ok to fill'. When a triangle defined by three consecutive vertices passes these tests, the coordinates of an interior point are calculated and stored as 'COLFILLX' and 'COLFILLY'. (These coordinates are relative to the start point of the shape.) The stored coordinates are subsequently used to calculate an interior point for every copy of the shape plotted in a tessellation.

The extensions in Program 5.9 colour the tiles in a tessellation

```
3190 'SUBROUTINE right
3200   X2 = X(V2)-X(V1) : Y2 = Y(V2)-Y(V1)
3210   X3 = X(V3)-X(V1) : Y3 = Y(V3)-Y(V1)
3220   LR = SQR(X2*X2+Y2*Y2)
3230   RIGHT = -Y2*X3/LR+X2*Y3/LR <= 0
3240 RETURN

3260 'SUBROUTINE ok to fill
3270   LOKV = NEXTV(NEXTL(V3))
3280   IF LOKV = V1 THEN OKTOFILL = TRUE : RETURN
3290   REENTRANT = FALSE
3300   X1 = X(V1) : X2 = X(V2) : X3 = X(V3)
3310   Y1 = Y(V1) : Y2 = Y(V2) : Y3 = Y(V3)
3320   X21 = X2-X1 : Y21 = Y2-Y1
3330   X31 = X3-X1 : Y31 = Y3-Y1
3340   TNUM = X21*Y31-Y21*X31
3350   WHILE NOT(REENTRANT) AND LOKV <> V1
3360     X = X(LOKV) : Y = Y(LOKV)
3370     D = X21*(Y3-Y)-(X3-X)*Y21
3390     IF ABS(D) < 1 THEN REENTRANT = FALSE
            ELSE S = (X31*(Y3-Y)-(X3-X)*Y31)/D :
                 T = TNUM/D : REENTRANT = (T > 1) AND (S > 0) AND (S < 1)
3400     LOKV = NEXTV(NEXTL(LOKV))
3410   WEND
3420   OKTOFILL = NOT(REENTRANT)
3430 RETURN

3440 'SUBROUTINE fill
3445   GOSUB 1190  'cursors
3450   FILLX = (X(V1)+X(V2)+X(V3))/3
3460   FILLY = (Y(V1)+Y(V2)+Y(V3))/3
3470   PAINT (FILLX,FILLY),1,1
3475   FILLED = TRUE
3476   COLFILLX = FILLX-STARTX : COLFILLY = FILLY-STARTY
3480 RETURN
```

alternately black and white. Pleasing results can be obtained with other colours and the results of colour experiments with the 'flying fish' tessellation can be seen in Colour Plate 9.

Adding tile decorations

The final program alteration that we present in detail (as Program 5.10) is the inclusion of a subroutine 'linedraw'. This is called from the main command loop in response to the command key 'l'. The basic structure of this procedure is the same as that of the line-drawing program described in Chapter 2. The main difference is that each time a point is fixed, the coordinates of the point are stored

```
  37 DMAX = 50
  38 DIM DECOP(DMAX),DX(DMAX),DY(DMAX)

 205 DECP = -1

 325 LCOMMS$ = LLEFT$+RRIGHT$+UP$+DOWN$+"mfp"

 360 COMMS$ = "qtpcadfl"

 546   IF DECP <= -1 THEN RETURN
 547   FOR P = 0 TO DECP
 548     IF DECOP(P) = 4 THEN PSET(SX+DX(P)*SCALE,SY+DY(P)*SCALE),1-COLOR
                         ELSE LINE -(SX+DX(P)*SCALE,SY+DY(P)*SCALE),1-COLOR
 549   NEXT P
 550 RETURN

 636   IF COMMAND$ = "l" THEN GOSUB 1190 : GOSUB 4000 : GOSUB 1190

4000 'SUBROUTINE linedraw
4010   IF DECP > -1 THEN LX = DX(DECP) : LY = DY(DECP) ELSE LX = 0 : LY = 0
4020   PX = LX : PY = LY
4030   GOSUB 4360  'lcursor
4035   COMMAND$ = INKEY$
4040   WHILE COMMAND$ <> "p"
4050     GOSUB 4120  'deccomm
4060     COMMAND$ = INKEY$
4070   WEND
4090   GOSUB 4360  'lcursor
4100 RETURN
```

Program 5.10 Line drawing extensions to Program 5.6 (to permit the decoration of tiles).

in two arrays, 'DX' and 'DY', and a code indicating the operation to be used at that point (4 = move or 5 = draw) is recorded in the array 'DECOP' (Figure 5.22). This information is used whenever a tile is drawn for planning or in a tessellation.

We use 4 and 5 as codes for move and draw for historical reasons – we originally developed these programs for a different computer on which 4 and 5 were the actual codes for move and draw.

5.5 FURTHER EXPLORATION OF THE WORLD OF ESCHER

In the preceding sections, we have presented in detail a program for designing interesting shapes that will tessellate. In the interests of clarity, we have restricted ourselves to shapes that tessellate by simple translation. In this section, we discuss further variations that could be programmed. Programming details are not included, but we do include photographs to illustrate the possibilities.

```
4120 'SUBROUTINE deccomm
4130   IF COMMAND$ = "" THEN RETURN
4135   IF LEN(COMMAND$) = 2 THEN COMMAND$ = RIGHT$(COMMAND$,1)
4140   IF INSTR(LCOMMS$,COMMAND$) = 0 THEN BEEP : RETURN
4150   GOSUB 4360  'lcursor
4160   IF COMMAND$ = "f" THEN DOP = 5 : GOSUB 4280  'fix
4170   IF COMMAND$ = LLEFT$ THEN PX = PX-XSTEP
4180   IF COMMAND$ = RRIGHT$ THEN PX = PX+XSTEP
4190   IF COMMAND$ = UP$ THEN PY = PY+YSTEP
4200   IF COMMAND$ = DOWN$ THEN PY = PY-YSTEP
4210   IF COMMAND$ = "m" THEN DOP = 4 : GOSUB 4280  'fix
4220   GOSUB 4360  'lcursor
4230 RETURN

4280 'SUBROUTINE fix
4290   IF DOP = 5 THEN LINE (LX,LY)-(PX,PY) ELSE PSET(PX,PY),0
4300   DECP = DECP+1
4310   DECOP(DECP) = DOP
4320   DX(DECP) = PX : DY(DECP) = PY
4330   LX = PX : LY = PY
4340 RETURN

4360 'SUBROUTINE lcursor
4370   PUT (PX-16,PY-16),BIGCURSOR
       'On the PCjr, use PUT (PX-16,PY+16),BIGCURSOR
4375   PUT (LX-8,LY-8),LITTLECURSOR
       'On the PCjr, use PUT (LX-8,LY+8),LITTLECURSOR
4380 RETURN
```

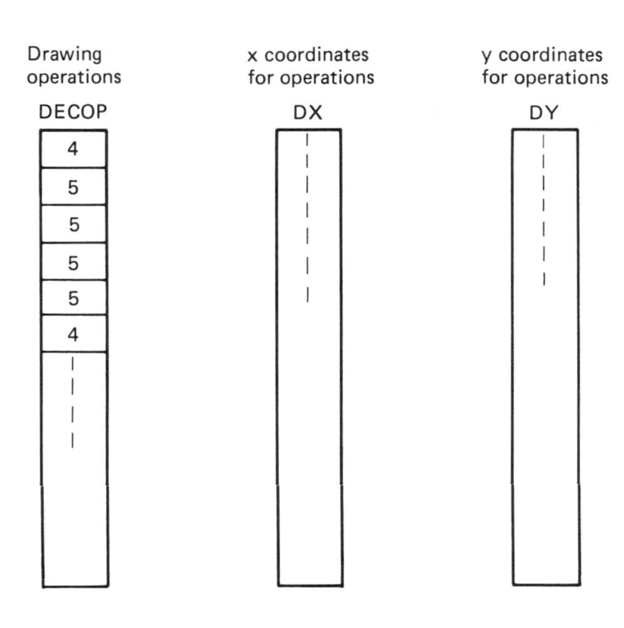

Figure 5.22
Data structure used for starting drawing operations and coordinates used in decorating a tile. Each drawing operation is either 4 (move) or 5 (draw)

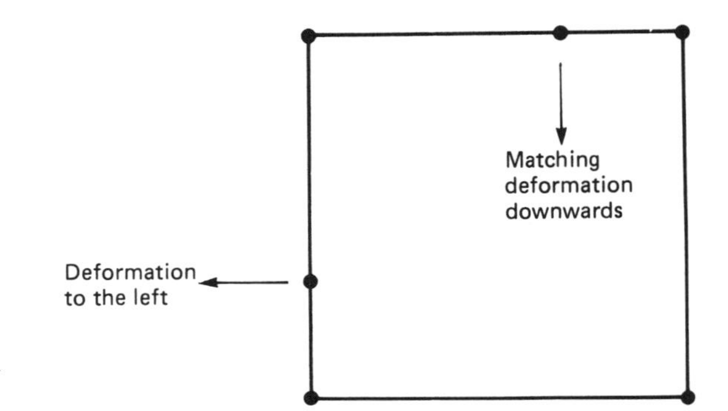

Figure 5.23
Deforming a tile that tessellates by translation and rotation

Figure 5.24
Stages in constructing a lizard tessellation

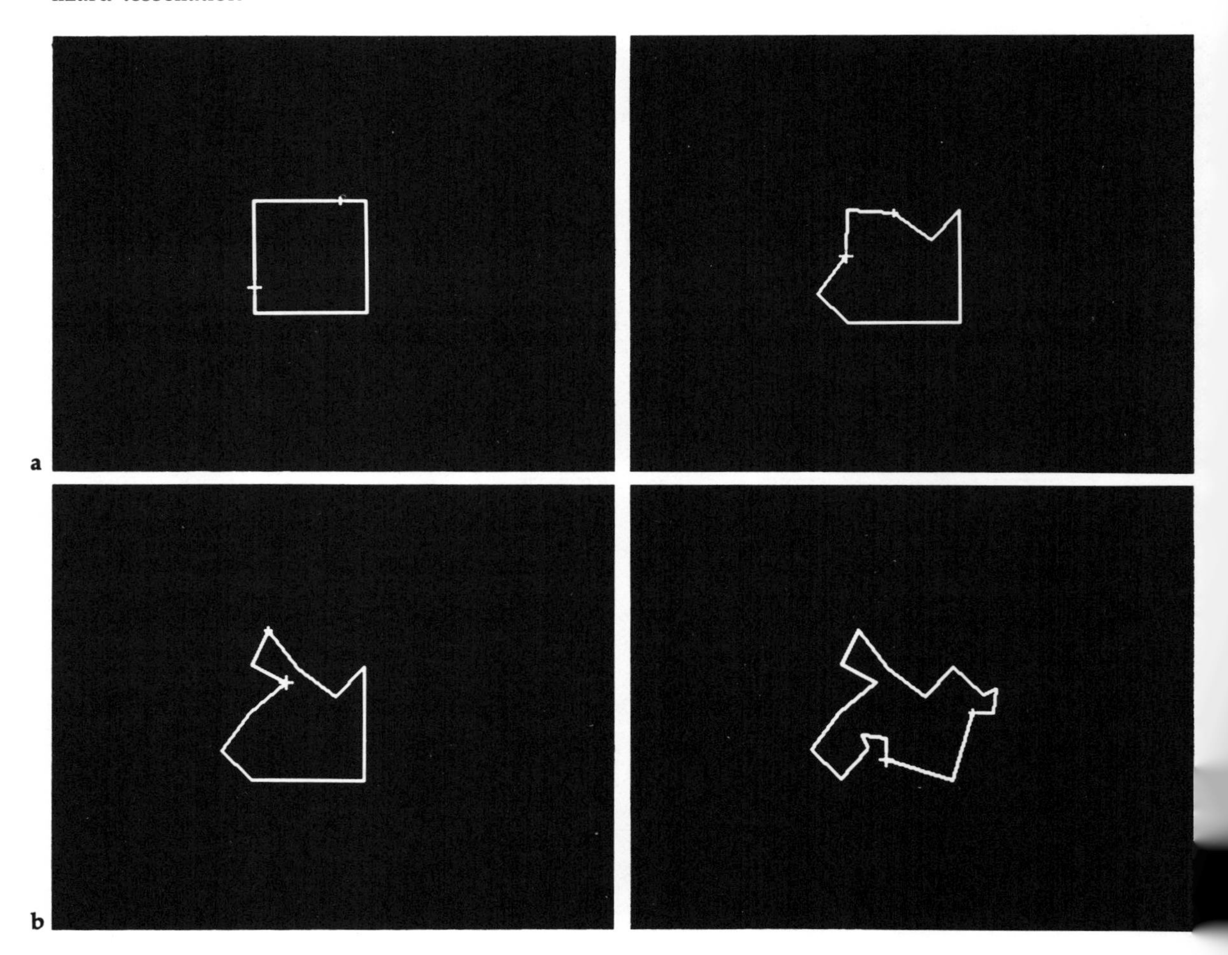

Tiles in different orientations

Figure 5.10, which was referred to in our introduction to the world of Escher, included a tessellation of a whale-like shape. However, this tessellation could not have been produced by the program that has been developed. The whale is not only translated in the tessellation, but is also displayed in different orientations. In order to design a tile that can be tessellated in different orientations, the design program would have to be extended to handle the rotations involved.

There are two aspects of the program's behaviour that would have to be modified to take account of rotations.

Firstly, the procedure that draws a tile would have to be supplied with extra information specifying the orientation of the tile it is to draw. This information could take the form of an angle of rotation or a transformation matrix. All the coordinates involved in drawing,

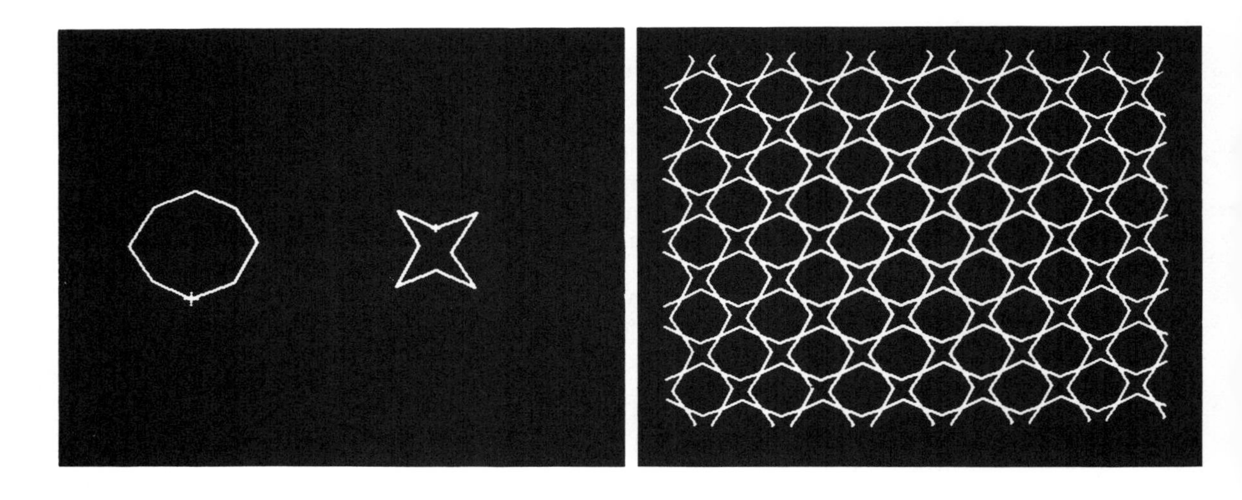

Figure 5.25
A simple pair of shapes that tessellate: they were produced by deforming a pair of squares

colouring and decorating the tile would have to be modified during the drawing process. The subroutine 'tessellate' would have to pass appropriate orientation information to each call of the tile drawing procedure.

The second point in the program at which rotations would have to be handled is in the tile deformation process. The whale tessellation was constructed from an initial square. However, it is no longer the case that opposite sides of the shape correspond. For example, the left side of a whale always meets the top of a whale in a tessellation. We can easily set up a structure of pointers to represent the new correspondences, but a difficulty now arises in implementing the deformation process. If a point on the left hand side of the shape is dragged to the left, then a corresponding point on the top has to be dragged downwards to maintain the tessellation property (Figure 5.23). This is because the two sides that correspond do not lie at the same orientation in the basic shape, but are at 90° to each other.

In more elaborate tessellations, corresponding sides could be at different angles to each other and a program would have to allow for this in the deformation process. The direction of any deformation carried out at the current point must be transformed appropriately before being applied to the corresponding side.

Figure 5.24 shows the build up of a lizard-like shape that tessellates by translation and rotation in the same way as the whale. This example is based on another of Escher's drawings (Colour Plate 10).

Multiple shapes

Figure 5.25 shows a simple example of a pair of shapes that together tessellate the plane. These were generated by deforming a pair of squares that alternate in a tessellation. Of course, a tessellation of the initial pair of squares is indistinguishable from a tessellation of a single square! To handle this, our data structure would need to be extended to contain information about two (or more) shapes each with their own vertices, lines and connectivity information.

Experiments with isosceles triangles

As a final example of further possibilities, Figures 5.26 and 5.27 demonstrate another type of tessellation layout involving rotations. We have already seen examples of these tessellation patterns in Figure 5.4. The basic patterns in Figure 5.4 were built up with copies of an isosceles triangle in different orientations.

The two equal sides of the initial triangle can be deformed in such a way as to maintain its tessellation property. Doing this

Figure 5.26
Tessellations with a deformed isosceles triangle

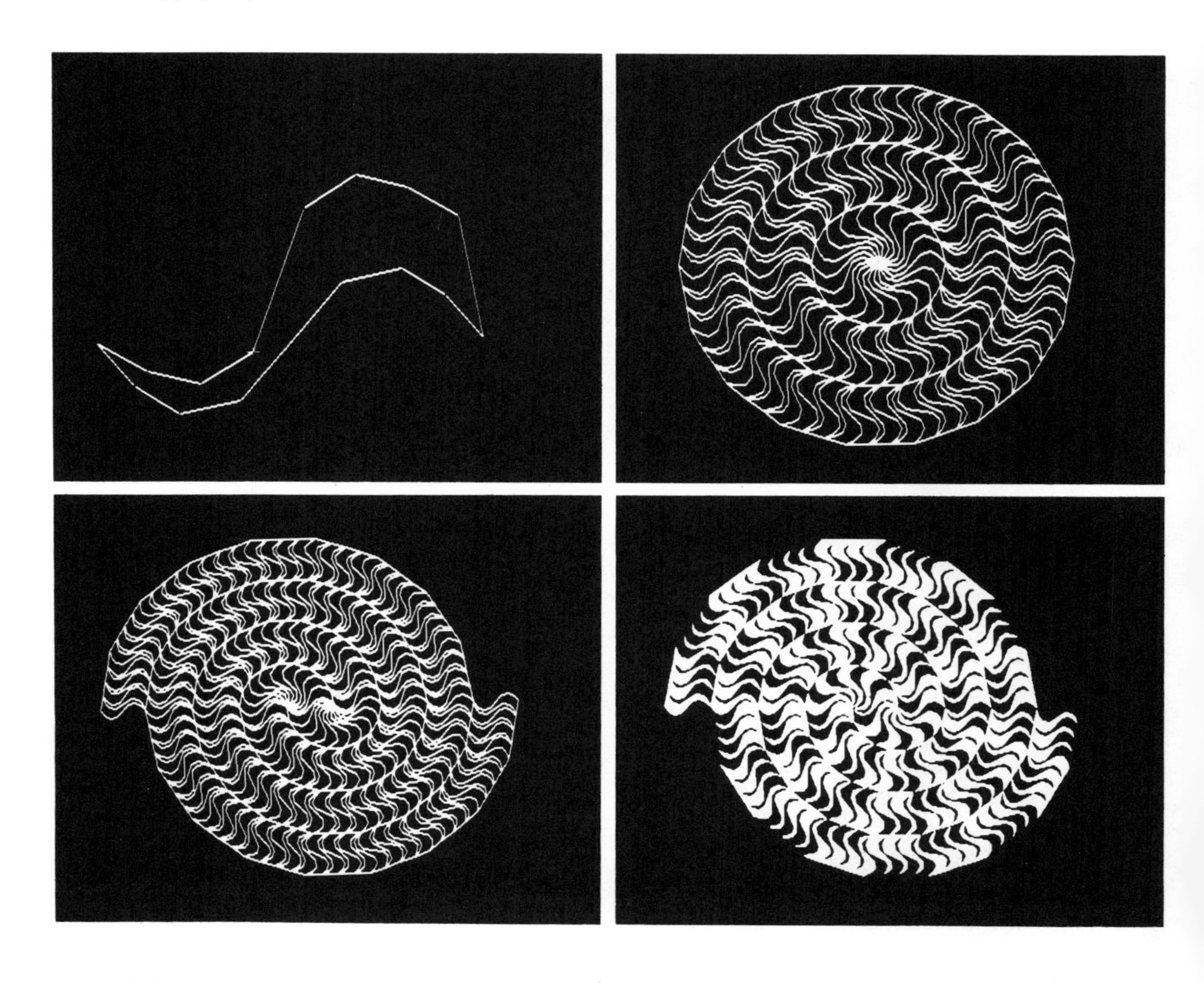

Figure 5.27
Tessellations with another deformed isosceles triangle

Figure 5.28
Deforming an isosceles triangle so that it will still tessellate in circular and spiral patterns

Matching deformation here
d
Deform side here
d
d
d
Matching deformation here
Matching deformation here

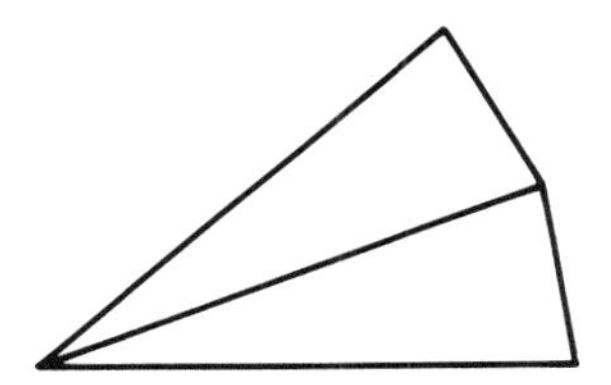

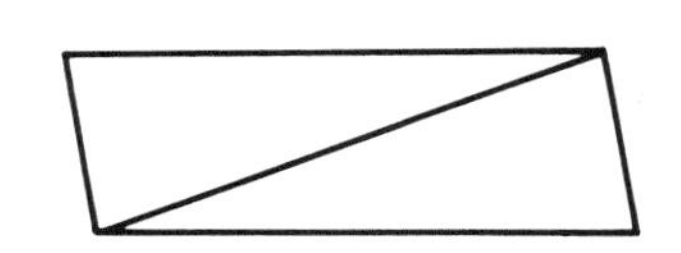

Figure 5.29
Two different ways in which isosceles triangles can meet in circular and spiral tessellations

automatically is rather trickier than it was in the examples that we have looked at so far. When a side is deformed at one point, matching deformations have to take place at three other points (Figure 5.28). This is because there are two different ways in which two copies of the initial triangle can meet in a tessellation (Figure 5.29).

6 *Recursion, fractals and natural patterns*

In this chapter we shall be looking at the fascinating application of recursive graphics. There are many complex patterns and curves that can easily be described recursively and recursion is a useful tool in computer graphics and computer-generated art. Recursive techniques can also be used to imitate natural patterns such as snowflakes, trees and coastlines. To use recursive graphics, we need an understanding of recursion as a programming process. We will start this chapter with a simple introduction to recursion that does not yet involve us in the extra complication of recursive graphics. Once recursion is understood as a process we can proceed to use it as a tool in graphics.

6.1 A SIMPLE INTRODUCTION TO RECURSIVE PROCESSES

In computing, a recursive process is one that is 'described in terms of itself'. A recursive subroutine is one that calls itself. Recursion is viewed with suspicion by beginners – how on earth can an operation be defined in terms of itself? One of our students recently remarked that writing a recursive program seemed like an act of faith. However, once mastered, recursion is a powerful tool and should not be neglected. There are many programming problems where a recursive solution is elegant and easy to write, and the non-recursive solution is difficult and tricky. Many human problem-solving activities are recursive in nature. For example, let us consider the problem of planning a route for walking through London from Trafalgar Square to the British Museum. One way of solving this problem might be to pick an intermediate landmark, such as Covent Garden, and break our original problem down into the problem of getting from Trafalgar Square to Covent Garden and from Covent Garden to the British Museum. A problem of navigation has been broken down into two easier subproblems, also of navigation.

This is the essence of recursion. The solution to a problem is described in terms of solutions to easier or smaller versions of the same problem. We could (rather fancifully) describe how to find a route between two points using the outline subroutine of Program 6.1. We shall not expand this into a complete BASIC program. In order to do so we would need to store a street map of London, lists of landmarks and their locations, a definition of what we mean by an 'easy' problem and so on. However, this outline subroutine describes a process with which we are all subconsciously familiar. It also exhibits the essential features of a recursive subroutine.

When a subroutine is called, the particular problem to be considered is specified by means of its parameters, A and B:

```
A$ = "Trafalgar Square" : B$ = "British Museum" : GOSUB ...
```

The first thing the subroutine does is to decide whether the problem represented by its parameters can be solved directly, without breaking it down into further subproblems. If this can be done, no recursion takes place. This is essential, otherwise the process of breaking the problem down into subproblems would never stop.

If the problem to be solved by the call of the subroutine is not an easy one, the subroutine breaks it down into easier subproblems, and requests the solution to each of these subproblems in turn. The solutions to the subproblems are requested by calling the same subroutine, but with different values for the parameters A and B. You might find it easier to think of the subproblems being solved by different copies of the subroutine; although it does not happen like this behind the scenes. This is the classic 'divide and conquer' approach to problem solving, so important in Artificial Intelligence.

On PC and PCjr BASIC, the user has to take extra steps to ensure that all the different sets of values for the parameters (A$ and B$ in this case) do not get confused. This will be covered shortly.

Learning to use recursion successfully means learning to recognize when a problem can be broken down into easier, or smaller, versions of itself and remembering to start a recursive subroutine with a test that recognizes when a given problem does not need to be further broken down. It is usually easier to write a recursive subroutine without worrying in detail about what the exact sequence of operations will be when the subroutine is called (an 'act

```
100 'SUBROUTINE find route between A$ and B$
110   IF GETTING FROM A$ TO B$ IS 'easy' (one street say) THEN print
        the route from A$ to B$ : RETURN
120   M$ = A LANDMARK APPROXIMATELY MIDWAY BETWEEN A$ AND B$
130   FIND ROUTE BETWEEN A$ AND M$
140   FIND ROUTE BETWEEN M$ AND B$
150 RETURN
```

Program 6.1 Recursive breakdown of the problem of finding a route between two points.

of faith' if you like). Just remember the two basic ingredients – the stopping condition and the breakdown into easier subproblems.

It is, of course, interesting to understand what does happen behind the scenes when we call a recursive subroutine. In fact, when a program does not work as intended, such an understanding is essential.

6.2 SOME EASY RECURSIVE PROGRAMS

Many of the programs presented in this section could very easily be written without recursion using simple loops. However, such 'inappropriate' use of recursion provides a useful introduction to the subject using problems with which we are familiar.

The first example (Program 6.2) simply prints the positive integers from 1 to N using a subroutine 'print up to'. We can break down the process of printing the numbers up to N into the problem of printing the numbers up to N – 1 followed by the use of a PRINT statement to print N. Of course if N = 0, then there are no values to be printed and this is the condition that we shall use to terminate the recursion.

The subroutine in Program 6.2 can be described in outline as:

```
'SUBROUTINE print up to N
  IF N = 0 THEN RETURN
  Call the subroutine to print up to N – 1
       (i.e. call the subroutine with N = N – 1)
  PRINT N (the original value of N)
RETURN
```

The extra details in Program 6.2 are concerned with keeping track of the various values of N required. At line 100, the subroutine is called

```
 10 DIM STACKN(20)
 20 INPUT N
 30 SP = 0
 40 GOSUB 60   'print up to N
 50 END

 60 'SUBROUTINE print up to N
 70   IF N = 0 THEN RETURN
 80   SP = SP+1
 90   STACKN(SP) = N
100   N = N-1 : GOSUB 60   'print up to N
110   N = STACKN(SP)
120   PRINT N
130   SP = SP-1
140 RETURN
```

Program 6.2 Recursively printing the numbers from 1 to N.

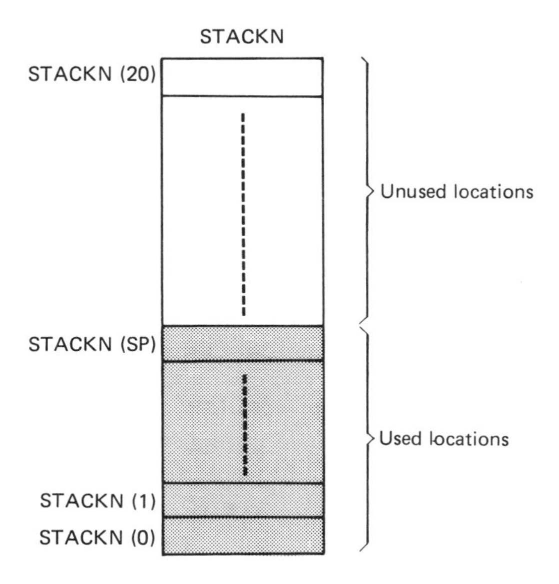

Figure 6.1
Use of an array to represent a stack for values of N (Note that location 0 has been drawn at the bottom – the convention for stacks)

recursively with a new value of N and, for the time being, we shall take on trust that this will succeed in printing all the integers up to N – 1. However, when this recursive subroutine call is complete, the PRINT statement has to print the old value of N. We must take a note of this old value of N before we change it and call the subroutine recursively. Also, we must restore this value of N after calling the subroutine.

In order to record an old value of N, we use a data structure known as a 'stack'. This is simply an array together with an integer that tells us the position of the last location that was used in the array (the 'stack pointer' SP). Figure 6.1 illustrates this. In order to remember a value of N so that it can be restored later, we use the recipe:

```
SP = SP + 1
STACKN(SP) = N
```

The value of N can then be changed for the recursive subroutine call. After the recursive subroutine call has been completed, N can be restored to its previous value by:

```
N = STACKN(SP)
SP = SP - 1
```

Note that it is necessary that the recursive subroutine call should leave the stack in exactly the same state as that in which it found it, so that the correct value for N is still at the top. This will certainly be the case, as any call of the subroutine 'print up to' adds 1 to SP and later subtracts 1.

In the next section we shall discuss in detail what happens behind the scenes when this program is obeyed.

In some programming languages, such as Pascal, and in some dialects of BASIC, the programmer does not have to concern himself or herself with organizing the stack. The stacking of parameters is handled automatically behind the scenes when a subroutine is called. In PC BASIC, however, this is not the case and we require the added complication of an explicit stack.

An interesting variation on Program 6.2 is to change it so that it prints the integers up to N, but in reverse order. In this case, the breakdown into an easier subproblem gives:

```
PRINT N
print numbers up to N - 1 in reverse order.
```

The complete program is given as Program 6.3. The main difference from Program 6.2 is that N is printed before the recursive call of our printing subroutine. Since nothing need be done with the old value of N after the recursive call, we can omit the stacking and unstacking process in this program.

Programs 6.2 and 6.3 are examples of a process sometimes called 'unary recursion' – a problem is broken down into one easier version of itself together with straightforward operations such as PRINT.

A simple example of 'binary recursion', where a problem is broken down into two simpler versions of itself, is provided by an alternative approach to printing the first N integers (Program 6.4). We can define a subroutine that prints the integers in a given range. For example:

```
I = 3 : J = 7 : GOSUB 100   'print between I and J
```

will print the integers 3, 4, 5, 6, 7.

```
I = 4 : J = 4 : GOSUB 100   'print between I and J
```

will print the single integer 4. This subroutine could be used to print the positive integers up to N by calling

```
I = 1 : J = N : GOSUB 100   'print between I and J
```

The subroutine 'print between' can be defined using binary recur-

```
10 INPUT N
20 GOSUB 40  'print up to N
30 END

40 'SUBROUTINE print up to N
50   IF N = 0 THEN RETURN
60   PRINT N
70   N = N-1 : GOSUB 40  'print up to N
80 RETURN
```

Program 6.3 Printing the numbers from 1 to N in reverse.

sion if we break down the problem of printing a given sequence into:

print the first half of the sequence
print the second half of the sequence

If only one value is to be printed, then this breakdown will not be needed. Again, we leave a detailed study of what happens when this program is run until the next section. For the time being, note that, when writing recursive programs, if a variable such as MID is going to be changed by a call of a subroutine, it may be necessary to stack the old value of MID at the start of the subroutine and restore it before returning from the subroutine. The value that MID had before entering the subroutine is then unchanged on exit.

The problem of printing the first N integers is, of course, a rather trivial problem. We finish this section with a simple recursive program that could not be so easily written without recursion. The problem we consider is that of printing a given positive integer in binary. For example,

```
N = 5 : GOSUB 60  'print binary N
```

should display

```
101
```

```
 10 DIM STACKI(20),STACKJ(20),STACKMID(20)
 20 SP = 0
 30 INPUT MAX
 40 GOSUB 60  'print up to MAX
 50 END

 60 'SUBROUTINE print up to MAX
 70   I = 1 : J = MAX
 80   GOSUB 100  'print between I and J
 90 RETURN

100 'SUBROUTINE print between I and J
110   IF I = J THEN PRINT I : RETURN
120   STACKMID(SP) = MID
130   SP = SP+1
140   MID = INT((I+J)/2)
150   STACKI(SP) = I : STACKJ(SP) = J
160   I = I : J = MID
170   GOSUB 100  'print between I and J
180   I = MID+1 : J = STACKJ(SP)
190   GOSUB 100  'print between I and J
200   SP = SP-1
210   MID = STACKMID(SP)
220 RETURN
```

Program 6.4 Using 'binary recursion' to print the numbers between two values.

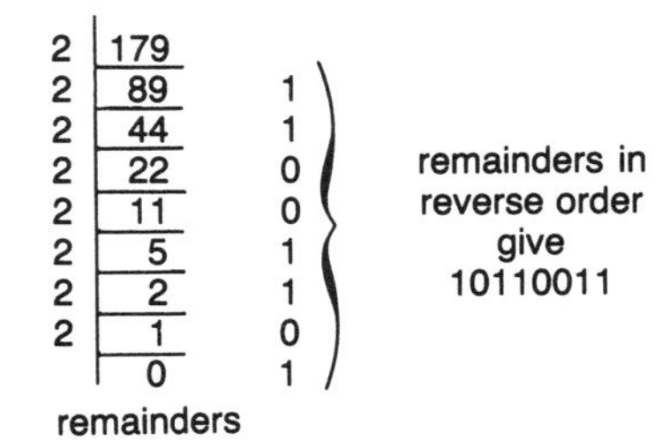

Figure 6.2
Converting a number into binary by successive division by 2

and

```
N = 179 : GOSUB 60  'print binary N
```

should display

```
10110011
```

The easiest way to convert an integer into binary is to keep dividing by 2 and collect all the remainders. The remainders represent the bits required, but they are generated in reverse order (Figure 6.2).

To treat this problem recursively, we break down the problem of printing the number N in binary:

```
print N DIV 2 in binary
PRINT ; N MOD 2;
```

where 'N MOD 2' is the last bit of the number (Program 6.5).

You might like to experiment with the effect of omitting some of the semicolons in this program. Changing line 70 affects only the first bit of the number printed while changing line 120 affects all the other bits apart from the first one.

```
10 DIM STACKN(20)
20 INPUT "Integer to be expressed in binary ";N
30 SP = 0
40 GOSUB 60  'print binary N
50 END

60 'SUBROUTINE print binary N
70   IF N < 2 THEN PRINT USING "#";N; : RETURN
80   SP = SP+1
90   STACKN(SP) = N
100  N = N\2 : GOSUB 60  'print binary N
110  N = STACKN(SP)
120  PRINT USING "#";N MOD 2;
130  SP = SP-1
140 RETURN
```

Program 6.5 Printing a number in binary.

Another experiment worth trying is to replace the stopping condition at line 70 with

```
70 IF N = 0 THEN RETURN
```

The program will then work correctly in all cases, except when the original input value is 0. Taking no action on a zero parameter is correct if the case 'N = 0' arises as a 'subproblem'. We do not want to print a leading zero at the start of a non-zero number. However, if the original number is zero, then this number must be printed. We must ensure that our subroutine correctly handles the case where the stopping condition is true on the first call of the subroutine, as well as the case where it is true for a subproblem.

6.3 HOW IT WORKS

We start this section by introducing a model – the 'tree of subroutine calls' – which will be valuable in understanding the behaviour of

```
 10 HEIGHT = 600 : HWIDTH = 1000
 20 SCREEN 2 : CLS : WINDOW (0,0)-(1279,799)
 30 GOSUB 60  'draw house
 40 INPUT ANY$
 50 END

 60 'SUBROUTINE draw house
 70   GOSUB 100  'draw front
 80   GOSUB 230  'draw roof
 90 RETURN

100 'SUBROUTINE draw front
110   LINE (0,0)-(HWIDTH,HEIGHT),,B
120   GOSUB 150  'draw windows
130   GOSUB 200  'draw door
140 RETURN

150 'SUBROUTINE draw windows
160   WW = 2*HWIDTH/10 : WH = HEIGHT/3
170   LINE (WW/2,WH)-(3*WW/2,2*WH),,B
180   LINE (7*WW/2,WH)-(9*WW/2,2*WH),,B
190 RETURN

200 'SUBROUTINE draw door
210   LINE (2*HWIDTH/5,0)-(3*HWIDTH/5,HEIGHT*2/3),,B
220 RETURN

230 'SUBROUTINE draw roof
240   LINE (0,HEIGHT)-(HWIDTH/2,4*HEIGHT/3)
250   LINE -(HWIDTH,HEIGHT)
260 RETURN
```

Program 6.6 House drawing program used to illustrate the idea of a tree of subroutine calls.

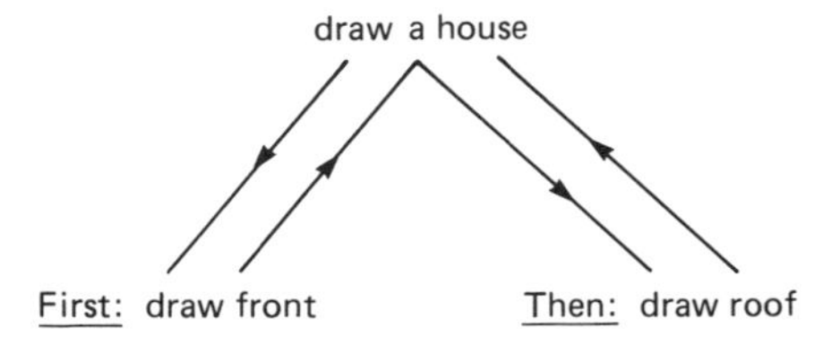

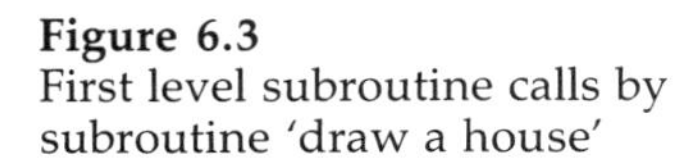
Figure 6.3
First level subroutine calls by subroutine 'draw a house'

recursive programs. To introduce this model, we first look at a program, Program 6.6, which involves subroutines, but no recursion. This program draws a simple house and is a much simplified version of Program 1.11. The process of drawing a house is broken down into the process of drawing a 'front' and then drawing a 'roof'. This is illustrated in Figure 6.3. Subroutine 'draw roof' is defined in terms of calls to LINE operations, but 'draw front' is broken down into further 'subproblems' (Figure 6.4). Subroutines 'draw windows' and 'draw door' are defined in terms of other calls to LINE. We can represent all this information as a complete 'tree of subroutine calls' for the program, together with arrows representing the 'flow of control' through the program (Figure 6.5). We have included calls to LINE in the tree of subroutine calls, because a call of LINE behaves just like a call of a subroutine.

Now let us consider the behaviour of the first recursive program of the last section. We can illustrate the behaviour of this program for a call of

```
N = 3 : GOSUB 40  'print up to N
```

by the 'tree' of subroutine calls shown in Figure 6.6. (The tree has only one branch at each level because we are using unary recursion.) Subroutine 'print up to' is called at several points with a different value for N each time. Successive calls of 'print up to' take place *before* the previous call has finished. The easiest way to understand what is happening is to imagine a separate copy of the subroutine being created each time it is called. Of course, such copying would be extremely wasteful of computer store (and time), and recursion is organized much more efficiently behind the scenes. However, in appreciating how a recursive subroutine works, it is convenient to imagine the whole subroutine being copied. We shall refer to these copies of a subroutine as 'activations' of the subroutine. We can expand the tree of subroutine calls in more detail (Figure 6.7).

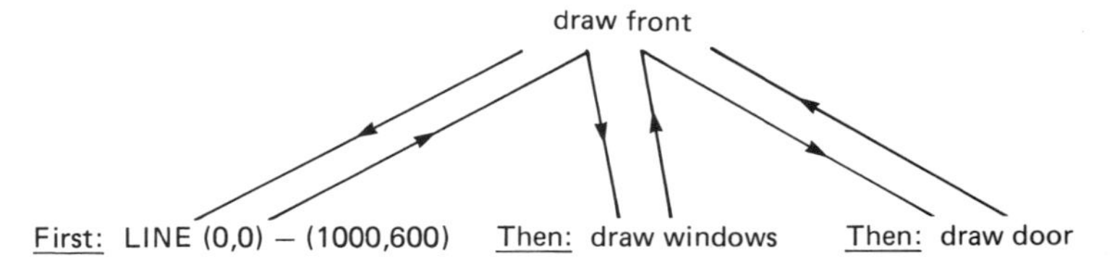

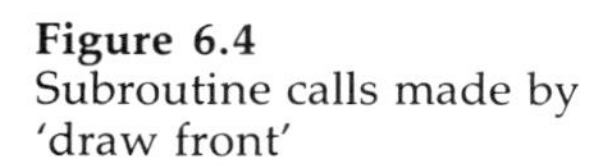
Figure 6.4
Subroutine calls made by 'draw front'

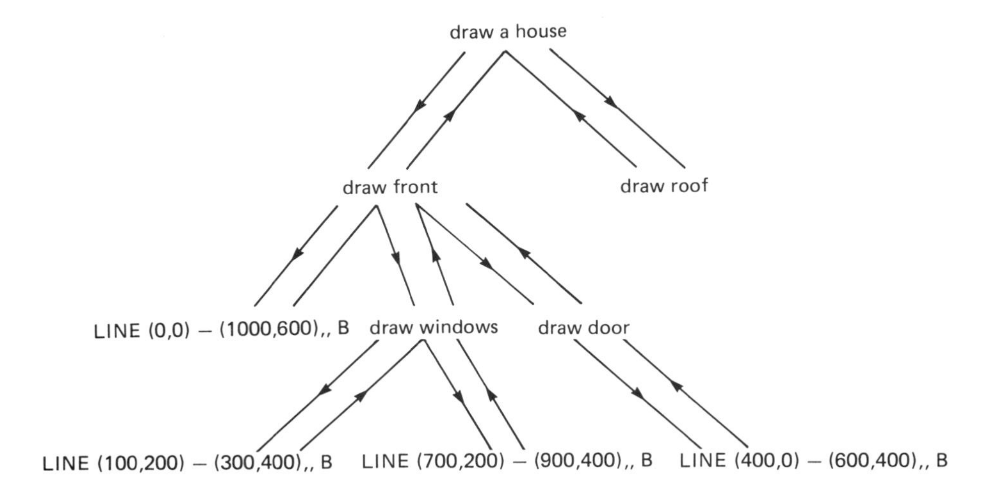

Figure 6.5
Full tree of subroutine calls for 'draw a house'

Now let us consider the behaviour of 'print between', the subroutine that used binary recursion. In Program 6.4, a call of

```
I = 1 : J = 5 : GOSUB 100  'print between I and J
```

executes the following:

```
stack old value of MID
MID = (1 + 5) DIV 2 i.e. MID = 3
I = 1 : J = 3 : GOSUB 100  'print between I and J
I = 4 : J = 5 : GOSUB 100  'print between I and J
```

Each of the two recursive calls of 'print between' behave in a similar way. You should now be able to follow the arrows through the tree in Figure 6.8 and see exactly how the sequence of subroutine calls results in the numbers being printed in the required order.

Note the importance of remembering the old value of MID on entering a call of the subroutine, and restoring it before returning. Thus, for example, when the subroutine call 'print between 1 and 3' is terminated, control returns to 'print between 1 and 5' and the value of MID has been restored to 3. The value 'MID = 3' is needed in 'print between 1 and 5' for calculating the first parameter (I) of the next recursive call (at line 180 of the program).

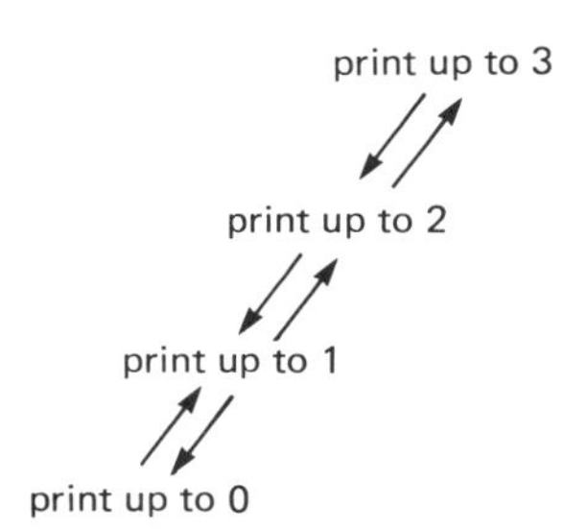

Figure 6.6
A non-branching tree for subroutine 'print up to'

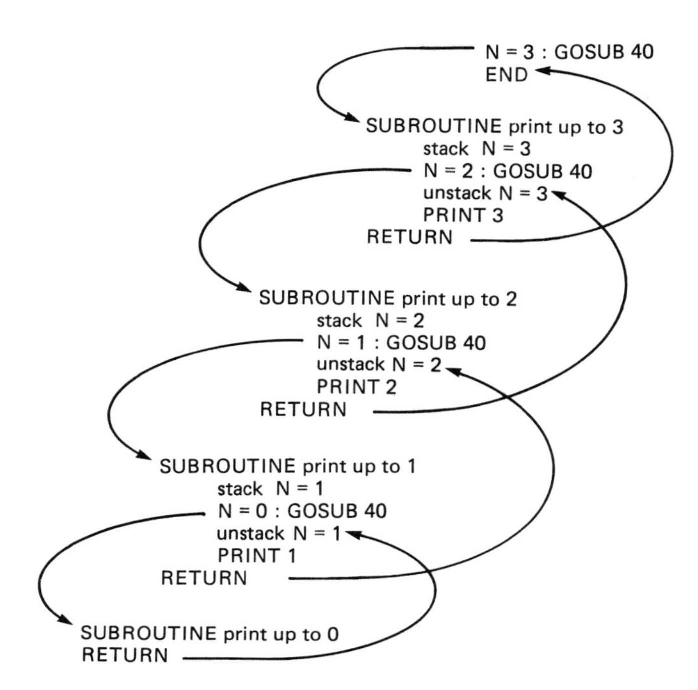

Figure 6.7
Detailed behaviour of subroutine 'print up to'

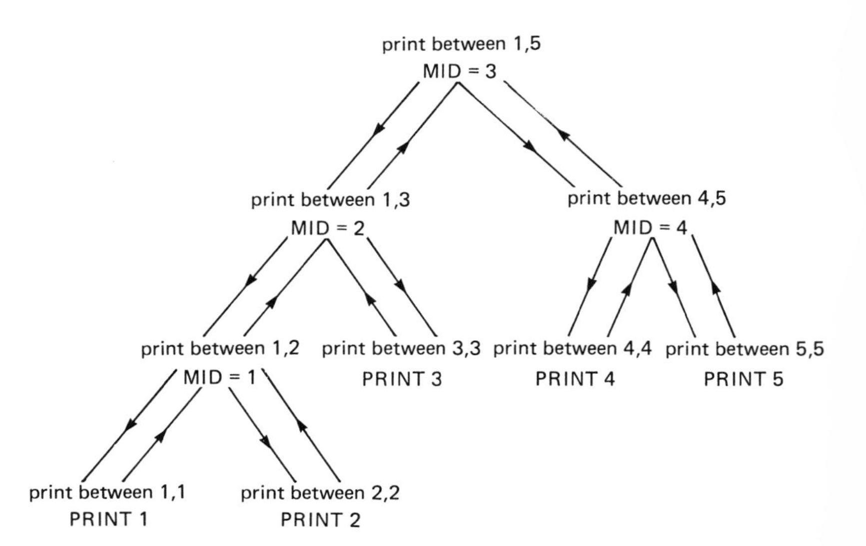

Figure 6.8
Tree of subroutine calls for 'print between'

```
10 DIM STACKR(20),STACKX1(20),STACKX2(20),STACKY1(20),STACKY2(20)
20 SP = 0
30 R = 192
40 SCREEN 2 : CLS
50 WINDOW (0,0)-(1279,799)
60 XC = 640 : YC = 400
70 GOSUB 100  'draw a square
80 INPUT ANY$
90 END

100 'SUBROUTINE draw a square
110   IF R < 10 THEN RETURN
120   STACKX1(SP) = X1 : STACKX2(SP) = X2
130   STACKY1(SP) = Y1 : STACKY2(SP) = Y2
140   SP = SP+1
150   X1 = XC-R : X2 = XC+R
160   Y1 = YC-R : Y2 = YC+R
170   PSET (X1,Y1)
180   LINE -(X1,Y2) : LINE -(X2,Y2)
190   LINE -(X2,Y1) : LINE -(X1,Y1)
200   STACKR(SP) = R
210   XC = X1 : YC = Y1 : R = R/2
220   GOSUB 100  'draw a square
230   XC = X1 : YC = Y2
240   GOSUB 100  'draw a square
250   XC = X2 : YC = Y2
260   GOSUB 100  'draw a square
270   XC = X2 : YC = Y1
280   GOSUB 100  'draw a square
290   R = STACKR(SP)
300   SP = SP-1
310   X1 = STACKX1(SP) : X2 = STACKX2(SP)
320   Y1 = STACKY1(SP) : Y2 = STACKY2(SP)
330 RETURN
```

Program 6.7 Recursive squares.

6.4 RECURSIVE SHAPES

Many beautiful patterns can be generated by drawing a basic shape and placing smaller recursive copies of the pattern at various points on the basic shape. We shall illustrate this technique first of all with a simple recursive square pattern and then with the snowflake pattern or Koch flake.

Recursive squares

Program 6.7 creates a pattern of recursive squares. The pattern consists of a square, together with a recursive half-size copy of the complete pattern centred on each corner of the main square.

Figure 6.9 shows the three stages in the build up for R = 192,

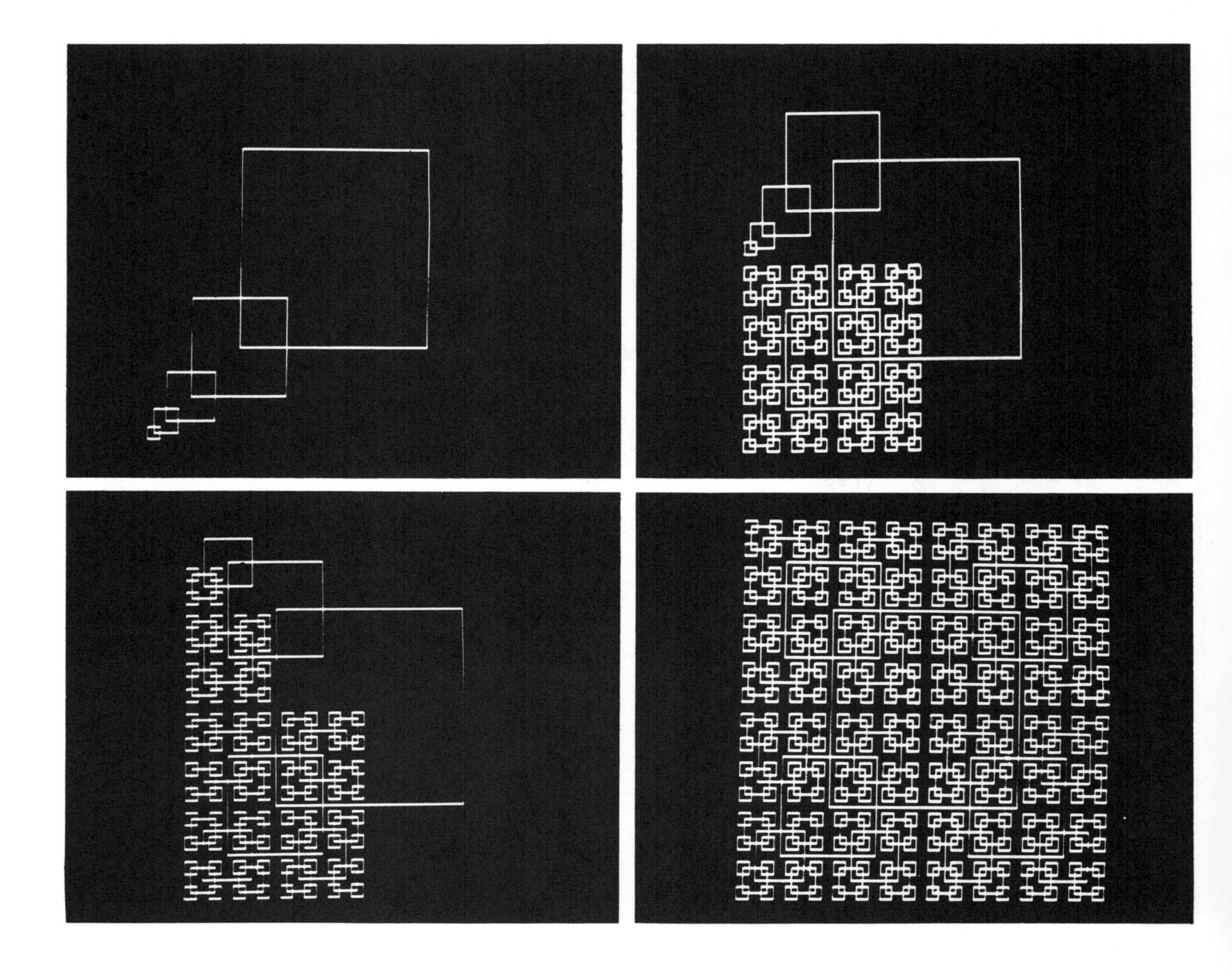

Figure 6.9
Building up a pattern of recursive squares

together with the complete pattern. For example, the first photograph illustrates the situation when the subroutine calls in Figure 6.10 have been activated. The last subroutine call triggers the stopping condition ($R < 10$) and terminates without drawing a square.

At the stage reached in the second photograph, the tree of subroutine calls that have been obeyed and terminated, together with the subroutine calls that are still active, has the form shown in Figure 6.11. (The active subroutine calls are down the right hand branch.)

Coloured squares

Recursive shapes like the squares can often be enhanced by colouring the basic shape each time it is plotted at all recursive levels. If different colours are used at adjacent levels, successively smaller copies of the shape will appear in different colours over the larger

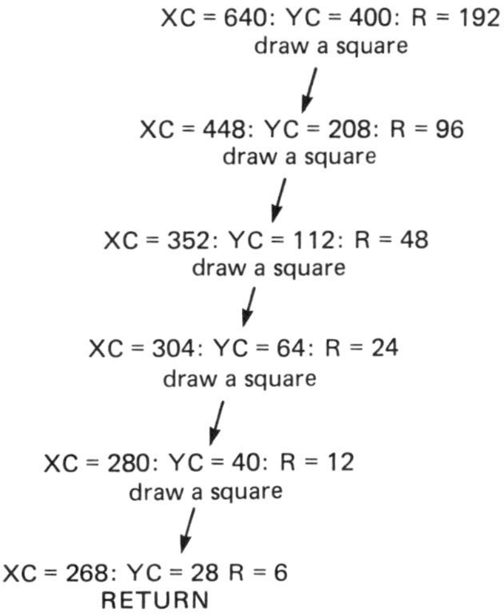

XC = 640: YC = 400: R = 192
draw a square
↓
XC = 448: YC = 208: R = 96
draw a square
↓
XC = 352: YC = 112: R = 48
draw a square
↓
XC = 304: YC = 64: R = 24
draw a square
↓
XC = 280: YC = 40: R = 12
draw a square
↓
XC = 268: YC = 28 R = 6
RETURN

Figure 6.10
Tree of subroutine calls in early stages of build-up of recursive square pattern

copies that have already been plotted. Program 6.8 does this for the recursive squares. (See Colour Plate 11.)

Snowflakes
The Koch flake consists of a pattern made up of two triangles that form a Star of David (Figure 6.12) together with smaller Koch flakes centred on each point of the star and possibly another flake in the centre of the star. Program 6.9 draws a Koch flake and some output is shown in Figure 6.13a.

There are many interesting variations that can be tried with this pattern. For example, the reduction factor used to determine the size of the smaller flakes can be varied. In Figure 6.13b, this was done and the central recursive flake was omitted (by leaving out the

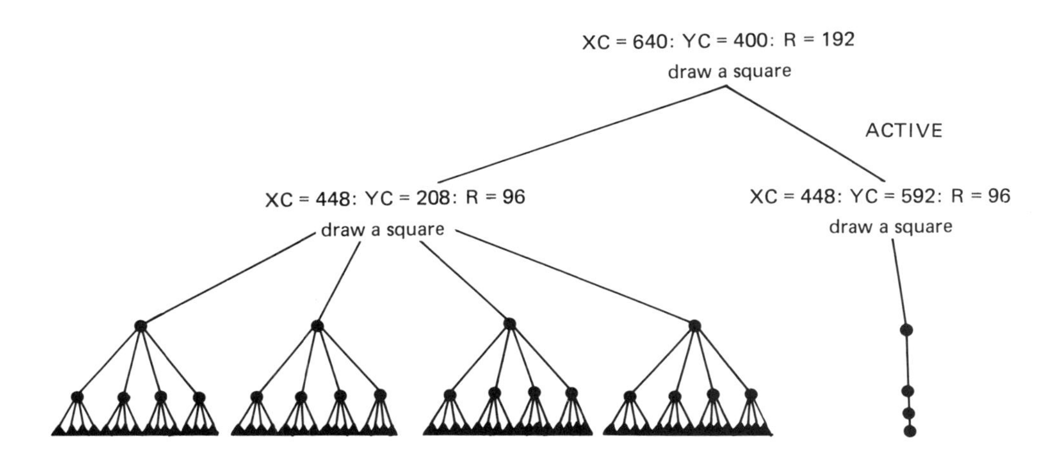

Figure 6.11
Shape of tree of subroutine calls during build-up of recursive square pattern

last recursive call in the definition of the subroutine). Using a different reduction factor for the central flake can also be effective (Figure 6.13c). Another interesting variation is to use two different reduction factors, one for the small flakes on the points of one of the triangles, and the other for the small flakes on the points of the other triangle. This replaces the six-fold symmetry with three-fold symmetry.

Finally, using colour in the same way as it was used in the recursive squares earlier produces striking effects. The result of using white only for colour fill is illustrated in Figure 6.13d. The result of changing colour at each recursive level is illustrated in Colour Plates 12 and 13. Program 6.10 produces coloured Koch flakes.

```
 10 DIM STACKR(20),STACKX1(20),STACKX2(20),STACKY1(20),STACKY2(20)
 15 DIM STACKCOL(20)
 20 SP = 0
 30 R = 192 : COLORS = 3
 40 KEY OFF
 50 SCREEN 1 : CLS
 60 WINDOW (0,0)-(1279,799)
 80 XC = 640 : YC = 400 : COL = 0
 90 GOSUB 120  'draw a square
100 INPUT ANY$
110 END

120 'SUBROUTINE draw a square
130   IF R < 4 THEN RETURN
140   STACKX1(SP) = X1 : STACKX2(SP) = X2
150   STACKY1(SP) = Y1 : STACKY2(SP) = Y2
160   SP = SP+1
170   X1 = XC-R : X2 = XC+R
180   Y1 = YC-R : Y2 = YC+R
190   LINE (X1,Y1)-(X2,Y2),COL+1,BF
200   STACKR(SP) = R : STACKCOL(SP) = COL
210   COL = (COL+1) MOD COLORS
220   XC = X1 : YC = Y1 : R = R/2
230   GOSUB 120  'draw a square
240   XC = X1 : YC = Y2
250   GOSUB 120  'draw a square
260   XC = X2 : YC = Y2
270   GOSUB 120  'draw a square
280   XC = X2 : YC = Y1
290   GOSUB 120  'draw a square
300   R = STACKR(SP) : COL = STACKCOL(SP)
310   SP = SP-1
320   X1 = STACKX1(SP) : X2 = STACKX2(SP)
330   Y1 = STACKY1(SP) : Y2 = STACKY2(SP)
340 RETURN
```

Program 6.8 Colour filled recursive squares.

```
 10 DIM STACKR(20),STACKX1(20),STACKX2(20),STACKY1(20),STACKY2(20)
 20 DIM STACKX(20),STACKY(20),STACKY3(20),STACKY4(20)
 30 SCREEN 2 : CLS
 40 WINDOW (0,0)-(1279,799)
 50 PI = 3.141593
 60 COS30 = COS(30*PI/180)
 70 SP = 0
 80 RESOLUTION = 8 : REDUCTIONFACTOR = 1/3
 90 X = 640 : Y = 400 : R = 256
100 GOSUB 130  'Koch flake
110 INPUT ANY$
120 END

130 'SUBROUTINE Koch flake
140   IF R < RESOLUTION THEN RETURN
150   STACKX1(SP) = X1 : STACKX2(SP) = X2
160   STACKY1(SP) = Y1 : STACKY2(SP) = Y2
170   STACKY3(SP) = Y3 : STACKY4(SP) = Y4
180   SP = SP+1
190   X1 = X-R*COS30 : X2 = X+R*COS30
200   Y1 = Y-R : Y2 = Y-R/2 : Y3 = Y+R/2 : Y4 = Y+R
210   LINE (X1,Y2)-(X,Y4) : LINE -(X2,Y2) : LINE -(X1,Y2)
220   LINE (X,Y1)-(X1,Y3) : LINE -(X2,Y3) : LINE -(X,Y1)
230   STACKR(SP) = R
240   STACKX(SP) = X : STACKY(SP) = Y
250   R = R*REDUCTIONFACTOR
260   X = X1 : Y = Y2
270   GOSUB 130  'Koch flake
280   X = STACKX(SP) : Y = Y4
290   GOSUB 130  'Koch flake
300   X = X2 : Y = Y2
310   GOSUB 130  'Koch flake
320   X = STACKX(SP) : Y = Y1
330   GOSUB 130  'Koch flake
340   X = X1 : Y = Y3
350   GOSUB 130  'Koch flake
360   X = X2 : Y = Y3
370   GOSUB 130  'Koch flake
380   X = STACKX(SP) : Y = STACKY(SP)
390   GOSUB 130  'Koch flake
400   R = STACKR(SP) : X = STACKX(SP) : Y = STACKY(SP)
410   SP = SP-1
420   X1 = STACKX1(SP) : X2 = STACKX2(SP)
430   Y1 = STACKY1(SP) : Y2 = STACKY2(SP)
440   Y3 = STACKY3(SP) : Y4 = STACKY4(SP)
450 RETURN
```

Program 6.9 Koch flake.

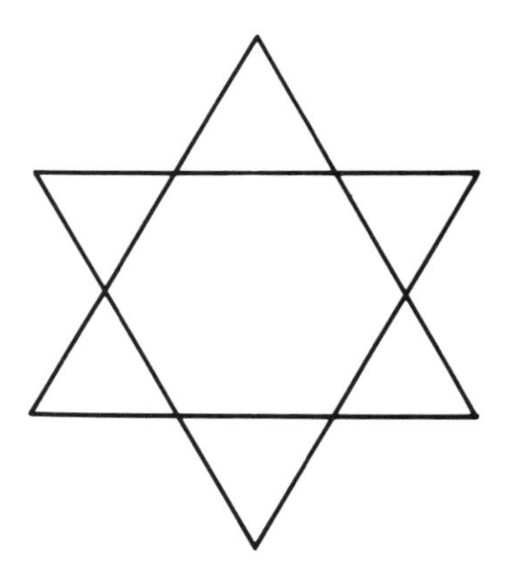

Figure 6.12
Star of David pattern from which Koch flake is developed

Figure 6.13
A selection of Koch flakes

```
 10 DIM STACKR(20),STACKX1(20),STACKX2(20),STACKY1(20),STACKY2(20)
 20 DIM STACKX(20),STACKY(20),STACKY3(20),STACKY4(20),STACKCOL(20)
 30 SCREEN 1 : CLS
 40 WINDOW (0,0)-(1279,799)
 50 PI = 3.141593
 60 COS30 = COS(30*PI/180)
 70 SP = 0 : COLORS = 3
 80 RESOLUTION = 8 : REDUCTIONFACTOR = 0.4
 90 X = 640 : Y = 400 : R = 256 : COL = 0
100 GOSUB 130  'Koch flake
110 INPUT ANY$
120 END

130 'SUBROUTINE Koch flake
140   IF R < RESOLUTION THEN RETURN
150   STACKX1(SP) = X1 : STACKX2(SP) = X2
160   STACKY1(SP) = Y1 : STACKY2(SP) = Y2
170   STACKY3(SP) = Y3 : STACKY4(SP) = Y4
180   SP = SP+1
190   X1 = X-R*COS30 : X2 = X+R*COS30 : XINC = R*COS30/3
200   Y1 = Y-R : Y2 = Y-R/2 : Y3 = Y+R/2 : Y4 = Y+R
210   LINE (X1,Y2)-(X,Y4),COL+1 : LINE -(X2,Y2),COL+1 : LINE -(X1,Y2),COL+1
220   LINE (X,Y1)-(X1,Y3),COL+1 : LINE -(X2,Y3),COL+1 : LINE -(X,Y1),COL+1
222   PAINT (X,Y),COL+1,COL+1
223   PAINT (X,Y3+R/4),COL+1,COL+1
224   PAINT (X2-XINC,Y3-R/4),COL+1,COL+1
225   PAINT (X2-XINC,Y2+R/4),COL+1,COL+1
226   PAINT (X,Y2-R/4),COL+1,COL+1
227   PAINT (X1+XINC,Y2+R/4),COL+1,COL+1
228   PAINT (X1+XINC,Y3-R/4),COL+1,COL+1
230   STACKR(SP) = R : STACKCOL(SP) = COL
240   STACKX(SP) = X : STACKY(SP) = Y
250   R = R*REDUCTIONFACTOR
255   COL = (COL+1) MOD 3
260   X = X1 : Y = Y2
270   GOSUB 130  'Koch flake
280   X = STACKX(SP) : Y = Y4
290   GOSUB 130  'Koch flake
300   X = X2 : Y = Y2
310   GOSUB 130  'Koch flake
320   X = STACKX(SP) : Y = Y1
330   GOSUB 130  'Koch flake
340   X = X1 : Y = Y3
350   GOSUB 130  'Koch flake
360   X = X2 : Y = Y3
370   GOSUB 130  'Koch flake
380   X = STACKX(SP) : Y = STACKY(SP)
390   GOSUB 130  'Koch flake
400   R = STACKR(SP) : X = STACKX(SP) : Y = STACKY(SP)
405   COL = STACKCOL(SP)
410   SP = SP-1
420   X1 = STACKX1(SP) : X2 = STACKX2(SP)
430   Y1 = STACKY1(SP) : Y2 = STACKY2(SP)
440   Y3 = STACKY3(SP) : Y4 = STACKY4(SP)
450 RETURN
```

Program 6.10 Coloured Koch flake.

```
 10 DIM STACKX(20),STACKY(20),STACKS(20)
 20 DIM STACKA(20),STACKB(20),STACKC(20),STACKD(20)
 30 DIM STACKS2(20),STACKS4(20)
 40 SCREEN 2 : CLS : WINDOW (0,0)-(1279,799)
 50 MINS = 300
 60 X = 2 : Y = 2 : S = 760
 70 A = 1 : B = 0 : C = 0 : D = 1
 80 GOSUB 100  'triomino
 90 END

100 'SUBROUTINE triomino
110   IF S < MINS THEN GOSUB 390 : RETURN  'draw tile
120   STACKS2(SP) = S2 : STACKS4(SP) = S4
130   SP = SP+1
140   S2 = S/2 : S4 = S/4
150   STACKX(SP) = X : STACKY(SP) = Y : STACKS(SP) = S
160   STACKA(SP) = A : STACKB(SP) = B : STACKC(SP) = C : STACKD(SP) = D
170   S = S2
180   'x = x : y = y : a = a : b = b : c = c : d = d
190   GOSUB 100  'triomino
200   X = STACKX(SP)+STACKA(SP)*S4+STACKB(SP)*S4
210   Y = STACKY(SP)+STACKC(SP)*S4+STACKD(SP)*S4
220   's = s2 : a = a : b = b : c = c : d = d
230   GOSUB 100  'triomino
240   's = s2
250   X = STACKX(SP)+STACKB(SP)*STACKS(SP)
260   Y = STACKY(SP)+STACKD(SP)*STACKS(SP)
270   A = STACKC(SP) : B = STACKD(SP) : C = -STACKA(SP) : D = -STACKB(SP)
280   GOSUB 100  'triomino
290   's = s2
300   X = STACKX(SP)+STACKA(SP)*STACKS(SP)
310   Y = STACKY(SP)+STACKC(SP)*STACKS(SP)
320   A = -STACKC(SP) : B = -STACKD(SP) : C = STACKA(SP) : D = STACKB(SP)
330   GOSUB 100  'triomino
340   S = STACKS(SP) : X = STACKX(SP) : Y = STACKY(SP)
350   A = STACKA(SP) : B = STACKB(SP) : C = STACKC(SP) : D = STACKD(SP)
360   SP = SP-1
370   S2 = STACKS2(SP) : S4 = STACKS4(SP)
380 RETURN

390 'SUBROUTINE draw tile
400   X1 = B*S : Y1 = D*S
410   X2 = A*S : Y2 = C*S
420   LINE (X,Y)-(X+X1,Y+Y1)
430   LINE -(X+X1+X2/2,Y+Y1+Y2/2)
440   LINE -(X+X1/2+X2/2,Y+Y1/2+Y2/2)
450   LINE -(X+X1/2+X2,Y+Y1/2+Y2)
460   LINE -(X+X2,Y+Y2)
470   LINE -(X,Y)
480 RETURN
```

Program 6.11 Triominoes.

6.5 REPTILES

In Chapter 5, we mentioned the subject of replicating tiles or 'rep-tiles'. These are tiles that can be tessellated into bigger and bigger copies of themselves. Now that we have recursion as a tool such shapes are easily produced.

Triominoes

Figure 5.5 showed how a simple triomino can be used as a reptile and Program 6.11 was used to produce these pictures. The subroutine 'triomino' is given (x,y) coordinates for the bottom left hand corner of the triomino shape and the overall size, S, of the shape to be drawn. (S is the length of the longest side.) Because a triomino may have to be drawn in several different orientations, we include four parameters (A, B, C, D) that represent a simple transformation matrix (Chapter 3). This matrix specifies the orientation of the shape.

If the size of shape specified to the subroutine 'triomino' is less than the value 'MINS' then a single triomino is drawn in the appropriate orientation. Otherwise, four recursive calls of the subroutine 'triomino' are used to draw four smaller triominoes that together will make up the triomino shape required. Drawing these smaller triomino shapes may involve further recursive calls.

Sphinx tiles

Figure 5.6 showed examples of tessellations with the Sphinx tile. These photographs were produced using Program 6.12. The overall structure of the program is the same as that of Program 6.11 (triominoes). Here, the size of the Sphinx shape, S, is given as the length of the shortest side of the shape as this makes the coordinate geometry a little more convenient.

6.6 SPACE FILLING CURVES AND FRACTALS

There are a large number of 'curves' that are variously described as 'space filling curves' or 'fractals'. The term 'fractal' has been recently coined to describe curves or surfaces that become more and more discontinuous the more closely we examine them. In computer graphics fractal surfaces have been used successfully to simulate natural landscapes. The more accurately we decide to plot a fractal curve, the longer it gets! Many naturally occurring curves and surfaces are fractals. For example, a sponge is a fractal surface, as is the surface of the Earth.

A coastline is a commonly quoted example of a naturally occurring fractal curve. Imagine approaching the planet from outer space. At first sight, a coastline would appear to be a fairly smooth curve. As we approach closer, indentations that were not previously apparent would begin to appear. As we come closer still, we would discover that the sides of these indentations themselves contained further irregularities. This increase in irregularity with every

```
 10 DIM STACKX(20),STACKY(20),STACKS(20)
 20 DIM STACKA(20),STACKB(20),STACKC(20),STACKD(20)
 30 DIM STACKS2(20)
 40 SCREEN 2 : CLS : WINDOW (0,0)-(1279,799)
 50 MINS = 50 : ROOT3 = SQR(3)
 60 X = 66 : Y = 120 : S = 384
 70 A = 1 : B = 0 : C = 0 : D = 1
 80 GOSUB 100  'sphinx
 90 END

100 'SUBROUTINE sphinx
110   IF S < MINS THEN GOSUB 440 : RETURN  'draw tile
120   STACKS2(SP) = S2
130   SP = SP+1
140   S2 = S/2
150   STACKX(SP) = X : STACKY(SP) = Y : STACKS(SP) = S
160   STACKA(SP) = A : STACKB(SP) = B : STACKC(SP) = C : STACKD(SP) = D
170   X = X+A*S*3/2 : Y = Y+C*S*3/2
180   S = S2
190   A = -A : B = B : C = -C : D = D
200   GOSUB 100  'sphinx
210   X = STACKX(SP)+STACKA(SP)*STACKS(SP)*3
220   Y = STACKY(SP)+STACKC(SP)*STACKS(SP)*3
230   's = s2
240   'a = -a : b = b : c = -c : d = d
250   GOSUB 100  'sphinx
260   X = STACKX(SP)+STACKA(SP)*STACKS(SP)+STACKB(SP)*STACKS(SP)*ROOT3
270   Y = STACKY(SP)+STACKC(SP)*STACKS(SP)+STACKD(SP)*STACKS(SP)*ROOT3
280   's = s2
290   A = -STACKA(SP)/2-STACKB(SP)*ROOT3/2
300   B = STACKA(SP)*ROOT3/2-STACKB(SP)/2
310   C = -STACKC(SP)/2-STACKD(SP)*ROOT3/2
320   D = STACKC(SP)*ROOT3/2-STACKD(SP)/2
330   GOSUB 100  'sphinx
340   X = STACKX(SP)+STACKA(SP)*STACKS(SP)+STACKB(SP)*STACKS(SP)*ROOT3/2
350   Y = STACKY(SP)+STACKC(SP)*STACKS(SP)+STACKD(SP)*STACKS(SP)*ROOT3/2
360   's = s2
370   A = STACKA(SP) : B = -STACKB(SP) : C = STACKC(SP) : D = -STACKD(SP)
380   GOSUB 100  'sphinx
390   S = STACKS(SP) : X = STACKX(SP) : Y = STACKY(SP)
400   A = STACKA(SP) : B = STACKB(SP) : C = STACKC(SP) : D = STACKD(SP)
410   SP = SP-1
420   S2 = STACKS2(SP)
430 RETURN

440 'SUBROUTINE draw tile
450   X1 = B*S*ROOT3/2 : Y1 = D*S*ROOT3/2
460   X2 = A*S : Y2 = C*S
470   LINE (X,Y)-(X+2*X1+X2,Y+2*Y1+Y2)
480   LINE -(X+X1+3*X2/2,Y+Y1+3*Y2/2)
490   LINE -(X+X1+5*X2/2,Y+Y1+5*Y2/2)
500   LINE -(X+3*X2,Y+3*Y2)
510   LINE -(X,Y)
520 RETURN
```

Program 6.12 Sphinx tiles.

increase in resolution could continue down to the level of individual grains of sand and even down to the molecular structure of matter itself.

When we draw a map of a coastline, the amount of detail that we can show depends on the scale of the map. Irregularities that would not appear on a small scale map would have to be included at a larger scale.

In this section, we look at a number of fractal curves that can be easily described recursively. In common with the coastline example, all of these curves share the property that, the more accurately they are plotted, the more variations will appear. The extent to which we can do this is, of course, limited by the resolution of the computer and the television or monitor. There will be a stage beyond which any attempts at greater accuracy will simply overwrite pixels that have already been plotted.

We first look at curves in which the variations are highly regular.

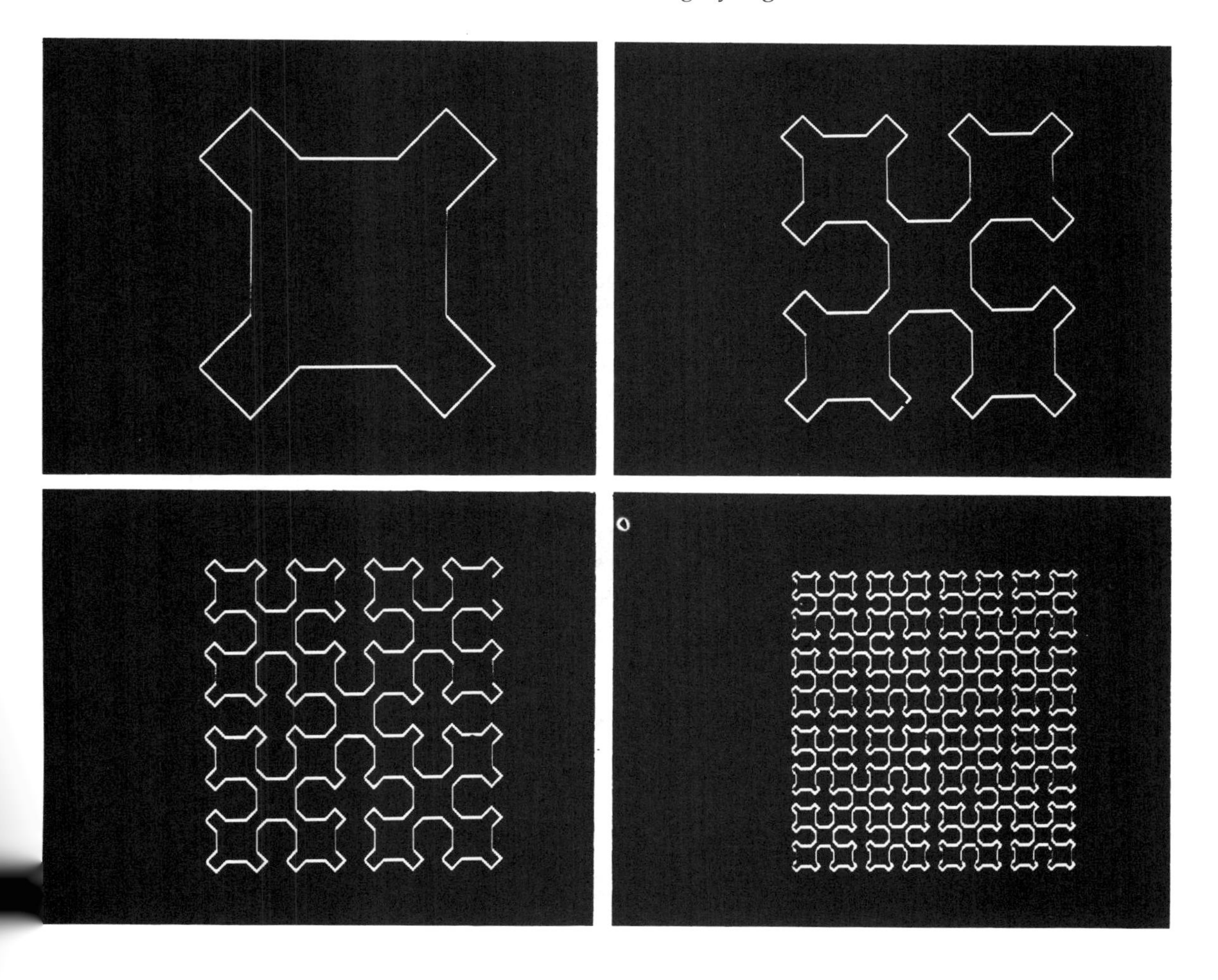

Figure 6.14
Sierpinski curves of orders 1 to 4

```
100 'SUBROUTINE sierpinski of order N centred at X,Y
120   IF N = 0 then draw a diamond and finish.
130   K = horizontal and vertical distances to the centres of the four
          subcurves.
140   Draw a sierpinski of order N-1 centred at X-K,Y-K
150   Draw a sierpinski of order N-1 centred at X-K,Y+K
160   Draw a sierpinski of order N-1 centred at X+K,Y+K
170   Draw a sierpinski of order N-1 centred at X+K,Y-K
180   Join these four subcurves at the centre.
230 RETURN
```

Program 6.13 Outline recursive subroutine for drawing a Sierpinski curve.

Later, we will show how the introduction of some degree of randomness allows us to use some of these curves to simulate the random variations in a coastline.

Sierpinski curves

Figure 6.14 shows the Sierpinski curves of orders 1 to 4. It is convenient to define a Sierpinski curve of order 0 which consists of a diamond (or a square rotated through 45°). Notice that each of these curves could be drawn as a continuous line, without lifting pencil from paper. We shall look at two ways of drawing these curves, where the second method draws the curve as a continuous line.

The first method is conceptually a little easier and for this approach we must first recognize that the Sierpinski curve of order 1 consists of four order 0 curves 'joined' at the centre. Similarly, the order 2 curve consists of four order 1 curves joined at the centre. In general, an order N curve consists of four order N – 1 curves joined at the centre. Note that when four subcurves are joined, this involves deleting four diagonal lines from the subcurves and joining the subcurves with two horizontal and two vertical lines. This suggests the outline given in Program 6.13 for a recursive subroutine to draw a Sierpinski curve of order N, centred at (x,y). In order to fill out this subroutine, we need to examine the geometrical details fairly carefully. Any curve of order 1 or more consists of

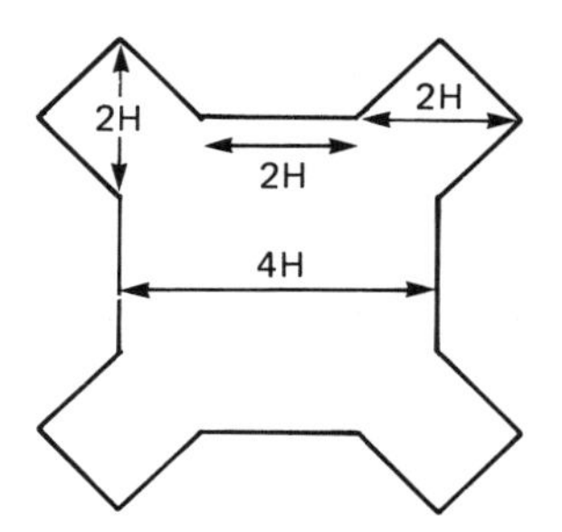

Figure 6.15 Dimensions of the basic shape in a Sierpinski curve

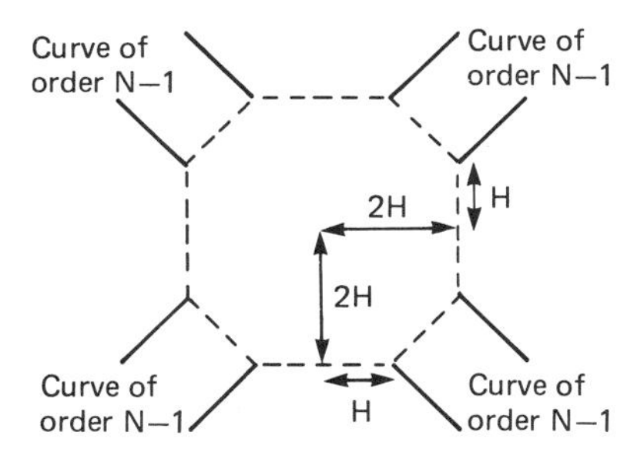

Figure 6.16
Dimensions at the centre of a Sierpinski curve of order N

```
 10 DIM STACKX(20),STACKY(20),STACKN(20),STACKK(20)
 20 CLS : LOCATE 1,1 : INPUT "Sierpinski curve: order (1..6) ";ORDER
 30 SIZE = (2^ORDER-1)*4+2
 40 H = INT(600/SIZE)
 50 H2 = H*2
 60 SCREEN 2 : WINDOW (0,0)-(1279,799)
 70 N = ORDER : X = 640 : Y = 400
 80 GOSUB 110  'sierpinski
 90 INPUT ANY$
100 END

110 'SUBROUTINE sierpinski
120   IF N = 0 THEN LINE (X-H,Y)-(X,Y+H) : LINE -(X+H,Y) :
                    LINE -(X,Y-H) : LINE -(X-H,Y) : RETURN
130   STACKK(SP) = K
140   SP = SP+1
150   K = 2^N*H
160   STACKN(SP) = N : STACKX(SP) = X : STACKY(SP) = Y
170   N = N-1
180   X = X-K : Y = Y-K
190   GOSUB 110  'sierpinski
200   X = STACKX(SP)-K : Y = STACKY(SP)+K
210   GOSUB 110  'sierpinski
220   X = STACKX(SP)+K : Y = STACKY(SP)+K
230   GOSUB 110  'sierpinski
240   X = STACKX(SP)+K : Y = STACKY(SP)-K
250   GOSUB 110  'sierpinski
260   X = STACKX(SP) : Y = STACKY(SP) : N = STACKN(SP)
270   LINE (X-H2,Y+H)-(X-H,Y+H2),0
280   LINE (X+H,Y+H2)-(X+H2,Y+H),0
290   LINE (X+H2,Y-H)-(X+H,Y-H2),0
300   LINE (X-H,Y-H2)-(X-H2,Y-H),0
310   LINE (X-H2,Y-H)-(X-H2,Y+H)
320   LINE (X-H,Y+H2)-(X+H,Y+H2)
330   LINE (X+H2,Y+H)-(X+H2,Y-H)
340   LINE (X+H,Y-H2)-(X-H,Y-H2)
350   SP = SP-1
360   K = STACKK(SP)
370 RETURN
```

Program 6.14 One way of drawing a Sierpinski curve.

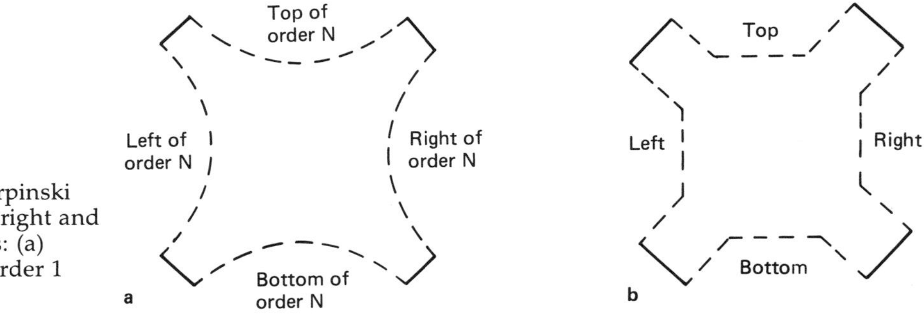

Figure 6.17
Breakdown of a Sierpinski curve into left, top, right and bottom components: (a) order N curve; (b) order 1 curve

repeated copies of the same basic shape and we shall name the various dimensions of this basic shape as in Figure 6.15. H is the smallest increment that will be required in our LINE statements. Thus the statements needed to draw a curve of order 0 (a diamond) centred at (x,y) are:

```
LINE (X-H, Y) - (X, Y+H) : LINE -(X+H, Y)
LINE -(X, Y-H) : LINE -(X-H, Y)
```

The distance from the centre of a curve of order N to the centre of one of its subcurves of order N – 1 is 2^NH. To convince yourself of this, you should mark the various distances on curves of different orders.

Finally, the situation at the centre of a curve of order N, when the four subcurves of order N – 1 have been drawn, can be illustrated as shown in Figure 6.16.

We need to delete the four dotted diagonal lines and draw the dotted vertical and horizontal lines. This can be easily accomplished by first plotting the diagonal lines in the background colour and then drawing the remaining lines. Program 6.14 is the complete program.

It is interesting to look at an alternative approach to drawing the Sierpinski curves by drawing the curve as a continuous line. This is the approach that would have to be used if the curve were to be drawn on a hard copy device (where lines cannot be deleted). This method is based on an algorithm described by Wirth (the inventor of the programming language Pascal).

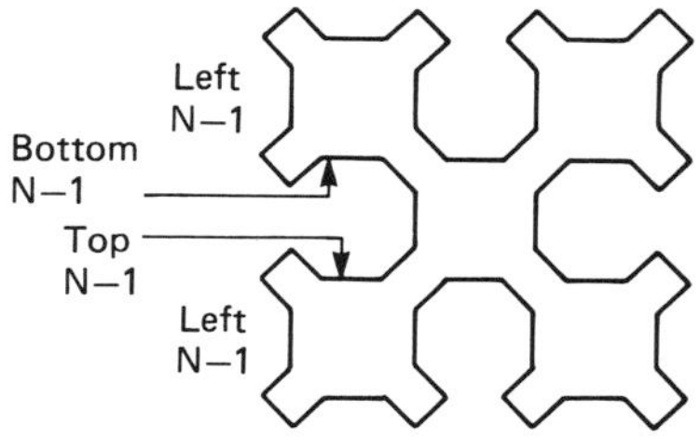

Figure 6.18
Composition of the 'left' component of an order 2 Sierpinski curve

We first observe that a curve of order N consists of four components connected at the corners – a left component, a top component, a right component and a bottom component (Figure 6.17a). For example, in the case of the order 1 curve, we have the curve shown in Figure 6.17b. The subroutine for drawing a Sierpinski curve of order N will be defined in terms of subroutines for drawing its four components. This is the subroutine 'sierpinski' in Program 6.15.

Now an order N *component* is made up of a sequence of order N – 1 components joined in a well-defined way. For example, a left component of order N consists of:

a left component of order N – 1
a diagonal line
a top component of order N – 1
a vertical line
a bottom component of order N – 1
a diagonal line
a left component of order N – 1

For example, with N = 2, we have Figure 6.18. If N = 0, the components are empty. (Joining four empty components diagonally

```
 10 DIM STACKN(20)
 20 CLS : LOCATE 1,1 : INPUT "Sierpinski curve: order (1..6) ";ORDER
 30 SIZE = (2^ORDER-1)*4+2
 40 H = INT(600/SIZE)
 50 H2 = H*2
 60 SCREEN 2 : WINDOW (0,0)-(1279,799)
 70 NX = 300 : NY = 100+H : PSET(NX,NY)
 80 N = ORDER
 90 GOSUB 120  'sierpinski
100 INPUT ANY$
110 END

120 'SUBROUTINE sierpinski
130   GOSUB 220  'left
140   NX = NX+H : NY = NY+H : LINE -(NX,NY)
150   GOSUB 350  'top
160   NX = NX+H : NY = NY-H : LINE -(NX,NY)
170   GOSUB 480  'right
180   NX = NX-H : NY = NY-H : LINE -(NX,NY)
190   GOSUB 610  'bottom
200   NX = NX-H : NY = NY+H : LINE -(NX,NY)
210 RETURN

220 'SUBROUTINE left
230   IF N = 0 THEN RETURN
240   SP = SP+1 : STACKN(SP) = N
250   N = N-1
```

Program 6.15 Drawing a Sierpinski curve as a continuous line. *continued*

```
260   GOSUB 220  'left
270   NX = NX+H : NY = NY+H : LINE -(NX,NY)
280   GOSUB 350  'top
290   NX = NX : NY = NY+H2 : LINE -(NX,NY)
300   GOSUB 610  'bottom
310   NX = NX-H : NY = NY+H : LINE -(NX,NY)
320   GOSUB 220  'left
330   N = STACKN(SP) : SP = SP-1
340 RETURN

350 'SUBROUTINE top
360   IF N = 0 THEN RETURN
370   SP = SP+1 : STACKN(SP) = N
380   N = N-1
390   GOSUB 350  'top
400   NX = NX+H : NY = NY-H : LINE -(NX,NY)
410   GOSUB 480  'right
420   NX = NX+H2 : NY = NY : LINE -(NX,NY)
430   GOSUB 220  'left
440   NX = NX+H : NY = NY+H : LINE -(NX,NY)
450   GOSUB 350  'top
460   N = STACKN(SP) : SP = SP-1
470 RETURN

480 'SUBROUTINE right
490   IF N = 0 THEN RETURN
500   SP = SP+1 : STACKN(SP) = N
510   N = N-1
520   GOSUB 480  'right
530   NX = NX-H : NY = NY-H : LINE -(NX,NY)
540   GOSUB 610  'bottom
550   NX = NX : NY = NY-H2 : LINE -(NX,NY)
560   GOSUB 350  'top
570   NX = NX+H : NY = NY-H : LINE -(NX,NY)
580   GOSUB 480  'right
590   N = STACKN(SP) : SP = SP-1
600 RETURN

610 'SUBROUTINE bottom
620   IF N = 0 THEN RETURN
630   SP = SP+1 : STACKN(SP) = N
640   N = N-1
650   GOSUB 610  'bottom
660   NX = NX-H : NY = NY+H : LINE -(NX,NY)
670   GOSUB 220  'left
680   NX = NX-H2 : NY = NY : LINE -(NX,NY)
690   GOSUB 480  'right
700   NX = NX-H : NY = NY-H : LINE -(NX,NY)
710   GOSUB 610  'bottom
720   N = STACKN(SP) : SP = SP-1
730 RETURN
```

Program 6.15 *continued*

at the corners gives a diamond shape.) This gives the subroutine 'left' for drawing a left component of order N. A similar breakdown can be achieved for the top, right and bottom components and the complete program is Program 6.15.

You should notice that there are two types of recursion involved in the last program. There is straightforward recursion where, for example, subroutine 'left' calls subroutine 'left'. There is also 'hidden' or 'mutual' recursion where, for example, subroutine 'left' calls subroutine 'top' which in turn calls subroutine 'left'.

You should run both Sierpinski programs and observe the differences in their behaviour.

```
 10 DIM STACKN(20)
 20 CLS : LOCATE 1,1 : INPUT "W-curve: order (1..6) ";ORDER
 30 SIZE = (2^ORDER+1)-1
 40 H = 300/SIZE
 50 SCREEN 2 : WINDOW (0,0)-(1279,799)
 60 NX = 300 : NY = 100+H : PSET(NX,NY)
 70 N = ORDER
 80 GOSUB 110  'w-curve
 90 INPUT ANY$
100 END

110 'SUBROUTINE w-curve
120   GOSUB 250  'left
130   NX = NX+H : LINE -(NX,NY)
140   NY = NY+H : LINE -(NX,NY)
150   GOSUB 400  'top
160   NY = NY-H : LINE -(NX,NY)
170   NX = NX+H : LINE -(NX,NY)
180   GOSUB 550  'right
190   NX = NX-H : LINE -(NX,NY)
200   NY = NY-H : LINE -(NX,NY)
210   GOSUB 700  'bottom
220   NY = NY+H : LINE -(NX,NY)
230   NX = NX-H : LINE -(NX,NY)
240 RETURN

250 'SUBROUTINE left
260   IF N = 1 THEN NY = NY+H : LINE -(NX,NY) : RETURN
270   SP = SP+1 : STACKN(SP) = N
280   N = N-1
290   GOSUB 250  'left
300   NX = NX+H : LINE -(NX,NY)
310   NY = NY+H : LINE -(NX,NY)
320   GOSUB 400  'top
330   NY = NY+H : LINE -(NX,NY)
340   GOSUB 700  'bottom
350   NY = NY+H : LINE -(NX,NY)
360   NX = NX-H : LINE -(NX,NY)
```

Program 6.16 Drawing a W-curve as a continuous line.

continued

```
370   GOSUB 250  'left
380   N = STACKN(SP) : SP = SP-1
390 RETURN

400 'SUBROUTINE top
410   IF N = 1 THEN NX = NX+H : LINE -(NX,NY) : RETURN
420   SP = SP+1 : STACKN(SP) = N
430   N = N-1
440   GOSUB 400  'top
450   NY = NY-H : LINE -(NX,NY)
460   NX = NX+H : LINE -(NX,NY)
470   GOSUB 550  'right
480   NX = NX+H : LINE -(NX,NY)
490   GOSUB 250  'left
500   NX = NX+H : LINE -(NX,NY)
510   NY = NY+H : LINE -(NX,NY)
520   GOSUB 400  'top
530   N = STACKN(SP) : SP = SP-1
540 RETURN

550 'SUBROUTINE right
560   IF N = 1 THEN NY = NY-H : LINE -(NX,NY) : RETURN
570   SP = SP+1 : STACKN(SP) = N
580   N = N-1
590   GOSUB 550  'right
600   NX = NX-H : LINE -(NX,NY)
610   NY = NY-H : LINE -(NX,NY)
620   GOSUB 700  'bottom
630   NY = NY-H : LINE -(NX,NY)
640   GOSUB 400  'top
650   NY = NY-H : LINE -(NX,NY)
660   NX = NX+H : LINE -(NX,NY)
670   GOSUB 550  'right
680   N = STACKN(SP) : SP = SP-1
690 RETURN

700 'SUBROUTINE bottom
710   IF N = 1 THEN NX = NX-H : LINE -(NX,NY) : RETURN
720   SP = SP+1 : STACKN(SP) = N
730   N = N-1
740   GOSUB 700  'bottom
750   NY = NY+H : LINE -(NX,NY)
760   NX = NX-H : LINE -(NX,NY)
770   GOSUB 250  'left
780   NX = NX-H : LINE -(NX,NY)
790   GOSUB 550  'right
800   NX = NX-H : LINE -(NX,NY)
810   NY = NY-H : LINE -(NX,NY)
820   GOSUB 700  'bottom
830   N = STACKN(SP) : SP = SP-1
840 RETURN
```

Program 6.16 *continued*

Figure 6.19
W-curves of orders 1 to 4

W-curves

Another curve that is closely related to the Sierpinski curve is the W-curve suggested by Wirth. Program 6.16 draws a W-curve and the results appear in Figure 6.19.

C-curves

The C-curve is a well-known fractal curve that can be easily generated recursively. Some C-curves are displayed in Figure 6.20, and the reasons for the name should be obvious. To see how it is constructed see Figure 6.21, which shows the first six generations of C-curves. The first generation C-curve is a straight line. The second generation C-curve is obtained from the first by replacing the line by an 'elbow' consisting of two equal lines at 45° to the original and at right angles to each other. Each generation of C-curve is obtained by replacing every straight line in the previous generation curve by an

```
10 DIM STACKX1(20),STACKX2(20),STACKY1(20),STACKY2(20)
20 DIM STACKMX(20),STACKMY(20)
30 THETA = 45 : PI = 3.141593
40 SINTH = SIN(THETA*PI/180) : COSTH = COS(THETA*PI/180)
50 SCREEN 2 : CLS : WINDOW (0,0)-(1279,799)
60 RESOLUTION = 15
70 RESSQ = RESOLUTION*RESOLUTION
80 X1 = 450 : Y1 = 300 : X2 = 830 : Y2 = 300
90 GOSUB 120  'ccurve
100 INPUT ANY$
110 END

120 'SUBROUTINE ccurve
130   XDIFF = X2-X1 : YDIFF = Y2-Y1
140   IF XDIFF*XDIFF+YDIFF*YDIFF =< RESSQ THEN LINE (X1,Y1)-(X2,Y2) : RETURN
150   STACKMX(SP) = MX : STACKMY(SP) = MY
160   SP = SP+1
170   STACKX1(SP) = X1 : STACKY1(SP) = Y1
180   STACKX2(SP) = X2 : STACKY2(SP) = Y2
190   XDIR = XDIFF/2/COSTH : YDIR = YDIFF/2/COSTH
200   MX = X1+XDIR*COSTH-YDIR*SINTH
210   MY = Y1+XDIR*SINTH+YDIR*COSTH
220   X2 = MX : Y2 = MY  'x1 = x1 : y1 = y1
230   GOSUB 120  'ccurve
240   X1 = MX : Y1 = MY : X2 = STACKX2(SP) : Y2 = STACKY2(SP)
250   GOSUB 120  'ccurve
260   X1 = STACKX1(SP) : Y1 = STACKY1(SP)
270   X2 = STACKX2(SP) : Y2 = STACKY2(SP)
280   SP = SP-1
290   MX = STACKMX(SP) : MY = STACKMY(SP)
300 RETURN
```

Program 6.17 C-curve.

elbow. Successive elbows are placed on the same side of the curve.

In Program 6.17, subroutine 'ccurve' joins two points with a C-curve. If the length of the line between the two points is less than 'RESOLUTION' then the C-curve is simply plotted as a straight line. Otherwise the coordinates of the 'elbow joint' are calculated and two recursive calls of 'ccurve' are used to join the first point to the elbow joint, and to join the elbow joint to the second point.

There are several parameters that can be varied in the C-curve program. The resolution can be varied to determine the generation of curve produced. This is how the six curves in Figure 6.21 were generated. Figure 6.20b shows a curve joining the same two points as were joined in Figure 6.20a, but at a different resolution.

Another variation that can be tried in Program 6.17 is to vary the angle that the two halves of the elbow make with the line joining the two end points. (The elbow will no longer be a right angle.) This is

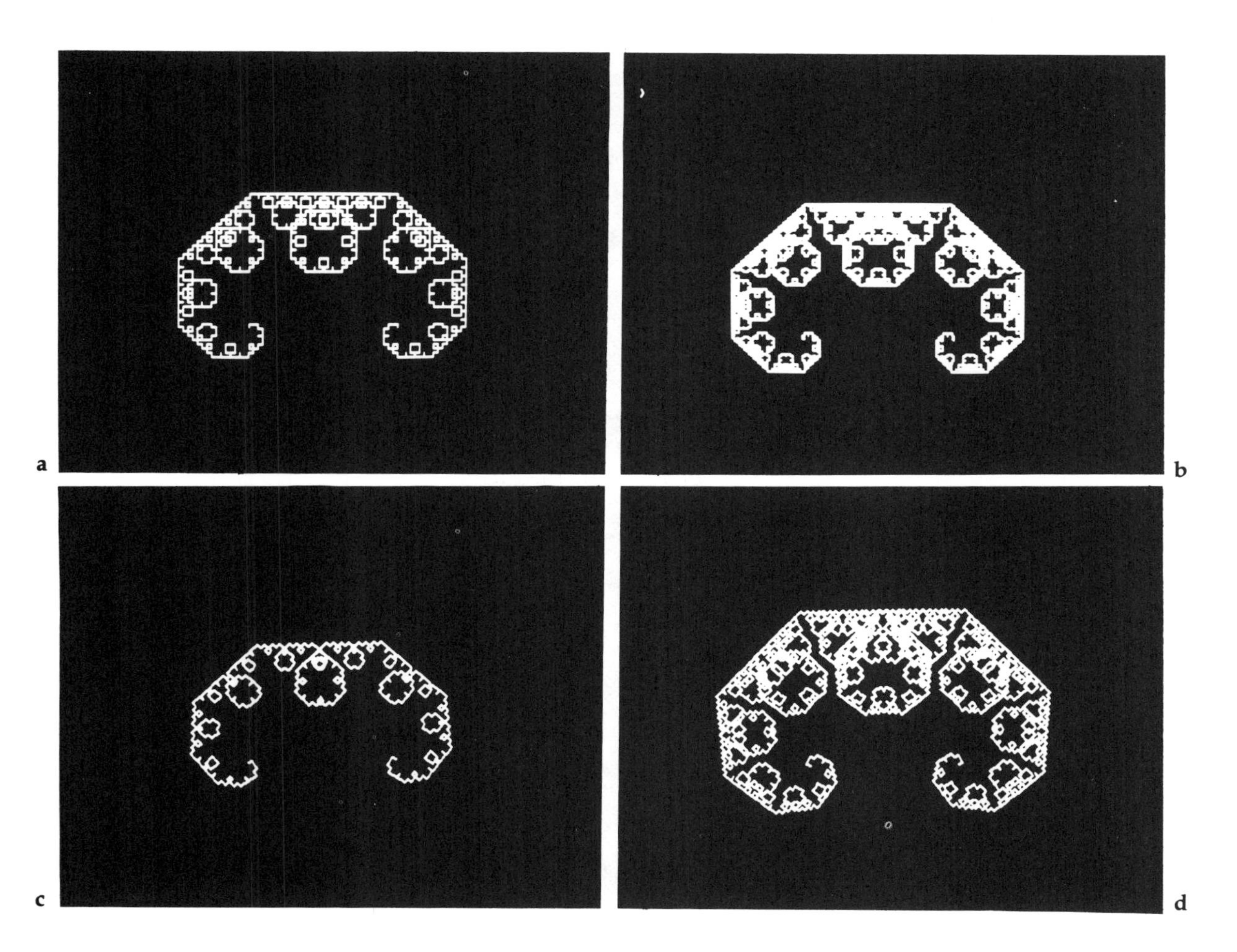

Figure 6.20
A selection of C-curves: (a) THETA = 45, RESOLUTION = 15; (b) THETA = 45, RESOLUTION = 8; (c) THETA = 43, RESOLUTION = 15; (d) THETA = 47, RESOLUTION = 1

done by varying the angle called 'THETA' in the program. The results of doing this are shown in the second pair of pictures in Figure 6.20. We will be saying more about such variations later.

Dragon curves

Another curve in the same family as the C-curve is the 'dragon curve', so called because its overall shape resembles a dragon. Figure 6.22 shows the first six generations of dragon curve. These are generated in a way that is very similar to the way in which the C-curves are generated. However, in this case, the elbows are placed on alternate sides of the curve. The curves in Figure 6.23 were generated by Program 6.18 using variations in the angle, 'THETA', that the sides forming an elbow make with the line they replace.

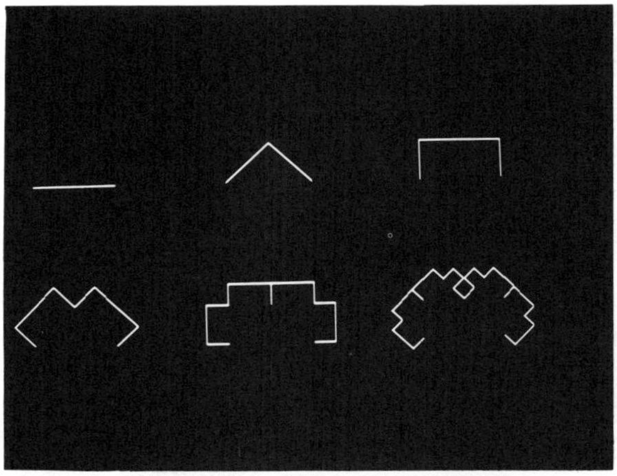

Figure 6.21
First six generations of C-curve

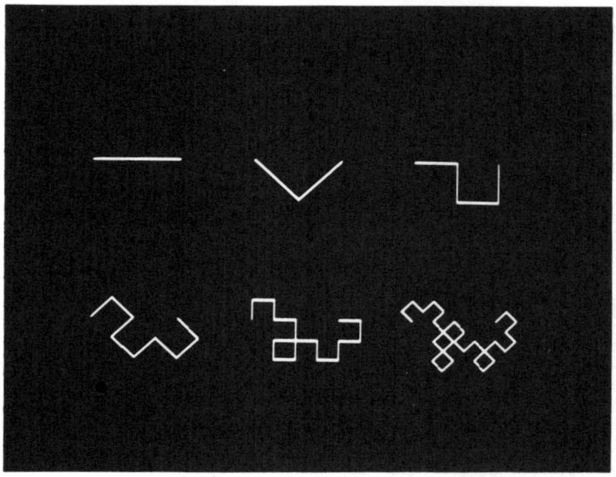

Figure 6.22
First six generations of dragon curve

Higher order line replacement in C-curves and dragon curves
The C-curves and dragon curves were generated by recursively replacing a line by two equal line segments. An interesting extension to this idea is to recursively replace a line by a sequence of more than two line segments. Program 6.19 does this, always making its replacement on the same side of the curve. Some of the results are shown in Figure 6.24a. We have had to use a GOTO loop instead of a FOR loop in subroutine 'fractal' in order to avoid the error message 'Out of memory' that can appear in some cases.

A simple variation to Program 6.19 can be used to make line replacement take place on alternate sides of the curve. (Subroutine 'fractal' needs an extra parameter whose sign indicates the side of the curve on which replacement should take place.) The results obtained are shown in Figure 6.24b.

Figure 6.23
A selection of dragon curves (RESOLUTION = 15): (a) THETA = 43; (b) THETA = 45; (c) THETA = 47; (d) THETA = 49

6.7 FRACTAL VARIATIONS – SIMULATING A COASTLINE

In this section, we will look at ways in which we can generate fractal curves that simulate naturally occurring silhouettes like coastlines or skylines. Techniques like those we describe can be generalized to three dimensions, and can be used for creating natural textures on surfaces in images generated as backgrounds in flight simulators, or in computer-assisted animation. The mathematics of fractal curves is complex, and we do not cover this in detail. As before, we adopt a straightforward recursive approach.

Natural outlines tend to connect points in a very definite way. The initial shape of a coastline is originally determined by the geological events that created the landmass. The action of sea and wind then generates random variations that are superimposed on this initial outline.

```
 10 DIM STACKX1(20),STACKX2(20),STACKY1(20),STACKY2(20)
 20 DIM STACKMX(20),STACKMY(20),STACKTHETA(20)
 30 POSTHETA = 45 : PI = 3.141593
 40 POSSIN = SIN(POSTHETA*PI/180) : COSTH = COS(POSTHETA*PI/180)
 50 SCREEN 2 : CLS : WINDOW (0,0)-(1279,799)
 60 RESOLUTION = 15
 70 RESSQ = RESOLUTION*RESOLUTION
 80 X1 = 300 : Y1 = 500 : X2 = 900 : Y2 = 500 : THETA = -POSTHETA
 90 GOSUB 120  'dragon curve
100 INPUT ANY$
110 END

120 'SUBROUTINE dragon curve
130   IF THETA > 0 THEN SINTH = POSSIN ELSE SINTH = -POSSIN
140   XDIFF = X2-X1 : YDIFF = Y2-Y1
150   IF XDIFF*XDIFF+YDIFF*YDIFF =< RESSQ THEN LINE (X1,Y1)-(X2,Y2) : RETURN
```

Program 6.18 Dragon curve.

What we will do here is describe how to make a program superimpose realistic random variations on what is initially a very simple outline. We will do this by replacing successive straight line segments in the original outline by fractal curves that exhibit some randomness.

```
 10 DIM STACKX1(20),STACKX2(20),STACKY1(20),STACKY2(20)
 20 DIM STACKPREVX(20),STACKPREVY(20),STACKNEXTX(20),STACKNEXTY(20)
 30 DIM STACKMIDX(20),STACKMIDY(20),STACKS(20)
 40 INPUT "Sides ";SIDES
 50 THETA = 180/SIDES : PI = 3.141593
 60 SINTH = SIN(THETA*PI/180) : COSTH = COS(THETA*PI/180)
 70 SCREEN 2 : CLS : WINDOW (0,0)-(1279,799)
 80 RESOLUTION = 15
 90 RESSQ = RESOLUTION*RESOLUTION
100 X1 = 450 : Y1 = 300 : X2 = 830 : Y2 = 300
110 GOSUB 140  'fractal
120 INPUT ANY$
130 END

140 'SUBROUTINE fractal
150   XDIFF = X2-X1 : YDIFF = Y2-Y1
160   IF XDIFF*XDIFF+YDIFF*YDIFF =< RESSQ THEN LINE (X1,Y1)-(X2,Y2) : RETURN
170   STACKMIDX(SP) = MIDX : STACKMIDY(SP) = MIDY
180   STACKPREVX(SP) = PREVX : STACKNEXTX(SP) = NEXTX
190   STACKPREVY(SP) = PREVY : STACKNEXTY(SP) = NEXTY
200   STACKS(SP) = S
210   SP = SP+1
```

Program 6.19 Higher-order C-curves.

```
160   STACKMX(SP) = MX : STACKMY(SP) = MY
170   SP = SP+1
180   STACKX1(SP) = X1 : STACKY1(SP) = Y1
190   STACKX2(SP) = X2 : STACKY2(SP) = Y2 : STACKTHETA(SP) = THETA
200   XDIR = XDIFF/2/COSTH : YDIR = YDIFF/2/COSTH
210   MX = X1+XDIR*COSTH-YDIR*SINTH
220   MY = Y1+XDIR*SINTH+YDIR*COSTH
230   X2 = MX : Y2 = MY : THETA = POSTHETA
240   GOSUB 120  'dragon curve
250   X1 = MX : Y1 = MY : X2 = STACKX2(SP) : Y2 = STACKY2(SP) : THETA = -POSTHETA
260   GOSUB 120  'dragon curve
270   X1 = STACKX1(SP) : Y1 = STACKY1(SP)
280   X2 = STACKX2(SP) : Y2 = STACKY2(SP) : THETA = STACKTHETA(SP)
290   SP = SP-1
300   MX = STACKMX(SP) : MY = STACKMY(SP)
310 RETURN
```

A completely random curve could be generated by repeatedly drawing a short line segment in a completely random direction.

```
WHILE TRUE : THETA = RND(360)
  LINE -(8*COS(RAD(THETA)), 8*SIN(RAD(THETA)))
WEND
```

```
220   STACKX1(SP) = X1 : STACKY1(SP) = Y1
230   STACKX2(SP) = X2 : STACKY2(SP) = Y2
240   XDIR = XDIFF/2 : YDIR = YDIFF/2
250   MIDX = X1+XDIR : MIDY = Y1+YDIR
260   PREVX = XDIR : PREVY = YDIR
270   S = 1
280     NEXTX = PREVX*COSTH-PREVY*SINTH
290     NEXTY = PREVX*SINTH+PREVY*COSTH
300     X1 = MIDX+NEXTX : Y1 = MIDY+NEXTY
310     X2 = MIDX+PREVX : Y2 = MIDY+PREVY
320     GOSUB 140  'fractal
330     PREVX = NEXTX : PREVY = NEXTY
340   S = S+1 : IF S <= SIDES GOTO 280
350   X1 = STACKX1(SP) : Y1 = STACKY1(SP)
360   X2 = STACKX2(SP) : Y2 = STACKY2(SP)
370   SP = SP-1
380   MIDX = STACKMIDX(SP) : MIDY = STACKMIDY(SP)
390   PREVX = STACKPREVX(SP) : PREVY = STACKPREVY(SP)
400   NEXTX = STACKNEXTX(SP) : NEXTY = STACKNEXTY(SP)
410   S = STACKS(SP)
420 RETURN
```

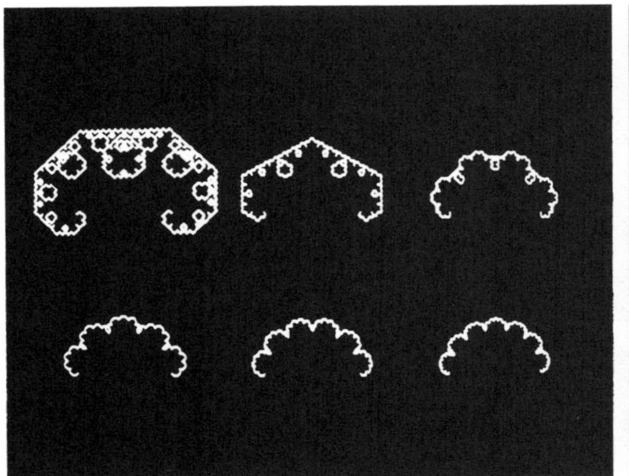

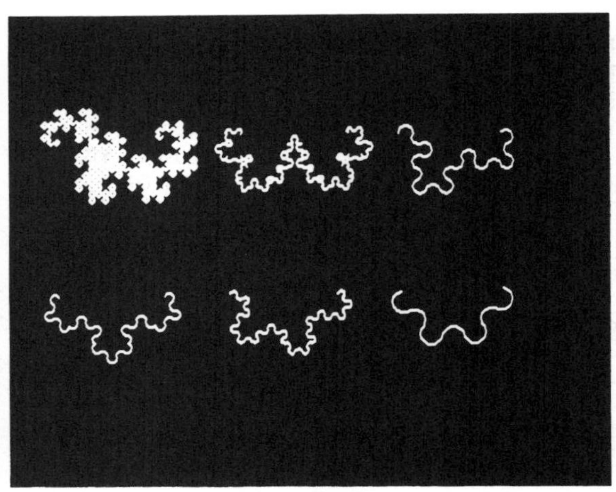

Figure 6.24
Higher order line replacement (a) in a C-curve (b) in a dragon curve

However, if you try this, you will find that the curve produced meanders aimlessly (with so-called Brownian motion).

We require a curve that connects two points, but exhibits random behaviour between the two points. To do this, we can add a random element to the process that was used to generate the C-curves and dragon curves described earlier. The operation used to introduce new levels of discontinuity into these curves was to recursively replace a line by an 'equilateral elbow', where the sides of the elbow made an angle 'THETA' with the line they replaced. We have found that the most effective way of generating a realistic 'coastline curve' that connects two points is to select 'THETA' at random at every replacement stage. We still use an equilateral elbow (Figure 6.25).

The range of values that 'THETA' is allowed to take determines the character of the coastline. Program 6.20 can be used to demonstrate this. It generates a random fractal curve between two points. At each recursive step, 'THETA' is selected randomly from the range

```
- MAXTHETA ... + MAXTHETA
```

Low values of 'MAXTHETA' result in minor variations in direction and larger values result in more violent fluctuations. This is illustr-

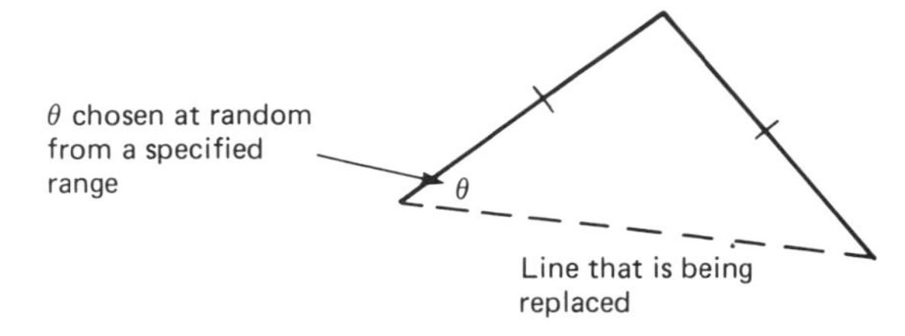

Figure 6.25
Recursive replacement of a line by an equilateral 'elbow' to generate random irregularities

ated in Figure 6.26 where the subroutine 'fractal' from Program 6.20 has been used to connect pairs of points for nine different values of 'MAXTHETA' ranging from 20° to 60°. With values of 'MAXTHETA' greater than 40° or 45°, there is a tendency for the curve to turn back on itself.

Figure 6.27a shows a map of Britain and Ireland that has been digitized fairly coarsely. For comparison, Figure 6.27b shows successive points on the coast connected by C-curves. Program 6.21 was used to add some realistic variations to the map's outline by generating random fractal curves between successive points round the coast, and the results are shown in the last two photographs in Figure 6.27. The best results were obtained by using 'MAXTHETA

```
  1 RANDOMIZE
 10 DIM STACKX1(20),STACKX2(20),STACKY1(20),STACKY2(20)
 20 DIM STACKMX(20),STACKMY(20)
 30 PI = 3.141593
 40 DEF FNRAD(DEGREES) = DEGREES*PI/180
 50 SCREEN 2 : CLS : WINDOW (0,0)-(1279,799)
 60 RESOLUTION = 10
 70 RESSQ = RESOLUTION*RESOLUTION
 80 MAXTHETA = 40
 90 X1 = 450 : Y1 = 500 : X2 = 830 : Y2 = 500
100 GOSUB 130  'fractal
110 INPUT ANY$
120 END

130 'SUBROUTINE fractal
140   XDIFF = X2-X1 : YDIFF = Y2-Y1
150   IF XDIFF*XDIFF+YDIFF*YDIFF =< RESSQ THEN LINE (X1,Y1)-(X2,Y2) : RETURN
160   STACKMX(SP) = MX : STACKMY(SP) = MY
170   SP = SP+1
180   STACKX1(SP) = X1 : STACKY1(SP) = Y1
190   STACKX2(SP) = X2 : STACKY2(SP) = Y2
200   THETA = MAXTHETA-RND*(2*MAXTHETA)+1
210   SINTH = SIN(FNRAD(THETA)) : COSTH = COS(FNRAD(THETA))
220   XDIR = XDIFF/2/COSTH : YDIR = YDIFF/2/COSTH
230   MX = X1+XDIR*COSTH-YDIR*SINTH
240   MY = Y1+XDIR*SINTH+YDIR*COSTH
250   X2 = MX : Y2 = MY  'x1 = x1 : y1 = y1
260   GOSUB 130  'fractal
270   X1 = MX : Y1 = MY : X2 = STACKX2(SP) : Y2 = STACKY2(SP)
280   GOSUB 130  'fractal
290   X1 = STACKX1(SP) : Y1 = STACKY1(SP)
300   X2 = STACKX2(SP) : Y2 = STACKY2(SP)
310   SP = SP-1
320   MX = STACKMX(SP) : MY = STACKMY(SP)
330 RETURN
```

Program 6.20 A random fractal curve.

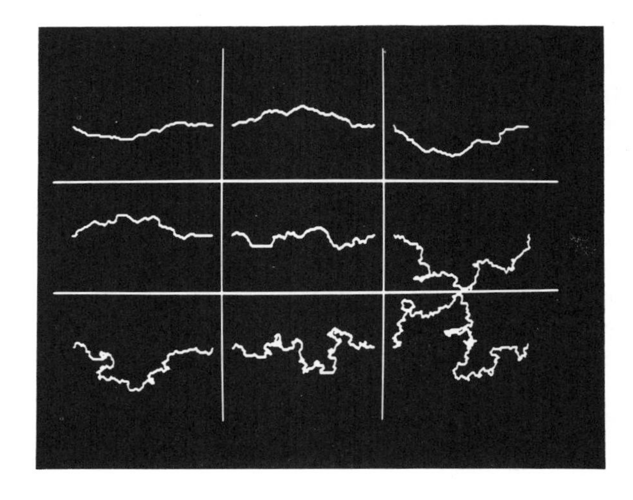

Figure 6.26
'Coastline' effects joining two points for various ranges of data: (values used for MAXTHETA range from 20 to 60 steps of 5°

Figure 6.27
Fractal variations on a map of Britain: (a) coarsely digitized; (b) filled in with C-curves; (c) MAXSTEP = 50, MAXTHETA = 40; (d) MAXSTEP = 30, MAXTHETA = 60

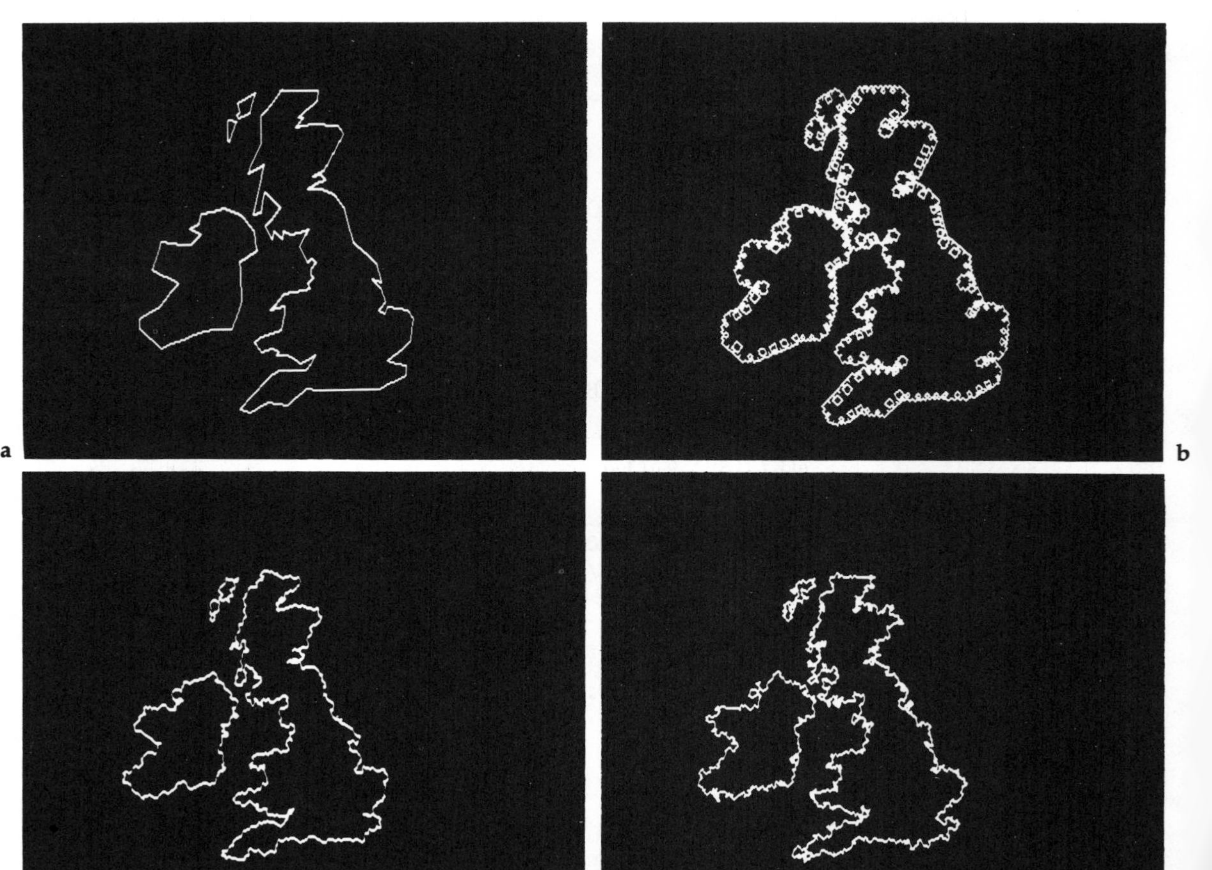

```
 10 DIM STACKX1(20),STACKX2(20),STACKY1(20),STACKY2(20)
 20 DIM STACKMX(20),STACKMY(20)
 30 MAXTHETA = 40
 40 DIM SINE(MAXTHETA),COSINE(MAXTHETA)
 50 PI = 3.141593
 60 KEY OFF
 70 FOR A = 0 TO MAXTHETA
 80   SINE(A) = SIN(A*PI/180)
 90   COSINE(A) = COS(A*PI/180)
100 NEXT A
110 RESOLUTION = 12
120 RESSQ = RESOLUTION*RESOLUTION
130 MAXSTEP = 50
140 SCREEN 2 : WINDOW (0,70)-(1279,869) : CLS
150 MAPFILENUM = 3
160 OPEN "MAP" FOR INPUT AS #MAPFILENUM
170 INPUT #MAPFILENUM, PLOTOP,X,Y
180 PREVX = X : PREVY = Y
190 PSET (PREVX,PREVY)
200 WHILE NOT EOF(MAPFILENUM)
210   INPUT #MAPFILENUM, PLOTOP,X,Y
220   IF PLOTOP = 5 THEN NEXTX = X : NEXTY = Y : GOSUB 270  'join
230   PREVX = X : PREVY = Y
240 WEND
250 CLOSE #MAPFILENUM
260 END

270 'SUBROUTINE join
280   LJXDIFF = NEXTX-PREVX : LJYDIFF = NEXTY-PREVY
290   LJSTEPS = INT(SQR(LJXDIFF*LJXDIFF+LJYDIFF*LJYDIFF)/MAXSTEP)+1
300   LJXSTEP = LJXDIFF/LJSTEPS
310   LJYSTEP = LJYDIFF/LJSTEPS
320   FOR LJS = 1 TO LJSTEPS
330     LJX = PREVX+LJXSTEP : LJY = PREVY+LJYSTEP
340     X1 = PREVX : Y1 = PREVY : X2 = LJX : Y2 = LJY : GOSUB 380  'fractal
350     PREVX = LJX : PREVY = LJY
360   NEXT LJS
370 RETURN

380 'SUBROUTINE fractal
390   XDIFF = X2-X1 : YDIFF = Y2-Y1
400   IF XDIFF*XDIFF+YDIFF*YDIFF =< RESSQ THEN LINE (X1,Y1)-(X2,Y2) : RETURN
410   STACKMX(SP) = MX : STACKMY(SP) = MY
420   SP = SP+1
430   STACKX1(SP) = X1 : STACKY1(SP) = Y1
440   STACKX2(SP) = X2 : STACKY2(SP) = Y2
450   THETA = INT(MAXTHETA-RND*(2*MAXTHETA)+1)
460   IF THETA < 0 THEN SINTH = -SINE(-THETA) : COSTH = COSINE(-THETA)
      ELSE SINTH = SINE(THETA) : COSTH = COSINE(THETA)
470   XDIR = XDIFF/2/COSTH : YDIR = YDIFF/2/COSTH
480   MX = X1+XDIR*COSTH-YDIR*SINTH
```

Program 6.21 Imposing fractal variations on a coarsely digitized map. *continued*

```
490    MY = Y1+XDIR*SINTH+YDIR*COSTH
500    X2 = MX : Y2 = MY  'x1 = x1 : y1 = y1
510    GOSUB 380  'fractal
520    X1 = MX : Y1 = MY : X2 = STACKX2(SP) : Y2 = STACKY2(SP)
530    GOSUB 380  'fractal
540    X1 = STACKX1(SP) : Y1 = STACKY1(SP)
550    X2 = STACKX2(SP) : Y2 = STACKY2(SP)
560    SP = SP-1
570    MX = STACKMX(SP) : MY = STACKMY(SP)
580 RETURN
```

Program 6.21 *continued*

= 40′ and by proceeding round the coast in steps of about 50 units of length at a time.

Finally, Figure 6.28 shows the results of colour filling a fractal map of Britain. This could be done using PAINT.

Recursively generated trees

Mathematically generated computer art can sometimes mean extracting as much variation as possible from a program by building into it suitable parameters for variation. The resulting variations in shape that are generated by the program can then be tuned to the desired result. This is nowhere better illustrated than in the tree-generating program that will generate a large variety of tree-like or plant-like forms.

The program is a simple example of recursion and uses the design statement:

'A tree is a branch with a tree on the end of it'.

To draw the tree we simply write a subroutine that draws a branch

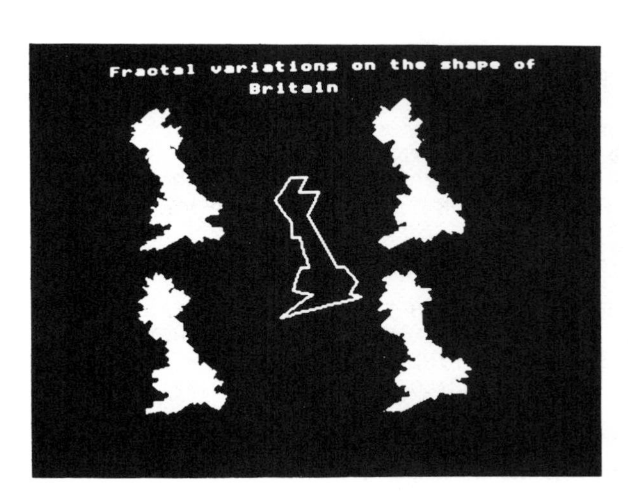

Figure 6.28
Colour-filled fractal variations on a map of Britain

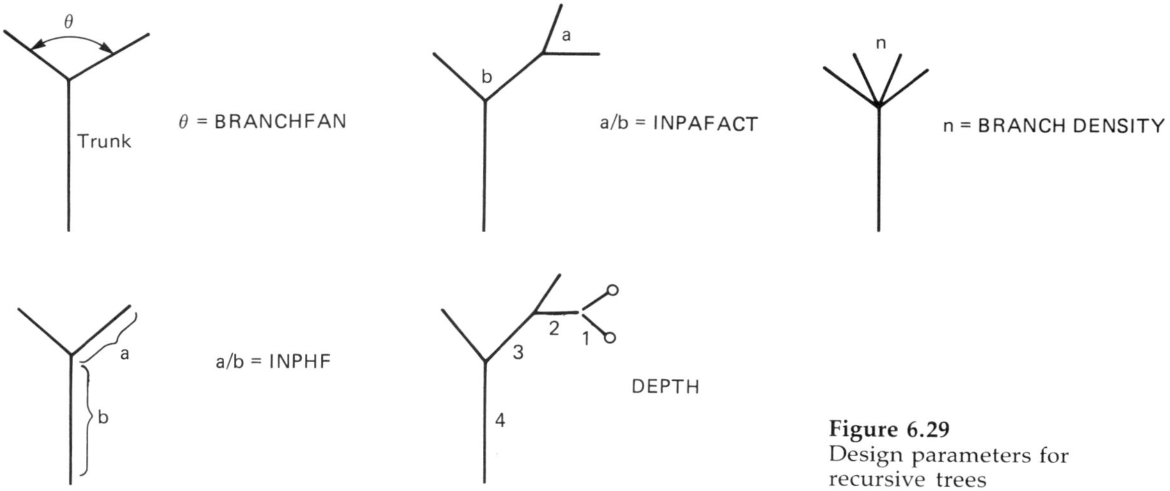

Figure 6.29
Design parameters for recursive trees

and then recursively calls itself. The variation parameters that we build into the program are shown in Figure 6.29, and the program is Program 6.22.

Six design parameters are used. The first parameter, 'RAND', is a randomizing parameter. If it is set to 0 there is no random element in the program. If it is set to 1 then the angle that each branch makes has a random perturbation added to it. Its length is also randomly perturbed. This means that the program will generate different trees using identical design parameters. The forms will, however, have an underlying 'sameness', the nature of which can be seen by examining Figure 6.30, which shows four executions of the program for identical parameters. Considerable aesthetic improvement results from the use of colour, and Colour Plate 14 is the output from a colour version of the program. One colour is used for the branches and one for the tips.

The next figure, Figure 6.31, contains three pairs of pictures. Each pair consists of a regular tree, together with its corresponding randomized version. The regular tree is generated with the randomizing parameter set to 0 and the randomized tree with the parameter set to 1. The remaining five parameters are identical for each pair.

The significance of the remaining five design parameters can be understood by studying Figure 6.29. These design parameters control the overall shape or 'look' of the tree. The first one is 'BRANCHFAN' and this is the angle between the first and last branches. The second parameter is 'INPAFACT' (input angle factor) and this determines the ratio between the branch angles at consecutive depths. The next parameter, 'BRANCHDENSITY', is the number of branches that emanate from a node. 'INPHF' (input height

Figure 6.30
Four trees generated with identical design parameters, but with the randomizing parameter set to 1

Figure 6.31 (opposite)
Regular and randomized trees: (a) 0, 120, 0.65, 2, 0.6, 6; (b) 1, 120, 0.65, 2, 0.6, 6; (c) 0, 70, 0.7, 3, 0.85, 5; (d) 1, 70, 0.7, 3, 0.85, 5; (e) 0, 110, 0.8, 3, 0.8, 5; (f) 1, 110, 0.8, 3, 0.8, 5

factor) is the ratio between branch lengths at consecutive depth levels. Finally, 'DEPTH' is the depth of recursion or the number of 'levels' in the tree.

The program can be further elaborated with more design parameters. For example, a finite branch thickness (proportional to branch length) could be incorporated. In the program the terminating 'leaves' are drawn as three extra pixels – this could also be changed. A windblown tree could be drawn by making the branches have a tendency to lean to the right or the left.

The subroutine 'tree' contains a FOR loop that controls the number of branches drawn at any level, each branch being drawn by a recursive call of 'tree'. The parameter 'RAND' controls the selection of one out of two 'tree' calls and you can see from the program the way in which the parameters are randomly perturbed.

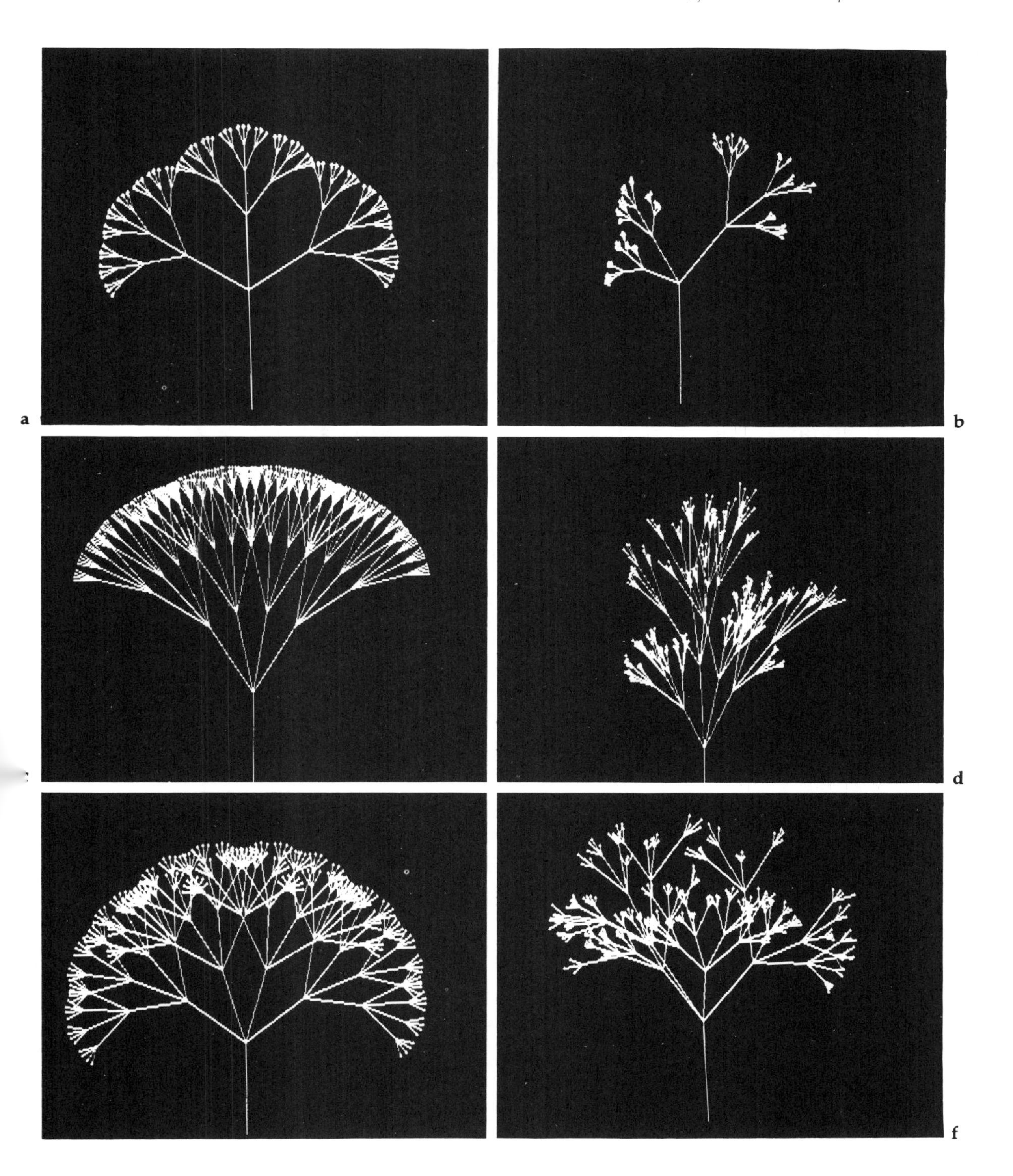
a
b
c
d
f

```
 10 DIM STACKI(20),STACKX(20),STACKY(20),STACKTHETA(20),STACKHF(20)
 20 DIM STACKANGLE(20),STACKBRANCHFAN(20),STACKHEIGHT(20),STACKDEPTH%(20)
 30 PI = 3.141593
 40 DEF FNRAD(DEGREES) = DEGREES*PI/180
 50 GOSUB 120  'initialise
 60 SCREEN 1 : CLS : WINDOW (0,0)-(1279,799)
 70 NX = 640 : NY = 100
 80 COLOR 0,0
 90 PSET (640,100),0
100 GOSUB 160  'tree
110 END

120 'SUBROUTINE initialise
130   INPUT RAND,BRANCHFAN,INPAFACT,BRANCHDENSITY,INPHF,DEPTH%
140 ANGLE = 90 : HEIGHT = 200
150 RETURN

160 'SUBROUTINE tree
170   IF DEPTH% = 0 THEN PSET (NX-2,NY),2 : PSET (NX,NY+4),2 :
                         PSET (NX+2,NY),2 : PSET (NX,NY),2 : RETURN
180   STACKI(SP) = I : STACKX(SP) = X : STACKY(SP) = Y
190   STACKTHETA(SP) = THETA : STACKHF(SP) = HF
200   SP = SP+1
210   '  STACKANGLE(SP) = ANGLE : STACKBRANCHFAN(SP) = BRANCHFAN
220   '  STACKHEIGHT(SP) = HEIGHT : STACKDEPTH%(SP) = DEPTH%
230   START = ANGLE-BRANCHFAN/2
240   THETA = BRANCHFAN/BRANCHDENSITY
250   IF DEPTH% <= 2 THEN HF = INPHF/2 ELSE HF = INPHF
260   X = HEIGHT*COS(FNRAD(ANGLE))
```

Program 6.22 Recursive trees.

```
270    Y = HEIGHT*SIN(FNRAD(ANGLE))
280    ANGLE = START
290    I = 1
300      NX = NX+X : NY = NY+Y : LINE -(NX,NY),3
310      IF RAND = 0 THEN GOSUB 420 : GOSUB 160  'tree
320      IF RAND = 1 THEN GOSUB 470 : GOSUB 160  'tree
330      ANGLE = STACKANGLE(SP) : BRANCHFAN = STACKBRANCHFAN(SP)
340      HEIGHT = STACKHEIGHT(SP) : DEPTH% = STACKDEPTH%(SP)
350      ANGLE = ANGLE+THETA
360      NX = NX-X : NY = NY-Y : PSET (NX,NY),2
370    I = I+1 : IF I <= BRANCHDENSITY+1 THEN 300
380    SP = SP-1
390    I = STACKI(SP) : X = STACKX(SP) : Y = STACKY(SP)
400    THETA = STACKTHETA(SP) : HF = STACKHF(SP)
410  RETURN

420  'SUBROUTINE for rand = 0
430    STACKANGLE(SP) = ANGLE : STACKBRANCHFAN(SP) = BRANCHFAN
440    STACKHEIGHT(SP) = HEIGHT : STACKDEPTH%(SP) = DEPTH%
450    BRANCHFAN = BRANCHFAN*INPAFACT : HEIGHT = HEIGHT*HF : DEPTH% = DEPTH%-1
460  RETURN

470  'SUBROUTINE for rand = 1
480    STACKANGLE(SP) = ANGLE : STACKBRANCHFAN(SP) = BRANCHFAN
490    STACKHEIGHT(SP) = HEIGHT : STACKDEPTH%(SP) = DEPTH%
500    ANGLE = ANGLE-THETA/2+RND*THETA+1 : BRANCHFAN = BRANCHFAN*INPAFACT :
       HEIGHT = HEIGHT*HF*(0.5+RND/1.5) : DEPTH% = DEPTH%-1
510  RETURN
```

7 The third dimension – representation

The aim of computer graphics is to present a pictorial representation of reality on a display screen. The picture presented is an abstraction or a model of reality generated by a computer program. At one end of the spectrum we may be presenting convenient summaries of numerical information, e.g. in graphs and bar charts, and the aim here is to enable the user to interpret numerical information more easily than if he or she was viewing long lists of figures. At the other end of the difficulty spectrum is one of the most impressive computer graphics projects: flight simulation. Here a three-dimensional world is presented on a screen and the trainee flies through it. The generating program responds to movements of the aircraft controls, speed, altitude, etc., and changes the view of the world accordingly. This complex animation requires considerable hardware resources and although the world models are stylized to a certain extent, the impression of reality is astonishing. In such a model the terrain that the pilot is flying over is generated to a quality that is a compromise between the cost of the hardware and the time available to generate an image (1/30th of a second).

If generation time is not critical then pictures can be generated that imitate reality to a degree of accuracy that is uncanny. These images are generated by using complex mathematical shading models to mimic reality.

Yet another approach is to mix reality and abstraction. This technique is currently popular in TV commercials and consists of mixing computer generated digital images with analogue images of reality from a TV camera.

Now the difference between attempting to model reality in a computer graphics image and two-dimensional line drawings such as graphs and bar charts is that we must represent the third dimension, depth, on the display screen. This immediately raises a number of significant problems many of which are the subject of computer graphics research activity in institutions all over the world. The main problems are as follows.

1. We need to be able to generate and represent three-dimensional models in a program so that they can be manipulated.
2. We need to be able to calculate a two-dimensional mapping of such models so that they can be displayed on the screen.
3. We need to take care of the hidden surface problem so that surfaces on an object that cannot be seen from a particular viewpoint are removed, and, that parts of objects obscured by other objects are not seen in the final display.
4. We need to colour each point on a surface taking into account an assumed light source and such factors as texture, transparency and reflectivity (see Colour Plate 17).

In this chapter and the next two, we will concentrate on the first three problems. At the moment hardware constraints of microcomputers are such that shading modelling is not practicable. Although we can set up the mathematics and calculate the exact colour value of a pixel we do not have the colour and spatial resolution to be able to display it.

Figure 7.1 shows three models of the same three-dimensional solid. The first is a so-called wireframe model. Here we do not implement hidden surface removal or shading. The model is defined as a list of vertices together with connectivity information. A two-dimensional representation of this model, as seen from a particular viewpoint, can then be drawn using line graphics to join the vertices together. The second model is identical to the first except that hidden lines are removed. You can see that the interpretation of the model is now considerably enhanced. In the third model, points on each of the visible surfaces are shaded. Each pixel in each surface is assigned a value or colour, taking into account the aforementioned factors. The final result is a careful imitation of reality. In fact mathematical shading models are now so accurate that when a three-dimensional solid is displayed on a screen of sufficiently high resolution it is almost impossible to tell if the resulting display is a real image, from a colour television camera, or a program generated model.

7.1 REPRESENTATION OF THREE-DIMENSIONAL MODELS

Three-dimensional graphics would be a simple extension of two-dimensional graphics, all our 3×3 transformations would become 4×4 transformations and that would be the end of the matter, if we had access to a three-dimensional display device. Of course the display device is two dimensional and the extra complication in three-dimensional graphics comes from the need to map the three-dimensional coordinates of the object to be displayed into the two-dimensional coordinates of the display system. It is convenient to express this as a combination of two transformations: the viewing transformation and the perspective transformation. This is needed

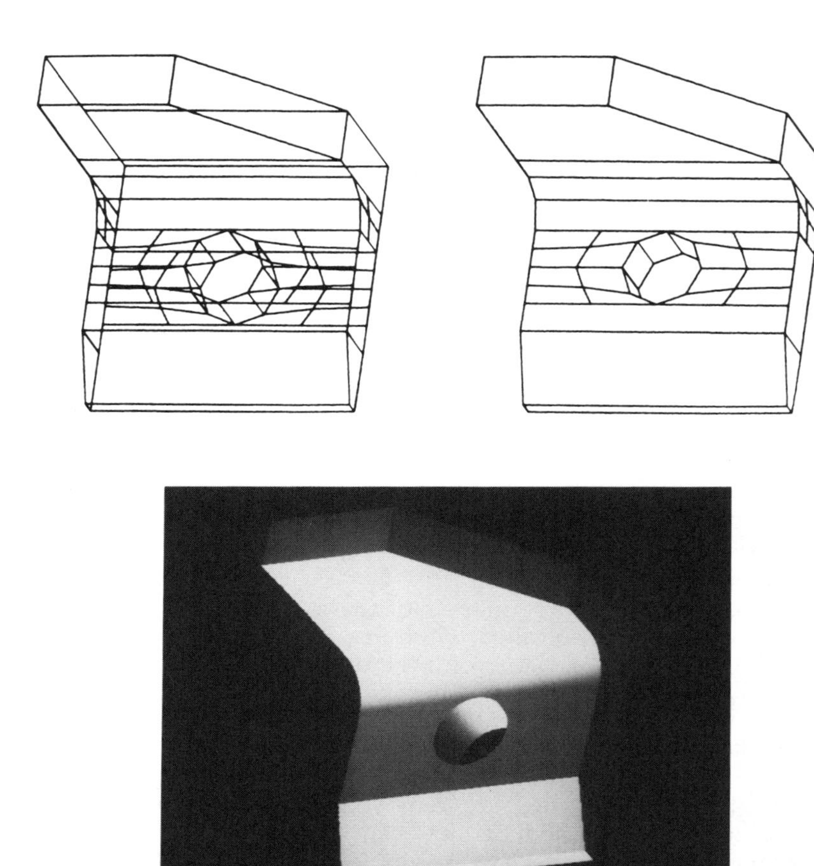

Figure 7.1
The three models used in computer graphics: wireframe, wireframe with hidden lines removed and shaded surface with hidden surfaces removed

in addition to any other of the transformations such as scaling, rotation and translation of the three-dimensional object.

We shall specify the coordinates of a three-dimensional object in a so-called world coordinate system. A house with a pyramidal roof could be specified in this system as a list of 9 (x,y,z) points in the world coordinate system (Figure 7.2).

Our intuition and visual experience with such abstractions as the wireframe model shown in Figure 7.1 enables us to realize the shape of the solid body that the model represents. Just as we would see different views of the real object as we moved our viewpoint around the sides and over the top, so we can construct two-dimensional representations of these different views from the original wireframe model (Figure 7.3). The views can be constructed from the original object by specifying a viewpoint in relation to the object. The so-called 'viewpoint transformation' converts the coordinates

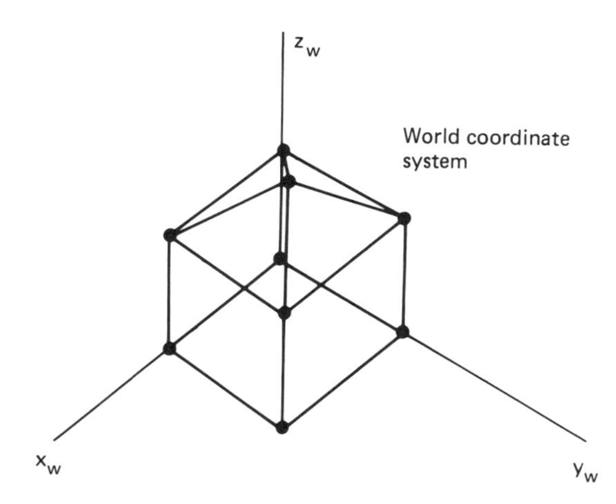

Figure 7.2
Three-dimensional world coordinate system

expressed in the world coordinate system into 'eye' coordinates expressed in a coordinate system centred at the viewpoint.

Having applied the viewpoint transformation we are still left with a list of three-dimensional coordinates. The transformation that produces a list of two-dimensional or screen coordinates from the viewpoint list is called the perspective transformation. These considerations together with three-dimensional manipulations that are analogous to the manipulations in two dimensions dealt with in Chapter 3 are the subject of the next chapter. For the remainder of this chapter we will be concerned with how we can represent three-dimensional structures in a program and how these can be generated.

The first thing that must be borne in mind is that although a wireframe model is just a collection of vertices joined by edges, such a representation in general is not sufficient in three-dimensional computer graphics. Although we require only the vertices and the connectivity information (which vertices are joined together) to draw a wireframe model on the screen, to remove hidden lines we need to consider the surfaces formed by the edges. We also need to consider surfaces, rather than vertices, for calculations in a shading model. This situation is summarized in Figure 7.4 for a wireframe cube. When we are performing three-dimensional linear transformations (see the next chapter) such as scaling, for example, then we

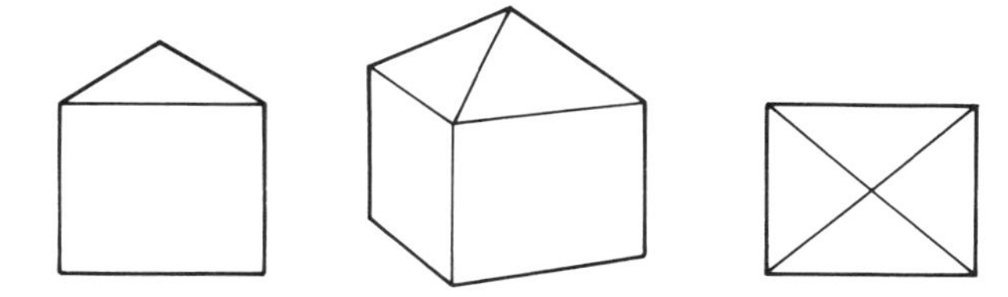

Figure 7.3
Different views of the same object

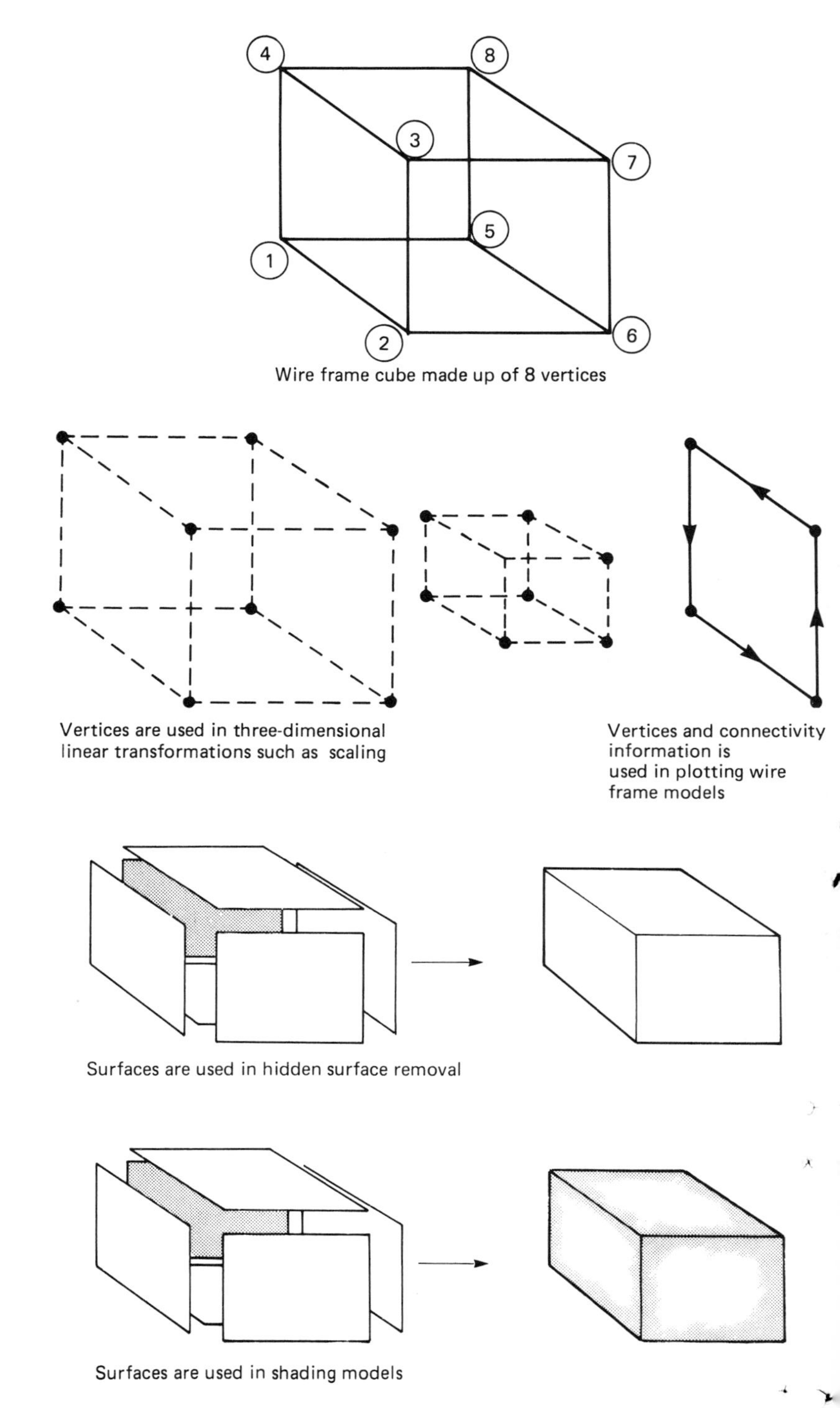

4
8
3
7
5
1
2
6
Wire frame cube made up of 8 vertices
Vertices are used in three-dimensional linear transformations such as scaling
Vertices and connectivity information is used in plotting wire frame models
Surfaces are used in hidden surface removal
Surfaces are used in shading models

Figure 7.4
Data entities used in computer graphic models

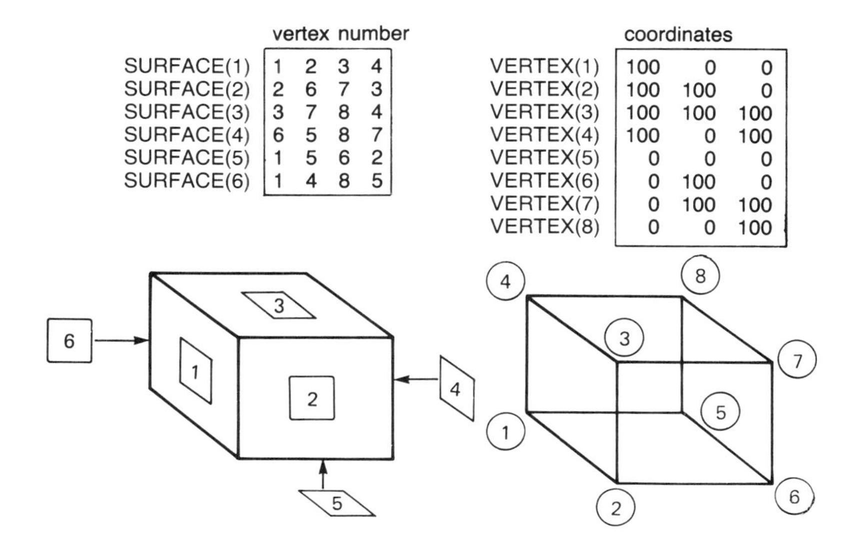

vertex number
SURFACE(1) 1 2 3 4
SURFACE(2) 2 6 7 3
SURFACE(3) 3 7 8 4
SURFACE(4) 6 5 8 7
SURFACE(5) 1 5 6 2
SURFACE(6) 1 4 8 5
coordinates
VERTEX(1) 100 0 0
VERTEX(2) 100 100 0
VERTEX(3) 100 100 100
VERTEX(4) 100 0 100
VERTEX(5) 0 0 0
VERTEX(6) 0 100 0
VERTEX(7) 0 100 100
VERTEX(8) 0 0 100
6
3
1
2
4
5
4
8
3
7
5
1
6
2

Figure 7.5
Data structure for surfaces using two arrays

simply operate on the eight vertices applying the same transformation to each. When we are plotting a wireframe model we need connectivity information. We need to know that to draw the cube we move to vertex 1, draw to vertex 2, draw to vertex 3, etc. This connectivity information can be expressed, generally but uneconomically, by explicitly storing representations of each of the six surfaces. The entity of a surface is needed for hidden surface removal and also for shading calculations. We are therefore led to a hierarchical data structure that allows a body to be specified as a collection of surfaces, each surface to be specified as a collection of vertices and each vertex to be specified as a set of three coordinates in world coordinate space.

A suitable data structure (Figure 7.5) is set up using two arrays 'SURFACE' and 'VERTEX'. The array 'VERTEX' contains a list of the coordinates of the eight vertices in the cube, and 'SURFACE' contains for each surface a list of vertex numbers that define the surface. This data structure means that we can deal with surfaces as entities.

A surface must contain (for reasons that will become clear later) vertices listed in counter-clockwise order as seen from outside the object. Thus the surface number 2 is specified in the second row of array 'SURFACE' which will contain the vertex numbers 2, 6, 7 and 3. Thus to access surface number 2 for calculation or plotting we would indirectly access the array 'VERTEX' as follows:

```
VERTEX(SURFACE(2,1))
VERTEX(SURFACE(2,2))
VERTEX(SURFACE(2,3))
VERTEX(SURFACE(2,4))
```

```
  10 DIM VERTEX(3,8), SURFACE(6,4)
        .
        .
        .
1000 'SUBROUTINE initialise
1020   FOR INITV = 1 TO 8
1030     READ VERTEX(1,INITV), VERTEX(2,INITV), VERTEX(3,INITV)
1040   NEXT INITV
1050   FOR INITSURFACENO = 1 TO 6
1060     FOR INITVERTEXNO = 1 TO 4
1070       READ SURFACE(INITSURFACENO,INITVERTEXNO)
1080     NEXT INITVERTEXNO
1090   NEXT INITSURFACENO
1100 RETURN

1110 DATA 100,0,0, 100,100,0, 100,100,100, 100,0,100
1120 DATA 0,0,0, 0,100,0, 0,100,100, 0,0,100
1130 DATA 1,2,3,4, 2,6,7,3, 3,7,8,4
1140 DATA 6,5,8,7, 1,5,6,2, 1,4,8,5
```

Program 7.1 Initialising a surface/vertex representation of a three-dimensional object (a cube).

Note that either the construction of surfaces in the object needs to be explicitly stated as here, or the method that constructs the solid must do so in such way that consecutive vertices relating to one surface are listed in counter-clockwise order (looking in from outside the object). For the cube the data structure is initialised by using a subroutine (Program 7.1).

A not insignificant disadvantage of this method is that it is not easy to find surfaces that share an edge. In the cube, for example, each edge is shared by two surfaces. This means that when the body is plotted each edge will be plotted twice over and the complete figure will take twice as long to be drawn. This is clearly a significant disadvantage in such applications as animation and the significance of this disadvantage increases with the complexity of the model. On the other hand, because each vertex is stored only once, memory space is saved. Also it is easy to change the coordinate values of a vertex (because there is guaranteed to be only one occurrence of a vertex in the list). This is important in interactive CAD where the user of an interactive data entry program may want to edit his or her model by changing a vertex.

Now this data structure must be extended in the more general case where different surfaces contain different numbers of vertices. In the 'church with steeple' example shown in Figure 7.6 there are 14 surfaces and 19 vertices. Each surface contains either 3, 4, 5, 6 or 8 vertices and we need an extra array, 'NOOFVERTICES', to hold this information. The alterations to the subroutine and the data structure are given in Program 7.2. The first five DATA statements list the

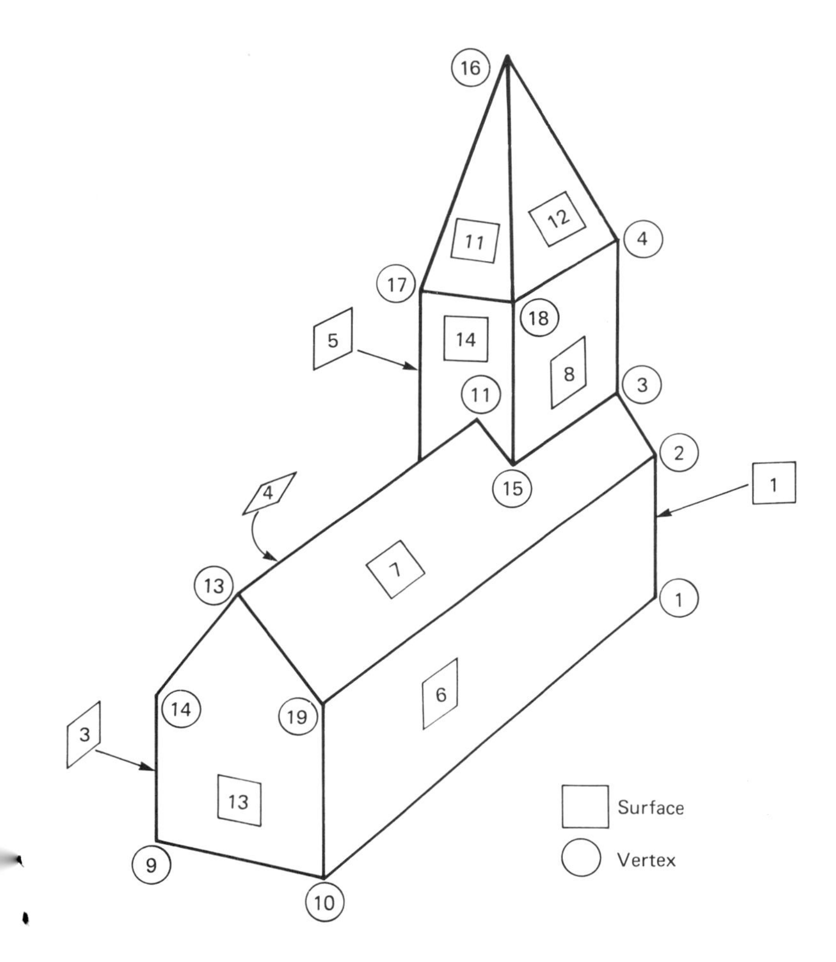

Figure 7.6
Surfaces and vertices for the church

19 vertices and the remaining 14 DATA statements give the surface information in the order specified in Figure 7.6. The first number in each of these DATA statements is the number of vertices in the surface and this is read into array 'NOOFVERTICES'. In this and subsequent programs in this chapter we use a standard viewpoint transformation that allows us to plot a particular view of the three-dimensional solid. The subroutines that perform this task should be accepted for the moment (they form the main topic of the next chapter).

Yet another extension that must be introduced is one to cope with multi-object scenes. Here we can introduce another two-dimensional array that lists the objects in the scene as sets of surfaces. This scheme is suggested by Figure 7.7 which shows the state of the data structure for the cube pyramid scene.

```
 10 DIM VERTEX(3,19),SURFACE(14,9),NOOFVERTICES(14)
 20 PI = 3.141593
 30 DEF FNRAD(DEGREES) = DEGREES*PI/180
 40 RHO = 700 : THETA = 45 : PHI = 60 : SCREENDIST = 2000
 50 GOSUB 2000  'init view transform
 60 SCREEN 2 : CLS : WINDOW (-640,-350)-(639,673)
 70 GOSUB 680  'initialise
 80 FOR SURFACENO = 1 TO SURFS
 90   GOSUB 500  'transform and plot
100 NEXT SURFACENO
110 END

500 'SUBROUTINE transform and plot
510   VERTEXNO = 1
520   GOSUB 600  'screen vertex
530   PSET (XS,YS) : TPSTARTX=XS : TPSTARTY=YS
540   FOR VERTEXNO = 2 TO NOOFVERTICES(SURFACENO)
550     GOSUB 600  'screen vertex
560     LINE -(XS,YS)
570   NEXT VERTEXNO
580   LINE -(TPSTARTX,TPSTARTY)
590 RETURN

600 'SUBROUTINE screen vertex
610   XW = VERTEX(1, SURFACE(SURFACENO,VERTEXNO))
620   YW = VERTEX(2, SURFACE(SURFACENO,VERTEXNO))
630   ZW = VERTEX(3, SURFACE(SURFACENO,VERTEXNO))
640   GOSUB 2100  'view transform
650   D = SCREENDIST
660   GOSUB 2150  'perspect transform
670 RETURN

680 'SUBROUTINE initialise
690   READ VERTS
700   FOR INITV = 1 TO VERTS
710     READ VERTEX(1,INITV), VERTEX(2,INITV), VERTEX(3,INITV)
720   NEXT INITV
730   READ SURFS
740   FOR INITSURFACENO = 1 TO SURFS
750     READ NOOFVERTICES(INITSURFACENO)
760     FOR INITVERTEXNO = 1 TO NOOFVERTICES(INITSURFACENO)
770       READ SURFACE(INITSURFACENO, INITVERTEXNO)
780     NEXT INITVERTEXNO
790   NEXT INITSURFACENO
800 RETURN
```

Program 7.2 Representing a more complex three-dimensional object (a church). The transformation to project an object on to the two-dimensional screen is explained in Chapter 8.

```
 810 DATA 19
 820 DATA 180,0,0,   180,0,50,   180,20,75,   180,20,120
 830 DATA 180,60,120,   180,60,75,  180,80,50,   180,80,0
 840 DATA 0,80,0,   0,0,0,   140,40,100,  140, 60, 75
 850 DATA 0,40,100, 0,80,50, 140,20,75,   160,40,250
 860 DATA 140,60,120,  140,20,120, 0,0,50
 870 DATA 14
 880 DATA 8,8,7,6,5,4,3,2,1
 890 DATA 4,1,10,9,8
 900 DATA 4,9,14,7,8
 910 DATA 6,14,13,11,12,6,7
 920 DATA 4,12,17,5,6
 930 DATA 4,1,2,19,10
 940 DATA 6,13,19,2,3,15,11
 950 DATA 4,3,4,18,15
 960 DATA 3,5,16,4
 970 DATA 3,17,16,5
 980 DATA 3,18,16,17
 990 DATA 3,4,16,18
1000 DATA 5,10,19,13,14,9
1010 DATA 5,15,18,17,12,11

2000 'SUBROUTINE init view transform
2010   SINTHETA = SIN(FNRAD(THETA)) : COSTHETA = COS(FNRAD(THETA))
2020   SINPHI = SIN(FNRAD(PHI)) : COSPHI = COS(FNRAD(PHI))
2030   VA = -SINTHETA : VB = COSTHETA
2040   VE = -COSTHETA*COSPHI : VF = -SINTHETA*COSPHI
2050   VG =  SINPHI
2060   VI = -COSTHETA*SINPHI : VJ = -SINTHETA*SINPHI
2070   VK = -COSPHI : VL = RHO
2080 RETURN

2100 'SUBROUTINE view transform
2110   XE  = VA*XW+VB*YW
2120   YE  = VE*XW+VF*YW+VG*ZW
2130   ZE  = VI*XW+VJ*YW+VK*ZW+VL
2140 RETURN

2150 'SUBROUTINE perspect transform
2160   XS = D*XE/ZE
2170   YS = D*YE/ZE
2180 RETURN
```

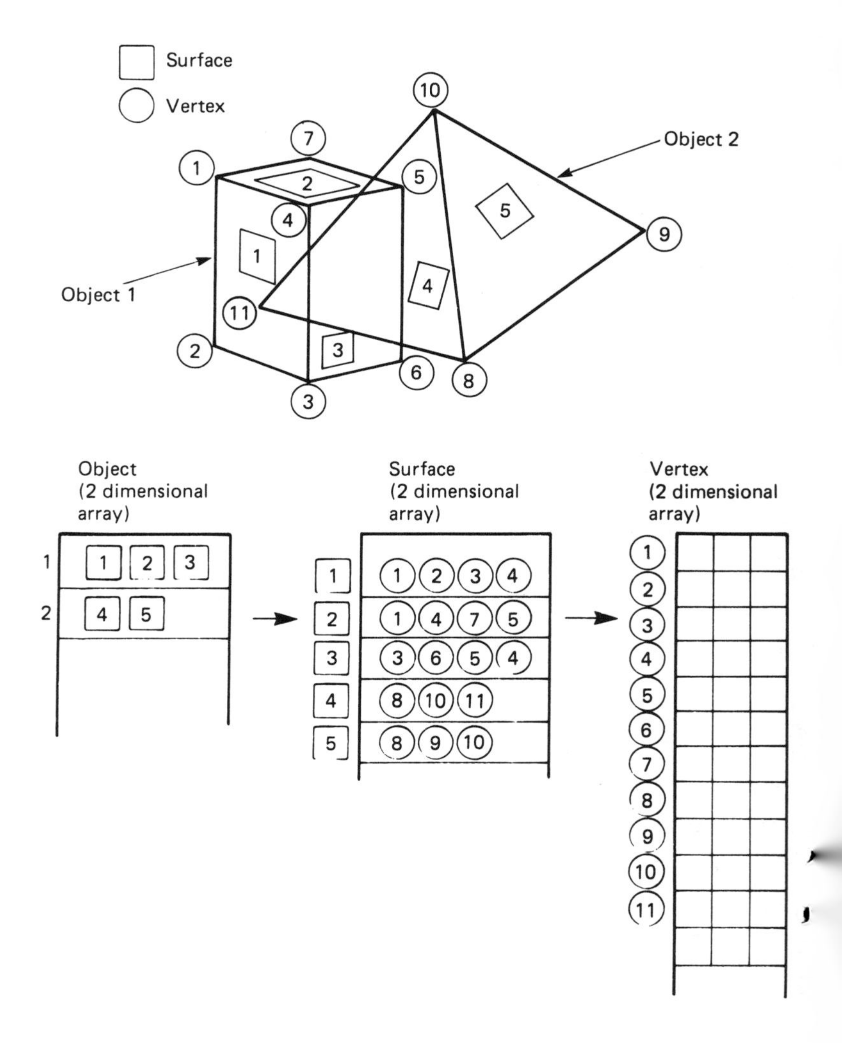

Figure 7.7
Data structure for multi-object scene

7.2 GENERATION OF THREE-DIMENSIONAL MODELS – PSEUDO THREE-DIMENSIONAL TECHNIQUES

We now move on to consider how three-dimensional models can be generated and we shall start by looking at some trivial but much used imitations of three-dimensional models. These are pseudo three-dimensional models because they are drawn by working entirely in two-dimensional coordinates. This is sometimes an acceptable shortcut for such applications as backdrops to arcade games. The limitations are obvious. The view of the scene is static, so the viewer cannot move around in the three-dimensional scene and the programming techniques are context dependent. To write a program to draw a particular scene the programmer simply sets up structures to draw a particular two-dimensional visualization or

```
 10 PI = 3.141593
 20 DEF FNRAD(DEGREES) = DEGREES*PI/180
 30 SCREEN 2 : CLS : WINDOW (0,0)-(1279,799)
 40 FOREVER = TRUE
 50 WHILE FOREVER = TRUE
 60   LOCATE 1,1 : INPUT "Centre and radius (x,y,r) ";XC,YC,R
 70   LOCATE 1,1 : PRINT SPC(60)
 80   GOSUB 110  'draw a sphere
 90 WEND
100 END

110 'SUBROUTINE draw a sphere
120   B = R
130   FOR A = 1 TO B+1 STEP B/5
140     GOSUB 210  'draw ellipse
150   NEXT A
160   A = B+1
170   FOR B = 1 TO A+1 STEP A/5
180     GOSUB 210  'draw ellipse
190   NEXT B
200 RETURN

210 'SUBROUTINE draw ellipse
220   PSET (XC+A,YC)
230   FOR THETA = 0 TO 360 STEP 10
240     COSINE = COS(FNRAD(THETA)) : SINE = SIN(FNRAD(THETA))
250     R = 1/SQR(COSINE*COSINE/(A*A)+SINE*SINE/(B*B))
260     X = R*COSINE : Y = R*SINE
270     LINE -(XC+X,YC+Y)
280   NEXT THETA
290 RETURN
```

Program 7.3 Pseudo three-dimensional spheres created using ellipses.

mapping of the scene. This is a trivialization of the general three-dimensional graphics model where we set up a three-dimensional data structure and are then able to construct from this model any view of the scene. The program works out a view for us. However, as already mentioned, we can use shortcuts in certain applications. Perspective is imitated in the usual way and hidden surface removal can be imitated by 'painting' (see later). Some generality can be built into the programs by using repetitions of models (suitably scaled) as we shall now illustrate. Again bear in mind that the diversity of the illustrative programs is unavoidable and the structure of each program is just a reflection of the structure of one particular view of the scene.

The first program, Program 7.3, draws pseudo three-dimensional spheres by drawing ellipses. The subroutine captioned 'draw

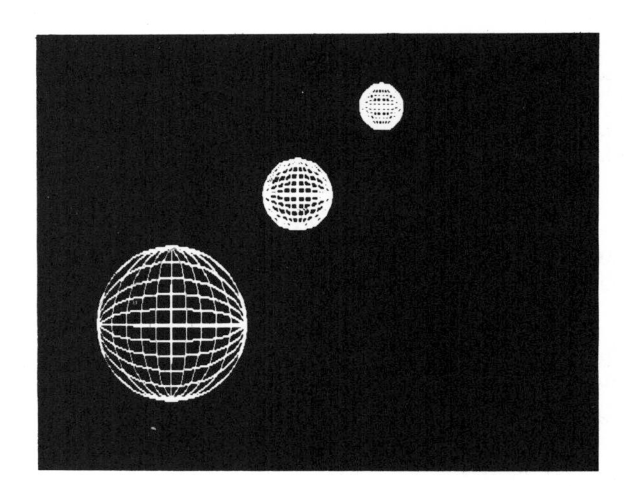

Figure 7.8
Pseudo three-dimensional techniques: spheres from ellipses

```
 10 PI = 3.141593
 20 DEF FNRAD(DEGREES) = DEGREES*PI/180
 30 SCREEN 1 : CLS
 40 SIDE = 50
 50 DX = SIDE*COS(FNRAD(35)) : DY = SIDE*SIN(FNRAD(35))
 60 FILLCOLOR1 = 2 : FILLCOLOR2 = 3
 70 GOSUB 230  'draw axes
 80 FOR X = 1 TO 10
 90   STARTX = -X*SIDE*COS(FNRAD(35))
100   STARTY = -X*SIDE*SIN(FNRAD(35))
110   PSET (STARTX,STARTY)
120   NEWX = STARTX : NEWY = STARTY
130   FOR Y = 1 TO 10
140     NEWX = NEWX+DX : NEWY = NEWY-DY
150     HT = RND*200 : IF HT < 20 THEN HT = HT+20
160     FILL$ = "true" : BORDERCOLOR = 1 : PSET (NEWX,NEWY),BORDERCOLOR
170     GOSUB 290  'draw bar
180     FILL$ = "false" : BORDERCOLOR = 0 : PSET (NEWX,NEWY),BORDERCOLOR
190     GOSUB 290  'draw bar
200   NEXT Y
210 NEXT X
220 END

230 'SUBROUTINE draw axes
240   WINDOW (-640,-600)-(639,199)
250   LINE (0,400)-(0,0),FILLCOLOR2
260   LINE -(600*COS(FNRAD(35)),-600*SIN(FNRAD(35))),FILLCOLOR2
270   LINE (-600*COS(FNRAD(35)),-600*SIN(FNRAD(35)))-(0,0),FILLCOLOR2
280 RETURN
```

Program 7.4 A pseudo three-dimensional bar chart (black and white).

ellipse' draws an ellipse centred at (xc, yc) and having axes a and b respectively. When $a = 0$ and $b = r$, a vertical straight line is drawn (an infinitely thin ellipse). When $a = r$ and $b = r$, a circle is drawn. To control the subroutine we thus need a structure that starts with $a = 0$ and increases a towards b, in other words a FOR loop. The program thus draws vertically aligned ellipses that get fatter and fatter and end up as a circle. A similar FOR loop controls the drawing of horizontally aligned ellipses and the net result is a figure that gives the impression of a sphere. Output from the program is shown in Figure 7.8.

The second program, Program 7.4, is a three-dimensional bar chart that uses an easy heuristic for hidden surface removal. The program draws pseudo three-dimensional bars whose heights represent particular values. The practical application is representation of a bivariate histogram (values are a function of two variables). For example, we may have data for ice cream sales together with date and the average temperature for that date. We could plot a bivariate histogram where the z-axis represented sales, the y-axis

```
290 'SUBROUTINE draw bar
300   NEWX = NEWX+DX : NEWY = NEWY+DY : LINE -(NEWX,NEWY),BORDERCOLOR
310   NEWY = NEWY+HT : LINE -(NEWX,NEWY),BORDERCOLOR
320   NEWX = NEWX-DX : NEWY = NEWY-DY : LINE -(NEWX,NEWY),BORDERCOLOR
330   NEWY = NEWY-HT : LINE -(NEWX,NEWY),BORDERCOLOR
340   IF FILL$ = "true" THEN
        PAINT (NEWX+DX/2,NEWY+(HT+DY)/2),FILLCOLOR1,BORDERCOLOR
350   IF FILL$ = "true" THEN
        PAINT (NEWX+DX/2,NEWY+(HT+DY)/2),FILLCOLOR2,BORDERCOLOR
360   PSET (NEWX,NEWY) : NEWX = NEWX-DX :
      NEWY = NEWY+DY : LINE -(NEWX,NEWY),BORDERCOLOR
370   NEWY = NEWY+HT : LINE -(NEWX,NEWY),BORDERCOLOR
380   NEWX = NEWX+DX : NEWY = NEWY-DY : LINE -(NEWX,NEWY),BORDERCOLOR
390   NEWY = NEWY-HT : LINE -(NEWX,NEWY),BORDERCOLOR
400   IF FILL$ = "true" THEN
        PAINT (NEWX-DX/2,NEWY+(HT+DY)/2),FILLCOLOR1,BORDERCOLOR
410   IF FILL$ = "true" THEN
        PAINT (NEWX-DX/2,NEWY+(HT+DY)/2),FILLCOLOR2,BORDERCOLOR
420   NEWY = NEWY+HT : PSET (NEWX,NEWY)
430   NEWX = NEWX-DX : NEWY = NEWY+DY : LINE -(NEWX,NEWY),BORDERCOLOR
440   NEWX = NEWX+DX : NEWY = NEWY+DY : LINE -(NEWX,NEWY),BORDERCOLOR
450   NEWX = NEWX+DX : NEWY = NEWY-DY : LINE -(NEWX,NEWY),BORDERCOLOR
460   NEWX = NEWX-DX : NEWY = NEWY-DY : LINE -(NEWX,NEWY),BORDERCOLOR
470   IF FILL$ = "true" THEN PAINT (NEWX,NEWY+DY/2),FILLCOLOR1,BORDERCOLOR
480   IF FILL$ = "true" THEN PAINT (NEWX,NEWY+DY/2),FILLCOLOR2,BORDERCOLOR
490   NEWY = NEWY-HT : PSET (NEWX,NEWY),BORDERCOLOR
500 RETURN
```

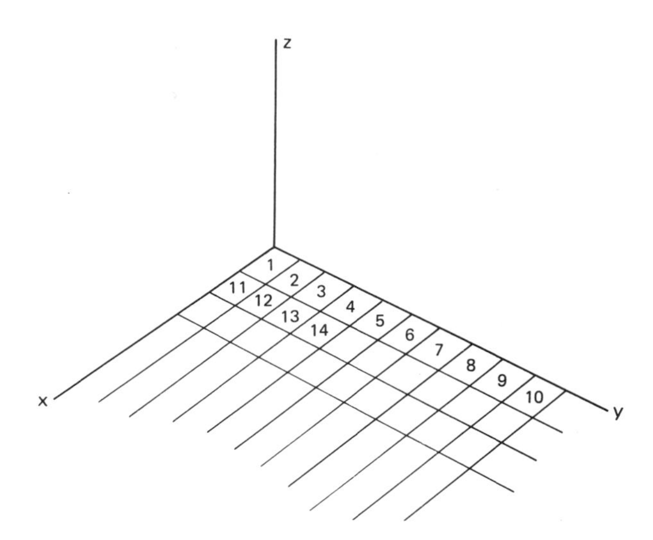

Figure 7.9
Plotting order in three-dimensional bar chart

temperature and the *x*-axis the date. Each sales value is plotted against two variables, temperature and date, and we need a three-dimensional graph.

Now because we are always going to view this model from exactly the same direction we can draw it in its entirety using a two-dimensional coordinate system. Another benefit of a fixed view-point is that we can adopt an easy hidden surface removal heuristic. The kernel of the program is the subroutine that draws a bar made up of three surfaces. This simply draws a box shape, in two dimen-

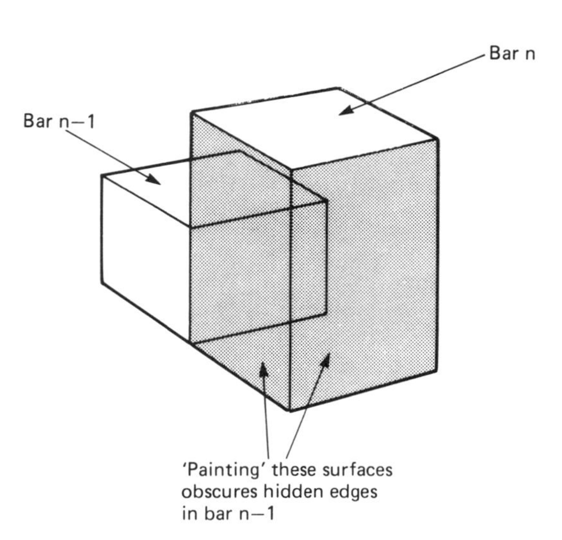

Figure 7.10
Painting method of hidden surface removal

Figure 7.11
Pseudo three-dimensional techniques: the three-dimensional bar chart

sions, of a given height. The subroutine is written in terms of relative coordinates and before the subroutine is entered the current position is reset. The subroutine is called twice for each bar and a painting algorithm, like that used in Chapter 3 for the outline characters, is used to fill the interior of each box. Remember that the interior fill is not just a straightforward application of PAINT because the box will contain detail from the previously drawn box. Now the structure of the program is such that the bars are drawn in the order shown in Figure 7.9. This means that if a surface in bar *n* obscures parts of edges in bar *n*–1, these are automatically removed by painting the surfaces of bar *n* (Figure 7.10). Again it is important to bear in mind that this simple method of hidden line removal is only possible because we have set up a fixed viewpoint. The output from the program is shown in Figure 7.11.

General hidden surface removal is one of the most difficult and costly operations in computer graphics. Some hidden surface algorithms, as we shall see later, use a painting technique as one of the methods in the algorithm. Program 7.5 is a colour version of Program 7.4 and uses exactly the same painting technique. Because we are now using more colours the organization of the subroutine is slightly different. The output from this program is shown in Colour Plate 15. In both programs the height of the bars was set using the random number utility.

Another common pseudo three-dimensional technique involves using scaling and diverging lines to represent perspective. Program 7.6 draws the road scene shown in Figure 7.12. This is made up of converging kerbs and road markers and trees that decrease in scale as the distance down the road increases. The same subroutine is used to draw every instance of an object. The object drawing subroutines are controlled from FOR loops. Each time an object, whether it is a tree or a road marker, is drawn it is suitably posi-

```
 20 SCREEN 1 : CLS
 30 PI = 3.141593
 40 DEF FNRAD(DEGREES) = DEGREES*PI/180
 50 SIDE = 50
 60 DX = SIDE*COS(FNRAD(35)) : DY = SIDE*SIN(FNRAD(35))
 70 FILLCOLOR1 = 3 : AXISCOLOR = 1
 80 FILLCOLOR2 = 1 : FILLCOLOR3 = 1
 90 FILLCOLOR4 = 2
100 GOSUB 260  'draw axes
110 FOR X = 1 TO 10
120   STARTX = -X*SIDE*COS(FNRAD(35))
130   STARTY = -X*SIDE*SIN(FNRAD(35))
140   PSET (STARTX,STARTY)
150   NEWX = STARTX : NEWY = STARTY
160   FOR Y = 1 TO 10
170     NEWX = NEWX+DX : NEWY = NEWY-DY
180     HT = RND*200 : IF HT < 20 THEN HT = HT+20
190     BORDERCOLOR = 3 : PSET (NEWX,NEWY),BORDERCOLOR
200     GOSUB 320  'draw bar
210     BORDERCOLOR = 0 : PSET (NEWX,NEWY),BORDERCOLOR
220     GOSUB 320  'draw bar
230   NEXT Y
240 NEXT X
250 END

260 'SUBROUTINE draw axes
270   WINDOW (-640,-600)-(639,199)
280   LINE (0,400)-(0,0),AXISCOLOR
290   LINE -(600*COS(FNRAD(35)),-600*SIN(FNRAD(35))),AXISCOLOR
300   LINE (-600*COS(FNRAD(35)),-600*SIN(FNRAD(35)))-(0,0),AXISCOLOR
310 RETURN

320 'SUBROUTINE draw bar
330   NEWX = NEWX+DX : NEWY = NEWY+DY : LINE -(NEWX,NEWY),BORDERCOLOR
340   NEWY = NEWY+HT : LINE -(NEWX,NEWY),BORDERCOLOR
350   NEWX = NEWX-DX : NEWY = NEWY-DY : LINE -(NEWX,NEWY),BORDERCOLOR
360   NEWY = NEWY-HT : LINE -(NEWX,NEWY),BORDERCOLOR
370   PAINT (NEWX+DX/2,NEWY+(HT+DY)/2),FILLCOLOR1,BORDERCOLOR
380   PAINT (NEWX+DX/2,NEWY+(HT+DY)/2),FILLCOLOR2,BORDERCOLOR
390   PSET (NEWX,NEWY) : NEWX = NEWX-DX : NEWY = NEWY+DY :
                         LINE -(NEWX,NEWY),BORDERCOLOR
400   NEWY = NEWY+HT : LINE -(NEWX,NEWY),BORDERCOLOR
410   NEWX = NEWX+DX : NEWY = NEWY-DY : LINE -(NEWX,NEWY),BORDERCOLOR
420   NEWY = NEWY-HT : LINE -(NEWX,NEWY),BORDERCOLOR
430   PAINT (NEWX-DX/2,NEWY+(HT+DY)/2),FILLCOLOR1,BORDERCOLOR
440   PAINT (NEWX-DX/2,NEWY+(HT+DY)/2),FILLCOLOR3,BORDERCOLOR
450   NEWY = NEWY+HT : PSET (NEWX,NEWY)
460   NEWX = NEWX-DX : NEWY = NEWY+DY : LINE -(NEWX,NEWY),BORDERCOLOR
470   NEWX = NEWX+DX : NEWY = NEWY+DY : LINE -(NEWX,NEWY),BORDERCOLOR
480   NEWX = NEWX+DX : NEWY = NEWY-DY : LINE -(NEWX,NEWY),BORDERCOLOR
490   NEWX = NEWX-DX : NEWY = NEWY-DY : LINE -(NEWX,NEWY),BORDERCOLOR
500   PAINT (NEWX,NEWY+DY/2),FILLCOLOR1,BORDERCOLOR
510   PAINT (NEWX,NEWY+DY/2),FILLCOLOR4,BORDERCOLOR
520   NEWY = NEWY-HT : PSET (NEWX,NEWY),BORDERCOLOR
530 RETURN
```

Program 7.5 A pseudo three-dimensional bar chart (colour).

tioned and scaled. Note that the shape of the road marker already includes convergence. We could if necessary employ the same painting algorithm as we used before if, for example, we wanted to draw overlapping trees. This would mean reversing the drawing order in Program 7.6 because we would have to draw the smallest first and work forwards.

```
 10 PI = 3.141593
 20 DEF FNRAD(DEGREES) = DEGREES*PI/180
 30 SCREEN 2 : CLS : WINDOW (-640,-512)-(639,287)
 40 LINE (-640,0)-(639,0)  'draw horizon
 50 LINE (0,0)-(300,-512)  'draw roadside
 60 LINE (0,0)-(-300,-512)  'draw roadside
 70 NEWDX = -300 : NEWDY = -512
 80 SCALE = 2 : DIST = 300 : THETA = 60
 90 FOR TREE = 1 TO 10
100   GOSUB 240  'draw a tree
110   NEWDX = NEWDX+DIST*COS(FNRAD(THETA)) :
      NEWDY = NEWDY+DIST*SIN(FNRAD(THETA))
120   PSET (NEWDX,NEWDY)
130   SCALE = SCALE/2 : DIST = DIST/2
140 NEXT TREE
150 NEWDX = 0 : NEWDY = -512 : PSET (NEWDX,NEWDY)
160 SCALE = 2 : DIST = 300
170 FOR MARKER = 1 TO 10
180   GOSUB 330  'draw markers
190   NEWDY = NEWDY+DIST*SIN(FNRAD(THETA))
200   PSET (NEWDX,NEWDY)
210   SCALE = SCALE/2 : DIST = DIST/2
220 NEXT MARKER
230 END

240 'SUBROUTINE draw a tree
250   RESTORE 310
260   FOR I = 1 TO 7
270     READ DX,DY
280     NEWDX = NEWDX+DX*SCALE : NEWDY = NEWDY+DY*SCALE
290     LINE -(NEWDX,NEWDY)
300   NEXT I
310 DATA -10,0, 0,30, -20,0, 25,120, 25,-120, -20,0, 0,-30
320 RETURN

330 'SUBROUTINE draw markers
340   RESTORE 400
350   FOR I = 1 TO 5
360     READ DX,DY
370     NEWDX = NEWDX+DX*SCALE : NEWDY = NEWDY+DY*SCALE
380     LINE -(NEWDX,NEWDY)
390   NEXT I
400   DATA -10,0, 4,50, 12,0, 4,-50, -10,0
410 RETURN
```

Program 7.6 A pseudo three-dimensional landscape.

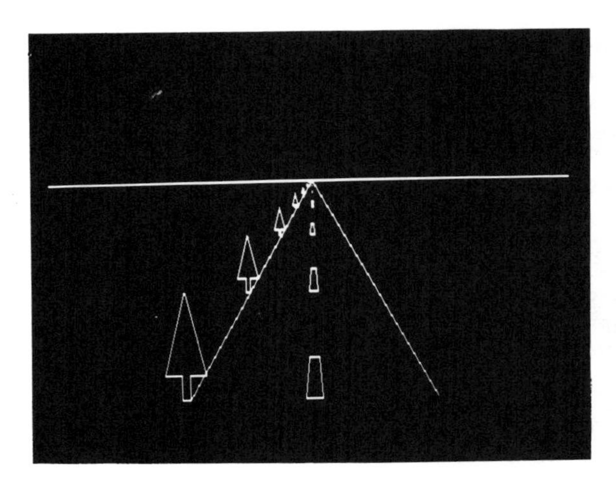

Figure 7.12
Pseudo three-dimensional techniques: converging lines

7.3 INPUT OF THREE-DIMENSIONAL DATA

Having defined a convenient way of representing three-dimensional data in a computer, we now move on to consider how such data can be generated or created. We will look at two methods of creating three-dimensional solids, firstly the input of three-dimensional data and secondly the generation of three-dimensional solids with mathematical assistance.

The creation of three-dimensional data is one of the most diverse areas in computer graphics. Certainly the art of creating realistic images of three-dimensional solids was at one time a Cinderella area of computer graphics that did not improve as rapidly as the other major areas. The difficulties are obvious. Whereas viewing techniques and surface shading techniques are more or less universal to all models, the most convenient method of input or creation is highly application dependent. The most obvious approach of typing three-dimensional coordinates from a keyboard is an accurate but hopelessly tedious method. Most approaches are interactive and the most sophisticated are based on methods that allow the construction of a solid from primitive elements such as cylinders, spheres, cubes, etc. Such methods are found in CAD where a common three-dimensional model may be a solid machine part. Such software is sometimes referred to as a graphics editor. The analogy is with a text editor which may take text from different sources, e.g. the keyboard, stored fragments, etc., and allow the user to put a new piece of text together and refine and change it. A graphics editor will allow a user to combine stored primitive elements, information from the keyboard, graphical information from a digitizer tablet or some other graphics input device. He or she will be able to view the model as it is being built up and to make refinements to it.

Another mainstream graphics input technique is to sculpt free form surfaces (surfaces that cannot easily be defined by mathematical equations) from a keyboard. The surface is defined by patches and as it is displayed the user can pull it this way and that, just as if he or she was modelling with a thin sheet of plasticine. This technique was originally developed to assist in the design of car bodies.

Now these techniques are beyond the scope of this text. Graphics editors are very complex and application dependent and interactive surface patching requires very advanced mathematics. An easy and widely used technique that we shall now look at is referred to as 'lofting'.

This means defining, via a digitizer tablet or some other interactive input device, a set of cross-sections of the object to be modelled. The best analogy is with a geographic contour map, where each contour traces the edge of a surface for a given height. If, for example, the object we wanted to define was a cone then we would input a set of concentric circles of decreasing radius. In practice of course cones can easily be defined analytically and the method is

```
 10 PI = 3.141593
 20 DEF FNRAD(DEGREES) = DEGREES*PI/180
 30 CLS
 40 INPUT "Contour file ";FILE$
 50 RHO = 2000 : THETA = 0 : PHI = 60 : D = 1500
 60 GOSUB 2000  'init view transform
 70 SCREEN 2 : CLS
 80 WINDOW (-640,-400)-(639,399)
 90 ZW = 0 : ENDOFCONTOUR = 9999
100 FILENUM = 3
110 OPEN FILE$ FOR INPUT AS #FILENUM
120 WHILE NOT EOF(FILENUM)
130   INPUT #FILENUM,XW,YW
140   GOSUB 250  'world to screen
150   PSET (XS,YS)
160   WHILE NOT EOF(FILENUM) AND NOT(XW = ENDOFCONTOUR)
170     INPUT #FILENUM,XW,YW
175     IF XW = ENDOFCONTOUR THEN 200
180     GOSUB 250  'world to screen
190     LINE -(XS,YS)
200   WEND
210   ZW = ZW+100
220 WEND
230 CLOSE #FILENUM
240 END

250 'SUBROUTINE world to screen
270   GOSUB 2100  'view transform
280   GOSUB 2150  'perspect transform
290 RETURN
```

Program 7.7 The creation of a three-dimensional object by 'lofting'. The screen projection procedures are as given in Program 7.2.

Figure 7.13
The lofting method of inputting three-dimensional data (a) the object defined as a set of height contours; (b)(c) the object as a three-dimensional solid

used where mathematical definitions are difficult or impossible. The general program structure is:

```
FOR CONTOUR = 1 TO NOOFCONTOURS
  GOSUB 100 'input contour at ht.z
  Z = Z + INTERVAL
NEXT CONTOUR
```

The next program, Program 7.7, is a simple demonstration of this technique. As it reads from a file that contains the contours it uses a nested WHILE structure. Figure 7.13 shows the input to and the output from the program.

Now an obvious disadvantage of this technique as it stands is that our three-dimensional model is not in the form of a collection of surfaces, but comprises a collection of contours at different heights.

```
 10 PI = 3.141593
 20 DEF FNRAD(DEGREES) = DEGREES*PI/180
 30 DEF FNDISTPQ = SQR(ABS((CURPX-NEXTQX)*(CURPX-NEXTQX)+
                   (CURPY-NEXTQY)*(CURPY-NEXTQY)))
 40 DEF FNDISTQP = SQR(ABS((CURQX-NEXTPX)*(CURQX-NEXTPX)+
                   (CURQY-NEXTPY)*(CURQY-NEXTPY)))
 50 DIM VERTEX(3,40),SURFACE(40,3)
 60 RHO = 250 : THETA = 15 : PHI = 28 : D = 600
 70 GOSUB 2000  'init view transform
 80 SCREEN 2 : CLS
 90 WINDOW (-640,-500)-(639,299)
100 GOSUB 350  'generate contours
110 GOSUB 510  'triangulate
120 PRINT "noofsurfaces is ",NOOFSURFACES
130 FOR SURFACENO = 1 TO NOOFSURFACES
140   GOSUB 170  'plot surfaces
150 NEXT SURFACENO
160 END

170 'SUBROUTINE plot surfaces
180   VERTEXNO = 1
190   GOSUB 280  'screen vertex
200   PSET (XS,YS) : STARTX = XS : STARTY = YS
210   FOR VERTEXNO = 2 TO 3
230     GOSUB 280  'screen vertex
240     LINE -(XS,YS)
250   NEXT VERTEXNO
260   LINE -(STARTX,STARTY)
270 RETURN

280 'SUBROUTINE screen vertex
290   XW = VERTEX(1, SURFACE(SURFACENO,VERTEXNO))
300   YW = VERTEX(2, SURFACE(SURFACENO,VERTEXNO))
310   ZW = VERTEX(3, SURFACE(SURFACENO,VERTEXNO))
320   GOSUB 2100  'view transform
330   GOSUB 2150  'perspect transform
340 RETURN

350 'SUBROUTINE generate contours
360   R1 = 150 : I = 0
370   FOR GCTHETA = -90 TO 90 STEP 9
380     I = I+1 : R11 = R1+(RND*16)-5 : THETAR = GCTHETA+(RND*3)-0.5
390     VERTEX(1,I) = R11*COS(FNRAD(THETAR))
400     VERTEX(2,I) = R11*SIN(FNRAD(THETAR))
410     VERTEX(3,I) = 0
420   NEXT GCTHETA
430   R2 = 80
440   FOR GCTHETA = -90 TO 90 STEP 10
450     I = I+1 : R22 = R2+(RND*12)-5 : THETAR = GCTHETA+(RND*2)
460     VERTEX(1,I) = R22*COS(FNRAD(THETAR))
470     VERTEX(2,I) = R22*SIN(FNRAD(THETAR))
```

Program 7.8 Triangulation between two contours. *continued*

```
480     VERTEX(3,I) = 100
490   NEXT GCTHETA
500 RETURN

510 'SUBROUTINE triangulate
520   I = 0 : P = 1 : Q = 22
530   CURPX = VERTEX(1,P) : CURPY = VERTEX(2,P)
540   CURQX = VERTEX(1,Q) : CURQY = VERTEX(2,Q)
550   NEXTPX = VERTEX(1,P+1) : NEXTPY = VERTEX(2,P+1)
560   NEXTQX = VERTEX(1,Q+1) : NEXTQY = VERTEX(2,Q+1)
570   WHILE NOT(P = 20) AND NOT(Q = 39)
580     IF FNDISTPQ < FNDISTQP THEN GOSUB 630 ELSE GOSUB 690
590 '                                fixpqq          fixqpp
600   WEND
610   NOOFSURFACES = I
620 RETURN

630 'SUBROUTINE fixpqq
640   I = I+1
650   SURFACE(I,1) = P : SURFACE(I,2) = Q : SURFACE(I,3) = Q+1
660   CURQX = NEXTQX : CURQY = NEXTQY : Q = Q+1
670   NEXTQX = VERTEX(1,Q+1) : NEXTQY = VERTEX(2,Q+1)
680 RETURN

690 'SUBROUTINE fixqpp
700   I = I+1
710   SURFACE(I,1) = Q : SURFACE(I,2) = P : SURFACE(I,3) = P+1
720   CURPX = NEXTPX : CURPY = NEXTPY : P = P+1
730   NEXTPX = VERTEX(1,P+1) : NEXTPY = VERTEX(2,P+1)
740 RETURN
```

Program 7.8 *continued*

Although the model is easy to plot in this form it is not suitable for processing by a hidden surface algorithm nor can it be applied to a shading model, which also requires a set of plane polygons. What we now need to do is develop a technique that will define a surface over the contours as a series of patches. This is called triangulation and standard mathematical techniques exist for finding the optimal surface between contours. We will adopt a much more straightforward approach to map our contour data into a collection of triangular surfaces and not concern ourselves with making sure that we achieve the optimal surface.

Program 7.8 incorporates a simple triangulation algorithm. It uses our standard surface-vertex data structure and for simplicity operates on two contours that are generated by the program. It is easily extended to the general case of many contours. The contours are just two semi-circles of different radii. These are generated in a subroutine. The lower contour is a semi-circle of radius 150 at a height of 0. The upper contour is a semi-circle of radius 80 at a height

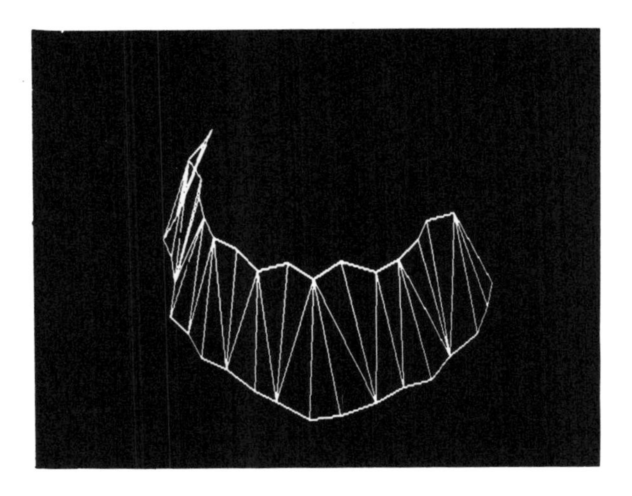

Figure 7.14
Output from simple triangulation algorithm operating on two semi-circular contours

of 100. These contours are generated by sweeping a radius through 180° in 10° intervals. The radius and the interval are both randomly perturbed so that a 'jagged' semi-circle is generated. This simulates the case of a general contour input from a digitizer. The vertices of these contours are loaded into array 'VERTEX'. In the general case, for n contours we would need a pointer to the start of each contour.

The only other subroutine that we are interested in at the moment is the one that performs the triangulation. This defines a surface of triangular patches between the two contours loading the results into array 'SURFACE'. The output from the program is shown in Figure 7.14. The algorithm implemented in this subroutine works by continually examining the relationship between four points (Figure 7.15). 'CURP' (i.e. 'CURPX' and 'CURPY') are the (x,y) coordinates of the current point on the lower contour. 'NEXTP' (i.e. 'NEXTPX' and 'NEXTPY') are the (x,y) coordinates of the next point on the lower contour. A similar convention is used for the current points

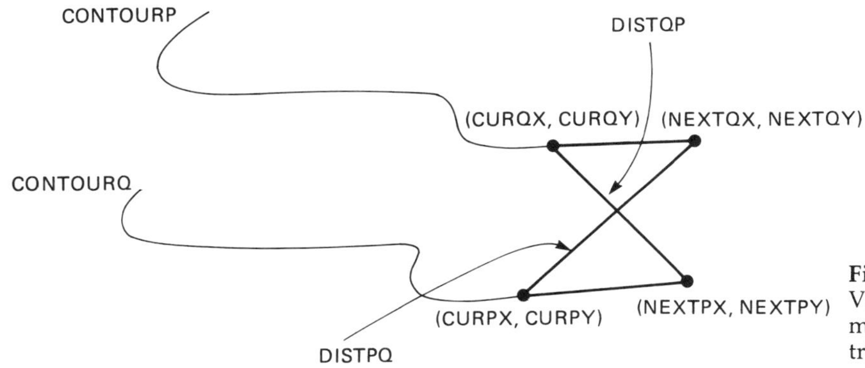

Figure 7.15
Variables and distance measures in the simple triangulations algorithms

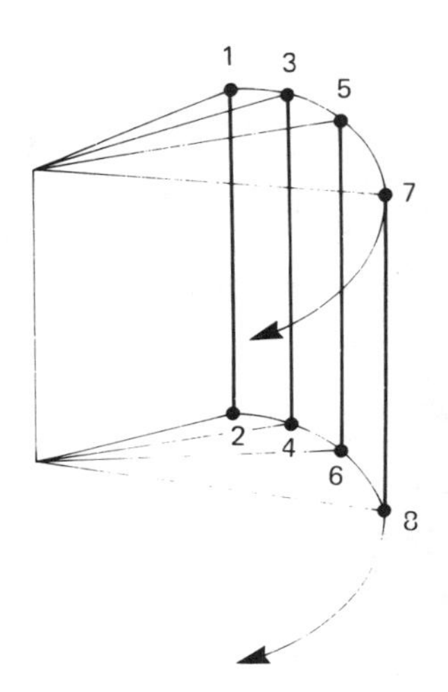

Figure 7.16
Generating a cylinder by 'sweeping' a line through 360°

on the upper contour. Given that the algorithm has triangulated to the current points it compares the distance from 'CURP' to 'NEXTQ' with the distance from 'CURQ' to 'NEXTP':

```
IF FNDISTPQ <= FNDISTQP THEN GOSUB 630 ELSE GOSUB 690
```

The subroutine captioned 'fixpqq' loads a surface into the data structure using one vertex from the lower (p) contour and two from the higher (q) contour. The subroutine captioned 'fixqpp' loads a surface using one vertex from the higher (q) contour and two from the lower (p) contour. The algorithm simply selects one from a choice of two distances and uses this criterion to select one of two subroutines.

A number of commonly used convex bodies can be generated by sweeping a line through 360° in intervals of say 10°. The simplest figure in this class is a cylinder. Cones and spheres can also be generated in this way although when a function, rather than a straight line, is swept we have the problem of triangulation again. This method is called rotational sweeping and is illustrated in Figure 7.16. This shows a cylinder being generated by sweeping a vertical line through 360°. The method can be generalized so that the swept line follows a profile that is input from a digitizer. This will generate bodies with translational symmetry and is appropriate in disciplines such as engineering and architecture.

Program 7.9 implements this idea. The contour shown in Figure 7.17a is input to the program. It is made up of vertices at the junction of two straight lines together with vertices every 10° on the curves which are all parts of circumferences of a circle. A three-dimensional model is easily constructed by considering a duplicate contour at some height above the original. Figure 7.17b and Figure 7.17c show two views of the object as generated by the program.

a

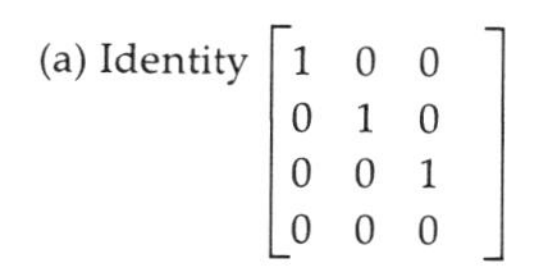

(a) Identity $\begin{bmatrix} 1 & 0 & 0 \\ 0 & 1 & 0 \\ 0 & 0 & 1 \\ 0 & 0 & 0 \end{bmatrix}$

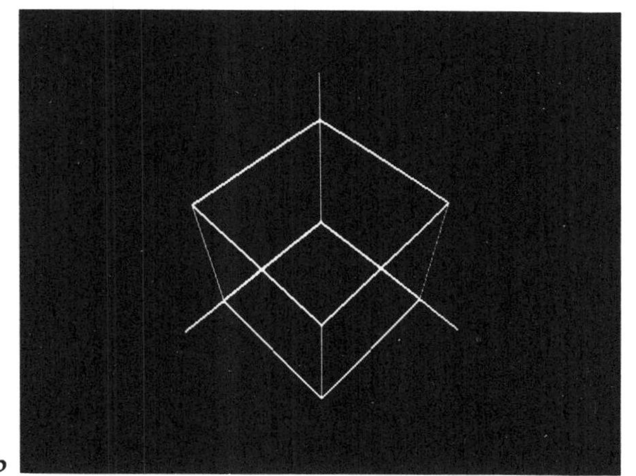

b

(b) Uniform scaling $\begin{bmatrix} 1.5 & 0 & 0 \\ 0 & 1.5 & 0 \\ 0 & 0 & 1.5 \\ 0 & 0 & 0 \end{bmatrix}$

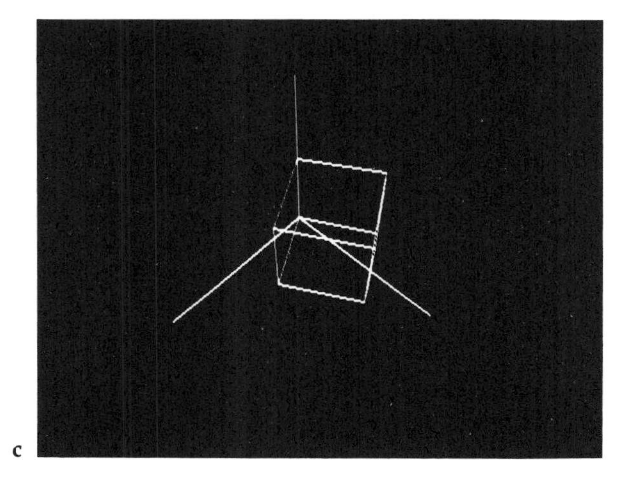

c

(c) Rotation (z-axis) $\begin{bmatrix} 0.866 & 0.5 & 0 \\ -0.5 & 0.866 & 0 \\ 0 & 0 & 1 \\ 0 & 0 & 0 \end{bmatrix}$

Figure 8.1
Using a general transformation procedure

(d) Rotation (*x*-axis)

$$\begin{bmatrix} 1 & 0 & 0 \\ 0 & 0.866 & 0.5 \\ 0 & -0.5 & 0.866 \\ 0 & 0 & 0 \end{bmatrix}$$

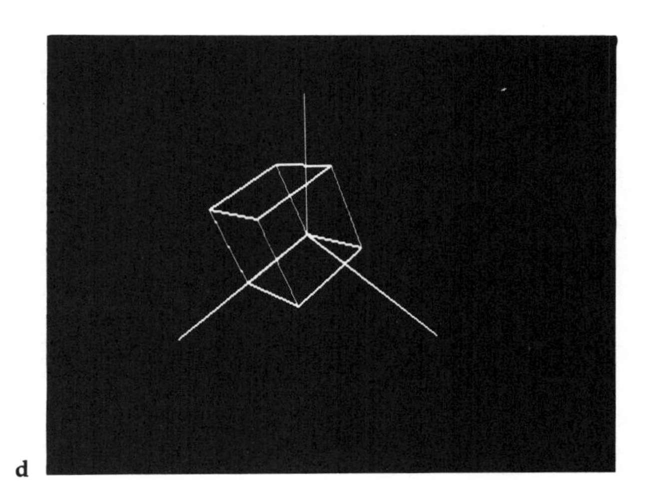

d

(e) Rotation (*y*-axis)

$$\begin{bmatrix} 0.866 & 0 & -0.5 \\ 0 & 1 & 0 \\ 0.5 & 0 & 0.866 \\ 0 & 0 & 0 \end{bmatrix}$$

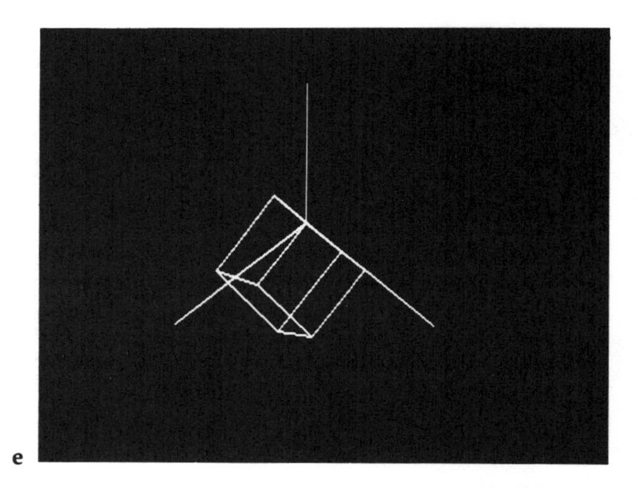

e

(f) *Y* shear

$$\begin{bmatrix} 1 & 0 & 0 \\ 0 & 1 & 0 \\ 0 & 1 & 1 \\ 0 & 0 & 0 \end{bmatrix}$$

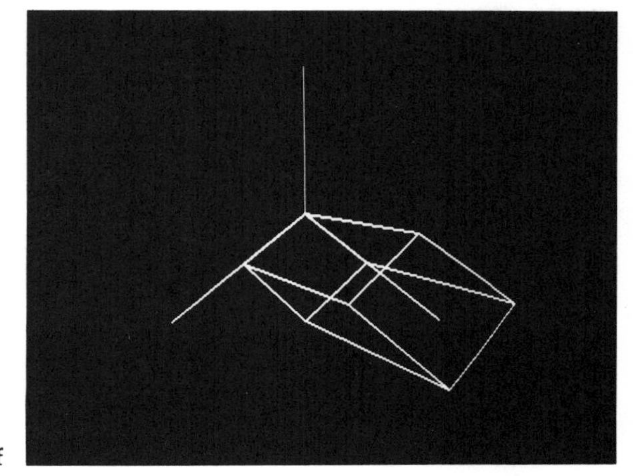

f

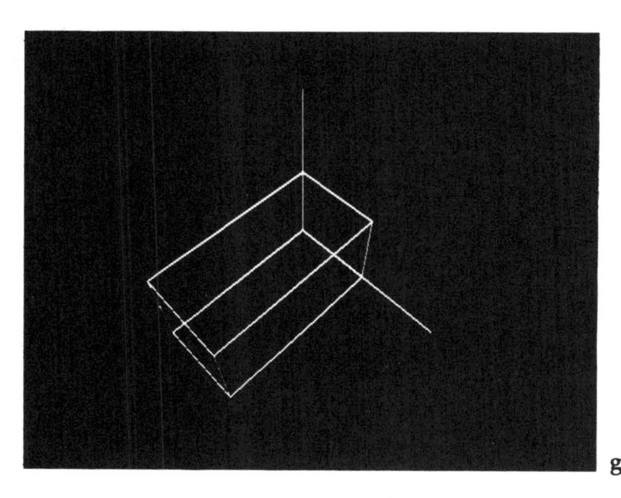

g

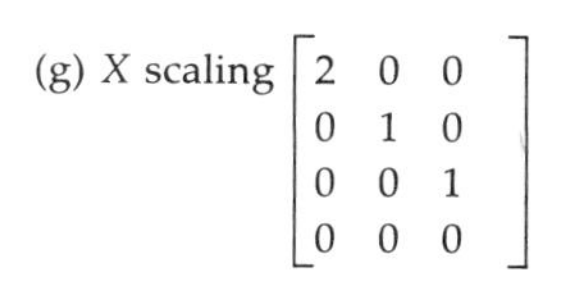

(g) X scaling $\begin{bmatrix} 2 & 0 & 0 \\ 0 & 1 & 0 \\ 0 & 0 & 1 \\ 0 & 0 & 0 \end{bmatrix}$

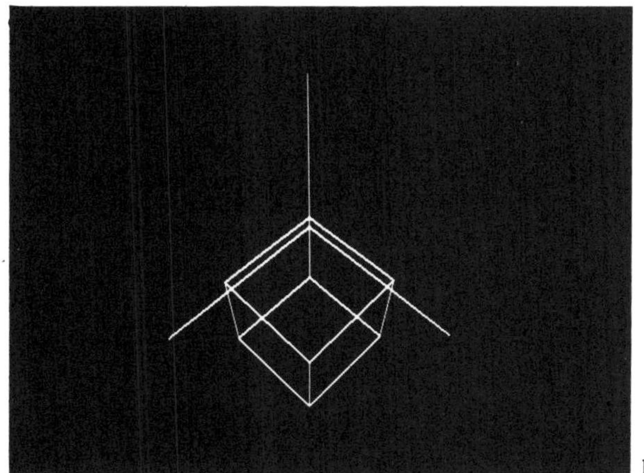

h

(h) Translation $\begin{bmatrix} 1 & 0 & 0 \\ 0 & 1 & 0 \\ 0 & 0 & 1 \\ 500 & 500 & 0 \end{bmatrix}$

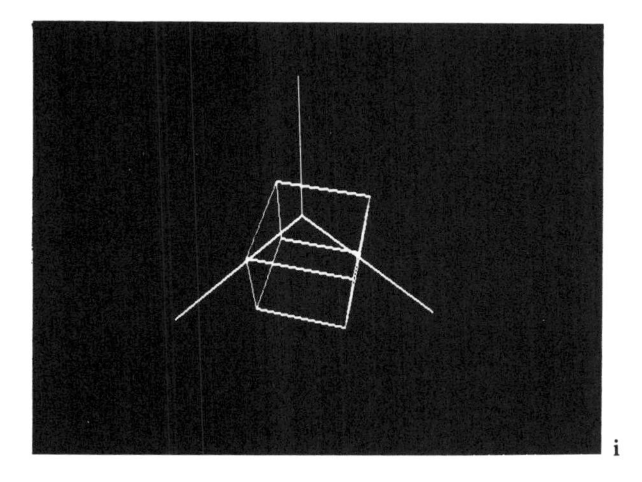

i

(i) Translation and rotation $\begin{bmatrix} 0.866 & 0.5 & 0 \\ -0.5 & 0.866 & 0 \\ 0 & 0 & 1 \\ 430.7 & 60.3 & 0 \end{bmatrix}$

World coordinates

vertex	x_w	y_w	z_w
1	100	0	0
2	100	100	0
3	0	100	0
4	0	0	0
5	100	0	100
6	100	100	100
7	0	100	100
8	0	0	100
9	50	50	150

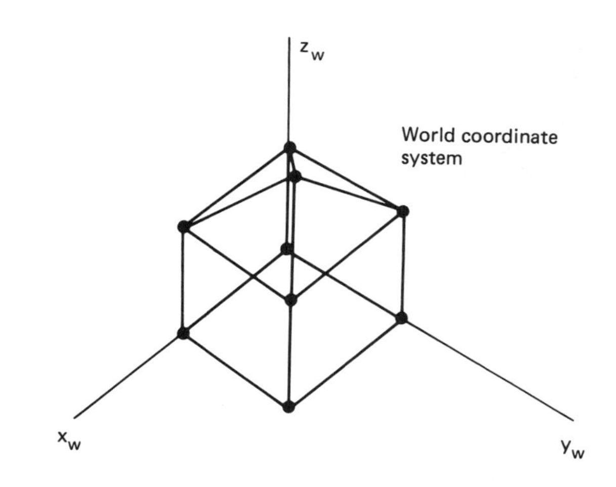

Figure 8.2
World coordinate system

For example, for a rotation of 30° about a point (50,50,0) we have

$$\begin{bmatrix} 0.866 & 0.5 & 0 & 0 \\ -0.5 & 0.866 & 0 & 0 \\ 0 & 0 & 1 & 0 \\ 31.75 & -18.25 & 0 & 1 \end{bmatrix}$$

8.2 WORLD COORDINATES TO SCREEN COORDINATES

In the previous chapter we introduced the idea of the viewpoint transformation and the screen transformation, and we have used

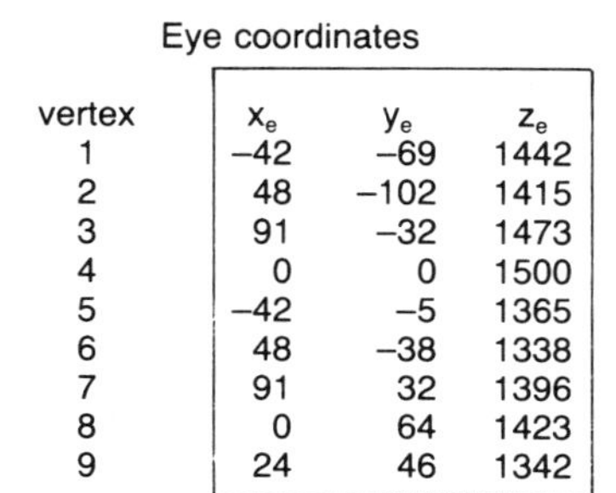

Eye coordinates

vertex	x_e	y_e	z_e
1	–42	–69	1442
2	48	–102	1415
3	91	–32	1473
4	0	0	1500
5	–42	–5	1365
6	48	–38	1338
7	91	32	1396
8	0	64	1423
9	24	46	1342

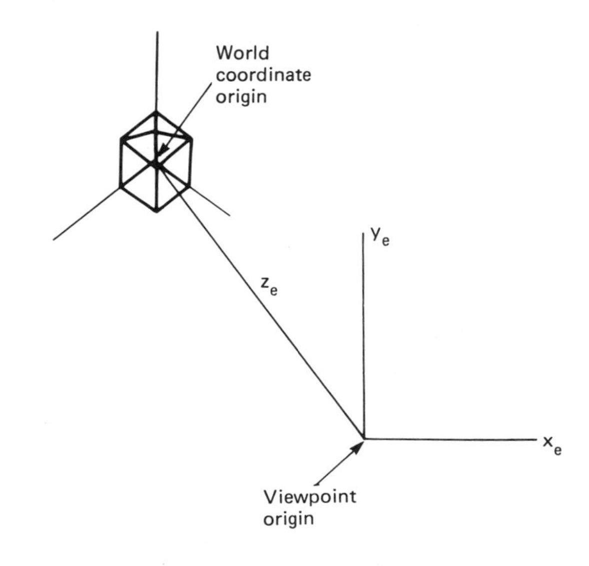

Figure 8.3
Eye coordinate system: the position of the eye is at the viewpoint origin

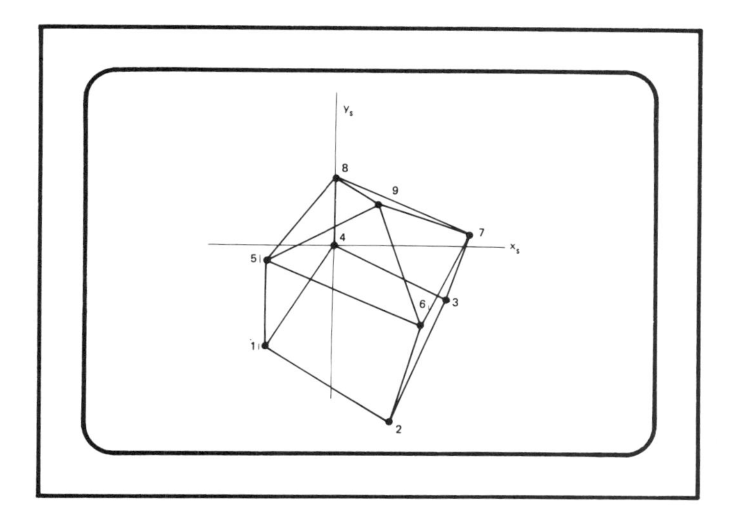

Screen coordinates

vertex	x_s	y_s
1	−88	−144
2	103	−216
3	185	−66
4	0	0
5	−93	−11
6	108	−84
7	195	69
8	0	135
9	54	102

Figure 8.4
Screen coordinate system

these transformations liberally in programs to display the results of various three-dimensional manipulations on a two-dimensional screen. In this section we will explain in detail how these transformations work. We will introduce the topic by looking at the whole process applied to a simple example and we will then examine each transformation in turn. As we described briefly in the previous chapter, going from the three-dimensional world coordinate space to two-dimensional screen coordinates takes us through two transformations. The process is illustrated in Figures 8.2, 8.3 and 8.4. Let us start with the cube and pyramid model shown in Figure 8.2. This has a list of world coordinates, showing that one edge of the cube is coincident with the *z*-axis. Now when we map this into screen coordinates we look at the model from a particular view. This means that we pretend that our eye is in a certain position in three-dimensional space. We then change our system so that the origin is centred at the viewpoint and the *z*-axis points towards the previous origin (the point (0,0,0) in the world coordinate system). This is shown in Figure 8.3. The *ze* coordinates are large because the viewpoint is a long way from the object. The list of coordinates are the three-dimensional eye coordinates for the object. These are the world coordinates after the origin is changed to the viewpoint (together with the other aforementioned transformations). Some of the *xe* and *ye* coordinates are now negative because the *ye* and *xe* axes are no longer aligned with the *xw* and *yw* axes (the precise reasons for this are explained later). The next transformation transforms the list of eye coordinates into a list of screen coordinates. Examination of Figure 8.4 will show that the screen coordinate list is related to the eye coordinate list. This relationship is specified by the perspective transformation described in the next section. Now that we have a list of two-dimensional screen coordinates these can be plotted on the screen.

It is important to bear in mind that both the viewpoint transformation and the perspective transformation are particular transformations, arbitrarily chosen for this example. There is an infinity of viewpoint transformations because there is an infinity of viewpoints. There is a large set of perspective transformations depending on the particular criteria that we wish to adopt to transform or map a three-dimensional point into a two-dimensional point.

8.3 THE VIEWING TRANSFORMATION

In this section we will deal with the first of the two transformations that take us from world to screen coordinates. This is called the viewpoint transformation. The mathematics of this transformation, although not particularly demanding, requires a firm appreciation of movements (rotations, etc.) in three-dimensional space and for this reason this has been isolated in Appendix 4. You can simply accept the result at this stage or work through Appendix 4. The derivation of the transformation is not important, but the interpretation of the parameters in the transformation is and this section will concentrate on that aspect.

The required operation is:

$$(xe,ye,ze,1) = (xw,yw,zw,1)\ V$$

where

$$V = \begin{bmatrix} -\sin\theta & -\cos\theta\cos\phi & -\cos\theta\sin\phi & 0 \\ \cos\theta & -\sin\theta\cos\phi & -\sin\theta\sin\phi & 0 \\ 0 & \sin\phi & -\cos\phi & 0 \\ 0 & 0 & \rho & 1 \end{bmatrix}$$

(xw,yw,zw) is the coordinate of a point in the world coordinate system, V is the viewpoint transformation and (xe,ye,ze) is the transformed coordinate. ρ (rho), θ (theta) and ϕ (phi) specify the position of the viewpoint in world coordinate space. Now the viewpoint is just a single point in three-dimensional world coordinate space and the viewpoint transformation converts the coordinates of the object in world coordinate space to coordinates in a system where the origin is moved to the viewpoint. This system is called the eye coordinate system. For mathematical convenience the viewpoint is specified in spherical coordinates (Figure 8.5). This means that we specify a point in three-dimensional space using two angles and a distance (instead of three distances). As well as simplifying the transformation mathematics, it is much easier and more natural to specify a particular viewpoint using two angles and a single distance. Figure 8.5 can be interpreted as follows. If we draw a line from the world coordinate origin to the viewpoint, ρ is the distance

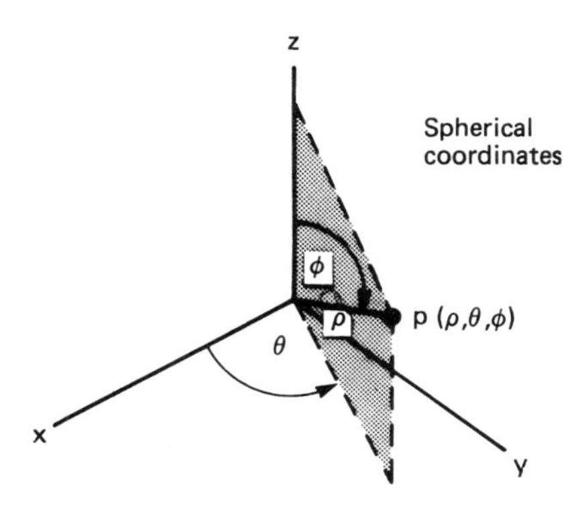

Figure 8.5
Spherical coordinate system

along this line, θ is the angle that the plane containing the line makes with the x-axis and φ is the angle that the line makes with the z-axis.

The BASIC implementation of the transformation is given as Program 8.2. Note that two subroutines are used in the implementation. The subroutine 'initialise view transform' would be called once for a given viewpoint and the subroutine 'view transform' would then be called once for each vertex in the object being viewed. The trigonometric calculations do not vary amongst vertices and it is important, for reasons of efficiency, that these are only carried out once.

As already mentioned the mathematics of the transformation is not important and we will now look at the effect of varying each parameter in turn while keeping the other two fixed. First of all let us consider the parameter φ, the inclination of the line from the origin to the viewpoint. Figure 8.6a shows two views of the wireframe

```
2000 'SUBROUTINE init view transform
2010   SINTHETA = SIN(FNRAD(THETA)): COSTHETA = COS(FNRAD(THETA))
2020   SINPHI = SIN(FNRAD(PHI)) : COSPHI = COS(FNRAD(PHI))
2030   VA = -SINTHETA : VB = COSTHETA
2040   VE = -COSTHETA*COSPHI : VF = -SINTHETA*COSPHI
2050   VG =  SINPHI
2060   VI = -COSTHETA*SINPHI : VJ = -SINTHETA*SINPHI
2070   VK = -COSPHI : VL = RHO
2080 RETURN

2100 'SUBROUTINE view transform
2110   XE  = VA*XW+VB*YW
2120   YE  = VE*XW+VF*YW+VG*ZW
2130   ZE  = VI*XW+VJ*YW+VK*ZW+VL
2140 RETURN
```

Program 8.2 The viewpoint transformation subroutines.

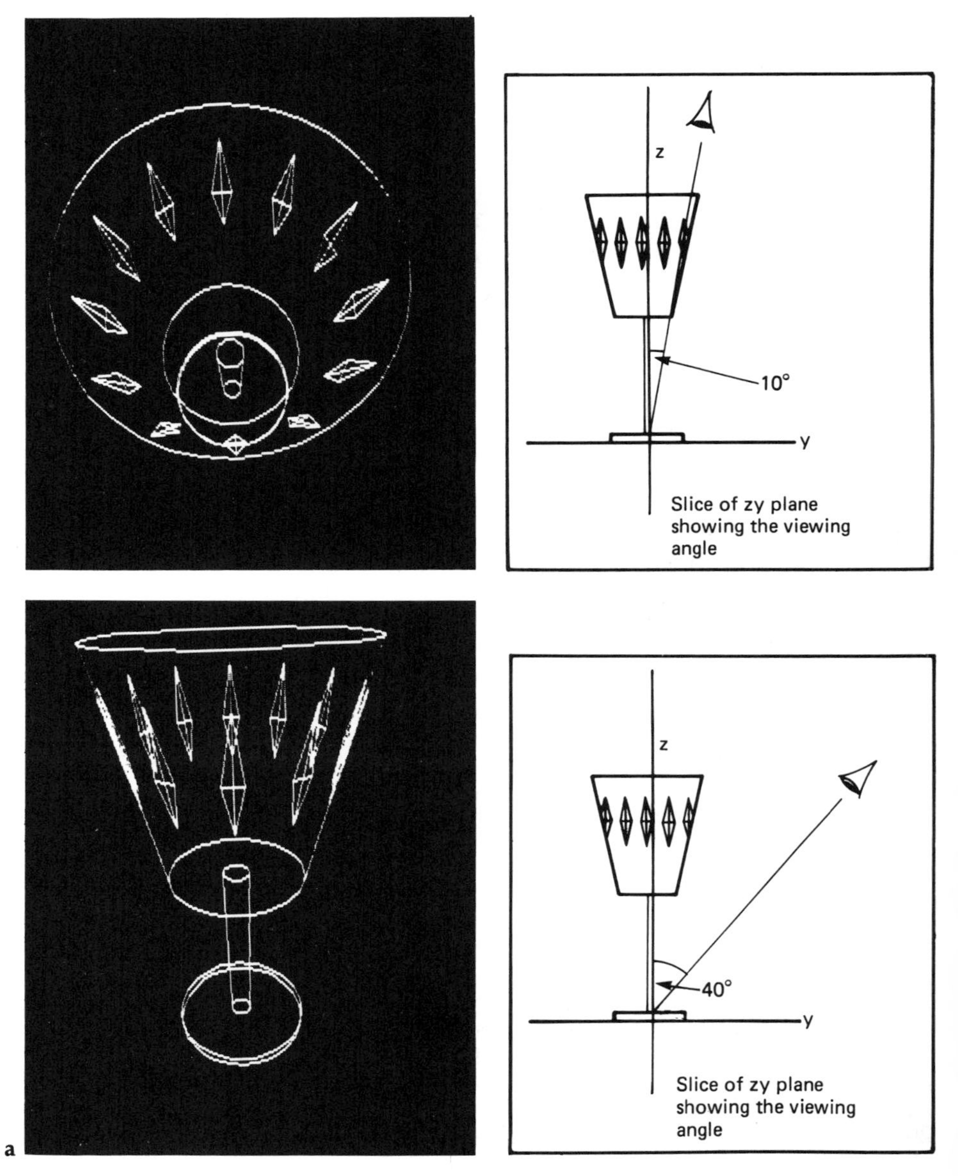

Figure 8.6
Wireframe wineglass
(a) illustrating the effect of the viewing angle φ;
(b) confusion at same viewing angles can be reviewed by adopting simple (and partial) hidden line removal

wineglass. In the first view φ is set to 10°. This is a very steep viewing angle and gives the illusion that we are looking down into the top section of the glass. The top rim is almost circular and contains the other three circles in the model. In the next view φ is set to 40° and you can see the effect that this has on the displayed object. Figure 8.6b shows a view that is difficult to interpret because of the confusion from lines from the far side of the glass. The second

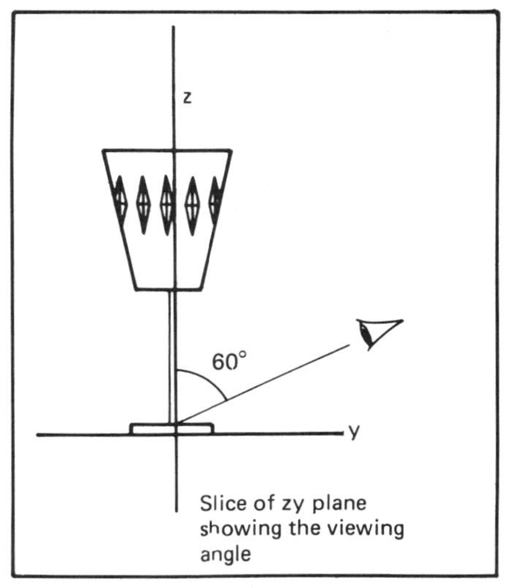

Difficulties arise in the example above. Here we are looking down on the base and up towards the rim.

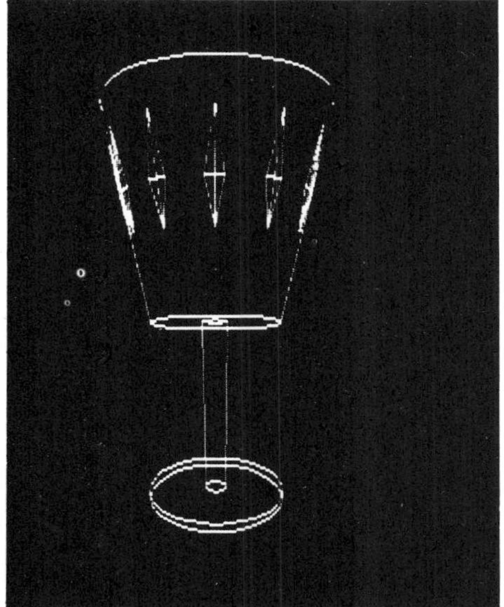

b

Ambiguity removed by removing both rim and motif.

illustration shows how, in this particular case, the application of simple alterations in the drawing subroutine can produce effective hidden line removal.

The next parameter to consider is θ, the rotation of the projection of the line in the (x,y) plane. Varying this parameter and keeping the others fixed will cause the viewer to 'fly around the object' as it were, at constant elevation. Thus the parameter ϕ fixes the height of the viewpoint with respect to the object and the parameter θ allows the viewpoint to be moved around the object in a horizontal plane. Now there is no point in moving around the wireframe wineglass because of its rotational symmetry and Figure 8.7 shows views of the 'church with steeple' for different values of theta. Program 8.3 was used to generate these illustrations from the data for the church. The inclination angle is fixed at 80° and the views are for θ set to 30°, 150°, –30° and 210° respectively. A hidden surface algorithm has been applied and this is explained in the next chapter. Note that the algorithm works on complete surfaces, and that parts of surfaces that are obscured from a certain viewpoint are not removed. Another way of putting it is to say that this algorithm only works for a convex polyhedron. The 'church with steeple' is not a convex polyhedron. Now as we have already mentioned this transformation will give us a list of three-dimensional coordinates in the eye coordinate system. What we now need is a perspective

Figure 8.7
Changing THETA to 'fly around' an object
(a) THETA = 30 (350,30,80,600)
(b) THETA = 150 (180,150,80,600)
(c) THETA = –30 (350, –30,80,600)
(d) THETA = 210 (180,210,80,600)

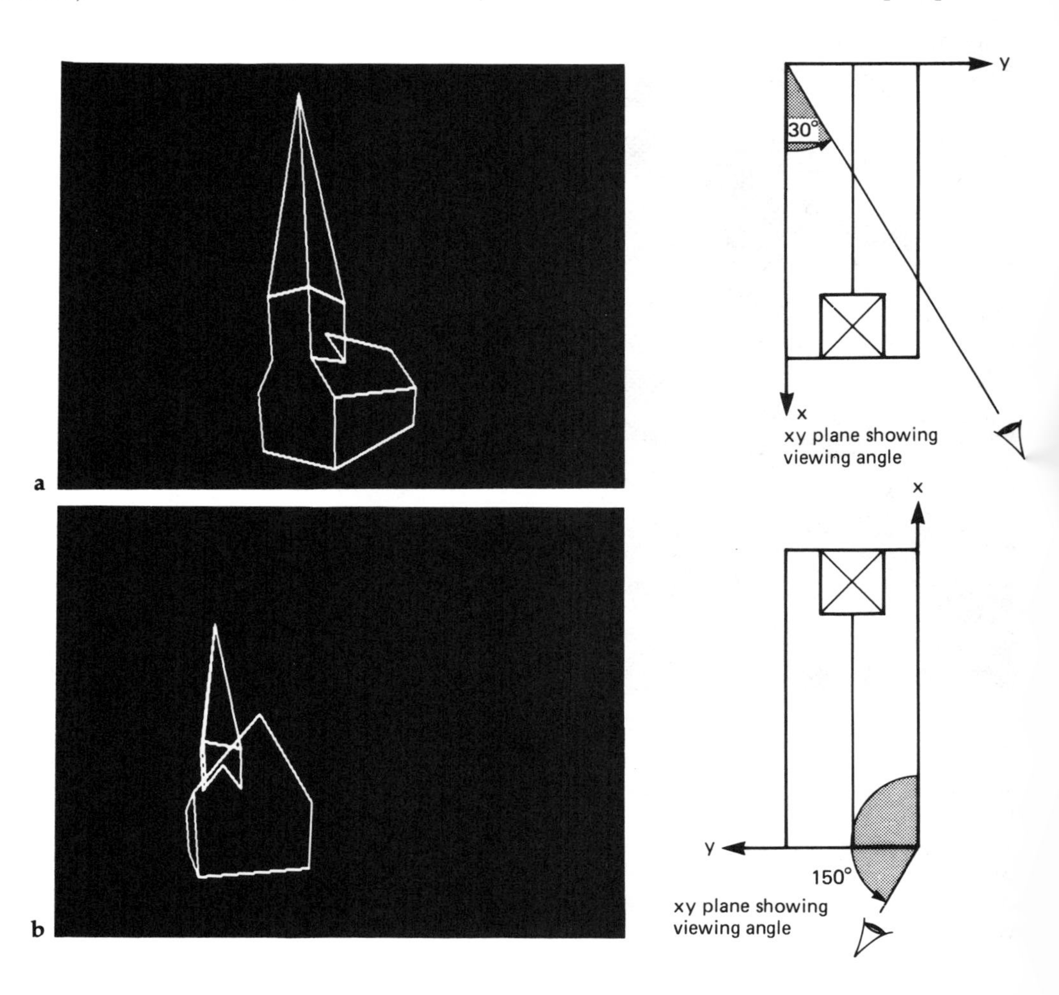

transformation that will produce screen coordinates. This is considerably easier to derive than the viewing transformation.

Perspective transformation

The perspective transformation from the eye coordinate system to the screen coordinate system is illustrated in Figure 8.8. Point p is a point in the eye system, p' is its mapping into the screen coordinate system and d is the distance of the eye from a screen. If we look at the illustration normal to the (ye,ze) plane we have Figure 8.9. It is easily seen that:

$$ys = d \times ye/ze$$

Similarly

$$xs = d \times xe/ze$$

We can imagine the process as follows. The screen is a plane parallel

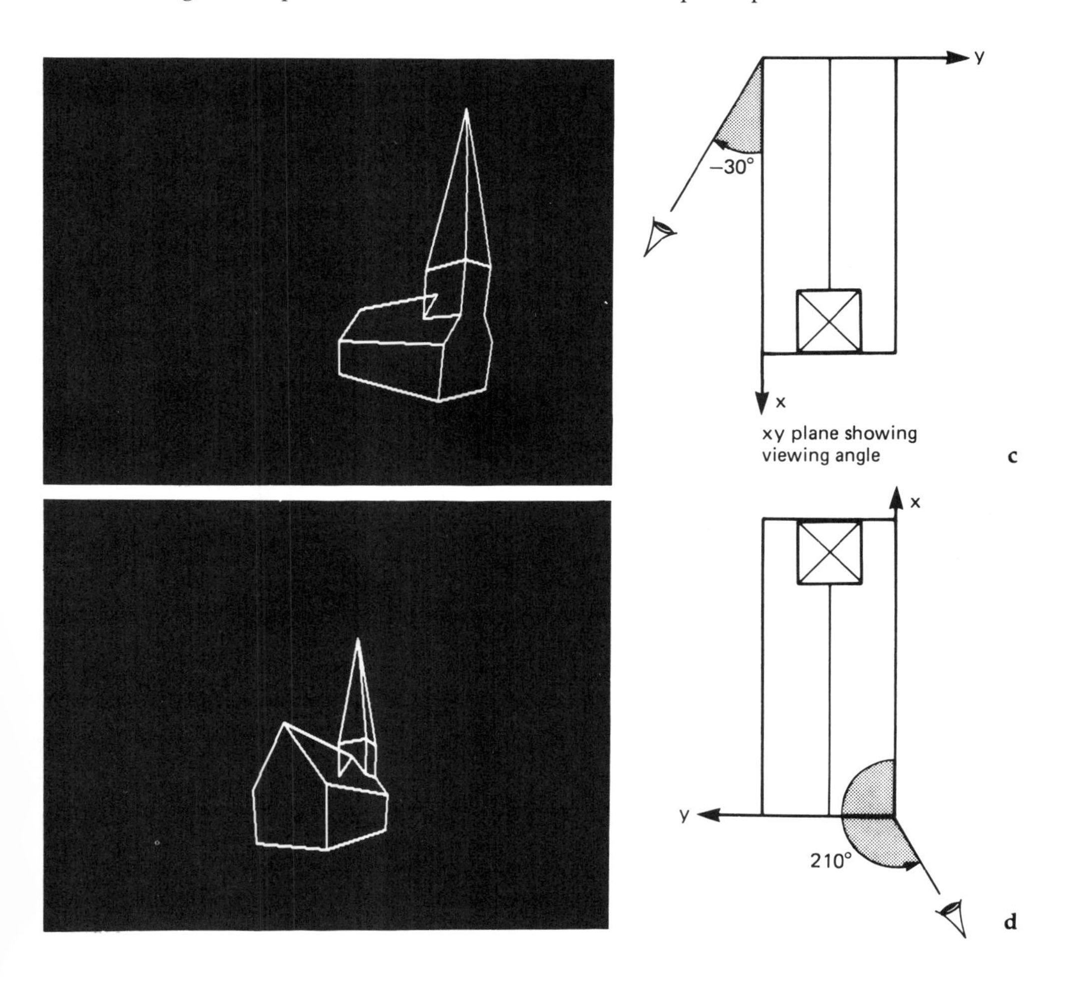

```
   5 DIM VERTEX(3,19),SURFACE(14,9),NOOFVERTICES(14)
  10 DIM VECTOR1(3),VECTOR2(3),VISIBLE(14)
  15 CLS
  20 PI = 3.141593
  25 DEF FNRAD(DEGREES) = DEGREES*PI/180
  30 PRINT " rho      theta    phi     screen dist"
  35 INPUT;" ";RHO : INPUT;"    ";THETA : INPUT;"     ";PHI :
     INPUT"    ";SCREENDIST
  40 GOSUB 2000  'init view transform
  45 SCREEN 2 : CLS : WINDOW (-640,-150)-(639,873)
  50 GOSUB 680  'initialise
  55 GOSUB 3000  'hidden face remove
  60 FOR SURFACENO = 1 TO SURFS
  70   IF VISIBLE(SURFACENO) THEN GOSUB 500  'transform and plot
  80 NEXT SURFACENO
  90 INPUT ANY$ : END
       .
       .
       .
3000 'SUBROUTINE hidden face remove
3030   XVIEW = RHO*SINPHI*COSTHETA
3040   YVIEW = RHO*SINPHI*SINTHETA
3050   ZVIEW = RHO*COSPHI
3060   FOR SURFACENO = 1 TO SURFS
3070     GOSUB 3130  'calculate surface vectors
3080     GOSUB 3190  'calculate normal vector
3090     GOSUB 3240  'calculate line of sight vector
3100     GOSUB 3290  'visibility test
3110   NEXT SURFACENO
3120 RETURN
```

Program 8.3 Generating different views of the church with steeple (Program 7.2). Hidden face removal is explained in Chapter 9.

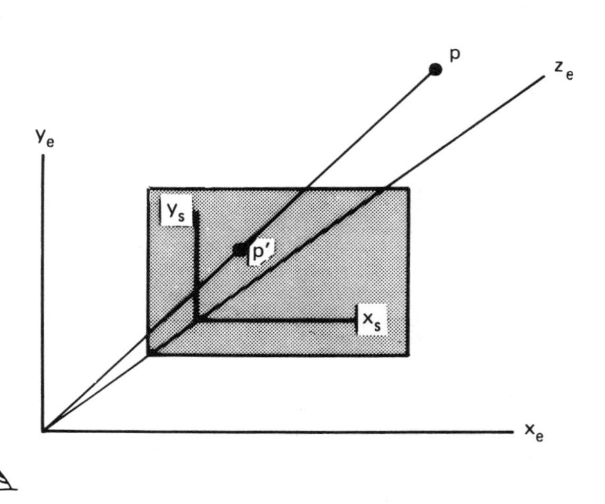

Figure 8.8
Perspective transformation details

```
3130 'SUBROUTINE calculate surface vectors
3140   FOR I = 1 TO 3
3150     VECTOR1(I) = VERTEX(I,SURFACE(SURFACENO,2))
                    - VERTEX(I,SURFACE(SURFACENO,1))
3160     VECTOR2(I) = VERTEX(I,SURFACE(SURFACENO,3))
                    - VERTEX(I,SURFACE(SURFACENO,1))
3170   NEXT I
3180 RETURN

3190 'SUBROUTINE calculate normal vector
3200   NORMALX = VECTOR1(2)*VECTOR2(3)-VECTOR2(2)*VECTOR1(3)
3210   NORMALY = VECTOR1(3)*VECTOR2(1)-VECTOR2(3)*VECTOR1(1)
3220   NORMALZ = VECTOR1(1)*VECTOR2(2)-VECTOR2(1)*VECTOR1(2)
3230 RETURN

3240 'SUBROUTINE calculate line of sight vector
3250   LINEOFSIGHTX = XVIEW-VERTEX(1,SURFACE(SURFACENO,1))
3260   LINEOFSIGHTY = YVIEW-VERTEX(2,SURFACE(SURFACENO,1))
3270   LINEOFSIGHTZ = ZVIEW-VERTEX(3,SURFACE(SURFACENO,1))
3280 RETURN

3290 'SUBROUTINE visibility test
3300   VISIBLE(SURFACENO) = NORMALX*LINEOFSIGHTX
                          + NORMALY*LINEOFSIGHTY
                          + NORMALZ*LINEOFSIGHTZ > 0
3310 RETURN
```

to the (xe,ye) plane. For every vertex in the object, a collection of points in the eye coordinate system, we can use a line to join the vertex to the origin (the eye). Where each line intersects the screen plane gives us the mapping from the vertex into the screen plane.

There is a family of perspective transformations available but this

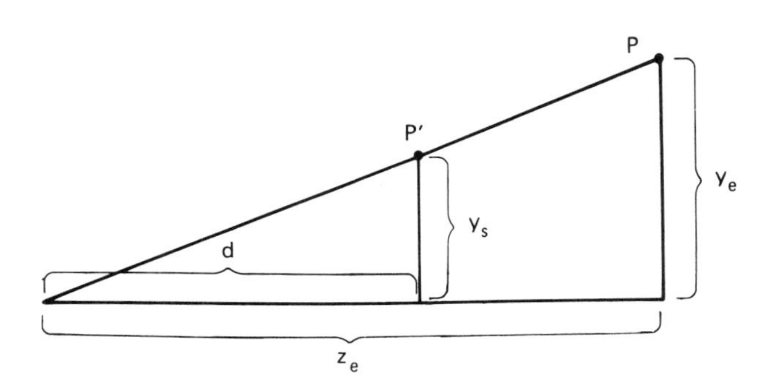

Figure 8.9
The y_e, x_e plane of Fig. 8.8

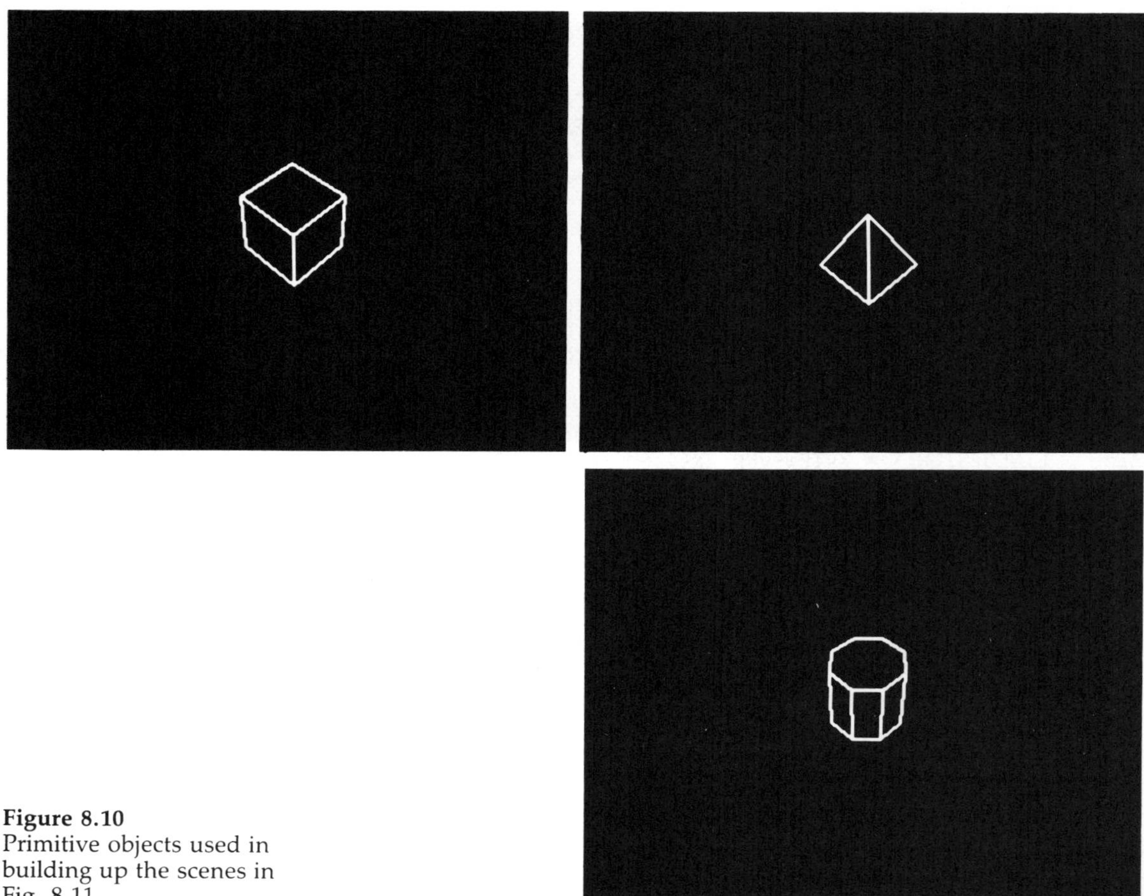

Figure 8.10
Primitive objects used in building up the scenes in Fig. 8.11

particular one is the easiest to compute and use, so we will restrict ourselves to it. It is categorised by having a single vanishing point and the *xs* and *ys* axes are parallel to the *xe* and *ye* axes.
The perspective transformation is implemented by:

```
2150   'SUBROUTINE perspect transform
2160     XS = D*XE/ZE
2170     YS = D*YE/ZE
2180   RETURN
```

and this is the transformation that we have used to generate the previous illustrations.

Building up multi-object scenes
In previous chapters we have made extensive use of two-dimensional linear transformations to build up two-dimensional composites

```
  10 DIM VERTEX(3,19),SURFACE(14,9),NOOFVERTICES(14)
  20 DIM VECTOR1(3),VECTOR2(3),VISIBLE(14)
  25 RHO = 3500 : THETA = 45 : PHI = 45 : SCREENDIST = 1500
  30 PI = 3.141593
  35 DEF FNRAD(DEGREES) = DEGREES*PI/180
  40 GOSUB 2000  'init view transform
  50 SCREEN 2 : CLS : WINDOW (-640,-512)-(639,511)
  60 FOR OBJECT = 1 TO 4
  65 PRINT OBJECT
  70   IF OBJECT = 4 THEN RESTORE 1210
  80   GOSUB 680  'initialise
  90   GOSUB 160  'transform verts
 100   GOSUB 3000  'hidden face remove
 110   FOR SURFACENO = 1 TO SURFS
 120     IF VISIBLE(SURFACENO) THEN GOSUB 500  'transform and plot
 130   NEXT SURFACENO
 140 NEXT OBJECT
 150 INPUT ANY$ : END

 160 'SUBROUTINE transform verts
 180   IF OBJECT = 4 THEN RESTORE 1290
 190   READ A,B,C,D,E,F,G,H,I,J,K,L
 200   FOR II = 1 TO VERTS
 210     X = VERTEX(1,II)
 220     Y = VERTEX(2,II)
 230     Z = VERTEX(3,II)
 240     GOSUB 280  'transform
 250     VERTEX(1,II) = XT : VERTEX(2,II) = YT : VERTEX(3,II) = ZT
 260   NEXT II
 270 RETURN

 280 'SUBROUTINE transform
 290   XT = A*X+B*Y+C*Z+D
 300   YT = E*X+F*Y+G*Z+H
 310   ZT = I*X+J*Y+K*Z+L
 320 RETURN
       .
       .
       .
1140 DATA 8, 400,0,400,  400,0,0,  400,400,0, 400,400,400
1150 DATA 0,400,0,  0,400,400,  0,0,400,  0,0,0
1160 DATA 6, 4,1,2,3,4,  4,3,5,6,4,  4,5,8,7,6,  4,8,2,1,7,
          4,4,6,7,1,  4,3,2,8,5
1170 DATA 1.7,0,0,0,  0,2.5,0,0,  0,0,1,0
1180 DATA 5,  400,0,0,  400,400,0,  0,400,0,  0,0,0,  200,200,400
1190 DATA 5,3,1,2,5,  3,2,3,5,  3,3,4,5,  3,4,1,5,  4,1,4,3,2
1200 DATA 0.5,0,0,200,  0,0.5,0,200,  0,0,0.5,400
1210 DATA 16, 117,0,0,  282,0,0,  400,117,0,  400,282,0
1220 DATA 282,400,0,  117,400,0,  0,282,0,  0,117,0
1230 DATA 117,0,400,  282,0,400,  400,117,400,  400,282,400
1240 DATA 282,400,400,  117,400,400,  0,282,400,  0,117,400
1250 DATA 10, 8,8,7,6,5,4,3,2,1,  8,9,10,11,12,13,14,15,16
1260 DATA 4,1,2,10,9,  4,2,3,11,10,  4,3,4,12,11,  4,4,5,13,12
1270 DATA 4,5,6,14,13,  4,6,7,15,14,  4,7,8,16,15,  4,8,1,9,16
1280 DATA 0.5,0,0,200,  0,0.5,0,600,  0,0,2,400
1290 DATA 0,0,1,400, 0,1,0,-1000, -1,0,0,0
       .
       .
       .
```

Program 8.4 Generating multi-object scenes.

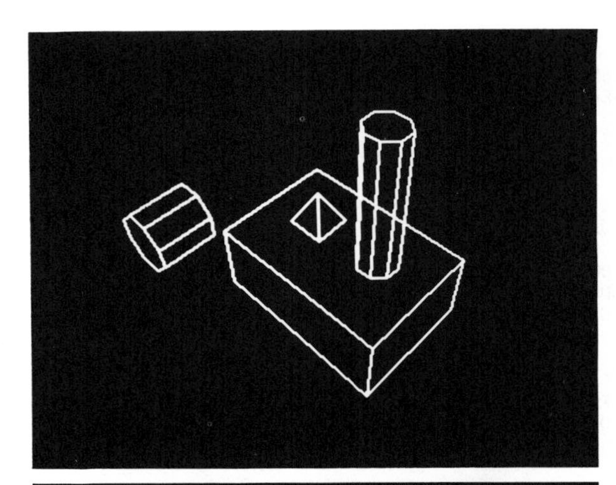

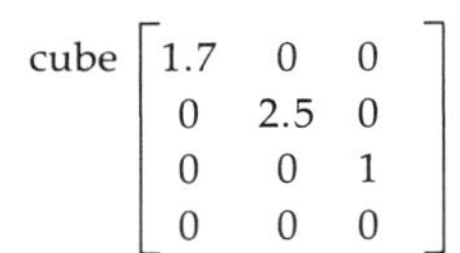

$$\text{cube}\begin{bmatrix} 1.7 & 0 & 0 \\ 0 & 2.5 & 0 \\ 0 & 0 & 1 \\ 0 & 0 & 0 \end{bmatrix}$$

$$\text{prism}\begin{bmatrix} 0.5 & 0 & 0 \\ 0 & 0.5 & 0 \\ 0 & 0 & 0.5 \\ 200 & 200 & 400 \end{bmatrix}$$

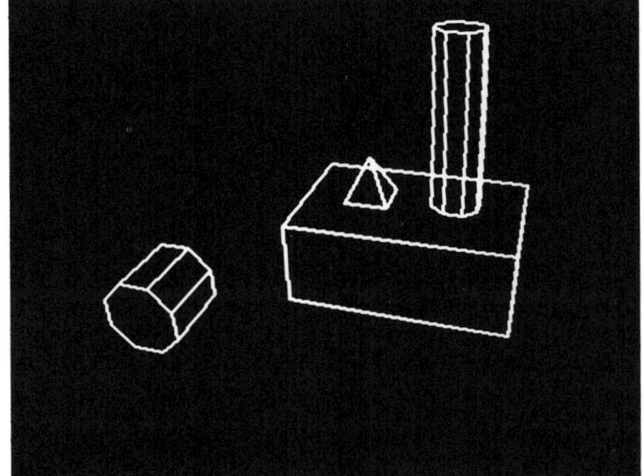

$$\text{octasolid}\begin{bmatrix} 0.5 & 0 & 0 \\ 0 & 0.5 & 0 \\ 0 & 0 & 2 \\ 200 & 600 & 400 \end{bmatrix}$$

$$\begin{bmatrix} 0 & 0 & -1 \\ 0 & 1 & 0 \\ 1 & 0 & 0 \\ 400 & -1000 & 0 \end{bmatrix}$$

a

Figure 8.11
A multi-object scene generated by applying transformations to the cube, prism and octasolid

that contain many instances of the same or different motifs. Starting with a set of standard two-dimensional motifs we can operate on these using translation, scaling and rotation, etc. We can perform the analogous operations in three dimensions. Figure 8.10 shows a set of three primitive objects. These objects can be moved around in three-dimensional space and used to build up multi-object scenes by using three-dimensional transformation matrices. This is analogous to the way two-dimensional designs were built up by moving motifs around in two-dimensional space.

Figure 8.11 shows views of two scenes generated in this way. The program that generated Figure 8.11 is Program 8.4. Both the transformation matrix parameters and the object vertices are given as data sets.

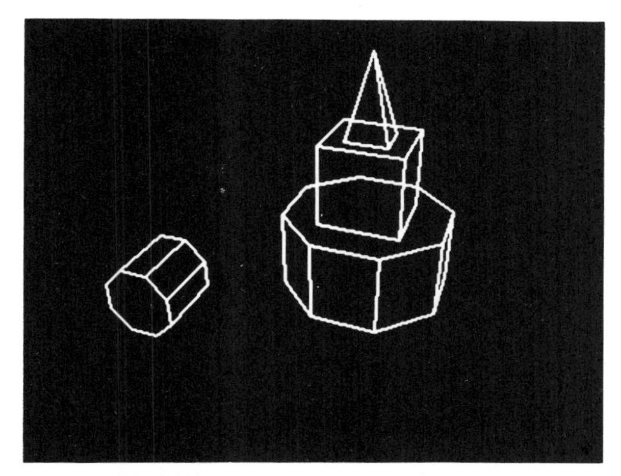

cube
$$\begin{bmatrix} 1 & 0 & 0 \\ 0 & 1 & 0 \\ 0 & 0 & 1 \\ 200 & 200 & 400 \end{bmatrix}$$

prism
$$\begin{bmatrix} 0.5 & 0 & 0 \\ 0 & 0.5 & 0 \\ 0 & 0 & 1 \\ 300 & 300 & 800 \end{bmatrix}$$

octasolid
$$\begin{bmatrix} 2 & 0 & 0 \\ 0 & 2 & 0 \\ 0 & 0 & 1 \\ 0 & 0 & 0 \end{bmatrix}$$

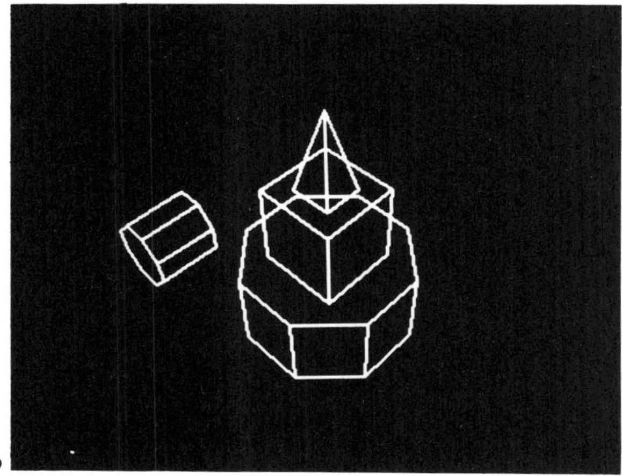

b

$$\begin{bmatrix} 0 & 0 & -1 \\ 0 & 1 & 0 \\ 1 & 0 & 0 \\ 400 & -1000 & 0 \end{bmatrix}$$

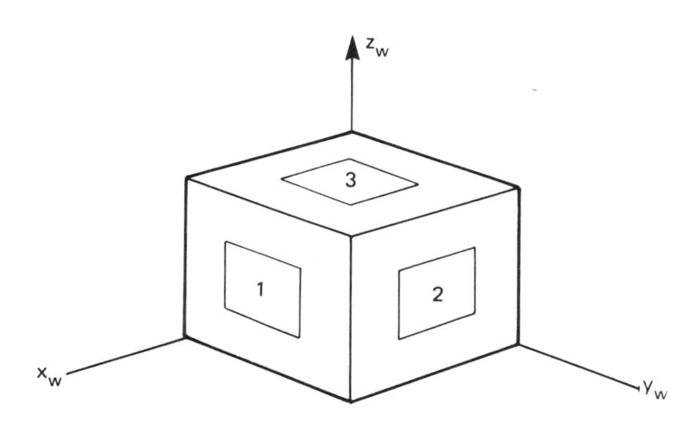

Figure 8.12
Three plane cube to be decorated

8.4 DECORATIVE TECHNIQUES IN THREE DIMENSIONS

A fascinating application of three-dimensional transformation techniques is the decoration of the surfaces of three-dimensional objects with the digitized motifs that we have used in earlier chapters. A two-dimensional motif or decoration is defined in the (x,y) plane. The operation of decorating a three-dimensional object with a two-dimensional motif is exactly equivalent to taking a piece of paper on which the motif is drawn and gluing it on to the surface of the object. If the surface on to which we are gluing the motif is flat then the required transformation is linear. If the surface is curved the required transformation is non-linear. The programming techniques for both the linear and non-linear processes are identical and quite easy. The mathematics of the non-linear transformation is a little more difficult. However, as always this can be ignored and the final results applied as a recipe.

```
  5 SCREEN 2 : CLS : WINDOW (-640,-460)-(639,339)
 10 OX = 640 : OY = 512
 15 PI = 3.141593
 20 DEF FNRAD(DEGREES) = DEGREES*PI/180
 25 RHO = 1100 : THETA = 45 : PHI = 55
 30 GOSUB 2000  'init view transform
 40 SCREENDIST = 900
 50 GOSUB 100  'draw cube
 60 FOR PLANE = 1 TO 3
 70   GOSUB 230  'draw squiral
 80 NEXT PLANE
 90 END

100 'SUBROUTINE draw cube
110   RESTORE 200
120   FOR PLANE = 1 TO 3
130     FOR VERTEX = 1 TO 5
140       READ XW, YW, ZW : GOSUB 2100  'view transform
150       GOSUB 2150  'perspect transform
160       IF VERTEX = 1 THEN PSET (XS,YS) ELSE LINE -(XS,YS)
170     NEXT VERTEX
180   NEXT PLANE
190 RETURN

200 DATA 400,0,0,400,400,0,400,400,400,400,0,400,400,0,0
210 DATA 400,400,400,400,400,0,0,400,0,0,400,400,400,400,400
220 DATA 400,0,400,400,400,400,0,400,400,0,0,400,400,0,400
```

Program 8.5 Placing a motif on the faces of a cube.

Linear decorative techniques in three dimensions

In this section we shall look at the simple problem of decorating a cube. We shall consider the cube to be made up of just three planes, plane1, plane2 and plane3. Note that this constrains the viewpoint to a certain region. As far as the model is concerned only three surfaces exist. If we attempt to view the object from a position that tries to 'see' the non-existent surfaces the results will be confusing. The plane scheme is shown in Figure 8.12. Program 8.5 produced the illustration Figure 8.13a which is the three planes of the cube decorated by a familiar mathematical motif. Figure 8.13b and c were produced using exactly the same technique but decorating with a motif rather than a mathematical pattern. The main program consists of a call to the subroutine 'draw cube' that draws the three surfaces and then a FOR statement that decorates each surface by calling the subroutine 'squiral' three times. The subroutine 'squiral' generates a motif as a function of x and y. The subroutine 'world to

```
230 'SUBROUTINE draw squiral
240   THETA = 0 : S = 1
250   FOR SQUARE = 1 TO 10
260     RESTORE 380
270     A = S*COS(FNRAD(THETA)) : D = S*SIN(FNRAD(THETA))
280     B = -D : E = A : C = 0 : F = 0
290     FOR VERTEX = 1 TO 5
300       READ X,Y
310       GOSUB 390  'transform
320       GOSUB 720  'world to screen
330       IF VERTEX = 1 THEN PSET (XS,YS) ELSE LINE -(XS,YS)
340     NEXT VERTEX
350     S = S*0.85 : THETA = THETA + 10
360   NEXT SQUARE
370 RETURN

380 DATA 200,200,-200,200,-200,-200,200,-200,200,200

390 'SUBROUTINE transform
400   XT = A*X+B*Y+C
410   YT = D*X+E*Y+F
420 RETURN

720 'SUBROUTINE world to screen
730   IF PLANE = 1 THEN ZW = YT : YW = XT : XW = 400 : YW = YW+200 : ZW = ZW+200
740   IF PLANE = 2 THEN ZW = YT : XW = XT : YW = 400 : ZW = ZW+200 : XW = XW+200
750   IF PLANE = 3 THEN XW = XT : YW = YT : ZW = 400 : YW = YW+200 : XW = XW+200
760   GOSUB 2100  'view transform
770   GOSUB 2150  PERSPECT TRANSFORM
780 RETURN
```

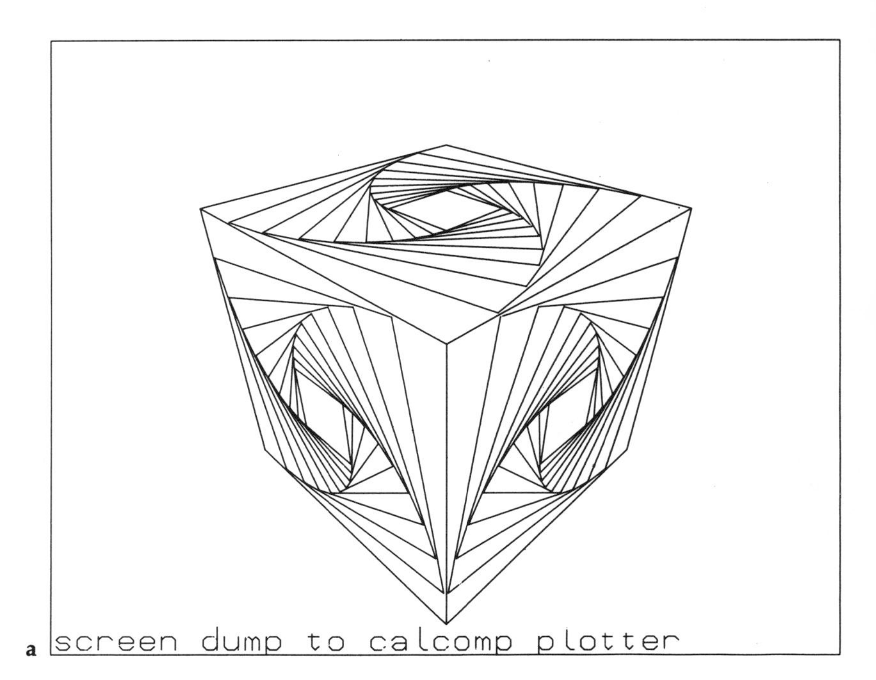

Figure 8.13
Decorating a cube

a

screen' is then called with *x,y* values for each point on the motif together with a plane number. Three IF statements in this subroutine 'glue' the motif to each of the three planes by performing a linear transformation. The transformation for plane1 for example is:

```
Z = Y
Y = X
X = 400
Y = Y + 200
Z = Z + 200
```

Here we have abandoned the more succinct matrix technique in favour of clarity. The first two assignments rotate the motif through 90° or make it stand up vertically (Figure 8.14). The next three assignments move it to the position of plane1 and centre it on plane1. This two step process is shown in Figure 8.14. Try running the program and experimenting with the viewpoint position bearing in mind the viewpoint restriction already mentioned.

Non-linear transformations

In Chapter 3 we dealt with non-linear transformations in two dimensions. Here we will extend this idea into three dimensions and look at transforming motifs so that they appear to lie on sur-

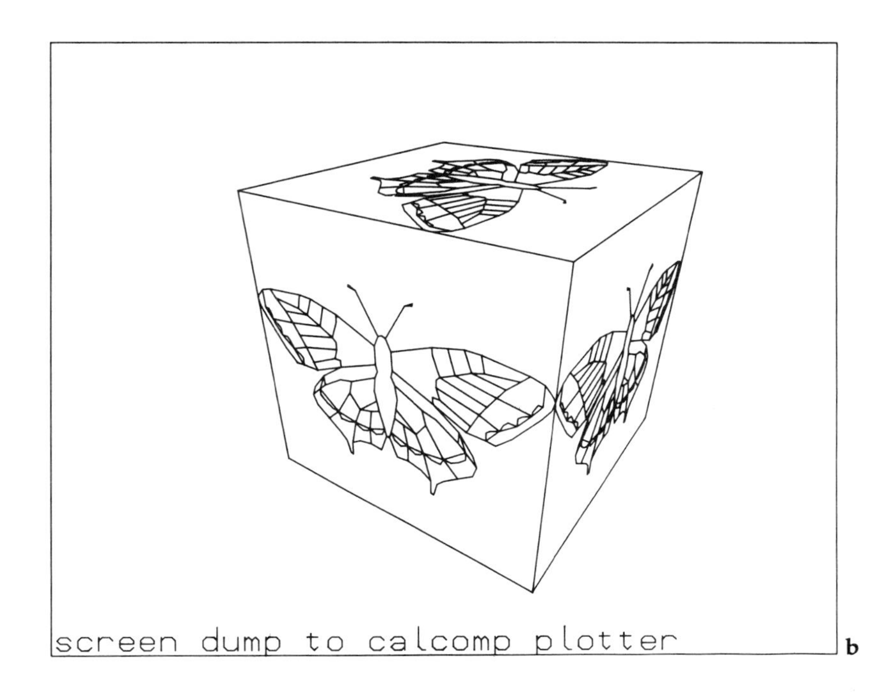
screen dump to calcomp plotter
b

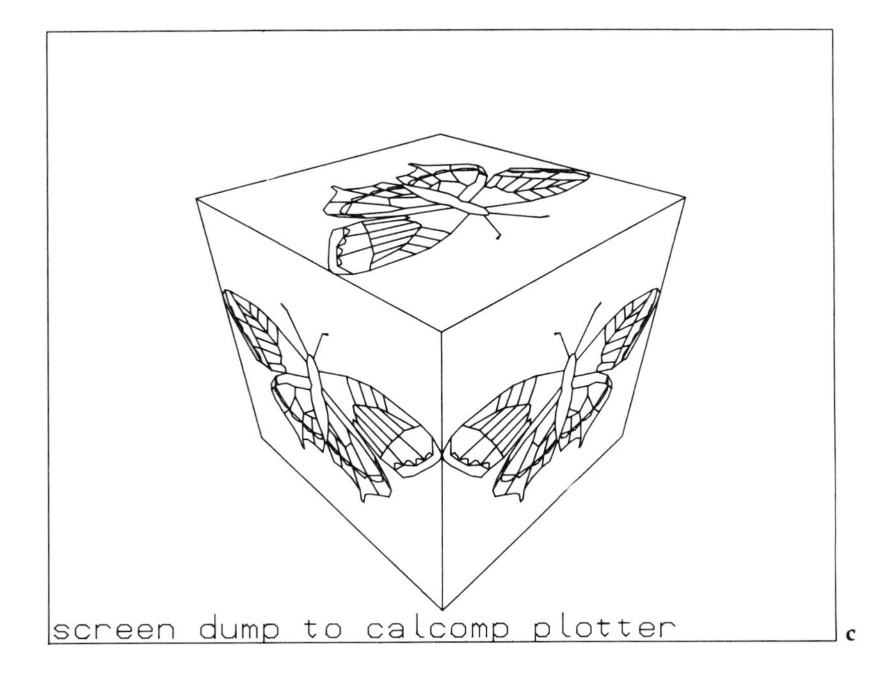
screen dump to calcomp plotter
c

faces. This idea is illustrated in Figure 8.15. Here every point in the flat shaded region in the (*xw*,*yw*) plane is to be transformed so that it lies on the surface of a cylinder. This is like taking a flat piece of paper containing the motif and sticking it around the cylindrical surface. Note that this is a transformation entirely in world coordinate space. After the transformation is complete we can view the object from any viewpoint as before. The transformation can be considered in two stages. First of all we make the motif upright again by rotating it through 90° about the *x*-axis. This is achieved by:

```
ZW = Y
```

Consider now Figure 8.16. Here we are looking down on a segment of the cylinder. The *xw*-axis contains a single line from the picture or

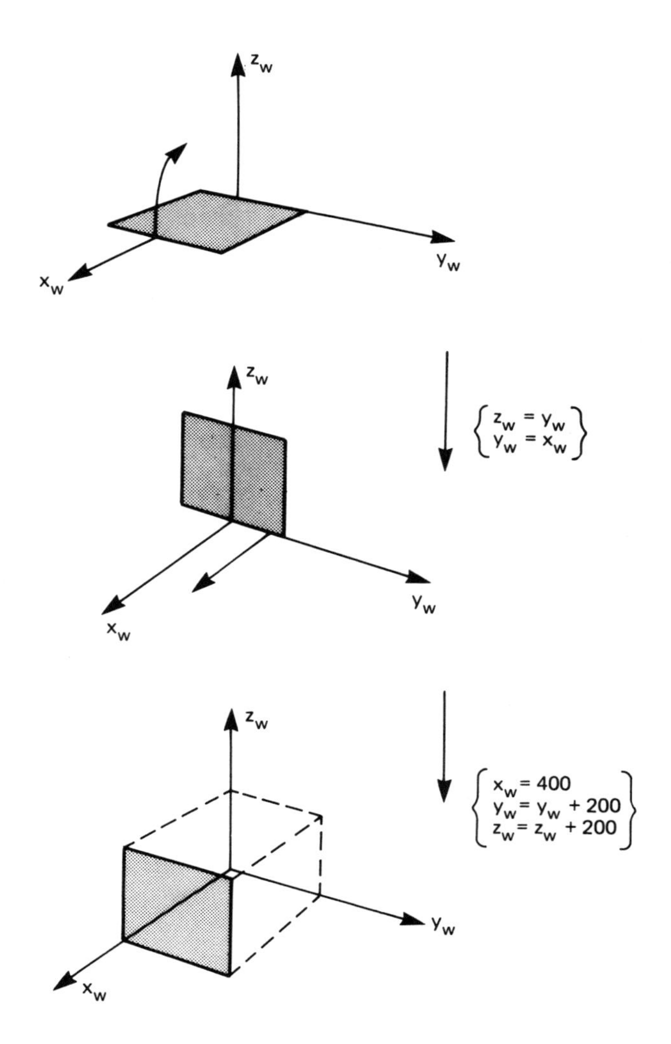

Figure 8.14
Moving the motif plane on to plane 1 of the cube

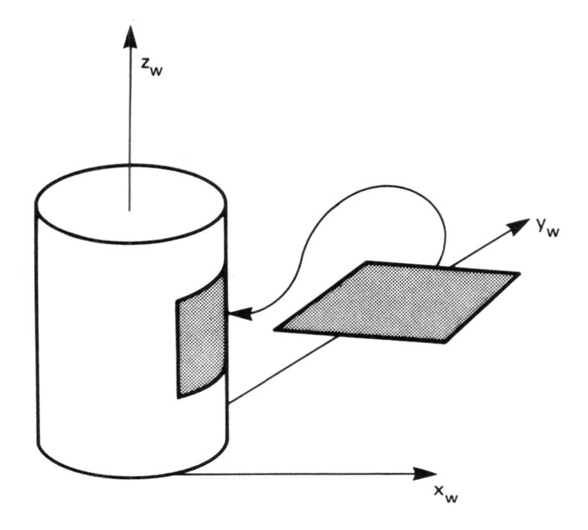

Figure 8.15
A motif defined in the (xw,yw) plane is wrapped around the surface of a cylinder

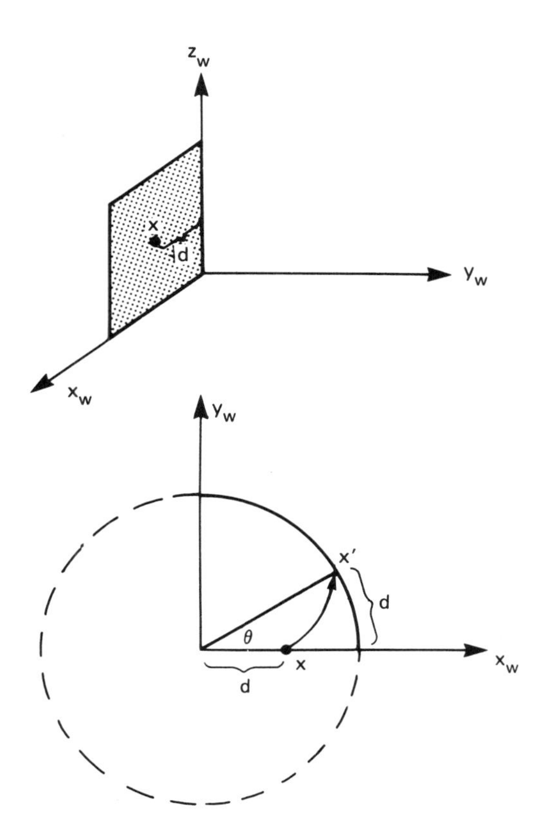

Figure 8.16
x transforms to x': note equal distances d

```
10 SCREEN 2 : CLS : WINDOW (-640,-335)-(639,469)
15 RHO = 2000 : THETA = 0 : PHI = 105
20 PI = 3.141593
25 DEF FNRAD(DEGREES) = DEGREES*PI/180
30 GOSUB 2000  'init view transform
35 R = 600 : SCREENDIST = 1000 : GRIDSIZE = 600
40 GOSUB 90  'draw grid
50 FOR GY = -GRIDSIZE TO GRIDSIZE-200 STEP 200
55 WORDY = GY : WORDX = -GRIDSIZE+150
60   GOSUB 210  'word
70 NEXT GY
80 INPUT ANY$ : END

90 'SUBROUTINE draw grid
100   FOR X = -GRIDSIZE TO GRIDSIZE STEP 100
105     Y = -GRIDSIZE
110     GOSUB 360  'screen
115     PSET (XS,YS)
120     FOR Y = -GRIDSIZE+100 TO GRIDSIZE STEP 100
130       GOSUB 360  'screen
135       LINE -(XS,YS),,,&HAAAA
140     NEXT Y
145   NEXT X
150   FOR Y = -GRIDSIZE TO GRIDSIZE STEP 100
155     X = -GRIDSIZE
160     GOSUB 360  'screen
165     PSET (XS,YS)
170     FOR X = -GRIDSIZE TO GRIDSIZE STEP 100
180       GOSUB 360  'screen
185       LINE -(XS,YS),,,&H8888
190     NEXT X
195   NEXT Y
200 RETURN
```

Program 8.6 Wrapping a motif or caption round a cylinder. (Use the caption DATA from Program 3.4.)

motif. The *zw*-axis is out of the paper. A point x in this line is mapped on to the circumference (a slice through the cylinder surface) in such a way that the distance from the origin to x is the same as the distance round the circumference from $(r,0)$ to the transformed point x'. Given that:

```
THETA = X/R
```

(remember that we are working in radians) the transformed point is given by:

```
XW = R*COS(THETA)
YW = R*SIN(THETA)
```

Thus all we need do is to apply this transformation (Program 8.6)

```
210 'SUBROUTINE word
220   RESTORE
230   READ LETTERS
240   FOR LETT = 1 TO LETTERS
245     X = WORDX : Y = WORDY
250     GOSUB 360  'screen
255     PSET (XS,YS),0
260     READ POINTS
270     FOR P = 1 TO POINTS
280       READ OP,RX,RY
290       X = X+RX : Y = Y+RY : REM coordinates in caption DATA are relative.
300       GOSUB 360  'screen
310       IF OP = 1 THEN LINE -(XS,YS) ELSE PSET (XS,YS),0
320     NEXT P
330     WORDX = WORDX+200
340   NEXT LETT
350 RETURN

360 'SUBROUTINE screen
380   GOSUB 420  'cylinder
390   GOSUB 2100  'view transform
400   GOSUB 2150  'perspect transform
410 RETURN

420 'SUBROUTINE cylinder
430   THETA = X/R
440   ZW = Y
450   XW = R*COS(THETA) : YW = R*SIN(THETA)
460 RETURN
```

prior to our normal viewpoint transformation and this gives us a motif in the shape of a cylinder. Figure 8.17 shows two views of such an object. One object was constructed from the butterfly motif and the other from outline characters. Note that it is the points or vertices of each figure that are transformed and not the lines con-

```
420 'SUBROUTINE sphere
430   THETA = X/R : PHI = Y/R
440   PROJR = R*COS(PHI) : ZW = R*SIN(PHI)
450   XW = R*COS(THETA) : YW = R*SIN(THETA)
460 RETURN
```

Program 8.7 The transformation for placing a motif on the surface of a sphere.

necting them. Although we place the points on the surface of a cylinder the lines between the points do not follow this surface and the transformation will not 'work' for figures with large distances between points.

The next example deals with sticking a motif on a spherical surface. This transformation is a little more difficult to understand. Basically it is the cylinder transform applied twice over. The first transform takes the motif on to the surface of the cylinder containing the sphere. The second application of the transform wraps the vertical lines that lie along the surface of the cylinder on to the surface of the sphere (Figure 8.18). The subroutine that implements this transform is given as Program 8.7 and this generates the output shown in Figure 8.19. This transformation is in fact the reverse of the familiar Mercator projection which is used to transform shapes on the surface of a sphere or globe and display them as two-dimensional maps.

8.5 STEREO EFFECTS

As a final example of the use of three-dimensional transformations, we present Program 8.8 which generates a stereo image of a three-dimensional object. The image produced on the screen consists of two views of the object seen from two slightly different viewpoints. One view is displayed in red and the other in green. The idea is that the red image represents what should be seen by the left eye and the green image what should be seen by the right eye. To see the stereo effect, the screen must be viewed through a pair of stereo red-green filter glasses.

To generate the two images, Program 8.8 applies only one viewpoint transformation and then perturbs the x (eye) coordinates obtained, first in one direction and then in the other, when applying

a

Figure 8.17
Mapping on to a cylindrical surface: (a) captions (two viewpoints); (b) a motif (two viewpoints)

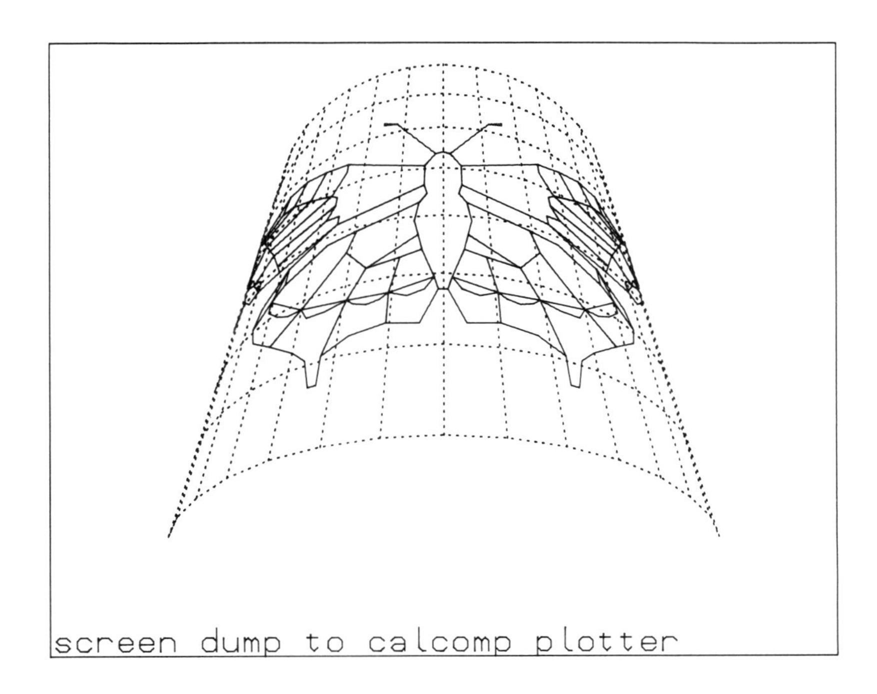
screen dump to calcomp plotter

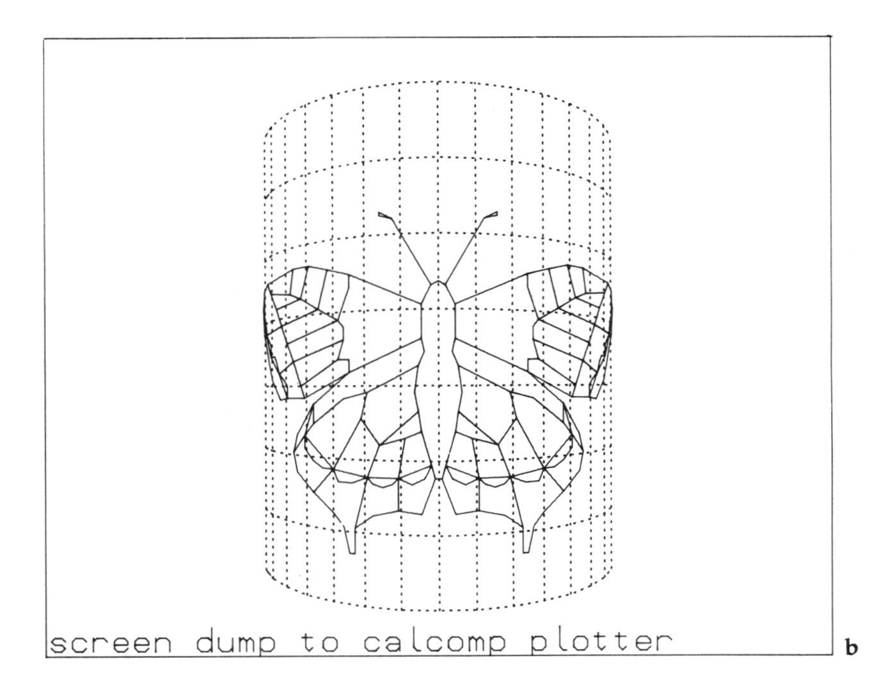
screen dump to calcomp plotter

b

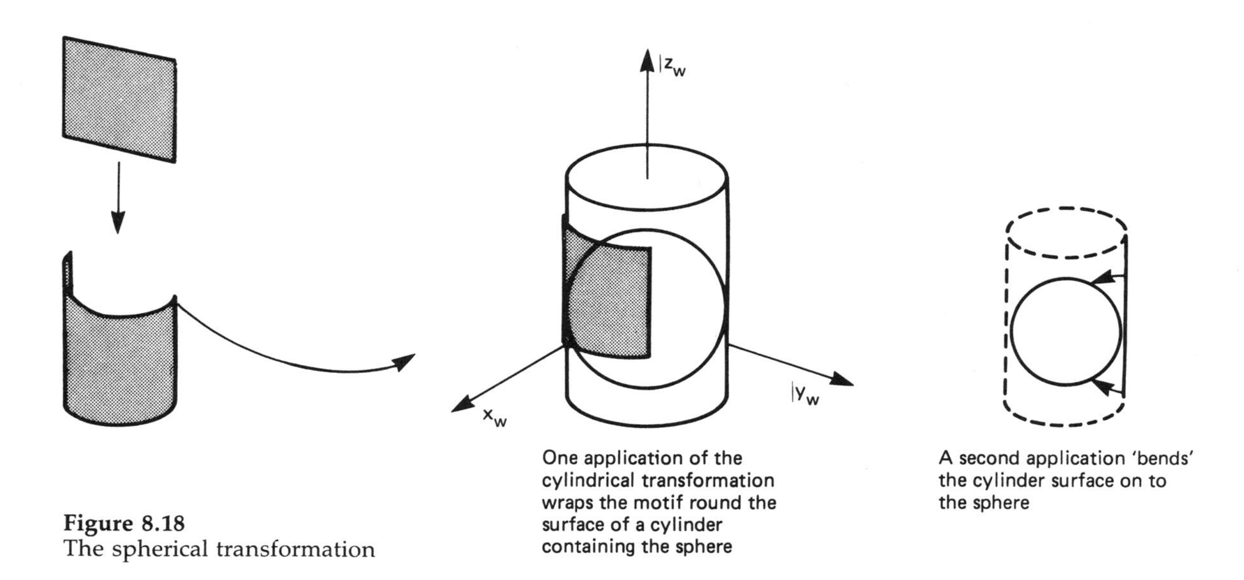

z_w
x_w
y_w
One application of the cylindrical transformation wraps the motif round the surface of a cylinder containing the sphere
A second application 'bends' the cylinder surface on to the sphere

Figure 8.18
The spherical transformation

the perspective transformations. Because the two eyes are close together, this approximation is adequate to mimic the binocular disparity that human beings perceive in a scene. Colour Plate 16 shows the wireframe wineglass after the stereo transformation has been applied. This is organized in the program by using GET on the two separate images and then using PUT with the OR action to combine them on the screen. Points where the two images intersect are then displayed in brown. A practical point demonstrated in this illustration is that where lines from each stereo image intersect a mixture of the two colours must be used. The brown is sufficiently

Figure 8.19
Mapping on to a spherical surface: (a) captions (two viewpoints); (b) a motif (two viewpoints)

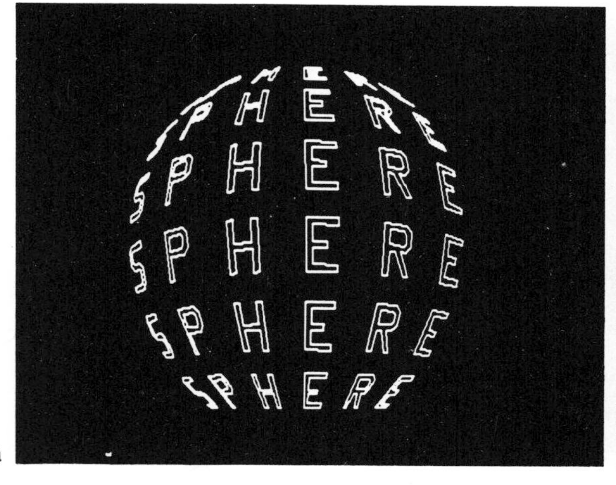

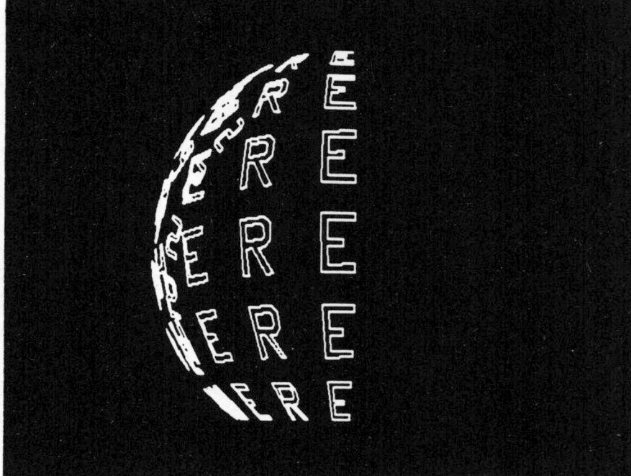

a

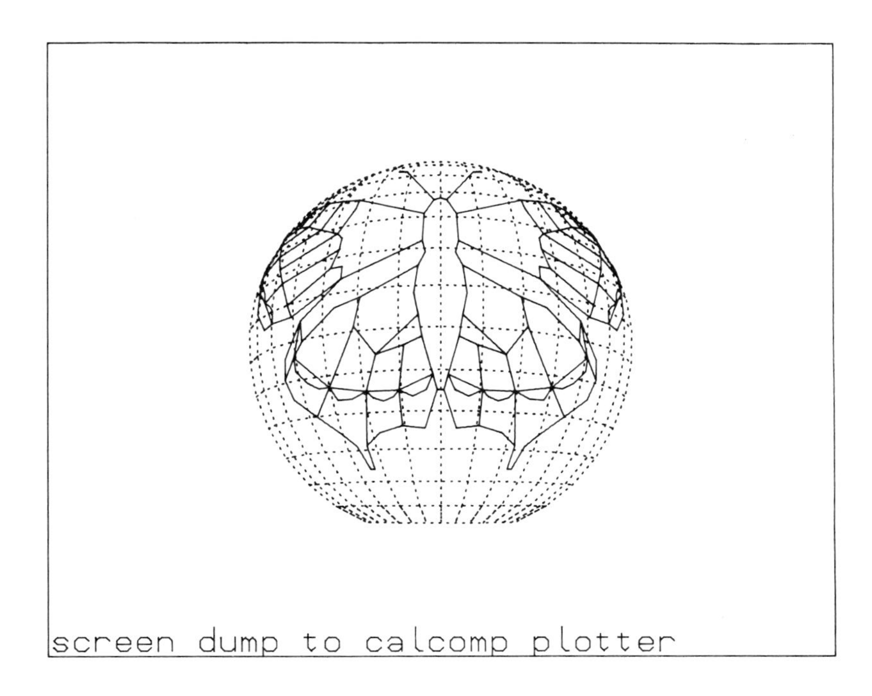
screen dump to calcomp plotter

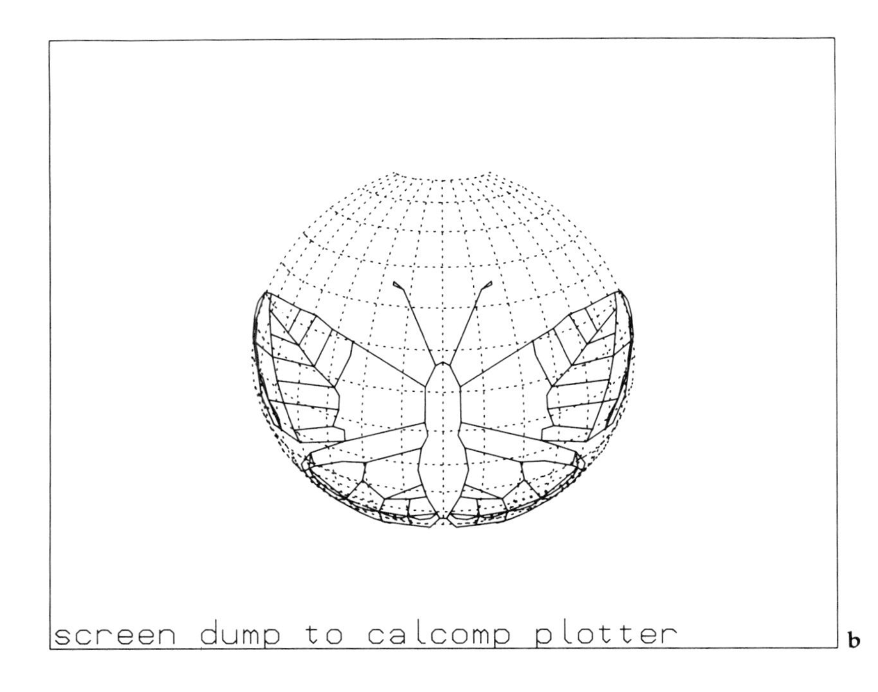
screen dump to calcomp plotter

b

```
  5 PI = 3.141593
 10 DEF FNRAD(DEGREES) = DEGREES*PI/180
 15 DIM SX(2,8),SY(8)
 20 DIM IMAGEA(8002)
 25 RHO = 5000 : THETA = 45 : PHI = 40 : SCREENDIST = 1500
 30 HALFEYE = 175
 35 SCREEN 1 : CLS
 40 COLOR 0,0
 50 GOSUB 2000  'init view transform
 60 FOR FIG = 1 TO 9
 70   ON FIG GOTO 71,72,73,74,75,76,77,78,79
 71   RESTORE 1001 : GOTO 80
 72   RESTORE 1002 : GOTO 80
 73   RESTORE 1003 : GOTO 80
 74   RESTORE 1004 : GOTO 80
 75   RESTORE 1005 : GOTO 80
 76   RESTORE 1006 : GOTO 80
 77   RESTORE 1007 : GOTO 80
 78   RESTORE 1008 : GOTO 80
 79   RESTORE 1009 : GOTO 80
 80   READ A,B,C,D,E,F,G,H,I,J,K,L
 90   RESTORE 220
100   FOR VERTEX = 1 TO 8
105     READ X,Y,Z
110     GOSUB 500  'transform
115     XW = XT : YW = YT : ZW = ZT
120     GOSUB 2100  'view transform
125     GOSUB 2150  'perspect transform
130     SX(1,VERTEX) = XS1 : SX(2,VERTEX) = XS2 : SY(VERTEX) = YS
135   NEXT VERTEX
140 WINDOW (-640,-500)-(639,299)
145 CLS : GOSUB 240  'draw axes
150 EYE = 1 : COL = 2
155 GOSUB 340  'draw cube
160 WINDOW
165 GET(0,0)-(319,199),IMAGEA
170 WINDOW (-640,-500)-(639,299)
175 CLS : GOSUB 240  'draw axes
180 EYE = 2 : COL = 1
185 GOSUB 340  'draw cube
190 WINDOW
195 PUT (0,0),IMAGEA,OR
200 INPUT ANY$
205 NEXT FIG
210 END
```

Program 8.8 Alterations to Program 8.1 to produce red-green stereo pairs.

```
220 DATA 1000,0,0,  1000,1000,0,  0,1000,0,  0,0,0
230 DATA 1000,0,1000,  1000,1000,1000,  0,1000,1000,  0,0,1000

240 'SUBROUTINE draw axes
250   RESTORE 330
260   FOR AXIS = 1 TO 3
270     READ XW,YW,ZW : GOSUB 2100  'view transform
280     GOSUB 2150  'perspect transform
285     AXISX1 = XS1 : AXISX2 = XS2 : AXISY = YS
290     READ XW,YW,ZW : GOSUB 2100  'view transform
300     GOSUB 2150  'perspect transform
305     LINE (AXISX1,AXISY)-(XS1,YS),2
306     LINE (AXISX2,AXISY)-(XS2,YS),1
310   NEXT AXIS
320 RETURN

330 DATA 0,0,0,2000,0,0,0,0,0,0,2000,0,0,0,0,0,0,2000

340 'SUBROUTINE draw cube
350   PSET (SX(EYE,1),SY(1)),COL
360   FOR VERTEX = 2 TO 4
370     LINE -(SX(EYE,VERTEX),SY(VERTEX)),COL
380   NEXT VERTEX
390   LINE -(SX(EYE,1),SY(1)),COL
400   LINE -(SX(EYE,5),SY(5)),COL
410   FOR VERTEX = 6 TO 8
420     LINE -(SX(EYE,VERTEX),SY(VERTEX)),COL
430   NEXT VERTEX
440   LINE -(SX(EYE,5),SY(5)),COL
450   FOR VERTEX = 2 TO 4
460     PSET (SX(EYE,VERTEX+4),SY(VERTEX+4)),COL
470     LINE -(SX(EYE,VERTEX),SY(VERTEX)),COL
480   NEXT VERTEX
490 RETURN
      .
      .
      .
2150 'SUBROUTINE perspect transform
2160   XS1 = SCREENDIST*(XE+HALFEYE)/ZE-HALFEYE
2165   XS2 = SCREENDIST*(XE-HALFEYE)/ZE+HALFEYE
2170   YS = SCREENDIST*YE/ZE
2180 RETURN
```

close to the yellow for it to act as a combination of red and green. If this is not done then intersecting areas are plotted in whatever colour is used second. In the fused image this results in blank areas.

8.6 THE USE OF COLOUR IN TRANSFORMATIONS

Colour can be used effectively in any of the two-dimensional or three-dimensional transformations just described. A motif can be manually coloured in its original form before the transformation takes place. The colouring information is then transformed along with the vertices. This means that a motif need be coloured once only irrespective of how many times it is transformed or the nature of the transformation. All we have to do after a set of vertices has been transformed is to ensure that the transformed areas are coloured in the correct colour. We can do this by storing the start coordinates given to PAINT in the original or untransformed version of the motif. These are stored as a list of coordinate pairs and associated colour code. When the motif is transformed the list of coordinate pairs is subjected to the same transformation and the transformed coordinate list, together with the colour codes, are used in PAINT.

9 *Reality in computer graphics*

Reality in computer graphics is a goal that is very near to fulfilment. The ultimate aim is to present a computer-generated image that looks so real that a viewer is unable to tell whether it is a real image or a generated image. The two major techniques that contribute to this goal are the removal of hidden surfaces and the shading of visible surfaces. Both techniques are computationally expensive.

Shading means considering every pixel in a two-dimensional representation of a surface and allocating a colour and an intensity to it according to a number of factors. These factors change over a surface as the position of the point that the pixel represents in three dimensions changes. The colour of a pixel representing a point on a surface depends both on the nature of the surface and the nature of the illumination that is assumed to be falling on it. The illumination may consist of diffuse light (uniform in all directions) and point source light from one of a number of point sources. Diffuse illumination considered on its own is not enough to make a scene realistic. Complete diffuse lighting rarely occurs naturally and the shade of a point, in diffuse light, does not change when its orientation changes. Point source lighting adds more realism, giving specular reflections or highlights.

The surface properties that determine how a pixel is coloured are reflectance (in effect the colour of the object), transparency (how much light is reflected and how much light passes through the object) and texture (a perfectly smooth object looks different from a coarsely textured object of the same colour).

Two examples of shapes that have been shaded using a shading model based on such factors are shown in Colour Plate 17. Such models are generated on high resolution displays with eight or more bits available for each pixel.

A more recent development that allows transparent and semi-transparent surfaces to be modelled is ray tracing. This accommodates shadows and the distortion of parts of a scene viewed through a transparent object. Currently, this is so computationally expensive that it is used only in research.

With a small micro we are limited by practical considerations to the wireframe models discussed in previous chapters. In high resolution mode, although the spatial resolution is reasonable, each pixel at this resolution can have only one of four values in the screen memory. Four colours are insufficient for realistic surface modelling, which requires at least 256 values per pixel. Although the effective colour range on the IBM PC can be extended by defining patterns to be used by PAINT, it is difficult to relate different patterns to different shades of one colour, and even with this extension we are far short of the colour range required for shading. So in this chapter we will restrict our discussion to the technique that can be implemented – hidden surface removal.

9.1 HIDDEN SURFACE REMOVAL

Although we cannot embark on surface shading we can enhance our wireframe models by removing hidden surfaces (or hidden edges). We are going some way towards realism by making the three-dimensional relationships amongst objects, and the three-dimensional relationships amongst surfaces within an object easier to interpret. The effect of ambiguities, such as the well-known Necker cube illusion, are diminished. There are many algorithms for hidden line removal used in different contexts; there is no standard approach or algorithm, the algorithm used depends on the application. One thing is certain: hidden line removal will add an execution-time penalty to your program.

Another problem that needs to be carefully considered is storage limitation. Effective hidden surface removal algorithms are large programs operating in graphics modes that themselves make large memory demands. This means that there is little space left for data structures and the remaining graphics programs. Memory space management is a separate topic and various techniques can be employed. For example, program compression, splitting the program into a 'common' segment plus a number of segments that chain each other and using separate programs and diskette files are three possibilities.

Before describing hidden surface algorithms we should mention one of the important factors that distinguish the algorithms. Algorithms can operate either in object space, where the calculations are carried out in the world coordinate system, or in display space, where the calculations are carried out in the screen coordinate system. Hybrid algorithms use information from both the object and the image space domain.

The remainder of this chapter is devoted to the discussion of three algorithms. The first cannot be implemented on a small PC, but is very easy to understand. It may eventually be possible to implement this algorithm on future generations of micros as their memory capacity grows.

The second and third algorithms are implemented using a simple scene as an example. These two algorithms are the most common in use and they are easy to understand and implement. Both use direct application of geometric principles.

9.2 DEPTH BUFFER ALGORITHM

One of the most direct approaches to the problem of hidden surface removal is the depth buffer or z-buffer algorithm. In this algorithm we keep a record of the intensity of a pixel together with its depth or value of its ze coordinate (depth information comes from object space and the algorithm, although primarily a display space algorithm, needs some information from the object domain). The need for a two-dimensional buffer to store the 'depth' of each pixel gives the algorithm its name and of course is the major disadvantage of the technique as it requires considerable extra storage. Each pixel now needs memory space, not only for its colour, but for its depth in the scene. To store a depth in the range 0–1023 would require 10 extra bits per pixel. This algorithm trades simplicity and ease of implementation against heavy memory requirement. The algorithm operates on the polygons that delineate the boundary of a surface that has been mapped into the screen coordinate system. It can be stated as:

1. Initially set depth(x,y) to a large value and intensity(x,y) to the background for every screen pixel (x,y).
2. For every polygon in the scene find all the pixels that lie within the polygon

   For each pixel within the polygon:

   (a) Calculate its z value and its screen coordinates (x,y).

   (b) If the z value $<$ depth(x,y) (eye coordinates) then depth(x,y) becomes the z value and intensity(x,y) becomes the intensity of the pixel, otherwise leave depth(x,y) and intensity(x,y) unaltered.

The process is exactly equivalent to searching through all the z values that a point (x,y) can have, assuming that a number of polygons overlap on (x,y) and assigning to the pixel (x,y) the appropriate value from the polygon that has the smallest z value.

Now although this algorithm is easy to understand we cannot implement it on the IBM PC because of memory limitations. It is worth mentioning that if sufficient memory was available, this is an extremely good algorithm. Not only is it easy to implement, but, unlike all other hidden surface algorithms, its execution time does not increase as a function of the complexity of the scene (the number of surfaces it contains). We shall look at another algorithm that can be implemented. Before we do this, however, we will look at back surface elimination or 'culling'. This removes those faces of a single object that cannot be seen because they face away from the viewpoint. The algorithm will do this for each object in the scene. Thus if the scene is a single convex polyhedron, the hidden surface problem is solved by this one operation. It cannot, however, deal with multi-object scenes where one object may partially obscure the other, nor with single non-convex objects. However, removing back faces in every case will cut down on the work to be done by the hidden surface algorithm and we will deal with this first. Back face removal typically removes half of the polygons in a scene. We will develop an algorithm to remove back faces, then a complete hidden surface algorithm to be applied to the scene after it has had its back faces removed.

9.3 BACK SURFACE ELIMINATION

Back surface elimination is not really an algorithm but a straightforward application of vector mathematics. It can be used as the basis of a more general algorithm that will deal with scenes containing many convex polyhedral objects. It is an object space procedure and although we are removing edges in a wireframe model, paradoxically it is the surfaces defined by the edges that we consider.

Given a viewpoint, we determine whether or not a face is visible from that viewpoint. Consider Figure 9.1 showing a cube decomposed into six surfaces. Pointing out of each surface we have a line that is normal or perpendicular to the surface. This line or vector determines the orientation of the plane. As the orientation of a plane changes, so does the orientation of this vector. It is called a surface normal vector. From the viewpoint we can construct 'line of sight' lines or vectors to any point on each surface. If we construct a line of sight vector to meet the surface normal vector, then the angle

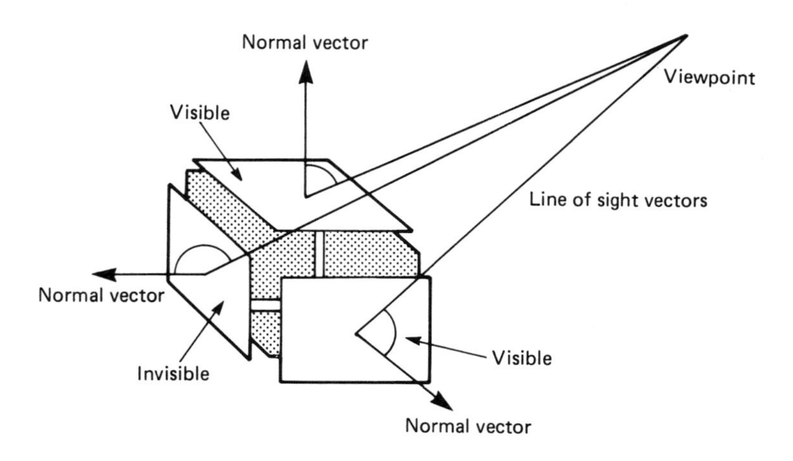

Figure 9.1
Three surfaces of a cube, their normal vectors and line of sight vectors

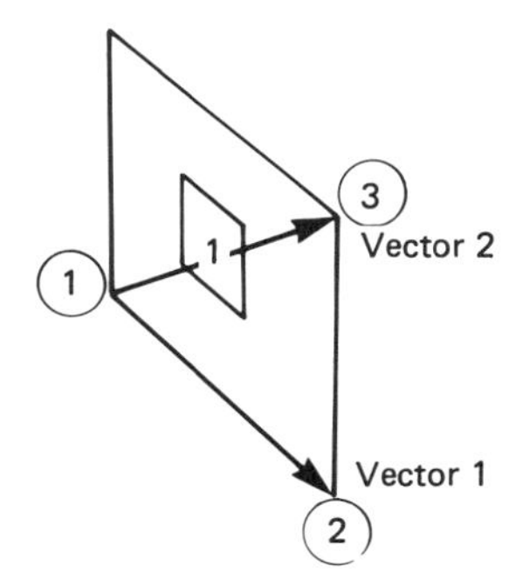

Figure 9.2
Two surface vectors calculated from the first three vertices of a surface

between these two vectors gives us a visibility test. The surface is visible from the viewpoint if, and only if, the angle between these two vectors is less than 90°.

In Program 9.1 we have implemented back surface elimination for the wireframe cube. Subroutine 'hidden face remove' tests each of the six surfaces for visibility. If a surface is visible its edges are plotted. We have used the hierarchical data structure introduced in Chapter 7 and subroutine 'initialise', which sets up a cube in this data structure, is reproduced for convenience.

Subroutine 'hidden face remove' lists the method broken down into further subroutine calls. Although it adds nothing to the method it is always desirable to break up complex algorithms into as many steps as possible.

The first thing that we do is to calculate the components of a pair of vectors lying in the surface. To do this we need to use some vector mathematics. Algebraically this is very simple as can be seen from the subroutines. It is best simply to accept these. Alternatively, you can consult a textbook: they are very common vector operations. These are two vectors emanating from the first vertex. We do this for each surface and calculate the components of vector 1 and vector 2, storing them in arrays 'VECTOR1' and 'VECTOR2'. This is shown in Figure 9.2 and is done by subroutine 'calculate surface vectors'.

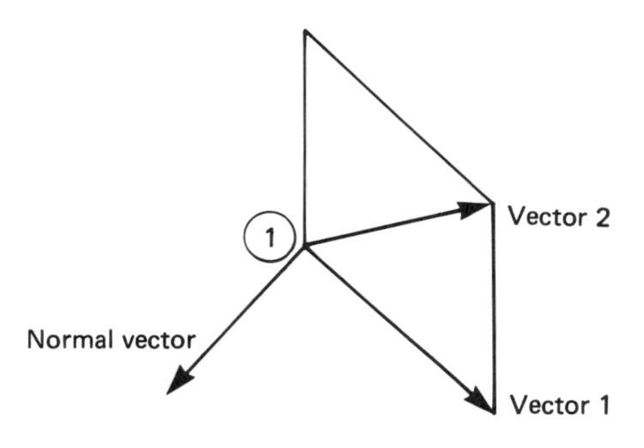

Figure 9.3
The normal vector calculated from the surface vectors by cross-product multiplication of vector 1 and vector 2

```
 10 PI = 3.141593
 20 DEF FNRAD(DEGREES) = DEGREES*PI/180
 30 DIM VERTEX(3,8),SURFACE(6,4)
 40 DIM VECTOR1(3),VECTOR2(3)
 50 DIM VISIBLE(6)
 60 CLS : PRINT : PRINT : INPUT "Viewing distance, rho ";RHO
 70 PRINT "Viewing angles:" : INPUT "theta ";THETA
 80 INPUT "phi ";PHI
 90 INPUT "screen dist ";SCREENDIST
100 GOSUB 790  'init view transform
110 XVIEW = RHO*SINPHI*COSTHETA
120 YVIEW = RHO*SINPHI*SINTHETA
130 ZVIEW = RHO*COSPHI
140 SCREEN 2 : CLS : WINDOW (-640,-400)-(639,399)
150 GOSUB 210  'initialise
160 GOSUB 350  'hidden face remove
170 FOR SURFACENO = 1 TO 6
180   IF VISIBLE(SURFACENO) THEN GOSUB 620  'transform and plot surfaceno
190 NEXT SURFACENO
200 INPUT ANY$ : END

210 'SUBROUTINE initialise
220   FOR INITV = 1 TO 8
230     READ VERTEX(1,INITV),VERTEX(2,INITV),VERTEX(3,INITV)
240   NEXT INITV
250   FOR SURFACENO = 1 TO 6
260     FOR VERTEXNO = 1 TO 4
270       READ SURFACE(SURFACENO, VERTEXNO)
280     NEXT VERTEXNO
290   NEXT SURFACENO
300 RETURN

310 DATA 100,0,0,  100,100,0,  100,100,100,  100,0,100
320 DATA 0,0,0,  0,100,0,  0,100,100,  0,0,100
330 DATA 1,2,3,4,  2,6,7,3,  3,7,8,4
340 DATA 6,5,8,7,  1,5,6,2,  1,4,8,5

350 'SUBROUTINE hidden face remove
360   FOR SURFACENO = 1 TO 6
370     GOSUB 430  'calculate surface vectors
380     GOSUB 490  'calculate normal vector
390     GOSUB 540  'calculate line of sight vector
400     GOSUB 590  'visibility test
410   NEXT SURFACENO
420 RETURN

430 'SUBROUTINE calculate surface vectors
440   FOR I = 1 TO 3
450     VECTOR1(I) = VERTEX(I,SURFACE(SURFACENO,2))
                   -VERTEX(I,SURFACE(SURFACENO,1))
460     VECTOR2(I) = VERTEX(I,SURFACE(SURFACENO,3))
                   -VERTEX(I,SURFACE(SURFACENO,1))
470   NEXT I
480 RETURN

490 'SUBROUTINE calculate normal vector
```

Program 9.1 'Culling' or back surface elimination.

```
500   NORMALX = VECTOR1(2)*VECTOR2(3)-VECTOR2(2)*VECTOR1(3)
510   NORMALY = VECTOR1(3)*VECTOR2(1)-VECTOR2(3)*VECTOR1(1)
520   NORMALZ = VECTOR1(1)*VECTOR2(2)-VECTOR2(1)*VECTOR1(2)
530 RETURN

540 'SUBROUTINE calculate line of sight vector
550   LINEOFSIGHTX = XVIEW-VERTEX(1,SURFACE(SURFACENO,1))
560   LINEOFSIGHTY = YVIEW-VERTEX(2,SURFACE(SURFACENO,1))
570   LINEOFSIGHTZ = ZVIEW-VERTEX(3,SURFACE(SURFACENO,1))
580 RETURN

590 'SUBROUTINE visibility test
600   VISIBLE(SURFACENO) = NORMALX*LINEOFSIGHTX
                         + NORMALY*LINEOFSIGHTY
                         + NORMALZ*LINEOFSIGHTZ > 0
610 RETURN

620 'SUBROUTINE transform and plot surfaceno
630   VERTEXNO = 1
640   GOSUB 720  'screen vertex
650   PSET (XS,YS) : STARTX = XS : STARTY = YS
660   FOR VERTEXNO = 2 TO 4
670     GOSUB 720  'screen vertex
680     LINE -(XS,YS)
690   NEXT VERTEXNO
700   LINE -(STARTX,STARTY)
710 RETURN

720 'SUBROUTINE screen vertex
730   XW = VERTEX(1,SURFACE(SURFACENO,VERTEXNO))
740   YW = VERTEX(2,SURFACE(SURFACENO,VERTEXNO))
750   ZW = VERTEX(3,SURFACE(SURFACENO,VERTEXNO))
760   GOSUB 880  'view transform
770   GOSUB 930  'perspect transform
780 RETURN

790 'SUBROUTINE init view transform
800   SINTHETA = SIN(FNRAD(THETA)) : COSTHETA = COS(FNRAD(THETA))
810   SINPHI = SIN(FNRAD(PHI)) : COSPHI = COS(FNRAD(PHI))
820   VA = -SINTHETA : VB = COSTHETA
830   VE = -COSTHETA*COSPHI : VF = -SINTHETA*COSPHI
840   VG = SINPHI
850   VI = -COSTHETA*SINPHI : VJ = -SINTHETA*SINPHI
860   VK = -COSPHI : VL = RHO
870 RETURN

880 'SUBROUTINE view transform
890   XE = VA*XW+VB*YW
900   YE = VE*XW+VF*YW+VG*ZW
910   ZE = VI*XW+VJ*YW+VK*ZW+VL
920 RETURN

930 'SUBROUTINE perspect transform
940   XS = SCREENDIST*XE/ZE
950   YS = SCREENDIST*YE/ZE
960 RETURN
```

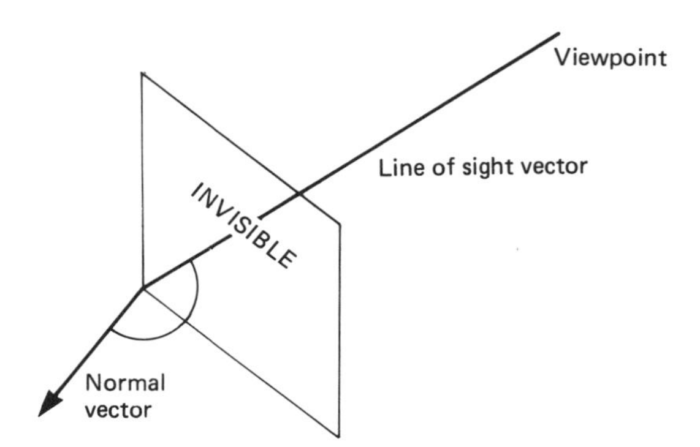

Figure 9.4
Comparing the normal vector with the line of sight vector to determine the visibility of a surface

The 'cross-product' of vector 1 and vector 2 gives a normal vector or a vector perpendicular to the surface and joining the surface at the first vertex. Vector multiplication differs from ordinary multiplication. The product can be another vector whose orientation depends on the type of the multiplication. A cross-product gives a vector normal to those two vectors that make up the product. This has components 'NORMALX', 'NORMALY' and 'NORMALZ'. This is shown in Figure 9.3 and is done by subroutine 'calculate normal vector'.

We can then calculate the components of the vector that joins the viewpoint to the vertex containing the normal vector and apply the visibility test. This vector is called the line of sight vector (Figure 9.4). The subroutine that calculates the vector is subroutine 'calculate line of sight vector'. Subroutine 'visibility test' calculates the 'dot product' of the line of sight and normal vectors. If the magnitude of the dot product is less than zero the the angle between the two vectors is greater than 90°.

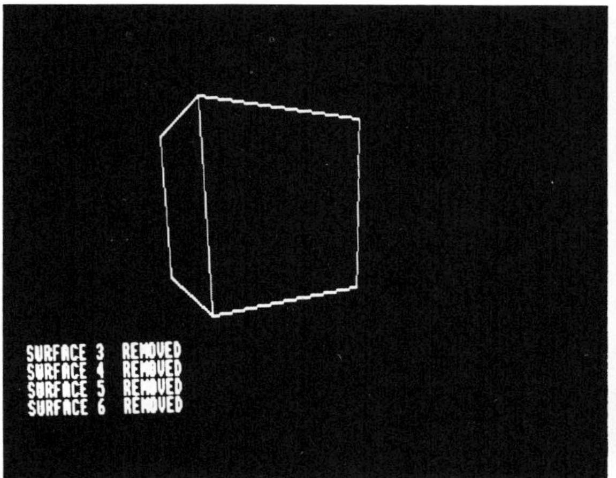

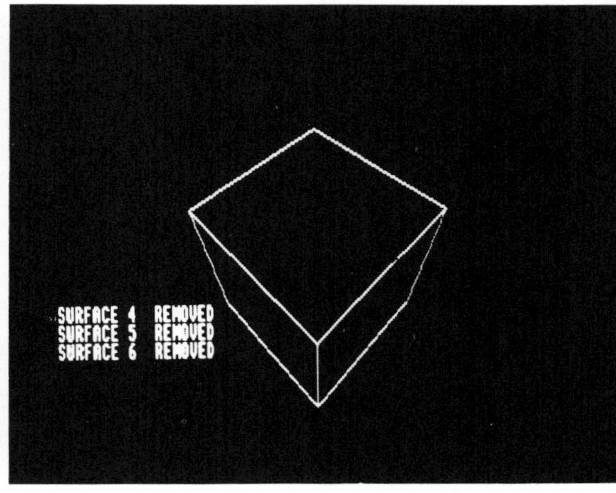

Figure 9.5
Output from the complete back-face elimination program showing a cube from different viewports

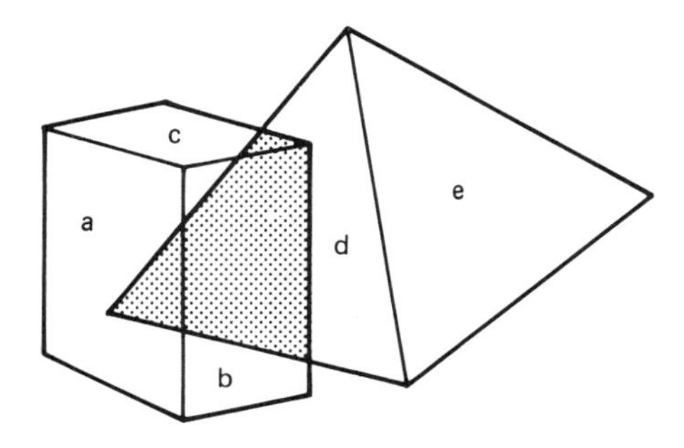

Figure 9.6
Two convex solids after back-face elimination – five polygon scene

Finally, we need a standard transformation and plotting subroutine for a surface (subroutine 'transform and plot').

Figure 9.5 shows views of the cube together with a list of the surfaces removed for two different viewpoints.

9.4 DEPTH SORT ALGORITHM

This is a hidden surface algorithm that can be applied after back surface removal to resolve any remaining problems. It is also known as the Newell, Newell and Sancha algorithm. It is a good algorithm to implement on a micro because it is relatively fast for a small number of surfaces. It does, however, demand a fine understanding of three-dimensional coordinate geometry and it is the longest program in the book. As always, if you are not happy with the mathematics then just use the subroutines and get used to what they do.

Like the depth buffer algorithm this is a priority algorithm. However, we now work on the priority of a complete surface rather than the priority of a single pixel. We store only a priority ordering for the surfaces rather than a depth (equivalent to a priority) for each pixel. Bear in mind that back surface elimination removes complete surfaces. What we now have to do is to remove parts of surfaces where appropriate. In the five polygon scene in Figure 9.6, for example, we need to remove the areas of polygon *d* that are obscured by polygons *a*, *b* and *c*. To do this we have to compare each polygon with every other. This problem, of surfaces nearer the viewpoint overlapping other surfaces, occurs, not only with sets of convex polyhedra, but also within a single polyhedron that is not convex. For example, in the church scene used in Chapter 7 certain viewpoints reveal a 'clash' between surface *A* and surface *B* (Figure 9.7).

Removing 'parts of a surface or polygon' means, in the case of a wireframe model, removing parts of the edge of a polygon, since the colour of all the surfaces is the same: the background colour. Thus what we are doing in this case is really hidden line removal. However, the algorithm will work equally well for shaded or filled surfaces. In fact, if we have only two colours available, we can use the background colour to eventually fill each polygon.

The basis of the algorithm is quite simple and we shall discuss the principles in outline before looking at how the algorithm is implemented in detail. There are three major steps in the algorithm and the second step resolves into four further steps. The major steps are:

1. Tentatively depth sort all polygons in the scene.

   This means allocating a priority to a polygon according to its distance from the viewpoint. Polygons furthest from the viewpoint get a lower priority than those near. Initially, this is done on the basis of the maximum z (eye) coordinate of each polygon.

2. If the depth extent of polygons overlap then resolve these ambiguities.

   This means that if the minimum z distance of a (lower priority) polygon is less than the maximum z distance of a

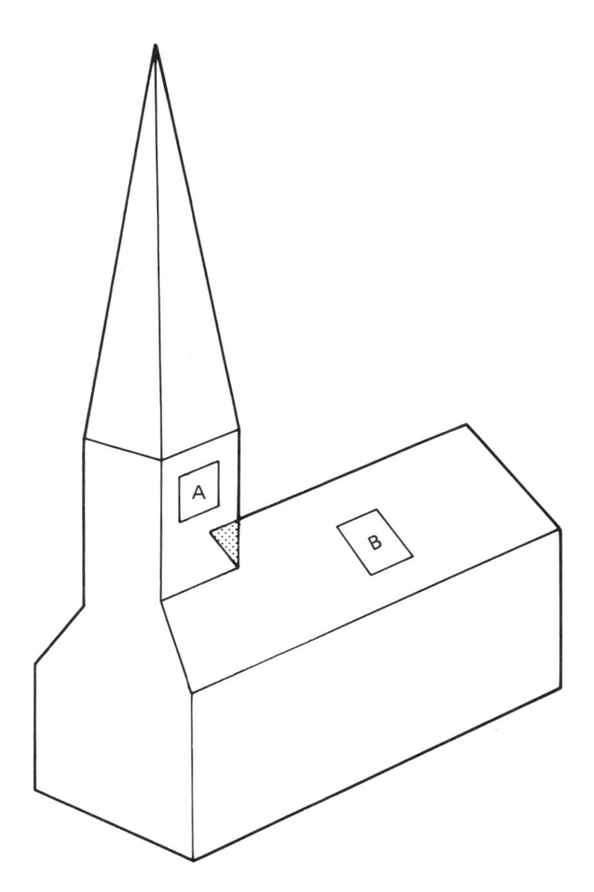

Figure 9.7
View of the church scene that reveals a clash between surfaces A and B

(higher priority) polygon, then these two polygons must be examined in further detail and their priorities swapped if necessary.

3. Colour fill each polygon in the background colour starting with the lowest priority polygon and going through the others in order of ascending priority.

Step 3 is easiest to understand and we will explain it first. Say, for example, in the five polygon scene, steps (1) and (2) produce the priority list e, d, b, c, a. We plot the polygons in that order and colour fill each polygon before drawing its outline. The scene is then built up on the screen as shown in Figure 9.8. Each time a polygon is filled, this erases those lines that are edges of a polygon of lower priority. In the case of a wireframe model, this process (filling all of the polygon with background colour when most of it is already in background colour just to delete part of an edge) may seem rather extravagant, but two points need to be made. First of all, the depth sort algorithm is a hidden surface removal algorithm and will work on models where the surfaces are shaded in a complex way. Secondly, the depth sort algorithm is the most efficient hidden surface algorithm for scenes containing up to many thousands of polygons. It is only for scenes more complex than this that other algorithms are more efficient. If you doubt this and can come up with a more efficient algorithm then you can name it after yourself and a place in history is assured!

To colour fill a polygon we use PAINT. This requires finding an interior point, a non-trivial task because of the ways in which some polygons are split up and because we allow a completely general viewpoint. A separate algorithm for this problem is developed and described at the end of the chapter.

The final step is sometimes called the painter algorithm. It is like the process of oil painting where a background can be painted in first. Figures in the image nearer the foreground can then be painted over the background obscuring it. Those figures can themselves be painted over and the process is continued until the foreground figures are finally painted.

We will now return to the algorithm and look at steps 1 and 2 in more detail. Step 1 is

1. Depth sort all the polygons in the scene.

For each polygon in the scene we find its maximum z coordinate. The polygons are then sorted initially on this basis. We then examine all pairs of polygons looking for a z extent overlap. For the cube-pyramid scene we would perhaps expect an overlap between polygons c and d. This is illustrated in Figure 9.9 which shows the scene in the (x,z) plane (eye coordinates). The second part of the figure shows how the objects would have to be positioned for there to be no z extent overlap. If there is an overlap between two polygons then we cannot say at this stage which polygon obscures which and we must enter step 2 to resolve this ambiguity. Step 2 is:

2. If the z extent of a pair of polygons overlap then resolve this ambiguity.

This is generally done by entering four subsidiary checks. We call

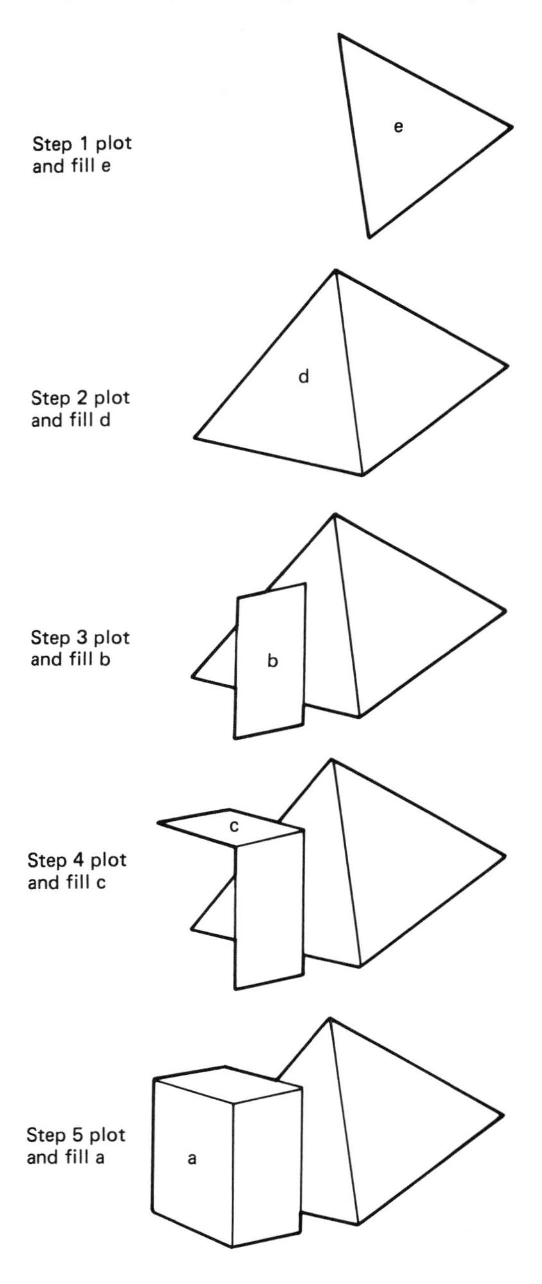

Figure 9.8
The five steps in building up the five polygon scene assuming a priority order a,c,b,d,e

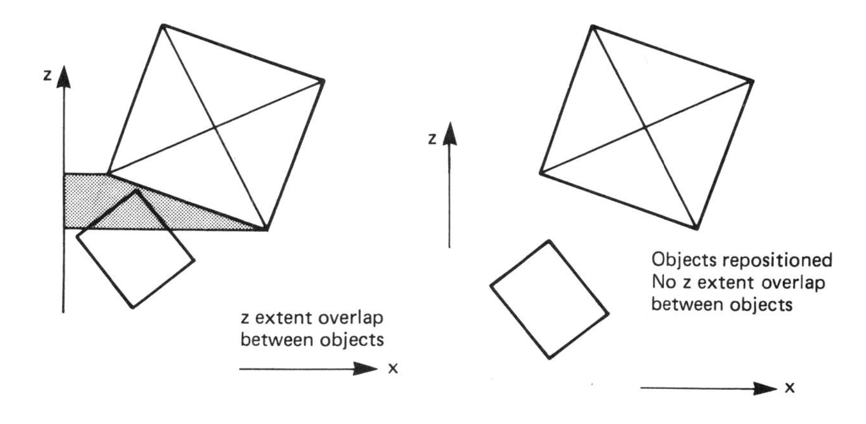

Figure 9.9
Five polygon scene with overlap and without overlap (The shape of the figures' cross-sections depends on the viewport)

the lower priority polygon *P* and the higher priority polygon *Q*. Whenever a check succeeds we assume the polygons *P* and *Q* are in the correct priority order and we can proceed to compare polygon *P* against other polygons in the list. If all four checks fail, then the last two checks are re-applied to see if *Q* has a lower priority than *P*. If the tests fail again, then we have a commonly occurring special case that must be dealt with by another subroutine. If any test on the

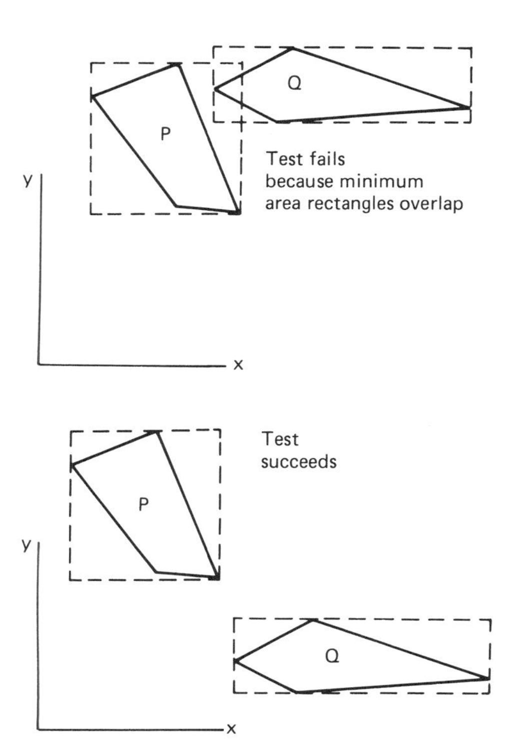

Figure 9.10
Minimax test for polygons – test for an overlap between the x extent and the y extent of the minimum area rectangles that enclose each polygon

re-application succeeds, then we can resolve the ambiguity by swapping the priorities of P and Q.

The checks are

(i) Minimax in x–y (screen coordinates)

This is illustrated in Figure 9.10. We surround each polygon with its minimum area rectangle and check to see if there is any overlap in the x extent or y extent of the rectangle. The name derives from the way in which these distances are checked. For example, we would check the minimum x coordinate of one polygon against the maximum x coordinate of the other. If this test succeeds, then the polygons do not overlap in x,y in screen coordinates. They therefore cannot obscure each other from the viewpoint under consideration. The test applied to polygons a and d in the five polygon scene is shown in Figure 9.11.

(ii) Full overlap test in x–y (screen coordinates)

This test, a more rigorous test than the minimax, is illustrated in Figure 9.12. It resolves polygons that do not overlap but fail the simple minimax test.

(iii) P is wholly on that side of the plane of Q which is further from the viewpoint.

This test is illustrated in Figure 9.13. We carry out this test by

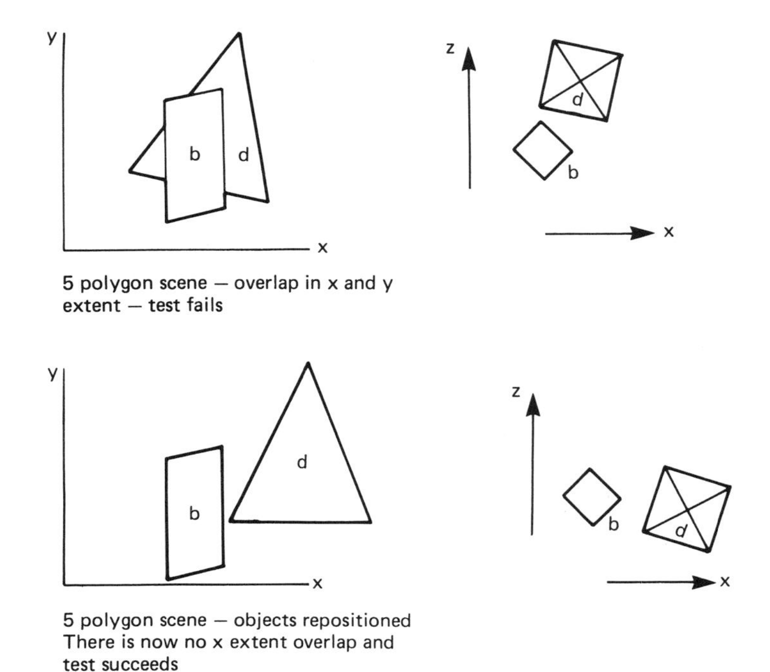

Figure 9.11
Minimax overlap – test applied to polygons b and d

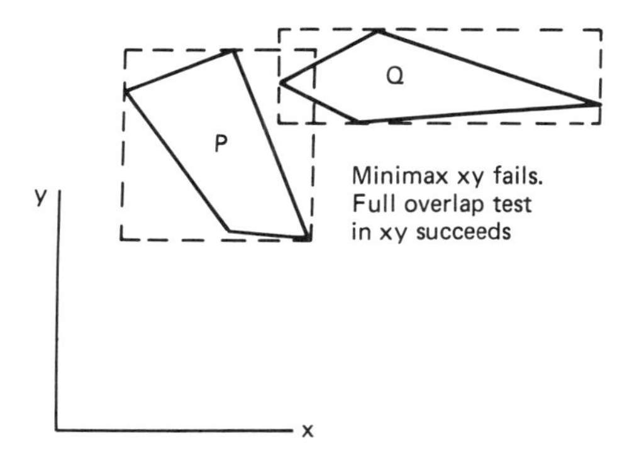
Q
P
Minimax xy fails.
Full overlap test
in xy succeeds
y
x

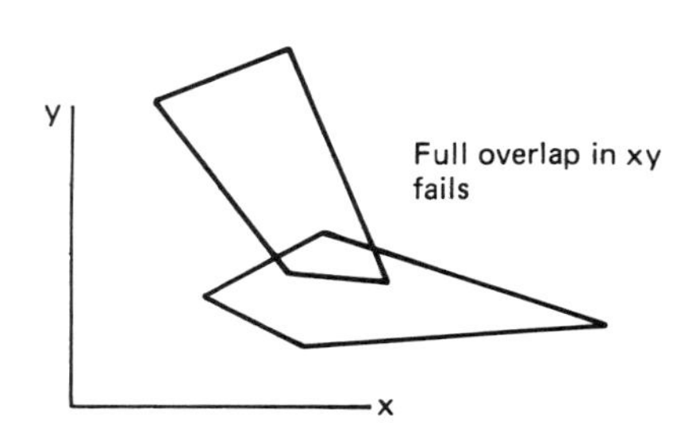
y
Full overlap in xy
fails
x

Figure 9.12
Full overlap test in xy

substituting each vertex in P into the equation for the plane of Q. Whenever a result of the wrong sign is obtained the test fails. For the test to succeed all vertices in P must give a result that has the opposite sign to the result obtained if the origin (the viewpoint) is substituted in the equation for the plane of Q. The mathematics of this is best accepted on a formula basis. Alternatively, any book on three-dimensional coordinate geometry will contain all the necessary material.

(iv) Q is wholly on that side of the plane of P which is nearer the viewpoint.

The reason for having both these tests should become clear if you examine some of the examples. If all four tests fail then we re-apply the last two tests, this time testing Q against P. If the tests now succeed, then P and Q must be swapped in the priority list. If they fail again we have encountered a commonly occurring looping

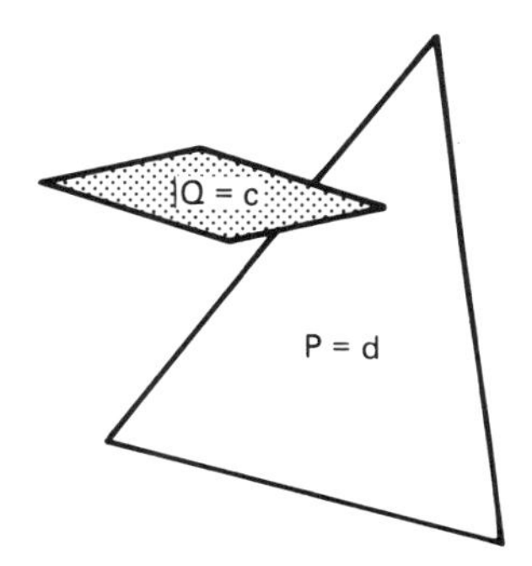
Q = c
P = d
P is not wholly on that side of
the plane of Q which is further from
the viewpoint – test fails
Q is wholly on that side of
the plane of P which is
nearer the viewpoint

Figure 9.13
Applying test (iii) in the five polygon scene

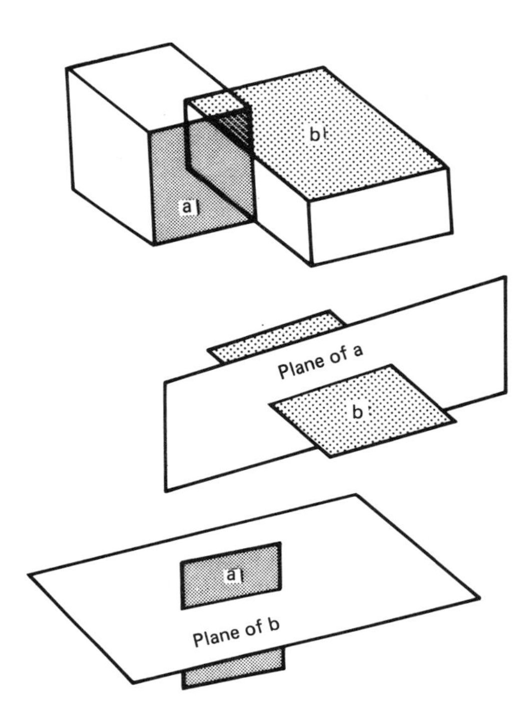

Figure 9.14
The looping situation that the algorithm must cater for

situation. Look at the situation in Figure 9.14. This illustrates the case of two rectangular solids (the easiest to consider). Say we are comparing surfaces *a* and *b*. They will fail tests (iii) and (iv). When they are tested the other way round, they will fail again and the algorithm will loop forever. This is because the plane of *a* cuts polygon *b* and the plane of *b* cuts polygon *a*. So if tests (iii) and (iv) fail again it is because of the mutual plane cutting property of *P* and *Q*. Clearly, the situation depicted in Figure 9.14 is not uncommon and we must deal with it. We do this by choosing one of the pair of conflicting polygons and splitting this polygon into two. Re-application of the algorithm should now succeed. Things are not quite as simple as this, however, and further problems can occur. These are explained later when the main program structure is discussed. In Figure 9.15 surface *b* has been split by the plane of *a* into two

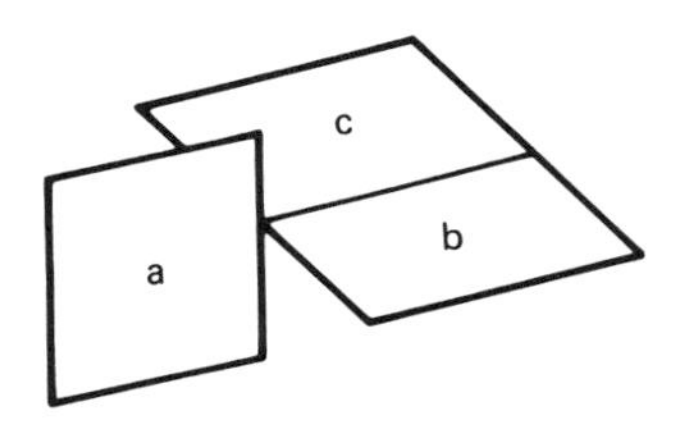

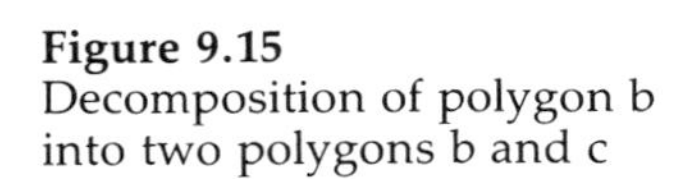

Figure 9.15
Decomposition of polygon b into two polygons b and c

polygons b and c. The algorithm now proceeds and a will end up with a priority intermediate between b and c. Note that if the solids in Figure 9.14 are well separated, then the situation would be resolved by a full x–y overlap test and there would be no need for plane splitting. This situation is shown in Figure 9.16.

Now the cost (in computing time) of applying each of the foregoing tests varies tremendously. The cheapest is the x–y minimax test and the most expensive (and complex) is the full x–y overlap test. For this reason, an efficient implementation of the algorithm would not necessarily apply them in the order discussed. In fact, our version of the algorithm will be structured so as to render the full x–y overlap test unnecessary. Whenever a test succeeds, a 'clash' is resolved. This means that it is better to apply the 'cheaper' tests first.

9.5 PROGRAM IMPLEMENTATION OF THE DEPTH SORT ALGORITHM

We now move on to the implementation of the algorithm. Both back face elimination and the depth sort algorithm are long programs with large associated data structures. For a picture of any complexity they will also take a long time to execute. For the purposes of this text we will split the program into a two-pass system. The image is 'passed' through the first program, back face elimination, generating an image with hidden faces removed which is stored on file. The second program, the depth sort algorithm, is then loaded and the output from the first pass used.

The effects of back face elimination can then be seen almost immediately, without having to wait for the full hidden surface removal part to execute. This part of the algorithm takes many times as long as back face elimination. In practice, the two parts can be joined together.

Data structure and programming scheme

It is convenient to re-use the data structure used in back face elimination. It must also allow new vertices and surfaces to be added when an existing polygon has to be split into two. The previous data structure was convenient and economical. There are many shared vertices in a scene consisting of convex polyhedra. We can simply extend this by setting up a two-level pointer system for representing the priority ordering. This is shown in Figure 9.17.

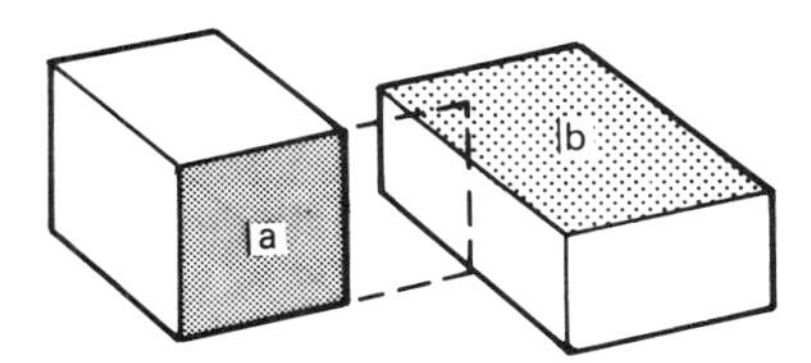

Figure 9.16
As Figure 9.14 but the solids no longer overlapping in the x–y plane. The looping situation is avoided by a full xy overlap test

This structure, with some wastage, will easily allow new surfaces to be added. For example, in the scene of Figure 9.14, surface *b* will eventually be split by surface *a*, generating two new surfaces and deleting one old surface. To keep the data structure and associated programming as simple as possible we will deal with single (non-convex) objects. The algorithm can easily be extended to deal with multi-object scenes involving an object array as suggested in Chapter 7.

Although the algorithm will work more quickly if we first apply back face elimination, then apply the depth sort algorithm to the remaining faces, this will make the program very long. We will therefore use the depth sort algorithm to remove back faces. In practice, it is best to make up a program by merging both algorithms, perhaps by using an intermediate file as suggested above.

Again to keep the program short we will completely omit the full x–y overlap test. Any problems that would be resolved by the full x–y overlap test are resolved by extra plane splitting. We adopt this approach because the full x–y overlap test is extremely complex. It is also very expensive and the algorithm needs careful structuring to make its use cost effective. Again in this check we could adopt a hierarchy of tests invoking a minimax check on individual lines before moving on to a full boundary intersection check. Also, there are numerous special cases where this is not enough.

Depth sort algorithm – main program structure

We start by transforming the vertices into eye coordinates and screen coordinates. This is done exactly as before but the transformed vertices are loaded into array 'EYEVERTEX'. The first three columns in this array contain the x, y and z eye coordinates. The next two columns contain the x and y screen coordinates. Another function that we perform once only is to evaluate the coefficients of the plane equation for each surface. Even when a surface is split, the two parts retain the same plane coefficients.

The various initialisation subroutines together with the overall structure of the algorithm appear as Program 9.2.

The program manipulates a priority list of surfaces in the array 'PRIORITY'. The first entry in this array will eventually be the number of the surface that should be plotted first; the second entry will be the number of the surface that should be plotted second, and so on. Initially, the surfaces are simply listed in numerical order.

The main program loop repeatedly calls subroutine 'select next surface' (always preceded by a preliminary sort of the surfaces on the basis of their maximum z coordinates). At each execution of this loop, the variable 'NEXT' is increased by 1 and subroutine 'select next surface' then ensures that the location 'PRIORITY(NEXT)' contains the number of a surface that is lower in priority than all the surfaces whose numbers are in the following locations. This involves comparing the surface that was initially placed in that

```
  5 PI = 3.141593
  6 DEF FNRAD(DEGREES) = DEGREES*PI/180
  7 FALSE = 0 : TRUE = -1
  8 DEF FNZEXTENTOVERLAP(P,Q) = LARGESTZ(Q) > SMALLESTZ(P)
 10 MAXVERTS = 30 : MAXSURFS = 20 : MAXEDGES = 9
 20 DIM EYEVERTEX(5,MAXVERTS),VERTEX(3,MAXVERTS),SURFACE(MAXSURFS,MAXEDGES)
 30 DIM LARGESTZ(MAXSURFS),SMALLESTZ(MAXSURFS)
 40 DIM NOOFVERTICES(MAXSURFS),PRIORITY(MAXSURFS)
 50 DIM A(MAXSURFS),B(MAXSURFS),C(MAXSURFS),D(MAXSURFS)
 60 DIM PREVIOUSLYMOVED(MAXSURFS)
 70 DIM OLDVERT(MAXEDGES),OLDDUMMY%(MAXEDGES)
 80 DIM SUCCEEDED%(MAXSURFS,MAXSURFS),DUMMYEDGE%(MAXSURFS,MAXEDGES)
 90 ROUNDOFF = 1
100 GOSUB 710  'initialise
110 GOSUB 1050  'init view transform
130 XVIEW = RHO*SINPHI*COSTHETA
140 YVIEW = RHO*SINPHI*SINTHETA
150 ZVIEW = RHO*COSPHI
170 FOR VERTEXNO = 1 TO VERTS
180   GOSUB 1150  'transform vertex
190 NEXT VERTEXNO
200 THENEXT = 0
210 GOSUB 1280  'initialise priors
220 GOSUB 1480  'initialise planecoeffs
230 WHILE THENEXT <> SURFS
240   THENEXT = THENEXT+1
245   START = THENEXT
250   GOSUB 1760  'z sort
260   GOSUB 320  'select next surface
270   PRINT "Surface priority list after pass "; THENEXT
280   PRINT TAB(2); : GOSUB 1700  'print priority list
290 WEND
300 GOSUB 3340  'save
310 END

320 'SUBROUTINE select next surface
330   GOSUB 650  'mark surfaces
340   P = PRIORITY(THENEXT) : QNEXT = THENEXT+1
350   WHILE QNEXT <= SURFS
360     Q = PRIORITY(QNEXT)
370     IF FNZEXTENTOVERLAP(P,Q) THEN GOSUB 400 ELSE QNEXT = QNEXT+1
380   WEND
390 RETURN

400 'SUBROUTINE resolve overlap
410   IF SUCCEEDED%(P,Q) THEN QNEXT = QNEXT+1 : RETURN
420   GOSUB 1930  'xy mimimax
430   IF SUCCEED THEN SUCCEEDED%(P,Q) = TRUE :
         SUCCEEDED%(Q,P) = TRUE : QNEXT = QNEXT+1 : RETURN
440   SURFACEP = P : SURFACEQ = Q : GOSUB 2070  'pq test
450   IF SUCCEED THEN SUCCEEDED%(P,Q) = TRUE : QNEXT = QNEXT+1 : RETURN
```

Program 9.2 Initialisation of data structures and main program structure for the depth sort algorithm.

continued

```
460   GOSUB 2110  'qp test
470   IF SUCCEED THEN SUCCEEDED%(P,Q) = TRUE : QNEXT = QNEXT+1 : RETURN
480   SURFACEP = Q : SURFACEQ = P : GOSUB 2070  'pq test
490   IF SUCCEED THEN IF NOT(PREVIOUSLYMOVED(Q)) THEN GOSUB 570 : RETURN
495 '                                                  priority swap
500   PQTESTRESULT = SUCCEED
510   GOSUB 2110  'qp test
520   IF SUCCEED THEN IF NOT PREVIOUSLYMOVED(Q) THEN GOSUB 570 : RETURN
530   IF SUCCEED AND PQTESTRESULT THEN GOSUB 570 : RETURN
540   IF SUCCEED THEN SURFACE1 = Q : SURFACE2 = P ELSE SURFACE1 = P :
                      SURFACE2 = Q
545   GOSUB 2300  'plane split
550   GOSUB 650  'mark surfaces
560 RETURN

570 'SUBROUTINE priority swap
580   PREVIOUSLYMOVED(P) = TRUE
590   PRIORITY(THENEXT) = Q
600   PRIORITY(QNEXT)= P
610   P = Q : Q = PRIORITY(QNEXT)
620   QNEXT = THENEXT + 1
630   SUCCEEDED%(P,Q) = TRUE
640 RETURN

650 'SUBROUTINE mark surfaces
670   FOR N = THENEXT TO SURFS
680     PREVIOUSLYMOVED(PRIORITY(N)) = FALSE
690   NEXT N
700 RETURN

710 'SUBROUTINE initialise
730   READ VERTS,SURFS
740   RHO = 700 : THETA = 45 : PHI = 60 : SCREENDIST = 700
750   FOR INITV = 1 TO VERTS
760     READ VERTEX(1,INITV),VERTEX(2,INITV),VERTEX(3,INITV)
770   NEXT INITV
780   FOR SURFACENO = 1 TO SURFS
790     READ NOOFVERTICES(SURFACENO)
800     FOR VERTEXNO = 1 TO NOOFVERTICES(SURFACENO)
810       READ SURFACE(SURFACENO,VERTEXNO)
820     NEXT VERTEXNO
830   NEXT SURFACENO
840 RETURN

850 DATA 19,14
860 DATA 180,0,0,   180,0,50,   180,20,75,   180,20,120
870 DATA 180,60,120,   180,60,75,  180,80,50,   180,80,0
880 DATA 0,80,0,   0,0,0,   140,40,100,  140, 60, 75
890 DATA 0,40,100, 0,80,50, 140,20,75,   160,40,250
900 DATA 140,60,120,  140,20,120, 0,0,50
910 DATA 8,6,5,4,3,2,1,8,7
```

Program 9.2 *continued*

```
 920 DATA 4,1,10,9,8
 930 DATA 4,9,14,7,8
 940 DATA 6,12,6,7,14,13,11
 950 DATA 4,12,17,5,6
 960 DATA 4,1,2,19,10
 970 DATA 6,15,11,13,19,2,3
 980 DATA 4,3,4,18,15
 990 DATA 3,5,16,4
1000 DATA 3,17,16,5
1010 DATA 3,18,16,17
1020 DATA 3,4,16,18
1030 DATA 5,10,19,13,14,9
1040 DATA 5,11,15,18,17,12

1050 'SUBROUTINE init view transform
1070   SINTHETA = SIN(FNRAD(THETA)): COSTHETA = COS(FNRAD(THETA))
1080   SINPHI = SIN(FNRAD(PHI)) : COSPHI = COS(FNRAD(PHI))
1090   VA = -SINTHETA : VB = COSTHETA
1100   VE = -COSTHETA*COSPHI : VF = -SINTHETA*COSPHI
1110   VG = SINPHI
1120   VI = -COSTHETA*SINPHI : VJ = -SINTHETA*SINPHI
1130   VK = -COSPHI : VL = RHO
1140 RETURN

1150 'SUBROUTINE transform vertex
1155   VW = VERTEXNO : XW = VERTEX(1,VERTEXNO)
1156   YW = VERTEX(2,VERTEXNO) : ZW = VERTEX(3,VERTEXNO)
1160   GOSUB 1190  'view transform
1165   VPE = VERTEXNO : XE = EYEVERTEX(1,VERTEXNO)
1166   YE = EYEVERTEX(2,VERTEXNO) : ZE = EYEVERTEX(3,VERTEXNO)
1170   GOSUB 1240  'perspect transform
1180 RETURN

1190 'SUBROUTINE view transform
1200   EYEVERTEX(1,VW) = VA*XW+VB*YW
1210   EYEVERTEX(2,VW) = VE*XW+VF*YW+VG*ZW
1220   EYEVERTEX(3,VW) = VI*XW+VJ*YW+VK*ZW+VL
1230 RETURN

1240 'SUBROUTINE perspect transform
1250   EYEVERTEX(4,VPE) = SCREENDIST*XE/ZE
1260   EYEVERTEX(5,VPE) = SCREENDIST*YE/ZE
1270 RETURN

1280 'SUBROUTINE initialise priors
1300   FOR SURFACENO = 1 TO SURFS
1305     SURFACEN = SURFACENO : COORD = 3 : GOSUB 1360  'largest xyz
1310     LARGESTZ(SURFACENO) = MAX
1315     SURFACEN = SURFACENO : COORD = 3 : GOSUB 1420  'smallest xyz
1320     SMALLESTZ(SURFACENO) = MIN
1330     PRIORITY(SURFACENO) = SURFACENO
```

continued

```
1340   NEXT
1350 RETURN

1360 'SUBROUTINE largest xyz
1370   MAX = -10000
1380   FOR I = 1 TO NOOFVERTICES(SURFACEN)
1390     IF EYEVERTEX(COORD,SURFACE(SURFACEN,I)) > MAX THEN
           MAX = EYEVERTEX(COORD,SURFACE(SURFACEN,I))
1400   NEXT I
1410 RETURN

1420 'SUBROUTINE smallest xyz
1430   MIN = 10000
1440   FOR I = 1 TO NOOFVERTICES(SURFACEN)
1450     IF EYEVERTEX(COORD,SURFACE(SURFACEN,I)) < MIN THEN
           MIN = EYEVERTEX(COORD,SURFACE(SURFACEN,I))
1460   NEXT I
1470 RETURN

1480 'SUBROUTINE initialise planecoeffs
1500   FOR S = 1 TO SURFS
1510     GOSUB 1540  'plane coeffs
1520   NEXT S
1530 RETURN

1540 'SUBROUTINE plane coeffs
1560   X1 = EYEVERTEX(1,SURFACE(S,1))
1570   X2 = EYEVERTEX(1,SURFACE(S,2))
1580   X3 = EYEVERTEX(1,SURFACE(S,3))
1590   Y1 = EYEVERTEX(2,SURFACE(S,1))
1600   Y2 = EYEVERTEX(2,SURFACE(S,2))
1610   Y3 = EYEVERTEX(2,SURFACE(S,3))
1620   Z1 = EYEVERTEX(3,SURFACE(S,1))
1630   Z2 = EYEVERTEX(3,SURFACE(S,2))
1640   Z3 = EYEVERTEX(3,SURFACE(S,3))
1650   A(S) = Y1*(Z2-Z3)+Y2*(Z3-Z1)+Y3*(Z1-Z2)
1660   B(S) = -X1*(Z2-Z3)-X2*(Z3-Z1)-X3*(Z1-Z2)
1670   C(S) = X1*(Y2-Y3)+X2*(Y3-Y1)+X3*(Y1-Y2)
1680   D(S) = -X1*(Y2*Z3-Y3*Z2)+X2*(Y1*Z3-Y3*Z1)-X3*(Y1*Z2-Y2*Z1)
1690 RETURN

1700 'SUBROUTINE print prior list
1720   FOR I = 1 TO THENEXT
1730     PRINT; PRIORITY(I);" ";
1740   NEXT : PRINT
1750 RETURN
```

Program 9.2 *continued*

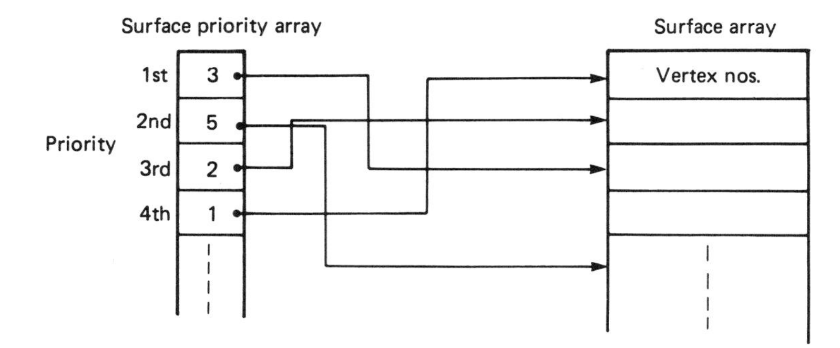

Figure 9.17
Simple data structure used to indicate surface priority

location (by subroutine 'z sort') with all the surfaces in locations 'NEXT+1' onwards. This process is organized by the loop in subroutine 'select next surface'. This loop repeatedly compares the surface in 'PRIORITY(NEXT)', surface *P* say, with the surface in 'PRIORITY(QNEXT)', surface *Q*, say. If all goes well, then 'QNEXT' will increase steadily until all comparisons with surface *P* have been made and we have confirmed that *P* is indeed the next surface in the priority ordering.

Success in any one of three tests will confirm that *P* has lower priority than *Q*. These tests are implemented by subroutine 'xy minimax', subroutine 'pq test' and subroutine 'qp test'. As soon as one of these tests is successful, 'QNEXT' is increased ready for testing *P* against the next surface. In addition, a successful test result is recorded in the array 'SUCCEEDED%'. This is used to prevent the same tests from being repeated later after any reordering.

If all three tests fail, then there are two possibilities: either the surfaces are in the wrong order and must be interchanged in the priority list, or one of the surfaces must be split in two by the plane defined by the other surface. To decide which action is appropriate, subroutine 'pq test' and subroutine 'qp test' are applied to the two planes in reverse order. If both of these retests fail, then the two surfaces, *P* and *Q*, have the mutual cutting property described earlier, and one of them must be split in two by a call of subroutine 'plane split'.

If one of the two retests succeeds, then an 'obvious' course of action would be to exchange *P* and *Q* in the priority list and check the surface now in the 'NEXT' position against all the surfaces that now come after it in the list. This would involve resetting 'QNEXT' to 'NEXT+1'. However, this could result in a continuous loop with several surfaces cycling in the 'NEXT' position. Such a situation is illustrated in Figure 9.18. For this reason, we keep a record (in array 'PREVIOUSLYMOVED') of any surface that is swapped out of the 'NEXT' position. If there is an attempt later to move this surface back into the 'NEXT' position, then we must consider whether this is appropriate.

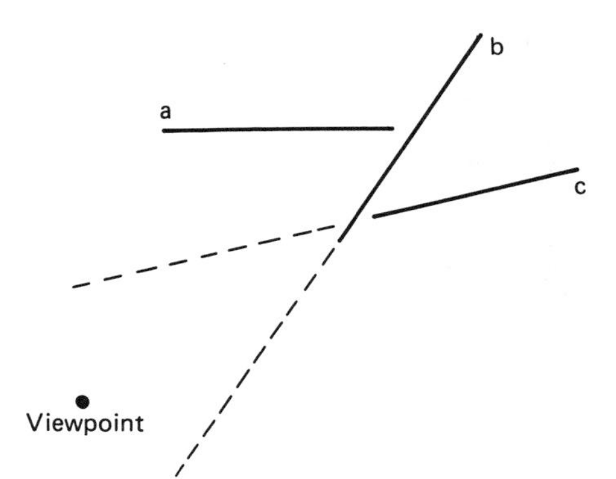

Figure 9.18
Mutually intercepting planes in the church scene

Such cycling situations could be resolved by using a full x–y overlap test, but we prefer to resolve them by further plane splitting. This is what is done, unless the two surfaces do not cut one another. (This is the case if both the *pq* test and the *qp* test succeed.) In this situation, swapping is allowed with a view to applying plane splitting at another point in the cycle.

Figure 9.19 shows stages in priority plotting for the church scene, which, as we have already discussed, is a non-convex solid. For this particular viewpoint two extra surfaces are generated making a total of 16. The unusual viewpoint ($\phi = -140$, $\theta = 10$) is a 'worm's eye' view and was chosen because it graphically illustrates the way in which the lower priority surfaces are eliminated, leading to a final object that paints out the first 13 surfaces plotted. In (a) to (d), parts of the steeple are visible and we are looking up into it. In (e) and (f) all of the steeple and the roof are obscured by the final three surfaces.

Figure 9.19 (opposite)
Various stages in the depth sort algorithm: 'the worm's eye' viewpoint is $\phi = -140°$, $\theta = 10°$

Finally, we will explain the detailed operation of each of the important subsidiary subroutines used in our implementation of the algorithm.

```
1760 'SUBROUTINE z sort
1780   LAST = SURFS
1790   WHILE LAST > START
1800     LASTMOVED = 0
1810     FOR J = START + 1 TO LAST
1820       IF LARGESTZ(PRIORITY(J)) > LARGESTZ(PRIORITY(J-1)) THEN
              TEMP = PRIORITY(J) : PRIORITY(J) = PRIORITY(J-1) :
              PRIORITY(J-1) = TEMP : LASTMOVED = J-1
1830     NEXT J
1840     LAST = LASTMOVED
1850   WEND
1860 RETURN
```

Program 9.3 Subroutine to sort surfaces on largest z-coordinates.

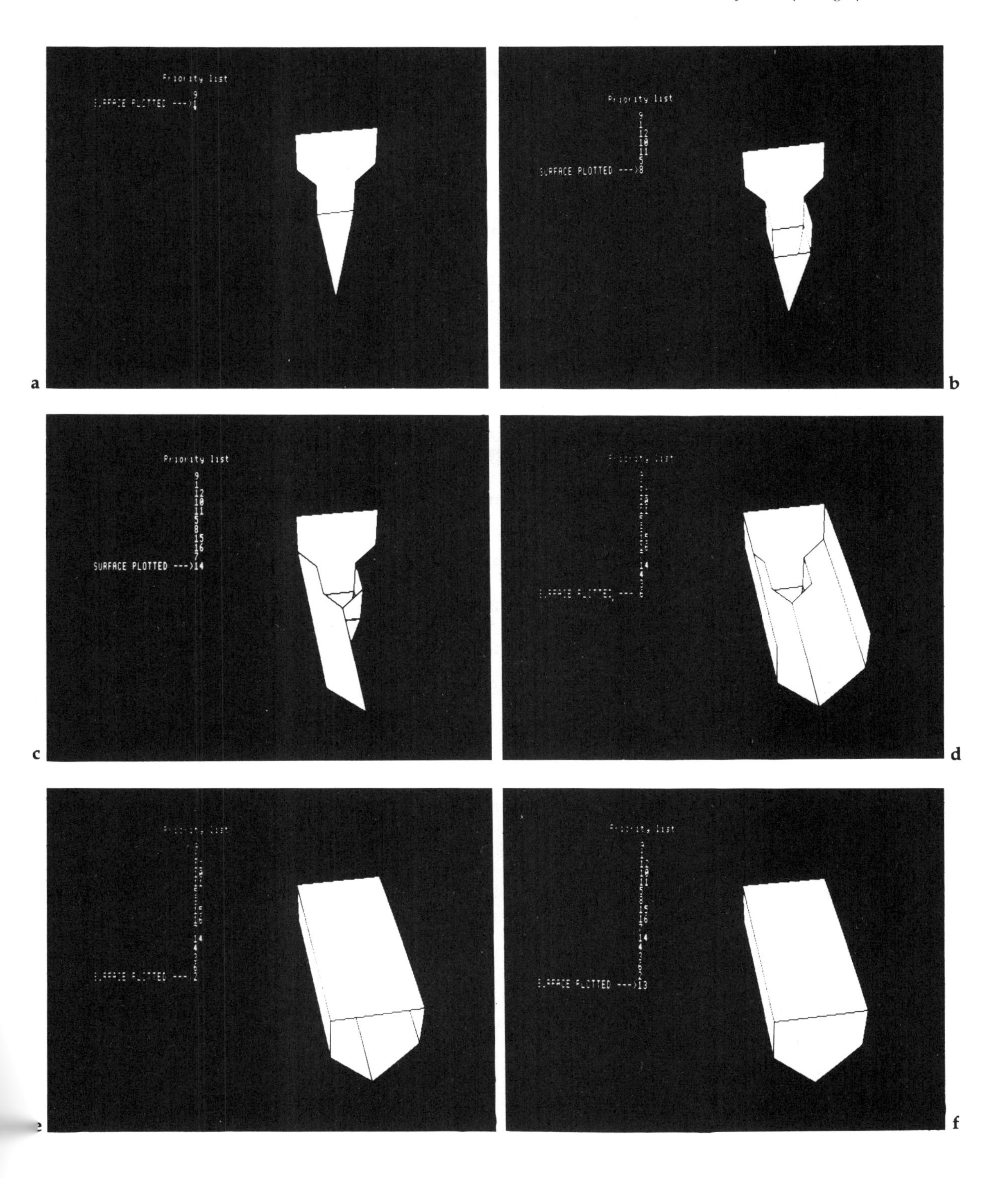
a
Priority list
9
SURFACE PLOTTED --->1
b
Priority list
9
1
12
10
11
5
SURFACE PLOTTED --->8
c
Priority list
9
1
12
10
11
5
8
15
16
7
SURFACE PLOTTED --->14
d
14
4
e
14
4
f
Priority list
14
4
SURFACE PLOTTED --->13

Depth sort algorithm – initial depth sort

To sort the surfaces into order we proceed as follows. For every surface we find the largest z coordinate (eye system) and sort the surface numbers in the array 'PRIORITY' on the basis of these values (Figure 9.17). This is a simple ordering exercise carried out in subroutine 'z sort' (Program 9.3). In this subroutine we use a bubble sort.

Depth sort algorithm – *z*-extent overlap

During the course of the algorithm, the check for possible z extent overlap is carried out by 'FNZEXTENTOVERLAP' (defined at the start of Program 9.2). Largest z values for each surface are held in array 'LARGESTZ' and smallest z values in array 'SMALLESTZ'. Note that in a convex polyhedron with a small number of faces there will be a large percentage of adjacent faces where the z extent overlap condition applies.

Depth sort algorithm – *xy*-minimax

This is implemented as subroutine 'xy minimax' (Program 9.4). Note that this test must be applied to the screen coordinates that were obtained from the eye coordinates using subroutine 'perspect

```
1930 'SUBROUTINE xy minimax
1945   SURFACEN = P : COORD = 4 : GOSUB 1420  'smallest xyz
1950   SMALLESTXP = MIN
1955   SURFACEN = P : COORD = 5 : GOSUB 1420  'smallest xyz
1960   SMALLESTYP = MIN
1965   SURFACEN = P : COORD = 4 : GOSUB 1360  'largest xyz
1970   LARGESTXP = MAX
1975   SURFACEN = P : COORD = 5 : GOSUB 1360  'largest xyz
1980   LARGESTYP = MAX
1985   SURFACEN = Q : COORD = 4 : GOSUB 1420  'smallest xyz
1990   SMALLESTXQ = MIN
1995   SURFACEN = Q : COORD = 5 : GOSUB 1420  'smallest xyz
2000   SMALLESTYQ = MIN
2005   SURFACEN = Q : COORD = 4 : GOSUB 1360  'largest xyz
2010   LARGESTXQ = MAX
2015   SURFACEN = Q : COORD = 5 : GOSUB 1360  'largest xyz
2020   LARGESTYQ = MAX
2030   IF LARGESTXP > LARGESTXQ THEN
         DIFFX = SMALLESTXP-LARGESTXQ
         ELSE DIFFX = SMALLESTXQ-LARGESTXP
2040   IF LARGESTYP > LARGESTYQ THEN
         DIFFY = SMALLESTYP-LARGESTYQ
         ELSE DIFFY = SMALLESTYQ-LARGESTYP
2050   SUCCEED = DIFFX >= 0 OR DIFFY >= 0
2060 RETURN
```

Program 9.4 Subroutine to carry out the x–y minimax test on surfaces.

transform'. Initially this finds, for each surface, the smallest *x*, smallest *y*, largest *x* and largest *y* values for the two surfaces being compared. These searches are carried out by subroutines 'smallest xyz' and 'largest xyz' respectively. (These were defined in Program 9.2.) Once these values have been found, a pair of IF statements is all that is required to implement the test.

Depth sort algorithm – pq **and** qp **tests**

These tests are 'symmetrical' and we can use the same subroutine for each, providing the order of the pair of surfaces is swapped, and, the sign of the fail condition is changed. This initial manipulation is carried out in subroutine 'pq test' and subroutine 'qp test' (Program 9.5), both of which call subroutine 'plane test'. This subroutine evaluates the coefficients of the plane of the second surface. It then checks the position of every vertex in the first surface to see which side of the plane the vertex is on. The equation of the plane of the second surface is obtained from the arrays *a*, *b*, *c* and *d* that were initialised at the start of the program. Substituting each vertex from the other surface into this equation determines on which side of the plane the vertex lies. The loop should terminate immediately a test fails. If all the vertices in a surface pass the test it succeeds.

```
2070 'SUBROUTINE pq test
2080   FAIL = +1
2090   SURFACE1 = SURFACEP : SURFACE2 = SURFACEQ : GOSUB 2150  'plane test
2100 RETURN

2110 'SUBROUTINE qp test
2120   FAIL = -1
2130   SURFACE1 = SURFACEQ : SURFACE2 = SURFACEP : GOSUB 2150  'plane test
2140 RETURN

2150 'SUBROUTINE plane test
2170   A = A(SURFACE2) : B = B(SURFACE2)
2180   C = C(SURFACE2) : D = D(SURFACE2)
2190   FAIL = FAIL*D
2200   I = 0
2220      I = I+1
2230      X = EYEVERTEX(1,SURFACE(SURFACE1,I))
2240      Y = EYEVERTEX(2,SURFACE(SURFACE1,I))
2250      Z = EYEVERTEX(3,SURFACE(SURFACE1,I))
2260      RESULT = A*X+B*Y+C*Z+D
2270      IF ABS(RESULT) < ROUNDOFF THEN SUCCEED = TRUE
             ELSE SUCCEED = (SGN(RESULT) <> SGN(FAIL))
2280   IF  I <> NOOFVERTICES(SURFACE1) AND SUCCEED THEN 2220
2290 RETURN
```

Program 9.5 Subroutines to carry out *pq* and *qp* tests for surface priority.

Note the way in which the test at the end of subroutine 'plane test' has been structured to avoid problems because of round-off errors. If a point is close to the surface (on either side) it passes, regardless of sign. For shared vertices, of which there are many in typical scenes, 'result' should evaluate to zero. However, due to round-off errors it may go slightly negative when it is supposed to be consistent with a set of positive numbers, or, vice versa. The only safe course of action is to accept any result near zero (to within a round-off error) as passing the test and this is exactly what we do.

Now the second application of the *pq* and *qp* tests can be accomplished by using the same subroutine, subroutine 'plane test', but this time swapping the parameters in the main program.

The complete program is tested on the church scene used in Chapter 8. As well as being a non-convex object, it also exhibits,

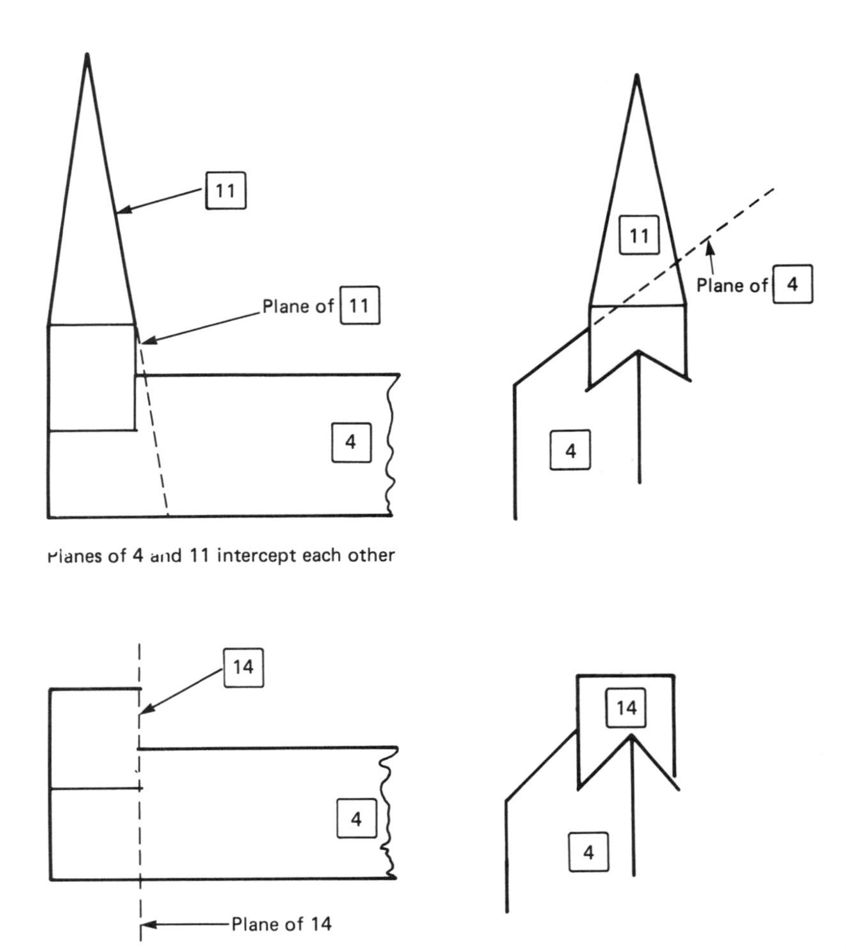

Figure 9.20
Mutually intercepting planes in the church scene

from certain viewpoints, mutually intercepting planes. Some of these possibilities are shown in Figure 9.20 and are resolved, as we have already discussed, by plane splitting.

Depth sort algorithm – plane splitting

If a plane has to be split into two we add one new surface into the data structure. The other new surface replaces the original surface in its original position in the data structure. We also have to find new vertices for each new surface in general, although very often a plane will split through existing vertices.

Subroutine 'plane split' calls a number of subsidiary subroutines whose function should be obvious from the subroutine names. These are listed together with subroutine 'plane split'. The sense of subroutine 'plane split' should be studied in conjunction with Figure 9.21, which shows the scheme used and the associated variables. Surface 1 is the surface that is being split by surface 2. We travel through the vertex list of surface 1 and compare each vertex with the plane coefficients of surface 2. (subroutine 'compare plane and verts'). When a change of sign is encountered we know that we have crossed over from one side of surface 2 to the other. This technique defines the pairs of vertices nearest to the intersection points – nearest 1, nearest 2, nearest 3 and nearest 4. The actual points of intersection (newx 1, newy 1, newz 1 and newx 2, newy 2, newz 2), which form the new vertices, are found by defining

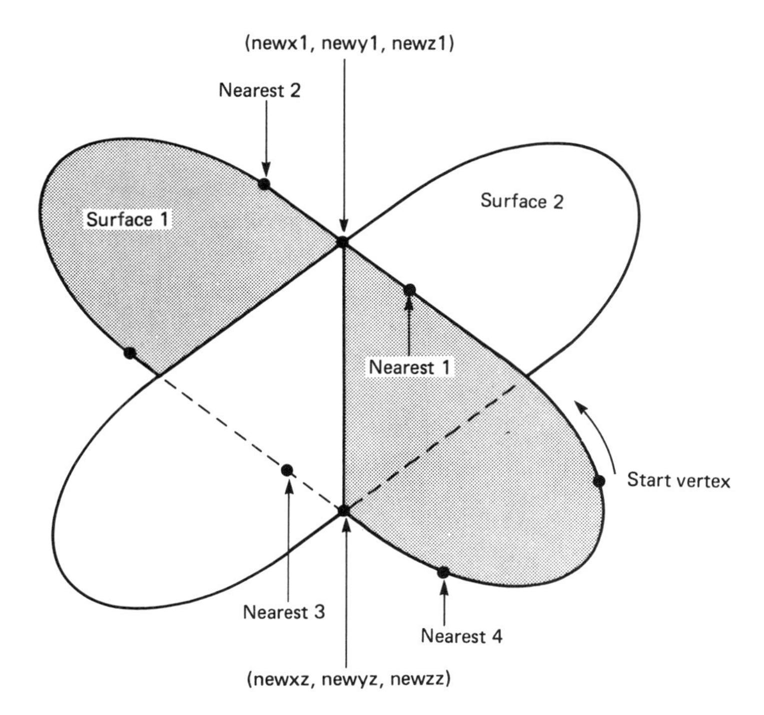

Figure 9.21
The plane-splitting scheme used by 'plane split': surface 1 is split by surface 2

```
2300 'SUBROUTINE plane split
2320   OLDVERTS = NOOFVERTICES(SURFACE1)
2330   FOR I = 1 TO OLDVERTS
2340     OLDVERT(I) = SURFACE(SURFACE1,I)
2350     OLDDUMMY%(I) = DUMMYEDGE%(SURFACE1,I)
2360   NEXT I
2370   A = A(SURFACE2) : B = B(SURFACE2)
2380   C = C(SURFACE2) : D = D(SURFACE2)
2390   X = EYEVERTEX(1,OLDVERT(1))
2400   Y = EYEVERTEX(2,OLDVERT(1))
2410   Z = EYEVERTEX(3,OLDVERT(1))
2420   OLDRESULT = A*X+B*Y+C*Z+D
2430   START = 1 : GOSUB 2570  'compare plane and vert
2440   NEAREST1 = REACHED-1 : NEAREST2 = REACHED
2450   START = REACHED : GOSUB 2570  'compare plane and vert
2460   IF REACHED = 1 THEN NEAREST3 = OLDVERTS ELSE NEAREST3 = REACHED -1
2470   NEAREST4 = REACHED
2480   V1 = NEAREST1 : V2 = NEAREST2 : GOSUB 2730  'find new vertex
2490   NEWV1 = NEWVERTEX
2500   V1 = NEAREST3 : V2 = NEAREST4 : GOSUB 2730  'find new vertex
2510   NEWV2 = NEWVERTEX
2520   ORIGINAL = SURFACE1 : GOSUB 2920  'add new surface
2530   GOSUB 3180  'replace original surface
2540   PRINT "Surface ";SURFACE1;" split by surface ";SURFACE2
2550   PRINT TAB(5)"New surfaces: "; SURFACE1;",";SURFS
2560 RETURN

2570 'SUBROUTINE compare plane and vert
2590   SIGNCHANGE = FALSE
2600   I = START
2610   WHILE NOT(SIGNCHANGE)
2620     I = I+1
2630     IF I > OLDVERTS THEN I = 1
2640     X = EYEVERTEX(1,OLDVERT(I))
2650     Y = EYEVERTEX(2,OLDVERT(I))
2660     Z = EYEVERTEX(3,OLDVERT(I))
2670     RESULT = A*X+B*Y+C*Z+D
2680     IF ABS(OLDRESULT) >= ROUNDOFF THEN
         IF ABS(RESULT) >= ROUNDOFF THEN
         SIGNCHANGE = SGN(RESULT) <> SGN(OLDRESULT)
2690     IF ABS(RESULT) > ROUNDOFF THEN OLDRESULT = RESULT
2700    WEND
2710    REACHED = I
2720  RETURN

2730 'SUBROUTINE find new vertex
2750   X1 = EYEVERTEX(1,OLDVERT(V1))
2760   Y1 = EYEVERTEX(2,OLDVERT(V1))
2770   Z1 = EYEVERTEX(3,OLDVERT(V1))
2780   IF ABS(A*X1+B*Y1+C*Z1+D) < ROUNDOFF THEN NEWVERTEX = OLDVERT(V1) :
         RETURN
```

Program 9.6 Subroutines for splitting a surface into two.

```
2790    X2 = EYEVERTEX(1,OLDVERT(V2))
2800    Y2 = EYEVERTEX(2,OLDVERT(V2))
2810    Z2 = EYEVERTEX(3,OLDVERT(V2))
2820    S = (-D-A*X1-B*Y1-C*Z1)/(A*(X2-X1)+B*(Y2-Y1)+C*(Z2-Z1))
2830    NEWX = X1+S*(X2-X1)
2840    NEWY = Y1+S*(Y2-Y1)
2850    NEWZ = Z1+S*(Z2-Z1)
2860    VERTS = VERTS+1 : NEWVERTEX = VERTS
2870    EYEVERTEX(1,NEWVERTEX) = NEWX
2880    EYEVERTEX(2,NEWVERTEX) = NEWY
2890    EYEVERTEX(3,NEWVERTEX) = NEWZ
2895    VPE = NEWVERTEX : XE = NEWX : YE = NEWY : ZE = NEWZ
2900    GOSUB 1240  'perspect transform
2910  RETURN

2920  'SUBROUTINE add new surface
2940    SURFS = SURFS+1 : S = SURFS
2950    SURFACE(S,1) = NEWV2
2960    DUMMYEDGE%(S,1) = TRUE
2970    J = 2 : I = NEAREST4-1
2980    WHILE I <> NEAREST1
2990      I = I+1 : IF I > OLDVERTS THEN I = 1
3000      SURFACE(S,J) = OLDVERT(I)
3010      DUMMYEDGE%(S,J) = OLDDUMMY%(I)
3020      J = J+1
3030    WEND
3040    PRIORITY(S) = S
3050    IF OLDVERT(NEAREST1) = NEWV1 THEN
          J = J-1
          ELSE SURFACE(S,J) = NEWV1 :
          DUMMYEDGE%(S,J) = OLDDUMMY%(NEAREST2)
3060    A(S) = A(ORIGINAL)
3070    B(S) = B(ORIGINAL)
3080    C(S) = C(ORIGINAL)
3090    D(S) = D(ORIGINAL)
3100    NOOFVERTICES(S) = J
3105    SURFACEN = S : COORD = 3 : GOSUB 1360  'largest xyz
3110    LARGESTZ(S) = MAX
3115    SURFACEN = S : COORD = 3 : GOSUB 1420  'smallest xyz
3120    SMALLESTZ(S)= MIN
3130    FOR SNO = THENEXT TO SURFS-1 : OS = PRIORITY(SNO)
3140      SUCCEEDED%(S,OS) = SUCCEEDED%(ORIGINAL,OS)
3150      SUCCEEDED%(OS,S) = SUCCEEDED%(OS,ORIGINAL)
3160    NEXT SNO
3170  RETURN

3180  'SUBROUTINE replace original surface
3200    SURFACE(ORIGINAL,1) = NEWV1
3210    DUMMYEDGE%(ORIGINAL,1) = TRUE
3220    J = 2 : I = NEAREST2-1
3230    WHILE I <> NEAREST3
```

continued

```
3235      I = I+1
3240      IF I > OLDVERTS THEN I = 1
3250      SURFACE(ORIGINAL,J) = OLDVERT(I)
3260      DUMMYEDGE%(ORIGINAL,J) = OLDDUMMY%(I)
3270      J = J+1
3280    WEND
3290    IF OLDVERT(NEAREST3) = NEWV2 THEN J = J-1
          ELSE SURFACE(ORIGINAL,J) = NEWV2 :
          DUMMYEDGE%(ORIGINAL,J) = OLDDUMMY%(NEAREST4)
3300    NOOFVERTICES(ORIGINAL) = J
3305    SURFACEN = ORIGINAL : COORD = 3 : GOSUB 1360  'largest xyz
3310    LARGESTZ(ORIGINAL) = MAX
3315    SURFACEN = ORIGINAL : COORD = 3 : GOSUB 1420  'smallest xyz
3320    SMALLESTZ(ORIGINAL)= MIN
3330 RETURN
```

Program 9.6 *continued*

parametric equations for the lines defined by nearest 1 and nearest 2, and nearest 3 and nearest 4 (subroutine 'find new vertex'). Actually, if the plane of surface 2 was crossed at a vertex of surface 1, then the number of this vertex is returned by subroutine 'find new vertex'. In general, the point of intersection between the lines and the plane of surface 2 are calculated. The two new surfaces are thus defined by a list of vertices plus two new ones common to each half of the split plane. One new surface is added to the data structure in the original position (subroutine 'replace original surface') and the other is added as a new surface (subroutine 'add new surface'). The

```
3340 'SUBROUTINE save
3350    FILENUM = 3
3360    OPEN "dump" FOR OUTPUT AS #FILENUM
3370    WRITE #FILENUM,VERTS,SURFS
3380    FOR SAVEV = 1 TO VERTS
3390      FOR C = 4 TO 5
3400        WRITE #FILENUM,EYEVERTEX(C,SAVEV)
3410    NEXT C : NEXT SAVEV
3420    FOR S = 1 TO SURFS
3430      WRITE #FILENUM,NOOFVERTICES(S)
3440      FOR E = 1 TO NOOFVERTICES(S)
3450        WRITE #FILENUM,SURFACE(S,E),DUMMYEDGE%(S,E)
3460    NEXT E : NEXT S
3470    FOR P = 1 TO SURFS
3480      WRITE #FILENUM,PRIORITY(P)
3490    NEXT P
3500    CLOSE #FILENUM
3510 RETURN
```

Program 9.7 Subroutine to save the priority list produced by the depth sort algorithm.

plane splitting subroutine, together with its subsidiary subroutines, is presented as Program 9.6.

Saving and plotting the scene

The subroutine 'save' (Program 9.7) transfers various parts of the depth sort algorithm data structure into a file and the information in this file can then be used later by Program 9.8 to plot the surfaces in the correct order. In addition to the surface list and the priority list, the only vertex information needed is the list of screen coordinates from the last two columns of the 'EYEVERTEX' array.

One further piece of information needed in the plotting program is an indication of which edges were not present in the original object but have been introduced by plane splitting. This information is recorded by the plane splitting subroutine in the logical array 'DUMMYEDGE%', which has an entry for each edge in the scene.

The final part of the algorithm involves painting each surface in the order given in the priority list. As already mentioned it is a non-trivial task to find an interior point as a start point for PAINT. Remember that any scheme must be independent of the viewpoint and the shape of the polygon. We have taken a shortcut and used the 'centre of gravity' of the surface as the start point. This works satisfactorily in most cases. A more general solution would be to use an approach similar to that described in detail in Chapter 5.

```
 10 MAXVERTS = 30 : MAXSURFS = 20 : MAXEDGES = 9
 20 DIM X(MAXVERTS),Y(MAXVERTS),NOOFVERTICES(MAXSURFS),
        SURFACE(MAXSURFS,MAXEDGES),DUMMYEDGE%(MAXSURFS,MAXEDGES),
        PRIORITY(MAXSURFS)
 30 SCALE = 3
 50 GOSUB 290  'load
 52 FOR SS = 1 TO SURFS
 53 PRINT "priority ";SS;" vertices ";NOOFVERTICES(PRIORITY(SS))
 54 NEXT SS
 55 STOP
 60 SCREEN 1 : CLS
 70 WINDOW (-640,-400)-(639,399)
 80 GOSUB 100  'draw surfaces
 90 END

100 'SUBROUTINE draw surfaces
105   FILLCOLOR1 = 2 : FILLCOLOR2 = 3
110   FOR P = 1 TO SURFS
120     S = PRIORITY(P)
130     VERTS = NOOFVERTICES(S)
140     BORDERCOLOR = 1 : BACKGROUNDCOLOR = 0
150     PSET (X(SURFACE(S,VERTS)),Y(SURFACE(S,VERTS))),BORDERCOLOR
160     FOR E = 1 TO VERTS
```

Program 9.8 Program to draw the scene using the priority list created by the depth sort algorithm.

continued

```
170         LINE -(X(SURFACE(S,E)),Y(SURFACE(S,E))),BORDERCOLOR
180       NEXT E
190       GOSUB 470  'colorfill
210       BORDERCOLOR = 0
220       PSET (X(SURFACE(S,VERTS)),Y(SURFACE(S,VERTS))),FILLCOLOR2
230       FOR E = 1 TO VERTS
240         IF DUMMYEDGE%(S,E) THEN
               LINE -(X(SURFACE(S,E)),Y(SURFACE(S,E))),FILLCOLOR2
               ELSE LINE -(X(SURFACE(S,E)),Y(SURFACE(S,E))),BORDERCOLOR
250       NEXT E
260       PRINT S : INPUT;"",ANY$
270     NEXT P
280 RETURN

290 'SUBROUTINE load
300     FILENUM = 3
310     OPEN "dump" FOR INPUT AS #FILENUM
320     INPUT #FILENUM, VERTS,SURFS
330     FOR V = 1 TO VERTS
340       INPUT #FILENUM, X(V),Y(V)
350       X(V) = SCALE*X(V) : Y(V) = SCALE*Y(V)
360     NEXT V
370     FOR S = 1 TO SURFS
380       INPUT #FILENUM,NOOFVERTICES(S)
390       FOR E = 1 TO NOOFVERTICES(S)
400         INPUT #FILENUM,SURFACE(S,E),DUMMYEDGE%(S,E)
410       NEXT E : NEXT S
420     FOR P = 1 TO SURFS
430       INPUT #FILENUM,PRIORITY(P)
440     NEXT P
450     CLOSE #FILENUM
460 RETURN

470 'SUBROUTINE colorfill
480     TOTALX = 0 : TOTALY = 0
490     FOR E = 1 TO VERTS
500       TOTALX = TOTALX+X(SURFACE(S,E))
510       TOTALY = TOTALY+Y(SURFACE(S,E))
520     NEXT E
530     AVX = TOTALX/VERTS : AVY = TOTALY/VERTS
535     'PSET (AVX,AVY),FILLCOLOR1
540     PAINT(AVX,AVY),FILLCOLOR1,BORDERCOLOR
550     PAINT(AVX,AVY),FILLCOLOR2,BORDERCOLOR
560 RETURN
```

Program 9.8 *continued*

10 *A lexicon of mathematical shapes*

This chapter consists of a set of programs that produce shapes under control of a mathematical formula. Most of the programs contain parameters that vary some aspect of the shape of the function and allow experimentation. The functions are mainly 'circular' functions and an illustration or set of illustrations accompanies each program.

The mathematics is presented without detailed explanation, in the belief that even a person with little or no mathematical knowledge can easily experiment with the shapes and gain familiarity with the functions and how their form is controlled by running the programs. The mathematics is presented in a very non-rigorous manner and many of the formulae 'overlap'. This means that although, for example, a cardioid formula is used to generate a particular shape, it may well be possible to generate exactly the same shape using the Lissajous formula. This is because most of the functions are 'circular' or harmonic which means that they are based on sine waves.

Individual shapes can be used as motifs in the decorative techniques described in other chapters and the motifs can be combined in any way you choose. Again you are limited only by your imagination and can experiment freely with the variable parameters of each shape. One of the fascinating aspects of using mathematically generated shapes is that unless you are an expert mathematician, the outcome of using a certain formula with particular parameters is unknown at the outset. There is literally an infinite number of possible variations.

Finally the aesthetic appeal of the patterns can always be enhanced by using colour. This is dealt with at the end of the chapter where suggestions for introducing colour are given.

10.1 SINE WAVES

Program 10.1 displays the familiar function:

$$y = \sin \theta$$

```
 10 PI = 3.141593
 20 DEF FNRAD(DEGREES) = DEGREES*PI/180
 30 SCREEN 2 : CLS
 40 FOR WAVE = 1 TO 3
 50   READ SX,SY,F,S
 70   WINDOW (-SX,-SY)-(1279-SX,779-SY)
 80   FOR THETA = 0 TO 720 STEP 10
 90     IF THETA = 0 THEN PSET (0,0)
        ELSE LINE -(THETA,S*SIN(FNRAD(F*THETA)))
100   NEXT THETA
110 NEXT WAVE

120 DATA 100,500,3,100
130 DATA 100,200,4,150
140 DATA 100,700,1,50
```

Program 10.1 Simple sine waves.

The variable parameters in this function are the amplitude or height of the wave (s in the program) and the frequency or rate of undulation (variable f in the program). The equation used in the program is:

$$y = s \sin(f\theta)$$

Modulating the amplitude of a sine wave

One of the things we can do with periodic functions, such as sine waves, is modulate them with another function. A periodic function is one whose 'pattern' repeats itself over and over again. If in the

Figure 10.1 Sine waves of different frequency and amplitude

```
 10 PI = 3.141593
 20 DEF FNRAD(DEGREES) = DEGREES*PI/180
 30 SCREEN 2 : CLS
 40 FOR WAVE = 1 TO 3
 50   READ SX,SY,F1,F2,S
 70   WINDOW (-SX,-SY)-(1279-SX,799-SY)
 80   FOR THETA = 0 TO 1080 STEP 1
 90     IF THETA = 0 THEN PSET (0,0)
        ELSE LINE -(THETA,S*SIN(FNRAD(F1*THETA))*SIN(FNRAD(F2*THETA)))
100   NEXT THETA
110 NEXT WAVE

120 DATA 100,150,1,20,140
130 DATA 100,400,1,10,90
140 DATA 100,650,2,30,140
```

Program 10.2 Sine waves modulated by other sine waves.

case of the sine wave we replace *s*, a constant, with a function, then the amplitude of the sine wave will itself vary.

In Program 10.2 we have replaced *s* with another sine wave. The function is

$$y = s \sin(f1\theta) \sin(f2\theta)$$

In the bottom illustration of Figure 10.2 $f2 = 20f1$, in the middle illustration $f2 = 10f1$ and $f1$ is the same in both cases. The top example shows the effect of increasing both $f1$ and $f2$. Note the not unpleasing interference effect in the bottom example caused by the limited x resolution.

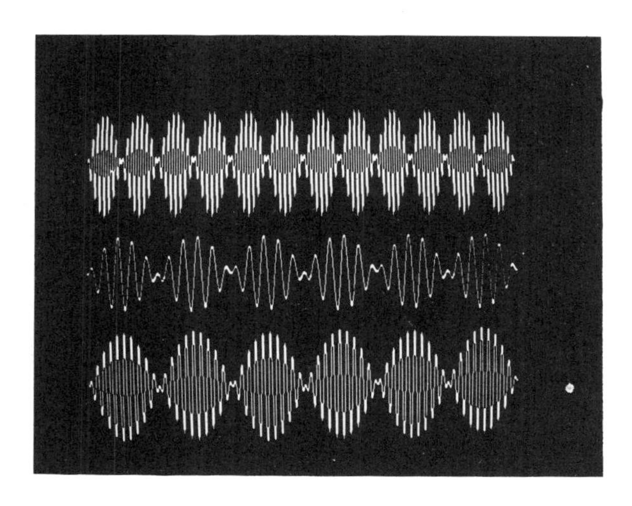

Figure 10.2
Modulating the amplitude of a sine wave

```
 10 PI = 3.141593
 20 DEF FNRAD(DEGREES) = DEGREES*PI/180
 30 SCREEN 2 : CLS
 40 FOR ELLIPSE = 1 TO 6
 50   READ PHI,XC,YC,A,B
 60   WINDOW (-XC,-YC)-(1279-XC,799-YC)
 70   X = A : Y = 0 : GOSUB 180  'transform
 80   PSET (XT,YT)
 90   FOR THETA = 5 TO 360 STEP 5
100     COSINE = COS(FNRAD(THETA)) : SINE = SIN(FNRAD(THETA))
110     R = 1/SQR(COSINE*COSINE/(A*A)+SINE*SINE/(B*B))
120     X = R*COSINE : Y = R*SINE
130     GOSUB 180  'transform
140     LINE -(XT,YT)
150   NEXT THETA
160 NEXT ELLIPSE
170 END

180 'SUBROUTINE transform
190   XT = X*COS(FNRAD(PHI))+Y*SIN(FNRAD(PHI))
200   YT =-X*SIN(FNRAD(PHI))+Y*COS(FNRAD(PHI))
210 RETURN

220 DATA 0,200,740,100,50
230 DATA 0,500,500,300,150
240 DATA 45,300,200,70,180
250 DATA -60,700,400,100,200
260 DATA 0,1100,500,50,300
270 DATA 0,700,730,70,70
```

Program 10.3 Ellipses.

Figure 10.3
Ellipses of different eccentricity and orientation

```
 10 PI = 3.141593
 20 DEF FNRAD(DEGREES) = DEGREES*PI/180
 30 SCREEN 2 : CLS
 40 FOR CIRC = 1 TO 4
 50   READ XC,YC,R,A
 60   WINDOW (-XC,-YC)-(1279-XC,779-YC)
 70   PSET (R,0)
 80   FOR THETA = 0 TO 360 STEP 1
 90     X = (R+A*SIN(FNRAD(10*THETA)))*COS(FNRAD(THETA))
100     Y = (R+A*SIN(FNRAD(10*THETA)))*SIN(FNRAD(THETA))
110     LINE -(X,Y)
120   NEXT THETA
130 NEXT CIRC

140 DATA 500,400,280,100
150 DATA 500,400,180,70
160 DATA 500,400,80,30
170 DATA 500,400,30,10
```

Program 10.4 Circles modulated by sine waves.

10.2 ELLIPSES AND CIRCLES

Program 10.3 generates ellipses. With an ellipse we can vary three parameters: *a*, the major diameter, *b*, the minor diameter, and 'phi', the orientation or slant of the figure. A circle is just a special case of an ellipse with *a* and *b* equal. The equation is

```
R = 1/SQR(COS(THETA)*COS(THETA)/(A*A)+SIN(THETA)*
    SIN(THETA)/(B*B))
```

Figure 10.4
Modulating the radius of a circle with an ellipse

```
 10 PI = 3.141593
 20 DEF FNRAD(DEGREES) = DEGREES*PI/180
 30 SCREEN 2 : CLS
 40 FOR CIRC = 1 TO 4
 50   READ XC,YC,R,A
 60   WINDOW (-XC,-YC)-(1279-XC,779-YC)
 70   PSET (R,0)
 80   FOR THETA = 0 TO 360 STEP 1
 90     IF THETA MOD 10 = 0 THEN A = A*(-1) : R = R+A
100     X = R*COS(FNRAD(THETA))
110     Y = R*SIN(FNRAD(THETA))
120     LINE -(X,Y)
130   NEXT THETA
140 NEXT CIRC

150 DATA 500,400,280,50
160 DATA 500,400,180,70
170 DATA 500,400,80,30
180 DATA 500,400,30,10
```

Program 10.5 Circles modulated by square waves.

Here we are generating an ellipse by sweeping r through 360°. For each value of 'THETA' we calculate x and y:

$$x = r \cos \theta$$
$$y = r \sin \theta$$

To generate a circle ($a=b$) our equation reduces to:

$$r = a$$

and if we wanted a program that would only generate circles, line 110 in the program would be omitted. The subroutine 'transform' rotates the ellipse through angle 'PHI'.

Figure 10.5 (below left) Modulating the radius of a circle with a square wave

Figure 10.6 (below right) 'Concentric' or 'linear' spirals

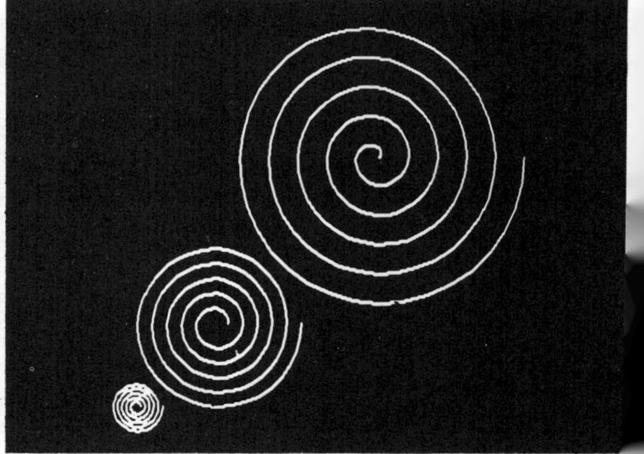

```
 10 PI = 3.141593
 20 DEF FNRAD(DEGREES) = DEGREES*PI/180
 30 SCREEN 2 : CLS
 40 FOR SPIRAL = 1 TO 3
 50   READ XC,YC,R,INC
 60   WINDOW (-XC,-YC)-(1279-XC,779-YC)
 70   PSET (R,0)
 80   FOR THETA = 0 TO 1800 STEP 10
 90     R = R+INC
100     X = R*COS(FNRAD(THETA))
110     Y = R*SIN(FNRAD(THETA))
120     LINE -(X,Y)
130   NEXT THETA
140 NEXT SPIRAL

150 DATA 320,270,25,.8
160 DATA 700,510,8,1.5
170 DATA 100,100,10,.3
```

Program 10.6 Simple spirals.

Modulating a radius

In Program 10.4 we generate a circle by sweeping a radius r through 360°. However, instead of keeping r fixed, we add a sine wave to r (lines 90 and 100). This means that we have taken a sine wave and twisted it into a circle. Making such patterns concentric at different radii produces a pleasing effect.

Program 10.5 uses the same idea but this time uses a square wave

```
 10 PI = 3.141593
 20 DEF FNRAD(DEGREES) = DEGREES*PI/180
 30 SCREEN 2 : CLS
 40 FOR SPIRAL = 1 TO 3
 50   READ XC,YC,R,INC
 60   WINDOW (-XC,-YC)-(1279-XC,779-YC)
 70   PSET (R,0)
 80   FOR THETA = 10 TO 1200 STEP 10
 90     R = R+R*INC/50
100     X = R*COS(FNRAD(THETA))
110     Y = R*SIN(FNRAD(THETA))
120     LINE -(X,Y)
130   NEXT THETA
140 NEXT SPIRAL

150 DATA 315,265,30,1
160 DATA 700,500,10,1.9
170 DATA 100,100,10,.7
```

Program 10.7 Non-uniform spirals.

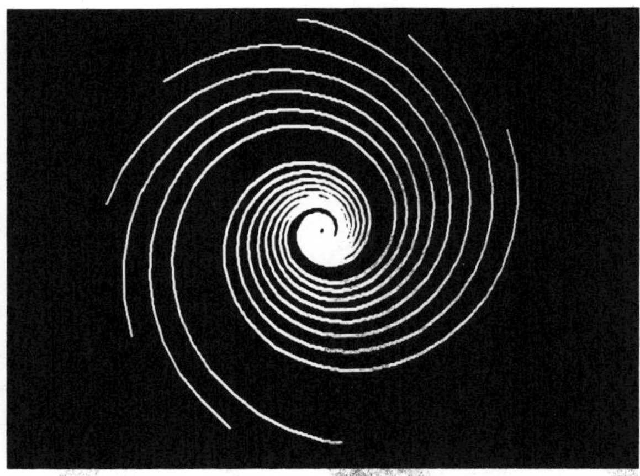

Figure 10.7 (above left) 'Non-linear' spirals

Figure 10.8 (above right) Spiral sets

as the modulating function (see line 90). This idea can, of course, equally be applied to an ellipse.

10.3 SPIRALS

Programs 10.6 to 10.9 generate different forms of spirals. Spirals are curves of the form:

$$r = k\theta$$

```
 10 PI = 3.141593
 20 DEF FNRAD(DEGREES) = DEGREES*PI/180
 30 SCREEN 2 : CLS
 40 READ XC,YC,RS,INC
 50 WINDOW (-XC,-YC)-(1279-XC,799-YC)
 60 FOR PHI = 0 TO 252 STEP 36
 70   X = RS : Y = 0 : R = RS : GOSUB 170  'transform
 80   PSET (XT,YT)
 90   FOR THETA = 0 TO 1000 STEP 10
100     R = R+R*INC/50
110     X = R*COS(FNRAD(THETA)) : Y = R*SIN(FNRAD(THETA))
120     GOSUB 170  'transform
130     LINE -(XT,YT)
140   NEXT THETA
150 NEXT PHI
160 END

170 'SUBROUTINE transform
180   XT = X*COS(FNRAD(PHI))+Y*SIN(FNRAD(PHI))
190   YT =-X*SIN(FNRAD(PHI))+Y*COS(FNRAD(PHI))
200 RETURN

210 DATA 640,400,10,1.9
```

Program 10.8 Rotating spirals.

```
10 PI = 3.141593
20 DEF FNRAD(DEGREES) = DEGREES*PI/180
30 SCREEN 2 : CLS
40 READ XC,YC,RS,INC
50 WINDOW (-XC,-YC)-(1279-XC,799-YC)
60 FOR PHI = 0 TO 360 STEP 28
70   X = RS : Y = 0 : R = RS : GOSUB 270  'transform
80   PSET (XT,YT)
90   FOR THETA = 360 TO 0 STEP -10
100    R = R+R*INC/20
110    X = R*COS(FNRAD(THETA)) : Y = R*SIN(FNRAD(THETA))
120    GOSUB 270  'transform
130    LINE -(XT,YT)
140  NEXT THETA
150 NEXT PHI
160 FOR PHI = 0 TO 360 STEP 28
170   X = RS : Y = 0 : R = RS : GOSUB 270  'transform
180   PSET (XT,YT)
190   FOR THETA = 0 TO 360 STEP 10
200    R = R+R*INC/20
210    X = R*COS(FNRAD(THETA)) : Y = R*SIN(FNRAD(THETA))
220    GOSUB 270  'transform
230    LINE -(XT,YT)
240  NEXT THETA
250 NEXT PHI
260 END

270 'SUBROUTINE transform
280   XT = X*COS(FNRAD(PHI))+Y*SIN(FNRAD(PHI))
290   YT =-X*SIN(FNRAD(PHI))+Y*COS(FNRAD(PHI))
300 RETURN

310 DATA 640,400,10,1.9
```

Program 10.9 Contra-rotating spirals.

Figure 10.9
Contra-rotating spirals

which means that as we sweep r through successive revolutions it gets bigger and bigger.

Program 10.6 increases r by an equal increment for each angular increment of 10°. Varying the program variable 'INC' has the effect shown. Note the concentric appearance of the spirals.

Program 10.7 is the same except that r is increasing non-linearly as a function of 'THETA' (look at line 90).

Program 10.8 generates sets of such spirals by applying a rotational transformation to each. In the illustration eight spirals are plotted. Each is subject to a rotation of 36° from the previous one. This pattern is used as a basis for some of the motifs in Chapter 4.

Program 10.9 generates two sets of contra-rotating spirals. A variation of this pattern abounds in nature as seed patterns, in, for example, fir cones and sunflowers. The natural pattern has different numbers of clockwise and counter-clockwise spirals. These are commonly 8,13 or 13,21 or 21,34 and these pairs of numbers are terms in a mathematical series known as the Fibonacci series. We have kept equal numbers of spirals in each set so that they join up.

Figure 10.10
Lissajous figures: (a) basic; (b) 5,1,5; (c) 11,5,3; (d) 5,9,6; (e) 17,13,9; (f) 31,27,23; (g) 71,67,63; (h) 9,19,19; (i) 5,17,17; (j) 71,19,19

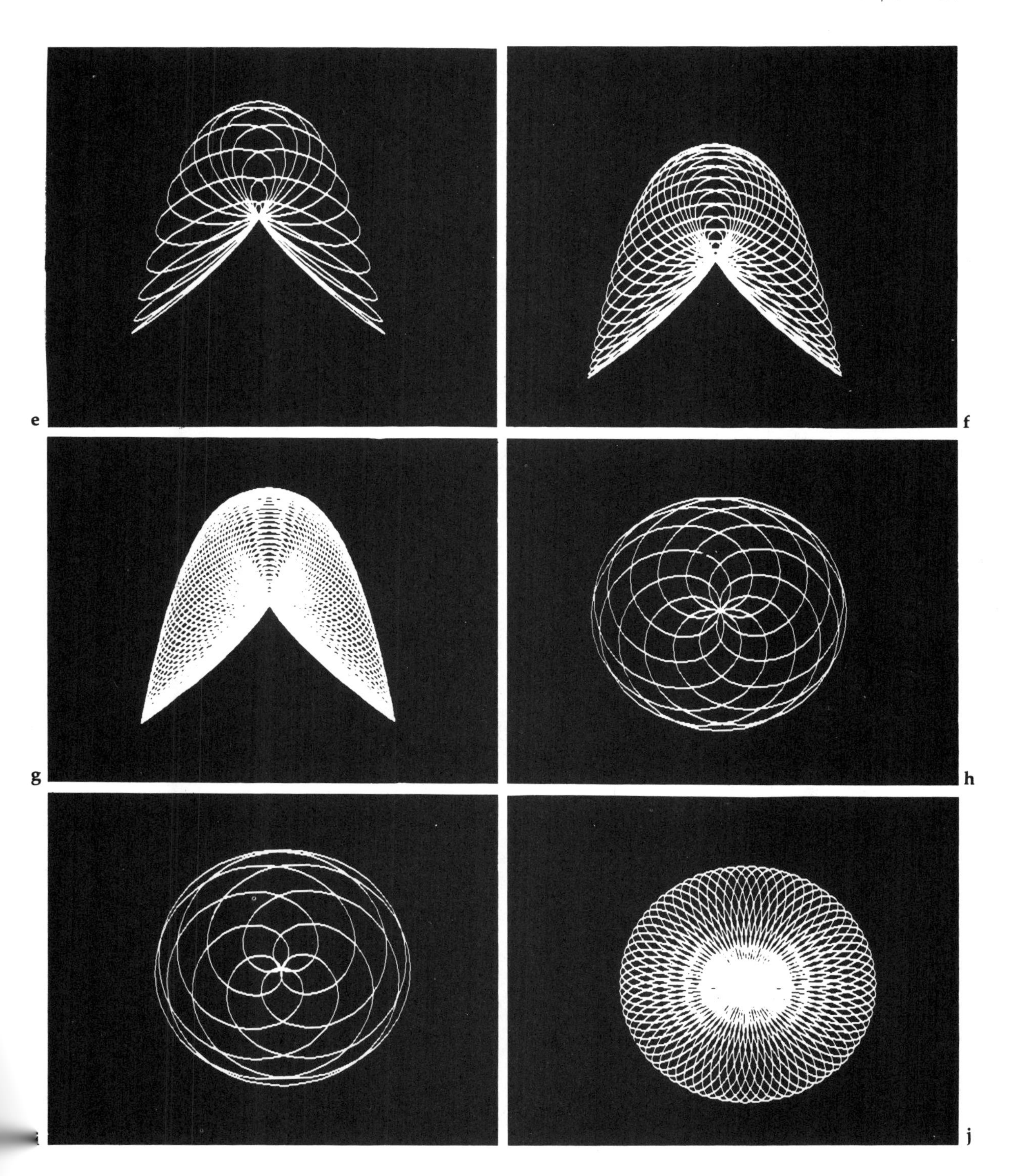
e
f
g
h
i
j

```
 10 PI = 3.141593
 20 DEF FNRAD(DEGREES) = DEGREES*PI/180
 30 SCREEN 2 : CLS
 40 FOR WAVE = 1 TO 6
 50   READ SX,SY,O,PHI,S
 60   WINDOW (-SX,-SY)-(1279-SX,779-SY)
 70   PSET (S*SIN(FNRAD(THETA)),S*SIN(FNRAD(O*THETA+PHI)))
 80   FOR THETA = 0 TO 360 STEP 5
 90     LINE -(S*SIN(FNRAD(THETA)),S*SIN(FNRAD(O*THETA+PHI)))
100   NEXT THETA
110 NEXT WAVE
120 END

130 DATA 200,600,1,90,100
140 DATA 550,600,2,0,150
150 DATA 950,600,3,90,150
160 DATA 200,200,4,0,150
170 DATA 550,200,4,45,150
180 DATA 950,200,5,90,150
```

Program 10.10 Basic Lissajous figures.

10.4 LISSAJOUS PATTERNS

Program 10.10 generates the basic Lissajous patterns of order 0,1,2,3,4,5 and 6 (Figure 10.10a). A Lissajous pattern is formed from two sine waves:

$$x = s1 \sin \theta$$
$$y = s2 \sin(o\theta + \phi)$$

where o is the order of the pattern. If the frequency of the sine waves is equal ($o = 1$) and $\phi = 90°$ then a circle results. If one sine wave is

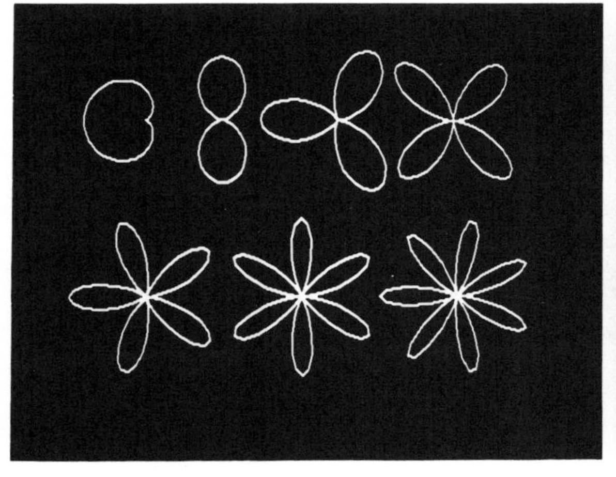

Figure 10.11 (below left) Basic cardiods

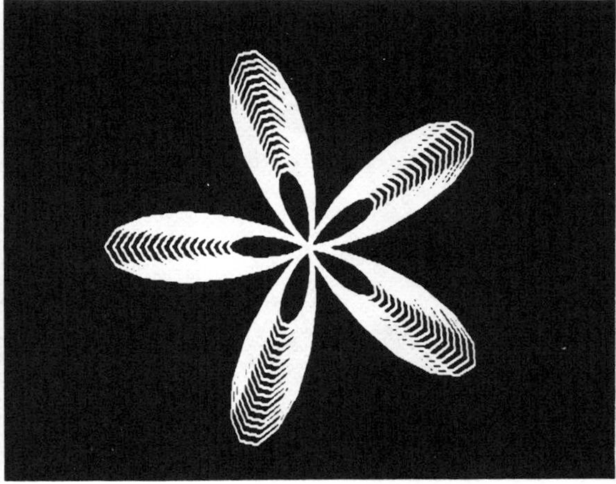

Figure 10.12 (below right) 'Concentric' 5-lobe pattern

```
10 PI = 3.141593
20 DEF FNRAD(DEGREES) = DEGREES*PI/180
30 SCREEN 2 : CLS
40 FOR CARDIOID = 1 TO 7
50   READ SX,SY,A,O
60   WINDOW (-SX,-SY)-(1279-SX,779-SY)
70   FOR THETA = 0 TO 360 STEP 5
80     R = A*(1-COS(FNRAD(O*THETA)))
90     X = R*COS(FNRAD(THETA)) : Y = R*SIN(FNRAD(THETA))
100    IF THETA = 0 THEN PSET (X,Y) ELSE LINE -(X,Y)
110  NEXT THETA
120 NEXT CARDIOID
130 END

140 DATA 200,600,80,1
150 DATA 400,600,80,2
160 DATA 700,600,100,3
170 DATA 1000,600,100,4
180 DATA 200,200,100,5
190 DATA 600,200,100,6
200 DATA 1000,200,100,7
```

Program 10.11 Basic cardioids.

twice the frequency of the other a figure of eight results. Making *o* equal to 0,1…6 and controlling 'PHI' produced Figure 10.10a.

By varying both frequencies simultaneously and making 'PHI' 90° gives:

$$x = s1 \sin(o1\theta)$$
$$y = s2 \cos(o2\theta)$$

Now making *s* itself a sine function, an astonishing variety of

```
10 PI = 3.141593
20 DEF FNRAD(DEGREES) = DEGREES*PI/180
30 SCREEN 2 : CLS
40 WINDOW (-640,-400)-(639,399)
50 FOR A = 70 TO 200 STEP 10
60   FOR THETA = 0 TO 360 STEP 5
70     R = A*(1-COS(FNRAD(5*THETA)))
80     X = R*COS(FNRAD(THETA)) : Y = R*SIN(FNRAD(THETA))
90     IF THETA = 0 THEN PSET (X,Y) ELSE LINE -(X,Y)
100  NEXT THETA
110 NEXT A
120 END
```

Program 10.12 Concentric 5-lobe pattern.

```
 10 PI = 3.141593
 20 DEF FNRAD(DEGREES) = DEGREES*PI/180
 30 SCREEN 2 : CLS
 40 WINDOW (-640,-400)-(639,399)
 50 S = 0.1 : A = 100
 60 FOR I = 1 TO 8
 70   FOR THETA = 0 TO 360 STEP 3
 80     R = A*(1-COS(FNRAD(5*THETA)))
 90     X = S*R*COS(FNRAD(THETA)) : Y = R*SIN(FNRAD(THETA))
100     IF THETA = 0 THEN PSET (X,Y) ELSE LINE -(X,Y)
110     S = S+1/360
120   NEXT THETA
130 NEXT I
140 END
```

Program 10.13 5-lobe cardioids with x scale manipulation.

```
 10 PI = 3.141593
 20 DEF FNRAD(DEGREES) = DEGREES*PI/180
 30 SCREEN 2 : CLS
 40 WINDOW (-640,-400)-(639,399)
 50 S = 0.1 : A = 100
 60 FOR I = 1 TO 8
 70   FOR THETA = 0 TO 360 STEP 3
 80     R = A*(2-COS(FNRAD(5*THETA)))
 90     X = S*R*COS(FNRAD(THETA)) : Y = R*SIN(FNRAD(THETA))
100     IF THETA = 0 THEN PSET (X,Y) ELSE LINE -(X,Y)
110     S = S+0.5/360
120   NEXT THETA
130 NEXT I
140 END
```

Program 10.14 Drawn out 5-lobe cardioids with x scale manipulation.

```
 10 PI = 3.141593
 20 DEF FNRAD(DEGREES) = DEGREES*PI/180
 30 SCREEN 2 : CLS
 40 WINDOW (-640,-400)-(639,399)
 50 S = 0.1 : A = 80
 60 FOR I = 1 TO 8
 70   FOR THETA = 0 TO 360 STEP 3
 80     R = A*(1-COS(FNRAD(3*THETA)))
 90     X = 0.5*S*R*COS(FNRAD(THETA)) : Y = S*R*SIN(FNRAD(THETA))
100     IF THETA = 0 THEN PSET (X,Y) ELSE LINE -(X,Y)
110     S = S+1/360
120   NEXT THETA
130 NEXT I
140 END
```

Program 10.15 3-lobe cardioids with x and y scale manipulation.

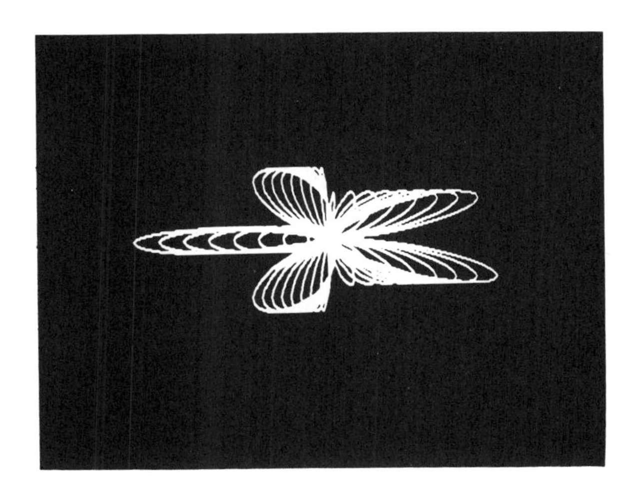

Figure 10.13
5-lobe cardiods with x scale manipulation

Figure 10.14
Drawn out 5-lobe cardiods with x scale manipulation

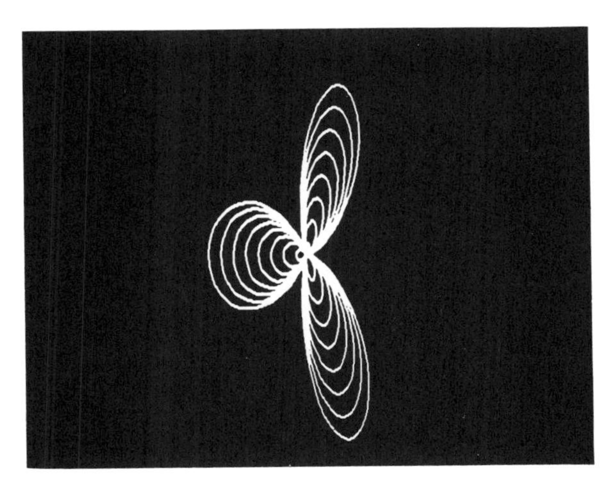

Figure 10.15
3-lobe cardiods with x and y scale manipulation

patterns results. Illustrations in Figure 10.10b to 10.10j show some of the patterns that can be obtained by:

$$x = 200 \sin(a\theta) \cos(o1\theta)$$
$$y = 200 \sin(a\theta) \cos(o2\theta)$$

The program used is given, with colour introduced, as Program 10.21. The values of 'A', 'O1' and 'O2' caption the illustrations.

Cardioid patterns

Although the Lissajous figures produce a wide variety of patterns, the control over individual lobes in the pattern is difficult. A pattern generating function where it is easier to control lobes is the cardioid. Program 10.11 generates seven basic cardioids from the formula:

$$r = a(1 - \cos(o\theta))$$

```
 10 PI = 3.141593
 20 DEF FNRAD(DEGREES) = DEGREES*PI/180
 30 SCREEN 2 : CLS
 40 WINDOW (-640,-400)-(639,399)
 50 S = 0.1 : A = 80
 60 FOR I = 1 TO 8
 70   FOR THETA = 0 TO 360 STEP 3
 80     R = A*(1-COS(FNRAD(3*THETA)))
 90     X = R*COS(FNRAD(THETA)) : Y = S*R*SIN(FNRAD(THETA))
100     IF THETA = 0 THEN PSET (X,Y) ELSE LINE -(X,Y)
110     S = S+1/360
120   NEXT THETA
130 NEXT I
140 END
```

Program 10.16 3-lobe cardioids with y scale manipulation.

```
 10 PI = 3.141593
 20 DEF FNRAD(DEGREES) = DEGREES*PI/180
 30 SCREEN 2 : CLS
 40 WINDOW (-640,-400)-(639,399)
 50 S = 0.1 : A = 80
 60 FOR I = 1 TO 8
 70   FOR THETA = 0 TO 360 STEP 3
 80     R = A*(2-COS(FNRAD(3*THETA)))
 90     X = R*COS(FNRAD(THETA)) : Y = S*R*SIN(FNRAD(THETA))
100     IF THETA = 0 THEN PSET (X,Y) ELSE LINE -(X,Y)
110     S = S+0.5/360
120   NEXT THETA
130 NEXT I
140 END
```

Program 10.17 Drawn out 3-lobe cardioids with y scale manipulation.

A cardioid of order 1 is the basic heart shape. Increasing *o* increases the lobes in the pattern as shown in Figure 10.11.

Program 10.12 takes the 5–lobe formula and varies the radius *a*.

Program 10.13 is another variation on the 5–lobe formula. Here we scale *x* with a scaling factor that is a function of 'THETA'. As the lobes are drawn their '*x*–magnification' is continually increased. This effect is best seen by watching the pattern build up.

In Program 10.14 we have 'drawn out' the cardioid from the centre by adjusting *r*. The effect of this can be seen by comparing Figure 10.13 and Figure 10.14 – the centre of the pattern is drawn out. Programs 10.15, 10.16 and 10.17 apply similar manipulations to a 3–lobe pattern. Again this is best seen by watching the pattern build up.

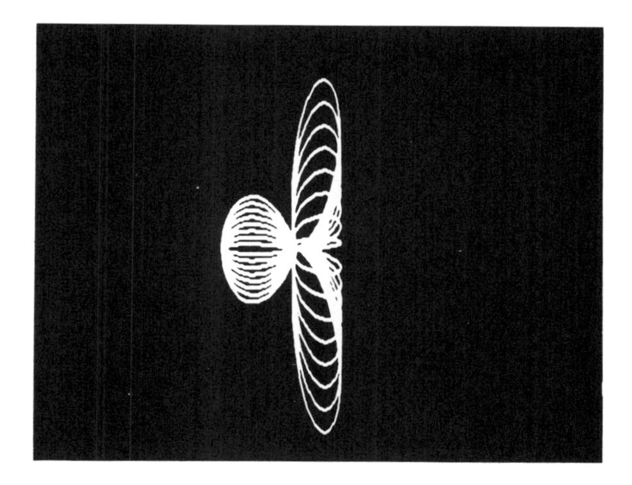

Figure 10.16
3-lobe cardiods wiht *y* scale manipulation

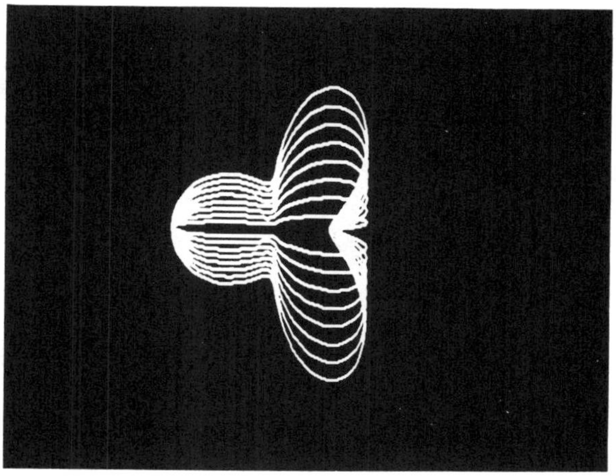

Figure 10.17
Drawn out 3-lobe cardiods with both *x* and *y* scale manipulation

```
10 PI = 3.141593
20 DEF FNRAD(DEGREES) = DEGREES*PI/180
30 SCREEN 2 : CLS
40 WINDOW (-640,-400)-(639,399)
50 S = 7 : THETA = 0
60 FOR SQUARE = 1 TO 15
70   GOSUB 120  'draw a square
80   RESTORE : THETA = THETA+15
90   S = S*0.82
100 NEXT SQUARE
110 END

120 'SUBROUTINE draw a square
130   FOR P = 1 TO 5
140     READ X,Y
150     GOSUB 200  'rotate
160     IF P = 1 THEN PSET (S*XT,S*YT) ELSE LINE -(S*XT,S*YT)
170   NEXT P
180 DATA 50,-50,50,50,-50,50,-50,-50,50,-50
190 RETURN

200 'SUBROUTINE rotate
210   XT = X*COS(FNRAD(THETA))-Y*SIN(FNRAD(THETA))
220   YT = X*SIN(FNRAD(THETA))+Y*COS(FNRAD(THETA))
230 RETURN
```

Program 10.18 Squiral – rotating and shrinking squares.

Figure 10.18
Squirals – rotating and shrinking squares

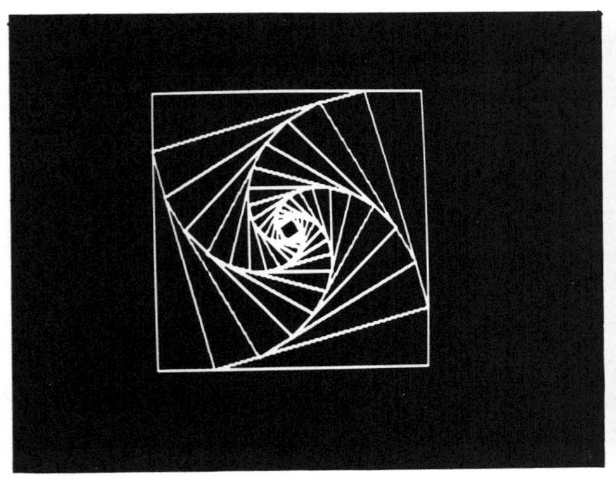

Figure 10.19
Rotating and shrinking hexagons

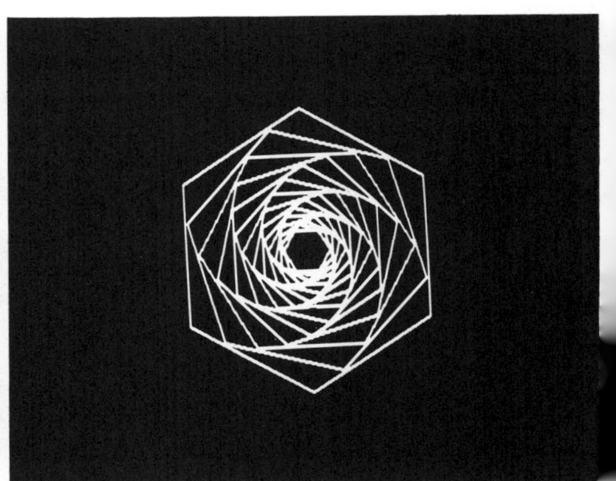

```
 10 PI = 3.141593
 20 DEF FNRAD(DEGREES) = DEGREES*PI/180
 30 SCREEN 2 : CLS
 40 WINDOW (-640,-400)-(639,399)
 50 S = 7 : THETA = 0
 60 FOR HEX = 1 TO 15
 70   GOSUB 120  'draw a hexagon
 80   RESTORE : THETA = THETA+15
 90   S = S*0.88
100 NEXT HEX
110 END

120 'SUBROUTINE draw a hexagon
130   FOR P = 1 TO 7
140     READ X,Y
150     GOSUB 200  'rotate
160     IF P = 1 THEN PSET (S*XT,S*YT) ELSE LINE -(S*XT,S*YT)
170   NEXT P
180 DATA 43.3,25,0,50,-43.3,25,-43.3,-25,0,-50,43.3,-25,43.3,25
190 RETURN

200 'SUBROUTINE rotate
210   XT = X*COS(FNRAD(THETA))-Y*SIN(FNRAD(THETA))
220   YT = X*SIN(FNRAD(THETA))+Y*COS(FNRAD(THETA))
230 RETURN
```

Program 10.19 Rotating and shrinking hexagons.

10.5 SQUIRALS

Program 10.18 produces a spiral effect by rotating and shrinking squares. This pattern is used for three-dimensional ornamentation in an earlier chapter. It is a popular microcomputer pattern because it is striking and effective but easy to draw quickly.

Program 10.19 is based on the same idea. This time a hexagon is used as the basic shape.

10.6 THE USE OF COLOUR IN PATTERNS

Another area worth exploration is the introduction of colour into these patterns. A number of schemes are possible. Firstly the obvious one: you can use different colours for the generating lines.

Secondly you can colour fill closed regions using PAINT as introduced in Chapter 2. This is far less predictable and will greatly extend the interest and appeal of the pattern. Closed regions will either occur as a consequence of the generated shape or they can be generated by overlapping two motifs – spirals, for example. The background should be coloured first so that a lot of time is not wasted by 'bleeds'. The colour fill scheme can be manual: you use an

```
10 PI = 3.141593
20 DEF FNRAD(DEGREES) = DEGREES*PI/180
30 CLS
40 INPUT "a,o1,o2 ",A,01,02
50 SCREEN 1 : CLS
60 WINDOW (-640,-400)-(639,399)
70 FOR THETA = 0 TO 360 STEP 1
80    X = 400*SIN(FNRAD(A*THETA))*COS(FNRAD(01*THETA))
90    Y = 400*SIN(FNRAD(A*THETA))*SIN(FNRAD(02*THETA))
100   IF THETA = 0 THEN PSET (0,0) ELSE LINE -(X,Y),C
110   IF 10*THETA MOD 10 = 0 THEN C = INT(RND*3+1)
120 NEXT THETA
130 END
```

Program 10.20 Coloured Lissajous patterns.

interactive program and choose colours for particular regions. Alternatively you can colour fill 'automatically'. This can be done by writing a program that scans the screen in the following way:

```
100 'SUBROUTINE color fill background
110    FOR I = -640 TO 639 STEP 4
120       FOR J = -400 TO 399 STEP 4
130          IF POINT(I,J) <> BACKGROUND COLOR THEN
             FILLCOLOR = INT(RND*3+1):
             GOSUB 1000 'color fill
140       NEXT J
150    NEXT I
160 RETURN
```

Thirdly the height of a two-dimensional function can be directly mapped into colour. This was done in Program 10.21 (see Colour Plate 18) which is just a colour plot of the function:

$$f(x,y) = \sin(x) + \cos(x)$$

This is a surface that has periodic humps and valleys. The height of the surface at a point (x,y) is simply mapped into one of four colours.

10.7 CYCLOIDS

In this final section we look at another powerful generator: cycloids. Like the Lissajous generator this method generates an astonishing variety of patterns. Some of the simpler patterns could be generated using techniques already given but the cycloid generator can produce complex circular patterns very easily (see Figure 10.21d, for example).

A cycloid is the curve traced out by a point on a circle as it rolls along another curve. The simplest cycloids are obtained when a

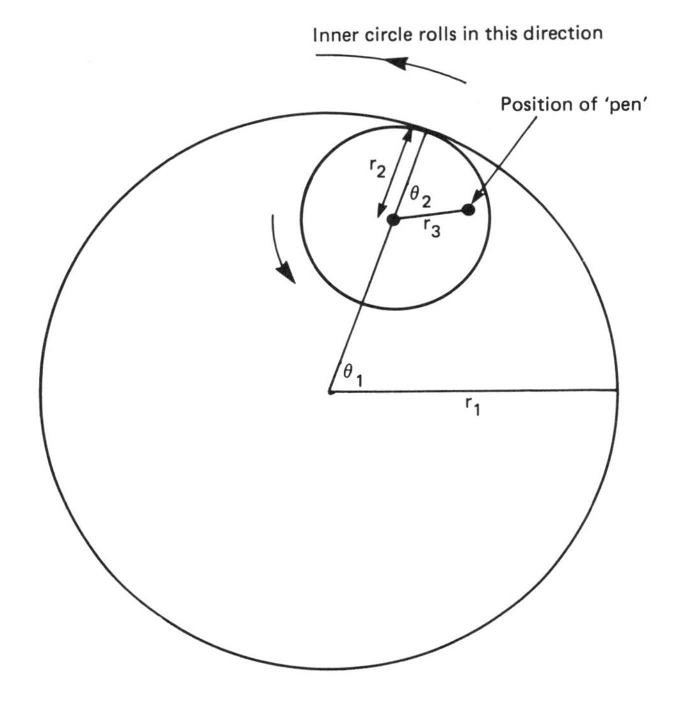

Figure 10.20
Parameters used in cycloid generation

circle rolls along a straight line, but much more interesting effects can be obtained by using a more complex surface such as another circle.

There are several well-known toys available that can be used to generate cycloids. These take the form of discs and other shapes

```
 10 DIM SINEVALUE(1000)
 20 PI = 3.141593
 30 DEF FNRAD(DEGREES) = DEGREES*PI/180
 40 DEF FNSINE(T) = SGN(T)*SINEVALUE(ABS(T))
 50 CLS : PRINT "Setting table of sines, WAIT..."
 60 FOR I = 0 TO 1000
 70   SINEVALUE(I) = SIN(FNRAD(I))
 80 NEXT I
 90 SCREEN 1 : CLS
100 WINDOW (-640,-400)-(639,399)
110 FOR X = -640 TO 640 STEP 4
120   FOR Y = -400 TO 399 STEP 4
130     C = ABS(INT(4.1*(FNSINE(X)+FNSINE(Y*1.5))) MOD 4 )
140     PSET (X,Y),C
150   NEXT Y
160 NEXT X
170 END
```

Program 10.21 A colour plot of a function of two variables.

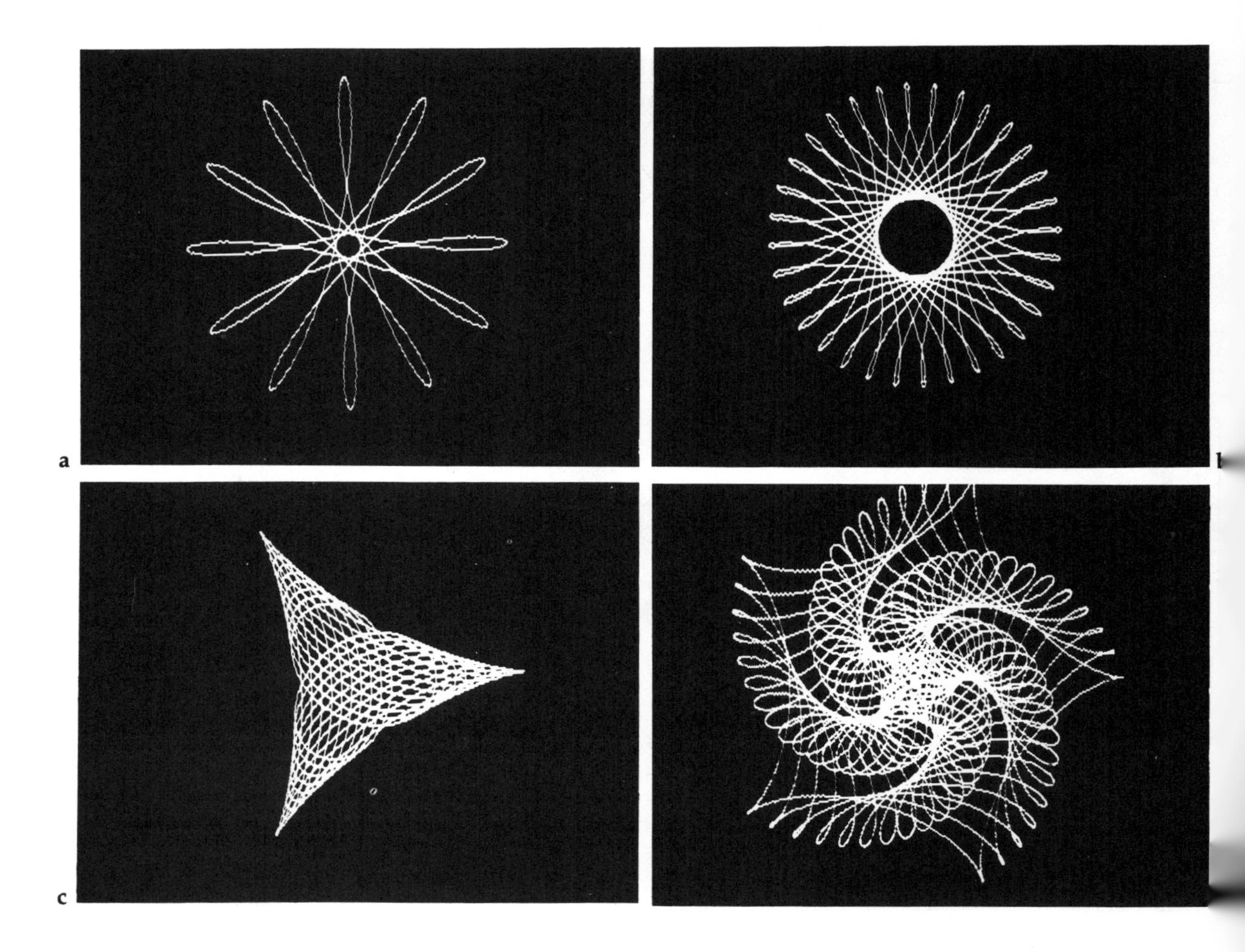

Figure 10.21
Cycloid patterns produced by varying parameters in subroutine 'pattern':
(a) 1,432,252,210,0,0;
(b) 1,384,252,224,0,0;
(c) 10,432,288,270,–24,0;
(d) 20,525,420,410,–20,7

with toothed edges. If one shape is pinned to the paper, a disc can be rolled along its edge and the teeth prevent slipping. A pen can be inserted in a hole in the moving disc and the path traced by the hole is marked out on the paper.

Program 10.22 generates cycloids of the type produced when a disc is rolled around the interior of a larger circle. These tend to produce the most pleasing patterns. A single such cycloid is illustr- ated in Figure 10.21a. This was produced by a call of the subroutine captioned 'pattern' with N = 1, R1 = 432, R2 = 252 and R3 = 210 The significance of the other parameters are not relevant in this case and will be explained shortly. Because N = 1, this results in a single call of the subroutine captioned 'cycloid' with 'THETA = 0' and R3 unchanged. R1 and R2 are the radii of the circle and R3 is the 'pen radius'. The significance of the radii R1, R2, R3 and the two angles 'THETA1' and 'THETA2' used during plotting are illustrated in

Figure 10.20. 'SIN' and 'COS' are very time consuming functions and before plotting starts the program initialises a table of values of 'SIN' and 'COS' for angles from 0° to 360°. The relative values of R1 to R2 determine the number of 'petals' a cycloid will have, and the value of R3 how fat and how long the petals are. Figure 10.21b shows a single cycloid with more petals.

Pleasing patterns can be obtained by superimposing several cycloids with different 'R3' values (Figure 10.21c) or different start-

```
 10 DIM SINE(360),COSINE(360)
 20 PI = 3.141593
 30 DEF FNRAD(DEGREES) = DEGREES*PI/180
 40 FOR T = 0 TO 90
 50   S = SIN(FNRAD(T)) : C = COS(FNRAD(T))
 60   SINE(T) = S : SINE(360-T) = -S
 70   SINE(180-T) = S : SINE(180+T) = -S
 80   COSINE(T) = C : COSINE(360-T) = C
 90   COSINE(180-T) = -C : COSINE(180+T) = -C
100 NEXT T
110 SCREEN 2 : CLS
120 WINDOW (-800,-512)-(799,511)
130 N = 1 : R1 = 432 : R2 = 252 : R3 = 210 : R3INC = 0 : THETAINC = 0
140 GOSUB 160  'pattern
150 END

160 'SUBROUTINE pattern
170   INC1 = 5 : INC2 = R1*INC1/R2
180   CR = R1-R2
190   THETA = 0
200   FOR I = 1 TO N
210     GOSUB 250  'cycloid
220     THETA = THETA+THETAINC : R3 = R3+R3INC
230   NEXT I
240 RETURN

250 'SUBROUTINE cycloid
260   THETA1 = THETA : THETA2 = 0
270   PSET ((CR+R3)*COSINE(THETA1),(CR+R3)*SINE(THETA1))
280   THETA1 = (THETA1+INC1) MOD 360
290   CX = CR*COSINE(THETA1)
300   CY = CR*SINE(THETA1)
310   THETA2 = THETA2+INC2
320   IF THETA2 > THETA1 THEN THETA2 = THETA2-360
330   THETA3 = (THETA1-THETA2+0.001) MOD 360
340   XINC = R3*COSINE(THETA3)
350   YINC = R3*SINE(THETA3)
360   LINE -(CX+XINC,CY+YINC)
370   IF (THETA1 = THETA) AND (THETA3 = THETA) THEN RETURN ELSE GOTO 280
380 RETURN
```

Program 10.22 A cycloid generator.

ing values for 'THETA1' (Figure 10.21d). The first parameter (n) supplied to the subroutine captioned 'pattern' selects the number of cycloids to be superimposed and the last two parameters 'R3INC' and 'THETAINC' determine the change in R3 and 'THETA' from one cycloid to the next.

You can see that this generator rivals the Lissajous generator in variety and at the same time gives much greater control over the design of the pattern.

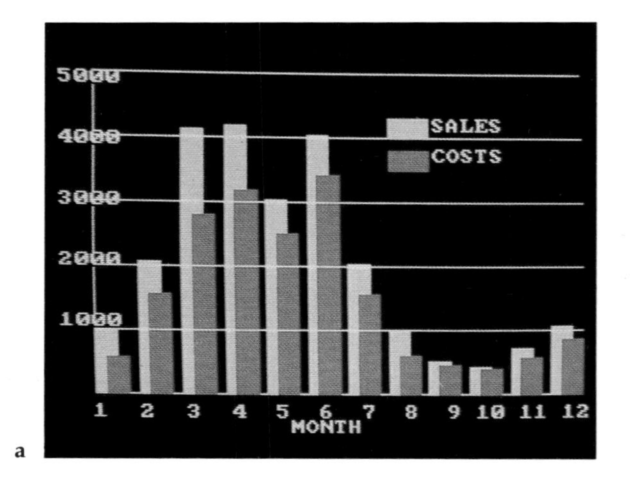

a

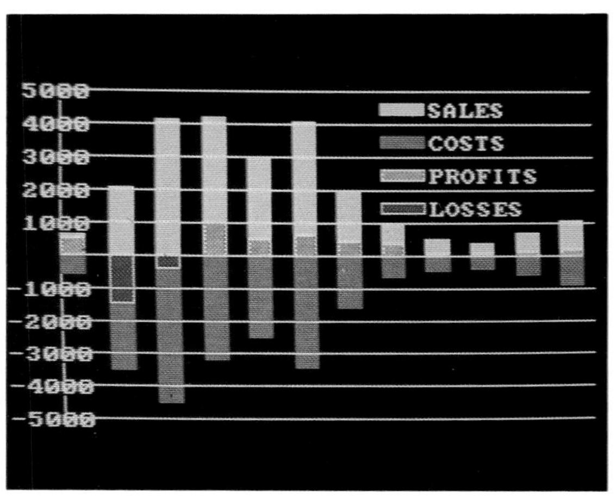

b

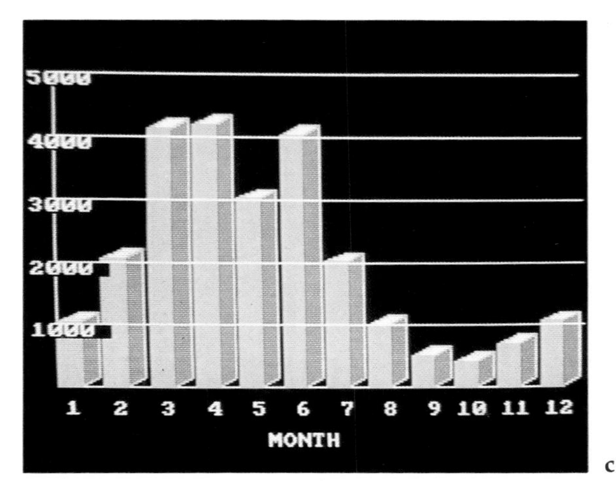

c

Plate 1 The use of colour in business graphics.

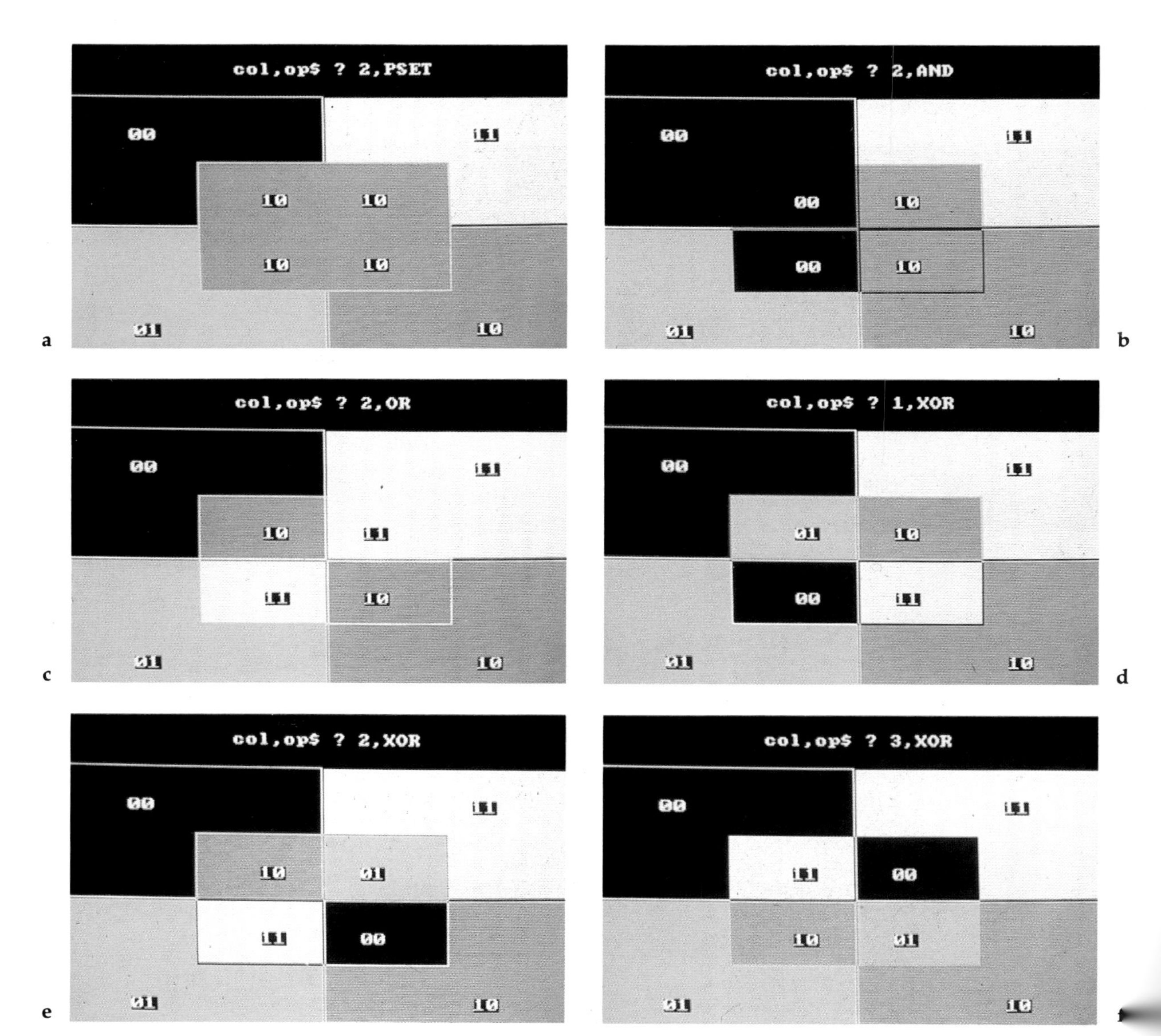

Plate 2 Illustration of the effect of plotting under the control of various logical actions in SCREEN 1. The screen originally contained four squares filled with the available colours. The four small squares in the centre of each figure were plotted by using the colour and logical action shown in the same figure. This shows how the colour laid down by PUT depends on the logical action, the colour sent and the colour already on the screen.

a

b

Plate 3 Using the screen memory to create four independent image planes with priority: (a) animated car is moving in the midground plane; (b) animated car is moving in the rear-ground plane.

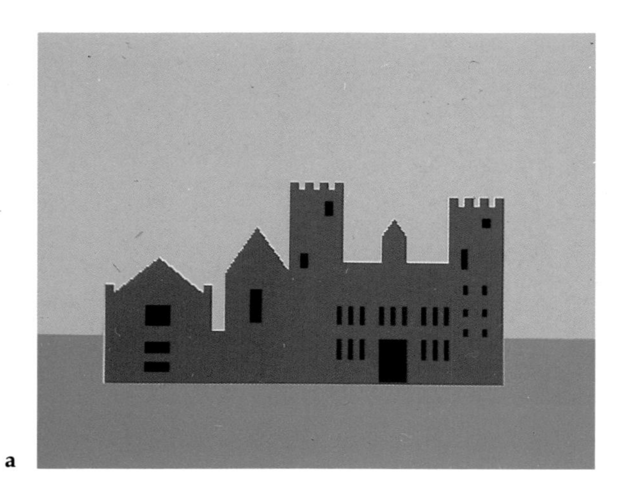
a

b

c

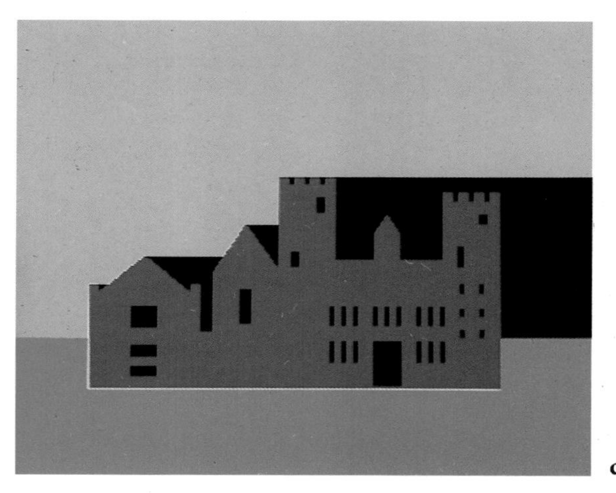
d

Plate 4 Three different flood-fill algorithms in progress: (a) filling regions that have convoluted shapes requires a general flood-fill algorithm; (b) simple point queueing algorithm showing diagonal 'wavefronts'; (c) queueing algorithm that works on horizontal rows of pixels; (d) recursive algorithm that works on horizontal rows of pixels.

Plate 5
A colour version of a caption effect suggested in Chapter 3. In this illustration three variables are used – scaling, rotation and translation.

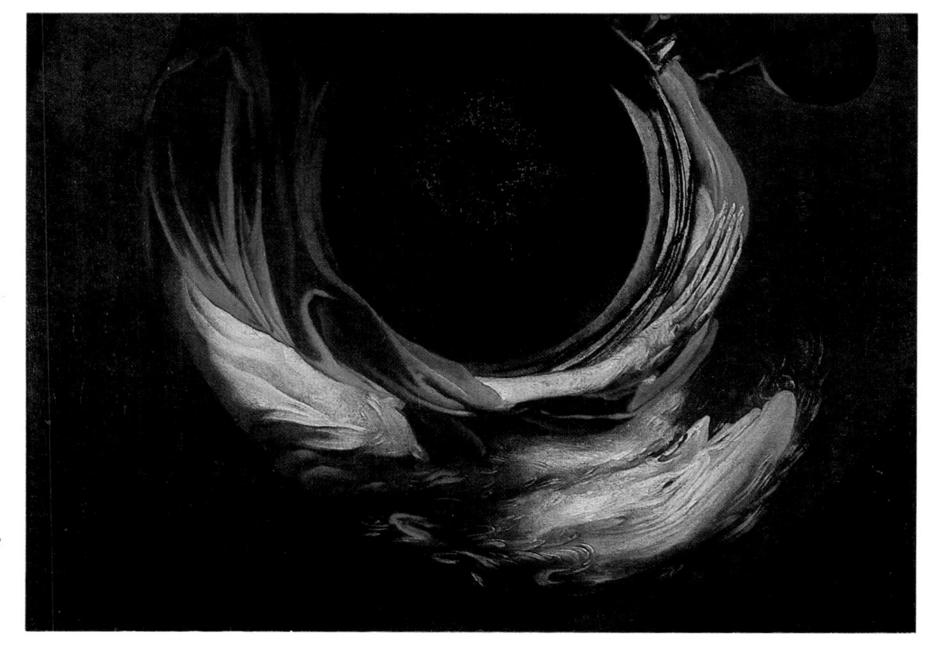

Plate 6
An anamorphic painting: 'St Jerome praying' c1635 by a French follower of Caravaggio.

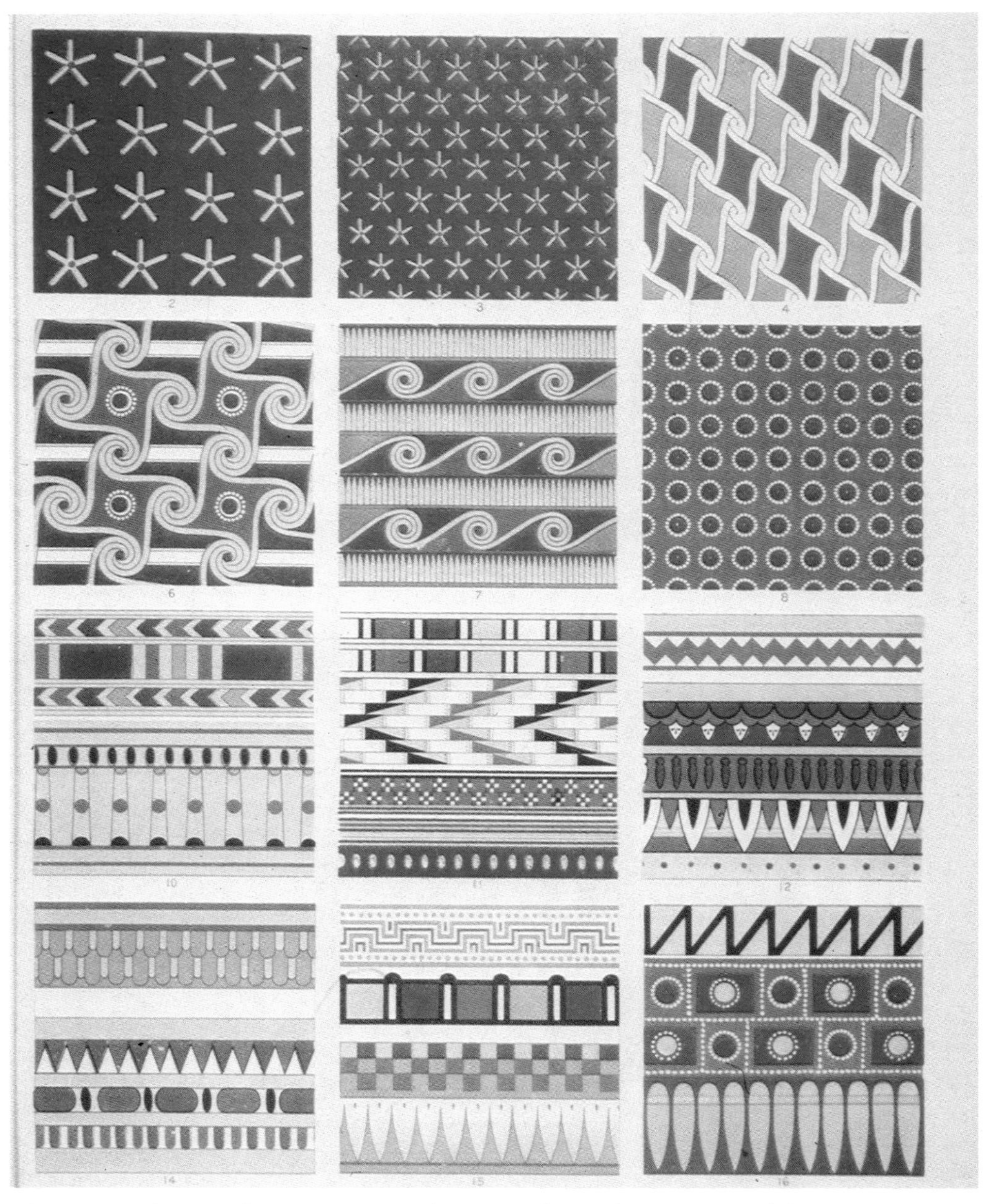

Plate 7 A selection of Egyptian network patterns from 'The Grammar of Ornament'.

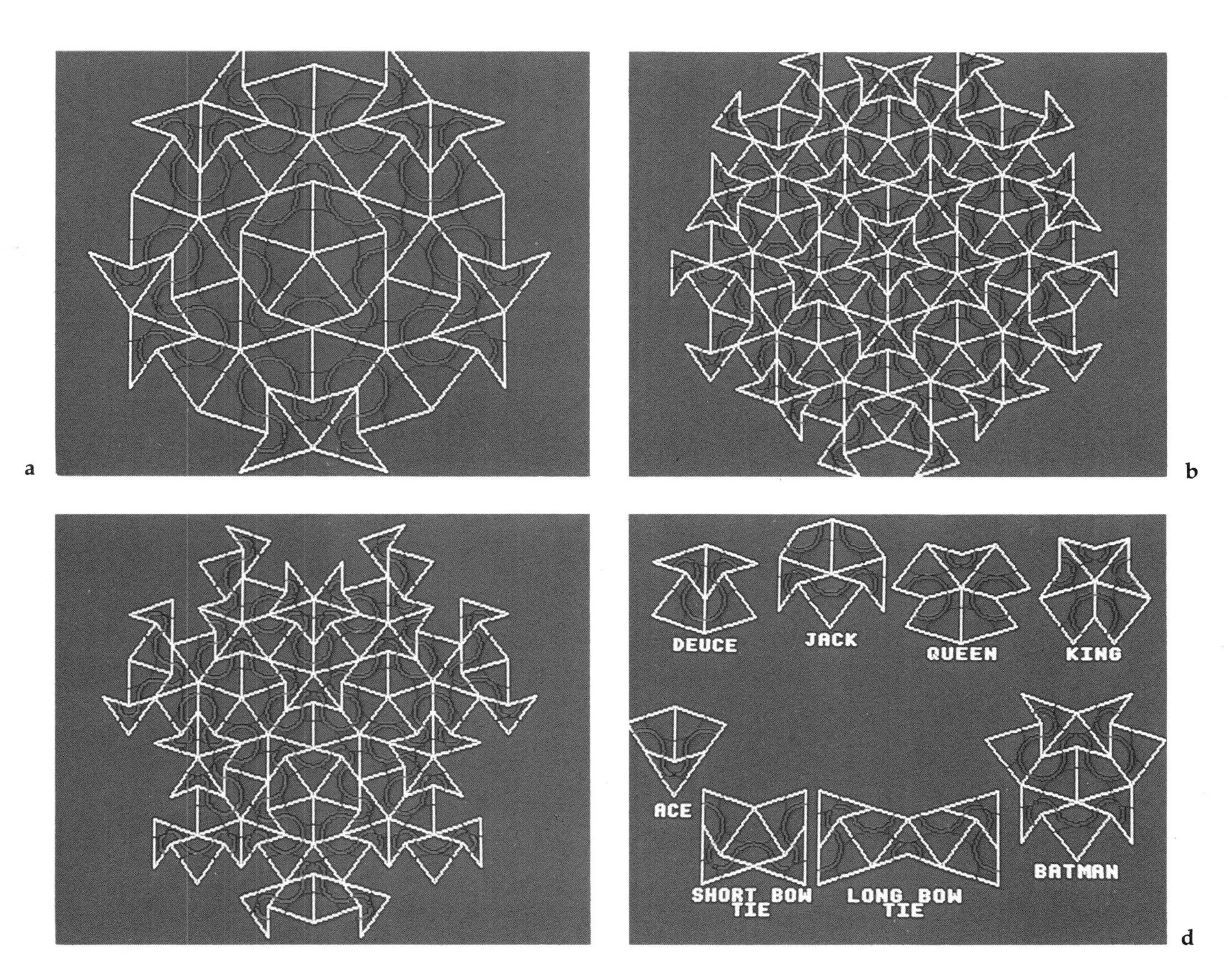

Plate 8 Penrose tessellations: non-periodic tessellations made from just two tiles – the Penrose kite and dart (white lines). The red and black lines show the permitted joinings: (a) the 'sun' pattern; (b) the 'star' pattern; (c) a pattern built around 'batman'; (d) a selection of single motifs with their popular names.

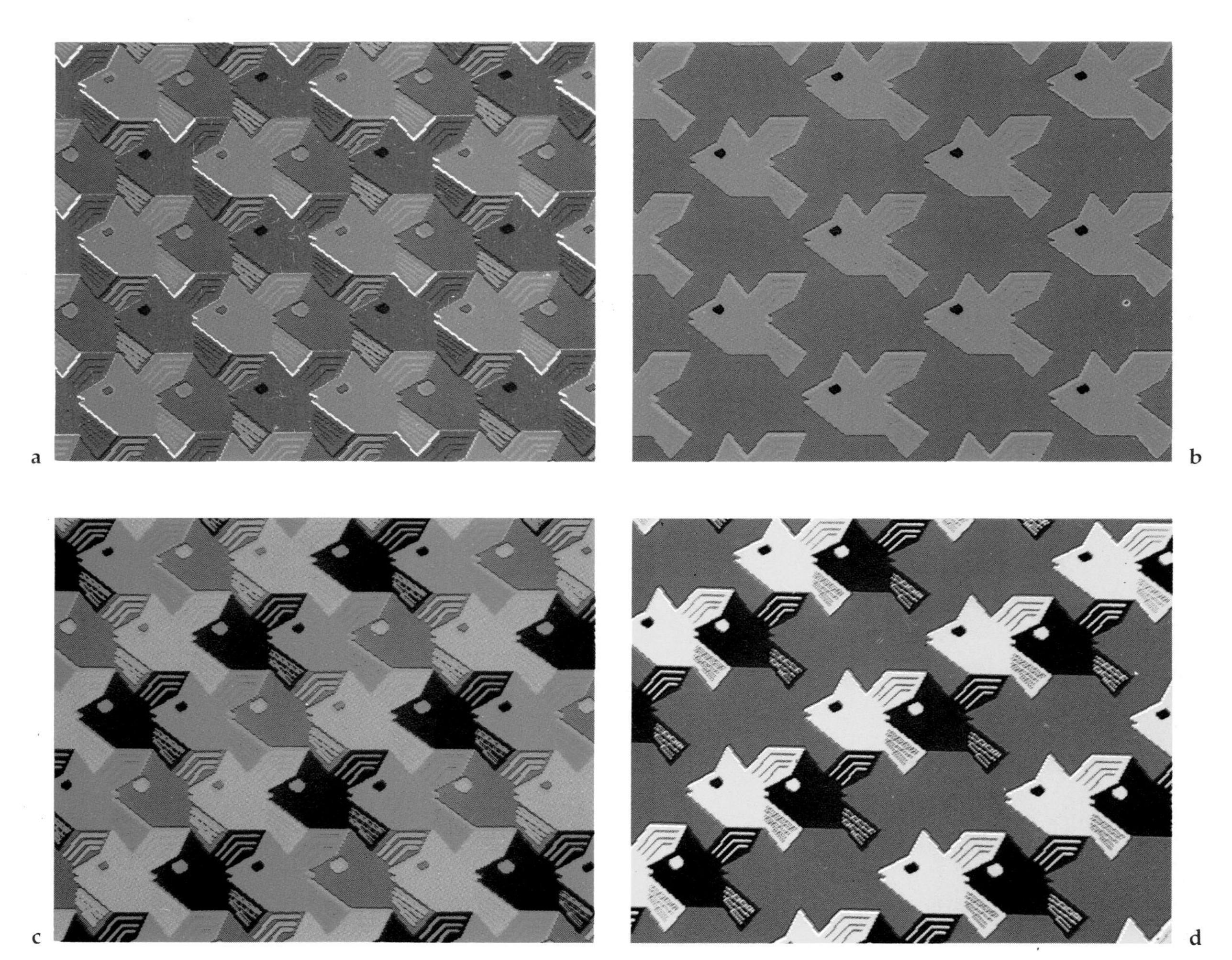

Plate 9 Colour variation of tessellation patterns: (a) the flying fish tessellation using three colours; (b) a two-colour version of 9a (after palette changes) converts the tessellation to a network pattern; (c) the flying fish tessellation using four colours; (d) a three-colour version of 9c (after palette changes).

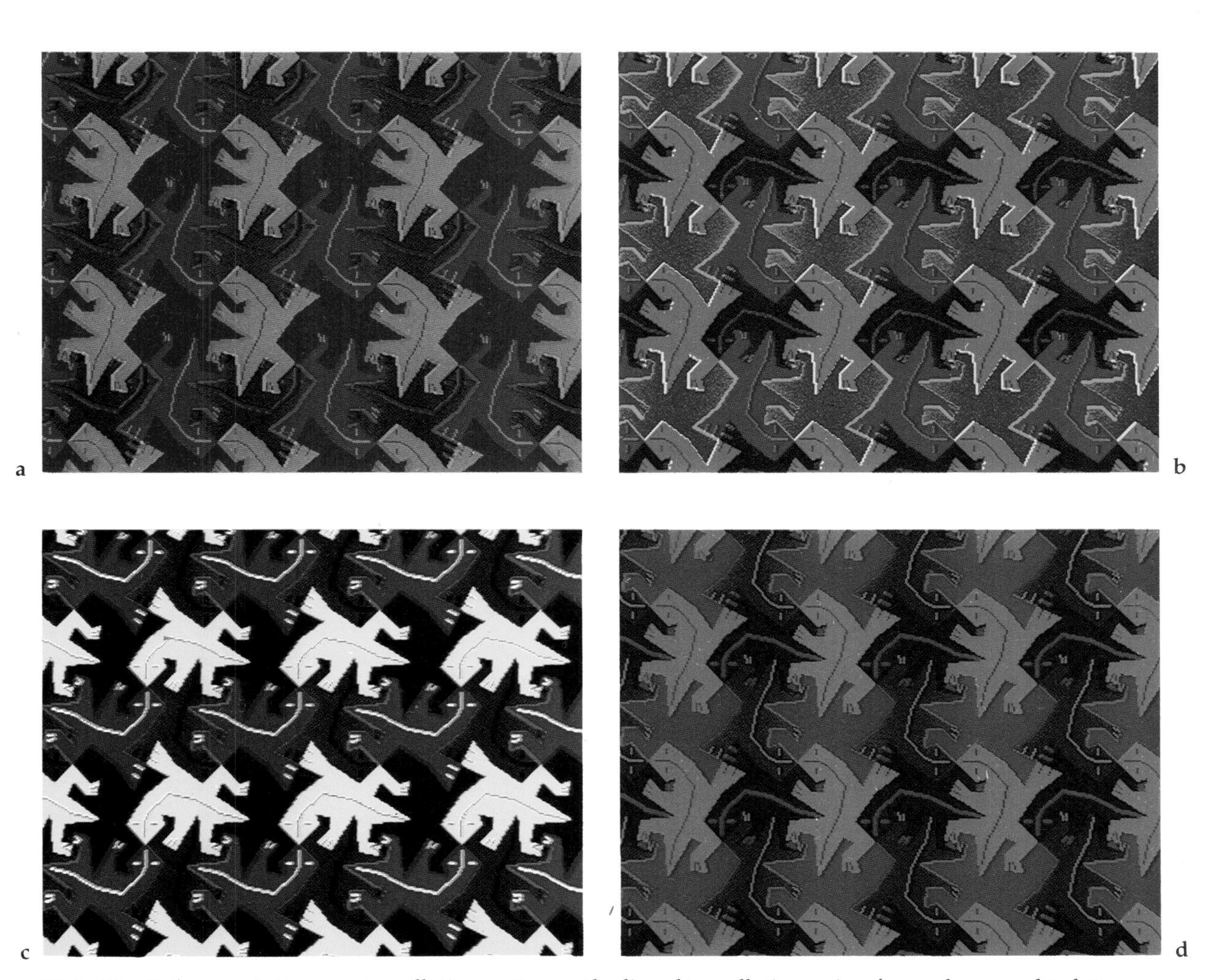

Plate 10 Colour variations on tessellation patterns: the lizard tessellation using four colours and palette changes.

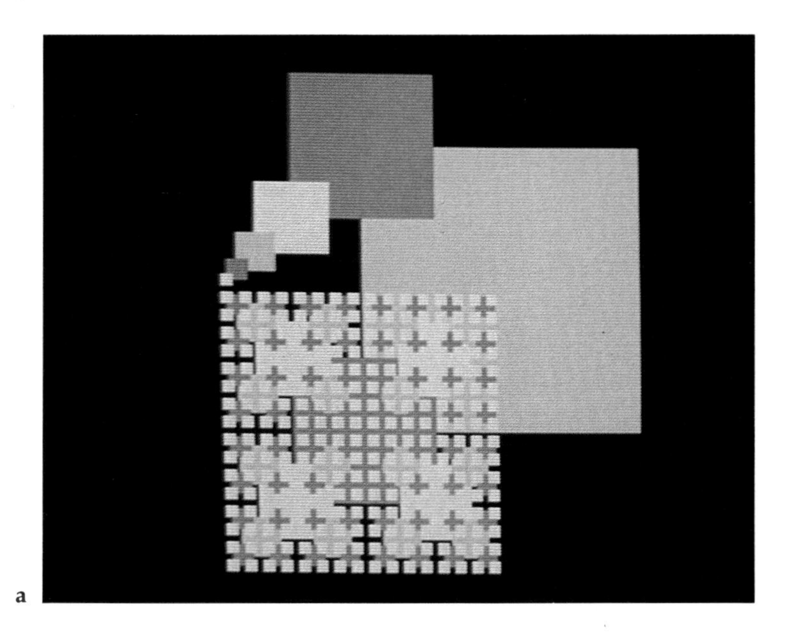
a

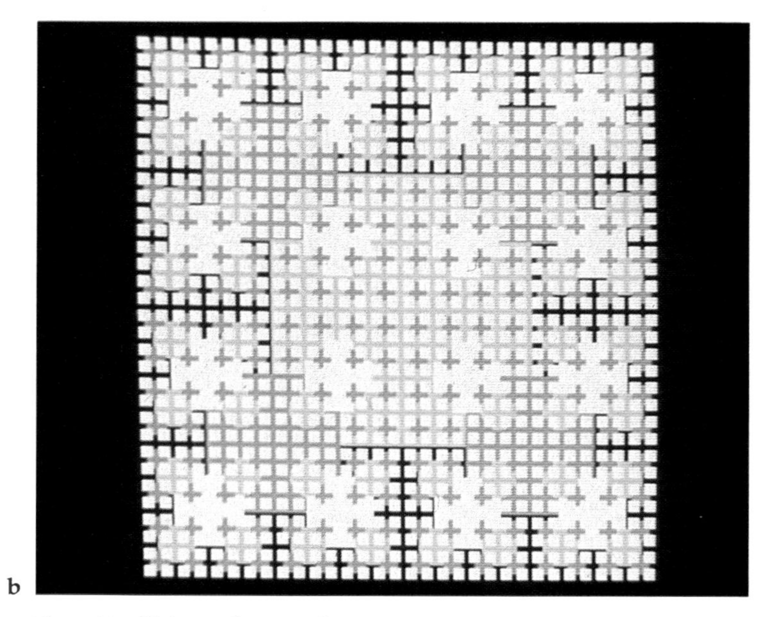
b

Plate 11 Using colour in the recursive square program: 11a shows the sequence in progress.

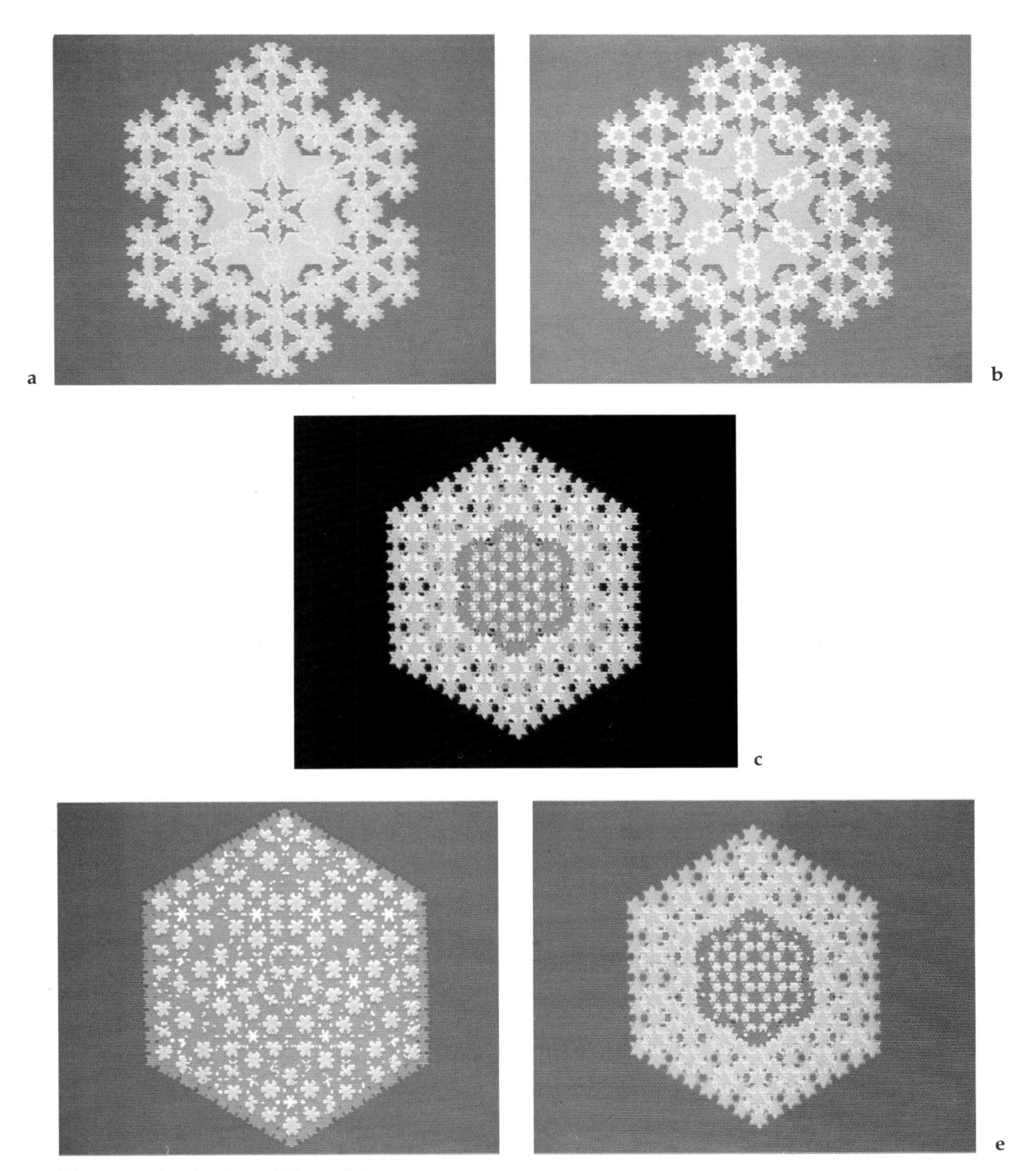

Plate 12 A selection of Koch flakes.

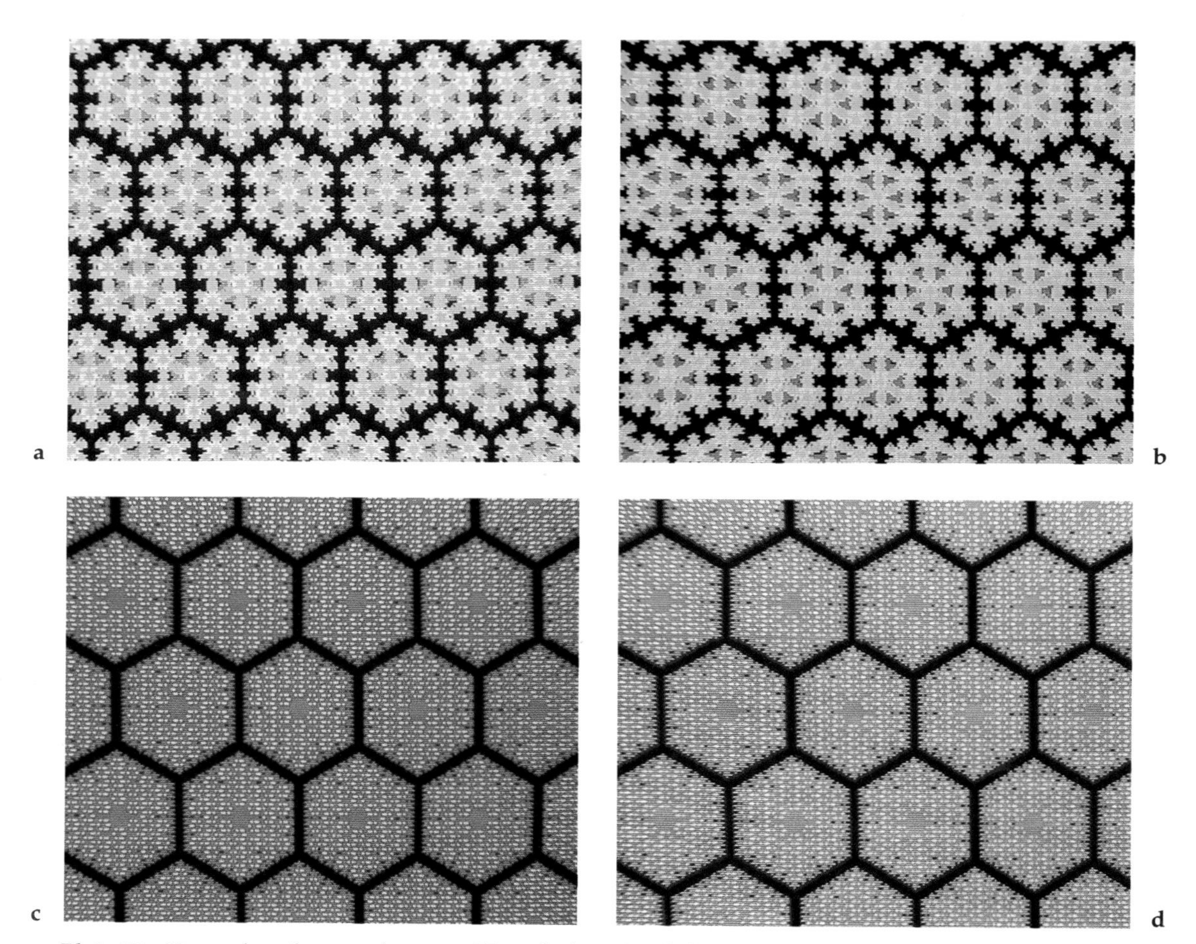

Plate 13 Examples of network group 17 made from Koch flakes: (a) and (b) are the same pattern, apart from palette changes, as are (c) and (d).

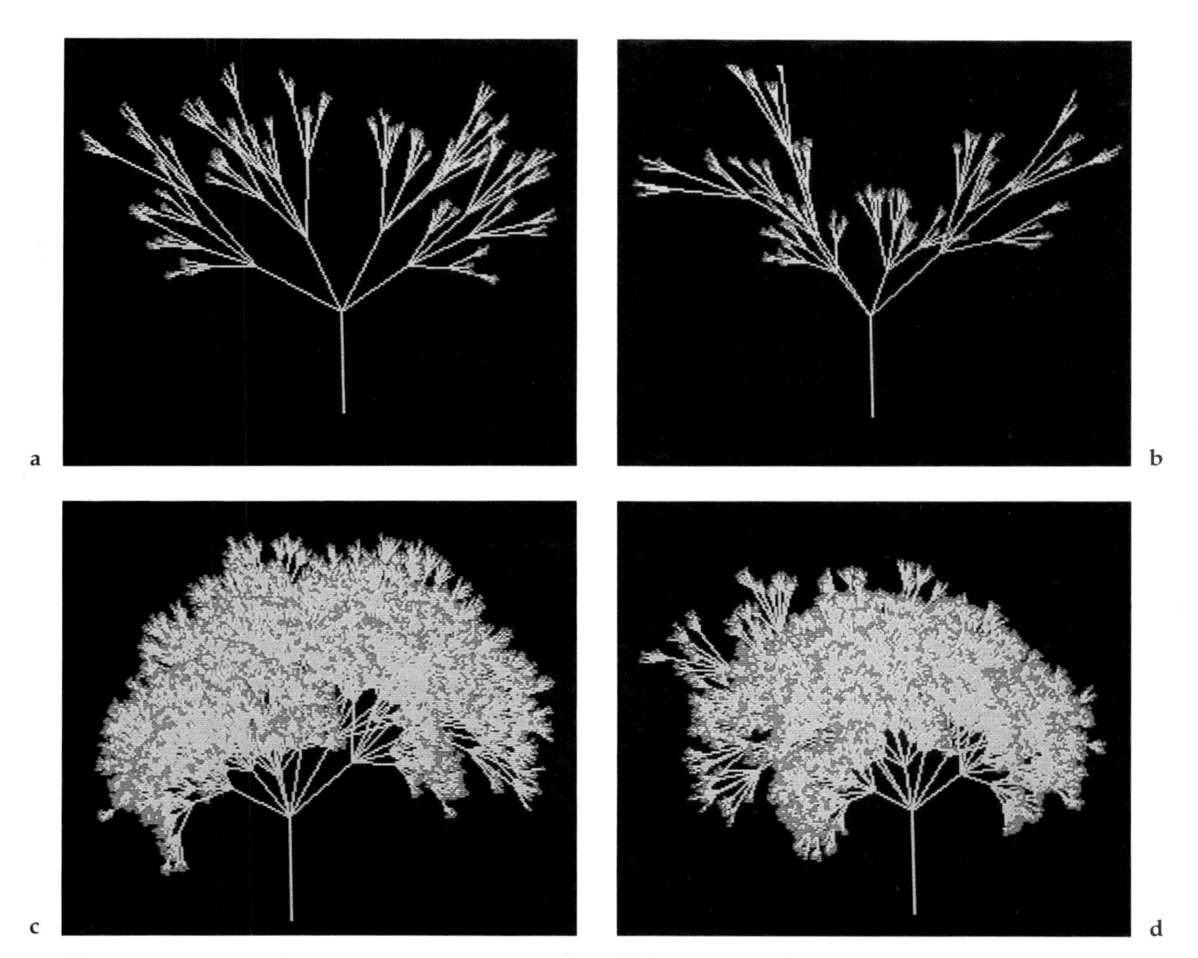

Plate 14 Recursively generated tree shapes: (a) and (b) two runs of the program using the same 'skeletal' parameters; (c) and (d) two runs of the program using the same 'bushy' parameters.

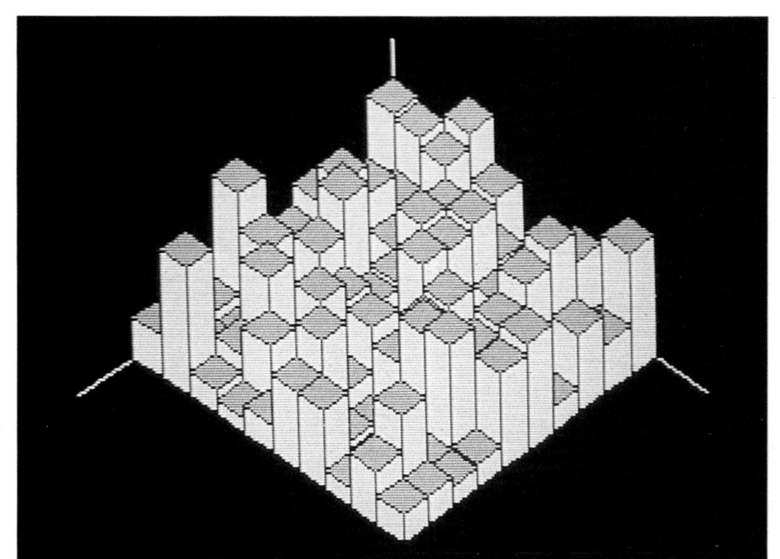

Plate 15
A common pseudo-three-dimensional image that uses simple priority painting to delete hidden surfaces.

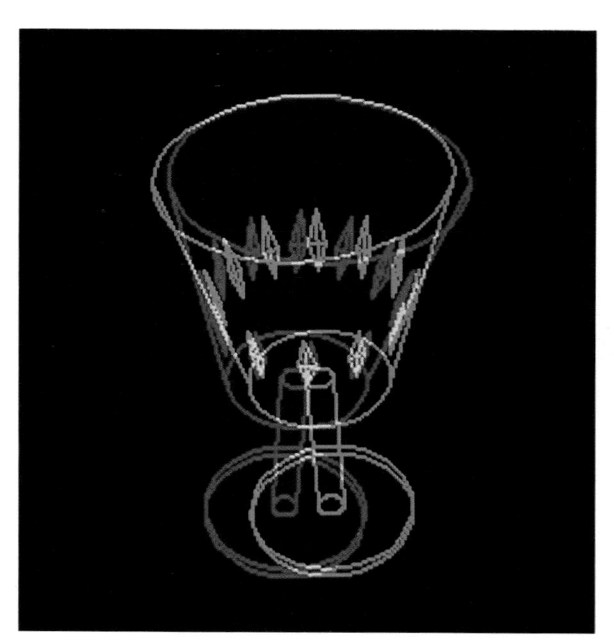

Plate 16
A stereo pair.

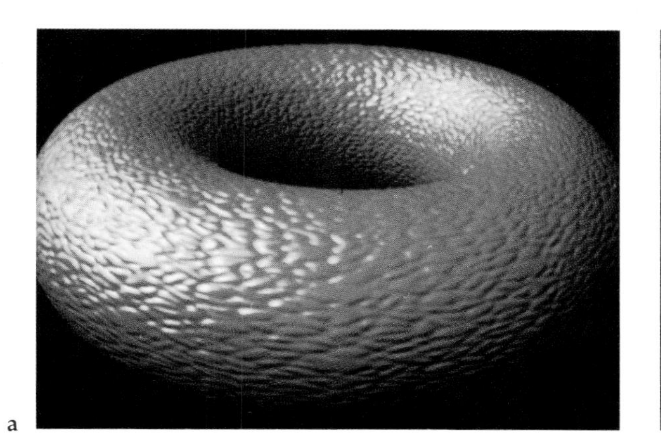

a b

Plate 17
Advanced computer-generated images by J. Blinn, courtesy of University of Utah: (a) a toroid whose textured surface shows both diffuse and specular reflection; (b) a strawberry showing both diffuse and specular reflection.

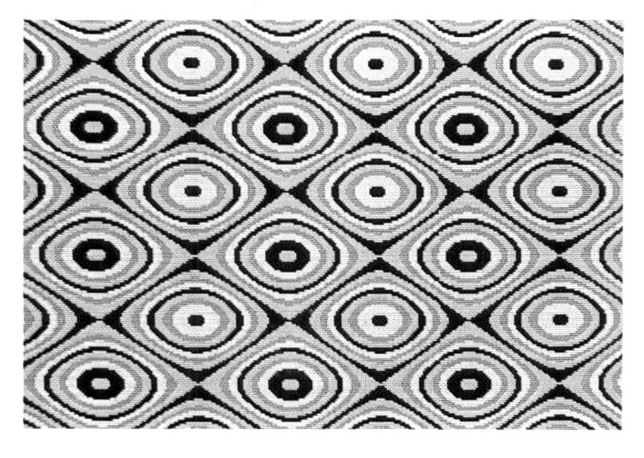

Plate 18 The function $f(x,y) = \sin(x) + \cos(y)$ using different colours to represent different function values.

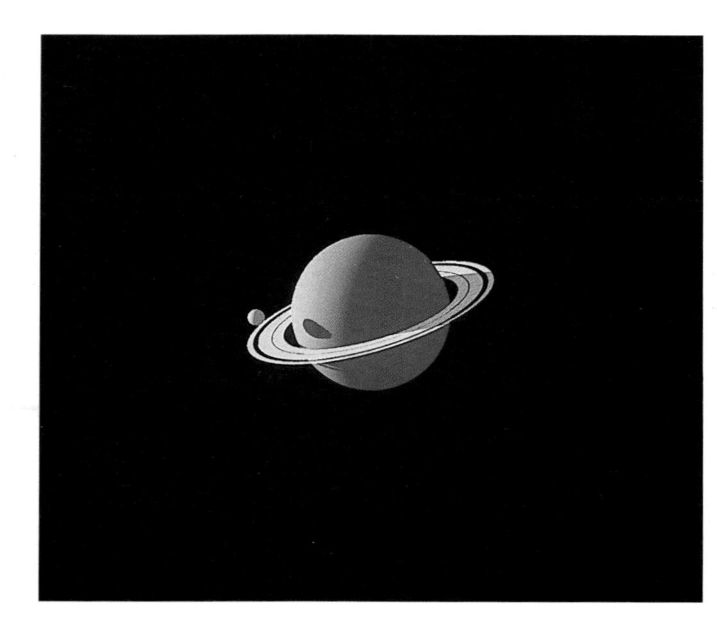

Plate 19
An elegant use of an 8-bit system and look-up table. Only a few colours are defined for the planetary rings and moon. The remainder of the rows in the look-up table are used to define a finely varying set for the planet. (By kind permission of the IBM UK Scientific Centre, Winchester.)

Plate 20
A frame-grabbed image showing the colour realism that can be attained with an 8-bit system. (By kind permission of the IBM Spain Scientific Centre, Madrid.)

Appendix 1 Summary of screen mode and colour facilities

TEXT FACILITIES AVAILABLE IN DIFFERENT SCREEN MODES

Screen	*Colours available*	*Characters per line*	*Lines*
0	16	40/80	24/5
1	4	40	24/5
2	2	80	24/5
3	16	20	24/5
4	4	40	24/5
5	16	40	24/5
6	4	80	24/5

GRAPHICS FACILITIES AVAILABLE IN DIFFERENT SCREEN MODES

Screen	*Colours available*	*Graphics resolution*
1	4	320 × 200
2	2	640 × 200
3	16	160 × 200
4	4	320 × 200
5	16	320 × 200
6	4	640 × 200

MEMORY REQUIREMENTS FOR DIFFERENT MODES

Screen	*Memory requirements*
0	2K/4K
1	16K
2	16K
3	16K
4	16K
5	32K
6	32K

OVERALL COLOUR RANGE

There are 16 actual colours available. These colours are numbered from 0 to 15.

Actual colour numbers and corresponding colours

Colour number	*Colour name*
0	black
1	blue
2	green
3	cyan
4	red
5	magenta
6	brown
7	white
8	grey
9	light blue
10	light green
11	light cyan
12	light red
13	light magenta
14	yellow
15	high-intensity white

COLOUR CODES IN DIFFERENT SCREEN MODES

In each screen mode colours are referred to by code numbers (attributes) from 0 upwards. The code numbers for a mode can be made to refer to any combination of actual colours (using PALETTE). There is an initial or default setting for each mode which specifies the colour that you get if you do not use PALETTE.

2 colour mode (SCREEN 2)

Colour code numbers	*Default actual colours*	
	colour	*number*
0	black	0
1	white	7

4 colour mode (SCREENs 1, 3 and 6)

Colour code numbers	*Default actual colours*	
	colour	*number*
0	black	0
1	cyan	3
2	magenta	5
3	white	7

In the 16-colour mode (SCREENs 0, 3 and 5) the colour codes are initially set to the corresponding actual colour numbers.

Appendix 2 Bits, bytes and hex

For the majority of straightforward programming applications, the user of the PC need not concern himself or herself with the details of how things like numbers and strings are represented inside the computer, but for some advanced applications a more detailed knowledge of the internal representation of information is required.

BITS

All information stored in a modern digital computer is held in the form of 'binary digits'. In this context, the word 'binary' means 'having two possible values', and a binary digit can thus be set to one of two possible values. We usually abbreviate the term binary digit to 'bit'.

When we write a bit on paper, we represent its two possible values as 0 or 1. Inside a computer, a bit might be represented by a magnetic field lying in one of two possible directions, or by an electronic voltage that can be positive or negative. The programmer, however, need not be concerned with the practicalities of representing a bit electronically or magnetically. When he or she needs to think in terms of the binary representation of information, he or she can think entirely in terms of ones and zeros.

With one bit, we can represent only two possible values, 0 or 1, and in fact some of the information in your PC is coded using only one bit. For example, in SCREEN 2, one bit is used to code the colour of each pixel on the screen. Each pixel can be one of two colours, colour 0 or colour 1.

Bit patterns

Bits are usually organized into groups or 'patterns'. With a group of two bits, each bit can be one of two values giving 2×2 possible different patterns.

First bit	*Second bit*	*Bit pattern*
0	0	00
0	1	01
1	0	10
1	1	11

A two-bit pattern is used to code the colour of each pixel on the screen in a four-colour mode such as SCREEN 1.

With three bits, there are 2×2×2 possible different patterns and so on:

No. of bits in pattern	*Example*	*No. of possible different patterns*
1	0	2
2	10	4 = 2×2
3	011	8 = 2×2×2
4	1010	16 = 2×2×2×2
5	10100	32 = 2×2×2×2×2
6	011010	64 = 2×2×2×2×2×2
7	1101001	128 = 2×2×2×2×2×2×2
8	11000101	256 = 2×2×2×2×2×2×2×2

Bit numbering

The bits in a bit pattern are usually referred to by numbering them from 0 upwards from right to left, bit0, bit1, bit2 and so on.

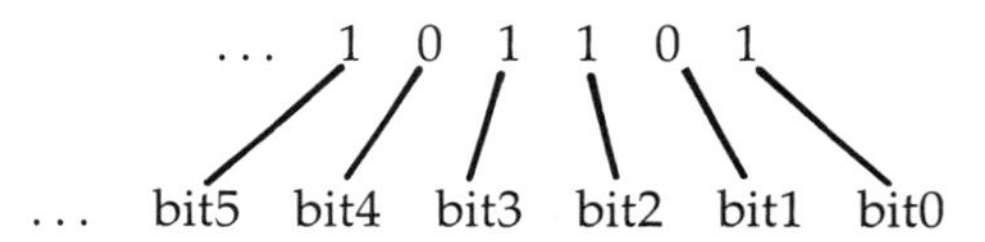

BYTES

A group of eight bits is called a 'byte'. One 'word' on your PC contains two bytes or one 16-bit pattern. The entire store that is accessible to the user might consist of 131 072 bytes. We usually quote storage capacity in 'K' where:

1K = 1024 $(1024 = 2^{10})$

Because we are working on a binary system, everything is organized behind the scenes in powers of 2. Thus we might say that a PC has 128 Kbytes of store, i.e. 128*1024 bytes or 128*1024*8 bits.

8-bit integers

When we use a group of decimal digits to represent a non-negative integer, each digit has a weight that is a different power of 10. For example, with five digits:

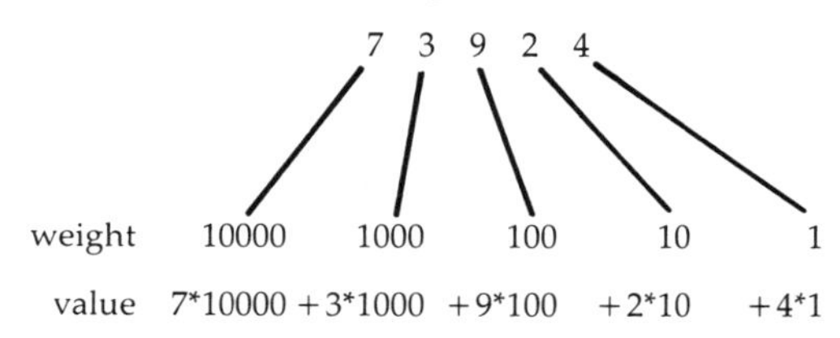

When we use a bit pattern to represent a non-negative integer, only two values are available for each digit, so we give each digit a weight that is a power of 2. For example, with a 6-bit pattern we might have:

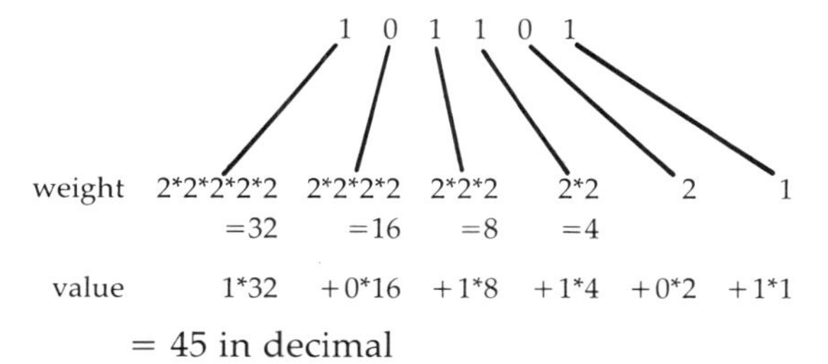

When we use a full byte to represent an integer in this way, we have:

Binary		*Decimal*
00000000	=	0
00000001	=	1
00000010	=	2
00000011	=	3
.		.
.		.
.		.
01111110	=	126
01111111	=	127
10000000	=	128
.		.
.		.
.		.
11111110	=	254
11111111	=	255

We saw earlier that there are 256 different 8-bit patterns and they can be used in this way to represent integers in the range 0 to 255. Because it contributes least weight to an integer, the rightmost bit, bit0, is usually called the least significant bit and the leftmost bit is called the most significant bit.

8-bit positive and negative integers

If we want to use bytes to represent both positive and negative integers, we have to define a different correspondence between the available bit patterns and the values they represent. The representation normally used is known as '2s complement' representation. A detailed description of this is beyond the scope of this book, but the next table shows how a byte would be used to represent negative as well as positive integers. The bit patterns that were previously used to represent positive integers from 128 up to 255 are now used *in the same order as before* to represent the negative integers from –128 up to –1. In particular, –1 is represented by a bit pattern that consists entirely of ones. This representation for negative numbers may seem rather strange, but it has many advantages when the computer is doing calculations that involve positive and negative numbers.

Binary		*Decimal*
10000000	=	–128
10000001	=	–127
10000010	=	–126
.		.
.		.
.		.
11111110	=	–2
11111111	=	–1
00000000	=	0
00000001	=	1
00000010	=	2
.		.
.		.
.		.
01111110	=	126
01111111	=	127

Note that you cannot tell by looking at a bit pattern what sort of information it is being used to represent. This is determined by the context in which it is used and by the way it is processed by the circuits of the computer. For example, the same bit pattern might be used in different contexts to represent an integer or a character code.

HEXADECIMAL NOTATION

When we are working with bit patterns, it becomes very tedious having to write long sequences of ones and zeros when we want to specify a particular bit pattern. We could abbreviate a byte by writing it as the equivalent positive decimal number, such as 179, but it is not at all obvious if we write 179 that we are talking about the bit pattern 10110011. When we want to abbreviate a bit pattern in a way that is not too far removed from its binary form, it is usual to write it in 'hexadecimal' notation (or hex for short). The bit pattern is first divided into groups of four bits. There are 16 possible different patterns of four bits and each of these possible patterns can be represented by a single 'hexadecimal digit' as follows:

4-bit pattern	*Hexadecimal digit*	*4-bit pattern*	*Hexadecimal digit*
0000	0	1000	8
0001	1	1001	9
0010	2	1010	A
0011	3	1011	B
0100	4	1100	C

0101	5	1101	D
0110	6	1110	E
0111	7	1111	F

We can thus write the bit pattern 10100011 in hex as A3:

```
10100011
 A   3
```

In PC BASIC we can write numbers in a program in hex if we precede the number by the symbol '&H'. Thus we write &HB3. Here are some other examples of bytes and the corresponding hex and decimal numbers:

Byte	*Hex*	*Decimal*
00011111	&H1F	31
00101110	&H2E	46
01101001	&H69	105
11111111	&HFF	255

Note that &H69 is quite different from decimal 69 which would be represented by the bit pattern:

01000101 = &H45

Because one hexadecimal digit corresponds to four binary digits, it is easy to visualize the bit pattern corresponding to a hexadecimal number (provided that we are familiar with the 16 patterns that correspond to the 16 hex digits). Thus, for example, &HB7 is easily visualized as:

```
 &HB7
10110111
```

and &HFA is easily visualized as:

```
 &HFA
11111010
```

16-bit and 32-bit numbers

An integer variable in PC BASIC occupies two bytes or 16 bits. A number stored in such a variable is coded as a pattern of 16 bits. The way in which a 16-bit pattern is used to represent positive and negative integers is a simple extension of the 8-bit 2s complement representation introduced earlier. Note in particular that –1 is represented by a pattern of 16 ones. A single precision variable occupies four bytes and is represented by a pattern of 32 bits. Details of how real numbers are coded as bit patterns are beyond the scope of this book.

LOGICAL OPERATIONS ON BIT PATTERNS

The various logical plotting modes selected by PUT use logical operations on bit patterns when plotting new information on the screen. For this reason alone, some knowledge of these operations is necessary. The logical operators AND, OR, XOR and NOT treat the values to which they are applied as bit patterns and operate on the individual bits of these patterns. A detailed knowledge of how these operations work is occasionally useful in advanced programming applications.

When a logical operation is applied to a bit pattern or to a pair of bit patterns, the individual bits are handled separately in creating the resultant bit pattern. AND, OR and XOR are each applied to a pair of bit patterns of the same length and the result is another bit pattern of the same length. NOT is applied to a single bit pattern and the result is another bit pattern of the same length. We shall illustrate the behaviour of the logical operations on bytes, but they will behave in exactly the same way on shorter or longer bit patterns.

AND

Each bit in the new pattern is the result of 'ANDing' the two bits in the same position in the two given bit patterns according to the following table:

bit1	bit2	bit1 AND bit2
0	0	0
0	1	0
1	0	0
1	1	1

Thus, for example:

byte1	10110100
byte2	01100101
byte1 AND byte2	00100100

OR

Each bit in the new pattern is the result of 'ORing' the two bits in the same position in the given bit patterns according to the following table:

bit1	bit2	bit1 OR bit2
0	0	0
0	1	1
1	0	1
1	1	1

Thus, for example:

byte1	10110100
byte2	01100101
byte1 OR byte2	11110101

XOR

Each bit in the new pattern is the result of 'exclusive ORing' the two bits in the same position in the given bit patterns according to the following table:

bit1	bit2	bit1 XOR bit2
0	0	0
0	1	1
1	0	1
1	1	0

The name of the operator derives from the fact that it 'excludes' the case where both bits to which it is applied are 1. Thus, for example:

byte1	10110100
byte2	01100101
byte1 XOR byte2	11010001

NOT

Each bit in the new bit pattern is the result of 'negating' the same bit in the given bit pattern. NOT produces the 'logical inverse' of the given bit pattern by changing 0s to 1s and 1s to 0s.

bit	NOT bit
0	1
1	0

Thus, for example:

byte	10110100
NOT byte	01001011

Representation of TRUE and FALSE

In PC BASIC the value TRUE is represented by a bit pattern containing nothing but 1s and FALSE is represented by a bit pattern containing nothing but 0s. When these values are stored in numeric variables, they look like the numeric values –1 and 0. We have often introduced variables 'TRUE' and 'FALSE' set to these two values.

Appendix 3 Matrix notation and multiplication

In Chapter 3 we have made use of matrix notation in linear transforms. We say that a point (x,y) transforms to a point (xt,yt):

$$xt = ax + by$$
$$yt = cx + dy$$

Given that all our transformations are of this form we can say that the transform T can be represented by the matrix:

$$\begin{bmatrix} a & c \\ b & d \end{bmatrix}$$

Now using matrix notation to represent the above operation we rewrite the equations in the form:

$$(xt, yt) = (x, y) \begin{bmatrix} a & c \\ b & d \end{bmatrix}$$

On the right hand side we are multiplying a row matrix (representing a single point in two-dimensional space) by a 2×2 matrix. The equation specified in the matrix notation is identical in every respect to the non-matrix form of the equation. To obtain xt from the matrix form we multiply the row matrix (x,y) by the first column:

$$xt = (x, y) \begin{bmatrix} a & . \\ b & . \end{bmatrix}$$

$$= ax + by$$

and to obtain yt from the matrix form we multiply the row vector by the second column:

$$yt = (x, y) \begin{bmatrix} . & c \\ .. & d \end{bmatrix}$$

$$= cx + dy$$

The other context in which we used matrix multiplication was to concatenate transforms together.

$$T = T1*T2$$

$$= \begin{bmatrix} a & c \\ b & d \end{bmatrix} \begin{bmatrix} e & g \\ f & h \end{bmatrix}$$

$$= \begin{bmatrix} (ae + cf) & (ag + ch) \\ (be + df) & (bg + dh) \end{bmatrix}$$

$$= \begin{bmatrix} p & r \\ q & s \end{bmatrix}$$

p is formed by taking the sum of the products of the entries in the first row of $T1$ with the first column in $T2$. q is formed by taking the sum of the products of the entries in the second row in $T1$ with the first column in $T2$. Inspecting the other two entries r and s will show how these are similarly derived. In the general case:

$$C = A^*B$$

each entry C_{ij} of the product is the sum of the products of the entries of the ith row of A with the corresponding entries of the jth column of B. We could easily write a procedure to multiply two 3×3 matrices together and this follows. In Chapter 3 we multiplied matrices together manually.

```
100 'SUBROUTINE multiplies two matrices together
110   FOR I = 1 TO 3
120     FOR J = 1 TO 3
130       INPUT A(I,J)
140     NEXT J
150   NEXT I

160   FOR I = 1 TO 3
170     FOR J = 1 TO 3
180       INPUT B(I,J)
190     NEXT I
200   NEXT J

210   FOR I = 1 TO 3
220     FOR J = 1 TO 3
230       SUM = 0
240       FOR K = 1 TO 3
250         SUM = SUM + A(I,K)*B(K,J)
260       NEXT K
270     C(I,J) = SUM
280     NEXT J
290   NEXT I
300 RETURN
```

Here we have used the usual convention when handling matrices – the first subscript is the row number, the second subscript is the column number (not to be confused with the convention for handling screen coordinates). Note that each matrix must be typed in row-wise.

Appendix 4 The viewing transformation

The viewing transformation, V, transforms points in the world coordinate system into the eye coordinate system:

$$(x_e, y_e, z_e, 1) = (x_w, y_w, z_w, 1)\ V$$

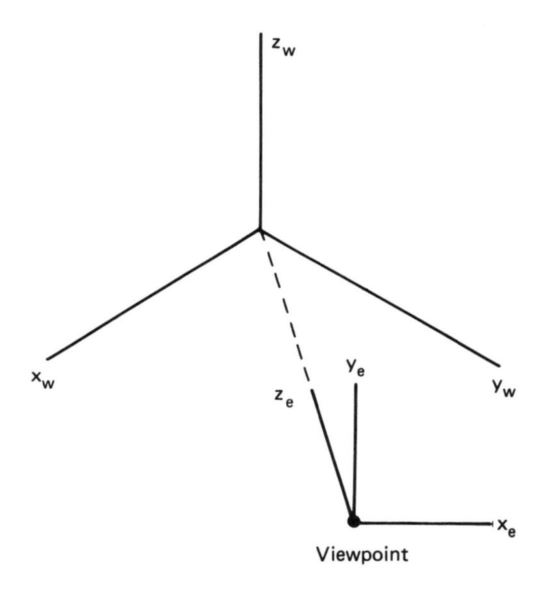

A viewpoint is given as a set of three coordinates specifying the viewpoint in the world coordinate system. An object described in the world coordinate system is viewed from this point along a certain direction. In the eye coordinate system, the z-axis points towards the world system origin and the x-axis is parallel to the x-y plane of the world system. It is standard to adopt a left-handed convention for the eye coordinate system. In the eye coordinate system the x and y-axes match the axes of the display system and the z_e direction is away from the viewpoint (into the display screen). World coordinates are normally right-handed systems so that in the computation of a net transformation matrix for the viewing transformation we would include a conversion to a left-handed system.

We can now specify the net transformation matrix as a series of translations and rotations that take us from the world coordinate system into the eye coordinate system, given a particular viewpoint.

These steps will be given as separate transformation matrices and the net transformation matrix resulting from the product will simply be stated. If you are unhappy with the derivation you can of course skip it and accept the final result – the net transformation matrix required for a viewing transformation.

Now the viewing transformation is best specified using spherical instead of cartesian coordinates. We specify a viewpoint in spherical coordinates by giving a distance from the origin ρ and two angles (θ and ϕ).

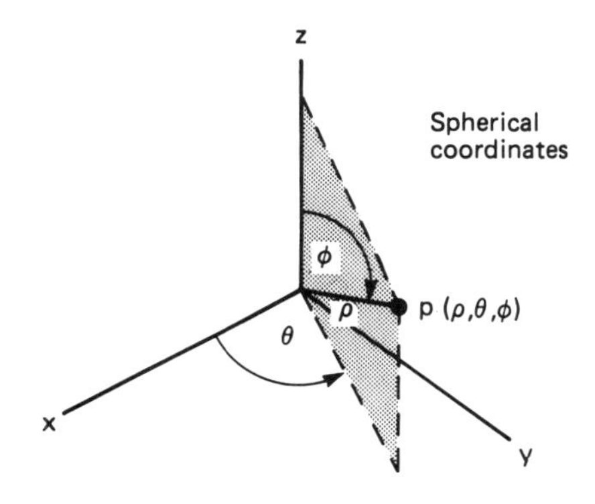

These are related to the viewpoint's cartesian coordinates as follows:

$$Tx = \rho \sin \phi \cos \theta$$
$$Ty = \rho \sin \phi \sin \theta$$
$$Tz = \rho \cos \phi$$

Another fact we require in this derivation is that to change the *origin* of a system from (0, 0, 0, 1) to (Tx, Ty, Tz, 1) we use the transformation:

$$\begin{bmatrix} 1 & 0 & 0 & 0 \\ 0 & 1 & 0 & 0 \\ 0 & 0 & 1 & 0 \\ -Tx & -Ty & -Tz & 1 \end{bmatrix}$$

Note that this is the *inverse* of the transformation that would take a point from (0, 0, 0, 1) to (Tx, Ty, Tz, 1).

The four transformations required to take the object from a world coordinate system into an eye coordinate system are:

1. Translate the world coordinate system to (Tx, Ty, Tz), the position of the viewpoint. All three axes remain parallel to their counterparts in the world system.

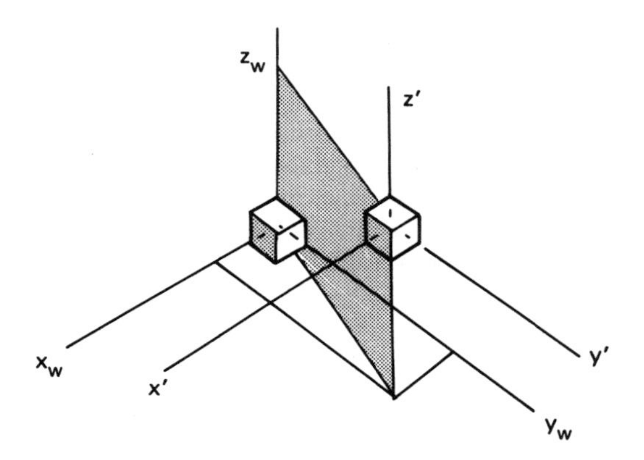

The cube in the diagram is not an object that is being transformed, but is intended to enhance an interpretation of the axes. Using spherical coordinate values for Tx, Ty, and Tz the transformation is:

$$T1 = \begin{bmatrix} 1 & 0 & 0 & 0 \\ 0 & 1 & 0 & 0 \\ 0 & 0 & 1 & 0 \\ -\rho \cos\theta \sin\phi & -\rho \sin\theta \sin\phi & -\rho \cos\phi & 1 \end{bmatrix}$$

2. The next step is to rotate the coordinate system through $(90° - \theta)$ in a *clockwise* direction about the z'-axis. The rotation matrices defined in Chapter 8 were for counter-clockwise rotation relative to a coordinate system. The transformation matrix for a clockwise rotation of the coordinate system is the same as that for a counter-clockwise rotation of a point relative to the coordinate system. The x''-axis is now normal to the plane containing ρ.

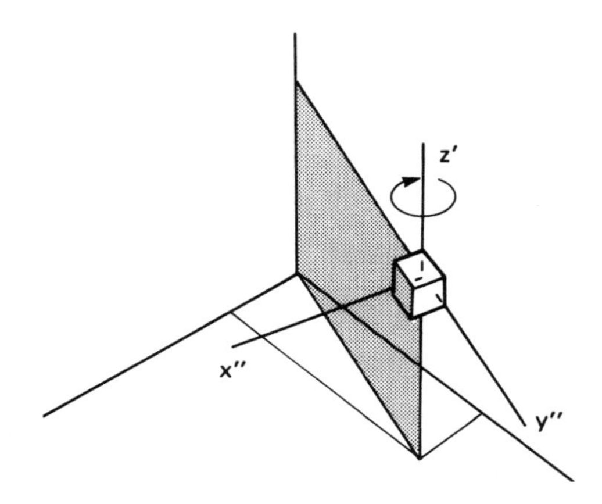

$$T2 = \begin{bmatrix} \sin\theta & \cos\theta & 0 & 0 \\ -\cos\theta & \sin\theta & 0 & 0 \\ 0 & 0 & 1 & 0 \\ 0 & 0 & 0 & 1 \end{bmatrix}$$

3. The next step is to rotate the coordinate system (180° – ϕ) counter-clockwise about the x'-axis. This makes the z'''-axis pass through the origin of the world coordinate system.

$$T3 = \begin{bmatrix} 1 & 0 & 0 & 0 \\ 0 & -\cos\phi & -\sin\phi & 0 \\ 0 & \sin\phi & -\cos\phi & 0 \\ 0 & 0 & 0 & 1 \end{bmatrix}$$

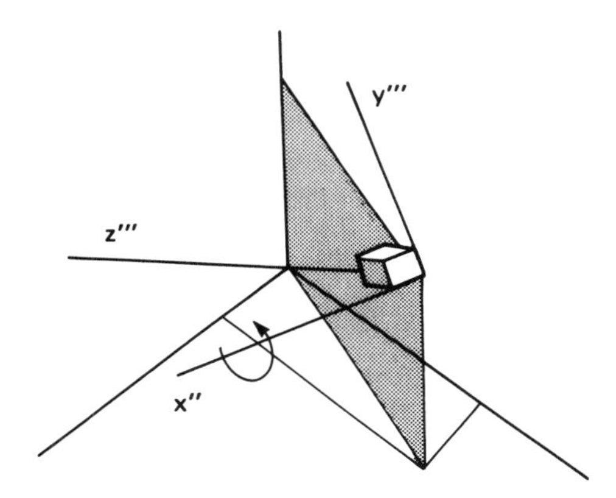

4. Finally we convert to a left-handed system as described above.

$$T4 = \begin{bmatrix} -1 & 0 & 0 & 0 \\ 0 & 1 & 0 & 0 \\ 0 & 0 & 1 & 0 \\ 0 & 0 & 0 & 1 \end{bmatrix}$$

Multiplying these together gives the net transformation matrix required for the viewing transformation.

$$V = T1{*}T2{*}T3{*}T4 = \begin{bmatrix} -\sin\theta & -\cos\theta\cos\phi & -\cos\theta\sin\phi & 0 \\ \cos\theta & -\sin\theta\cos\phi & -\sin\theta\sin\phi & 0 \\ 0 & \sin\phi & -\cos\phi & 0 \\ 0 & 0 & \rho & 1 \end{bmatrix}$$

where

$$[x_e\ y_e\ z_e\ 1] = [x_w\ y_w\ z_w\ 1]{*}V$$

Appendix 5 A brief description of IBM graphics enhancements

There are two enhancements to the Standard Color Graphics Adaptor, which is the normal colour graphics system on the IBM PC.

The objective of this appendix is to describe in general terms the hardware and software advantages of the IBM Professional Graphics Controller. The Enhanced Graphics Adaptor is also dealt with, but since this only differs slightly from the Standard Color Graphics Adaptor, most of the new information applies to the Professional Graphics Controller.

This appendix is not, of course, a programming manual for the device, but is intended to introduce the reader to the more advanced facilities available from this enhancement. The important differences between this device and the Standard Color Graphics Adaptor are explained and the information is given in the form of a technical/software overview. At the time of writing (late 1985) no textbooks have been published on this device and the information in this review is from IBM sources.

The text of this book has been written using a Standard Color Graphics Adaptor. The practical uses of such a device are numerous, but the limitations of the display hardware confine it to such major areas as business use, recreational or leisure use and educational use.

The attributes of the Standard Color Graphics Adaptor that exclude its use in advanced science and engineering applications are spatial resolution and colour range. As we have seen, both of these attributes depend mainly on memory capacity and the volume of a screen memory in bits is simply the product of the number of pixels on the screen and the number of bits per pixel. We have also seen that we can juggle with the screen memory and trade spatial resolution against colour. For example, with a fixed volume of 128 000 bits we can use the Standard Color Graphics Adaptor as:

1. A high resolution two-colour display (SCREEN 2):

   (640 × 200) pixels × 2 colours/pixel
   = 640 × 200 × 1 bits
   = 128 000 bits

2. A medium resolution four-colour display (SCREEN 1):

   (320 × 200) pixels × 4 colours/pixel
   = 320 × 200 × 2 bits
   = 128 000 bits

It is fairly obvious that spatial resolution places an upward limit on the complexity of line drawings that can be displayed. Fine detail in engineering drawings may be lost or distorted with a limited resolution device. On the other hand, the constraints that emerge from limited colour range are probably less important with current applications. A large number of computer graphics displays consist of line drawings together with text and (possibly) closed regions filled with flat colour. Such diagrams are abstractions that may model the behaviour of some kind of system, say an electrical circuit diagram or a printed circuit board diagram. In such cases displaying a large number of colours on the screen is confusing. When colour is used to represent functionality the golden rule is to keep the number of colours to a minimum (certainly 10 or less).

There are two contexts which demand a large number of colours. Firstly, in the shading of three-dimensional solid models such a facility is required. Here the goal is to increase the realism of the object appearing on the screen by shading the surface according to its interaction with the light source that is assumed to illuminate it. An illumination model is used to calculate the effect of one of a number of light sources on a surface. A number of factors are taken into account. In a simple model, the surface normal, the surface reflectivity characteristics, the position of the light source and the position of the viewer are considered. This yields a highly realistic result but a large number of intensities may be required to render the effect of the gradation of light intensity across a surface. An example of a shaded surface using the Professional Graphics Controller is shown in Colour Plate 19. Even with 256 colours/pixel available, the shading is coarse and false contours are apparent in the variation of intensity over the surface of the sphere. Elimination of these requires yet more colours/pixel, and devices that render realistic shaded objects use up to 24 bits/pixel (over 16 million colours/pixel).

Another obvious application is image processing. Here an image from a TV camera is 'grabbed' or 'frozen', digitized and stored in the screen memory. Colour Plate 20 shows an example of such a use. To adequately reflect the reality of the scene viewed by the TV camera, a large number of colours/pixel are necessary. Image processing is, in a sense, the converse of computer graphics. Rather than a program producing an image, the program operates on an image already in the screen memory. Some applications, TV commercials for example, involve a mix of both computer graphics and image processing. An image grabbed from a TV camera may be mixed or combined with computer graphics to give a special effect.

For applications like these, or any other area that requires a large number of colours, two enhancements are available. Firstly, there is

Table 1 Screen memory characteristics

Device	*Pixels*	*Colours available*
IBM Colour Graphics Adaptor:		
High res.	640×200	2/2
Med. res.	320×200	4/16
IBM Enhanced Graphics Adaptor:		
Enhanced res.	640×350	16/64
High res.	640×200	16/64
Med. res.	320×200	16/64
IBM Professional Graphics Controller	640×480	256/4096

the IBM Enhanced Graphics Adaptor. This offers an increase in screen memory and makes 16 colours available in high resolution (640×350). However, the 'width' of the colour table or video look-up table is increased to 6 bits and the set of 16 screen colours can be any combination of 16 from 64.

The IBM Professional Graphics Controller can display a total of any 256 colours from a total menu of 4096. Both Colour Plate 19 and Colour Plate 20 were produced using this device. Table 1 summarizes the screen memory characteristics of both devices. The Professional Graphics Controller does more than offer more colours and higher spatial resolution. It is, in fact, an intelligent graphics terminal with its own on-board processor. This means that the PC's CPU is freed from the distinctly non-trivial calculations involved in graphics utilities. For example, the basic line drawing utilities, which cause selected pixels to 'bright-up' between two specified end points, needs a processing facility to calculate the position of these pixels. With the Standard Color Graphics Adaptor this task is undertaken by the PC's CPU. In the Professional Graphics Controller, the low-level pixel calculations are undertaken by the processor in the terminal. This frees the CPU from these calculations and the work done in a graphics application program is split into two. The calculations needed to determine the position of graphics primitives such as line end points, circle position and radius, etc., is undertaken in the CPU. The pixel calculations are carried out by the Professional Graphics Controller. The Professional Graphics Controller accepts high-level commands from the 'host' CPU in the form of character codes. A string of codes represents a command together with a list of parameters that the command is to operate on.

Another function performed by both these enhancements is to emulate the Standard Color Graphics Adaptor. This enables software that has been written to drive the Standard Color Graphics Adaptor to be run on a device that incorporates an enhanced graphics facility. The Professional Graphics Controller is in effect two devices, one of which is the Standard Color Graphics Adaptor emulator. Both devices are active at all times, but only one may be connected to the screen at any time.

In summarizing the characteristics of both enhancements (Table 1) we can view the Enhanced Graphics Adaptor as a kind of halfway house offering an extension in both spatial and colour resolution. The Professional Graphics Controller is, as the name implies, best viewed as a separate device, or graphics terminal, offering a much larger range of graphics utilities over the Standard Color Graphics Adaptor. The remainder of this discussion applies to the Professional Graphics Controller.

As we have already mentioned, the graphics utilities in the Professional Graphics Controller are activated by sending commands from the 'host' CPU in a string of characters or bytes. Of course this process is transparent to a high-level language user. Line drawing and other utilities are simply called up from a user application program in the normal manner. It should be mentioned at this stage that there are two methods of communicating with the Professional Graphics Controller from a high-level program. The 'naked' method involves sending the appropriate codes together with their parameters to activate the Professional Graphics Controller functions. Thus specific graphics subroutines can be set up for each utility and called from the main program. The subroutines then send the bytes to the device using a PRINT statement. The second method is through a software interface known as a standard graphics package. The *raison d'être* of such standards is to enable software writers to produce machine-independent graphics packages. The Graphical Kernel

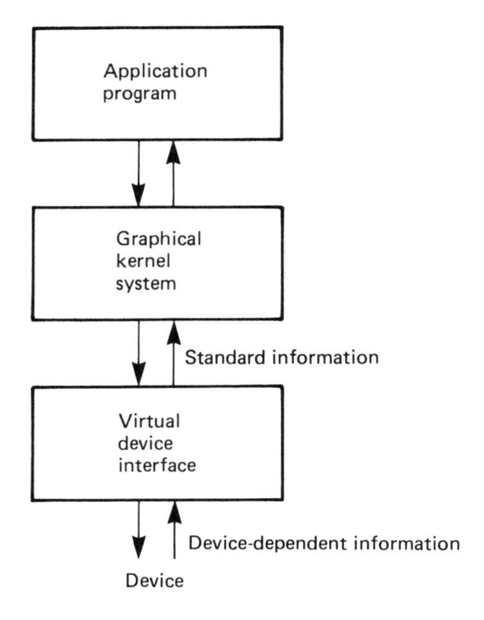

System (GKS) adopted in 1984 defines graphics functions at the programmer level. The Virtual Device Interface (VDI) takes the standard output from GKS and performs the necessary conversion for a particular display device.

An important programming strategy facilitated by the on-board processor is the ability to transmit lists of utilities, or commands, to the controller for subsequent execution. A list of commands set up in this way can then be executed by using a single command from the user program. This means that subpictures can be stored as command lists that are executed when required. Command lists may call each other. This facility, generally known as segmentation, is extremely important in professional graphics.

The range of colours offered by the Professional Graphics Controller means that the colour table can be sensibly organized. In fact the colour table consists of 256 rows, or entries, each of which are 12 bits wide. Each of these entries consists of 3×4 bit partitions which define the 12-bit colour as three 4-bit components – the red, green and blue components. A colour value is considered to be a triple of

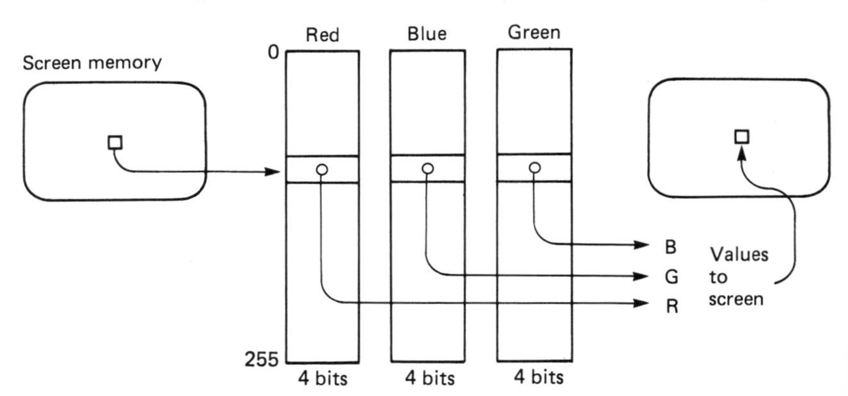

these three components. Each component is 4 bits and this defines a colour component to an accuracy of one in 16. Used in this way, the colour space of the Professional Graphics Controller can be viewed as a cubic grid of $16 \times 16 \times 16$. Each point on the grid specifies one of the 4096 colours. How a subset of these colours is selected, and the corresponding way in which the values are loaded into the colour table, depends on the application. If, for example, we have an application in which the colour is to be specified in the program as a triple (red, green and blue components), then we can only sensibly use six values per component:

$$6 \times 6 \times 6 = 216$$

because 6 is the largest number whose cube is less than or equal to 256. If the colour table is loaded as shown in Table 2, then points in cubic $16 \times 16 \times 16$ RGB colour space would be selected by the logical colour codes, or index values, as shown below. Codes 216 to 255 are unused.

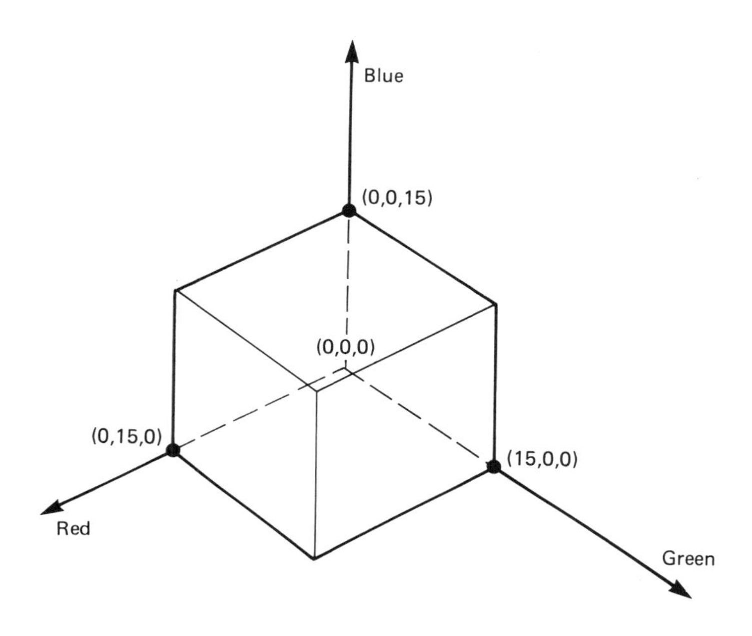
Blue
(0,0,15)
(0,0,0)
(0,15,0)
(15,0,0)
Red
Green

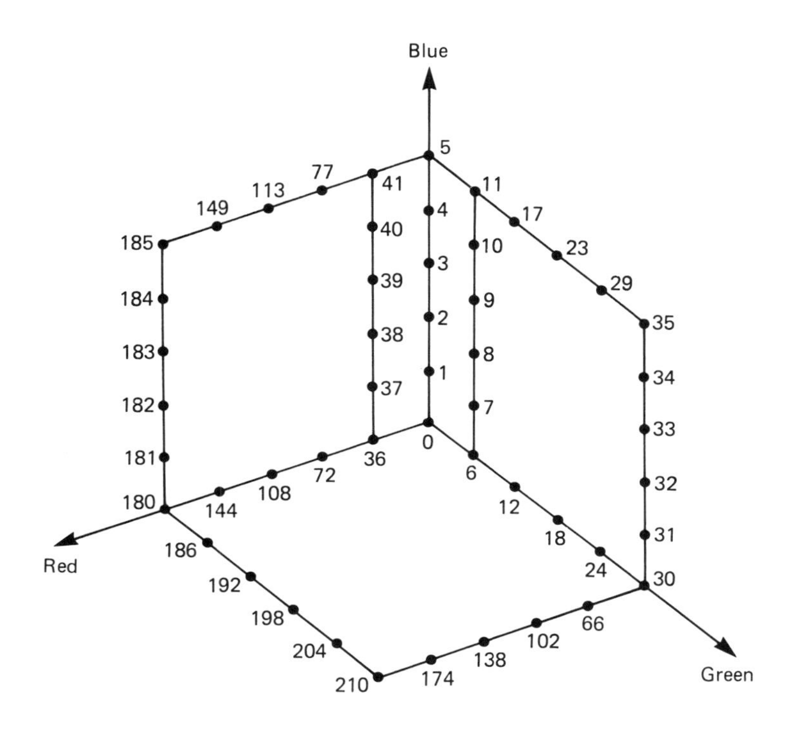
Blue
5
4
3
2
1
0
41
40
39
38
37
36
11
10
9
8
7
6
17
23
29
35
34
33
32
31
30
77
113
149
185
184
183
182
181
180
72
108
144
12
18
24
186
192
198
204
210
174
138
102
66
Red
Green

Table 2 A scheme for loading the colour table

	Red	*Green*	*Blue*
0	0	0	0
1	0	0	1
2	0	0	2
3	0	0	3
4	0	0	4
5	0	0	5
6	0	1	0
7	0	1	1
8	0	1	2
9	0	1	3
10	0	1	4
11	0	1	5
12	0	2	0
13	0	2	1
14	0	2	2
15	0	2	3
16	0	2	4
17	0	2	5
.	.	.	.
.	.	.	.
.	.	.	.
35	0	5	5
36	1	0	0
.	.	.	.
.	.	.	.
.	.	.	.
71	1	5	5
72	2	0	0
.	.	.	.
.	.	.	.
.	.	.	.
107	2	5	5
108	3	0	0
.	.	.	.
.	.	.	.
.	.	.	.
143	3	5	5
144	4	0	0
.	.	.	.
.	.	.	.
.	.	.	.
179	4	5	5
180	5	0	0
.	.	.	.
.	.	.	.
.	.	.	.
215	5	5	5

Another use of the colour table is to enable the screen memory to be viewed as eight separate bit planes, with the capability of storing eight separate (but single colour) images. (This is similar to the PCjr

Table 3 Loading the colour table to display prioritized images

Index value	*Table contents*
0	0
1	0
2	colour for plane 2
3	colour for plane 2
4	0
5	0
6	colour for plane 2
7	colour for plane 2
8	0
9	0
10	colour for plane 2
11	colour for plane 2
.	
.	
.	
254	colour for plane 2
255	colour for plane 2

techniques described in Chapter 2.) Each plane is identified by a value 1, 2, 4, 8, 16, 32, 64 or 128. Images can be drawn (or deleted) in one of these planes by using a masking command. The colour table is then used to make visible (or invisible) selected planes. For example, to display plane 2 only, we would load the colour table as shown in Table 3. Those rows, in which the value of the index is such that there is a 1 in the second least significant bit position, are set equal to the display colour. The images in each plane can be animated by reloading the appropriate entries in the colour table with the display colour for each plane in sequence. Alternatively, a static display of more than one plane can be produced with the planes appearing in their implied priority order. This implied priority (for example, 128 nearest the viewer and overlapping all other images) can be changed quickly by reloading the colour table. Incidentally, in the special case where images do not overlap, a total of 256 images can be stored.

The other distinguishing feature of the Professional Graphics Controller, provided by the on-board processor, is the extended command set. This provides a far greater set of graphics facilities than the Standard Color Graphics Adaptor. These can be categorised as follows:

1. Draw utilities (2D and 3D);
2. image transmission utilities;
3. two- and three-dimensional transformation facilities;
4. text utilities;
5. facilities to control the colour table;
6. flags or state indicators;

7. readback commands;
8. command list utilities; and
9. miscellaneous.

Drawing utilities are commands that draw shapes and these are generally a superset of the facilities available on the Standard Color Graphics Adaptor. The major difference is that three-dimensional drawing utilities are available. These are utilities that operate with three-dimensional coordinates or end points rather than two-dimensional points.

Image transmission utilities are used with units of scan lines, or parts of lines. These are used for fast transmission of blocks of the image from the application program to the screen memory, and in the opposite direction. A similar function is provided for in the Standard Color Graphics Adaptor by PUT and GET.

Certain three-dimensional transformations and the viewing transformations have explicit commands. These have been dealt with in earlier chapters and were set up then by user programming commands.

Text utilities include a selection of text sizes, the angle of the text and its justification about a current position pointer.

The colour table commands allow the user to load colours into any colour table entry, read the value of any entry and load pre-defined sets of colour table data. User-defined sets of colour table data can be saved.

Flags are registers that are used to set and test the current condition or state of the Professional Graphics Controller. These flags contain, for example, the attributes associated with the output functions such as current colour.

Readback commands allow the programmer to query the Professional Graphics Controller parameters. For example, we may wish to test the current value of a pixel in a certain position in the screen memory. Other readback facilities include querying the value of colour table entries and viewing matrix coefficients. A complete set of the Professional Graphics Controller commands is shown in Table 4. No parameters are given.

Table 4 Professional Graphics Controller primitives

Command code		
Long form	*Short form*	*Description*
ARC	AR	Draw arc
AREA	A	Fill area
AREABC	AB	Fill to specified colour
AREAPT	AP	Set fill pattern
CA	CA	Set ASCII mode
CIRCLE	CI	Draw circle

Command code		
Long form	*Short form*	*Description*
CLBEG	CB	Begin command list
CLDEL	CD	Delete command list
CLEARS	CLS	Clear screen
CLEND	CE	End command list
CLIPH	CH	Set hither clip mode
CLIPY	CY	Set yon clip mode
CLOOP	CL	Run command list (multiple times)
CLRD	CRD	Read command list
CLRUN	CR	Run command list
COLOR	C	Set current colour
CONVRT	CV	Convert coordinates
CX	CX	Set HEX mode
DISPLA	DI	Set display mode
DISTAN	DS	Set viewing distance
DISTH	DH	Set CLIPH distance
DISTY	DY	Set CLIPY distance
DRAW	D	Draw vector
DRAW3	D3	Draw vector in 3D
DRAWR	DR	Draw relative
DRAWR3	DR3	Draw relative 3D
ELIPSE	EL	Draw ellipse
FILMSK	FM	Set fill mask
FLAGRD	FRD	Read status flag
FLOOD	F	Flood viewport
IMAGER	IR	Read image line
IMAGEW	IW	White image line
LINFUN	LF	Set draw function
LINPAT	LP	Set draw pattern
LUT	L	Set LUT entry
LUTINT	LI	Initialise LUT
LUTRD	LRD	Read LUT entry
LUTSAV	LS	Save LUT setting
MASK	MK	Set draw mask
MATXRD	MRD	Read model matrix
MDIDEN	MDI	Initialise model matrix
MDMATX	MDM	Set model matrix
MDORG	MDO	Set model origin
MDROTX	MDX	Rotate model (x)
MDROTY	MDY	Rotate model (y)
MDROTZ	MDZ	Rotate model (z)
MDSCAL	MDS	Scale model
MDTRAN	MDT	Translate model
MOVE	M	Move drawing point
MOVE3	M3	Move 3D drawing point
MOVER	MR	Move drawing point (relative)
MOVER3	MR3	Move 3D (relative)
POINT	PT	Draw point
POINT3	PT3	Draw 3D point
POLY	P	Draw polygon

continued

Command code		
Long form	*Short form*	*Description*
POLY3	P3	Draw 3D polygon
POLYR	PR	Draw polygon (relative coordinates)
POLYR3	PR3	Draw 3D polygon (relative coordinates)
PRMFIL	PF	Set fill mode
PROJCT	PRO	Set projecting angle
RECT	R	Draw rectangle
RECTR	RR	Draw relative rectangle
RESETF	RF	Initialise status
SECTOR	S	Draw sector
TANGLE	TA	Set text angle
TDEFIN	TD	Define text character
TEXT	T	Draw text string
TEXTP	TP	Use programmed characters
TJUST	TJ	Set text justify
TSIZE	TS	Set text size
VWIDEN	VWI	Initialise viewing matrix
VWMATX	VMW	Set viewing matrix
VWPORT	VWP	Set viewport parameters
VWROTX	VWX	Rotate view (x)
VWROTY	VWY	Rotate view (y)
VWROTZ	VWZ	Rotate view (z)
VWRPT	VWR	Set view reference point
WAIT	W	Wait N frames
WINDOW	WI	Set window parameters

Bibliography

Ernst. B. *The Magic Mirror of M. C. Escher* Ballantine Books 1979

Foley J. D. and Van Dam A. *Fundamentals of Interactive Computer Graphics* Addison-Wesley 1982

Gardiner M. 'On Tesselating the plane with convex polygon tiles' *Scientific American* Vol. 233, No. 1

Gardiner M. 'Extraordinary nonperiodic tiling that enriches the theory of tiles' *Scientific American* Vol. 236, No. 1

Haeckel E. *Kunstformen der Natur* Leipzig 1904

Jones O. *Grammar of Ornament* London 1856

Mandelbrot B. *The Fractal Geometry of Nature* Freeman 1983

Martin G. E. *Transformation Geometry: An introduction to Symmetry* Springer-Verlag 1982

Newman W. M. and Sproull R. F. *Principles of Interactive Computer Graphics* McGraw-Hill International 1979

Shubnikov A. V. and Kopstik *Symmetry in Science and Art* Plenum Press 1974

Toth F. *Regular Figures* Pergamon Press 1964

Index